PARTNERS IN GOD'S LOVE

by

JOHN L. DAVEY

"Love, the many splendoured thing"

xulon PRESS

TABLE OF CONTENTS

DEDICATION

With love, to all my mentors in love.

John L. Davey – July, 1984

ACKNOWLEDGEMENTS

It's not very often that a son gets to critique his father's work.

I explored the possibility of getting Dad's handwritten manuscript published in 1984, shortly after his death, but quickly realized that the time and cost of typing, editing, proofreading and publishing would be prohibitive. So it was put on the "backburner" so to speak. In the ensuing years several events transpired (all part of God's plan!) to make the project feasible. One was the increasing use of personal computers and word processors. This solved the typing issue. A second one was the development of the internet, which made the research easier. The final event was personal, but was certainly ordained by the Lord, and that was my early retirement from work due to the onset of Parkinson's disease. This gave me the time to look after all the necessary details that go along with getting a book published.

By necessity, any major project involves teamwork. I must first give honour and thanksgiving to our wonderful Saviour, who through the leading of the Holy Spirit, led Dad to develop the theme of this devotional. My thanks go out to Kae Johnston, Phyllis Trim, and Verna and Clarence Becker, early missionary colleagues of my parents, whose prayer support has been invaluable. One runs the risk of missing someone here and it would be remiss not to thank Cornelia Martin, of Dominica, who influenced, in a positive way, my very early childhood values. I am grateful to Larry Dick, a long time friend of our family, for the foreword, and who was instrumental in choosing the hymnbook mentioned in the February 21 reading. Irvine McKee, my brother-in-law, spent countless hours doing the necessary work of proofreading and making editorial comments on the first draft. His insights were invaluable and I thank him for them. In closing, I would like to thank my wife, Sharon, whose quiet support and encouragement during the times when I got overwhelmed by the enormity of the project, brought me back to the task at hand.

I trust that the Lord will use the truths and principles in this book to enrich the life of the reader.

John T. Davey
January, 2007

FOREWORD

I first met John L. Davey in 1979, soon after his retirement from the mission field in the West Indies, where he had spent many years serving as the General Manager of the Christian Literature Crusade. He and his wife, Ethel, chose to retire in Edmonton, to be close to their family. Rather than return to the more familiar and established Beulah Alliance church, they joined a brand-new church in west Edmonton – Westland Baptist. This was to be their church home until John's death only a few years later. At Westland, John helped out in many different ways, but was most prominent in his role as a Bible teacher.

During those brief years, John seemed to have sense of urgency about completing his "book project" and his Bible classes often reflected the focus of the book he was working on. Partners in God's Love was not just a concept to be accepted and then largely ignored. Also, it wasn't something that was distant and understandable only in an impersonal or theoretical way. To John, God's love was an integral part of the very fabric of life and relevant to every experience and relationship throughout life.

John clearly felt that he had an assignment from God to write about his own experience with God's love. His book, therefore, while not biographical, offers many personal insights and stories from his own life, woven into the Bible's teaching about the many aspects of God's love. It is presented in the form of daily devotionals, one for each day of the year, so it can be absorbed slowly and savoured, just like a fine meal and indeed, life itself.

I commend this book to you, regardless of where you are in your own life journey and what has been your own experience with God's love. We can be grateful, too, that John was able to complete his notes for this book and share them with all of us before he was called to be with the Lord. It is my prayer that you will be blessed by reading this book as you experience God's love in your own life.

Larry Dick
Edmonton, Alberta
January, 2007

PREFACE

While this is but a minor work about a major subject it is my credo about love. It is the fruit of lifelong experience, observation, and meditation upon the Word of God. The page entitled "Something Personal" (January 2) tells of my introduction as a teenager, to the highest love, the God of love and the love of God. Five decades have come and gone since then and I am still learning its dimensions, effect on, and governance of all the other loves in my life. It has been life's major because it is listed as the "greatest" in the Scriptures of truth. It is also the New Commandment of Christ to His new creations, and the infallible indicator to the world that we are His disciples. His Word also points out that my love to Him, the Invisible One, is measured by my love to the visible ones, the people around me.

With such standards, it is hardly necessary to say I have frequently fallen far short and failed in the practice of them. This is not mock humility or pseudo confession God knows, and others know it is the truth. And the fault, without excuse, is all mine. Yet, all glory to Him, His love would not let me go. How grateful I am that His love in grace, found me early, and, when I strayed into "By-Path Meadows", early brought me back to His highway of love.

The listed loves in the following pages do not come in progressive, orderly, homiletic form. Life is not orderly and I thought the same non-pattern of the loves of life should be followed here. There will be odd juxtapositions: the loves will be frequently falling over each other; seeming to sometimes trip each other up or deliberately contradict each other. Yet, for those with eyes to see life steadily, and see it whole, there is a schema, a pattern. holy, heavenly love is always seeking a way to invade and conquer, for their perfecting, all the other lesser loves.

Substance has always been given precedence over style; sustenance over system. The balance of truth has been aimed at and illustrations are intermixed with exposition. This is a collection of essays, reflexions, reminiscences, self-portraiture, and Scriptural teaching. Old Testament and New Testament "love" teachings will augment each other. It darts to and fro in time. Millennia will change from 2000 B.C. to 1900 A.D. In the space of a sentence or two centuries will be telescoped. The manners, morals, and mores of bygone days will coalesce with todays. East and West, despite Kipling, meet here. England finds itself alongside Australia; the West Indies close to Canada; the U.S.A. with India, Africa. All join here under his glorious banner of love.

His love is sovereign, silent, permeating and, where there is any opening, or willingness to respond, there the revolutionary encounter happens. It is my hope that for all who read these pages there will be many such encounters.

JANUARY 1 – LOVE GREETS THE NEW YEAR

On this first day of another New Year, no better thought could greet our waking minds than that which is the theme of these pages: "God is Love."[1] At the dawning of this morning no happier feeling could bless us than that which is the title of this book: "Partners in God's Love." And, should we have a companion of the Way, who is with us, and awake in the dawn's early light, there could be no warmer greeting than "I love you." What a lovely beginning for this New Year, and for the rest of the 365 or 366 days, should we be allowed to see them. If otherwise, for those who know and love Him it will be even better; the revelation of heavenly love at the dawning of eternal day will amaze us. The many splendoured thing, the divine love, is now beyond our full comprehension, but not our contemplation. Then, faith will be lost in sight; hope will be realized and love be forever. Oh, what a day that will be...!

But now, what a day this will be! John Keble (1792 – 1866) expresses beautifully what I am feeling about His love, and all the other loves that beset, benefit and bless my way and your way.

"New every morning is the love
Our wakening and uprising prove,
Through sleep and darkness safely brought
Restored to life, and power, and thought.

New mercies each returning day
Hover around us while we pray;
New perils past, new sins forgiven,
New thoughts of God, new hopes of heaven.

Old friends, old scenes, will lovelier be,
As more of heaven in each we see;
Some softening gleam of love and prayer
Shall dawn on every cross and care.

The trivial round, the common task,
Will furnish all we ought to ask;
Room to deny ourselves, a road
To bring us daily nearer God.

Only, Oh Lord, in Thy great love,
Fit us for perfect rest above;
And help us, this and every day,
To live more nearly as we pray." Amen

We "...have not passed this way before"[2] but love has: Love's foreknowledge, foresight, forethought, and foreplanning goes before. His love dwells in us, energizes, elevates, and enables us for Keble's "trivial round, the common task;" – practical down to earth living and loving and loving. Or the large, the difficult , the sufferings, and the other services His love has planned for this New Year's day; microcosm of all the other new days of this year. We will also find His love not only enabling, but ennobling. We are uplifted by His love, and when it has its way, and sway, in us He is honoured and glorified, others are blessed and we are better people.

JANUARY 2 – LOVE: SOMETHING PERSONAL

I received, in my youth, what the early Methodists described as a baptism of heavenly love. I had, at about fourteen years of age, become converted, baptized, and a church member. Yet for five of my teen-age years I drifted spiritually even as I developed physically and mentally. But at nineteen my life was revolutionized as I discovered that the divine love was a many splendoured thing in itself as well as irradiating all other loves.

The circumstances were these. I received a short letter inviting me to a Saturday night meeting at a farm home about thirty miles from Sydney, Australia. The date was December 7, 1935. Somewhat against my will I went. The messenger of God, whose name I have forgotten, spoke to a small group that hot summer night on John 3:16.

At first, as I sat on that veranda I didn't pay much heed for "I knew it all." But as he continued to speak of the love of God in giving His Son, the Spirit of God began a dialogue with my spirit. It went something like this as I remember:

"So you know all about John 3:16 and you believe it?"
"Yes."
"Well, what have you done about it since you believed it?"
"Nothing much."
"Why not?"
"I suppose I have been too concerned with my own affairs and pleasures."
"Tonight you are at a crossroad. Why don't you make a complete commitment of your life to Christ who loved you so?"

This silent interior conversation concluded with the conviction that I ought to make that whole hearted commitment and I did so, sincerely, within my heart. Immediately, that very moment, without any outward manifestations, I received that baptism of love. At the close of the meeting, when public opportunity was given for testimonies, I told briefly what had happened and said:

"From tonight, by the grace of God, things will be different."

And they have been different for almost fifty years.

Power was given to witness of the love of God in Christ to my workmates, family, and friends. Wrongs were righted. His love led me to a Keswick convention. There, Dr. Mowill, the then Archbishop of Sydney, at the conclusion of his address on Missionary Day, said:

"We will sing the hymn: "When I survey the wondrous Cross..." Then when we come to the last verse: "Were the whole realm of nature mine, That were an offering far too small; Love so amazing, so divine Demands my soul, my life, my all." Change "Demands" to "Shall have" if you are willing for the mission field should He call you."

I did so, and that many splendoured love led me on to Bible College, to the mission field, and all the other loves. Friendship love. Romantic love. Marital love. Family love. Brotherly love.

JANUARY 3 – GOD IS LOVE – Part One

"Come, let us all unite to sing,
God is love, God is love.
Let heav'n and earth their praises bring;
God is love, God is love.
Let ev'ry soul from sin awake,
Each in his heart sweet music make,
And sing with us, for Jesus' sake,
God is love! God is love!"
Howard Kingsbury (1842 – 1878)

This is the supreme love song we once couldn't sing, for sin had silenced us, but now with heart and mind and mouth, because of Jesus, we, with all the saved on earth can sing "God is Love." Just three monosyllables to describe His nature and His character. Three little words to indicate the source, substance, and splendour of God who is love. Three mighty words, majestic words. "God;" only comprehensible because He chose to reveal Himself in creation and redemption. "Is;" present tense of the verb "To Be;" God always "Is", and again, as He revealed, this is His name: "I AM" – "Who was, Who is and Who is to come." "Love;" His first, last, best, and greatest name of all.

He is Spirit; He is life; He is holy; He is light; He is consuming fire and because He is all these, and through all these attributes, He is love. Geddes Macgregor says:

"Either it is nonsense, to say nothing of maudlin humbug, or else it is by far the most exciting statement about God to be found in either the Bible or any other literature in the world."

How true. "God is love" does not describe his activities but his nature. Taking the other aspects and attributes mentioned above, we have a comprehensive view of the divine nature and of the character of divine love. This is most important for though incomplete and false views of God and love have always been present they are increasing today.

God is not a loving, doting old grandpa or Father Christmas as some by their words and actions seem to indicate. He us not a "Patsy" or "Pushover" to be pushed around, or to obey the whim, will, or wishes of fallen, finite man. He is not soft or sentimental – He is holy heavenly love. This love is strong, steady, and substantial. This love is wonderful, awe-inspiring, and worship producing. It should cause us to fall on our faces for it combines Mount Sinai and Mount Calvary: God is law and God is love. Easy grace and easy believism have produced an easy love. Easy grace results in antinomianism rebuked by Paul. Easy believism results in false security revealed by James. Easy love results in lying rebutted by John.

God, whose nature is love, created in love, rules in love, judges in love, and redeemed us with costly love. All His attributes combined in Calvary love – grace love. We are called to real repentance and true faith in our Lord Jesus Christ. We are saved by grace through faith that results in works, believing we have assurance of eternal life now. It is for the world.

These three words must occupy us again.

JANUARY 4 – GOD IS LOVE – Part Two

Monosyllables are marvellous words. They are not only snappy, short, and simple words, but they are very much more. They often contain profound thoughts that confound the intellects of the worldly wise. They can stretch the minds of ordinary believers and illumine the hearts of the humble. The three that concern us again are amazing examples. "Multum in parve" – "much in little" – is another way of stating the truth concerning them.

John uses them twice to describe the nature and character of God who revealed Himself in the person of His Son. Without this self revelation we finite beings could not have known the infinite, heavenly, and eternal Father and His infinite, heavenly, and eternal love. But we have been shown Him, as the Son, the Christ, the Saviour, the Lord, became Jesus, who lived amongst sinful humanity. We have seen Him! The Lord of creative love; the Lord of redemptive love. "God is love". Let us consider and savour more fully these amazing monosyllables. (It takes a polysyllabic word to describe and define a one-syllable word!)

"God" – "In the beginning God…"[1] God is only comprehensible because He revealed Himself and must be accepted by faith. For "…without faith it is impossible to please Him, for he who comes to God must believe that He is and that He is a rewarder of those who seek Him."[2] One of the tests I use to try the accuracy of new translations is to check the way in which the letters are used in the spelling of the names of deity. In Genesis 1, "God" is used many times. This first primary name is a uniplural noun ("Elohim"- sometimes El or Elah) from "El" – strength and "Alah" – to swear, bind with an oath. It contains the first hint of the Trinity in its plurality: "And God said. 'Let us make man in Our image'…" and yet its unity is never in doubt. So "God created man in his own image…"[3]

"Is" introduces the second primary name of Deity. It is always spelled with capitals, usually Lord, sometimes God. In Genesis 2 onwards we are introduced to the composite title "Lord God". It is then used regularly. Lord is Jehovah "Yahweh" in Hebrew, meaning "the self-existent One" who literally is spoken of as "I AM WHO I AM" or just "I AM". He is the eternally self-contained, self-sufficient, and self-existing One who continually and progressively reveals Himself, as He did in Jesus Christ, who took upon himself the "I Am" title. "Is" is the present tense of the verb "To be". The one Who was; Who is; and Who is to come. God the Lord "Is" – Father, Son, and Holy Spirit. "Jehovah", "Yahweh", "Yhwh", derived from the verb "Hayah" - to be.

"Agapé" is the main Greek word used in the New Testament to describe the love of the Triune God, who is self-giving, self-sacrificing, serving love. And this love is given irrespective of merit in the object. It was given fully and freely on the Cross, and is given by His Spirit now. It is profound and yet a child can say and believe: "Jesus loves me this I know, For the Bible tells me so…"

JANUARY 5 – GOD IS LOVE – Part Three

"God is love" is the third of John's great statements concerning the nature of God. He said in his gospel "God is Spirit"; he has already said in this first letter "God is Light" and now he completes his trilogy by saying twice, "God is love."[1] The repetition is not an aid to remembrance; it is to indicate the superiority and supremacy of love. "God is Spirit" does not describe Him wholly, for there are evil spirits in the world. "God is light", while indicating superiority over darkness, still does not fully picture Him. But "God is love" qualifies Spirit, governs light and wholly, fully, and completely describes the one, the only, the unique God. In all the pantheons of mythology and all the religions of antiquity and modernity, there is no God, like our Lord, Jehovah, - Jesus is [4] His name, and He is love. John, in this first letter, concentrates his teaching on love into three chapters. Introducing the theme in chapter two; developing and applying it in chapter three; expanding, consolidating, and climaxing it in chapter four, with his repeated statement "God is love".

The writer, under the guidance of the Spirit, did not say: "God is the love." That would mean that love is a quality, which God possesses. But the absence of the article emphasizes that love is what God is in His essential nature. Further, because God is love, love which He shows is occasioned by Himself only and not by any outside cause.

"The love of God"[2] does have the definite article, which also indicates that the statement "God is love" is not reversible; it must never be read as "Love is God." This error is being proclaimed as today's "liberating" truth! I will enlarge on this later. (January 19)

Three words, statements, and chapters; trilogies of Trinitarian truth about Trinitarian love. The supreme manifestation of "God is love", and that the love of God is for us, is seen in His Son's coming into the world and His death on the Cross. "By this the love of God was manifested in us, that God has sent His only begotten Son into the world so that we might live through Him. In this is love, not that we loved God, but that He loved us and sent His Son to be the propitiation for our sins."[3] We did not love God; we cannot appease Him nor avoid His wrath. The Son, our Saviour by His sacrifice, did what we could never do. In the words of Thomas Kelly (1769 – 1855)

"We sing the praise of Him who died,
Of Him who died upon the Cross;
The sinner's hope let men deride
For this we count the world but loss.

Inscribed upon the Cross we see
In shining letters, God is love.
He bears our sins upon the tree;
He brings us mercy from above.

The Cross: it takes our guilt away;
It holds the fainting spirit up;
It cheers with hope the gloomy day,
And sweetens ev'ry bitter cup."

To a world without hope and without God, and to the saints, the message of cheer is "God is love." "We know love by this, that He laid down His life for us..."[4] The supreme proof that "God is love."

JANUARY 6 – "I LOVE YOU" – Part One

Another three monosyllables which rank high in language and importance. I have placed them as "follow-ons" from the first three. We must start with further thoughts on that theme. We saw that "God is love" is a statement concerning His nature and character. But love is also evidenced in His acts and here we come to the love of God. This is not a reversal of the monosyllables but an extension of truth. Because He is love, in nature and character, it follows that all He does will be motivated by love, and will in the end prove to be the fruit of eternal love purposed for our earthly and eternal welfare.

When God says "I love you" we should rethink the expression by considering it word by word. "I love you." We have already seen a little of the depth of love contained in the names of Deity. As the Father loves the Son, so the Son loves us. He is uniquely the Beloved of His Father, and that word "agapetos" – dearly beloved – spoken of the Son, is applied to all His own children. The third primary name of Deity is "Lord" (Hebrew – Adon, Adonai) – meaning master. It first appears in Genesis, Lord God, Master. Or Lord Jehovah. While this name and title is applied to both God and man, it is carefully distinguished in the best translations by the use or omission of the capital letter. Lord, Master – speaking of Deity and lord, master – speaking of humanity. As applied to man, the word is used in the relationships of master and husband. This name and title and these two relationships, apply and exist in the person of our Lord and Master Jesus Christ who is our Master and Husband. He is the Bridegroom.

He says: "I love you." I died for you! I live for you!

The Father says in act, fact, and speech: "I love you." For I come in the person of my Son, to reconcile the world to myself. The Son says in act, fact, and word: "I love you." For I come in flesh to bear your sin in my body on the Cross. And the Spirit says in act, fact, and still, small whispered voice: "I love you." I come in fullness at Pentecost to make real within you, and to show through you the love of God. "…because the love of God has been poured out within our hearts through the Holy Spirit who was given to us."[1] We listen in awe, amazement, and adoration as we hear the Triune God with one accord whisper, speak, shout, and thunder across the ages to human beings everywhere: "I love you." He continuously says it and He consistently shows it.

Oh sinner believe it; Oh rebel receive it; Oh saint rejoice in it. To know we are loved personally, purposefully, and powerfully, with this divine enabling, ennobling love ought to bring glad acceptance and a reciprocal cry "Yes Lord and I love You, because You first loved me." And this response, which he loves to hear, carries with it far reaching implications and responsibilities. If I say "I love Him" in word, then I must show it by my acts here on earth. This demands further careful consideration: it has a lot to do with obedience.

JANUARY 7 – "I LOVE YOU" – Part Two

The words "I love you" are magnificent and mighty in their meaning when we realize that God is speaking them. He reminds Israel that He is their Creator, Redeemer, Sustainer, and Enabler. "But now, thus says the Lord, your Creator, O Jacob, And He who formed you, O Israel, 'Do not fear, for I have redeemed you; I have called you by name; you are Mine! When you pass through the waters, I will be with you; And through the rivers, they will not overflow you. When you walk through the fire, you will not be scorched, Nor will the flame burn you. For I am the Lord your God, The Holy One of Israel, your Savior; I have given Egypt as your ransom, Cush and Seba in your place. Since you are precious in My sight, Since you are honoured and I love you, I will give other men in your place and other peoples in exchange for your life. Do not fear, for I am with you; I will bring your offspring from the east, And gather you from the west. I will say to the north, 'Give them up!' And to the south, 'Do not hold them back.' Bring My sons from afar And My daughters from the ends of the earth, Everyone who is called by My name, And whom I have created for My glory, Whom I have formed, even whom I have made.'"[1]

The truths flowing from, surrounding, and underlying the divine declaration of love, become apparent when put in the above context. They apply first to Israel in Isaiah's time, as seen in the return and restoration after the Babylonian exile. Their final meaning will only become apparent at the return of Christ. But His "I love you" in Israel's past, is equally true of her present and of her future. The Abrahamic Love Covenant has been, is, and will be fulfilled, even to its bottom line: "…And in you all the families of the earth will be blessed."[2]

Secondly, it is this bottom line that concerns us here; for we Gentiles of all the families of the earth, are included in His "I love you". Don Richardson popularized this "bottom line" expression in his speaking and writing. His books: Peace Child, Lords of the Earth, and Eternity in Their Heart all illustrate the theme. All the families of the earth were to be blessed through the Christ who came as the Jewish Messiah but also as the Saviour of the world. "I love you" includes those in the East, the West, the North and the South, and it includes you and me. It is the all inclusive love of God for Gentile as well as Jewish sinners.

The psalmist caught the thought: "Oh give thanks to the Lord, for He is good, For His lovingkindness is everlasting. Let the redeemed of the Lord say so, Whom He has redeemed from the hand of the adversary And gathered from the lands, From the east and from the west, From the north and from the south."[3]

The Lord Jesus Christ Himself clarified, confirmed, and called for its fulfillment. When the Roman centurion called on Jesus, and had faith in Him and His authority and ability: "He marvelled, and said to those who were following: "…truly I say to you, I have not found such great faith with anyone in Israel. I say to you that many will come from east and west, and recline at the table with Abraham, Isaac and Jacob in the kingdom of heaven;"[4] And a little later He also said: "The harvest is plentiful, but the workers are few."[5] His "I love you" calls for "I love You" action from us.

JANUARY 8 – "I LOVE YOU" – Part Three

"…Therefore beseech the Lord of the harvest to send out workers into His harvest."[1] The divine "I love you" demanded the outpoured love and life of the Lord Jesus Christ to turn this tremendous truth into down to earth, person to person ministry. His request to His disciples that they pray for labourers shows that all kinds of serving went hand in hand with the preaching of the Gospel. His substitutionary work on the Cross made possible the Good News we proclaim. This is the only Gospel. There is again today the old heresy of the "social gospel." There are no other gospels. But there are social implications, and accompaniments of the Gospel. Let us be sure to keep the balance of truth here. His "I love you" stars with salvation from sin, and continues with everything necessary for life and godliness. Before all this, pre-venient grace (the grace that goes before), prepared the way, warned us, and gave good to us. For it is the "…riches of His kindness and tolerance and patience…" all this is the goodness and "the kindness of God" which leads us to repentance.[2] This is all included in his "I love you". From eternity past, into eternity future, this is what His "I love you" means. The worth of His love lies in this worthiness. We are all unworthy if it. The tragedy is that His self-less, self-sacrificing and serving love should go rejected.

Yet He goes on saying "I love you" in another way. He says "I love you" through His own children in whom His love has become personalized. He not only asks us to pray for loving labourers for His harvest field, He also uses these concerned people, these compassionate witnesses, these committed lovers, and sends them out with His "I love you" in their hearts, heads, and hands. Saying "I love you" with their whole being behind their love actions, and their whole personality behind their verbal witness.

> "You are writing a gospel, a chapter each day;
> By the deeds that you do; and the words that you say.
> People read what you write, whether faithless or true;
> Say what is the gospel, according to you?"
> Unknown

To say "I love you" by being, and doing love, is effective proclamation of Christ, and basic witness to Him. Yet it should not preclude "saying so" as the Psalmist exhorted. Sometimes, "witness of life alone," can be both a reason and an excuse for not speaking for Christ.

To whom and for how long are we going to say "I love you"? To all people as opportunity affords, and for as long as life lasts. To the nearest and dearest; to family and friends; to neighbours near and far; and to enemies, who hate us for Christ's sake, who despise us, run us down and would run us out of town if they could. Later we will consider what it means and what it costs to say "I love you" to all of these. In Dickens's great story Dombey and Son there is the touching story of Florence's love for the father who hated her. A love so steadfast and true that, Dombey lost his wealth and all his friends, Florence came again with the same love that he had despised and so callously rejected. This is what Christians are called to do continuously. Let the love of Christ within say "I love you" without and without ceasing.

JANUARY 9 – "GOD IS_____" "WE ARE"

In a European churchyard there is, on a tombstone, an epitaph by a poet to his wife; a lovely tribute stated by what he implied but did not say. The inscription reads:

"She was _____, but words are wanting to say what! Think what a wife should be and she was that."

This really sets our mind working, as the poet desired, about that paragon wife and her virtues. We will pursue this train of thought later in the Scripture passage which describes the perfect wife (October 4). Here we use the poet's words and apply them to God. "God is" and He is the eternally self-existing, self-sufficient One. "He is". "And without faith it is impossible to please Him, for he who comes to God must believe that He is…"[1]

God is holy. This is His essential nature and if we are in His family then "As obedient children, do not be conformed to the former lusts which were yours in your ignorance, but like the Holy One who called you, be holy yourselves also in all your behaviour; because it is written, 'You shall be holy, for I am holy.'"[2]

God is just. Because He is who He is, He is what He is: holy and just. Shall not the God of all the earth do right? Because He is faithful and just, as well as being loving and kind, Calvary became essential. As Scripture says, "…that He would be just and the justifier of the one who has faith in Jesus."[3] And being justified, we will be just – just as He is.

"God is ___" "We are___"! We have filled in the blank describing Him and ourselves, because we are in His Son. There are yet other words that could be used: Wisdom, truth, power, fire, wrath and so on but there is one that contains all these. Yes "God is love." The four letter word cries, demands to fill the blank space. Already we have given pages to it, and we will give many more. It thrills, fills, and spills out of me, since that memorable night when I first truly understood a little of its unlimited glory.

God is; God is holy: God is just. He is ___, but words are wanting to say what? Think about what a God should be and He is that! He is love, holy love, and just love.

God is love. In music just three beats, but these three mighty, majestic beats, were sufficient to inspire "The Messiah." Every time we hear it, we can hear sounding silently all through it the theme, God is love. Sometimes sounding gently in the pastoral passages, but then more urgently in the passion love passages. Then, in a haunting melody, our three beat theme, is the personal testimony of the soloist: "I know that my Redeemer liveth." Finally, choir and orchestra peak in the Hallelujah Chorus.

Just writing about it starts the goose pimples on my back and the shivers down my spine. Like the sound of many waters at Niagara, or the sea surging as we cross the mighty ocean, God is love. This can never be rightly described, All the artists of all the ages, could not do it justice. But you and I can experience what we can't really define. God is my love. God loved me at Calvary. God loves me eternally.

JANUARY 10 – GOD LOVES ME

When I am in London, England it brings back all sorts of memories. I was born in Rochester, Kent, another ancient city thirty miles south of London. In 1924 my father took me to the recently opened Wembley Stadium where the Empire Exhibition was being held. As I walked through the fascinating Australian and Canadian pavilions I couldn't foresee what these two countries were to mean in my life. One of my favourite walks is from Westminster Abbey, past the Houses of Parliament and Queen Boadicea's statue, along the Thames Embankment to Queen Cleopatra's Needle. That granite obelisk once stood in front of the great temple at Heliopolis in Egypt.

I have just been looking at some pictures I took of the Needle. One inscription at the base of the monument reads:

"This obelisk, prostrate for centuries on the sands of Alexandria, was presented to the British Nation A.D. 1819 by Mohamed Ali, Viceroy of Egypt. A worthy memorial of our distinguished countrymen Nelson and Abercromby."

On each of the four sides of the pillar, the hieroglyphics are still as strong and clear as when they were cut over three thousand years ago.

The city of the sun, Heliopolis has long since vanished. Egyptian dynasties and civilizations have come and gone as ours will also perish, but the stones still speak. When I look at the monument I always focus on the base. For there, buried from sight, are artifacts from the past for future archaeologists to unearth, should London perish as Heliopolis did.

"It's a strange list: A set of coins; specimens of weights and measures; a London directory; a bundle of newspapers; photographs of the twelve most beautiful women of the period; a box of hairpins; articles of feminine adornment; a razor; a parchment containing a translation of the hieroglyphics on the obelisk."

So writes Dr. Frank W. Boreham, D.D.(1871 – 1959), who as a small boy, watched the "needle" being raised.

But there is something else there also; of more value than all the other items. The Word of God is there. The British and Foreign Bible Society supplied it and one special text in 215 languages. Surely you can guess what that text is. Yes of course. "For God so loved the world that He gave His only begotten Son, that whosoever believeth in Him should not perish, but have everlasting life." John 3:16 as it is called from its location in the Gospel of John. A buried text in ten score and fifteen tongues for some future delver in the dust and detritus of London to discover.

But it's the truth contained in the text that needs to be buried in the heart thus affecting the living. The truth in five great couplets: God and the world; love and giving; the Son and whosoever; believing and living; unbelieving and perishing.

I have told what effect the truths of this verse had upon me nearly fifty years ago. It was no passing experience. From that day to this – God's love and the gift of His love, his Son – has controlled my life and given me peace.

"By Christ on the Cross Peace was made.
My debt, by His death, was all paid;
No other foundation is laid
For Peace: the Gift of God's Love."
Peter Bilhorn (1861 – 1936)

JANUARY 11 – LOVED! WHY ME, OH LORD?

"Amazing love! How can it be, That Thou, my God, should'st die for me!" Charles Wesley (1707 – 1788) I am loved! What heart-warming knowledge. What assurance to my soul. What stability it brings to life. What a glorious experience on the earthly level and oh, so much greater on the heavenly. I often ask myself the question: Why me oh Lord? In thinking of all the human love I have known, I marvel and I'm grateful. But it's still a puzzle. Knowing myself and knowing that God knows me through and through with even truer knowledge, I'm more amazed than ever at His love for me.

I am not alone in this kind of thinking. The poet Daniel Whittle (1840 – 1901) wrote what I and many others have felt but can't put into words:

"I know not why God's wondrous grace
To me He hath made known;
Nor why, unworthy as I am,
He claimed me for His own.

I know not how the Spirit moves,
Convincing men of sin;
Revealing Jesus thro' His Word,
Creating faith in Him.

I know not what of good or ill
May be reserved for me;
Of weary ways or golden days
Before His face I see.

I know not when My Lord may come;
I know not how nor where;
If I shall pass the veil of death,
Or meet Him in the air."

There is much I don't know about His reasons for loving me. But in the case of Israel, she was chosen because God from a heart of love chose to do so. In His holy love He dug them from the pit of Ur of the Chaldees. He loved Terah and Abraham and led them out to become faith pilgrims. He loved crooked Jacob into straitness and integrity. He loved Joseph and sent him to Egypt to prepare for them. He loved Moses who played his part in the making of a nation. He loved Joshua who completed the first stage of the possession of the promised land. He executed His grand love design in sending His Son, via Israel, to be the Saviour of the world.

Why? Why them oh Lord? The reply comes loud and clear: "The Lord did not set His love on you nor choose you because you were more in number than any of the peoples, for you were the fewest of all peoples, but because the Lord loved you..."[1] Unexplainable. He loved because He would love. The cynic may say: "How odd of God to choose the Jews." "Love chose Israel" we reply. That is also why He loved the church which He is building. That is why He loves you and me, and gave Himself for us. He loves because He is Love; He wills to love; He must love. Let us spend no more time on the reason why but enjoy the assurance, certainty, comfort, and blessing of knowing we are loved. We have left until the end the chorus refrain. Go back and quote it after every verse. "But I know whom I have believed; And am persuaded that He is able To keep that which I've committed unto Him against that day."[2]

JANUARY 12 – GOD'S LOVE FOR THE WORLD

John 3:16 says: "For God so loved the world, that He gave His only begotten Son, that whoever believes in Him shall not perish, but have eternal life." This has been called the Gospel in a nutshell. It is also an in-depth digest of Biblical doctrine. God; God's love; the world; His unique Son; the gift of that Son; the Cross; all mankind; the individual; believing in Christ; salvation from; salvation to; eternal lostness and eternal life. It is the Bible condensed to one verse.

The word "so" seems simple but it isn't. It describes the love of God which is indescribable. We can never fully comprehend "What is the breadth and length and depth and height and know the love of Christ which passeth knowledge." This is what the little word "so" seeks to do. It is trying to open our finite eyes to the infinite love of God. So "so" is, while seemingly simple, really profound and exceedingly difficult to translate as missionaries tell us. They sometimes have to use several words in place of "so." "So fully," "So freely," etc. One missionary waited on the Lord and listened long and closely to tribal conversations. Finally he had to settle for four words to replace "so." This translation when translated back into English reads: "God loved the world to such an extent that He gave ..."

The word "whoever" carries no such problems. A little boy in Sunday School, when asked what it meant replied immediately: "You, me, and anyone else." An apt answer. We can all put our names in place of "whoever." I remember some boys in my first Sunday School class literally doing that.

The word "believe" has been difficult to understand in English let alone translate it into another language. It is not only mental assent to truth about Christ but heart trust in Him. Reception of Him into our lives with obedience. It is commitment to Christ Jesus as Lord and Saviour. Another missionary seeking the equivalent for "believe" in the language of his area found it in this fashion. He was once travelling with the tribe when the chief, with his small son by his side, came to a deep gully. The only crossing was by way of a slippery log. The little boy was fearful and held back. The missionary, observing the scene heard the following conversation: "Come" said the father "climb on my back and just lean your whole weight on me." Eureka, thought the missionary. There's the commitment and obedient trust of true believing. Translated back into English it reads: "...that who leans his whole weight on Him shall not perish..."

Reading John 3:16 with these three thoughts we have this real expression of truth. "For God loved the world to such an extent that He gave His only begotten Son, that you, me, or anyone else who leans his whole weight on Him should not perish but have everlasting life."

JANUARY 13 – LOVE'S SECOND "3:16"

John's first "3:16" in his Gospel is well known to most of us. But we are not so well versed, either mentally or experientially, with this second "3:16" in his Epistle. "We know love by this, that He laid down His life for us; and we ought to lay down our lives for the brethren."[1] We have no problem with the first truth expressed here as this is the known Gospel, John 3:16 expressed in shorter form with added emphasis. "We know love by this…" God's love, in the gift of His Son, and the Son's love in the gift of His life, reveal, to all who have their eyes opened what divine love in its breadth and depth really means. This knowledge has brought us salvation through grace and by faith's acceptance. Subjects for great personal gratitude and rejoicing. His costly Cross provided us redemption "…without money and without cost."[2] We rejoice in this message.

However, the cost accounting doesn't end there – the last half of John's second "3:16" reminds us of consequential love, not comparable to His love, but costly just the same. "…and we ought to lay down our lives for the brethren." Aye, here's the rub and maybe the reason why this second John 3:16 is hardly known and rarely quoted. One consequence of this divine loving-giving is a demand for discipleship which counts the cost and a willingness to pay it. "Truth and Consequences" is not a game, this is life; the Christian life, the Christ life and Christlikeness constrains us to lay down our lives for others. Do we delight in this method?

What does this include? It may mean martyrdom for Christ, His church or fellow Christians. A young man named Bill McChesney did this for a brother missionary during the Congo (Zaire) revolution of the 1960's. He could have saved his life but chose to stay with his friend, knowing the cost. The mocking words of the crowd to Christ on the cross: "…He saved others; let Him save Himself…"[3] unwittingly described what neither He nor Bill, nor any other saint can do. If we would save others, we cannot save ourselves. While His saving work was unique and special, saving others is still a Scriptural statement for us. While we may think it optional (and it is) there is an inner compulsion, that is an imperative, compelling us to stay with a situation as Bill did. Another paradox – we can and yet we can't! Never forget that we are his "means", and also what this means. Not many of us will be called to literally lay down our lives. However the world situation is beginning to indicate that much more persecution and many more martyrdoms may be in the making. Be that as it may, love that lays down its life for others is living martyrdom.

Lest this conjure up an altogether false and joyless picture of "pickled" people, sour saints etc., let me hasten to clarify. "Martyr" is a transliteration of the Greek word for "witness." We are all to be his living, loving witnesses with all the power, joy, and strength given by the Spirit for the continual sacrifice and laying down of our lives that this entails. John 3:16 is the Gospel in a nutshell. 1 John 3:16, as someone said: "Shows we are the nutshells that must be broken."

JANUARY 14 – THIS IS MY BELOVED SON

Beloved is an admirable adjective, delightfully descriptive of someone greatly loved and dear to the heart. Agapé is the word we will be using to describe the holy, heavenly love of God. It has become reasonably well known in Christian circles in recent years with books about agapé and a TV programme named "Agapé." Then just a few days ago we went to a summer vacation Bible camp finale where our beloved granddaughter was, with many others, singing the songs and choruses she had learned. I noted, in the dialogue the leader had with these little ones, that he made special reference to God's love as Agapé. I was impressed. As long as it is explained to them, children quickly learn there is something very special and different about God's love. It's all connected with our adjective. "Agapetos" – beloved, is from the verb "agapao" – "to love." So we have this lovely family of words, verb, noun, and adjective, all love words which are used regularly in the New Testament, about His heavenly and earthly families.

The Father spoke from heaven expressing His love for and delight in His Son with these words: "…This is My beloved Son, in whom I am well-pleased."[1] The occasion was the public baptism of Jesus by John in the Jordan river. This marked the commencement of our Saviour's final three years of intense ministry culminating with His death and resurrection. At His baptism the heavens were opened and the symbolic dove descended upon Him, a sign of the Holy Spirit anointing the Son for service. These miraculous signs preceded the Voice, acknowledging with affection, the relationship of the Father to the Son. God loved His Son and wanted the entire world to know it; for it was for the world He had been given. Agapé's heart and home is in heaven and now heaven attests that the Beloved has come to earth.

It happened again at the Son's transfiguration. This was a metamorphosis (the word actually used in the text). It was a transformation of His essential form, proceeding from within. It was a brief and glorious unveiling of His eternal glory. In the blinding sunlight of His face and the shining white as light garments, the three disciples were silent in their awe. Except for Peter! Moses and Elijah appeared also from heaven but again were overshadowed by the Voice saying: "This is My beloved Son, with whom I am well-pleased; listen to Him!"[2] No wonder the three fell on their faces in awesome wonder and worship.

We will do the same, and we will listen to Him. After the beloved Son completed his work of redemption and returned to the glory from whence He had come, these prophetic words were fulfilled as they will be fully consummated at His second coming. "Lift up your heads, O gates, And be lifted up, O ancient doors, That the King of glory may come in! Who is the King of glory? The Lord strong and mighty, The Lord mighty in battle."[3] The beloved Son, the King of glory, had returned victorious from the battle. "To the praise of the glory of His grace, wherein He hath made us accepted in the beloved."[4]

JANUARY 15 – THE LOVE OF GOD

I recently made a serendipitous discovery. A book amongst <u>The Classics of Faith and Devotion</u> series entitled <u>On the Love of God</u> by that lover of God, of the Middle Ages, St. Bernard of Clairvoux (1090 - 1153). He was certainly clear sighted in this area and reiterates truth about the love of God that needs reemphasis today.

"Love is the fountain of life, and the soul which does not drink from it cannot be called alive."

Writing in his treatise <u>On the Love of God</u> says editor Dr. James M. Houston:

"Bernard, in the twelfth century, had already begun his theology of love. Love is the beginning and the end of life, for God is love. Since love is of God, the experience of love in God can only come through Jesus Christ His Son. It is the gift of love that orients the soul to God. Thus love is not something that is just desirable and pleasant to experience, as one option among others. It is man's whole reason for existing at all. That is why the figure of the bride in the Canticles (Song of Songs) appealed to these theologians of love. It is the proper imagery of the soul before God."

Moving on from the source and satisfaction of divine love, through the sacrifice of the Son, Bernard examines:

"our universal obligation to love God because He is God, and he finds that the measure of our love is to love Him without measure. If a man is to be made a lover, then that means he is created free, free to choose. But by reason of the fall of man, man chooses the wrong things in idolatry, worshiping the creation instead of the Creator. He loves also selfishly, loving himself in the place of God. Man, therefore, has by grace to grow out of such baser and perverted forms of love and come to love God for His own sake and also to love himself as God loves him. Then he shall relate to God not by fusion, as water may identify in a barrel of wine but as a bride to a bridegroom, free to choose the one loved."

Bernard teaches us more about the essential place of the will in love in his treatise <u>On Free Will and Grace</u>. This is only another way of seeing once more that man is made to love God. But to love God with disinterested love, he must first be free. Relating to God, then, becomes a progressive growth in freedom. William of St-Thiery (1085 – 1148?) sees:

"…that the exercise of love lies in the will. But in the wilfulness of sin and its rebellion against God, love is impure and deflected from loving God. Only those who humbly obey God are really docile to love. It needs the Will or Spirit of God to transform our own wills in order to love God as we should…that we might realize the love 'being shed abroad in our hearts by the Holy Spirit.'"

"We shall then begin to find that love and reason give us bi-focal vision on life; we are given depth to reality that is beyond mere intellectualism as love enlightens reason and reason instructs love. Without love, reason leads only to pride, while love without reason is passion. This bi-focal view then provides wisdom."

We are grateful to Dr. Houston and Multnomah Press for reintroducing us, eight hundred years after his death, to Bernard <u>On the Love of God</u>.

JANUARY 16 – LOVE, "A" MANY SPLENDOURED THING

Francis Thompson (1859 – 1907), one of England's great poets, lived but a short life. A sad, rebellious life, until divine love, shown through human love, rescued him. We tell more of his story later (November 11) in "Flying from Love", which is the title I give to Thompson's life as is told in <u>The Hound of Heaven</u>. There he describes his futile flight "from this tremendous Lover."

Here, however, I want to give the source of the sub-title of this book "Love, the many-splendoured thing." It derives, as the Epigraph tells, from Francis Thompson and his poem <u>The Kingdom of God</u> and is found in the line which speaks regretfully of those "…that miss the many-splendoured thing." To quote it more fully:

> "The angels keep their ancient places;
> Turn but a stone and start a wing!
> 'Tis ye, 'tis your estranged faces
> That miss the many-splendoured thing."

We are told that to estrange, is to turn away in feeling or affection; to alienate the affections of someone, or to cause to be strange or as a stranger. "Estranged faces" are turned away from affection, friendship, human love, and worst of all divine love. Yet, as Thompson found out to his eternal benefit, God's face was not estranged from him. That tremendous lover and His many-splendoured love hounded him until he about faced and came home.

Long after the poet's home-call another writer borrowed Thompson's line "The many-splendoured thing", changing the article from definite to indefinite. Chinese doctor, Han Suyin wrote a highly acclaimed book <u>A Many-splendoured Thing</u> published in 1952. This is her personal story, when as a widow after eight years of marriage, with her daughter, Mei, she goes to Hong Kong after completion of her medical studies in Britain. It begins in 1949 about the time of the exodus of missionaries from China. She gives, not unsympathetic, but unflattering, portraits of some of the missionaries with whom she came in contact. Her first chapter is called "Exodus from China" and her second is entitled (shades of Thompson) "The Kingdom of God." But <u>A Many-splendoured Thing</u> does not major on missionaries, the "Kingdom of God", or divine love. It is a human love story, an interracial one, described thus when published:

> "In the cosmopolitan surroundings of Hong Kong she meets and falls in love with Mark Elliott, the correspondent of a British newspaper. The book is a singularly frank memorial to their love, for Mark is killed in Korea. The happiness it diffuses is a measure of their courage and faith for both know from the first that everything is against them…With her unfaltering honesty, fine balance and astonishing feel for the English language she has written an outstanding love story."

The author writes a requiem for a love that was doomed from the outset. The supreme sorrow is something we, with regret, have to state; sadly Han Suyin did not come to know "the" many-splendoured love. Natural love is for mutual comfort, the continuation of the race, and the nurturing care of the family. It is "a" many-splendoured thing and when coupled with "the" many-splendoured thing, which is the love of God, then earthly blessing and heavenly bliss, which is God's will for us, become reality. Suyin, like so many others, seems to have missed it.

JANUARY 17 – LOVE, "THE" MANY SPLENDOURED THING

Dr. Leon Morris, in his book <u>The Testaments of Love</u>, (which is a study of love right through the Bible) shows what "the" many-splendoured thing, divine love, really is. These splendours include studies of the love of God; friendship love; romantic love; natural affection and other aspects of this greatest of all subjects. Each has its own special colour and radiance; combined they form an arc of prismatic colours, a rainbow; dissolved they emerge as the one white light, and one word, love.

Here we are going to examine the major love; God's love. To use the word minor, of the other loves is misleading for each has its own importance. Natural or lesser loves would perhaps be more appropriate. These loves are categorized in these pages but life's loves are not segregated in boxes; they flow from and into one another and are gloriously mixed at times, like pigments on a painter's palette. We needn't stop loving to ask ourselves: "Am I engaged in agapé, philia, eros or charity?" That would be foolish. We are seeking enlightenment along the lines of Paul's prayer: "…that you, being rooted and grounded in love may be able to comprehend with all the saints what is the breadth and length and height and depth, and to know the love of Christ which surpasses knowledge..."[1] To do this we need to know about love in its varied forms – the right and good loves and wrong and inordinate loves.

So, first things first. The love of God – the love of Christ – the love of the Spirit, Trinitarian love is my name for it. The Greek term is agapé. Dr. Morris says:

"An interesting feature of the New Testament is that even though so many words for love were available and in common use, the Christians preferred to use another one – namely agapé. This word is not entirely new but it was not common before the New Testament."

Agapé is, as it is specially demonstrated in the gift of His Son, a self-giving, self-sacrificing and serving love, given irrespective of merit in the object.

Agapé is God's gift love; as He gave Himself in His Son for the reconciliation of the world; as the Son gave Himself on the cross for our redemption; as the Spirit gives Himself in our regeneration and sanctification and pours out the Love of God in our hearts. Agapé is trinitarian, self-giving, objective, holy, "earthed", and mostly unrequited love.

It is "earthed" love because the Son came to earth to manifest it in loving concrete fashion. Now it is "earthed" in and through us, his born-again, Spirit controlled people. It is for the whole world and only "gets there" by us. This many-splendoured love of God is freely and fully given to us and we by thanksgiving and "thanksliving" share it, and show it to others.

JANUARY 18 – G – I – L GOD IS LOVE

From the book <u>The Wall of Partition</u> we here introduce its hero Rodney Steele. He had travelled the world in despair after being estranged from the woman he loved. He had been absent from London for ten years but, now returned, the text and the truth, "God is love" kept being brought before him. As he reflected in sadness that love had failed him, he also saw that he had rejected God's love. He was, at that time, living in Harley Street, and in the lower apartment of that same building was the widow of a Bishop. He met Mrs. Bellamy and in the course of conversation they discussed a novel which had captured the London public. The widow condemned the book, (not knowing that Steele was the author), because it portrayed bitterness; betrayed ideals and dismayed her by its disbelief in love. Altogether it was a book that would not only depress people but make them sour and cynical. One can imagine how the author felt as Mrs. Bellamy gave her opinions, still in ignorance that Steele was the author.

She then went on to tell him, in contrast, of her own and her late husband's experience. They had been living and ministering in a rural area of Surrey County. The village in which they were based had experienced an epidemic of scarlet fever and diphtheria. Both had worn themselves out in attending the stricken children and then, just as the epidemic was abating, their own three little ones were suddenly smitten. Within two weeks Griselda, Irene and Launcelot were dead.

When his last child died, Bishop Bellamy led his heartbroken wife into the garden that soft summer evening. Speech was difficult for sorrow was sore! Out of his grief the loving husband and father sought to comfort his wife. He finally whispered, rather than spoke to her:

"My wife, there is one rope to which we must cling steadfastly, in order to keep our heads above water amid these overwhelming waves of sorrow. It has three golden strands. It will not fail us. God – is – love."

The widow stopped, still living that long ago grief. Then continued, saying to Steele:

"The house was empty. There was no more patter of little feet; no children's voices merrily shouting about the house. The three little graves in the churchyard bore their names and on each we put the text, spelt out by the initials of our darling's names: G-od and G-riselda; I-s and I-rene; L-ove and L-auncelot. We were sustained by the certainty of the love of God. God – is – love on each grave."

What a thought! G – I – L

This telling, by the widowed lady, of their loss and God's love to the little ones in calling them home early, and of His succouring love to the parents left behind, became the means God used to force Steele to face himself, his past, and his lost love of a woman, and of God. Rodney Steele repented and was saved.

The purposes of God in the lives of the Bellamys, their children, and Steele merged and emerged again in that rope of three golden strands of which the Bishop had spoken. God – is – love. Three monosyllables; three beats, three notes of music; three golden strands; the threefold cord: God – is – love.

JANUARY 19 – LOVE IS NOT GOD!

This title is purposefully put in this provocative form to remind us of the whole statement: God is love but love is not God. This is the grave error of the misguided in love, of all ages; especially it would seem today when what passes for love is defied. Hit parades parade the travesty, look at any list of titles; theatre marquees market the money making lie, while newspapers, books, radio and television all trumpet the untruth: "Love is god." The whole media world, with few exceptions, seems bound in a latter day conspiracy to ridicule, deny or decry the truth that God is, and God is love. They scream God isn't; God certainly isn't love. Love is; love is the only god. While we have really been indicting "lust" as the four letter substitute for the right "love", it should never be forgotten, what we will be saying in a dozen different ways that even the good loves: friendship, brotherly, philanthropic, family, patriotic etc. can also be deified. We shall also see that deity can turn out to be a demon.

Friendship love can become any one of several abominations such as lesbianism or homosexuality. Brotherly love can be a limited fraternity indeed; politically, socially, economically, and religiously. Philanthropic love is seen today in the paradox of millionaire politicians calling for the redistribution of wealth while jealously guarding, by every tax dodge possible, their own patrimony. The Scriptural caution about the rich must have an added weight of judgment today. Family love can turn into a tyrannous demand of parents or children of others, ruining all in the process. When given, or demanded, like this it can destroy for it is a "smother" love. Patriotic love can be as Samuel Johnson (1709 – 1784) said:

"The last refuge of a scoundrel."

But all this is talking of the debasement of right, good, proper, and lovely loves. Any one can see that in that form, they are demon possessed, self destroying like the lunatic among the tombs. But we hardly believe that in their highest forms, they can also be called demons. The devil dresses "as an angel of light to deceive"[1] and likewise his demons do his deadly soul destroying work not with pitchforks, forked tails, and fiery blasts from the pit, but with the seduction of loves divorced from the control of the love of God, the God who is love.

M. Denis de Rougement (1906 – 1985), earlier in this century, wrote that:

"Love ceases to be a demon only when he ceases to be a god"

which sums up this page. It reminds us of the epigraph of John Donne (1573 – 1631):

"That our affections kill us not, nor dye."

Our frequent mentor in love, C. S. Lewis (1898 – 1963), points out that Rougement's remark can be restated in the form:

"Love begins to be a demon the moment he begins to be a god."

This balance seems to me an indispensable safeguard. If we ignore it, the truth that God is love may slyly come to mean the inverse, that love is god.

JANUARY 20 – IS GOD ALWAYS LOVE?

Some of us have memories which go back to the days of "samplers"; of children using coloured threads at school to pick out texts and mottoes. Now the wheel has turned a half century and many adults and children are engaged in similar arts today. Petit-point, cross stitch, tatting, and weaving are all in vogue again. Perhaps they always have been, but I was too busy about other things to notice.

I do remember an early sample of a bookmark, hand done, which I carried in a Bible years ago. On the underside it was a mess. A jumble of colours and a jungle of letters. It had no aesthetic appeal and no legible message. The top side, the right side, the true side, was beautiful in choice of coloured threads and clarity of message. The truth shone out in the words, the oh so familiar words: "God is love."

It was in the last century, in Durham County (in the North of England where my parents lived as children at that same time), that the beloved Dr. Handley Moule (1841 – 1920), Bishop of Durham, an outspoken evangelical Anglican, made effective use of such a bookmark and its message. The coalfields of Durham County and the City of Newcastle-on Tyne, were conversation topics of my parents after they had moved to the South of England. I remember Dad talking of the "banks of the coaly Tyne" and "where there's muck there's money." He and mother, when young, I'm sure heard the Bishop speak for they were brought up in the evangelical, Anglican, low church tradition.

They may have been living near there when the tragic West Stanley colliery disaster took place in 1909. Dr. Moule went there immediately and spoke to the anxious crowd of waiting relatives and friends gathered at the pit-head wheelhouse. With entombed miners below, the Bishop dared to speak on the subject: "God is love."

"It's very difficult for us to understand why God should let such an awful disaster happen, but we know Him, and trust Him, and all will be right. I have at home an old bookmark given me by my mother. It is worked in silk, and, when I examine the wrong side of it, I see nothing but a tangle of threads crossed and re-crossed. It looks like a big mistake made by someone who did not know what she was doing. But, when I turn it over and look at the right side, I see there beautifully embroidered, the letters 'God is love'. We are looking at all this today from the wrong side. Some day we shall see it from another standpoint, and shall understand."

Years later, some who were present said they had been unforgettably helped and comforted by his message.

It is a text, a truth, and a theme which stands the tests of time, of tragedy, and of triumph. There is no occasion, circumstance or happening of good or ill, that is outside the omnipresence, omniscience, and omnipotence of the God who is love. These three big O's of love's presence, prescience, and power become more relevant when we put the "Omni" before them. "God is love" means He is present at all times: He is omnipresent. "God is love" means He always knows all about everything: He is omniscient. "God is love" means he has all power, in heaven and earth: He is omnipotent. Read Psalm 139 in the light of these words.

JANUARY 21 – LOVING THE UNSEEN ONE

In September 1938, as I was about to leave Sydney, Australia for the beginning of my missionary calling, a group of friends gave me a wrist watch. I had spent two or three years with them in fellowship and Christian work and their farewell gift marked this association. On the back of the watch were the words:

"Presented to Mr. J. L. Davey as a love token from Bolgowlah Prayer Meeting, 12.9.38. 1 Peter 1:8."

Of course I quickly checked the reference and read "Whom having not seen, ye love; in whom, though now ye see Him not, yet believing ye rejoice with joy unspeakable and full of glory." I still have that watch and for forty-five years have consulted the back on occasions, more meaningfully than I have glanced at the front. When the "seen things" pressed me sore, that word on my wrist has helped me to look off by faith to the "Unseen One" I love. His unseen presence has been with me all the days and in all my ways.

To buy something sight unseen is a risky business. One might well end up, if it's a land purchase, with a swamp in Florida, as some speculators have. To love unseen, on the human level, is even more risky, though Isaac and Rebekah did. But to love the risen Lord demands only an act of faith. Multitudes of witnesses tell of His love and of their experience of that love.

Once when wearing a witness badge in my lapel with the words:

"What think ye of Christ?" on it I was cheered when a man reading it said:
"He is altogether lovely. He is the fairest of ten thousand to my soul!"

He had experienced unseen love, and so was I, and as we talked, we found this "unsubstantial" love, wonderfully solid and satisfying.

"How sovereign, powerful and free,
Has been His love to sinful me."
Samuel Medley (1738 – 1799)

When our Lord walked this earth He was the unknown One, now He is the unseen One – seen by the eye of faith. After his resurrection He was often seen but unrecognized even by His own. "…Jesus came and stood in their midst, and said to them, 'Peace be with you.' And when He had said this He showed them both His hands and His side. The disciples therefore rejoiced when they saw the Lord[1]…But Thomas, one of the twelve, called Didymus, was not with them when Jesus came. The other disciples therefore were saying to him 'We have seen the Lord!' But he said to them 'Unless I see in His hands the imprint of the nails…I will not believe.'"[2] Thomas was like those today from the state of Missouri: "I'm from Missouri; you've got to show me!" The Lord showed Thomas and lovingly rebuked him and lovingly encourages us the same time. "Because you have seen Me, have you believed? Blessed are they who did not see, and yet believed."[3] As we go on not seeing but believing, and by faith finding substance and pleasing God we also find inexpressible joy as a corollary. "…the proof of your faith, being more precious than gold…may be found to result in praise and glory and honor at the revelation of Jesus Christ; and though you have not seen Him, you love Him, and though you do not see Him now, but believe in Him, you greatly rejoice with joy inexpressible and full of glory."[4]

JANUARY 22 – LOVE CHOOSING

As we saw earlier, in the history of Israel it was divine love, unwarranted and unmerited, that prompted the choosing of that nation for His sovereign purposes. Israel was chosen not to be a pet, but a pattern of righteousness in the earth. Scripture makes clear that she failed, but she did not fail in God's prime purpose: that through her His righteous one would come the Christ, the Saviour, Jesus.

Joshua in his deathbed speech, at 110 years of age, reviews the story of the nation from the time of God's choice of Abraham until the then present. Now he changes the emphasis. It is their responsibility, having been chosen by God to now choose him. Love chose – love chooses. Joshua, who had led the way in this, did it again before he died, in the memorable words: "…as for me and my house, we will serve the Lord."[1] That generation that knew Joshua and the elders and had seen the loving goodness, severity, and power of God, did make the reciprocal response of love, choosing, serving and loving the Lord. Succeeding generations did not. We won't pursue that sad catalogue of events but make some applications for ourselves.

We are living today with the consequences of choices, right or wrong, made not by us, but by our parents and fore parents back to Adam. He, with Eve, made the original wrong choice, bringing sin and death into the world and tainting us with the bias toward self will and wrong choices.

It is the choices we make that concern us here, for God has provided the last Adam, Christ, to come in grace and undo the results of the first Adam's fatal choice. We won't be doomed by Adam's choice but by our own choice or rejection of Christ. Love found a way to redeem us through the gift of His Son who chose to offer Himself to the death on the cross for sin and sinners. My decision will determine my destiny. My discipleship will determine the eternal destiny of others.

For a number of years we have had the text: "As for me and my house, we will serve the Lord" in the entrance of our apartment. It is a testimony and an expression of our desire to keep on making the love choices that glorify Him, bring good to others, and blessing to ourselves and families.

The most important love choice was His in choosing us in His Son. The next most important was our love choice of Him. Third in the scale of love choices was that of choosing a marriage partner. As will later be specifically pointed out, we should ask our heavenly Father to choose the suitable life companion. Then we should wait and watch and when the signs are evident, then make the love choice of whom He has chosen. It is not as simple as it sounds but it is possible. These three choices of love have eternal results in the lives for which we are further responsible. An important truth is frequently missed by the omission of a few words at the end of a well known verse: "Believe in the Lord Jesus, and you will be saved, you and your household…"[2] Love choosing right includes the promise of household salvation.

JANUARY 23 – LOVING AND LIKING

The English language is fortunate to have the verbs to love and to like. This is very useful when we wish to distinguish having pleasure in, or liking, and having a deep affection for, or loving. Most often liking has to do with things, but it's also frequently used of people, while loving usually has to do with people, but is frequently used of things. To confuse things more, we who have an English heritage and language, often use the one verb when we should be using the other.

C. S. Lewis (1898 - 1963), as to be expected, and with his usual clarity, has something to say about these two verbs and the way we interchange them.

"Most of my generation were reproved as children for saying that we loved strawberries, and some people take a pride in the fact that English has the two verbs love and like while French has to get along with aimer for both. But French has a good many other languages on its side too. Nearly all speakers, however pedantic, or however pious, talk every day about loving a food, a game, or a pursuit. And in fact there is a continuity between our elementary likings for things and our loves for people. Since the highest does not stand without the lowest we had better begin at the bottom, with mere likings; and since to like anything means to take some sort of pleasure in it, we must begin with pleasure."

Here we must leave him as he goes on to describe need-pleasures and need-loves and our loving and liking them.

I wish to introduce here a Scriptural happening in which both loving and liking are seen. Each rightly descriptive of both person's emotions and feelings for the other but where the use of one verb was entirely inappropriate. I speak of the after breakfast one on one conversation, and in effect, counselling session our Lord had with Peter. The point of that dialogue is frequently lost because most translations don't differentiate between the two Greek words agapé and philia. J. B. Phillips translation is quoted fully and deliberately, because he makes the play as the Lord does on the two words. It opens up the meaning of the dialogue and shows the difference between liking and loving.

But hear the Word of God: "When they had finished breakfast Jesus said to Simon Peter, 'Simon, son of John, do you love me more than these others?' 'Yes, Lord,' he replied, 'you know that I am your friend.' 'Then feed my lambs,' returned Jesus. Then he said for the second time, 'Simon, son of John, do you love me?' 'Yes, Lord,' returned Peter. 'You know that I am your friend.' 'Then care for my sheep,' replied Jesus. Then for the third time, Jesus spoke to him and said, 'Simon, son of John, are you my friend?' Peter was deeply hurt because Jesus' third question to him was 'Are you my friend?', and he said, 'Lord, you know everything. You know that I am your friend!'"[1] This dialogue, in this translation, clarifies everything for me. It is the difference between lover and friend; between loving and liking. Later we will return to Peter and see what a difference Pentecost made.

The next time you hear someone say "I like that person but I didn't love him or her." think again of Peter, and apply the truth. Ask yourself the questions: "Do I like the Lord Jesus or do I really love Him?" "Is it friendship or love?" It can be, and is, according to the New Testament both; but mere friendship alone is a level too low for our Lord.

JANUARY 24 – LOVE FOR CHRIST – AND A LIKING FOR CRICKET

Cricket, lovely cricket! Canadians and Americans might think this heading refers to that lively and noisy little insect. But it's the name of a game I have in mind. While the editorial in today's "Edmonton Journal" (June 2, 1984) refers to "the arcane rituals of cricketers" we who know England, Australia, New Zealand and the West Indies know better.

As a schoolboy in England I played cricket and "soccer" football. As a young man in Australia I spent a weeks vacation at the Sydney Cricket Ground watching the final game of the 1931,'32 series between England and Australia. Then, when in the West Indies, what a wonderful time we had when the visiting teams came. We would pack a lunch basket and relax by going to watch a few hours of play.

In 1965 when the Australians were in Barbados, we were privileged to have Brian Booth (1933 -), Christian cricketer, gentleman and captain of their team, visit and have a meal with the family. What a happy time that was as we talked of Christ and cricket.

Now I am enjoying reading Brian's cricket autobiography Booth to Bat. More than thirty years ago Brian was led to Christ by a former cricketer, then minister at St. George's Church, Hurtsville. Brian tells the story in his chapter: "New Captain – New Rules."

"The parson had impressed me by his friendliness and sincerity but I had no idea he was a cricketer. He continued to take an interest in my cricket. I heard some of his exploits from Arthur Morris, who told me: 'Roy Gray could have played Sheffield Shield if he hadn't gone in the ministry.'"

This godly minister, lover of Christ, lover of souls, and liker of cricket tackled Brian directly about the claims of Christ. But let Brian tell it like it was.

"One particular evening he came directly to the point. 'Brian, do you know Jesus Christ in a personal way?' I was speechless. The colours of the St. George Club are red and white. That night my face was true to club colours. No one had ever asked me a question like that before. I stammered out: 'I believe in God, if that's what you mean.' 'Well, partly, but it's more than a belief that God exists. Look.' He opened a Bible and read from John's Gospel Chapter 3 Verse 16. 'God loved the world so much that He gave His only Son, that everyone who believes in Him should not be lost, but have eternal life...' he read the verse again and personalized it. 'God loved Brian Booth so much that he gave His only Son, so that if Brian Booth believes in Him he will not be lost but have eternal life.'"

That's how Brian came to Christ. Through the best known and loved verse in the Bible. A lover of Christ with a liking for cricket led to Christ a lover of cricket, who in turn became a lover of Christ, with a still strong liking for cricket. They have their verbs and priorities right.

JANUARY 25 – LOVING GOD AND OBEDIENCE

In the Old Testament, as far as Israel obeyed God, in that measure she loved God. Obedience and love are eternally linked in the Scriptures, and what God has united let no one separate. "You shall therefore love the Lord your God, and always keep His charge, His statutes, His ordinances, and His commandments."[1] "It shall come about, if you listen obediently to my commandments which I am commanding you today, to love the Lord your God and to serve Him with all your heart and all your soul, that He will give the rain for your land in its season, the early and late rain..."[2] "For if you are careful to keep all this commandment which I am commanding you to do, to love the Lord your God, to walk in all His ways and hold fast to Him, then the Lord will drive out all these nations from before you...Every place on which the sole of your foot treads shall be yours."[3] These are the promises of omnipotent love to obedient love.

This threefold iteration of the truth that love and obedience are indissoluble goes further in showing, by the repeated "Ifs" and "Thens", the personal and national consequences of this loving obedience. Obedient love is responsible, accountable, and has built in rewards. His love producing and resulting in obedience is the really personal, truly practical and Biblically normal love. He chose Israel because He loved, and as Israel responded properly and practically to His love, the rewarding "Thens" followed the conditional "Ifs". Conversely, "If" they ceased to love and obey Him, "Then" evil consequences would follow automatically.

The history of Israel, measured by millennia, has been a constant illustration of these truths that flow from the major promise. Loving God means obeying Him. The history of the Church, churches, and individuals illustrate the theme. He loved and obeyed His Father. He loved and became obedient unto death for you and me.

"I stand amazed in the presence of Jesus the Nazarene,
And wonder how He could love me, A sinner, condemned, unclean.
O how marvellous! O how wonderful! And my song shall ever be:
O how marvellous! O how wonderful is my Saviour's love for me!"
Charles Gabriel (1856 – 1932).

He says "Show me." He tells me: "If you love Me, you will keep My commandments"[4] "He who has My commandments and keeps them is the one who loves Me..."[5] "...if anyone loves Me, he will keep My word; and My Father will love him, and We will come to him and make Our abode with him. He who does not love Me does not keep My words..."[6] This is clear and unequivocal.

Love to Christ is equated with obedience to Him, to the keeping of His commandments, and the hearing and reading of His word. It is repeated three times in the same chapter just as Israel was reminded of the same truth three times.

We should sit up, take stock, and start to love Him personally and practically by the loving giving of ourselves and substance to people we can see. C. T. Studd (1860 - 1931), a wealthy sportsman, searched his New Testament to see if he was obeying all the commands of Christ. He read of the rich young man who was told to give away his fortune but disobeyed. Studd obeyed, gave his fortune away and went away rejoicing the rest of the way.

JANUARY 26 – TO LOVE GOD IS TO OBEY HIM

There are several emphases of love which will become apparent through this book. One is the transfiguration of all the natural loves by agapé – holy, heavenly love. Another is the process of purifying and perfecting the lesser loves by death in life, and death at the end of life. The third emphasis that is repeatedly stressed is this: We love God in the same measure that we obey Him. Old and New Testament Scriptures are used to show the connection between love to God and doing what He commands. Agapé demonstrated by and resulting in action. I illustrate it again by pointing out an important book with the same emphasis.

I have heard the author speak on how it came to be possible for him to write such a story. The book is Charles Colson's (1931 -) <u>Loving God</u>. Colson, of Nixon's Watergate infamy, went to prison because of that criminal conspiracy. He was converted and wrote that story in his autobiographical <u>Born Again</u>. <u>Loving God</u> is his first doctrinal book, in which he teaches in various ways, and by numerous stories, the central theme that we only love God truly as we obey Him.

Colson and his colleagues are practising this in their work of Prison Ministries and Prisoner Fellowships. Having been a prisoner himself Charles Colson knows the needs of prisoners. Their supreme need is to know Christ as Saviour and Lord, and to be nurtured and helped afterwards. Colson not only preaches and writes about loving God, he practices it in obedience by helping to free prisoners from the inner bondage of Satan and sin, and caring for them. The numerous illustrations in the book make arresting impact; for they are true life stories of people whose love-obedience brought others into the light and life of love-obedience, and made others practitioners of it also.

One such story is the obscure Christian in the Russian prison system, the Gulag as it is called, and who lovingly and obediently bore his witness for Christ in that awful place. He spoke one day to a fellow prisoner, and it was almost his last witness on earth for he was killed shortly afterwards, never knowing that he was an instrument used in the conversion of Alexander Solzhenitsyn (1918 -).

The book of Deuteronomy was often quoted by our Lord, frequently referred to by other New Testament writers, and we need to read and heed it's repeatedly stressed theme: "To love God is to obey Him." Moses emphasizes it again as he draws to the close of his life. He introduces his subject with a few verses which are taken up by Paul in Romans. Heart faith. Heart obedience. Heart love like Jude's word in the New Testament: "keep yourselves in the love of God…"[1] This is a command and a choice like Moses. "I call heaven and earth to witness against you today, that I have set before you life and death, the blessing and the curse. So choose life in order that you may live, you and your descendants, by loving the Lord your God, by obeying His voice, and by holding fast to Him; for this is your life…"[2]

JANUARY 27 – LOV'ST THOU ME?

"Hark, my soul! It is the Lord;
'Tis thy Saviour, hear His word;
Jesus speaks, and speaks to thee:
"Say, poor sinner, lov'st thou Me?

Can a woman's tender care,
Cease toward the child she bare?
Yes, she may forgetful be;
Yet will I remember thee.

Mine is an unchanging love,
Higher than the heights above:
Deeper than the depths beneath,
Free and faithful, strong as death.

Lord, it is my chief complaint
That my love is weak and faint;
Yet I love Thee, and adore:
Oh, for grace to love Thee more."

William Cowper, (1731 – 1800) poet, "the singer of the dawn", as Dr. Arnold of Rugby used to call him, poses the question as if put by the Lord: "Say, poor sinner lov'st thou Me?" And answers it honestly and with a prayer: "Oh, for grace to love Thee more." This "singer of the dawn" sang his songs out of darkness and dearth. This poet, when a little lad of six was deprived of mother love when he was most in need of it. Late in life he was presented with a picture of her and turned the occasion into poetry.

"Oh that these lips had language! Life has passed
With me but roughly since I heard thee last
These lips are thine – thy own sweet smile I see,
The same that oft in childhood solaced me.

My mother, when I learn'd that thou wast dead,
Say, wast thou conscious of the tears I shed?
Perhaps thou gavs't me, though unfelt, a kiss;
Perhaps a tear if souls can weep in bliss.

I heard the bell toll'd on thy burial day;
I saw the hearse that bare thee slow away.
Thy maidens, grieved themselves at my concern,
Oft gave me promise of thy quick return.

Thus many a sad tomorrow came and went,
Till, all my stock of infant sorrow spent,
I learn'd at last submission to my lot,
But, though I less deplored thee, ne'er forgot."

"Mother," he seems to say "I know you loved me; and you know I loved you."

JANUARY 28 – HOW DO I LOVE THEE, LORD?

At best inadequately. At worst deplorably. Is this a wrong answer to the question or an honest evaluation? It is given in light of the Lord's question to Peter: "…do you love me more than these?"[1] and Peter's honest answers. And in the context of His other words: "So you too, when you do all the things which are commanded you, say, 'We are unworthy slaves; we have done only that which we ought to have done.'"[2] in the blinding light of His love, and His new commandment that we should love as He loved; which of us does not need to ask forgiveness for sins of omission and commission in all the loves, especially the highest, love for God?

Gerhard Tersteegen (1697-1769) wrote some glorious, though little known or sung hymns. We are thankful to those who translated them from the German to the English Methodist hymn book for perpetuating them. John Wesley (1703 – 1791) translated some of these hymns including the one that is relevant to our theme.

> "Thou hidden love of God, whose height,
> Whose depth unfathomed no one knows,
> I see from far Thy beauteous light,
> And inly sigh for Thy repose;
> My heart is pained, nor can it be
> At rest, till it finds rest in Thee.
>
> O hide this self from me, that I
> No more, but Christ in me, may live!
> My vile affections crucify,
> Nor let one darling lust survive
> In all things nothing may I see,
> Nothing desire or seek, but Thee!
>
> Each moment draw from earth away
> My heart that lowly waits Thy call;
> Speak to my inmost soul and say,
> "I am thy love, thy God, thy all!"
> To feel Thy power, to hear Thy voice,
> To taste Thy love, be all my choice."

Tersteegen states that his will seems fixed on this goal and his choice is for it. Surely God will make the lordship of love supreme in his life. God has done His part, Ours is to respond, initially confessing Jesus as Lord, because His Spirit has prepared the way. "…no one can say, 'Jesus is Lord,' except by the Holy Spirit.."[3] Many will say Lord, Lord and He will respond I never knew you. The lordship of love in our lives depends on the Spirits full control.

JANUARY 29 – HOW DO I LOVE THEE, LORD JESUS?

"Fairest Lord Jesus,
Ruler of all nature,
O Thou of God and man the Son:
Thee will I cherish,
Thee will I honour.
Thou my soul's glory joy and crown."

"I will." When we say it at the marriage ceremony and to Christ, our heavenly Bridegroom, we are willing ourselves to love. Thee will I worship, honour and cherish. Despite failures in the earthly fulfillment of our vows and worse of our pledges to our heavenly Lover we still say "I love you Lord Jesus," and He who knows the heart knows that this is our dearest deepest will.

Three times we have asked ourselves and sought to answer the question: How do I love Thee? How do I love Thee Lord? How do I love Thee Lord Jesus? We have listened to several witnesses give a self analysis of their love in the lesser, greater, and greatest loves. We heard a German lover of the Lord speak of his lack and his longing.

"Jesus, Thy boundless love to me
No thought can reach, no tongue declare;
Unite my thankful heart with Thee
And reign without a rival there.
To Thee alone, dear Lord, I live;
Myself to Thee, dear Lord, I give.

In suffering be Thy love my peace,
In weakness be Thy love my power;
And when the storms of life shall cease,
Jesus, in that important hour,
In death as life be Thou my guide,
And save me, Who for me hast died."
Paulus Gerhardt (1607-1676)

It is over 300 years since the death of Gerhardt and we stand in our mind's eye before another grave. It is July 1931 and the scene is in the then Belgian Congo, Africa. It is vivid to me because I have been reading a copy of the Worldwide Evangelization Crusade magazine for September and October 1931 which describes the homegoing of that lover of the Lord, Charles T. Studd (1860 - 1931). How did Studd love the Lord Jesus? The cover states: "A great innings ended." "And they overcame him because of the blood of the Lamb and because of the word of their testimony, and they did not love their life even when faced with death."[1] Inside the cover there is a picture of a balding, bearded, beak nosed, haggard looking man who had loved the Lord Jesus, by giving up his family, fame, and fortune to serve Christ in China, India, and Africa. Underneath the picture are the words:

"...We thank God...he has had such a death as he desired, preaching the Gospel up to the end, and his grave surrounded by hundreds of his native converts."

I turn to the back cover where Studd gives another answer to our question.

"Oh this Jesus, this marvellous Being, this wondrous Name above every other Name, to whom all shall presently bow; but it is our joy, our everlasting honour to bow to Him now, but in utter love and obedience and glorious abandonment."

"How do I love Thee, Lord Jesus?"

"That's how", said C. T. Studd.

JANUARY 30 – "DEUS CARITAS EST"

"God is love" in any language. A very special love, agapé which has been explained. The King James Version translation of agapé in 1 Corinthians 13 as charity needs clarification. Almost four hundred years ago the word charity – from the Latin caritas (dearness, love) - was carried over from the Latin Vulgate version and transliterated into English and was well understood. Four centuries later charity means almsgiving; the private or public relief of the poor, or other charitable acts, which may be prompted by love, or not. "Cold as charity" shows how far the word has been devalued. Rightly, in most modern translations, charity has been replaced by love. God today is not today's charity – God is love – and we have seen that this describes His nature, His essential being. Thus His love is holy love; His love is a consuming fire; His love is tender and severe; His love is terrible and comforting.

Is this confusing and contradictory? No, it is a Biblical explanation of those monosyllables "God is love." George MacDonald (1824 – 1905) calls this "Inexorable Love."

"Nothing is inexorable but love…For love loves unto purity…therefore all that is not beautiful in the beloved, all that comes between and is not of love's kind, must be destroyed. And our God is a consuming fire…When we say that God is love, do we teach men that their fear of Him is groundless? No, as much as they fear will come upon them, possibly more…Escape is hopeless…for love is inexorable."

Shall we flee from this holy, heavenly love? No! Fly to it, in repentance and faith, and find forgiveness and the fellowship of love. Thomas Merton (1915 – 1968), in his autobiography, <u>The Seven Storey Mountain</u>, tells of such a flight. First away from God into the morass of false philosophies, loves and lusts. Then of the reverse journey to find, as he calls it:

"this free gift of sanctifying grace…The real work is the work of grace and the infused gifts of the Holy Ghost. What is 'grace'? It is God's own life, shared by us. God's life is love. Deus caritas est. By grace we are able to share in this infinitely self-less love of Him…transfigured and transformed when the love of God shines in. The life of the soul is not knowledge, it is love…"

In 1938 Merton bowed to this inexorable love.

"I became more and more conscious of the necessity of a vital faith, and the total unreality and insubstantiality of the dead, selfish rationalism which had been freezing my mind and will for the last seven years…"

Merton's journey in life and love started that August and September.

Meanwhile, the winds of war were beginning to blow. The Munich crisis of September 1938 coincided with the start of my missionary vocation. That month I sailed from Sydney, Australia on the French steamer "Pierre Loti", bound for Neumea, New Caledonia. During the three week wait for the mainline ship to France I went up country in that large island to visit French missionaries. In one native village, when asked to give a message, I told the story of a man who built a wind direction indicator with "God is love" on it. That village church had a weather vane pointing North. That night my key comment was: whichever way the wind blows – God is love. Whatever kind of wind blows, God is love; inexorable love.

JANUARY 31 – GOD IS UNCHANGING LOVE

I now will tell the whole story of "Whichever way the wind blows, God is love. Whatever wind blows, God is love." On that long ago night, under the stars on the tropical island of New Caledonia, with a soft wind blowing, and the weather vane moving on the top of the village church, I told the crowd of islanders the story of the wind indicator on which was written: "God is love." These words I pointed out, could well be, in our imagination, on the weather vane above our heads. It was a quite ordinary weather van but typically French, being surmounted with a Gallic rooster. Fixing their attention on it, with the balmy breezes wafting to us the scent of frangipani, I added to the text "God is love" another one "…the wind blows where it wishes…"[1] for my message on God's unchanging love. Come wind, come weather: God is love.

The critic of the weather vane illustration might say: "But God and His love aren't changeable like the wind!" To which I reply: "the point of the story is that whatever kind of wind blows, God is love; from zephyr to hurricane. He is the unchanging God. No matter from which direction the wind blows, be it North, South, East, West or any of the compass points between God's love is steadfast, unchangeable."

The applications made that night in the South Pacific, before WWII, were suited to my audience's circumstances. I little knew that one year from that 1938 September (it was the month of the Munich crisis from which Chamberlain with his peace umbrella, returned from appeasing Hitler, waving his piece of paper – 'Peace in our time'), the cyclones of war would begin blowing in Europe and later in the Pacific. I have often wondered whether any of my congregation later, with the hurricane howling around them, remembered our open air meeting and the message. At the conclusion of the meeting the French missionary told me the theme had inspired him to replace the Gallic rooster with "God is love." I wonder did he ever do it? Some poet who signs himself only as J.H.S. wrote the substance of it all:

"God is love – whatever happens,
God is love – in Him we rest,
Tho' the wind around be blowing
From the North, South, East or West.

God is love – oh, grave it clearly
High across life's weather vane,
For in spite of outward seeming,
Naught God sends can be our bane.

God is love – then let us trust Him
Whether skies be dark of fair,
From all points of heaven's compass
The four winds His love declare."

"…and He appeared on the wings of the wind."[2] During our more than thirty years in the Caribbean, as every hurricane season approached, we wondered which of the West Indian islands would be in the path of the storm. Our dear Dominica was devastated in 1979. We were not there but "family" was. Like Paul in his storm they proved in reality, whatever wind blows: "God is love."

FEBRUARY 1 – "GOD, THOU ART LOVE!"

If I forget,
Yet God remembers! If these hands of mine
Cease from their clinging, yet the hands divine
Hold me so firmly that I cannot fall;
And if sometimes I am too tired to call
For Him to help me, then He reads the prayer
Unspoken in my heart, and lifts my care.

I dare not fear, since certainly I know
That I am in God's keeping, shielded so
From all that else would harm, and in the hour
Of stern temptation strengthened by His power;
I tread no path in life to Him unknown;
lift no burden, bear no pain, alone.
My soul a calm, sure hiding place has found:
The everlasting arms my life surround.

God, Thou art love! I build my faith on that.
I know Thee who has kept my path, and made
Light for me in the darkness, tempering sorrow
So that it reached me like a solemn joy;
It were too strange that I should doubt Thy love..."
Robert Browning (1812 – 1899)

The love of God was the foundation of Browning's being. We will be seeing this in more detail later in these pages. He not only talked of it in his poetry and conversation, but he practiced it in living, in this "dance of plastic circumstance" as he called it. It governed his romance with Elizabeth Barrett (1806 – 1861), one of the great love stories of the 19th century. The love of God carried him from youth to old age.

"My times be in Thy hand!
Perfect the cup as planned!
Let age approve of youth, and death complete the same!"

Browning saw life steadily, whole, and for the believer, as being held in the hands of love divine. He committed himself unreservedly to those compassionate controlling hands, and trusted, even when forgetful, tired, lonely the One who knew all and cared. "God, Thou art Love!"

In the above poem of that name, the poet introduces two areas where the love of God has sustained him. In the realm of prayer and the arena of temptation. We will be looking later at "The Love of God and Prayer" (April 28) and "The Love of God and Temptation." (February 2)

"And if sometimes I am too tired to call
For Him to help me, then He reads the prayer
Unspoken in my heart, and lifts my care."

How truly expressive of both what prayer can be and what the love of God is. The silent, burdened desire and need of the heart, read and responded to by divine love.

FEBRUARY 2 – THE LOVE OF GOD AND TEMPTATION

The distinction, often made between divine testing in love and devilish temptation in hate, is valid, but an oversimplification in some ways as we shall see. In a good sense it is said of Christ and his believers. "For since He Himself was tempted in that which He has suffered, He is able to come to the aid of those who are tempted."[1] The context shows that the temptation was the cause of suffering to Him, not a drawing away to sin, so that believers have the sympathy of Christ as their High Priest in the suffering which sin occasions to those who are in the enjoyment of communion with God. As evidenced by: "For we do not have a high priest who cannot sympathize with our weaknesses, but One who has been tempted in all things as we are, yet without sin."[2] There was no sinful infirmity in Him. W. E. Vine in his Expository Dictionary of New Testament Words comments on the word "tempt":

"in all the temptations which Christ endured, there was nothing within Him that answered to sin. There was no sinful infirmity in Him. While He was truly man, and His Divine nature was not in any way inconsistent with His Manhood, there was nothing in Him such as is produced in us by the sinful nature which belongs to us."

"...for the ruler of the world is coming, and he has nothing in Me; but so that the world may know that I love the Father, I do exactly as the Father commanded Me..."[3] Love led Jesus by the Spirit into the wilderness to be tempted by the devil, just as divine love would lead Him later to the Garden tests from which He emerged victorious. The love of God allowed the Son to be tempted to prove that as the last Adam He would triumph in the power of the Spirit and the Word.

In Eden, Satan, by his implied doubt of the loving benevolence and word of God, had gained the dominion. That Satanic solicitation to self-will against the will of God; that devious devilish attack on the obedience of love led to the fall of man. Contrasting the temptation of the "first man Adam" and the "last Adam" we see it as the temptation of the lordship of love. The first Adam lost out by listening to the siren call, and listening to the voice of Eve. Human love can often be the enemy of the highest love. Adam should have responded to his wife, as the Lord did to Peter, by saying "Get thee behind me Satan." But he didn't. Thank God, the last Adam, in all His temptations and tests of His loving obedience, regained by love and obedience all that the first Adam had lost.

We have discussed the original temptation in Eden and its counterpart in the wilderness because in them we have the essence of all devilish temptation. The three elements in Eve's temptation have been classified for all time as "...the lust of the flesh and the lust of the eyes and the boastful pride of life..."[4] These lusts used constantly by the prince of this world, are the enemies of love. His threefold temptation of Jesus was his effort to induce Jesus to act independently of His Father and in disobedience to the Father's love.

Here is where temptation and testing merge. God in love can over-rule devilish temptation and turn it into loving testing. The temptation of Christ became a test of love. Remember, "No temptation has overtaken you but such as is common to man; and God is faithful...will provide the way of escape."[5] Love will enable us to stand and resist or provide a way of escape.

FEBRUARY 3 – ANOTHER ONE OF LOVE'S TESTS

This was originally given to Israel, but has special relevance to the church and Christians today. ""If a prophet or a dreamer of dreams arises among you and gives you a sign or a wonder, and the sign or the wonder comes true, concerning which he spoke to you, saying, `Let us go after other gods (whom you have not known) and let us serve them,' you shall not listen to the words of that prophet or that dreamer of dreams; for the Lord your God is testing you to find out if you love the Lord your God with all your heart and with all your soul."[1]

Discernment of the Spirit is especially needed today when there are a multitude of "prophets," "prophecies," "visions" and "dreams" being given in the name of the Lord. How can we distinguish between the spurious, flesh generated, satanically originated and the truly Spirit inspired prophetic word? Especially, when the false is accompanied by "lying wonders" which are fulfilled! What the false prophet said came true! Isn't this the usual and conforming fact that indicates a true prophet and prophecy? Yes, it often is, but not always as our introductory Scriptures indicate.

All prophecies, by anyone, must be in line with Scripture and its spiritual and moral tenor and teaching. "To the law and to the testimony: if they speak not according to this word, it is because there is no light in them."[2] In these days of increasing Biblical ignorance among evangelicals it is little wonder that such are easily led astray by seducing spirits using seeming spiritual prophets. Some even to the road to Endor where like Saul they "...Consult the mediums and the spiritists who whisper and mutter..."[3]

Even those who know the Word are not immune to satanic temptation and deception especially when he comes disguised as an "angel of light."[4] Humility, holiness, control by the Spirit, awareness of satanic wiles plus spiritual discernment are pre-requisites for prevention of deceit. Knowing God and the Word and having on the whole armour of God helps us to overcome in the struggle "...against the rulers, against the powers, against the world forces of this darkness, against the spiritual forces of wickedness in the heavenly places.,"[5] and against all his schemes and flaming missiles. What we infrequently realize, while all the above is going on is that something else is taking place as well. Not only the testing of our faith but the testing of our love; in other words the testing of love: obedience.

We have seen that scripturally, love to God is linked with obedience to God and this is illustrated in the opening verses. When the false prophets seek to seduce us away from God, "to go after other gods," by the use of deceiving messages and miracles, let us also discern the testing of God in the tempting of the devil. In love God is permitting Satan to do this in order that we might be enabled to grow and show love in obedience. "...for the Lord your God is testing you to find out if you love the Lord your God with all your heart and with all your soul."

FEBRUARY 4 – LOVE'S BUFFETINGS

"Batter my heart, three person'd God; for, you
As yet but knocke, breathe, shine, and seeke to mend;
That I may rise, and stand, o'erthrow mee,'and bend
Your force, to breake, blowe, burn and make me new.
I, like an usurpt towne, to'another due,
Labour to'admit you, but Oh, to no end,
Reason your viceroy in mee, mee should defend,
But is captiv'd, and proves weake or untrue.
Yet dearely'I love you,'and would be loved faine,
But am betroth'd unto your enemie:
Divorce mee,'untie, or breake that knot againe;
Take mee to you, imprison mee, for I
Except you'enthrall mee, never shall be free,
Nor ever chast, except you ravish mee..."
John Donne (1573 – 1631)

The erudite Doctor, dean, preacher, poet and teacher, who wrote the above truths, knew what he was writing about. He had been badly battered about by life, love and death. He knew they were indivisible and inescapable and knew God used them to bring souls to Himself. Now he asks for more. Donne is either a masochist or a spiritually enlightened man. Does he take pleasure in pain or is he deeply learned in the divine ways of deliverance through destruction and life through death. He is well taught, and able to teach us, these paradoxical ways of God's perfecting of the saints. He knew to rise he must fall; to be mended he must first be rent; to be free he must be imprisoned; to live he must die and to be pure he must be ravished by eternal love.

God, using the battering ram of love, has broken into many a well guarded "city of man-soul." That citadel of the proud Pharisee Paul was breeched by all powerful love on the Damascus Road, nigh on two thousand years ago. Millions since, buffeted by "the slings and arrows of outrageous circumstance" have been humbled, brought to repentance and found, in retrospect, that love had engineered the "batterings" and enable them to sing the song of the soul set free:

"Make me a captive, Lord, and then I shall be free.
Force me to render up my sword, and I shall conqueror be.
I sink in life's alarms when by myself I stand;
Imprison me within Thine arms, and strong shall be my hand."
George Matheson (1842 – 1906)

Millennia have separated Paul and the preacher of St. Paul's yet both had been brought to their senses by blows. These bruisings brought them to Christ and now they are linked in their longings and writings for a deeper experience of liberating love. "I find then the principle that evil is present in me, the one who wants to do good. For I joyfully concur with the law of God in the inner man, but I see a different law in the members of my body, waging war against the law of my mind and making me a prisoner of the law of sin which is in my members. Wretched man that I am! Who will set me free from the body of this death?"[1]

How good to know that love is perfecting His perfect work. The God who did not hesitate to "batter" His own Son for the world of battered sinners will not hesitate to batter His Son's followers for their own good. Paul experienced these buffetings; "...a thorn in the flesh, a messenger of Satan to torment me..."[2] an incredible list of batterings for Christ's sake and some self buffeting to discipline his own body. Donne and Paul are on the same wavelength; the truth that love's buffetings are essential to love's blessings.

FEBRUARY 5 – LOVE'S SUFFERING

Frances Ridley Havergal's (1836 – 1879) well known hymn "Like a River Glorious" was announced in a service. All went well until we came to a stanza which had been rearranged, with credit lines, and no doubt the best of motives, to modernize it for this generation. It started me thinking: a) Do we have the right to alter a dead poet's poetry? b) Does the alteration improve it? c) Is there something lost in the new lines? For myself in answer to: a) I feel we don't have the license to alter. b) I think it weakens it and c) I give an unequivocal yes. First the original stanza:

"Every joy or trial
Falleth from above,
Traced upon our dial
By the Sun of Love.
We may trust Him fully
All for us to do,
They who trust Him wholly
Find Him wholly true."

Evidently, "Traced upon our dial By the Sun of Love" was the problem. Obscure at best? Obsolete at worst? Our lives are like the old fashioned sundials. The joys and trials of our daily lives are all sent from heaven. Then traced upon the dial of our lives – the face of our experience. The shadow is cast by the Son of love, reflecting from the fixed reference point of this truth: "Beloved, think it not strange concerning the fiery trial which is to try you."[1] Here is the altered stanza:

"Every joy or testing
Comes from God above,
Given to His children
As an act of love;
We may trust Him fully
All for us to do
They who trust Him wholly
Find Him wholly true."

In the end both come down to this one truth: Divine love suffers and because He does, He permits it in the children He loves. All loves have suffering built into them. If the Son of His love learned obedience through the things which He suffered and He who was perfect was perfected through suffering for His work as High Priest, how much more do we need it.[1]

If part of His love suffering is long suffering, enduring the contradictions of sinners, then trials, tests and tribulations will be part of the sent suffering of love. Tribulation works, brings about patience. Suffering is a gift. Don't run from it, nor seek to be released from it, until it has done its perfecting work. All will be well, because perfect love is in control. That woman of great faith, at her son's death, said "Shalom – peace."

FEBRUARY 6 – LOVE AND THE AFFLICTIONS OF GOD

Lenore Grubert is a multiple sclerosis patient. As a Christian afflicted like this, and accepting it with grace, she is a living witness to her Lord. A visitor asked: "If God is a God of love, why does He permit so much suffering in the world?" Lenore said later:

"These words, spoken more in bewilderment, than an inquiry, were prompted by the state of my health. With the poet, Elizabeth Barrett Browning (1806 - 1861), I can say:

"I have lost oh, many a pleasure,
Many a hope, and many a power
Studious health, and merry leisure..."

"However I believe that my life, so circumscribed by an affliction, is controlled by God. Because I accept existing physical conditions as His will, I have no feelings of resentment with my lot in life; any suggestion of pity is a welcome opportunity to tell of God's love and purpose in permitting my nerve disease. By means of this trouble God drew me closer to Himself."

Mrs. Grubert, of White Plains, New York, is a graduate of the University of Wisconsin and has a master's degree in fine arts from Columbia University. She goes on to say:

"My years of physical disability (more than twenty) have resulted in spiritual progress by the grace of God...I have learned the need and joy of showing love to God and fellow men; therefore I am a better person because I have had this debility. Certainly, through the power of the Holy Spirit, affliction can enrich the inner life, thus contributing to the eternal welfare of the soul. Over and over again, Scripture substantiates my trust that God, with love, oversees my physical burden. These two passages concerning affliction are my favourites: 'Behold, I have refined thee, but not with silver; I have chosen thee in the furnace of affliction. For mine own sake, even for mine own sake, will I do it...' 'For our light affliction, which is but for a moment, worketh for us a far more exceeding and eternal weight of glory'"

She then says a startling thing:

"Affliction is like a two-edged knife in the hand of a loving God."

Mrs. Grubert who entitled her article (from the "Alliance Witness"): God's Love in Affliction" wrote it in gratitude and for the glory of God. She goes on to explain her two-edged knife statement.

"This spiritual approach to affliction, where God's will is accepted and His underlying purpose of love is understood, has brought sustaining courage and lasting comfort. Indeed, the difference between victory and defeat in trouble is an unshakable trust in the goodness of God; a firmly grounded belief that God is a God of love...Having gained enlightenment as to God's love and purpose in permitting my physical burden, I have come to sense another value of affliction which goes beyond personal edification...It may be God would have infirmity contribute to the spiritual growth of the well...How? Vicarious experience of bodily distress offers individuals a chance to show love to the burdened one, which is the essence of love for God. Here is offered an opportunity to grow in His love. '...if we love one another God abides in us, and His love is perfected in us.' 'Now we who are strong ought to bear the weaknesses of those without strength and not just please ourselves.'"

She quotes Mrs. Browning again:

"Can I love thee my Beloved; can I love Thee? And is this like love to stand with no help in my hand?"

FEBRUARY 7 – DIVINE LOVE AND CANCER

"Canon David Watson died on February 18, 1984. He had cancelled all his engagements since December because cancer of the liver had again become active. He wrote then of his realization, 'that all my preaching, writing and other ministry was absolutely nothing compared with my love relationship with Him.'"

This religious news item is stark but it also shines with glorious radiance in the circumstances of David Watson's dying statement, that nothing matters, compares nor can alter "my love relationship with Him." How glorious, triumphant and God honouring. Divine love conquers cancer; sometimes by healing it, more often by not healing it, but allowing it to be the final healer. I once heard a Pentecostal preacher say so truly:

"Death is the final healer."

David Watson's autobiography <u>You are My God</u> tells how he was converted at Cambridge under John Collins, followed by David Sheppard and how he discovered in his first two curacies a deepening commitment to evangelism and a new experience of the Holy Spirit. Then he found himself in York, with an almost empty church. Prayer and fasting led to conversions and growth, transforming the church into a pioneer renowned worldwide. The story of his spiritual pilgrimage, the growth of his marriage, and the transformation of the church make for compelling reading. But the testimony is never truimphalistic.

"The Christian gospel is not about superstars. It is rather about God's extraordinary grace in spite of very ordinary human faults and failing...I have tried to write honestly, in my life, my marriage and the church, about the pains and joys we have experienced. No human frailty need be a hindrance to God's infinite grace."

Note these last two sentences. Pain and joy; human frailty. God is glorified in the frailty of the human frame and its pains and joys. The pains and joys are given to us by divine love in proportion to our individual needs and in the end-view Christlikeness.

"And we know that God causes all things to work together for good to those who love God, to those who are called according to His purpose. For those whom He foreknew, He also predestined to become conformed to the image of His Son, so that He would be the firstborn among many brethren."[1] These verses have been quoted frequently and should not be separated. God's purposes in love are outlined here for all those who love Him. We are predestined to be like Christ and He causes all things to work to this desired end. Joys and sorrows; health and sickness; cured or uncured cancer; all things are working to that one end. The means He uses to that end should not be our concern. Recognition of what, and why, He is allowing all these things is what we need today. Jacob said "...all these things are against me."[2] Joni Eareckson Tada, David Watson and a great cloud of witnesses say: "All these things are for me." They are the means divine love uses for our eternal good and God's eternal glory.

FEBRUARY 8 – NO EASY LOVE

The word easy is found only once in the New Testament and then in connection with the yoke of Christ. This may seem contradictory to the title for today's reading but it is not. Easy has the connotation of useful, good, kind, even comfortable; not "easy-cheap", nor "easy come – easy go." New Testament love is difficult, hard and costly. In fact all real love has its price; and therein lies its value and splendour. Even romantic love, which seems so easy that you fall into it, demands its down payment of time, energy and even money. The costs escalate as you follow through into marital love. What about family love, filial love and fraternal love and all the others on the list? Easy is not the word, difficult better describes the effort and hard will be some of the decisions. We are not bemoaning these facts of love; rather we are glorying in their values and virtues. This love is a many splendoured thing.

The cross, synonymous with death, is at the center of all real love whether we realize it or believe it. Love yourself is pop theology based on our Lord's teaching that we should love our neighbours as we love ourselves. As we have said before, we are not knocking proper self-esteem or self-worth but we do need the right emphasis and balance of all the other Scriptural teaching on the subject.

What was our Lord's emphasis? Love to our neighbour should be at least equal with self-love. Is He commanding self-love? No. He is commanding neighbourly love. "If anyone comes to Me, and does not hate…even his own life, he cannot be My disciple. Whoever does not carry his own cross and come after Me cannot be My disciple." "He who loves his life loses it, and he who hates his life in this world will keep it to life eternal."[1] This is no easy love. What does He mean? The terms "hate" and "love" in these passages are comparative. The believer's love for himself, when compared with his love for Christ, is as if it were hate. Our Lord applied the same truth to Himself, when He dealt with earthly relations and relationships. "…Who is My mother and who are My brothers?"[2] In the Lord the natural loves are sanctified and lifted to the level of holy heavenly love and that is no easy love. This is the way difficult love is transcended and glorified.

The same comparisons apply to wife and family. "So husbands ought also to love their own wives as their own bodies. He who loves his own wife loves himself; for no one ever hated his own flesh, but nourishes and cherishes it, just as Christ also does the church."[3] Our Lord and Paul take self-love as universally believed and then use this as a starting point to move from this easy love to the hard teachings of difficult love. Denial and death of self-love is the emphasis. To love our neighbours and our wives truly is to love them as Christ did the church. He laid down His life for it. Cross love is the "I crossed out" love. Cross love is costly love. We are always at the cross roads; we must choose – easy or hard love.

FEBRUARY 9 – DIVISIVE LOVE

I have spent time in showing how love unites in all the loves and now I use a contradictory term! 'Tis deliberately done for life is contradictory and so is love. In these pages I have also used some odd conjunctions in the titles: "Love Plus Hate" (February 11), "Love – A Severe Mercy" (February 14) etc. In fact "Love's Conjunctions" could be a subtitle for this book. I have not avoided love's dichotomies but I have tried to point out false ones, such as the pious divorcing of the natural loves from super-natural love. I have deliberately mixed the loves, watching them flow into and out of each other as they do in life with each nourishing, enlarging, energizing and controlling the other.

Now "Divisive Love" the true not the false; the inescapable not the avoidable. Some of these hard truths inherent in true love, and often implied, if not stated, have been seen in "No Easy Love" (February 8) and now here is another of the same kind. "Do not think that I came to bring peace on the earth; I did not come to bring peace, but a sword. For I came to set a man against his father, and a daughter against her mother, and a daughter-in-law against her mother-in-law; and a man's enemies will be the members of his household."[1] This is the balance of truth about the family aspects of love. Good as all the God given family loves are they can be the enemy of the best and highest love.

We all know the truth of the Lord's statement, some by very difficult personal experience. Just this week, while attending an Asian Christian Conference, held in the city of Edmonton, Alberta, Canada, I heard a young Trinidadian give his testimony. He said:

"I came from a wealthy Hindu family in South Trinidad and at 16 years of age had to choose between Hinduism and Christ; between my family and Christ; between riches and Christ. His grace enabled me to choose Christ but it was not easy."

Later I met and talked with him and he said:

"First generation Christians are cut off, in some cases, completely, permanently; most of us have had a very hard time but there was no other way."

Here no hint of compromise, nor avoidance of the cross and death in this conflict of loves. I asked him if he had had contact with his family since then.

"Yes, and some have been converted."

My heart rejoiced. Faithfulness in carrying out this truth of "Divisive Love" has resulted in family being united in heavenly love.

There is the paradox, divided to unite. There is division between the lower and the higher; between the lesser and the greater; between the good and the best. When this hard truth about the loves is accepted, the natural loves are enhanced and, as in the case of the young Trinidadian, the family is united in Christ and love. But it is not always the case. Happy endings in love are not always the norm down here, even in the lesser loves. But "Divisive Love" must still be followed and the Lord's compensations are found in the eternal union with the beloved.

FEBRUARY 10 – LOVE VERSUS HATE

"As soon," Dr. Thomas Chalmers (1780 – 1847) used to say, "as soon as a man comes to understand that God is love, he is infallibly converted."

As we saw (January 18), Florence Barclay (1862 – 1921) wrote a book The Wall of Partition to show how her hero, Rodney Steele, made this tremendous and transfiguring discovery. This handsome, rich and well travelled man seemed to have everything going his way, but closer contact with him revealed a turned off, sour spirited man. A probing psychiatrist would have discovered that years earlier he had loved a beautiful girl.

In his book A Handful of Stars, Dr. Frank W. Boreham, D. D. (1871 – 1959) tells the story under the title Rodney Steele's text.

"But an unscrupulous and designing woman had gained his sweethearts confidence and had poisoned her heart by pouring into her ear the most abominable scandals concerning him. She had returned his letters; and he, in the vain hope of being able to forget, had abandoned himself to travel and literature. But on whatever shores he wandered, and on whatever seas he sailed, he nursed in his heart a dreadful hate – a hate of the woman who had so cruelly intervened. And, cherishing that hate, his heart became hard and bitter and sour. He lost faith in love, in womanhood, in God, in everything. And his books reflected the cynicism of his soul. This is Rodney Steele as the story opens..."

On the natural level in some cases losing love can lead to losing heart and then losing the desire to live. In Steele's case, loss of love led to hate of the one who caused the loss. This kind of hate is a hellish thing destroying self and others. It is not our plan to follow Steele here, but in fortuitous ways the text "God is love" kept confronting him and in the end triumphed in his life. God's love broke down the dividing wall of hate, that "Wall of Partition."

Christians, while being hated by all, (as they were in the first century, and will be again in the last) for Christ's sake must themselves love all, as well as one another. Despite this worldly hatred we are to rightly love the world. The one who says he loves God while hating his brother is not only a liar and a murderer but is in darkness, not light. Christians are not even to hate their enemies as the old dispensation allowed. God, who is love, enshrined in the heart and loosed in the life, can conquer hate and everything else.

As Emmet Fox (1886 – 1951) says:

"There is no difficulty that enough love will not conquer; no disease that enough love will not heal; no door that enough love will not open; no gulf that enough love will not bridge; no wall that enough love will not throw down; no sin that enough love will not redeem. It makes no difference how deeply seated may be the trouble, how hopeless the outlook, how muddled the tangle, how great the mistake; a sufficient realization of love will dissolve it all..."

We were once on the wrong side "...spending our life in malice and envy, hateful, hating one another. But when the kindness of God our Savior and His love for mankind appeared, He saved us..."[1] and put us on the right side.

FEBRUARY 11 – LOVE PLUS HATE

We continue with more of these hard sayings concerning love some of which I learned the hard way. While preparing for the mission field I was told by a missionary friend as being "Too loving!" Twenty five years later while on the mission field I was challenged by a young missionary with these words: "John, there's not a bit of love in you!" "Too loving!" "Not a bit of love in you!" Who was right? Had I changed for the worse? The first, older man saw me as too soft in my love. The second, younger man saw me as too hard. The former thought I needed to know and show what today has been called "tough love." The latter thought I needed "tenderizing." Probably both were right and as usual the wise middle way between extremes is desirable.

Love and hate are strong words, are closely connected and are amongst the strongest of the passions and emotions. In the space of a quarter of a century I had learned some lessons on "Love plus hate." I learned the truth of "Ye that love the Lord, hate evil…"[1] in those years on the foreign field. Obviously there are right and wrong kinds of hate but this is one of the necessary and proper kinds. Lovers of the Lord must be haters of the evil one and all evil.. Our Lord Jesus, lover of souls, showed holy anger, righteous indignation against evil and evil men. Because we hate evil and its consequences we love to call sinners to repentance and faith in Christ. This is how we sought on the mission field to show "love plus hate." We were once amongst the lovers of iniquity but now we hate the things we once loved and love the things we once hated.

There is another area where love plus hate is called for, and it is one of the hardest to learn and practice. Our Lord said: "If any man come to me, and hate not his father, and mother, and wife, and children, and brethren, and sisters, yea, and his own life also, he cannot be my disciple"[2] The context shows that this hard saying was deliberately intended to find from the attendant multitudes those who would be disciplined, dedicated disciples. Those who would count the cost and be willing to take up the cross and follow the Lord wherever He led. Analysis of the Lord's statement makes it obvious that hate here is not malice, ill will or evil intent towards our loved ones. Hatred here is used as comparative. The Lord is not contradicting Himself when He said: "Love one another." Our right love for our families when compared to our love and devotion to Him can be justly termed hate.

I knew the theory before I went as a missionary but my mother knew the reality. As I sailed from Sydney, Australia, on September 15, 1938 my mother left a letter for me in the cabin. It was to be read "at sea." In it she said:

"Son it is not a sin to love. I love you and I'll miss you. In my own quiet way I give you to God for others need you."

This is love for the Lord which would hate to be selfish and keep a loved one from the will of God. Years later we understood "love plus hate" when we fare welled our own children.

FEBRUARY 12 – "JACOB I LOVED, BUT ESAU I HATED"[1]

This statement has been a problem and stumbling block to many. If God is love how can He hate? That, as we have seen, is no great problem. He is true to His own nature which loves righteousness and hates evil. The more frequently heard criticism today is:

"If God is love, then why does He allow all this pain and suffering?"

One newspaperman and TV talker prominent in Canada for many decades was Gordon Sinclair – an elderly curmudgeon who died in his eighties, in May 1984. I heard him say that he was an atheist because no one who sees children suffer could believe in the Christian God who is supposedly a God of love. The problems of pain, sickness, suffering and death have troubled many honest thinkers through the ages. The root problem, and cause of much suffering in the world, is sin. God answered the sin problem by giving Himself, and suffering in the Person of His Son, on the Cross for our sins. That coming again will one day be the final eradicator of tears and pain and suffering and death.

But the problem before us concerns His loving and choosing the devious, unworthy and crooked schemer Jacob, while hating and rejecting the honest, earthy, open and straight shooting Esau. The first and essential thing to do is read the source history in the Bible, of the birth of these twins, of their subsequent lives and deaths. Almost half of Genesis is taken to tell of Jacob and his progeny and the story of Esau, his older brother, is wrapped up with him. Then we need to read the New Testament references to both of them; the comments, particularly Paul's, will be illuminating and help in solving the problem. The whole context of Romans 9 needs study for it gives not only the antecedents and consequences but reveals the consistent principles which God applies to not only Jacob and Esau but to Jews and Gentiles. His purposes in salvation are also revealed. Love governs all his dealings while hate is the other, and necessary side of love. Paul is emphatic in stating this other truth: "There is no injustice with God." He also warns us not to be presumptuous little beings criticizing their Creator; "On the contrary, who are you, O man, who answers back to God? The thing moulded will not say to the moulder, 'Why did you make me like this,' will it?" Yet we presume to do so!

The answers to the problem of love plus hate, of Jacob being loved and Esau being hated, will be found in the Scriptures, not in the reasonings and philosophies of men who deny the existence of God and then turn around and criticize Him and His Word. Pharaoh is a case in point, and also illustrates the divine principles. He denied the God of Israel; he hardened his heart at every request to "Let my people go." Then God hardened the attitudes already there. The same sun that melts wax hardens clay.

In the case of the brothers, God sees the possibility of spiritual perception and development in Jacob but none in Esau. He was a "despiser" of his birthright and counted a bowl of beans of more worth. He was a man of time and sense and of the earth earthy. God had to hate his attitudes and actions but gave him an earthly inheritance and blessed him as far as He could thus fulfilling the second rate blessing Esau's father Isaac gave to him. There are lessons for us in this love-hate story.

FEBRUARY 13 – A TIME TO LOVE...

"A time to love and a time to hate"[1] is the full quotation from that memorable list that says there is a time for opposites, and a time for almost everything. We will here discuss a time for, timeliness of and timing in love. Is there any time when the lesser loves are not in season; spring, summer, fall and winter? In season and out of season, romantic love, marital love, friendship love, brotherly-sisterly love, humanitarian love, patriotic love and all the other loves, paternal, maternal, filial etc. are in season.

But note another: "There is a time to embrace and a time to shun embracing." The emphasis is of course appropriateness There is a right time for the expression of romantic love, just as there is a right time and place for the intimate acts of physical marital love. The timeliness is governed by modesty, decorum, morals, mores, and manners of couples just getting together, engaged or married. Biblical principles will govern the time and place for right and proper physical love, from touching and kissing to petting and intercourse. These things are intended by God but controlled by propriety and spirituality.

Is there, in like fashion, an appropriate time for the other loves, or are they on a full time basis? It would seem that 24/7 is the norm for friendship, brotherly, humanitarian, philanthropic and other similar loves. When the Good Samaritan came upon the man in need, he didn't consider the time of day. Neighbourly love went into action immediately. Compassionate love punches no time clock. Likewise when enemies need food or drink, should this only be done during working hours? These are twenty-four hour responsibilities. There is no other time like the present for manifesting the love of Christ, at home, in the family or elsewhere. Our Lord manifested His love in time, but He is love all the time, as we know personally. There is no place, no time, no season, when His love is not in season. He loves us still and until the end. This is so eloquently expressed:

"Loved! then the way will not be drear;
For One we know is ever near,
Proving it to our hearts so clear,
That we are loved.

Loved when our sky is clouded o'er,
And days of sorrow press us sore;
Still we will trust Him evermore,
For we are loved.

Time, that affects all things below,
Can never change the love He'll show;
The heart of Christ with love will flow,
And we are loved.

Loved in the past of yesterday,
And all along our future way,
And in the present of today,
For ever loved.

Loved when we sing the glad new song
To Christ for whom we've waited long,
With all the happy, ransomed throng;
For ever loved."
Grace Pennell

His time for love is all the time. Past time, present time, future time. Across all the sweep of time to eternal time "when time will be no more." Respond to it! Be in time!

FEBRUARY 14 – LOVE - A SEVERE MERCY

The one theme constantly recurring in these pages is that love and death and death and love are inseparable. All the lesser loves, the natural loves, are destined for death which, for the Christian, purifies, elevates and completes them. Things are different in the heavenly love land. There we know as we are known; there we do not marry or give in marriage, we are all wedded to the Bridegroom. There, friendship love, brotherly love, will be cleansed and again completed in the Friend above all others. Every love we have known that was right and proper on earth will be found again but on a higher plane. Death is working now in all our natural loves. It is the final healer, the last liberator into the love that knows no end. It is perpetually remembered in the higher love. "Lord, lift me up and let me stand By faith on heaven's tableland…" John Oatman Jr. (1856 – 1922) He is in the process of doing it.

In one of the great contemporary love stories, A Severe Mercy, Sheldon "Van" and Jean "Davy" Vanauken move from passionate pagan love, with its natural happiness and fulfilment, to its purification and ultimate completeness in Christian love. They move in time and space from the Eastern seaboard of the United States to the West Coast and Pearl Harbour, in World War II. Then on to England and Oxford. But let Van tell of Davy and their love.

They met in a department store and Van writes:

"Thus began what I must call, judging by all others I've known, a remarkable love. Its remarkableness lay, not in our falling quite desperately in love – many have experienced that glory – but in what we made of that love. The pagan love made invulnerable by means of the "Shining Barrier.""

He quotes from an unknown author to describe what falling in love meant to him, and, with a change of pronouns, to her – for they read and discussed it together.

"To hold her in my arms against the twilight and be her comrade forever – this was all I wanted so long as my life should last…And, this, I told myself in a kind of wonder, this was what love was; this consecration, this curious uplifting, this sudden inexplicable joy, and this intolerable pain."

Together they composed a poem expressing what they believed about love. This they called "The Shining Barrier."

"This present glory, love, once given grace
The sun of blessing in a sure embrace
Must not in creeping separateness decline
But be the centre of our whole design…"

The rest of the book centres on another design. Their invulnerable "Shining Barrier" of pagan love was to be broken down by divine love, and in the process transformed by death. At Oxford, C. S. Lewis (1898 - 1963) was instrumental in counselling them regarding Christ and the faith. Finally Davy first and then Van found the Lord. The chapter "Thou Art the King of Glory" tells it all. Then Davy fell prey to a mysterious illness resulting in her early death. Van was continuously, in his faith and sorrow, helped by Lewis whose line in a letter gave the truth and true consolation:

"You have been treated with a severe mercy."

FEBRUARY 15 – LOVE'S SEVERITY

As a young Christian worker I was involved in tent campaigns conducted by Irish evangelist W. P. Nicholson (1876 – 1959) and old time American revivalist E. E. Shelhamer (1869 – 1947). These men are long gone to glory and their names will stir only faint echoes in the memories of some saints still living in Australia, Ireland and America. As I think of these campaigns, the smell of sawdust and wood shavings is almost as strong as the memories of nights and days under these canvas tops. For I was the watchman-doorkeeper in these flapping cathedrals. I was on duty night and day sleeping in the tent after the service and the last soul had been dealt with. I got to know the speaker's styles and sermons very well. They were both old time "fire and brimstone" preachers, yet loving men. They preached a balance of "the kindness and severity of God."[1] They had both suffered. Shelhamer in his book <u>Sixty Years of Thorns and Roses</u> tells how he used to preach. "I would skin people alive…" until suffering, the loss of his wife early in marriage, did its softening sweetening work. I observed that their preaching produced disciples. The number was not large nor was the "slippage". Many of those converted went on to become missionaries.

Today the preaching on the wrath of God is rarely heard. A sermon on hell is as rare as preachers like Nicholson and Shelhamer. Sermons on love are frequent today and this is good as these pages have stressed. But what kind of love? Biblical and balanced? That stresses both the goodness, kindness and longsuffering of God and the holiness, righteousness, justice and severity of God? Some ill informed critics have said that Jesus' preaching was gentle, kindly and loving while Paul's was hard, harsh and judgmental. C. S. Lewis points out how erroneous this is; saying that our Lord's teaching on the fire that is not quenched…where their worm does not die…where hell is a reality, is more severe than Paul's. Our Lord also taught that Hades is not oblivion, but conscious agony of guilt and remorse; there is torment in that place, and that it is a fixed destiny from which could come no message of hope or return. He also said that the eternal fire was prepared for the devil and his angels, and the "accursed ones" would be commanded to depart from Him and join the devil in eternal punishment.

These truths cannot be evaded, ignore them though we do. The Lord of love and truth is issuing love's warnings. God does not will the death of the wicked. He is not willing that any should perish. He wants His "watchmen on the walls" to warn of impending danger. There is guilt if we don't. Surely this is a ministry of love, to warn the wicked, to flee from the wrath to come.

But let this be clear; no one can speak, teach or preach "Love's Severity" without a weeping heart or tearful eye like our Lord himself – love weeping for the lost.

FEBRUARY 16 - THE ANATHEMA OF LOVE

"If any man love not the Lord Jesus Christ, let him be Anathema..."[1] "If anyone does not love the Lord, he is to be accursed..."[2] "But even if we, or an angel from heaven, should preach to you a gospel contrary to what we have preached to you, he is to be accursed!... so I say again now, if any man is preaching to you a gospel contrary to what you received, he is to be accursed!"[3] Here, three times in the original the word anathema is used, and usually translated accursed. Only in one New Testament reference is it kept, in the King James Version (K.J.V.), in the original language. Elsewhere the K.J.V. translates it accursed.

This is strong language for love! If you don't love Christ you are accursed! If you dilute, tamper with or substitute any other gospel for the Gospel as defined clearly in Scripture then you are accursed. Anathema has been transliterated from Greek to English and while not commonly used, it is still understood. It has the general meaning of disfavour of the Lord. This disfavour is traceable back to the "curse" after the fall in Genesis and was indicated in the reference in Deuteronomy "he who is hanged is accursed of God."

Our Lord Jesus Christ bore this double curse, the curse of sin and the curse of the criminal tree for us. "Christ redeemed us from the curse of the Law, having become a curse for us—for it is written, 'Cursed is everyone who hangs on a tree.'"[4] Here a different word for curse is used, meaning the righteous judgment of God upon sin, as borne by our Substitute on the Cross. This is the terrible background of "The Anathema of Love." He, in His love, submitted to the curse of sin borne on the accursed tree, the Cross of Calvary. Love bore the curse. And that is how the Gospel of love was forged; out of the fires of the righteous curse of love on sin. No wonder this holy, righteous Gospel must be kept inviolate.

I have only known one man who closed his proclamation of the Gospel of the love of Christ with the warning anathema, and that man was the Australian apostle of love, John G. Ridley, MC (1896 – 1974) He did it in the memorable message on "Caught in a Cloudburst" – the cloudburst of love – to which further reference will be made (November 9). He concludes by solemnly and faithfully warning everyone in his hearing of their responsibility to receive Christ and not to reject Him and His love. Then, like the weeping prophet Jeremiah, he says with tears "If any man love not the Lord Jesus Christ, let him be anathema." You have to have a deep understanding of, and experience of, Calvary love to preach like John did.

Paul, under the direction of the Holy Spirit, wrote the anathema of love and also 1 Corinthians 13. In Romans he had just finished writing nothing "will be able to separate us from the love of God, which is in Christ Jesus our Lord" then carries straight on to "I am telling the truth in Christ, I am not lying, my conscience testifies with me in the Holy Spirit, that I have great sorrow and unceasing grief in my heart. For I could wish that I myself were accursed, separated from Christ for the sake of my brethren, my kinsmen according to the flesh."[5] This is the broken weeping, heart of love, identified with his Lord and the lost.

FEBRUARY 17 – LOVE WEEPING

Loves weeps from the beginning to the ending of life. We are born to the sound of our mother's tears of anguish, joy and love, but we never knew it. Some mothers mourn like Hagar over her dying child or like the mothers of Bethlehem bereft of their children by that butcher Herod. "…A voice is heard in Ramah, Lamentation and bitter weeping. Rachel is weeping for her children; She refuses to be comforted for her children, Because they are no more."[1] When love took the form of a baby and entered the world via Mary's womb it caused weeping by all the other mothers of Bethlehem. Great is the mystery behind that combined event of love and weeping. Mary had already been told "a sword will pierce even your own soul." Prophetic of the time, thirty three years in the future, when she would know love's mourning at the Cross. All His life that Cross loomed over Him. He was "…A man of sorrows and acquainted with grief…Surely our griefs He Himself bore, and our sorrows He carried…"[2]

All love has sorrow, suffering and tears inherent in it; each life is apportioned its share. His love bore the world's sorrow, suffering and sin. His love, born to the sound of weeping, entered its last three years with the certainty that "Those who sow in tears shall reap with joyful shouting. He who goes to and fro weeping, carrying his bag of seed, Shall indeed come again with a shout of joy, bringing his sheaves with him."[3] Three years of watering the good seed with His tears. Three days of being that corn of wheat falling into the ground and dying and then the harvest. It was the way the Master went; shall not the servant tread it still?

His love was called to the hard task of wakening a sleeping people, wooing a recalcitrant nation and warning a wayward and wilful city. "O Jerusalem, Jerusalem, the city that kills the prophets and stones those sent to her! How often I wanted to gather your children together, just as a hen gathers her brood under her wings, and you would not have it! "Behold, your house is left to you desolate; and I say to you, you will not see Me until the time comes when you say, `Blessed is he who comes in the name of the Lord!'"[4] And still, twenty centuries later that city, nation and state has not said it. They rejected their Messiah then, and still do.

Later, on another visit to Jerusalem "He saw the city and wept over it, saying 'If you had known in this day, even you, the things which make for peace! But now they have been hidden from your eyes…because you did not recognize the time of your visitation." Paul loved and wept and warned Ephesus in the same way – for three years.

But it was in the Garden of Gethsemane that love's weeping reached a peak that none can dare to know. "…being in agony He was praying very fervently; and His sweat became like drops of blood falling down upon the ground being in agony He was praying very fervently; and His sweat became like drops of blood, falling down upon the ground."[5] This is love weeping bloody tears. His weeping heart, His tear filled eyes and His bloody sweat show what it costs love to woo, to warn and to win the wicked.

FEBRUARY 18 – A SAD SONG OF LOVE'S EXPECTATIONS, UNFULFILLED

"Let me sing now for my well-beloved A song of my beloved concerning His vineyard. My well-beloved had a vineyard on a fertile hill. He dug it all around, removed its stones, And planted it with the choicest vine. And He built a tower in the middle of it And also hewed out a wine vat in it; Then He expected it to produce good grapes, But it produced only worthless ones…the vineyard of the Lord of hosts is the house of Israel.."[1]

Not all love songs are happy ones. Sad songs of love are also standard. Love's expectations in this case were unfulfilled because Israel lacked the desire, the will, the obedience and the response of love. Divine love supplied all the requisite conditions for a wonderful love relationship which was not realised. The woes that followed were inevitable. Six are listed in the rest of the chapter and describe Israel's sins, while a seventh woe is given from Isaiah himself.

The sad circumstances were the death of King Uzziah, who had started, in his youth, to love and obey the Lord but, becoming arrogant with power, was struck down with leprosy and lived segregated for the rest of his life. Isaiah was in the temple of the Lord at the time of the king's death and saw a vision of the Lord of glory in all His exalted holiness. Seeing Him, he also saw himself crying out "…Woe is me, for I am ruined! Because I am a man of unclean lips, And I live among a people of unclean lips; For my eyes have seen the King, the Lord of hosts"[2] Uzziah's sad life story of love's expectations unfulfilled were echoed in this confession of the prophet who did love the Lord, who was serving him, yet indicts himself. Honest confession was followed by real cleansing and recommissioning. Isaiah went on to become the Gospel prophet of divine love foretelling the birth, death and resurrection of the Lord Jesus Christ. In Isaiah's case the sad story of love's expectations not lived up to was changed into the joyous new song which he sang and reminded Israel that they too should "Sing to the Lord a new song, Sing His praise from the end of the earth!..."[3]

From Isaiah's prophecy concerning the Lord comes the fulfillment in the New Testament. This is the Lord whom the prophet had seen 700 years before and as in Isaiah's time, so in the Lord's time, surrounded by unbelief and unrequited love the Lord sorrowfully indicts His generation. "But though He had performed so many signs before them, yet they were not believing in Him. This was to fulfill the word of Isaiah the prophet which he spoke: 'Who has believed our report? And to whom has the arm of the LORD been revealed?' For this reason they could not believe, for Isaiah said again, 'He has blinded their eyes and He hardened their heart, so that they would not see with their eyes and perceive with their heart, and be converted and I heal them.'"[4] The portions quoted here are from Isaiah 53:1 and Isaiah 6:10, with John making the link to Christ.

Isaiah's day; our Lord's day; our day. 2,700 years from Isaiah to us. We hear the lament of love still; only believe and you will sing the glad new song.

FEBRUARY 19 – SOME PSALM-SONGS OF LOVE, CONCERNING CHRIST

The five books of Psalms were the inspired love, prayer and praise book of Israel. For two thousand years they have also been the private love songs of Christians and part of the public corporate devotional worship of the church. This was established early by those first Spirit filled Christians of those first Spirit-filled churches. The Psalms have been the love story book of the church in the wilderness of both covenants. And rightly so, for in these five volumes, truths distilled from human experience, revelations direct from heaven and the commands and communications of love are seen and felt by the people of God of all ages.

So these Psalm books, these songs of love books, have inspired other hymn writers, and hymn compilators, and hymn book producers, in a long and Godly line from the first century to the twenty first. The Scottish Presbyterians gave the whole church the Psalter in metric; we are indebted to them.

The inspired writers of the Psalms portray the truths of God, sometimes in the abstract, but mostly in the concrete terms of human life and experience. These truths are wrought into, and wrung out of, the emotions, desires, hopes and sufferings of the saints by the circumstances of their lives. These providential circumstances are engineered by divine love and as such are analogous, and prophetically anticipatory, of the conditions, circumstances, sufferings and triumphs of love in the incarnate Christ.

Look at three of these best known and best loved, love songs, concerning Christ crucified, Christ caring and Christ crowned. Three psalms; prophetic of the good Shepherd dying for His sheep; the great Shepherd living for his sheep; and the chief Shepherd coming for His sheep. The cross, the crook and the crown are the symbols in this trilogy of Psalms and the New Testament descriptions of Him and His shepherd love ministries. Now let's behold the Lamb of God; the Lord of all being; and the lion of the tribe of Judah. There is a love song in all three of these titles.

In Psalm 22 Calvary love is portrayed in all its stark suffering. Death by crucifixion is graphically, horribly and truly pictured. There for sinners was love beyond compare.

In Psalm 23 caring love is pictured as He guides and provides everything His children need in their earthly pilgrimage. Seven of the compound Jehovah titles are indicated in the short compass of six verses. The Lord my Shepherd, Peace, Healer, Righteousness, Banner, Provider and Presence.

In Psalm 24 coming, crowning love is prophesied. "The earth is the Lord's…who is worthy to rule over it? The Lord! Who is the Lion-Lamb! Who is the King of glory? The Lord strong and mighty. The Lord mighty in battle."

FEBRUARY 20 – ANOTHER PSALM-SONG OF LOVE CONCERNING CHRIST

Psalm 45 is introduced as "A song celebrating the King's marriage." I have often wondered if this is in any way connected with the Song of Songs, that superlative love song. Whoever wrote it, it was sent to "the choir director." Whatever the literal and historical reference, and whomever the earthly king, our concentration is upon our heavenly King and His kingdom. It is a song of love to our King of Kings and His glorious advent. It is one of the sixteen Messianic Psalms, so called because of the prophetic references to the coming Messiah. They are all fulfilled and quoted in the New Testament. So let us, with Charles S. Horne (1865 – 1914), join in anticipatory celebration of this coming event.

"Sing we the King who is coming to reign,
Glory to Jesus, the Lamb that was slain,
Life and salvation His empire shall bring,
Joy to the nations when Jesus is King.

All shall be well in His Kingdom of peace,
Freedom shall flourish, and wisdom increase,
Foe shall be friend when His triumph we sing,
Sword shall be sickle when Jesus is King.

Souls shall be saved from the burden of sin.
Doubt shall not darken His witness within,
Hell hath no terrors, and death hath no sting;
Love is victorious when Jesus is King.

Kingdom of Christ, for Thy coming we pray,
Hasten, O Father, the dawn of the day
When this new song Thy creation shall sing,
Satan is vanquished and Jesus is King."

This song, popular in my youth, has been one of favourite second coming hymns; learned from my father and associated in my mind with Psalm 45. Let us now look again at this love song concerning Christ. This Psalm was probably connected with the Passover season and was a reminder of that momentous time when Israel was spared and saved by the blood of the lamb. It is a reminder of redemption and release from bondage. This background, with its updating of "…Christ our Passover also has been sacrificed."[1] for us, gives us an apt reminder of His wonderful love which underlies this love song Psalm. No wonder the writer begins with "My heart overflows with a good theme; I address my verses to the King; My tongue is the pen of a ready writer. You are fairer than the sons of men; Grace is poured upon Your lips; Therefore God has blessed You forever."[2] Thus he is addressed with praise and adoring love. Then the king's crusade, the king's enemies and the king's throne and kingdom are mentioned. His love of righteousness, and hatred if evil, is proclaimed and amplified by the writer of Hebrews. The oil of joy, and the fragrant garments, occupy more of this love poem and the king's daughter, the king's desire and the king's palace all have verses dedicated to them.

The typology of this love song supreme is all fulfilled in our Lord, in His two comings, in His bride the church and in all believers from east, west, north and south.

FEBRUARY 21 – MORE SONGS OF LOVE

For the last few years my wife and I have been attending, and assisting, a new extension church that meets in a school in a section of the City of Edmonton that was bush just a decade ago. In fact, I went one winter's day for a cross country walk on snow shoes, across the very spot where Westland Baptist Church now gathers. We were introduced by this congregation to a hymn book called <u>Hymns for the Family of God</u>, a compilation of some of the timeless hymns of the church universal, plus some of the better hymns and choruses born in our day and generation. <u>Hymns for the Family of God</u> is the only song book of today's church of which I have knowledge, that is built around the theme of God's love.

Published in 1975 the Preface states:

"We have divided our hymnal into four major sections: God's Love for Us; Our Love for God; Our Love for the Family of God; and Our Love for Others. This seems a logical and theologically oriented sequence. As we are made aware of God's love for us, we respond to His love with our own love. Once we know His love and acknowledge it by giving Him our love, we are then free to love each other and those beyond the family of God. It is our hope that this plan will help us all to know why we are singing, and to whom we are singing."

This is admirably stated, and, consciously or unconsciously, those who made this selection were led along the lines of the great Scripture truth which emphasizes the main message of this book: "You shall love the Lord your God with all your heart, and with all your soul, and with all your strength, and with all your mind; and your neighbour as yourself."[1] This pivotal truth and epitome of all of God's commands is given major consideration later. Here we mention it again as a summation of this new hymnal.

A few selections from the four sections, amplify the two commands upon which all the others depend. The first 300 or so hymns emphasize the major theme "God's Love for Us" and illumines for worship the love work of God the Father, God the Son and God the Holy Spirit. A truly trinitarian love section. The second 200 hymns follow on with "Our Love for God" shown in adoration, thanksgiving, commitment, submission, confession, repentance, invitation, prayer, intercession, dedication, aspiration, inner peace, stewardship etc. Then another 100 or so hymns show "Our Love for the Family of God" with the last 100 emphasizing "Our Love for Others." Testimony, witness, evangelism missions, concern for others outside the church. 700 hymns for the church of the last part of the 20th century. Of course, there are some favourites that are not there on this great love subject, but on the whole it is a balanced collection of songs and hymns.

Fred Bock of the editorial board has this very personal thing to say about the love that helped produce this hymnal.

"The love of my wife Lois and of our family is evidenced in how supportive they've been toward this endeavour, allowing me many hours away from them...while they kept everything running smoothly at home. They love me, I know that, and I love them for giving me this freedom."

Practical love produced these songs of love and it is most encouraging to see how the publisher has blended and brought out the treasures of "Things new and old." This is also scriptural.

FEBRUARY 22 – SPOKEN SONGS OF LOVE

As the Psalms are sometimes read and sometimes sung, so do we with the songs of the faith. Scripture says we are to speak our love songs to the Lord as well as sing them. "Speaking to one another in psalms and hymns and spiritual songs, singing and making melody with your heart to the Lord;."[1] While, as we have previously seen (February 21), singing is here, so also is speaking. Both should be heart felt praise to the Lord. In fact, when you come to think of it, love songs are frequently spoken to the beloved. To burst out into song is possible only to a few; while saying "I love you" is possible to all. Singing can be a performance whether solo or in company. There comes to me, a mind picture of an operatic tenor, or chorus, declaiming love in loud song. While this is right for public consumption, in private adoration, speaking our love is quite in order for both heavenly and earthly loves. All that to point out that in the new hymnal, previously described, there are interspersed readings amongst the hymns and their melodies. These authors range from St. Patrick to Solzhenitsyn; from John Bunyan to Gloria Gaither; and from Francis Xavier to Billy Graham. Let's listen to one or two of the readings; a couple or so on love, which is the theme of the hymnbook Hymns for the Family of God.

Hear John Bunyan (1628 – 1688) speak his love song, and perhaps the reader can speak it aloud and thus praise the Lord also.

"The love of Christ. Here is love, that God sent His Son, His Son that never offended, His Son that was always His delight. Herein is love, that He sent Him to save sinners; to save them by bearing their sins, by bearing their curse, by dying their death, and by carrying their sorrows. Here is love, in that while we were yet enemies, Christ died for us; yes, here is love, in that while we were yet without strength, Christ died for the ungodly."

If we personalize this, substituting personal pronouns, I, me, for me etc. we will benefit and the Lord will be honoured and truly worshipped.

Gloria Gaither's reading on "His love…Reaching" should be personalized also and thus we will be led deeper, and with more gratitude, into the love of God.

"Right from the beginning God's love has reached, and from the beginning man has refused to understand. But love went on reaching, offering itself. Love offered the eternal…we wanted the immediate. Love offered deep joy…we wanted thrills. Love offered freedom…we wanted license. Love offered communion with God Himself…we wanted to worship at the shrine of our own minds. Love offered peace…we wanted approval for our wars. Even yet, love went on reaching. And still today, after two thousand years, patiently, lovingly. Christ is reaching out to us today. Right through the chaos of our world, through the confusion of our minds. He is reaching…longing to share with us…the very being of God. His love still is longing, His love still is reaching, right past the shackles of my mind. And the Word of the Father became Mary's little Son. And His love reached all the way to where I was."

And to where I am now. Thank you Lord for your longing, understanding and reaching love.

FEBRUARY 23 – LOVE SINGING

"…singing and making melody in your heart to the Lord."[1] This has been a key verse through this section. We have previously discussed the "Speaking to one another in psalms and hymns and spiritual songs" part of the verse and now we will review "Singing and making melody in your heart to the Lord." Creation was ushered on with joyous singing as the Lord reminded Job: "Where were you when I laid the foundations of the earth?…When the morning stars sang together and all the sons of God shouted for joy?"[2] This must be the first reference to angels singing at creation. We, like Job, were not there, but the Lord gives us the joyous picture of love singing and worshipping.

Men were there when the angels sang again, when the Son of God was born into the world. "And when He again brings the firstborn into the world, He says, 'And let all the angels of God worship Him.'"[3] The awestruck shepherds were reassured, and joined in that first great glory song of loving worship at the birth of the saviour. The love singing, the melody making in the heart to the Lord, that has flowed from that nativity is only matched and surpassed by the legion of love songs, and love singing that surrounds his passion. The cross and the resurrection have inspired the greatest volume of love singing the world has ever known; from simple heart born hymns to great oratorios. Angels again announced the joyous news: "He is risen" and that dispirited band began singing again. Peter was there and never forgot it. Later he wrote that he was a "…witness of the sufferings of Christ, and a partaker also of the glory that is to be revealed."[4] So many others were there. And we were there! As He prayed for us, who down the centuries would believe, so He bore our sins in His own body on the tree. And the love singing has gone on in earth, and in heaven, for over two thousand years.

> "There is singing up in Heaven such as we have never known,
> Where the angels sing the praises of the Lamb upon the throne,
> Their sweet harps are ever tuneful, and their voices always clear,
> O that we might be more like them while we serve the Master here!
>
> But I hear another anthem, blending voices clear and strong,
> "Unto Him Who hath redeemed us and hath bought us," is the song;
> We have come through tribulation to this land so fair and bright,
> In the fountain freely flowing He hath made our garments white.
>
> Then the angels stand and listen, for they cannot join the song,
> Like the sound of many waters, by that happy, blood washed throng,
> For they sing about great trials, battles fought and vict'ries won,
> And they praise their great Redeemer, Who hath said to them, "Well done."
>
> So, although I'm not an angel, yet I know that over there
> I will join a blessed chorus that the angels cannot share;
> I will sing about my Saviour, Who upon dark Calvary
> Freely pardoned my transgressions, died to set a sinner free."
> Johnson Oatman, Jr. (1856 -1922)

And that is the redeemed sons of God singing the song of love. Will you be able to do so?

FEBRUARY 24 – THE POET OF DIVINE LOVE

The poems of American poet of divine love John Greenleaf Whittier (1807 – 1892) are rarely read in these days of false TV, stage, screen, book, magazine and press presentations of love. Nor are his hymns sung much, even in so called evangelical churches, which seem to prefer the trite, and watered down themes of the holy, heavenly, warm, wistful, wooing, harsh and hard love of God. How refreshing to read the following excerpts:

"Immortal love, forever full,
Forever flowing free,
Forever shared, forever whole,
A never ebbing sea!

Our outward lips confess the name
All other names above;
Love only knoweth whence it came,
And comprehendeth love.

In joy of inward peace, or sense
Of sorrow over sin,
He is His own best evidence,
His witness is within.

But warm, sweet, tender, even yet,
A present help is He;
And faith still has its Olivet,
And love its Galilee." Our Master

"Who fathoms the Eternal Thought?
Who talks of scheme and plan?
The Lord is God! He needeth not
The poor device of man.

I know not what the future hath
Of marvel or surprise,
Assured alone that life and death
His mercy underlies.

And if my heart and flesh are weak
To bear an untried pain,
The bruised reed He will not break,
But strengthen and sustain.

I know not where His islands lift
Their fronded palms in air;
I only know I cannot drift
Beyond His love and care."

FEBRUARY 25 – BLIND, BUT SEEING, SINGING LOVERS

The story of the man born blind and his journey to double sight is an enthralling one. His story is introduced by a query of the disciples "…'Rabbi, who sinned, this man or his parents, that he would be born blind?' Jesus answered, 'It was neither that this man sinned, nor his parents; but it was so that the works of God might be displayed in him.'"[1] There are other considerations raised by their question. To the disciples the blind man was the occasion for theological speculation; to Jesus he was a human being to be pitied and helped. The question of the disciples was grounded in the belief that bodily infirmity or suffering was due to sin[2] whether of his parents or his own. And based on the view (which some Jews held) of the soul's pre-existence. Jesus dismissed the thought of any special sin on the part of the man or his parents and invited consideration of an entirely different approach. God had permitted this condition to demonstrate His glory, as His power would become operative in this case. To see the love that allowed this condition and the love that dealt with it, bringing good and glory to God, is so helpful.

Unbalanced teachings on God's love, in first permitting the sickness, and the healing or not healing, are prevalent today. There is sickness which is the result of original sin and we are all dying from it. There is sickness which is the result of the individuals own sin. This sin, when repented of and forsaken, can be forgiven and sometimes, but not always, the physical and psychological results are healed. Then there are the physical sicknesses to which we are all heir; God in grace sometimes heals these and sometimes not – we are told to live with them, His grace will be sufficient, and, in victory, God will be greatly honoured.

Then there are sicknesses sent for the sole purpose of glorifying God, whether by healing in life or the final healing of death. Fanny Crosby (1820 – 1915) lived blind for her whole long life. She loved the Lord and wrote several thousand hymns despite and because of her affliction. "I Am Thine O Lord", "Blessed Assurance", "All The Way My Saviour Leads Me" to name but three. And George Matheson (1842 – 1906), whose finance broke the engagement because he was going blind which resulted in the glorious lines: "O Love that wilt not let me go…O Cross that liftest up my head…" These like the blind man who was given double sight, worshipped the love that had permitted their blindness, and gave themselves in grateful praise.

"O Love, Who formedst me to wear
The image of Thy Godhead here;
Who soughtest me with tender care
Thro' all my wanderings wild and drear;
O Love, I give myself to Thee,
Thine ever, only Thine to be.

O Love, who thus hast bound me fast,
Beneath that gentle yoke of Thine;
Love, who hast conquer'd me at last
And rapt away this heart of mine;
O Love, I give myself to Thee,
Thine ever, only Thine to be."
Johann Scheffler (1624 – 1677)

FEBRUARY 26 – "AMADEUS"

"Amadeus" in Latin means "Loved of God." Parents who would bestow this name upon a child must have loved him with a noble love that proclaimed, by faith, that their beloved was also loved of God. And of course they were right. Jesus love for children is shown in Scripture and sung in our hymns.

"When mothers of Salem
Their children brought to Jesus,
The stern disciples drove them back
And bade them to depart:
But Jesus saw them ere they fled,
And sweetly smiled, and kindly said,
"Suffer little children to come unto Me."
William Hutchings (1827 – 1876)

But who is this "Amadeus?" He was a special child as far as gifts went. A musical prodigy whose lovely melodies move us still. His life was like Dante Alighieri's (1265 – 1321) poem "Divine Comedy." Wolfgang Amadeus Mozart (1756 – 1791) whose parents gave him a middle name from two Latin words "Amer" – love and "Deus" – God. Conjucted as "Ama-deus" – loved of God. There is a modern play of this name professing to portray the character of Mozart. It claims to be thoroughly documented by eyewitness accounts, as well as by his own correspondence and other writings. The producers call it a cosmic comedy that is ultimately played on God's great stage, and where God has the last great laugh. They go on to say:

"'Amadeus' reflects an ever present conflict: the envy of the mediocre for those of genius and talent. 'Amadeus' also has something to do with what and whom we choose to idolize: our heroes mirror the values our society celebrates – it is a reflection of our real selves. There are more mediocrities in the world than there are geniuses. Mediocrity is exposed by true talent. Hence the murderous envy…The passion for celebrity, for fame, for the gift of uniqueness is everywhere. But God favours whom He chooses. In 'Amadeus' we see a betrayed lover of God…God had His own plans for the world through His gift to the world of Wolfgang Amadeus Mozart."

Whatever we may make of Mozart's life we know how his music makes us feel. I soar when I sing with a congregation Samuel Medley's (1738 – 1739) hymn set to the magnificent music of "Amadeus" as adapted by Lewis Mason. The tune is known as "Ariel."

"O could I speak the matchless worth,
O could I sound the glories forth which in my Savior shine!
I'd sing His glorious righteousness, and magnify the wondrous grace
Which made salvation mine…

Soon, the delightful day will come
When my dear Lord will bring me home, and I shall see His face;
Then with my Savior, Brother, Friend, a blessed eternity I'll spend,
Triumphant in His grace…"

Such words, such music, sets our simple souls mounting and makes us mediocre folks grateful to God for gifted geniuses such as Amadeus. Loved of God and so are we. Do we, likewise, love Him?

FEBRUARY 27 – SONGS OF LOVE

Through these pages many references have been made about, and quotes taken from poems, songs and hymns about love. Love songs, concerning any of the loves, from Solomon's through David's, Mary's and on to the song of the redeemed in Revelation always stir me and bless my soul. We have mentioned the fact that Psalms, hymns and spiritual songs welling up in our hearts and being shared with others are a mark of the Spirit's moving in us. Martin Luther (1483 – 1546) wrote:

"I wish to see all arts, principally music, in the service of Him who gave and created them. Music is a fair and glorious gift of God. I would not for the world forego my humble share of music. Singers are never sorrowful, but are merry, and smile through their troubles in song. Music makes people kinder, gentler, more staid and reasonable. I am strongly persuaded that after theology there is no art that can be placed on a level with music; for besides theology, music is the only art capable of affording peace and joy of the heart. The devil flees before the sound of music almost as much before the Word of God."

Luther wrote from experience. That sorely tried man, who had taken his stand for the great Biblical truth he had found "The just shall live by faith", was tested not only by his opponents but often by his friends, and more often still by his own temperament, and the devil's opposition. He once flung his inkpot at the presence of that evil spirit who seemed to fill his chamber. This symbolic act, while portraying the power of ink, really only splattered the wall. His writings did so much more to counteract the devil. Reading Luther's introduction to the Epistle to the Romans, a group of Moravian Christians in London little knew that a seeking Anglican clergyman had been constrained by divine love to attend their meeting. That night John Wesley's heart was "strangely warmed" by the Holy Spirit using that writing. Luther's best known hymn "A Mighty Fortress Is Our God" from Psalm 46, tells of conflicts of all kinds but is a triumphant poem of praise and love to "the right Man on our side, The Man of God's own choosing; Dost ask who that may be? Christ Jesus, it is He; Lord Sabaoth, His name, From age to age the same, And He must win the battle." Luther wrote many songs of love to his Lord, most of them little known or sung now. His Christmas love song includes the verse:

"Glory to God in highest heaven,
Who unto us His Son hath given!
While angels sing with pious mirth
A glad new year to all the earth."

But it is with the song of love wrung from his own heart when in depression and despair that we will leave him:

"Out of the depths I cry to thee,
Lord God! O hear my prayer!
Incline a gracious ear to me,
And bid me not despair:…

Though great our sins and sore our wounds,
And deep and dark our fall,
His helping mercy hath no bounds,
His love surpasseth all…"

FEBRUARY 28 – SONGS OF LOVE FROM THE 18th CENTURY

John Wesley (1703 – 1791) and his brother Charles (1707 – 1788) pretty well spanned the 18th century with its beginning of the industrial revolution and the American and French revolution. In the midst of turmoil and transition, these men, with George Whitefield (1714 – 1770) and others, were used of God to bring revival to Britain and save her from bloody revolution. Revival, revolution, through the new outpouring of the Holy Spirit brought regeneration to individuals, who in the aggregate, became a multitude affecting the manners, morals and mores, not only of their own century, but with marked effect on the 19th and even into our own.

Holy Spirit revival, as it always does, brought with it a creative outburst of praise to the Lord, and an amazing output of hymns by many writers of different persuasions. Charles Wesley alone wrote hundreds of hymns. "My heart overflows with a good theme…"[(1)] John Wesley had one major premise which he stated in his preface to the 1779 edition of <u>A Collection of Hymns for use of the People Called Methodists</u>: "That which is of infinitely more moment than the spirit of poetry is the spirit of piety…" What a contrast with some today who seem to care little for the spirit of poetry and even less for the spirit of piety. The spirit of popularity is the goal in certain religious musical circles today, with the spirit of pelf (love of money) governing. What a contrast to the love for Christ and love for souls which prompted the Wesley's and other great hymn writers of their day. Hear John again: "Many gentlemen have done my brother and me (though without naming us) the honour to reprint many of our hymns. Now they are perfectly welcome to do so, provided they print them just as they are…" Copyright laws were not in vogue then, but even had they been, John and Charles would have refused to hinder the spread of the Gospel via their love songs to the Lord. "Freely you received, freely give"[(2)] was their Scriptural guideline. Wesley lived on a few pounds a year (the spirit of poverty) and gave thousands to the Lord's work of evangelism and to the poor. Songs of love, real love, come from the motivation of a love quickened and love responding heart.

Charles's hymns have always blessed me. Among my favourites are: "Come, let us all unite and sing – God is love!" with that great gospel hymn "And can it be that I should gain an interest in the Saviour's blood?...Amazing love! How can it be…". "Depth of mercy! Can there be Mercy still reserved for me…God is love…" is another that still blesses my soul. From my boyhood days, in a primitive Methodist Sunday School in England, these songs of love well up from my subconscious. But it was from Mr. Roy Gordon of the Open Air Campaigners, Australia in the 1930's that I learned this gem:

"My God, I am thine,
What a comfort divine,
What a blessing to know that my Jesus is mine!
In the heavenly Lamb Thrice happy I am,
And my heart it doth dance at the sound of his name."

Charles majored on love and we leave him on that note:

"'Tis Love! 'tis Love! Thou diedst for me,
Hear Thy whisper in my heart;
The morning breaks, the shadows flee:
Pure, universal Love Thou art;
To me, to all Thy mercies move;
Thy nature and Thy name is Love."

FEBRUARY 29 – LOVE AND REVIVAL

"…that you have left your first love"[1] is an apt description of both churches and individuals that need revival. The prayer of Kenneth Lorne Cober that the Lord might renew His church and restore her ministries is especially relevant today. He emphasizes three main areas: Teach us Thy Word; Teach us to pray; Teach us to love. These are not only essentials for maintaining personal and corporate closeness to Christ; they are indispensable for revival of God's people and the church. A revival of personal Bible study and church Bible teaching, a revival of personal prayer and church prayer meeting and a revival of personal love and church loving is needed.

"Renew Thy church, her ministries restore:
Both to serve and adore,
Make her again as salt throughout the land,
And as light from a stand.
'Mid somber shadows of the night,
Where greed and hatred spread their blight,
O send us forth with power endued:
Help us, Lord, be renewed!

Teach us Thy Word, reveal its truth divine;
On our path let it shine.
Tell of Thy works, Thy mighty acts of grace;
From each page show thy face.
As Thou has loved us, sent Thy Son,
And our salvation now is won,
O let our hearts with love be stirred:
Help us, Lord, know Thy Word.

Teach us to pray, for Thou are ever near;
Thy still voice let us hear.
Our souls are restless til they rest in Thee:
This our glad destiny.
Before Thy presence keep us still,
That we may find for us Thy will,
And seek Thy guidance every day:
Teach us, Lord, how to pray!

Teach us to love, with strength of heart and mind,
Everyone, all mankind.
Break down old walls of prejudice and hate;
Leave us not to our fate.
As Thou hast loved and given Thy life,
To end hostility and strife,
O share Thy grace from heaven above:
Teach us, Lord, how to love!"
Kenneth Lorne Cober

God will answer prayers like these but there are certain things we must do before He can do His part. These are clearly shown in the conditional "If" and the "Then" of promise in the Scripture which says: "If my people, which are called by my name, shall humble themselves, and pray, and seek my face, and turn from their wicked ways; then will I hear from heaven, and will forgive their sin, and will heal their land."[2] These are the first steps of love and revival.

MARCH 1 – LOVE IS THE GREATEST

D. L. Moody (1837 – 1899) wrote:

"I was staying with a party of friends at a country house during my visit to England in 1884. On Sunday evening, as we sat around the fire, they asked me to read and explain some portion of Scripture. Being tired after the services of the day, I told them to ask Henry Drummond (1851 – 1897), who was one of the party. After some urging he drew a small Testament from his hip pocket, opened it at the 13th chapter of 1st Corinthians, and began to speak on the subject of love. It seemed to me that I had never heard anything so beautiful, and I determined never to rest until I had brought Henry Drummond to America to deliver that address."

Thus Mr. Moody started Henry Drummond on his world mission of witness on the theme of love and made him an author. In 1889 his address was published and became a best seller. Millions of copies of The Greatest Thing in the World were sold and it has gone on selling for over a century. It was the first book that opened up that chapter to me.

It was not only the exposition; I also sensed his example. The writer believed in and lived the love of God. Mr Moody confirmed this. He also wrote about the man as well as his message.

"Some men take an occasional journey into the 13th of 1st Corinthians but Henry Drummond was a man who lived there constantly, appropriating its blessings and exemplifying its teachings."

Listen to another contemporary witness, Sir William Robertson Nicol:

"The real secret of his charm lay in his passionate devotion to Jesus Christ."

And yet another, Dr. Frank Boreham, D. D. (1871- 1959).

"Henry Drummond really loved his Lord; loved Him naturally, intensely, increasingly. A woman…explained the work of grace in her soul by saying that she had once heard Mr. McCheyne exclaim in prayer, 'O Lord, Thou knowest that we love Thee!' and she could see by his shining face that he meant it. Henry Drummond affected men very similarly. "Love is everything!' he exclaims, in his eloquent exposition of his text. 'Love is life; to love abundantly is to live forever.'"

Dr. Boreham, to whom we are indebted for this biographical sketch of Drummond, also tells us how it all began.

"His spiritual pilgrimage began early…At the age of nine he attends a little meeting for children…The teacher tells the story of the Cross…a little fellow remains sobbing on the sofa. 'Why, whatever's the matter, Henry?' asks the teacher. 'I'm crying to think that, in spite of all He's done for me, I don't love Him!' replies the distressed boy. The teacher talked with him and prayed with him; and years afterwards, Henry Drummond told the students of Amherst College that it was at that meeting in his uncle's home that his Christian life began. 'It was then,' he said, 'that I first began to love the Saviour.'"

Drummond was found by Calvary love; thus he practiced and proclaimed it until he was forever enfolded by the Christ whom having not seen he loved.

MARCH 2 – THE EXCELLENCE OF AGAPÉ - Part One

The finest and fullest description of this supreme love is given in the thirteen verses of the thirteenth chapter of 1st Corinthians. It is also the best known, with the accompanying dangers of over-familiarity. Its context between chapters 12 and 14 is not without significance, not only to that gifted but carnal church, but to churches since. However the emphasis is for us personally as the last words of the preceding chapter indicate "And I show you a still more excellent way."

This individual emphasis forms the introduction to the subject in verses 1 – 3. It is easily remembered by the five "Ifs". "If I speak with tongues…If I have the gift of prophecy…If I have all faith…If I give all and If I deliver my body…" The gift of tongues without love is reverberating noise. The prophetic gift, the gift of knowing all the mysteries and all knowledge, plus mountain removing faith, without love leaves me but a cipher – a zero – nothing. If I give away all I have and suffer martyrdom, without love it is all pointless. The supreme gift is missing – holy heavenly love - the love of God in Christ poured into our hearts by the Holy Spirit. Any good gift ungoverned by this supreme gift is not only worthless but dangerous. Any results, produced apart from this love, do not remain.

In verses 4 – 7 we have the description and definition of this special love. It is a 15 fold illustration and demonstration of the excellencies of agapé. Some are positive, some are negative. Love is patient. This patience in the original is a macro word – long or large. Long-suffering – suffereth long as the old version says. Love is kind. Paul's is the only comment needed here. Love is not jealous – envious. Not resentful, grumbling but the opposite – generous and genial. Love does not brag – does not vaunt itself – but is self-effacing. This kind of love is not arrogant – not puffed up – not proud but humble, lowly and meek. Love does not act unbecomingly – does not behave unseemly – but correctly, suitably, decently and decorously. Love does not seek its own – its own way – its own selfish interests but is rightly interested in the welfare of others. Love is not provoked but is quiet, peaceable, tranquil and serene. Love does not take into account a wrong suffered – love thinketh no evil – but rather faces, forgives and forgets it. Love does not rejoice in unrighteousness – rejoiceth not in iniquity – because love rejoices with, and in the truth. Love is joyful when righteousness prevails and faith triumphs. Love bears all things. Love carrying capacity is shown in bearing not only our own burdens but the burdens of others.

Love believes all things - all things concerning Christ; all good things concerning others but believing love is discerning – it is not blind nor gullible. Love hopes all things. Like the faith which works by love. So love governs all hopes as well as inspiring all hopes. Love does not hope that all things will work out – love's hope lies in the certainty that all God's promises in Christ for the future are fulfilled. Love endures all things. The enduring capacity of this holy, heavenly love is exemplified in the life of our Lord; to hold up courageously and continuously under suffering. These four "all things" of verse 7 climax the description of this supreme love and still there's more to come.

MARCH 3 – THE EXCELLENCE OF AGAPÉ – Part Two

The first seven verses of this unparalled exposition of holy, heavenly and Calvary love have shown us the desirability and given us a detailed description of this divine dynamic. Following that definition and demonstration we now come to the durability and destiny of this eternal love. The last six verses and chapter 14 verse 1 complete the exposition. Verse 8 says "Love never fails." It doesn't, because its source is the unfailing, eternal God Himself. It is now contrasted with other gifts that finally cease. Note the use of "If" once again. "If there are gifts of prophecy, they will be done away; if there are tongues, they will cease; if there is knowledge, it will be done away." These three examples include the most important gift – prophecy; the most controversial gift – tongues; the most universal gift – knowledge. Like all the other gifts they are temporal, while self-giving, serving love alone is eternal. Love, serving, giving and flowing from the Throne of God ministers on earth then returns to its source enhanced, enriched and still serving. "…and His bond-servants will serve Him; they will see His face, and His name will be on their foreheads."[1] One likes to think that that name will be His first, best name of love.

1 Corinthians 13:9-12. This shows us the durability, as well as the desirability and superiority of love. Again note the emphasis and contrasts. Part – Partial – Perfect. During this church age we know partially, not perfectly. Though perfect love has come and we know Him who personifies it, yet at best, we portray Him and it imperfectly. However we are to grow and mature in love. We are to move on from childhood and childishness to full manhood in Christ and His love. Now we see in and through the looking glass dimly and imperfectly. Then we will see fully face to face.

"See how great a love the Father has bestowed on us, that we would be called children of God; and such we are…. Beloved, now we are children of God, and it has not appeared as yet what we will be. We know that when He appears, we will be like Him, because we will see Him just as He is."[2] We will see perfect love. We will be like Him in perfect love. Meanwhile the purifying and perfecting work goes on. We are becoming what we are – Christ-like lovers. "But now faith, hope, love, abide these three; but the greatest of these is love." Faith will be lost in sight; hope will be realized; but love remains eternally – for God is eternal love.

So the chapter ends but its actual conclusion is in chapter 14 verse 1. "Pursue love" – two words. A fitting and final conclusion for us. If we are in Christ we have been found by perfect love and He indwells us. Now comes the paradox: go in pursuit of love which has already pursued and captured us. Having found us we are now to follow after it. This is a lovely, life-long quest, learning more, living more, of that love which passes all knowing and understanding.

MARCH 4 – A PARAPHRASE OF THE LOVE CHAPTER

Ken Taylor (1917 – 2005), whom I have been privileged to know since his days as director of Moody Press, started to write a simplified version of Scripture portions to read at the breakfast table with his family of then small children. He did this translation work each morning while taking the train to work. The children were enthusiastic in their response to what I have heard him describe as a "thought translation" where he tried to catch the thought of the writer. For instance: there are fifteen words in this verse. "Many plans are in a man's heart, but the counsel of the Lord will stand."[1] Taylor caught the thought with five words. "Man proposes, but God disposes." So he continued his private translation for his family and like Topsy it grew into the Living Bible. Remember its purpose; remember it is a paraphrase, and remember to use it with discrimination and with other literal translations. It makes easy reading here, but as we study it literally and practice it, it will be hard. From my own copy of the Living Bible, personally autographed by Ken, read again and be blessed by this paraphrase of 1st Corinthians Chapter 13.

"If I had the gift of being able to speak in other languages without learning them, and could speak in every language there is in all of heaven and earth, but didn't love others I would only be making noise. If I had the gift of prophecy and knew all about what is going to happen in the future, knew everything about everything, but didn't love others, what good would it do? Even if I had the gift of faith so that I could speak to a mountain and make it move, I would still be worth nothing at all without love. If I gave everything I have to poor people, and if I were burned alive for preaching the Gospel but didn't love others, it would be of no value whatever. Love is very patient and kind, never jealous or envious, never boastful or proud, never haughty or selfish or rude. Love does not demand its own way. It is not irritable or touchy. It does not hold grudges and will hardly ever notice when others do it wrong. It is never glad about injustice, but rejoices whenever truth wins out. If you love someone you will be loyal to him no matter what the cost. You will always believe in him, always expect the best of him, and always stand your ground in defending him. All the special gifts and powers from God will someday come to an end, but love goes on forever. Someday prophecy, and speaking in unknown languages, and special knowledge – these gifts will disappear. Now we know so little, even with our special gifts, and the preaching of those most gifted is still so poor. But when we have been made perfect and complete, then the need for these inadequate special gifts will come to an end, and they will disappear. It's like this: when I was a child I spoke and thought and reasoned as a child does. But when I became a man my thoughts grew far beyond those of my childhood, and now I have put away the childish things. In the same way, we can see and understand only a little about God now, as if we were peering at his reflection in a poor mirror; but some day we are going to see Him in His completeness, face to face. Now all that I know is hazy and blurred, but then I will see everything clearly, just as clearly as God sees into my heart right now. There are three things that remain – faith, hope and love and the greatest of these is love."

MARCH 5 – LOVE IS PATIENT

The definitive words "Love is," "Love is not," in 1st Corinthians Chapter 13 makes quite clear what is, and what is not expected in the life of one who claims to know Christ personally and to show Him to others. The first attribute of love mentioned here is patience. This is another word with many depths some of which we will explore later. Today's reading is merely an introduction to the subject. Patience has to do with waiting, or moving calmly, quietly, not being hasty in decision or precipitate in action. Not losing one's cool or blowing one's top. Patient love is enduring love. It is steadfast love; love which perseveres. My father jokingly urged me, when a boy, to get to know a fellow named Percy Verance. Dad's jokes usually had a point to them. I've often thought how wise, and how right he was. This then is love enduring, going on, going through, and going up. Sustaining afflictions with the fortitude and courage that love supplies. That love of God poured out in our hearts by the Holy Spirit. "May the Lord direct your hearts into the love of God and into the steadfastness of Christ."[1]

The realities, purposes and rewards of this kind of love-patience are shown in the life of our Lord and some of the saints. It was the way the Master and His servants went in previous ages and, we are still called to this Via Dolorosa – this way of grief, sorrow, pain and suffering. The words "dolours" and "dolorous" are not used much today although the girl's name Dolores is still in vogue. The dolours of disciplined scourging, sent, or permitted, as corrective chastisement by the Lord, must be borne patiently. "For those whom the Lord loves He disciplines...it is for discipline that you endure..."[2]

Then there is the love-perseverance connection with hope. "...we exult in hope of the glory of God. And not only this, but we also exult in our tribulations, knowing that tribulation brings about perseverance; and perseverance, proven character; and proven character, hope; and hope does not disappoint, because the love of God has been poured out within our hearts through the Holy Spirit who was given to us."[3] What an amazing and progressive list, with tribulation working patience-perseverance and the love of God controlling all by the Spirit. "And let endurance have its perfect result, so that you may be perfect and complete, lacking in nothing."[4] Patient, persevering and enduring love is one of the marks of Christian character on the way to completeness and perfection. Fellowship in this patience-perseverance of Christ is the key to keep believers from the hour of testing and to share in the kingdom. "Because you have kept the word of My perseverance, I also will keep you from the hour of testing..." and "I, John, your brother and fellow partaker in the tribulation and kingdom and perseverance which are in Jesus..."[5]

MARCH 6 – LOVE IS KIND

While long-suffering patience is often regarded as one of the passive virtues of love, we will see later that there is activity going hand in hand with the patient waiting for Christ. Attitudes and actions are connected. However we can also say that kindness is the active outworking of love. Here is the inner attitude producing the outer actions. That inner control is exercised by the Holy Spirit of love and kindness, as He forms Christ in us. This month's readings conclude with two pages on His lovingkindness towards us, and it is because He loves, and He is kind, that we too can love and be kind. "…for He Himself is kind to ungrateful and evil men."[1] His children should show that they are in the family of God by their kindness to ungracious, ungrateful and ungodly people.

Love manifests itself in kindly words and loving deeds not only to the unsaved, but also to the family of God as we are individually able. "Be kindly affectioned one to another with brotherly love…"[2] One can feel the warmth of the loving benevolent nature of Paul, a seemingly austere man, yet whose kind concern for individuals and churches is apparent again and again. This whole love chapter was written with them in mind and again we see the applicability to situations in Corinth. Paul's love and kindness to them demanded that certain sins be dealt with and wrongs righted. In the particular case of the one excommunicated restoration is the goal, and with love and kindness Paul pleads for this. From a kind heart flows kind writing, kind words and kind actions. Paul didn't only write "love is kind" he practiced it. "For out of much affliction and anguish of heart I wrote to you with many tears; not so that you would be made sorrowful, but that you might know the love which I have especially for you."[3] Regarding the disciplined brother, Paul continues: "…forgive and comfort him…urge you to reaffirm your love for him."[4] We are to be kind to all but I think there are several groups who need special love and kindness.

"Let us be kind; the way is long and lonely,
And human hearts are asking for this blessing only –
That we be kind.

We cannot know the grief
That men may borrow;
We cannot see the souls
Storm-swept by sorrow;
But love can shine upon the way
Today, tomorrow;
Let us be kind.

To age and youth let gracious words be spoken,
Upon the wheel of pain so many weary lives are broken,
We live in vain who give no tender token.
Let us be kind.

Let us be kind; the setting sun will soon be in the west,
Too late the flowers are laid upon the quiet breast.

Let us be kind." Anon.

MARCH 7 – LOVE IS NOT JEALOUS

We used to, while on beach missions with the Open Air Campaigners in Sydney, Australia, teach the children a chorus which I haven't heard for almost 50 years. It started out with rabbits. Something Australian children of those days knew, not as cuddly little pets, but as the major pest to agriculture. Millions of them were destroying drought ridden pasture whose scarce pickings might have kept sheep and cattle alive. So the chorus began:

"Seek them out; Get them gone;
All the little rabbits in the fields of corn…"

And then after drawing the scene on the sketch board we would again draw hearts which were put alongside the fields of corn. Keep those rabbits out! And in like fashion:

"Envy, jealousy, malice and pride,
These must never in our hearts abide."

The children all knew about rabbits; putting names on them helped us to teach abstract truths. These four are connected but we deal with only one now: jealousy.

Jealousy is the noun which indicates mental uneasiness due to suspicion or fear of rivalry. It develops into envious resentment against a successful rival or the possessor of any coveted advantage. Jealous is the adjective that describes the person holding these resentments. Saul, the first king of Israel, was such a person. He was jealous of David's successes, accomplishments and of the acclaim given the youth. "…Saul has slain his thousands, And David his ten thousands."[1] His jealousy increased as fears of losing his kingdom increased. This led on to hatred and hatred brought forth the murderous attempts on David's life. Jealousy wants to destroy rivals with suspicion, fear, resentment, hatred, and murder. What a dreadful downward progression is brought about by this multiplying brood from the pit of hell. The Williams translation of "Love is not jealous" says "Love never boils with jealousy." Jealousy boiled over into murder as Cain killed his brother Abel. Jealousy instigated the first murder and it has been responsible for many others. Jealousy can destroy reputations and character. The jealous tongue slanders and wrecks careers, lives and families.

In contrast to jealous Saul we will later (June 1) take a long look at his non-jealous, very loving son Jonathon. What a contrast! If there is one Old Testament character above another who is the perfect illustration of "Love is not jealous" then it is this noble, non-jealous son of a jealous father. Heredity gave place here, as it always will, to the power of love. Jealousy, that green eyed monster, allied to envy, sought to murder Joseph, but later, when the tables were turned, love triumphed again. Joseph was not vindictive. Joseph loved his formerly jealous, but now fearful brothers.

Jonathon and Joseph. Their attitudes and actions come to us clearly over the millennia saying "Love is not jealous." Over these same millennia is wafted the sweet perfume, the lovely fragrance from these lives that knew not envy, jealousy, malice or pride; the sweet smelling savour of pure love.

Jealousy is wrong and evil. Love is not jealous. True, but there is a right jealousy connected to love.

MARCH 8 – LOVE'S JEALOUSY

"Put me like a seal over your heart, Like a seal on your arm. For love is as strong as death, Jealousy is as severe as Sheol; Its flashes are flashes of fire, The very flame of the Lord. Many waters cannot quench love, Nor will rivers overflow it; If a man were to give all the riches of his house for love, It would be utterly despised."[1]

There are several great statements here concerning love. We have noted elsewhere that the source, strength and standing of love is based on sacrifice. Here the lover is the seal, privately kept in the heart and publicly shown like a bracelet. There is a time for the private sealing of love and a time for its life long public display 'till death – "for love is as strong as death." But "strong as death" has more to it than 'till death do us part. Death's strength is part of the warp and woof process of love-life itself. That weaving, viewed from the underside, seems but a snarl of knots and colours. Seen from the topside – His side – it spells "God is love." "And we know that God causes all things to work together for good to those who love God…"[2] This is the ordained spiritual death process whose strength is seen all through the New Testament. The dying to self; the dying for the beloved; the dying for the spouse. How strong is love? That's how strong it is.

But loves strength evidenced in jealousy is what concerns us here. We know that properly understood, right jealousy walks close to the natural loves. But can it legitimately be found in conjunction with spiritual, heavenly and holy love? Yes it can. But this demands a right understanding and evaluation of jealousy. There is a wrong kind, condemned in Scripture, and there is a right kind, commended in Scripture.

Jealousy and envy are close relations. The distinction, as noted by W. E. Vine in his <u>Expository Dictionary of New Testament Words</u> is:

"that envy desires to deprive another of what he has, while jealousy desires to have the same or the same sort of thing for itself."

"Phthanes," envy, is the feeling of displeasure produced by witnessing or hearing of the advantage or prosperity of others. This word, frequently used in the New Testament, always has an evil connotation attached to it. The word "Zelos" translated jealousy also has the meaning zeal and indignation. The context helps us differentiate between right and wrong jealousy. "For zeal for Your house has consumed me…"[3] was an Old Testament prophecy concerning Christ which the disciple remembered when He cleansed the temple. He was rightly jealous and justly zealous. Holy love is as strong as death with a jealousy as severe as Sheol; its flashes are flashes of fire, the very flame of the Lord. This is heavenly love shown in holy jealousy. If it seems too reminiscent of Mount Sinai it is meant to be so. For Sinai was not annulled by Mount Calvary; it was vindicated and fulfilled there. Holy, heavenly love is holy, righteous love. This generation has not only removed "Holy" from the cover of the Bible it is in the process of removing holiness from love. The result is tragedy on many levels. But nothing can quench true love.

MARCH 9 – LOVE IS NOT BOASTFUL

"Love vaunteth not itself." "Love does not brag." "Love does not boast." The Berkeley Version renders these thoughts as: "Love is not out for display." Moffatt's translation says: "Love maketh no parade."

"Love makes no self-exalting display. It does not desire to show off, It never seeks to glorify itself. The one who loves is truly self-effacing. He feels unworthy. Not so the braggart. In his heart he feels that other people are fortunate to have his love. All his attention is focused on himself, not upon others. The one who truly loves does not seek the spotlight." Richard W. DeHaan (1923 – 2002)

As is our custom in this series on what love is and is not, we again take the text and view it in the light of happenings in the church at Corinth. Paul intends 1st Corinthians Chapter 13 to be the standard against which their problems and disorders, as well as all that was praiseworthy, should be judged. In the section of the letter leading up to the love criteria we have an example of the kind of boastful display that denigrates the lesser, humbler and self-effacing members of the body.

This charismatic church had members with the more spectacular gifts and others with the less spectacular ones. The tendency is, and it is not limited to this first century church, for superiority to breed disdain and cause division by self-exalting displays of these spiritual gifts by super-spiritual people. This destroys the harmony, unity and wholeness of the body which is His church. In the analogy of the body, Paul points out that no member can say: "I have no need of you. On the contrary, it is much truer that the members of the body which seem to be weaker are necessary; and those members of the body which we deem less honorable, on these we bestow more abundant honor…but God has so composed the body, giving more abundant honor to that member which lacked, so that there may be no division in the body, but that the members may have the same care for one another."[1] Divisions were rife in this gifted church and it is obvious from the opening of Chapter 13 that lack of love by the gifted was one of the causes. The gifts of tongues, prophecy, knowledge and faith are singled out and shown to be worthless without love. Saints with true gifts are governed by love and are humble. They do not vaunt themselves or their gifts. They do not brag or boast about them. They don't make ostentatious display of them. They don't parade them or use them as ego boosters. They don't use them for self-aggrandisement. They don't feel superior to the inferior members. For God, as we have read, gives greater honour to the lowly members. He apportions gifts for His Sovereign purposes throughout the body for the mutual service and benefit of all. All for one and one for all.

Love cares; love cares for all, without respect for persons or gifts. The gifted should not brag for love is not boastful. The primacy of love over gifts is made very clear. There is a loving rebuke implied also in the words: "Love vaunteth not itself." "Where then is boasting? It is excluded…"[2]

MARCH 10 – LOVE IS NOT PROUD

"Love is not puffed up." "Love is not proud." "Love is not arrogant." Pride is the foremost of the deadly sins. Pride, of the wrong kind, is marked by arrogance, egotism, conceit, self-importance and is usually headed for a fall. The first sin in the universe was pride in Lucifer. "How you have fallen from heaven, O star of the morning, son of the dawn! You have been cut down to the earth, You who have weakened the nations! But you said in your heart, 'I will ascend to heaven; I will raise my throne above the stars of God, And I will sit on the mount of assembly…I will ascend above the heights of the clouds; I will make myself like the Most High.'"[1] This prophecy against the King of Babylon contains also the history of Satan, his pride, self-will and God's response. This created being, anointed, exalted cherub, was blameless until the day he ceased to love honour and obey God. His five-fold "I will" was met by God's four-fold "I have."[2] Lucifer was deposed; his pride destroyed him. Later in Eden, he used the same appeal to pride and self-will to destroy the love, trust and obedience of our forefathers. That's what pride did to the cherub-angel and Adam and Eve and has been doing ever since.

"Pride goeth forth on horseback grand and gay,
But cometh back on foot, and begs its way."
The Bell of Atri – Henry Wadsworth Longfellow (1807 – 1882).

Self-love and pride are intimately connected, it is difficult to say which comes first. They move together like Siamese twins. In the case of the Corinthians to whom this word "Love is not proud" was first addressed we can well see why! This word indicts them, as it does us, for it was also given that we might honestly examine ourselves. Pride and self-will increase by the same amount that our love for God decreases. Any increase in pride of place, race, face and worst of all grace, results in God exposing, chastising and purging it out of us. When we get puffed up He will burst our balloon. If we become arrogant with haughty attitudes and wield power without love and humility then God will bring us down. The way down is up and the way up is down.

The first sections of 1st Corinthians describe the problems produced by pride. After commending all that is praiseworthy the apostle condemns all that is unworthy. Like his Lord did in dictating the messages to the seven churches in Asia, Paul first gives positive praise, thus building up in love, before giving negative criticism which, though constructive and also given in love, is not always welcome. Here Paul indicts them for disagreements and divisions; for glorying in men rather than God; for their fleshly follies and childishness; for their worldly wisdom as opposed to the heavenly; for their conceit and opposition to Paul; and for the permitted immorality on their midst.[3] "…why do you boast?…we are fools for Christ's sake, but you are prudent in Christ; we are weak, but you are strong…I do not write these things to shame you, but to admonish you as my beloved children…now some have become arrogant…I will come to you soon, if the Lord wills, and I shall find out…shall I come to you with a rod, or with love and a spirit of gentleness?"[4] Love as exemplified by Paul was not proud. They needed his exhortation by word and letter.

MARCH 11 – LOVE DOES NOT ACT UNBECOMINGLY

"Love does not behave itself unseemly." Unseemly behaviour covers a lot of attitudes, actions and answers that are the antithesis of love in attitude, action and answers. "Love does not act unbecomingly." Unbecoming behaviour does not become a Christian; is not worthy of a follower of Christ. "Love is not rude" says another version. A rude person, originally had a different connotation. Our rude forefathers meant in their natural state, rather rough and wild perhaps, but real men, unsophisticated, untutored, unformed by artifice or art. Rude today means discourteous, uncivil, coarse and uncouth. I have never seen the verse translated "Love is not uncouth." While rude and uncouth are included in unseemly behaviour, they by no means explain the deeper meanings of the verse. To be couth is, amongst other things, to be friendly, kind and pleasant; like those barbarians on Malta, two thousand years ago, were to the weary shipwrecked sailors. "The natives showed us extraordinary kindness; for because of the rain that had set in and because of the cold, they kindled a fire and received us all."[1] Rude natives who were not rude. Non-Christians showing what love is as well as what it is not. The short, simple translations, while helpful, do not give all the meanings.

We note that the words uncomely, unbecoming and unseemly, while not in vogue today, are expressive of the truths in other parts of this letter to the Corinthians and in particular the advice given in Chapter 7. The Corinthian Christians had evidently sent Paul a questionnaire on romance, sex, love and marriage including a few curveball questions. Celibacy, what about it? Fornication is common in Corinth, what about it? Marriage, is it a may or a must? Problems facing the married and unmarried are evident. Paul seeks to answer all in the light of the Gospel and Christian love. The following statement to parents or guardians shows the pertinence of Paul's phrase "Love does not act unbecomingly." "But if any man thinks that he is acting unbecomingly toward his virgin daughter, if she is past her youth, and if it must be so, let him do what he wishes, he does not sin; let her marry."[2] Due to the distresses and uncertainties of the times Paul is urging the single state. Here he goes on to say: "So then both he who gives his own virgin daughter in marriage does well, and he who does not give her in marriage will do better."[3] That's what "love does nit act unbecomingly" means in attitude, answers and actions.

Is this relevant to us today when marriage customs have changed so much? Christian love in parents will still advise, answer and act on behalf of their children in teaching the principles of God's Word concerning love, sex and marriage. We are accountable until our children are of age or remain under our roof. Love will act becomingly by watching, praying, weeping and warning about "unequal yokes." Love will behave, believe and urge the children to wait on the Lord for a Christian life partner.

MARCH 12 – LOVE IS NOT SELF-SEEKING

"Love is swift, sincere, pious, pleasant, gentle, strong, patient, faithful, prudent, long-suffering, manly and never seeking her own; for wheresoever a man seeketh his own, there he falleth from love."

The writer who dared to describe love with a dozen or more words and then to put his finger on the cause of falling from love, has to be an intimate of the Lord. The humble practitioner of love was Thomas à Kempis (1380 – 1471) and the quote is from his classic The Imitation of Christ. Thomas was not a self-seeker. The lowliest position and the humblest service in the kitchen was where self was abnegated and love practised. With him it was not less of self and more of Christ, but none of self and all of Christ.

"Love seeketh not her own" was the answer to several of the problems in the Corinthian church. The problem of liberty of conscience in the matter of eating meat sacrificed to idols; the question of marital rights, material rights and ministerial rights, plus all other just claims; and finally the relationship with weaker brethren. Like Thomas à Kempis, Paul could write "Love does not seek its own" self interests, because he sought always the interests of others. If eating meat sacrificed to idols would be a stumbling block to any soul, then he would not eat that meat. This is love practicing what it preaches. The same was true with all his rights and privileges as an apostle and preacher of the Gospel. Love led him to forego all the lawful marital, material and ministerial rights that he was entitled to. Paul exercised his right to do this because his love sought the glory of God and the salvation of souls. Love seeketh higher ends. "Whether, then, you eat or drink or whatever you do, do all to the glory of God. Give no offense either to Jews or to Greeks or to the church of God; just as I also please all men in all things, not seeking my own profit but the profit of the many, so that they may be saved."[1]

Thus in his own life he did not seek his own profit but always the profit of others. By foregoing his rights, he received the moral right to exhort by his example. There is no wrong exaltation of self or false humility here. His personal seeking the glory of God and the eternal good of all men indirectly encouraged the Corinthians to cease giving offense by their carnal selfishness.

The threefold division of the whole world, seen in Jews, Gentiles and the church is right at the Corinthians door. What a mission field was Corinth. Paul, motivated by non self-seeking love, became a Jew to win Jews. He went outside the Jewish law to win Gentiles. He became weak to win the weak. He made himself a slave to all that he might win the more. "...I have become all things to all men, so that I may by all means save some."[2] Paul is the best expositor of his own texts. He illumines the truth that "Love is not self-seeking." His life majors on the theme that love seeks the salvation of others.

MARCH 13 – LOVE IS NOT PROVOKED

"Love is not provoked" say some of the modern translations. The King James Version, which we memorized, is "Love is not easily provoked." We love the excuse provided by that adverb. I do not propose a discussion on the background of the texts used or consulted in these versions. I want to apply here what my Principal, Rev. C. Benson-Burnett, used to advise when in Bible College.

"Gentlemen, when you have a choice to make, you will usually find in the end, it is the wisest and best course to choose the hardest. It most frequently leads to the highest good."

So we will take the harder of these two versions.

"Love is not provoked."
"But Lord that is too hard! Lord that doesn't work in the everyday world!"
"Oh Lord I hear You; You are getting to me; I will be honest; I love that left out word; easily eases my conscience."
"I am touchy, irritable, grouchy and easily exasperated."
"But Lord, I have a good excuse – I'm a choleric-melancholic! That's why I'm temperamental with a temper!"

Let's cease this self-justifying monologue of reasonable excuses and excusable reasons and face up to the fact that where heavenly love is given control in a life, that love is not provoked. Short fuses, blowing one's top and loosing one's cool are out. All the other modern jargon buzz phrases that mean I'm provocable are out!

"Hold on, you are preaching sinless perfection!"
"No, I'm just holding up to myself the standard of God's Word that love is not provoked."

I confess that failure here has been frequent. Why should this be the case? "The fault, dear Brutus, is not in our stars, but in ourselves…" Julius Caesar by William Shakespeare (1564 – 1616). Accept that this practical outworking of Christian love is the norm. Wycliffe Bible Commentary says, à propos of our choosing the harder translation, that we were right to do so.

"Is not easily provoked is not strong enough; there is no easily in the Greek text. A translator with a short temper must have been responsible for the A.V. rendering!"

So I am left without excuse. I will find that the way of victory is Christ in me. All of God's commands and demands are to the Christ-life in me, not to the old me. He is the unprovocable One; the One who didn't answer back. The silent, serene One living and loving fully in me will be cool, calm and collected through me. Love provokes others to love and good works. The word provoked means to be greatly excited. It is the word paroxysm in Greek. My paroxysms of love make others rightly and greatly excited.

The text is applicable to the Corinthians' tendency to rush off to the pagan law courts at the slightest provocation. Like them today we too are a litigious race thinking that litigation is the way. For Christians love is the answer, not the law. Paul advises the Corinthians, and us, that it is better to suffer wrong, to suffer loss in these areas, than to wash dirty Christian laundry in the public pagan judicial systems. These are some of the sad and shameful results where love is not ruling paramount in our lives.

MARCH 14 – LOVE KEEPS NO RECORD OF WRONGS

The comparison of translations is a useful exercise. The King James Version says love "…thinketh no evil." The New International Version "…it keeps no record of wrongs." The New American Standard Bible "…does not take into account a wrong suffered." The living bible paraphrase states "Love does not hold grudges and will hardly even notice when others do it wrong." Taken together they show that when agapé controls that marvellous bookkeeping computer, our mind, then the "forget it" button will be in constant use. The Greek word "logizomai" in the text is a term that was in constant use by bookkeepers and accountants. The background thought is of ledger keeping in the old B.C. (Before Computer) days. If we let our imagination loose a little we can picture, in the negative and wrong sense, a Scrooge pouring over his columns! It is a sad fact that on the one hand some professing Christians, hold grudges, keep records of wrongs and have their lists of grievances which fester in their minds. Suddenly something triggers the outpouring of all these to the shock and surprise of the poor ignorant accused. On the other hand the one who really loves "keeps no record of wrongs," score-cards, charge cards or calling to account cards. All wrongs are quickly dealt with or written off immediately while all rights, or good things done by others, are recorded for edification and praise. That is positive divine love in action. Keep the credit side of the ledger in good order. Write off the debit side and, though this is contrary to worldly business principles, we will find, that in the spiritual realm, it will make and not break us.

In the Corinthian context we saw that lawsuits before secular courts were prevalent among these gifted yet carnal Christians. Carnality and fleshliness marred their testimony in other areas also. Paul, in grief, writes to them: "And I, brethren, could not speak to you as to spiritual men, but as to men of flesh, as to infants in Christ. I gave you milk to drink, not solid food; for you were not yet able to receive it. Indeed, even now you are not yet able, for you are still fleshly. For since there is jealousy and strife among you, are you not fleshly, and are you not walking like mere men?"[1] This love chapter was written in this context and for the express purpose of showing that the dynamics of holy, heavenly love would meet every situation and provide power to do whatever was right. Every one of the fifteen statements in verses four through seven are written first to address the local situation. Then the principles are of universal application meeting us where we live today. Love "thinketh no evil," "…keeps no record of wrongs." "…does not take into account a wrong suffered." "…does not hold grudges and will hardly even notice when others do it wrong." This truth was first for Corinthian Christians and has still been the truth for all children of God for over 2,000 years. This teaching has immediate personal and practical relevance for us believers today. How am I working it out in my circumstances right now?

MARCH 15 – LOVE DOES NOT REJOICE IN UNRIGHTEOUSNESS

Righteous love is never glad about any evil or injustice nor does it rejoice in iniquity or unrighteousness. It faces up to them and, when necessary, deals with them. The case of the incestuous sinner in the Corinthian church this gross wickedness was not winked at nor covered up. It was exposed by Paul, the church was exhorted to put away the sinning brother, and Paul himself dealt with him in the Spirit, disciplining him by giving him over to Satan for a period, "...for the destruction of his flesh, so that his spirit may be saved in the day of the Lord Jesus."[1] This immorality amongst the Corinthian Christians was unbelievable. "...immorality of such a kind as does not exist even among the Gentiles..."[2] Paul writes with anguish of heart and Godly grief. Love "...does not rejoice in unrighteousness"[3] but rebukes, rejects and prays for its destruction. Love also prays for the unrighteous one's repentance, return and restoration to the fellowship of the body.

All this is why Dr. Moffatt, in his commentary on 1st Corinthians Chapter 13 and this verse love "...does not rejoice in unrighteousness," likens the lyric to a surgeon's lancet. "The lyric is like a lancet" and love's scalpel with its hard, sharp cutting edge does its cutting, cleansing, healing work. Divine love, as we have seen and will consider at much greater length, is not a soft and sentimental love. It is pure, clear, clean and powerful; grounded in and a producer of God's righteousness. In the light of holy, righteous love like this, our sins and self-righteousness are cut away, like filthy clothes are cut away, before the surgeon cuts again. We know His are not unkind cuts; they are the necessary wounds for our welfare. The divine Surgeon's scalpel is wielded by the hands of love. Our great Physician practises preventative as well as restorative medicine. He loves righteousness, hates evil, and seeks the sinner's salvation.

The press and the immoral media of all kinds are symptomatic of our sick society. The whole communication system seems set on the promotion of sin, sex, scandal, crime, violence and unrighteousness of every kind. Is this a too sweeping and scathing indictment? Look at the headlines. What sells papers? Despite editorial denials of these things the media give what the masses want. Perversions and pornography; the facts of a declining society are prominently displayed with the sanctimonious cry:

"Freedom of the Media – No Censorship."

No doubt that was the cry of Sodom and Gomorrah. They were destroyed and we are so doomed. A society that rejoices in unrighteousness has no future. In the midst of all this darkness there still shines God's saints who are a Godly remnant that do not rejoice in unrighteousness. Love rebukes unrighteousness and rejoices with the truth.

MARCH 16 – LOVE REJOICES IN, WITH THE TRUTH

In contrast to March 15 where, "Love does not rejoice in unrighteousness," we now discuss the positive side of the truth. Love rejoices in, and with, the truth. Paul has been at pains, in the build up to the love section of the letter to the Corinthians, to expose wrong thinking, to point out wrong attitudes, to rebuke sin and to deal with errors of many kinds. He is also careful to keep the balance of truth by praising what is good in them, and rejoicing with the saints in the truths they enjoy and hold. His introduction to the letter is a beautiful illustration of love rejoicing with the truth. "Paul…To the church of God which is at Corinth, to those who have been sanctified in Christ Jesus, saints by calling…I thank my God always concerning you for the grace of God which was given you in Christ Jesus, that in everything you were enriched in Him, in all speech and all knowledge, even as the testimony concerning Christ was confirmed in you, so that you are not lacking in any gift, awaiting eagerly the revelation of our Lord Jesus Christ, who will also confirm you to the end, blameless in the day of our Lord Jesus Christ."[1]

Does that leave you breathless? The length of the last quote, five verses long, is exceeded only by the length, breadth, depth and height of the love that rejoices in the truth. Paul loved these Corinthians; he loved that church, as he loved all the churches and people under his care. He commends them as a graciously gifted (charis – grace; charisma – a gift involving grace) church; a richly endowed church in gifts of speech and knowledge; in fact not lacking in any gifts. They were eagerly awaiting the coming of the Lord Jesus Christ. What a eulogy, a eucharistic tribute of praise and gratitude to God for these, saints by calling, these sanctified in Christ, believers. Paul was no flatterer. He spoke sober truth always, and he spoke it in love. We never need to go beyond the bounds of the two letters to the Corinthians to find what Paul meant by every single one of the thirteen verses in 1st Corinthians Chapter 13. Every one of these verses contains other amplifications and applications of holy, heavenly love. So here, as we noted, by his introductory commendation, he illustrates what he means by love rejoicing in, and with, the truth.

He emphasizes it again in the second letter to them. After the heart searching, caused by all the true love rebukes of the first letter, Paul's pastor-heart overflows as he recalls and rejoices at what the truth spoken in love had wrought. "But thanks be to God, who always leads us in triumph in Christ, and manifests through us the sweet aroma of the knowledge of Him in every place."[2] "You are our letter, written in our hearts, known and read by all men; being manifested that you are a letter of Christ, cared for by us, written not with ink but with the Spirit of the living God, not on tablets of stone but on tablets of human hearts."[3] That is love rejoicing with the truth.

MARCH 17 – TRUTH AND LOVE

Truth can expel error and true love can be the expulsive power that drives out false affections.

"False ideas can be refuted by arguments, but by true ideas alone are they expelled."

Walter Harper, one-time secretary to the late C. S. Lewis (1898 - 1963), describes Lewis's work as follows:

"Lewis's genuine and enduring value – that which continues to endear him to a growing number of readers – lies in his ability not only to do combat but to cleanse: to provide for the mind an authentic vision of the faith which purges and replaces error, uncertainty and especially the presumptuousness of those who, as Lewis says… 'claim to see fern-seed and can't see an elephant ten yards away in broad daylight.'"

Lewis had a special ability to dissect and dispel the enthusiasms and follies of the twentieth century. He exposed lying philosophers and their philosophies by introducing them to God's eternal truth. He was not afraid to battle in the arena of the schools and intellectuals.

He did the same thing in the realm of love versus the false loves and affections that destroy. His book The Four Loves is an exposition of agapé, only he uses the old English word charity. The love of God is the purgative power that ejects the false affections and retains the true. He exposes, by holding up to the light of truth, the rights and wrongs of friendship and family loves and of eros and sexual love.

Now look at them united; the dynamic of truth and love, or love and truth. Truth balances love in the sense that it keeps it from the errors of romanticism, false sweetness and the abominations and perversions so prevalent today. Love balances truth in the area of the heart, mind and mouth speaking it. Or, to change the figure, it controls the hand that wields the sword of truth and ensures that "…my sword shall be bathed in heaven…" as the King James Version has it. The modern translation says: "For My sword is satiated in heaven, Behold it shall descend for judgment…The sword of the Lord is filled with blood…"[1] "…the sword of the Spirit, which is the word of God."[2] and it "…is living and active and sharper than any two-edged sword, and piercing as far as the division of soul and spirit, of both joints and marrow…"[3] We are not advocating soft blows with "this right good Jerusalem Blade" as Bunyan (1628 – 1688) called it; rather we are tempering judgment with mercy, and remembering we sever to unite and cut to heal.

We should not forget that it is a two edged sword; with both edges to be applied to myself. Circumstances alter cases and both our Lord and Paul laid the truth side of the sword very heavily on hypocrisy while using the two sides on repentant sinners and ignorant unbelievers. Two sides united in one sword. Two truths united in Scripture. "…speaking the truth in love, we are to grow up in all aspects into Him…"[4] We are to warn the wicked who are perishing "…because they did not receive the love of the truth so as to be saved."[5] We must look further at love and truth.

MARCH 18 – LOVE AND TRUTH

Aletheia is another of those lovely Greek words literally lifted into English as a girl's name. It is not so common today when names are chosen less for meaning and relevance than for family reasons etc. Aletheia means truth and when coupled with love, as it often is in Scripture, it makes the ideal combination. Which governs which? A good question, answered I think by our theme verse "But speaking the truth in love, we are to grow up in all aspects into Him who is the head, even Christ."[1] Love governs. "I love you truly" is a common expression in the language of love, whether of natural love or spiritual, but the implications and real meaning occupy a lifetime. As we mature in life, love happily tends to grow up, becomes more outgoing, less possessive, more truthful and realistic, savouring less of fantasy and more of fact. This is the context of the verse "until we all attain to the…knowledge of the Son of God, to a mature man, to the measure of the stature which belongs to the fullness of Christ…"[2]

It is written: "For of His fullness we have all received, and grace upon grace. For the Law was given through Moses; grace and truth were realized through Jesus Christ."[3] By receiving Him, we received all of Him, His fullness, His grace, His love and His truth, and we also see the interlocking relationship between grace and truth, love and truth. When He quoted the Scriptures and applied them to Himself "…all were speaking well of Him, and wondering at the gracious words which were falling from His lips…"[4] When He quoted some more and applied the truth to these same hearers "…all the people in the synagogue were filled with rage…"[5] and tried to kill Him. All this was in His hometown of Nazareth where His ministry was Scriptural and was in the power of the Spirit.

We are also called to Spirit filled service. He is the Spirit of love, truth and holiness, and these all work together through us. The righteousness and holiness of God demand, and produce truth in our "…innermost being."[6] This is exemplified in us, not in any arrogant attitude or action, by being guided by the goodness which is the fruit of the Spirit of love. Those who observe and listen to us, will see and hear Him and "Behold then the kindness and severity of God…"[7] The latter is almost lost today. "So have I become your enemy by telling you the truth?"[8] Without the truth people perish being open to deception and lies. "…in accord with the activity of Satan, with all power and signs and false wonders, and with all the deception of wickedness for those who perish, because they did not receive the love of the truth so as to be saved."[9]

Truth alone and apart from love can be harsh, hard and unholy. Love alone and apart from truth can be sentimental, soft and soul destroying. Together they glorify God, deliver souls and do good to all.

MARCH 19 – GAIUS: BELOVED IN TRUTH

The apostle John had some favourite words such as life, light, love and truth. They were all linked and exemplified in Christ. John's concern is that we might know Him so truly that we will also exemplify these four attributes in our lives and generation. Having the Son we have the life. Walking in his light we have the light. Abiding in his love we have the love. Knowing the truth we have the truth. All four together are invincible.

One of John's favourite couplings was love and truth. "Little children, let us not love with word or with tongue, but in deed and truth."[1] "The elder to the chosen lady and her children, whom I love in truth…"[2] "The elder to the beloved Gaius, whom I love in truth."[3] Gaius is a living illustration of someone walking in love and truth. A concrete example of love and truth aids the abstract teaching. Not like the man pouring a concrete sidewalk who started chasing some children. A parent said:

"Don't you love children?"
"Yes," he replied "I do, but in the abstract not in the concrete!"

John loved Gaius in the concrete. He called him beloved four times and loved him in the truth and "…was very glad when brethren came and testified to your truth, that is, how you are walking in truth.":[4] John also praised his faithfulness in service to the brethren and strangers, especially in giving aid to them on their journeys. "…they have testified to your love before the church."[5] Gaius was one of the "…fellow workers with the truth."[6] What a great leader in the local church. He was a beloved, true, faithful and loving man. These first century lay persons walked in love and truth. Thank God there are still such in today's churches. John and Gaius both practiced what they preached, and so do many today.

Unfortunately, then as now, there are also members and leaders of another kind. Diotrephes, (whose name it has been suggested means "nourished by Zeus") was not marked by Christian love and truth. He demonstrated more of the pagan than the puritan. His ambition bred arrogance and his little brief authority puffed up into that well known type of church and mission leader, or layman, who becomes dictatorial. John described his domineering personality and self love thus: "…Diotrephes, who loves to be first among them, does not accept what we say. For this reason, if I come, I will call attention to his deeds which he does, unjustly accusing us with wicked words; and not satisfied with this, he himself does not receive the brethren, either, and he forbids those who desire to do so and puts them out of the church."[7] John was rejected and vilified and the Lord's presence was dishonoured and downgraded by this usurper's unloving and untruthful words and deeds.

The darkness of this life contrasts with the love and truth that dominated and regulated Gaius' life. Truth and love were beautifully balanced and were inseparably united in his doctrine and practice. Love, as we have so often seen, is demanded in all doctrines and is to be practiced by all of us, in all situations, all the time. Gaius, in the Darby Version of "…speaking the truth in love…"[8] was "…holding the truth in love…" This combination was also holding him.

MARCH 20 – LOVE ALWAYS PROTECTS

William Evans, in his book <u>Romans and Corinthians</u>, made the following comment about this phrase:

"The word "beareth" means "outroofeth", but it has no English equivalent. It means to prevent the storms from getting at those who were on the inside of the building, and keeps the occupants dry and warm. Love is such a protection. It is tolerant, enduring and covering…"

In this, the first of this quartet of "alls" ("bears all things, believes all things, hopes all things, endures all things")[1] the New International Version says "It always protects" and finishes the quartet thus: "always trusts, always hopes, always perseveres." Love "always protects." It protects not only the physical body but also the mind. It guards "mind-gate" on the way to the citadel of "man-soul" in Bunyan's (1628 – 1688) picturesque terminology. The one who is controlled by love is protected morally and love also seeks to give moral protection to others through those who have been so safeguarded.

Charles Simeon (1759 – 1836) in his <u>Expository Outlines</u> writes:

"Where love does not exist, there will be a readiness to spy out evil, and to spread the report of it far and wide; but where it reigns, there will be a disposition rather to cast a veil over our brother's faults, yes, and over his sins too; according as it is written 'love shall cover the multitude of sins.' Where the revealing of what we know is necessary for the maintenance of public justice, there love to the community will supersede the obligation of which we are now speaking; but where no necessity exists for exposing the shame of our brother; we ought as far as possible to conceal it, and to cast over it the mantle of love."

Love protects spiritually. While bodies, despite love, will decay; and minds, protected by love, will deteriorate; the spirit, kept protected by the love of God, will go on from strength, increasing and abounding in love. Love will see our soul safely across the final river, not Charon the mythological ferryman who conveyed the souls of the dead across the river Styx. The Lord of love will escort us across old Jordan's swelling tide. Perfect love keeps us spiritually in all our ways and in all our conflicts for all our days here below. Love will keep us from that enemy who prowls as a roaring lion seeking prey; love will guard us from all the wiles and snares Satan sets; love will protect us from fear of failure, from fear of the future and from fear of that last enemy, death.

This love is personified in our Lord Jesus Christ. As He in love protected Peter by prayer, when Satan desired to have him, so He in His love is exercising day and night watch-prayer care for us from the throne. Watch-care like this is a protective cover. This is what the verb "stego" means primarily; to protect or preserve by covering. In the Nestlé Greek literal translation it is rendered "Love all things covers." It is a beautiful thought; covered by love; what a covering! "…his banner over me is love."[2] He interposed His Person covering and saving us, by bearing our sins as He now bears our burdens. Love protects, covers, bears and forbears; all-inclusive love.

MARCH 21 – LOVE ALWAYS TRUSTS

There is a lovely illustration of this trusting belief in the following description of a person who is not named. Reference is made to this anonymous one by Arthur Pridham in his <u>Notes and Reflections on First Corinthians</u>.

"If he had heard good tidings of his brethren, he believed it to the full, counting no measure of grace improvable where the giver is the Lord. If an ill report was brought to him, he believed it but in part. His knowledge of man forbade him to discredit any authentic rumour of disorder in the church; while his knowledge of God, of His power and His faithfulness, still kept his truth from failing, even where the work of grace seemed ruinously marred. Love's sympathies are ever with the truth. It rejects, therefore, nothing, whether welcome or unwelcome, that is credible."

This balance of truth about "Love believing all things" and "Love trusting always" is needed to correct our thinking where we tend to be gullible, and to equally correct it where we tend to be cynical. Love believes all things because all things, good or bad, are possible. Love trusts always that God will over-rule in all things. Love believes that the best is ahead, despite the increasing darkness. Love trusts that backsliders will be restored. Love-belief, love-trust will always triumph for it is moving in the train of His triumph. Love-belief, love-trust, is always optimistic about all things. Love-belief, love-trust, is always positive while having to deal negatively in some situations. Love-belief, love-trust, like this is perfectly displayed only in the life of our Lord. However, I think Paul would come first amongst us sinners.

Paul, in exemplifying these truths of love believing and trusting, had this to say when evil reports came to him. "For I have been informed concerning you, my brethren, by Chloe's people, that there are quarrels among you."[1] Knowing the Corinthians, he believed the report and acted immediately in love to deal with the problem of incipient denominationalism. "Now I mean this, that each one of you is saying, "I am of Paul," and "I of Apollos," and "I of Cephas.'..."[2] All three are only ministers. Paul rebukes the following of man. One sows, another waters, God gives the increase.

He again had the same kind of experience with them later: "…when you come together as a church, I hear that divisions exist among you; and in part I believe it."[3] This had to do with disrespect at the love-feasts and at the Lord's Table which followed. Believing the reports, he again acted swiftly to deal with these things. He did it by writing a letter of love which benefited them and us today. Love-belief, love-trust, always has to accept the truth whether good or bad.

Praise the Lord, for when the next reports came they gave Paul cause for great rejoicing as he also believed the news of repentance, restoration and renewal in the lives of the Corinthian believers. The second letter to them is one of thanksgiving. Love believing and trusting all things brought a double blessing to them and to Paul.

MARCH 22 – LOVE AND FAITH

We have seen why love is the greatest of the threesome of faith, hope and love. Although faith runs all through these readings, I would like to discuss it again especially in its connection with love. It is linked with hope also, not only in the great love chapter, but in the commencement of the great faith chapter. "Now faith is the assurance of things hoped for..."[1] Paul uses faith, hope and love quite often, though not always in this order. For instance he writes to the Thessalonian church: "We give thanks to God always for all of you...constantly bearing in mind your work of faith and labor of love and stead-fastness of hope in our Lord Jesus Christ."[2] Then he goes on to explain: "...how you turned to God from idols..."[3] – that is the work of faith "...to serve a living and true God..."[3] – that is the labour of love, "and to wait for His Son from heaven..."[4] - that is the steadfastness of hope. These three, faith, hope and love are positive comparatives, with love as the superlative.

In 1st Corinthians 13 we are told that we can be possessed of "all faith" yet if that is severed from love we have nothing and are nothing. A strong statement which shows not only the supremacy of love but stresses the importance of the connection. This holy, heavenly love can stand alone, as it does in the Trinity, but faith cannot. Its "Modus Vivendi – mode of living – is stated thus: "...faith working through love."[5] The context concerns the Galatian Christians who had begun so well by love and faith in Christ; who had run so well "...through the Spirit, by faith, are waiting for the hope of righteousness."[6] but were now turned back to justification by law. The apostle Paul describes them as "...fallen from grace."[7] We should take the warning to heart. "Faith working through love" is the only way to keep running well, to keep obeying the truth, to keep standing firm and to keep from deserting Christ.

For my own understanding I have made a personal definition of faith.

"Faith is my personal, positive and present response to the Word of God, written and living."

I have also a personal definition of love.

"Love is the Christ life formed in me and poured out through me by the Holy Spirit."

I should complete this personal trilogy of definitions with hope.

"Hope is my confident certainty that what God has promised in Christ for the future He will perform."

Love and faith working together (according to these definitions) in me and through me are, the supernatural gifts of love and faith given by Christ through His Spirit, enabling me to live and love, walk and work, and believe and behave in a supernatural way in this natural world. It is a high and holy calling made possible only because of His indwelling, infilling and outpouring.

Oswald Chambers (1874 – 1917), in his book <u>My Utmost for His Highest</u> (my first copy of which was given to me by Mrs. Gertrude Chambers (? – 1966) his widow), sums it up for us in words which enable us to live the life of love and faith.

"God's commands are made to the life of His Son in us and not to our human nature. What He commands may be humanely difficult, but behind our obedience is the all omnipotent power of God."

MARCH 23 – LOVE AND HOPE

A lot has been said so far in these readings about faith and love. Faith which works by love is a Biblical thought which occurs often, but not much has been written here about love and hope and their connection in the spiritual scene. The poets have plenty to say about passionate love, particularly hopeless love. Robert Graves (1895 – 1985) has a few lines on "Love Without Hope" in the once impossible area of class and station. The note of humour softens the hopelessness here.

"Love without hope, as when the young birdcatcher
Swept off his tall hat to the squire's own daughter,
So let the imprisoned larks escape and fly
Singing about her head, as she rode by."

In the arena of romantic love, in all ages of history, hopeless love has often led to depression, despair and even death. I once worked, in my youth, with a young man who took his own life because of a hopeless love affair. Mutual suicides by thwarted lovers haunt the pages of the past and present. These sad, shocking events, point up the importance of hope in life and love. The star crossed lovers lament:

"When hope is gone, everything is gone."

Yet is it necessarily true? "While there's life there's hope" is a general statement applicable in many areas including love. For the majority seem to survive the pain of impossible and unrequited love and find that time heals and another love comes along. Hope springs eternal, at least in some human breasts.

In the kingdom of eternal, spiritual love, "While there's life there's hope" is accompanied by another important statement: Where there's love; there's hope. For in a world that is loved by God, and still has the Gospel of the love and grace of God preached to it, none need despair and we should despair of none. Note the eleventh hour conversion of an apparently hopeless case, the thief dying for murder. He was seized of hope when he heard the words of Christ on the cross, "…Father, forgive them; for they do not know what they are doing…"[1] He dared to hope that these words of love and forgiveness could include him. His hopes were realized so swiftly and so gloriously above and beyond the "remembrance" he had asked. "…Truly I say to you, today you shall be with Me in Paradise."[2] Natural hope was transmuted by love into spiritual hope. This hope is the confident assurance that what Christ has promised He will perform and He did and He will. But don't presume upon or spurn love-hope. "…For unless you believe that I am He, you will die in your sins."[3]

A woman's hope-chest is really a love-hope chest. A chest full of love promise, packed with love-hope expectations. The Christian's love-hope chest is the Word of God with its plenitude of love-hope promises for the future; all contained in this tremendous word: Love "…hopes all things…"[4] Love-hope looks forward to the return of the Love-Hope Himself. Love-hope anticipates the resurrection of the body. Love-hope expects the reign and rule of righteousness. Love-hope is confident that the regeneration and restoration of all creation will take place. This love, that hopeth all things, will never be confounded. We need to look further at this.

MARCH 24 – LOVE HOPES ALL THINGS

"Now may our Lord Jesus Christ Himself and God our Father, who has loved us and given us eternal comfort and good hope by grace, comfort and strengthen your hearts in every good work and word."[1] Hope is a grace gift for eternal comfort and encouragement. He has loved us and gifted us with good hope. What a love gift. Perhaps the discoverers of the cape at the extreme southern end of Africa knew this verse when they rounded it and named it the Cape of Good Hope. Whether they did or not, we revel in the thought of that blessed hope, that good hope, that hope within the veil, that anchor of hope our Lord Jesus Christ Himself, who is Himself our hope. It is because of Him and His redemption and resurrection we have been given this living, loving hope; the love that now enables us to hope all things.

The more I read the Scriptures the more I am amazed at the place given to, and the part hope plays in theory and practice; in teaching and action. Hope in doctrine is prominent in Romans, particularly in the life of Abraham, whom we mostly associate with faith. Hope affected his behaviour. Hope in action is very prominent in that book of the Acts of the Holy Spirit, as one would expect. He is the power of hope, and the outpourer of the love of God that enables us to hope all things. Love not only undergirds and upholds hope, it energizes and expands it, making us a people who are lovingly hopeful and hopefully loving in increasing measure.

"Love always hopes even when certain facts might seem to point in the other direction. In spite of disappointments it keeps its eye on the prospect of a good outcome. The realities of the moment do not dim the desire for future victory and glory. True love hopes for the best in others, regardless of what the present circumstances might be..." Richard W. DeHaan (1923 - 2002)

"Upheld by hope, a glorious hope
As days and years roll by;
The coming of our Lord and King
Is surely drawing nigh.

Upheld by hope, all toil is sweet
With this glad thought in view,
The Master may appear tonight
To call his servants true.

Upheld by hope, that wondrous hope,
That I shall see His face,
And to his likeness be conformed
When I have run the race.

Upheld by hope, in darkest days
Faith can the light descry:
The deepening glory in the East
Proclaims deliverance nigh.

Upheld by hope, 'Beloved one'
I hear the Bridegroom say,
'Awake arise! Go forth to meet
My chariot on the way.'

Upheld by hope, how glad the heart,
My soul is on the wing:
E'en now His hand is on the door,
He comes, my glorious King"
E. May Grimes (1868 – 1927)

"Now may the God of hope fill you with all joy and peace in believing, so that you will abound in hope by the power of the Holy Spirit."[2] Here, in this lovely benediction, we have God the Father, and the Holy Spirit joining Christ the Son in trinitarian love and hope. By this trinity of love and hope we are filled with the love that hopes all things.

MARCH 25 – LOVE ALWAYS PERSEVERES

There will be a much fuller consideration of patience, perseverance and endurance in the series love's gifts (May 4) and love's graces (May 17). Here we want to use the thought brought out by The Berkeley Translation which says ""Love endures without limit." Whatever the load given by holy, heavenly love, that limitless love will enable perseverance to the end of even limitless suffering. We have, in this series, frequently used the context of the Corinthian letters to aid us in the interpretation of these love statements. Here we see in Paul's life, as he tells the Christians in Corinth, illustrations of love enduring all things. What follows is an unbelievable catalogue of awe-inspiring sufferings. Paul endured all of these with perseverance, though strained to the limits and pressed out of measure. Divine love's enabling brought him through, not just somehow, but victoriously and praisefully.

He is defending his apostleship to the gainsayers in Corinth. "I wish that you would bear with me[1]... for I am jealous for you with a godly jealousy[2]... I am afraid that, as the serpent deceived Eve by his craftiness, your minds will be led astray from the simplicity and purity of devotion to Christ[3]... I consider myself not in the least inferior to the most eminent apostles[4]... I more so..."[5] Then follows a list of endured sufferings. "...in far more labors, in far more imprisonments, beaten times without number, often in danger of death. Five times I received from the Jews thirty-nine lashes. Three times I was beaten with rods, once I was stoned, three times I was shipwrecked, a night and a day I have spent in the deep. I have been on frequent journeys, in dangers from rivers, dangers from robbers, dangers from my countrymen, dangers from the Gentiles, dangers in the city, dangers in the wilderness, dangers on the sea, dangers among false brethren; I have been in labor and hardship, through many sleepless nights, in hunger and thirst, often without food, in cold and exposure. Apart from such external things, there is the daily pressure on me of concern for all the churches."[6]

This list has been given in its entirety because, next to the sufferings of our Lord, the sufferings endured by Paul are almost without parallel in the history of the church. I know of none equal to his. He persevered through all that long list for long years, enduring without limit all that love laid on him. That love enabled him to endure right to the end of life in Rome. "For I am already being poured out as a drink offering, and the time of my departure has come. I have fought the good fight, I have finished the course, I have kept the faith."[7]

We will have only a short list of suffering at the end of our race but long or short "...let us run with endurance the race that is set before us, fixing our eyes on Jesus, the author and perfecter of faith..."[8]

MARCH 26 – LOVE NEVER FAILS

I believe that Paul is, in this phrase, as well as introducing another truth about love, expressing a hope that the Corinthians will also see in their circumstances, that love is the answer and will never fail them in all their sorry situations. We have previously (March 15) quoted from Dr. Moffatt where, in his commentary on 1st Corinthians Chapter 13, he describes "The lyric is like a lancet." Paul lanced and probed into all the festering sores of that first century church. A surgeon's scalpel can be beautiful to the eyes of the one helped to healing by it. We generally read this beautiful description of love without reference to its context and in so doing we miss the lancet in the lyric. This passage has a beauty of words and composition that makes it an extraordinary love poem. It also has other more permanent beauties. It is the beauty of love in pursuit of sinners and backsliders. It is the beauty of love producing holiness. It is the beauty of love reconciling, restoring and renewing.

The context has already shown love's permanence in comparison with the impermanent gifts. They will cease to exist and will be done away with. But love remains, for love is eternal. "Love never fails; but if there are gifts of prophecy, they will be done away; if there are tongues, they will cease; if there is knowledge, it will be done away. For we know in part and we prophesy in part; but when the perfect comes, the partial will be done away."[1] Until the perfect One comes to set up His reign of perfect love, joy and permanent peace we have the love of God poured into us continually by the Holy Spirit. In the meantime this love controls us and governs the use of all the gifts.

Love didn't fail in Corinth. Love never fails, never falters, never ceases to have force, never loses its mighty authority and never falls. The use of the word fail, as it is translated in most of the versions, is actually the verb for fall. The Nestlé Greek New Testament literally translates it "Agapé never falls." W. E. Vine in his Expository Dictionary of New Testament Words tells us that the verb "pipto" meaning "to fall," is used of the Law of God in its smallest detail, in the sense of losing its authority or ceasing to have force. "But it is easier for heaven and earth to pass away than for one stroke of a letter of the Law to fail."[2] Our Lord didn't come to destroy the law but to fulfill it and usher in the higher law of love.

Let us make all this personal. As W. E. Littlewood (1831 – 1886) in his hymn so aptly says:

"There is no love like the love of Jesus
Never to fade or fall
Till into the fold of the peace of God
He has gathered us all.

There is no heart like the heart of Jesus,
Filled with His tender love,
No throb can throw that our hearts can know,
But He feels it above.

Jesus' love, precious love,
Boundless and pure and free;
O turn to that love, weary, wand'ring soul:
Jesus pleadeth with thee!"

Forgetting the Corinthians for a moment and putting aside theoretical study let us hear love personified calling us to Himself. Let us respond and receive afresh the fullness of that love that will never fade, fail or fall.

MARCH 27 – LOVE GROWING OLDER AND GROWING UP

To grow older is not necessarily to grow wiser, better or more loving. What is worse some seem to have a wish for permanent Peter Pan'ism or perpetual youth along the lines of Ponce de Leon's (1460 – 1521) alleged search for the fountain of youth in what is now called Florida. Such desires are doomed. "…it is appointed for men to die once…"[1] Meanwhile let's live for love, for love outlasts this body, outlives us and is transcendent. It is transfigured by death and transferred to that higher realm where our saved spirits have gone to be with Him. Love can be allowed to decay in us, and it can be lost; aging with love, can be like aging in wine where the bouquet is enhanced. Love matures as we grow older, or at least it ought to do so, but the process has to be started when we are young.

In the great love chapter we are reminded that "When I was a child, I used to speak like a child, think like a child, reason like a child; when I became a man, I did away with childish things."[2] Love's developing maturity in us starts with speaking as a child. While children in our day are usually pre-teens the Biblical child normally included the teenager. The usual worldly-wise youth talk about love need not detain us here as it can be candidly summed up as eroticism gone wrong with lust often the four letter substitute for love. This is fostered by aging stage and screen stars and their cynical "cashing in on it" companies. What we are concerned about is that Christian young people are speaking this way, singing these songs or their supposedly Christian substitutes.

Wrong speaking about love of course flows from the wrong thinking and wrong reasoning about love as the text states. The natural man, young or old, can never think straight or reason correctly about moral and spiritual things, because these faculties have been doubly blinded by the god of this world and the sinful desires of the human heart. This veiling is also evident in the religious but unregenerate Scripture quoters. Our children, taught by dedicated Christian parents and Sunday School teachers, are still babes in the knowledge of Christian love's delights and demands. They can be subverted and their minds hardened by the false ideas of love around them. How we really need to pray for them and love them to maturity.

What can we as parents and teachers do about it? First pick up, pack up and put away the childish notions thinking, reasoning, speaking and acting concerning love. Then concentrate on heavenly love and its applications in our hearts and homes. It's saddening and frightening to be growing older but not growing up in the knowledge of God who is love. Maturity in theses matters does not come by the aging of years but by thinking as He thinks; reasons as He reasons; speaking as He speaks about love. Every act of obedience to Him develops us. Youth can outgrow greybeards if they will hear and heed and trust and obey the Lord of love in their relationships at school, at home and at work. "We ought always to give thanks to God for you, brethren, as is only fitting, because your faith is greatly enlarged, and the love of each one of you toward one another grows ever greater."[3]

MARCH 28 – LOVE'S BOUNDARIES

A reader of 1ˢᵗ Corinthians Chapter 13 would say this love has, like space, no boundaries. It is limitless, always enlarging as the American poet Edwin Markham (1852 – 1940) tells us:

"He drew a circle that shut me out
Heretic, rebel, a thing to flout
But love and I had the wit to win;
We drew a circle that took him in."

While this is true there is another side of the subject that must not be avoided. Divine love has boundaries that exclude. The balance of Scriptural truth compels us to mention this. There is a circle of fiery love that bars entrance.

A modern commentary, by Lewis B. Smedes (1921 – 2002) entitled Love Within Limits, is recommended reading. As the author says:

"The purpose of this book is to explore how ideal love – selfless love – can take root in the crevices of real life. I want to see in a realistic way how the power of love can reshape our lives…But ideal love does not work in an ideal world. It works within the limits of our ordinary lives…we must let it work within the limits set by all the other legitimate claims and pressing needs of our humanity."

It will help us to look at love as practiced by Paul. Knowledge of what prompted his two letters to the Corinthians will show this love-governed man moving within the parameters of love. This love saw the evil in the Corinthian church, rebuked it and called for repentance and excommunication of the evil doer. This love is not blind or tongue tied for love speaks the truth. This speaking the truth in love was effective in producing remorse and repentance in the church, and the restoration of the excommunicated one, with resultant rejoicing and glory to God. Thus Paul practiced ideal love in the real world. When his fellow Jews refused the Good News he left them and went to the Gentiles. When Peter and other leaders were partial and hypocritical love rebuked them. Agapé is not silent, it is outspoken and severe. It is true, tough, bold, brave and balanced.

A Scripturally balanced view of the love of God demands that His holiness, righteousness and justice be included with it. "Behold then the kindness and severity of God…"[1] Rejecters of Calvary love will themselves be rejected. The divine long-suffering has its limits as Peter is at pains to tell us. We all know that our Lord Jesus is divine love perfectly personified. The record of the Gospels, His life, and His works perfectly portray this balance of truth. Limitless love has its limits. His indictments and woes do not deny love, they only enhance and clarify it.

MARCH 29 – "IFS" OF LOVE

Captain Reginald Wallis was an inspiration to me as a young man growing up in Australia. He was an indefatigable Christian worker, constantly travelling and speaking for His Lord at conferences, conventions and Keswick deeper Life meetings. He combined his spoken witness with frequent writings in the "Christian Herald" and other magazines. The Captain was a Christian soldier who fought courageously on many fronts. He died suddenly and, according to his son, prematurely early. He didn't just rust out, he loved out!

Rudyard Kipling's (1865 – 1936) "If" had challenged me in my teens. My father had given me a copy which I framed and put on my wall in the men's hostel on the then Lord Mayor of Sydney's farm, "Navua," Groseweld . N. S. W. where I worked. Captain Wallis's "If" inspired me when, at "Navua" I made a complete commitment of my life to Christ. The Captain's poem for Christians begins with apologies to Kipling, for his poem inspired the form for Wallis's "If".

If you can keep "the faith" when those about you
Are losing it and seeking something new;
And stand the firmer though they flout you
As being simple and old fashioned too;

If you can put your hand in Christ's, and feeling
The marks of Calvary's scars upon your palm,
Can gladly say "Amen" to all his dealing,
Or change the sigh into a joyous psalm.

If you can laugh when human hopes are banished,
When castles fall and cherished prospects die;
And just keep on, tho' earthly props have vanished,
Content to see the pattern by and by.

If you can meet abuse without complaining,
And greet your unkind critic with a smile,
If, conscious that your human love is waning,
You claim a Calvary love that knows no guile;

If you can bear the unjust imputation
Without reviling or revengeful thought,
And even forfeit rights and reputation,
Because His glory is the one thing sought;

If you can give an honest commendation
To him whose work is larger than your own,
Or scorn to speak the word of condemnation
To him who falls or reaps what he has sown.

If you can give consent to Calvary's dying,
To live anew in resurrection power,
And so gain victory, not by personal trying,
But by resting in his triumph every hour;

If you can be content with His provision,
Though others seem to prosper and succeed,
Nor let repining mar the heavenly vision,
And simply trust in God for every need.

If you can let the mind of Christ possess you,
To think on "things of good report" and true;
And ever let the love of Christ obsess you,
Constraining everything you say and do;

If you can find in Him your highest treasure,
Let Him hold sway over heart, soul and limb,
Then life is yours, blessing without measure,
And, what is more, you'll reign with Him.

These "Ifs" cover many areas of the Christian life and the last verse crowns them all. If we are living like this we are obsessed by love. The great Scriptural "Ifs" of our Lord are being fulfilled in and through us. "If you know these things, you are blessed if you do them…"[1] "…If anyone loves Me, he will keep My word; and My Father will love him…"[2] "If you keep My commandments, you will abide in My love…"[3]

MARCH 30 – HIS LOVINGKINDNESS

"Give thanks to the Lord, for He is good, For His lovingkindness is everlasting. Give thanks to the God of gods, For His lovingkindness is everlasting. Give thanks to the Lord of lords, For His loving-kindness is everlasting."[1] Psalm 136 is one of the most memorable in the five books of Prayers, Praises and Songs known to us as the one Book of Psalms. It is memorable, not only because in the space of twenty-six verses it uses one phrase twenty-six times, but because of the emphasis this places on the truth in the text. It reveals the character and conduct of our God, by the use of an adjective and noun joined in one word, and stresses His unchanging nature in the final word. "His lovingkindness is everlasting." The phrase is prefaced by another "Give thanks to the Lord" and bridged by the word "For." We ought to be a perpetually praiseful people because of who and what He is. "Give thanks to the Lord, for He is good, For His lovingkindness is everlasting."

We can follow the pattern given by the Psalmist in our own thanksgivings for this unique and extra special lovingkindness. In verses one through three he begins his portrayal of the triune God and His trinitarian lovingkindness. As we have seen before, the three primary names of God are (El, Elohim) God; (Jehovah) Lord; and (Adonai) Lord. Each is deliberately distinguished by upper and lower case spelling. Jehovah, our Jesus is good; "His lovingkindness is everlasting;" for he came, and died, and lives for us. Elohim is God of gods; "His lovingkindness is everlasting;" for He so loved us, and the world that He gave His unique Son. Adonai, Lord; "His lovingkindness is everlasting;" for he is our Master, Teacher, Head and Husband. In his careful use and emphasis of these three names, the Psalmist glorifies the triune God and praises the trinitarian love displayed therein, if wee have eyes to see. Bible reading must be Bible meditation and study, not mere Bible racing through the per diem number of verses. So let's stop and be thankful for the truths of love and lovingkindness revealed in the first three verses.

The writer devotes the next six uses of "For His lovingkindness is everlasting" to extol God's goodness in all His creative wonders. Reflect on verses four through nine and give thanks for sun, moon and stars; for the heavens, and land and sea and all that is on and in them. Therein the creator is revealed. This is creative lovingkindness.

Redemptive lovingkindness is shown in verses ten through twenty-two. These give the history of Israel from Egypt to Canaan and thirteen more illustrations of His everlasting lovingkindness, his mercy that endureth for ever. They describe forty years of His story and forty years of His lovingkindness in redeeming them.

The last four verses become more personal. He remembers us… He rescued us through His everlasting lovingkindness. So:

"I will tell the wondrous story,
How my lost estate to save,
In His boundless love and mercy,
He the ransom freely gave."
Philip P. Bliss (1838 – 1876)

Let us all "Give thanks to the God of heaven, For His lovingkindness is everlasting."[2]

MARCH 31 – THY LOVING KINDNESS

"Because Your lovingkindness is better than life, My lips will praise You. So I will bless You as long as I live; I will lift up my hands in Your name."[1] One of the precious fruits of the moving of the Spirit in our times has been the setting to music of Scripture verses, of which the Scripture just quoted is one. This is always a mark of the Spirit's filling and overflowing. Being continually filled with the Spirit ensures that we will be "speaking to one another in psalms and hymns and spiritual songs, singing and making melody with your heart to the Lord."[2] So we sing today:

"Thy loving kindness is better than life
Thy loving kindness is better than life
My lips shall praise Thee..."
Hugh Mitchell

Two tremendous nouns combine in this composite word, embodying all the benevolent grace of the Trinity. Lovingkindness; love and kindness; each word is great in itself. Together they are greater still. This combination, manifesting God's nature and His acts, is described by the Psalmist as being "better than life." For love is the greatest, most excellent, eternal force in the universe. It is the benevolent affection of God for His creation and creatures, all of them, for He makes His sun, His rain, His air available to all. It is the moral, judicial, merciful and gracious redemptive giving that brought His Son to earth and salvation to the world. That love and kindness is reproduced in those who receive Him and is shown by their reverential affection for Him. That same benevolent lovingkindness is shared with others in the human family. "...love one another..."[3] "Be kind to one another, tender-hearted, forgiving each other, just as God in Christ also has forgiven you."[4]

His lovingkindness guides and governs all my ways and all my days. Love and kindness have led me and supervised me these fifty years. As the Psalmist praised that blessed benevolence, so do I, and so should we. Let it be our daily prayer and praise theme. "Make me know Your ways, O Lord; Teach me Your paths. Lead me in Your truth and teach me, For You are the God of my salvation; For You I wait all the day. Remember, O Lord, Your compassion and Your lovingkindnesses, For they have been from of old. Do not remember the sins of my youth or my transgressions; According to Your lovingkindness remember me, For Your goodness' sake, O Lord. Good and upright is the Lord; Therefore He instructs sinners in the way. He leads the humble in justice, And He teaches the humble His way. All the paths of the Lord are lovingkindness and truth To those who keep His covenant and His testimonies."[5]

Over the years we have participated in a practical manner in these blessings as we have walked the paths of love, humility, holiness and obedience. When we wandered, sometimes wilfully, from the Way, then His love and kindness directed us back. How good, how gracious, how glorious and how great Thou art, my Lord and my God. "Surely goodness and lovingkindness will follow me all the days of my life, And I will dwell in the house of the Lord forever."[6]

APRIL 1 – LOVE'S EASTER

The word Easter is found only once in the King James Version but it is a substitution by the translators for the word Passover. Easter, despite its heathen background and connections, is now part of the Christian calendar while Passover remains the prized possession of the Jews. And that's a pity. Why? Because they hold to the historical setting of the word and have missed its fulfillment in the verse: "…For Christ our Passover also has been sacrificed."[1]

"Paschal Lamb by God appointed,
All our sins were on Thee laid,
By almighty love appointed,
Thou hast full atonement made:

Every sin may be forgiv'n
Thro' the virtue of Thy blood,
Open'd is the gate of Heaven,
Peace is made 'twixt man and God."
John Bakewell (1721 – 1819)

As Calvary covered it all so the opened tomb justified all who believe in Him, "…who was delivered over because of our transgressions, and was raised because of our justification."[2] The joyful cry "He lives!" took a few days to penetrate the shock and grief of the disciple present at the Crucifixion. Friday was a dark day but Sunday is coming! The gloom of the tomb will be dispelled by resurrection life and light and love.

Because He lives we too now live in newness of life and love. Paul, in his first prayer for the Ephesians having heard of their faith in the Lord and love for all the saints, makes several petitions, one of which was that they might know "…what is the surpassing greatness of His power toward us who believe…in accordance with the working of the strength of His might which He brought about in Christ, when He raised Him from the dead…"[3] Mighty resurrection power. The power of the risen, ascended Christ and the descended Spirit, bursting forth in an explosion of love. Paul prayed that they might experience this when he petitioned for them a second time. Cause and effect are here; resurrection life resulting in resounding love.

"Buried with Christ and raised with Him too
What is there left for me to do?
Simply to cease from struggling and strife
Simply to walk in newness of life."
T. Ryder.

This walk in newness of life and love entails suffering. "That I may know Him and the power of His resurrection and the fellowship of His sufferings, being conformed to His death; in order that I may attain to the resurrection from the dead."[4] Dare we pray Paul's personal prayer? To know Him is to experience the power that flows from the union with the risen Christ and to enter into fellowship with His sufferings, These are two aspects of the same experience. Being conformed to His death is the cause-way to being conformed to His life. The continuous experience of dying out to self. An expression of humility not uncertainty. The resurrection "from the dead" is the resurrection of the believers, not a general resurrection. The overall story of love's Easter is so comprehensive: beginning at the Garden tomb and continuing through the experiences of His people through two thousand years with its climax at the rapture resurrection of His own people.

APRIL 2 – THE LOVE OF CHRIST

Charles Simeon's (1759 – 1836) name stirs few memories today. Most people now have very little time to read current evangelical literature or articles on the lives of contemporary Christian workers, let alone reading about the life of a man born in 1759! Religious television programmes meet the needs for inspiration and information for many in this generation. To their loss I believe. To read widely, wisely and well, in Christian history and biography not only expands our understanding but challenges us to deeper devotion and love for Christ. I make no apologies for illustrating from lives that are past. At least they have finished their courses, have fought a good fight and kept the faith. Some, still alive, whom we could note and quote, have not done so well.

Simeon found Christ on Easter Day, 1770. He wrote:

"On Easter Sunday, April 4, I awoke early with these words upon my heart and lips: 'Jesus Christ is risen today; Hallelujah!' I had as full a conviction that I relied on the Lord Jesus Christ alone for my salvation as I had of my own existence. The love of Christ overwhelmed me by its incomprehensible grandeur."

As a young man entering the ministry after college he started at Holy Trinity, Cambridge, and was still serving there when he died fifty-four years later. Lord Macaulay, the statesman, said of him:

"If you knew what his authority and influence were, and how they extended from Cambridge to the most remote corners of England, you would allow that his real sway in the church was far greater than that of any Primate."

Simeon was a contemporary of another lover of the Lord, William Wilberforce (1759 – 1833), who showed the love of Christ in his practical and political work for the emancipation of slaves.

"Charles Simeon is staying with us, his heart glowing with the love of Christ. How full he is of that love! Oh, that I might copy him as he copies Christ!"

So attested Wilberforce, giving us the key to Simeon's long faithful ministry. He never faltered in fifty years. Love for, and the love of Christ sustained him.

The love of Christ in his life was also contagious. The others who caught it from him affected England and in some cases blessed the ends of the earth. For years he gave a tea party once a week to which all young men from the university were welcome. As an old man of seventy, he looked over a list of the names of men, who during the forty years between 1789 and 1829, had been successful missionaries. "Why," he exclaimed with delight, "they are all of them my tea party men!" Henry Martyn (1781 – 1812), who translated the New Testament into Hindi and Persian as a chaplain in India, was one of them. Simeon became one of the founders of the Church Missionary Society.

Dr. Frank Boreham D. D. (1871 – 1959) says that:

"Charles Simeon's text is the text of the four magnitudes: '...to know the love of Christ which surpasses knowledge...' Wide as the limits of the universe; long as the ages of eternity; deep as the abyss from which it has redeemed us; and high as the throne of God itself. Immensity is the only adequate symbol of its vastness. Charles Simeon explored all four of these dimensions."

APRIL 3 – FOUR DIMENSIONAL LOVE

"The love of God is greater far
Than tongue or pen can ever tell;
It goes beyond the highest star,
And reaches to the lowest hell;

O love of God, how rich and pure!
How measureless and strong!
It shall forevermore endure
The saints' and angels' song.

When years of time shall pass away,
And earthly thrones and kingdoms fall,
When men, who here refuse to pray,
On rocks and hills and mountains call,

God's love so sure, shall still endure,
All measureless and strong;
Redeeming grace to Adam's race
The saints' and angels' song.

Could we with ink the ocean fill,
And were the skies of parchment made,
Were every stalk on earth a quill,
And every man a scribe by trade,

To write the love of God above,
Would drain the ocean dry
Nor could the scroll contain the whole
Though stretched from sky to sky."
Frederick W. Lehman (1868 – 1953)

This great hymn introduces the four dimensional love that Paul prayed might be understood by the Ephesian Christians and all who have read that prayer from that day to this. "so that Christ may dwell in your hearts through faith; and that you, being rooted and grounded in love, may be able to comprehend with all the saints what is the breadth and length and height and depth, and to know the love of Christ which surpasses knowledge, that you may be filled up to all the fullness of God."[1]

The indwelling Spirit and the indwelling Christ are one and the same and their goals for our inner life are one. Christ dwells in our hearts by faith and the Holy Spirit is increasingly forming Him in us. Paul prays for enabling for us to comprehend the incomprehensible. We can never fully know the breadth of His love. It is broader than our mind's imagination. It is wider than the oceans and the limitless reach of space. It is broad enough to include every tongue and tribe and nation; yes, even the crowds today on the broad way to destruction.

Who can understand the length of the love of Christ? How long is long? How long is time? How long is eternity? This love has neither beginning nor ending. "…I have loved you with an everlasting love; Therefore I have drawn you with lovingkindness."[2]

The height of the love of Christ is higher than the birds and the air which is the first heaven. It is higher than the planets and the sun of our solar system and the stars of the universe which is the second heaven. It is as high as the heights of the holy throne of the One high and lifted up which is the third heaven where Paul was caught up and saw things indescribable and secret and heard inexpressible words. This is where language fails us as we contemplate the height of His holy, heavenly love. How do we in the Northern latitudes think of up? And those down under where to go down is up? How can we know that which surpasses knowledge? Paul caught up into Paradise couldn't – how can we?

APRIL 4 – THE LENGTHS OF HIS LOVE

How long is long? The length of His love is immeasurable. We will not attempt to measure it, except by thinking of the length which is unthinkable – the length of the life and love of the eternal God, and of the lengths to which He went in order to save us. With this, another immeasurable in mind, we will rather concentrate on the effect of this dimension on the lives of a few, who in their day were called fanatics, in the lengths to which they went in response to His length of love. These people were the Scotch covenanters of some centuries ago. For Christ and the Covenant they suffered long. They suffered the loss of all, for they were "…rooted and grounded in love."[1] They did what they had to do with comprehension, seeking "…to comprehend with all the saints what is the breadth and length and height and depth, and to know the love of Christ which surpasses knowledge…"[2] We will, from these persecuted saints, single out but two; two women, one young, one old, who loved as long as life lasted, and laid down their lives in lengthy dying. By doing so they entered into the length of days and length of life and love that has no ending. From A Handful of Stars by Dr. Frank Boreham, D. D. (1871 – 1959) we hear the story.

"It was a beautiful May morning when Major Windrom rode into Wigton and demanded the surrender, to him and his solders, of two women who had been convicted of attending a conventicler. One of them was Margaret Wilson, a fair young girl of eighteen. She was condemned to be lashed to a stake at low tide in such a way that the rising waters would slowly overwhelm her. In hope of shaking her fidelity, and saving her life, it was ordained that her companion should be fastened to a stake a little farther out. 'It may be,' said her persecutors, 'that, as Mistress Margaret watches the waves go over the widow before her, she will relent!' The ruse, however, had the opposite effect. When Margaret saw the fortitude with which the older woman yielded her soul to the incoming tide, she began to sing a paraphrase of the 25th Psalm, and those on the beach took up the strain. The soldiers angrily silenced them, and Margaret's mother, rushing into the waters, begged her to save her life by making the declaration that the authorities desired. But, tantalized and tormented, she never flinched; and as the waves lapped her face she was heard to repeat, again and again, the triumphant words 'For I am persuaded, that neither death, nor life, nor angels, nor principalities, nor powers, nor things present, nor things to come, Nor height, nor depth, nor any other creature, shall be able to separate us from the love of God, which is in Christ Jesus our Lord.'"

That is the length of the love of God in Christ, as Margaret Wilson, eighteen years of age, described it from drowning lips. That is the length of her love in response to the length of His. The finite and measurable is caught up into the infinite and immeasurable dimension of eternal love, the length of His love.

APRIL 5 – THE BREADTHS OF HIS LOVE

In this series we have told a little of Charles Simeon's (1759 – 1836) story and how on Easter Sunday he found full assurance of salvation.

"The love of Christ overwhelmed me by its incomprehensible grandeur."

That line is worth repeating for it was that love in all its four dimensions that kept him serving Christ for half a century and used him to urge young university students to go to the ends of the earth, and proclaim four dimensional love. And many did. One special portion of Scripture dominated Simeon's life for almost six decades. He repeated the rapturous words he had used previously of the love of Christ, when he described the passage and "its overwhelming and incomprehensible grandeur." He loved it; quoted it; preached on it and wrote of it. It occurs repeatedly in his correspondence. In a letter to a Miss Elliott he writes:

"My dear Ellen…Only get your soul deeply and abidingly impressed with the doctrine of the Cross and everything else will soon find its proper place in your system. Labour from day to day to comprehend the breadth and length and depth and height, and to know the love of Christ which passeth knowledge. That is all I want…"

Later, in writing in response to a minister's letter which had outlined a number of problems, Simeon urges him to get comprehensive views of the breadth and length and depth and height and to know the love of Christ which passeth knowledge.

The breadth of Simeon's ministry in preaching, writing, assisting in the founding of the Anglican Church Missionary Society, and sending out missionaries attests to his love for Christ. His breadth of compassion included encouragement for William Wilberforce (1759 – 1833) in his political efforts to free the slaves. Simeon stayed occasionally at the emancipator's home. The abolition, first of slavery and the slave trade itself, was followed by the emancipation of the slaves themselves. He also encouraged Henry Martyn (1781 – 1812), noble missionary to the Muslims, calling him "one of my tea party men." The breadth of his interests and the breadth of his love were all the result of the breadth of Christ's love for him.

Canon Carus wrote a definitive story on Simeon's life and in an appendage to that biography the Canon tells that as soon as he began to fail, his mind turned to his text.

"I am fully determined to begin at once a set of sermons on that grand subject in Ephesians: 'That ye may be able to comprehend what is the breadth and length and depth and height, and to know the love of Christ which passeth knowledge.' I don't expect or desire to preach them; but, if my life be spared write them I will!"

Two weeks before his death his mind was still full of it. The Canon tells us:

"During the greater part of Thursday his whole mind was absorbed upon his favourite passage" and again it is quoted in full. "It is the grandest subject I can conceive of. I should think a life well spent in which one wrote four sermons on that passage in a manner worthy of it!"

And so he died. His life was the best commentary on that portion. Better than any four sermons. He illustrated all the four dimensions, but for me, Simeon illumines best the breadth of His love.

APRIL 6 – THE DEPTHS OF HIS LOVE

A brilliant, witty, author and playwright, Oscar Wilde (1854 – 1900), destroyed himself, his family, his life and his career through pederasty. This perversity was exposed and Wilde was brought to trial, found guilty, and sentenced to prison. Today he would be acclaimed! In jail he wrote one of the saddest books I have ever read. I picked up my copy, many years ago in a New Zealand second hand bookstore. The title is De Profundis literally "Out of the Depths" with sub-title "The Ballad of Reading Gaol." Here is one quote:

"Yet each man kills the thing he loves,
By each let this be heard.
Some do it with a bitter look,
Some with a flattering word,
The coward does it with a kiss,
The brave man with a sword."

Wilde through his sin, killed the love of his wife and many friends. Yet, many years later, his son, wrote a book of affectionate understanding and forgiveness about his father. As I read De Profundis I was struck by two things: the depth of Wilde's remorse and regrets (God alone knows if it was repentance) and the closeness Wilde came to the knowledge of the truth in Christ (was it a conversion? – again God alone knows). This I do know, "Out of the Depths" made me better acquainted with the depths of the love of Christ for sinners.

There is a Psalm which possibly prompted Wilde's writing in Reading Jail, and almost certainly gave him the title for his book De Profundis. They are the literal, in Latin, opening words of the Psalm "Out of the depths". This Psalm belongs, curiously, to the series known as the "Songs of Ascents." Like Wilde in his depths of sin and despair the Psalmist also voices his hope in the Lord's forgiving love. "Out of the depths I have cried to You, O Lord. Lord, hear my voice! Let Your ears be attentive To the voice of my supplications. If You, Lord, should mark iniquities, O Lord, who could stand? But there is forgiveness with You…with the Lord there is lovingkindness, And with Him is abundant redemption…"[1] For the Psalmist whatever his sin, for Israel and their rebellion, for Wilde and his homosexuality, for you and me in our sins there is hope. "He made Him who knew no sin to be sin on our behalf, so that we might become the righteousness of God in Him."[2] Praise God for this exchange of sin.

"Oh, the deep, deep love of Jesus, vast, unmeasured, boundless, free!
Rolling as a mighty ocean in its fullness over me,
Underneath me, all around me, is the current of thy love.
Leading onward, leading homeward, to my glorious rest above.

Oh, the deep, deep love of Jesus, spread His praise from shore
How He loves us, ever loves us, changes never, never more.
How He watches o'er His loved ones, died to call them all His own.
How for them He's interceding, watches o'er them from the throne.

Oh, the deep, deep love of Jesus, love of every love the best!
Tis an ocean vast of blessing, 'tis a haven sweet of rest.
Oh, the deep, deep love of Jesus, 'tis a haven of heavens to me;
And it lifts me up to glory, for it lifts me up to thee."
S. Trevor. Francis (1834 – 1925)

APRIL 7 – LAUNCHING OUT INTO THE DEPTHS

"A little boy was playing by the shore of the broad blue sea
And oft he looked across the waves so wonderingly,
It was a new entrancing sight to him, this watery waste,
The rocky billows tossing with their foam wreaths graced,
And often in his inland home with childish glee
The lad would say to young and older folks 'I've seen the sea!'

And so he had, the boy made no mistake, his words were true;
But yet how much of oceans vast expanse had met his view?
Only the waves that beat upon the shore, while far away
The broad Atlantic in all its length and breadth before him lay.
And so we say 'We know the love of Christ' and so we do
'Tis no exaggeration or mistake but sweetly true.

But yet, how much of that great love do we yet know?
Only the waves that beat upon the shore that nearer flow.
The mighty ocean of redeeming love rolls deep and wide
Filling earth and heaven and eternity with its vast tide.
We know it by a sweet experience now, yet shall explore
Its height, its depth, its length and breadth for evermore."

Meanwhile, until that day of full revelation and realization, I must go on exploring this ocean of love, always conscious that there's more and I'll never discover it all. But it's my life goal and heart's desire to explore and experience all I can contain, "and to know the love of Christ which surpasses knowledge..."[1] To do this I have found one essential way. I must leave the shore of the known, move past the breakers on the edge, go to the back of the waves and "..."Put out into the deep water..."[2] as our Lord told Simon Peter. This entails leaving the shallows and exercising faith. I have found again and again during the past fifty years that this obedience of faith reveals new wonders in the ocean of love. I have proved, for more times than I can count, the reality of God's Word that."... faith working through love"[3] is the way of discovery, the explorers delight, and brings more experiential knowledge of the, never fully knowable, love of Christ. Leaving the shore and shallows means severing the lines and ties that would hinder and hold us back. "Let go the hawsers and springs" I have heard ship's captains say as I have sailed the seven seas.

Andrew Murray (1828 – 1917) has some pertinent things to say about this:

"As a Christian sees that, though he knows so little of his Lord's love, the Lord is ready to lead him on to it in a way he does not know. He becomes willing to turn away from everything that can occupy the heart, and to yield himself in patient obedient discipleship, to the influences of his relationship with his Lord. He learns to know that love can master him. The love of Christ asks and claims the whole heart and life...When the love of Christ becomes everything to any of us, and we yield ourselves to His love, demonstrated in dying for sinners, that love will teach us. It will constrain us, to part with all for this pearl of great price."

As we let go, launch out into the deeps of the will and love of God, and let Him have His way with us, we discover what those mariners of old found. The harvest of the sea, as Peter did. The wonders of the deep as the Psalmist sang. "Those who go down to the sea in ships, Who do business on great waters; They have seen the works of the Lord, And His wonders in the deep."[4]

APRIL 8 – THE HEIGHTS OF HIS LOVE

From the heights of heaven, to which John the beloved was to be caught up in the Spirit from his exile in the isle of Patmos, come these words of wonder and gratitude. "…To Him who loves us and released us from our sins by His blood—and He has made us to be a kingdom, priests to His God and Father—to Him be the glory and the dominion forever and ever. Amen."[1] The blood bought, blood washed throng around the Throne, seen from the ramparts of glory are a fit symbol to illustrate this last dimension.

Our present lofty position in Him is possible because God has "…raised us up with Him, and seated us with Him in the heavenly places in Christ Jesus."[2] It was love that wrought so effectively: "…God, being rich in mercy, because of His great love with which He loved us, even when we were dead in our transgressions, made us alive together with Christ…"[3] So, we like John, are already in the heights, with the throng around the Throne. What sights greet the eyes of anticipatory love. We see Him "face to face." We see the marks of love in His hands and feet and the scar in His side. We see so much now, by faith which works by love, but there will be so much more. "…things which eye has not seen and ear has not heard, and which have not entered the heart of man, all that God has prepared for those who love Him."[4]

The heights are exhilarating; the heights of His love are experientially wonderful as Charles Simeon (1759 – 1836) found out. He took the words that John heard from the heights and made them his motto, and held them before him as his ideal. Simeon has long since joined that multitude in the heights of heaven.

A contemporary of Simeon's, though from a different station in life, was John Nelson (1707 – 1774), the stone mason from Yorkshire, England, who was stirred to conviction by John Wesley's (1703 – 1791) preaching. In his journal Nelson tells how, at seven on the Sunday morning of June 17, 1739, John Nelson, among a crowd of six thousand, heard John Wesley. The thirty-two year old Nelson was converted three months later when as he tells us:

"In the afternoon, I opened the Book where it is written: 'Unto Him that loved us, and washed us from our sins in His own blood…' I was so affected that I could not read for weeping."

The new lover of the Lord, having been washed from his sins and been lifted to the heights, longed for others to find the Saviour. Upending an old washtub for his pulpit, he often preached with stones whistling past his head and sometimes blood streaming down his face when a rock found its mark. His journal tells of love's longings fulfilled.

"My wife began to be concerned…was thoroughly convinced and her heart was filled with peace and love… my own brother was brought to experience the redeeming love of Christ, My mother was the first ripe fruit that God gave me of my labour…Another of my brothers, my aunt and two cousins were converted…my grand-daughter rejoices in the Lord…"

Saved from the depths to the heights and from these same heights they will come with Him some day.

APRIL 9 – THE CORDS OF LOVE

When Abraham bound Isaac his son and laid him on the altar, these cords hardly seemed cords of love. Yet, as is so frequently the case in life, things are not what they seem. On Abraham's part they were the cords of loving obedience to the voice of God. On Isaac's part they were the cords of loving obedience to his father's will. On God's part they were the symbolic cords of His Son's loving submission to His Father's plan for the salvation of sinners. Isaac was not sacrificed; the Son of God was. Later, in the daily sacrificial animal offerings made by the children of Israel for the covering of sins, the cords of binding were again present. "…Bind the festival sacrifice with cords to the horns of the altar."[1] "…bind the sacrifice with cords, even unto the horns of the altar," says the King James Version in almost similar words. This scripture is a picture of what took place during the Levitical offerings and a prophetic portrayal of what would take place on the Cross of Calvary. It also reveals what that Cross meant to the Father who was bound to His Son by eternal cords of love, and it is also a full expression of what, on the Cross for a brief moment, it meant to the Son to have these cords of love severed as His soul was made an offering for sin. "…My God, my God, why…"[2] was wrung from Him in that moment of terrible forsaking. The cords were cords of love's obedience; cords of submission, love's submission; and cords of identification, love's identification of the Son with us sinners and our sins. "The cords of death encompassed me And the terrors of Sheol came upon me…"[3] as we were bound together on that Cross. His were the cords of love, ours the cords of sin and shame. "I have been crucified with Christ…the Son of God, who loved me and gave Himself up for me."[4] No Roman cords or nails could have bound Him, or kept Him there on that cruel and criminal cross. He set His face as a flint to go to Jerusalem and to that altar of sacrifice on Calvary. In gratitude I bind myself to Him with His own cords of love.

"I lift my heart to Thee, Savior Divine,
For Thou art all to me, And I am Thine;
Is there on earth a closer bond than this,
That my Beloved's mine, and I am His?

Thine am I by all ties, And chiefly Thine,
For through Thy sacrifice Thou, Lord, art mine;
By Thine own cords of love, so sweetly wound
Around me, closely I to Thee am bound.

To Thee, Thou Bleeding Lamb, I all things owe,
All that I have and am, And all I know;
All that I have is now no longer mine,
And I am not my own: Lord, I am Thine.

How can I, Lord, withhold Life's brightest hour
Thee; or gathered gold, Or any power?
Why should I keep one precious thing from Thee,
When Thou hast given Thine dear Self for me?

I pray Thee, Savior, keep Me in Thy love,
Until the world Thou sweep And me remove
To that fair realm, where, sin and sorrow o'er,
Thou and Thine own are one for evermore."
Charles Edward Mudie (1818 – 1890)

His own cords of love have drawn from all nations a people for Himself, and bound them to Himself for all time. We are bound to Him with the ties of our voluntary obedience and submission; bound by freedom's bonds and bound, above all, by those strong spiritual cords of love.

APRIL 10 – GIFT LOVE

"Love ever gives,
Forgives, outlives,
And ever stands
With open hands.

And, while it lives,
It gives.
For this is Love's prerogative,
To give, and give, and give."
William Arthur Dunkerley (1852 – 1941)

Love is no Dead Sea, always receiving never giving. Too low down to have an outlet it shrinks into itself with Sodom's salted ruins somewhere at its southern end. Love is like the sweet sea, or lake, of Galilee fed by the Jordan River. That river, rising in the springs of snow-capped Mt. Hermon, pours itself into Galilee which has provided a living to fisherman living around its shores. Galilee at its southern end pours the river out again in continuing blessing until it dies in the Dead Sea. This picture parable of giving love starts in the heights where in reality it all begins. Trinitarian giving love is divine love where the Father gives Himself in Christ reconciling the world unto Himself. The Son in love gives Himself in person and passion for the sins of the world. The Spirit pours himself in love into born again people who in turn give this love to others.

"…the free gift of God is eternal life in Christ Jesus our Lord."[1] This gift came as a baby, developed as a boy, matured as a man and died at thirty-three. All the time He was Immanuel – God with us. It had all been prophesied six hundred years before His birth. "For a child will be born to us, a son will be given to us…"[2] foretelling His humanity and His deity. The same prophet foresaw the great gift love of the Cross. "…He poured out Himself to death, And was numbered with the transgressors…"[3]

"O 'twas love, 'twas wondrous love,
The love of God to me;
It brought my Savior from above,
To die on Calvary!"
Martha M. Stockton (1821 – 1885)

"…the Son of God, who loved me and gave Himself up for me."[4] This is the love that lives and gives and forgives, me, now. My reaction should be the attitude of gratitude. How grateful I should be, in word and deed, in response to such giving. "Thanks be to God for His indescribable gift!"[5] Heart praise should flow and hand service should be given in return. "…Freely you received, freely give."[6] And still He gives, and gives, and gives again. "He who did not spare His own Son, but delivered Him over for us all, how will He not also with Him freely give us all things?"[7] His divine power has granted to us everything pertaining to life and godliness.

"Give of your best to the Master;
Naught else is worthy His love.
He gave Himself for your ransom,
Gave up His glory above.

Laid down His life without murmur,
You from sin's ruin to save.
Give Him your heart's adoration;
Give Him the best that you have.
Howard B. Grose (1851 – 1939)

So we but give Him back His own, hopefully with interest, when we give to others here below. In giving love to him and others we find that it boomerangs. "Give, and it will be given to you…"[8]

APRIL 11 – LOVE'S STRENGTH

"Measure thy life by loss instead of gain,
Not by the wine drink, but the wine poured forth;
For love's strength standeth in love's sacrifice,
And whoso suffers most has most to give."

These words by an unknown author contain an important Biblical principle illustrated and taught in both the Old and New Testaments.

David recognised this truth: that sacrifice provides and proves the strength of love. He in turn, by his action also showed that "love's strength standeth in love's sacrifice." David was hiding from Saul in the cave of Adullam. With him was a motley crowd of about four hundred men, including his family, and "everyone who was in distress, and everyone who was in debt, and everyone who was discontented gathered to him; and he became captain over them…"[1] With their families there were probably a thousand mouths to feed and water while moulding the men into a formidable fighting force. David, no doubt hot and thirsty, expressed a longing for a drink of water from the well of Bethlehem. So great was the love of his leading men for him that even a desire became a command. Three of his chiefs, willing to sacrifice their own lives, broke through the ranks of the Philistines and brought the water to him. He would not drink it but poured it out symbolically as a drink offering to the Lord, saying: "…Shall I drink the blood of these men who went at the risk of their lives?…"[2] He knew that "love's strength standeth in love's sacrifice," and knowing it showed it forever by his act. They gave; he gave.

When we, at the Lord's Table, partake of the wine, symbol of the blood Christ shed for us, we are remembering not a symbolic death, like David's three men, but a real one. Not symbolic blood but the real life substance of the Saviour. Not the strength and sacrifice of mighty men, but the strength of the heart and hands of Him who was without sin. The sacrifice of the Lamb, Who was without spot or blemish, slain for the sins of the world. Not the love of finite men for a fine but flawed man, but divine love, not sentimental but a supremely strong and redemptive love for you and me. Great David's greater Son gave the greatest demonstration of love's strength standing in love's sacrifice, which the world has ever seen. He suffered most and has most to give.

"Greater love has no one than this, that one lay down his life for his friends."[3] Yet He laid down His life for His enemies. He died for the ungodly. "For one will hardly die for a righteous man; though perhaps for the good man someone would dare even to die.   But God demonstrates His own love toward us, in that while we were yet sinners, Christ died for us."[4] In the light of His love and in the standing we have because of His sacrifice "…we ought to lay down our lives for the brethren."[5] (Or at least be willing to.) This is John's second truth from his second "3:16." This is how we measure our lives. This is the loss that is all pure gain.

APRIL 12 – LOVE'S MEMORIAL FEAST

I have told elsewhere of standing beside Dr. Horatius Bonar's grave in Edinburgh, Scotland (December 8). In his long life (1808 – 1889), that lover of the Lord wrote some memorable hymns. For me, the following hymn is one of the deepest and loveliest that we sing at love's memorial feast.

"Here, O my Lord, I see Thee face to face;
Here would I touch and handle things unseen;
Here grasp with firmer hand eternal grace,
And all my weariness upon Thee lean.

Here would I feed upon the bread of God,
Here drink with Thee the royal wine of Heaven;
Here would I lay aside each earthly load,
Here taste afresh the calm of sin forgiven.

This is the hour of banquet and of song;
This is the heavenly table spread for me;
Here let me feast, and feasting, still prolong
The hallowed hour of fellowship with Thee."

I have no help but Thine; nor do I need
Another arm save Thine to lean upon;
It is enough, my Lord, enough indeed;
My strength is in Thy might, Thy might alone

Mine is the sin, but Thine the righteousness:
Mine is the guilt, but Thine the cleansing blood;
Here is my robe, my refuge, and my peace;
Thy Blood, Thy righteousness, O Lord my God!

These verses are usually sung at the commencement of the Feast of Remembrance; the memorial of the Lord's death celebrated by His people until He comes again. Following the first Passover supper our Lord instituted this new Lord's supper, or Lord's table. Hear His words: "…Jesus took some bread, and after a blessing, He broke it and gave it to the disciples, and said, "'Take, eat; this is My body.' And when He had taken a cup and given thanks, He gave it to them, saying, 'Drink from it, all of you; for this is My blood of the covenant, which is poured out for many for forgiveness of sins.'"[1] The symbolic breaking of bread typified, then and now, His body broken for us at Calvary, and the symbolic wine typified His blood shed for us on the cross. This was the first memorial love feast.

The early church held agapé feasts, love feasts, a communal meal followed by what we also now call communion. Shockingly, some of these meals developed into shameful drunken times, with resultant disorders and dire results. Paul, in love, rebuked these abuses; as he would have all the other abuses and misuses of "the table" and "the feast" which have since developed from this simple memorial and symbolic supper. Paul was also given the full revelation of the significance and meaning of it, summed up by three looks. The backward look: to the Crucifixion, His death, and all its implications. The second is the forward, upward look to His coming. "For as often as you eat this bread and drink the cup, you proclaim the Lord's death until He comes."[2] Then there is the inward look of self judgement. "…a man must examine himself…"[3] At the conclusion we read: "After singing a hymn, they went out…"[4] We will allow the last verse of Dr. Bonar's hymn to conclude this meditation on love's memorial feast.

"Feast after feast thus comes and passes by;
Yet, passing, points to the glad feast above,
Giving sweet foretaste of the festal joy,
The Lamb's great bridal feast of bliss and love."

APRIL 13 – LOVE FEASTS PERVERTED

The agapé feast was a communal meal which the early church celebrated and which usually concluded with the Lord's supper. This Christian community love feast was meant to be a convocation and manifestation of holy love in fellowship. Instead it degenerated into drunken feasts. It was marred and perverted by ungodly, unconverted professors of Christ who had infiltrated the membership and led astray some of the believers. The result was unbelievable debauchery and drunkenness at some of these "love ins" and a carry over of the disorders into the holy celebrations which followed. False prophets and pseudo-teachers had wormed their way in. Jude describes these charlatans, these pretentious impostors, in strong words. "These are the men who are hidden reefs in your love feasts when they feast with you without fear, caring for themselves; clouds without water, carried along by winds; autumn trees without fruit, doubly dead, uprooted; wild waves of the sea, casting up their own shame like foam; wandering stars, for whom the black darkness has been reserved forever."[1]

Peter also indicts the false prophets and teachers with their false ways and words corrupting many with their carnal carousing at the love feasts. "But false prophets also arose among the people, just as there will also be false teachers among you, who will secretly introduce destructive heresies, even denying the Master who bought them...Many will follow their sensuality, and because of them the way of the truth will be maligned; and in their greed they will exploit you with false words...They count it a pleasure to revel in the daytime. They are stains and blemishes, reveling in their deceptions, as they carouse with you, having eyes full of adultery that never cease from sin, enticing unstable souls..."[2] God's holy love standards are attacked by Satan from outside the assemblies of the saints but most frequently and successfully from within the church. He subverts and perverts the truth, turning Christian love festivals into carnal lust sessions. We can be sure, now as then, that the attack will be upon the high and holy heavenly love. The devil goes for the jugular; he destroys the greatest thing, love; he debases the lovely love feasts and, worst of all, undermines the witness of the Lord's Table.

Paul makes this very clear as he introduces and concludes the teaching and description of the communion love feast. "Therefore when you meet together, it is not to eat the Lord's Supper...and one is hungry and another is drunk. What!... do you despise the church of God..."[3] "But a man must examine himself, and in so doing he is to eat of the bread and drink of the cup. For he who eats and drinks, eats and drinks judgment to himself if he does not judge the body rightly. For this reason many among you are weak and sick, and a number sleep. But if we judged ourselves rightly, we would not be judged. But when we are judged, we are disciplined by the Lord so that we will not be condemned along with the world. So then, my brethren, when you come together to eat, wait for one another. If anyone is hungry, let him eat at home, so that you will not come together for judgment. The remaining matters I will arrange when I come."[4] There is something to be said for the old time Scotch system of "fencing the table." This love feast needs explaining and defending anew today.

APRIL 14 – LOVE'S MEMORIALS

In old Philadelphia, not far from Independence Hall and the building where the cracked Liberty Bell is enshrined, there is an old graveyard. There, on a stone set in the wall, is the epitaph of Benjamin Franklin (1706 – 1790), one of the memorable characters of the American revolution. This was composed by Franklin and here they are from a photograph I took of them on the wall.

"The body of Benjamin Franklin (like the cover of an old book, its contents torn and stript of its lettering and gilding) lies here, food for worms but the work itself shall not be lost for it will, as he believed appear once more in a new and more elegant edition revised and corrected by the Author."

Curiously, they are not on his tomb which merely reads:

"Benjamin and Deborah Franklin, February 1790."

I don't know if the stone with this epitaph once stood at his grave. This was Franklin's way of expressing his belief in the resurrection and a new redemptive body. Grave stones are memorials, many of them erected by loving family or friends and often expressing the departed's love and belief in the Saviour. Others leave their love memorials in letters.

I was privileged once, when in London, England, to see the salt-stained pages pencilled by Commander Allen Gardiner (1794 – 1851) as he lay dying of starvation on a lonely beach in Patagonia, South America. These pages are perhaps the most moving love memorials I have ever seen. Who was Commander Gardiner and why was he dying like that in Tierra del Fuego? He was a naval officer of Great Britain in the time of the Napoleonic Wars. He had turned his back on God in his youth but God hadn't turned His back on Allen. He was converted through correspondence. An old lady, a friend of his dead mother, was constrained to write to the young man about the claims of Christ. The letter reached him in 1820 as his ship, "H. M. S. Leander", lay at anchor in the Straits of Melacca. Gardiner dates his conversion to receipt of that letter. From then on he blazed trails for Christ all around the world. J. W. Marsh, his biographer, tells us that from the Falkland Islands he sailed with six companions to pioneer a mission in Patagonia; a land unknown and a people forgotten. Terrible storms and delays prevented supplies reaching the little party until too late. All were dead when the relief party reached them. Whether the Commander died last is not known but he recorded the story and it is a memorable memorial. His journal is full of jubilant joy and triumphant love.

"On the day that preceded his death he assures us that, though five days without food, he has no sensation of hunger. And here are the last sentences he ever penned. 'Yet a little while, and through grace we shall join that blessed throng to sing the praises of Christ throughout eternity. I neither hunger nor thirst though five days without food. Marvellous kindness to me a sinner.'"

Other missionaries carried on the work of love began by Gardiner and his band. Death is often the way love wins. Later Charles Darwin in his famous voyage in the "Beagle" testified of the changes the gospel had brought to Patagonia.

APRIL 15 – LOVE'S NEW LAWS

The more we look into love's ramifications the more amazed we are at the way it permeates the whole of our society and the way it has been to the fore from Eden to the world of our day. Secular writers from Ovid (43BC – 17AD) to television serialists today; saints as disparate as Paul of the first century to Bernard of Clairvoux (1090 – 1153) a thousand years later; Bishop Anders Nygren (1890 – 1978) and Oxford don C. S. Lewis (1898 – 1963) of the twentieth, have, with multitudes of others, attested to the importance of the subject. The more we think of it the more we find these loves intermingled in every area of life. The word is in every language, the meanings are many, and the implications far reaching. It undergirds the Ten Commandments and the Beatitudes of Jesus. His nine "blesseds" are but His new commandment of love seen as inner attitudes governing outer actions and producing reactions from others. Let us look at them in the light of love.[1]

"Blessed are the poor in spirit..." Happy are these poor paupers of the spirit; impoverished and knowing their inner need. Happy the humble, as opposed to the proud. The Lord of love loves such and makes them His heirs.

"Blessed are those who mourn..." Happy are those who mourn over sin. His love brought Him to Calvary. Past guilt is gone and sin's present dominion is broken and one day we will have deliverance from its very presence. Love found a way to comfort; the costly way of the Cross.

"Blessed are the gentle..." Happy are the mild and gentle. The Lover of our souls is the source and one day He and we in the strength of almighty meekness will inherit the earth. Love is gentle but not weak.

"Blessed are those who hunger and thirst for righteousness..." Eschewing the self-righteousness of the Pharisee and emulating the attitude and prayer of the Publican we are given His righteousness and a love for him and it. We who love the Lord and righteousness must conversely hate evil.

"Blessed are the merciful..." Happy are those who are full of mercy. This is another of these inner attitudes of love, born of His love, when we are born again. This is a boomerang of love when put into practice.

"Blessed are the pure in heart..." Happy are those whose hearts are cleansed by the blood; clear of guile and undivided in their love. Such see God now in loving control of their circumstances and in the future "face to face."

"Blessed are the peacemakers..." Happy are those engaged in love's ministry of making peace where divisions and barriers exist. He, in His loving role of making peace, led the way; we must follow and show we are also sons.

"Blessed are those who have been persecuted for the sake of righteousness..." A happy loving band, led on by holy love to heaven.

"Blessed are you when people insult you and persecute you, and falsely say all kinds of evil against you..." Happy are you who know suffering for love's sake as I loved and suffered for you.

You are part of a wonderful band of lovers. Lovers of the Lord; of poverty; of penitence; of gentleness; of righteousness; of mercy; of purity; of peace; of persecution; of false accusation. The new commandment of love has its ramifications in us, through us and brings reactions upon us. Happy are such lovers.

APRIL 16 – LOVE'S BOOMERANGS

Many, many years ago I was crossing, by train, the great Australian desert, called the Nullabor Plain. Nullabor means "No Tree" and it certainly had none. At a lonely station (as I remember called Oonadatta or something like that) a group of Australian aboriginals from a nearby reserve came to the train selling hand carved souvenirs. I bought three. A kangaroo, and an emu, carved out of mulga roots and a boomerang out of the same hardwood. I wondered at the time where they got the wood on "No Tree" plain. That boomerang, a real one, was a source of interest in other countries particularly when I used it to illustrate Scripture.

It was many years later that I found the word boomerang in the Bible; The Living Bible that is. Ken Taylor's (1917 – 2005) paraphrase says: "Because the wicked are unfair, their violence boomerangs and destroys them."[1] This boomerang effect of returning to us what we throw is equally applicable whether we dispatch evil or good. The Ten Commandments of the Old Covenant are ten boomerangs still returning woes to the lives of those who break them. The Beatitudes of the New Covenant are nine boomerangs which come back with big blessings.

Here is a portion from His Word which lists six more similar ones: "…love your enemies…and your reward will be great…be merciful, just as your Father is merciful. Do not judge, and you will not be judged…do not condemn, and you will not be condemned; pardon, and you will be pardoned. Give, and it will be given to you…"[2] Loving; being merciful; not being judgemental; uncondemning; forgiving; giving. Two have a negative emphasis while four accentuate the positive. These boomerangs were born of love. Obviously they need a page each, but as that is not possible here, we will confine ourselves to the theme title. Love is the begetting power and propulsive force of these six boomerangs.

Look now at loves control of these boomerangs. As the love of God is the source and control of His grace and mercy so that same love in us propels the boomerang of mercy in our daily dealings. It returns. "Blessed are the merciful, for they shall receive mercy."[3] Love governs our discerning and critical faculties ensuring righteous judgments; not self –righteous and condemnatory as the Pharisees were in their demand that the woman caught in adultery be dealt with by the Law. Our Lord did not condone her sin and neither did He condemn her. We are condemned already if we don't believe. He did not come to condemn but to save. Love not only originates forgiveness but forgives at great length; up to "seventy times seven."[4] Our own forgiveness for Christ's sake demands that we forgive others. If we don't it will boomerang; if we do it will return with recompense. "Love must give" is a truism. We have discussed this elsewhere but here we will emphasize the rewarding return of this boomerang. "Give, and it will be given to you…pressed down, shaken together, and running over…"[5] We do not give to get but we can't give without getting.

APRIL 17 – LOVE AND FORGIVENESS

"Forgiveness doesn't mean that you can become some sort of a wimp and forgive without some kind of demand. We are responsible for what we have done."

This comment, by Father Robert Friday, professor of religion at the Catholic University of America, was made à propos of some headlines concerning Pope John Paul II (1920 – 2005). The background is as follows: In St. Peter's Square, Rome, Italy on May 13th, 1981 the Pope was shot by Mehmet Ali Agca (1958 -). The Pope recovered and pardoned his would be assassin. In January 1984 the Pontiff gave a public demonstration and lesson in personal forgiveness as he went to the terrorist's cell in Rome's Rebibbia prison and "held the hand that had held the gun that was meant to kill him." "Time" January 9, 1984. The television cameras were in the cell publicly recording the event for their viewers and posterity. Another Italian writer commented:

"The Pope intends to say, 'If we really want peace we must make the first step, we must forget offences and offer the bread of love and charity.'"

These are worthy sentiments and a worthy act.

However, we do need to take a closer look at love and forgiveness. First let's note a fundamental fact. Our Lord is the only One Who, in the essential, eternal and divine sense, can forgive sins. While on earth Christ did this, saying: "...Son, your sins are forgiven."[1] This raised the wrath of the scribes who rightly said: "...who can forgive sins but God alone?"[2] but who wrongly called Jesus a blasphemer. They refused to recognize Him as God, the Messiah, the Christ. This authority to finally forgive sins is still His, though He has given to all His children the power to proclaim the message of forgiveness and to declare to sinners that if they will repent and believe, they will be saved and forgiven. This is how Peter, Paul and all New Testament preachers proclaimed the love and forgiveness of God, Our Lord purchased forgiveness by His blood; we declare it.

Secondly, it would be beneficial to review what our prerogative is in the matter of personally forgiving those who sin against us. We are to "Be kind to one another, tender-hearted, forgiving each other, just as God in Christ also has forgiven you."[3] Does our personal love exhibited in forgiveness of the wrongdoer equate with divine forgiveness? No! We must be careful to distinguish between divine and human forgiveness. Human forgiveness sometimes includes the remission of penalty. Divine forgiveness follows the execution of the penalty. God could be just and justify the sinner by exacting the penalty from His Son, our Substitute and Saviour. Thus He can be "...faithful and righteous to forgive us our sins..."[4] and not only loving and kind.

Where does love and forgiveness on the personal level run counter to law and justice on the government level? The Italian authorities didn't free Ali Agca who now seems repentant. The Pope forgave him on a human basis but left him locked in prison to carry out the rest of his sentence. The Christian spirit of love and forgiveness cannot be the basis of public policy. It cannot open prison doors and loose all the convicts. This would result in anarchy and mayhem. Restraint and punishment are necessary even for forgiveness. There are two orders: the law and the Gospel. We forgive because of the Gospel, but the criminal still spends time in jail.

APRIL 18 – THE FIRST GREAT COMMANDMENT ON LOVE

The Scriptures from which our Lord constantly quoted were the Old Testament. The law which is quoted here consisted of the five books of Moses: Genesis, Exodus, Leviticus, Numbers and Deuteronomy. "One of them, a lawyer, asked Him a question, testing Him, 'Teacher, which is the great commandment in the Law?' And He said to him, 'You shall love the Lord your God with all your heart, and with all your soul, and with all your mind. This is the great and foremost commandment. The second is like it, You shall love your neighbour as yourself. On these two commandments depend the whole Law and the Prophets.'"[1] In this portion the lawyer, an expert in Mosaic Law, questions the Lord. In a similar case described by Luke, another, or the same lawyer, asks a leading question concerning eternal life. This is answered by our Lord with another question: "...'What is written in the Law? How does it read to you?'"[2] The lawyer answered in almost identical words that the Lord had given in Mathew. Both the Lord and the lawyer are quoting from the Old Testament. Deuteronomy for the great and foremost commandment, and Leviticus for the second.[3]

Dealing with first things first, we look at this great and foremost commandment which covers and fulfills, the first four commandments of the Decalogue. All of these have to do with our relationship to God. "a) You shall have no other gods before Me. b) You shall not make for yourself an idol...You shall not worship them or serve them...c) You shall not take the name of the Lord your God in vain...d) Remember the sabbath day, to keep it holy."[4] God only; not only first. God worshipped; not idols. God's name honoured. God's day observed. If we love God supremely we will acknowledge him uniquely; we will worship Him only; we will magnify His name and we will honour His day. Thus love is the following of these laws. One law of love covers these four. As always the lesser is contained in the greater.

The kind, quality, amplitude and duration of love required to do this is expressed in four ways. You and I must love God with all our heart...all our soul...all our strength...all our minds. With such a requirement, like the lawyer, we begin to wriggle. We are convicted by the questions and the answers. Can I do this? Have I done it? The lawyer hadn't nor can any natural man. So not only have I not kept these four commandments, I have not kept the one on which they depend. I cannot inherit eternal life this way. I am condemned already. If one link is broken then the whole chain is broken. But what I cannot do, He Himself can do for me, and in me, and through me.

Is there a resolution of these problems? Yes, there is and it lies in this same love; the love of God in the Person of His Son. "...God has sent His only begotten Son into the world so that we might live through Him. In this is love, not that we loved God, but that He loved us and sent His Son to be the propitiation for our sins."[5] He died for us. By this means we are brought from death to life. His divine love is the love in us that loves Him; the new law of life that fulfills the law.

APRIL 19 – THE SECOND GREAT COMMANDMENT ON LOVE

"Owe nothing to anyone except to love one another; for he who loves his neighbor has fulfilled the law. For this, 'You shall not commit adultery, you shall not murder, you shall not steal, you shall not covet,' and if there is any other commandment, it is summed up in this saying, 'You shall love your neighbour as yourself.' Love does no wrong to a neighbor; therefore love is the fulfillment of the law."[1] We have seen our Lord confirming the Scriptural statements of the Old Covenant, that the Ten Commandments can be reduced to two; love God and love your neighbour. Paul, in the quote above, confirms what has been said and enlarges on the second great commandment on love. The last six, of which Paul quotes four, deal with human relationships. We have noted that the first four deal with our relationship to God.

The fifth is called "...the first commandment with a promise."[2] "Honor your father and your mother, that your days may be prolonged..."[3] The New Testament interprets "honour" as "obedience." This is the first requisite of love in children. Love is the fulfilling of this law.

The sixth commandment "Thou shalt not kill"[4] is better rendered, as it is in the more modern versions "You shall not murder." There is an important difference between the two words. Murderers, who are judicially executed after due process of law, as Scripture commands, are killed justly. The positive emphasis that Paul, our Lord and the lawyer all make is, if love for our neighbour controls us, there will be seen again that love is the fulfilling of this law.

So it is with the seventh "you shall not commit adultery." Our Lord refuted the men who demanded the death penalty for the adulterous woman. The men were guilty too, but, as is so often the case, the woman pays the price and the man gets off. Our Lord would not permit this double standard. He did not condemn the woman, nor condone her sin, but forgave her and said: "...Go. From now on sin no more."[5] It wouldn't be done at all if love controlled us, for love is the fulfilling of this law.

The eighth "you shall not steal" covers a wide range from petty pilfering through armed robbery to corporate crookedness. "He who steals must steal no longer..."[6] is one of the numerous New Testament comments on this command. If I love my neighbour, love is again the fulfilling of this law.

The ninth "You shall not bear false witness against your neighbor"[7] refers to legal lying in courts of law but is not limited to these places and people who are perjurers. As love will inhibit lying then the law will be fulfilled.

The tenth "You shall not covet" will be met if we follow the idea that love does not wrong a neighbour. Love therefore is the fulfillment of all these laws.

APRIL 20 – WE CAN LOVE OUR NEIGHBOURS

"…And who is my neighbor?"[1] This self-justifying question was asked by the lawyer to get himself off a hook. It didn't, for the Lord told him a story pointing out who and what a true neighbour was. My neighbour is anyone who crosses my path with a need that I can meet. Neighbourly love is that inward awareness of other's needs and is willing to get outwardly involved in helping to meet them. It is brotherly love in action.

It has been said that among the prevailing philosophies of life there are three constants. First is the robber philosophy which believes that:

"What's yours is mine and I mean to get it."

Then there is the philosophy of the officially religious Priest and Levite. They say in effect by their actions:

"What's mine is mine and I mean to keep it."

The third is the Good Samaritan philosophy which proclaims by its deeds:

"What's mine is yours if you need it."

All three are clearly depicted here by our Lord.

The first is practiced in various ways all of which are harmful and hurtful. "Dog eat dog" is widely prevalent in the cut-throat competition of the business world. Brotherly love is rarely seen there. But it's in the area of exploitation of people and prices that the big robberies take place. Few of the robber barons are caught and fewer jailed. The little personal robberies, though also devastating, as the case in this story, are at least in the open. They are not condoned but are condemned with the big boys by our Lord. There is no neighbourly love here. "What's yours is mine and I mean to get it."

The second also comes in many forms. The refusal to get involved by many neighbours who saw their neighbour being stabbed to death shocked the U. S. A. and the world a few years ago. The unwillingness to intervene through physical fear, or fear of being sued, is also seen today when streams of traffic will pass a wrecked or broken down vehicle, with none stopping to see if help is needed. Leave it to someone else as it will cost me time and maybe money. That mentality, even among Christians, is the philosophy of the Priest and Levite who passed by on the other side. "What's mine is mine and I mean to keep it" shows no practical knowledge of what neighbourly love means.

The practical assistance given by the despised Samaritan is in marked contrast to the others. This man had compassion. It is the missing word. Compassion, with passion, is more than pity; more than even sympathy; it is empathy with the needy and it stretches out its hand to help. It binds up wounds. It uses its own conveyance to carry the sick to shelter. It is the love that pays the present costs of care and future after care. This is what a true neighbour is and does. This is the brotherly love philosophy that says: "What's mine is yours if you need it."

APRIL 21 – LOVE DEMANDS THAT WE LOVE OUR ENEMIES

Our Lord in the Sermon on the Mount said: "You have heard that it was said, 'You shall love your neighbor and hate your enemy.' But I say to you, 'love your enemies and pray for those who persecute you, so that you may be sons of your Father who is in heaven...'"[1] One evidence of being a child of God, says our Lord, is that we love and pray for our enemies. As the Father impartially "...causes His sun to rise on the evil and the good, and sends rain on the righteous and the unrighteous"[2] so we His children must likewise behave. Anyone can love those who love them; the world does this. Even Gentiles and hated tax-gatherers practice this. Then we are challenged with the impossible: "Therefore you are to be perfect, as your heavenly Father is perfect."[3] The divine perfection is absolute. The divine love is perfect. We know we fall short. Yet the emphasis here is on the aspect of that perfect love which loves its enemies. This is attainable because "...He has granted to us His precious and magnificent promises, so that by them you may become partakers of the divine nature..."[4] What He promises He performs.

The Lord Jesus Christ not only taught us that we should love our enemies; He showed us how to do it. We see heavenly love in action on the Cross. "...Father, forgive them; for they do not know what they are doing..."[5] We also see love doing its divine work in the personal pardon and promise of immediate paradise to the repentant thief by loving our enemies and forgiving and saving those responsive to hear and heed its call. The centurion on guard at the foot of the Cross responded: "...'Truly this was the Son of God'..."[6] he began praising God, saying, 'Certainly this man was innocent.'"[7]

Stephen followed in His train. Now we see that when God commands He enables His own children to do as the Saviour did; to follow His example and love enemies. Spirit filled Stephen preached a powerful sermon in Acts 7 which raised the ire of his religious hearers. Very Scriptural truth was very personally applied. The bitter hatred, even of the truth spoken in love and in the Spirit, resulted in the murder of the speaker. As he was being stoned to death the Spirit enabled him to emulate His Lord by praying for and forgiving his enemies. "But being full of the Holy Spirit, he gazed intently into heaven and saw the glory of God, and Jesus standing at the right hand of God..."[8] They went on stoning Stephen as he called on the Lord and said, 'Lord Jesus, receive my spirit!' Then falling on his knees, he cried out with a loud voice, 'Lord, do not hold this sin against them!' Having said this, he fell asleep."[9]

God is glorified as we love our enemies and sometimes enemies are convicted and converted. Young Saul, the persecutor and murderer's accomplice guarded the clothes of the killers. Maybe that scene, so indelibly impressed in his memory, became the first step towards the Damascus Road where the enemy of Christ became transformed by divine love into a lover of his enemies.

APRIL 22 – WE CAN LOVE OUR ENEMIES

A lady died on Friday, April 15, 1983. This was remarkable, not because she died on her ninety-first birthday, but because she loved her enemies. During World War II this Dutch Christian lady, Miss Corrie ten Boom (1892 – 1983), her father and her family helped and hid many Jews from the Nazis. Her efforts saved the Jews from the horrors of Hitler's extermination camps, but she could not save herself. She saw her family taken to concentration camps and she, with her sister, was sent to Ravensbruck Prison near Paris, France. She watched her sister die yet through the love of God was able to forgive the captors and murderers of her family. She loved her enemies and ministered amongst them after the war.

Cpl Jacob De Shazer was one of the American airmen who flew on April 18, 1942 in B25 bombers from the heaving deck of the carrier "Hornet," for an air raid on Japan. They became known as General Jimmy Doolittle's Raiders (1897 – 1993). When their gasoline ran out over China, De Shazer was ordered to jump. Parachuting in fog, he cracked some ribs as he landed in a cemetery and was later captured by Japanese soldiers who were occupying that part of China. He was condemned to be executed with the other airmen but this was later commuted to life imprisonment. In May 1944, in solitary confinement in prison in Nanking, China, De Shazer obtained the use of a Bible for three weeks from a prison guard and through it he was converted. Love one another was a new commandment to this man who hated the Japanese. But he was enabled to love brutal guards and later determined to serve God in Japan. In December 1945 he, with his family, returned as a missionary. His leaflet "I Was a War Prisoner of Japan" was widely distributed and read. Through it Captain Mitsuo Fuchida (1902 – 1976), leader of the Japanese squadron which bombed Pear Harbour, was brought to Christ in April 1950. These two former enemy aviators learned that they could love their enemies.

June 30, 1960 was the day the Belgian Congo became independent. Almost immediately anarchy, revolution and bloodshed burst out. The story of the Congo Christian martyrs, both national and foreign, is well known and is another illustration in our lifetime, of this super-natural love which can love its enemies. One example only among many is the story of a young missionary doctor who was brutalized and shockingly abused by the "Simbas" in 1964. Dr. Helen Roseveare (1925 -), of the Worldwide Evangelization Crusade, demonstrated this love both during and after the revolution. She returned to Zaire, as it is now called, continued her medical and evangelistic work, and also the training of national staff. This story is told in full by Alan Burgess in the book Daylight Must Come.

These three modern illustrations of the dynamic love that can love enemies are but the continuation of the first century Acts of the Apostles, from Stephen onwards.

APRIL 23 – LOVE AT PRAYER

Prayer can be selfish.

"Lord bless me and my wife; my son John and his wife, us four, no more."

It is not as blatantly selfish as that obvious exaggeration but prayer coverage is sometimes only umbrella sized. It covers me and mine. They say love begins at home and that is true. It must start there but not stop there. We have sadly seen that concern and love for other people and their children can mean neglect of our own at home. While trying to save other people we lose our own. The premise of loving service will take care of that, as it does in the case of prayer.

We move on and out in prayer coverage. Love in prayer includes the near at hand, our neighbours, after our own. This is community coverage.

Then we move farther afield as we pray for our local, national and international rulers to provide righteous government and incorrupt leadership. This is done "...so that we may lead a tranquil and quiet life in all godliness and dignity. This is good and acceptable in the sight of God our Saviour, who desires all men to be saved and to come to the knowledge of the truth."[1] This is continental coverage.

Love at prayer moves wider still. Now its coverage is only encompassed by the blue black dome of the sky, the stars and the Throne of heaven itself. We cannot all be witnesses to the ends of the earth except by love giving and love praying. Physically we are limited to some end, or at most a few ends of the earth but love at prayer is like a rainbow, a many splendoured thing, encompassing the whole globe, encircling the Throne. This is global coverage.

All of these are achieved by intercessory prayer. For the perfect example of love at prayer we look at the Lord's Prayer, which should be called the disciple's prayer. This prayer has elements of intercession in it. Love at prayer like this moves in the parameters of the will of god. It rightfully imposes itself into situations that the Spirit of God has identified and indicated for our individual involvement. Intercession, love at prayer, is the intervention in the affairs of the earth through the "groaning" within us of the Holy Spirit; sometimes inarticulate and sometimes expressed by tears as well as words. It begins in heaven and affects earth. All these elements are seen in the life of love at prayer either in John's Gospel, chapter seventeen, or in His other intercessory prayers. One practical example of this while He was on earth is: "Simon, Simon, behold, Satan has demanded permission to sift you like wheat; but I have prayed for you, that your faith may not fail..."[2]

Finally, a personal one for you and me; "Therefore He is able also to save forever those who draw near to God through Him, since He always lives to make intercession for them."[3] Love is still at prayer!

APRIL 24 – LOVE AND THE UNVEILED CHRIST

"Once our blessed Christ of beauty,
Was unveiled from human view,
But through suffering, death & sorrow,
He has rent that veil in two.

O, behold the Man of Sorrow,
O, behold Him in plain view,
There He stands, the mighty Conqueror,
Since He rent that veil in two.

Yes, He is with God, the Father,
Interceding there for you;
For He is the Well beloved
Since He rent the veil in two.

Holy angels bow before Him,
Men of earth give praises due;
For He is the mighty Conqueror
Since He rent the veil in two."
The Unveiled Christ
N. B. Herrell (1879 – 1954)

He who was from eternity veiled in light too bright for earthly eyes, was unveiled in love as a baby that all could see, and seeing, believe. A few who loved Him saw an unveiling of His glory on the Mount when He was changed before their eyes. Peter never forgot this occasion. Years later he wrote: "…we were eyewitnesses of His majesty. For when He received honor and glory from God the Father, such an utterance as this was made to Him by the Majestic Glory, 'This is My beloved Son with whom I am well-pleased' and we ourselves heard this utterance made from heaven when we were with Him on the holy mountain."[1]

On the Cross the mighty Conqueror defeated sin and Satan and there His love was unveiled. There His deity was unveiled as the centurion acknowledged. "When the centurion, who was standing right in front of Him, saw the way He breathed His last, he said, 'Truly this man was the Son of God!'"[2] "And Jesus uttered a loud cry, and breathed His last. And the veil of the temple was torn in two from top to bottom."[3] As dying love uttered this cry from the Cross, undying love by a symbolic act, from heaven downwards, split the great Temple veil from top to bottom. The way into the Holy of Holies had been opened by the One Who is our great High Priest, Advocate and Intercessor. He now invites us to come gladly, with confidence and boldly to the throne of grace. "For we do not have a high priest who cannot sympathize with our weaknesses, but One who has been tempted in all things as we are, yet without sin. Therefore let us draw near with confidence to the throne of grace, so that we may receive mercy and find grace to help in time of need."[4]

As He walked unrecognized on the Emmaus Road with the two despondent disciples, the risen Christ unveiled Himself to them firstly through the Scriptures. The gloom was fully dispelled at the meal where He revealed Himself, secondly in the breaking and blessing of the bread. This double unveiling of Himself, made their hearts burn within them, and opened their mouths in joyful loving witness, "…The Lord has really risen…"[5]

Finally from heaven, where His loving ministry continues, He will fully unveil Himself to the waiting saints in love's reunion in the skies. Later, his unveiling to an unbelieving world will be awesome in its power when He rends the skies in two.

APRIL 25 – THE MYSTERY AND MASTERY OF AGAPÉ

The mystery and mastery of agapé in our Lord's life is revealed in the love section of His high priestly prayer uttered at the conclusion of the Last Supper. He was loved by His Father and so are we. "I in them and You in Me, that they may be perfected in unity, so that the world may know that You sent Me, and loved them, even as You have loved Me…for You loved Me before the foundation of the world."[1] The love-life in the Trinity is complete in itself and completely selfless. It is self-giving service and sacrifice for the world that it created and the world that rejected it. This triune agapé of Father, Son and Holy Spirit was manifested in all its fullness at Calvary and Pentecost.

This fellowship of love has incorporated itself into every true believer. "I in them and You in Me… You sent Me, and loved them, even as You have loved Me." Mystical union is the term often used to describe this indwelling. We are an integral part of Him as He is of us. We recognise, but will never fully understand it until glory, the mystery of it in ever increasing measure even as we submit to the mastery of it in every area of our lives. Submission to the mastery of His love is the prerequisite to entry into the mystery of His love. If we are willing to do His will, then we shall know of His teaching. This is always the divine order. True belief and true love obeys; real belief and real love know, and know that they know and show that they know.

The very down to earth outworking of this eternal mystery and spiritual mastery of agapé is shown when there is unity amongst the Lord's people. This in turn is a testimony to the world. He has chosen to manifest Himself to the world since Calvary and Pentecost through His children. This mystery is not comprehended by the world, but they do see and understand the mastery of His supernatural love in ordinary, believing men and women. At the risk of repetition we say again that the mystical union is known and shown by the Master's control in the love life of His own. "…That the world may know that You sent Me, and loved them… although the world has not known You, yet I have known You; and these have known that You sent Me… that the love with which You loved Me may be in them, and I in them."[2]

"We are one in the bond of love;
We are one in the bond of love.
We have joined our spirit with the Spirit of God;
We are one in the bond of love.

Let us sing now, everyone;
Let us feel His love begun.
Let us join our hands that the world will know
We are one in the bond of love."
Otis Skillings (1935 – 2004)

APRIL 26 – LOVE'S UNITY

While still upon this earth, our Lord Jesus in His prayer of intercession made requests for the unity of His disciples then, and for all His people since. "…Holy Father, keep them in Your name, the name which You have given Me, that they may be one even as We are."[1] "do not ask on behalf of these alone, but for those also who believe in Me through their word; that they may all be one; even as You, Father, are in Me and I in You, that they also may be in Us, so that the world may believe that You sent Me. The glory which You have given Me I have given to them, that they may be one, just as We are one; I in them and You in Me, that they may be perfected in unity, so that the world may know…"[2]

This prayer for the unity of believers begins with recognition of the need of it and that God's keeping power is necessary to maintain it. The Name is also a preserver of unity. God's protective oversight and His holy name and nature, which is love, reflects the oneness between the Father and the Son which is the standard for the disciples. This bond, this binding force, is His love. "…put on love, which is the perfect bond of unity."[3] This is the way that His prayer is answered: "that they may be perfected in unity" and that this loving unity may be a powerful witness to the world.

The early church manifested this unity in oneness of mind; in corporate assembly; in communion, communication and a common-wealth; and in accord in teaching, fellowship and prayer. The result was that people were being saved and added to the church daily "but none of the rest dared to associate with them; however, the people held them in high esteem."[4] When later, Christians were torn and devoured by wild animals to make a Roman holiday at the Coliseum, even the mob there marvelled at their devotion and love for the Lord and one another. This love was so obvious that a man named Tertullian in about 192AD wrote down:

"Behold how these Christians love one another!"

Today, in many places, because of our divisions and lack of love, the world says the same thing as the Roman world but with a mocking sneer on their lips. Our witness has been rendered powerless because of our lack of real unity producing love.

It would be wrong to paint the picture of the first century church as flawless and perfected in unity. Any reader of the Acts and Epistles knows of their disputes, disagreements and yes, even divisions. But they did work at maintaining unity. How? They did it by facing up to the causes of disunity and dealing with them quickly and in the spirit of love. They chose Spirit filled men to defuse racial disharmony; they rebuked, in the spirit of love, error and evil. They dealt face to face, speaking the truth in love to each other. This is how they maintained the unity of the Spirit in love.

APRIL 27 – LOVE AND INTERCESSION

There are a few words that open up this great subject. The first is information. Loving intercession is impossible without information. We must be an informed people. How that information comes need not detain us here. But come it does, via any of the media or by direct impression of the Spirit. Once the needs are known there must be individual acceptance of the responsibility to do something about it. The state of my love relationship with the Lord, and people, now begins to determine what I do with the information that is calling me to the ministry of intercession. I can identify myself with the person, the problem, whatever it is or I can in effect say, "Pray have me excused." Lovelessness, resulting in a lack of response or withdrawal, will refuse this identification. This lack of love will see, or sense, the word that is coming next and back off even further.

Intervention, is not only the next word, it is the next step in intercession. Not only will love identify, it will, with sympathy, empathy and compassion truly intervene; put itself between; as an intervener in prayer to heaven and, if able, an intervener on earth. In logical sequence the loving and informed intercessor is now completely involved in terms of the cost of time, sweat, money, tears and even blood. This is the path the Lord trod in intercession. We have seen our Lord in His prayers on earth and on the throne in heaven interceding for us. He calls us to share in this ministry. All can engage in it. It is not platform work, but mostly private toil. Yet it is a most productive and fruitful service when engaged in under the direction and power of the Spirit. In wonderment the Lord sees so few willing to devote themselves to it. I surmise that a lack of love for God and souls must be the main reason. "And He saw that there was no man, And was astonished that there was no one to intercede…"[1]

To get practical with these abstract concepts, let us look at an intercessor in action. Several strikes are against him. He is an exile; a slave; but he has been placed in a strategic spot, at a crucial time in the history of his homeland. He has not only patriotic love, but this expatriate has a concerned, compassionate and loving heart towards God and His people. Who is he? Nehemiah! Read his book for the full story; a thriller indeed; far better than the poor picture given here. He sought information. He accepted personal responsibility. He identified himself with the need back in his homeland. He intervened, as God gave him access to a ruler's ear: "…So I prayed to the God of heaven. I said to the king…"[2] He became completely involved as he was given a leave of absence and royal support to go and build the walls of Jerusalem. Nehemiah's intercessory prayer should be carefully read and his life of intercession, with all its elements, should be emulated. Intercession like this has an eye to see, a mind to think, a heart to feel and a hand to execute. This is love at work in the ministry of intercession.

APRIL 28 – THE LOVE OF GOD AND PRAYER

There are some Scriptures which open up the vital subject of love and prayer. Paul, moved by gratitude for past and present memories, prayed: "I thank my God in all my remembrance of you, always offering prayer with joy in my every prayer for you all[1]...For it is only right for me to feel this way about you all, because I have you in my heart[2]... For God is my witness, how I long for you all with the affection of Christ Jesus. And this I pray, that your love may abound still more and more..."[3] The love of God prompts Paul's prayer for the Philippian church and individuals; loving memories take him down the past to their first meeting, first converts and first church in Philippi and to Lydia whose heart the Lord opened at the prayer meeting by the riverside. Her love for the Lord prompted her to open her home as a place of hospitality for Paul and the team, and later as a place of meeting. The love of God ruled in the hearts of Paul and Silas in prison in Philippi. With backs, bloody and bruised from the beatings, they prayed and sang hymns of praise to God at midnight. What a difference in our world of today! Often the saints are so in the world, and loving the world wrongly, that midnight finds them watching the late show! The love of God in praise and prayer was seen and heard by other prisoners, and after the earthquake, the love of God prevailed in preventing a suicide and saving the jailer and his family. Memories such as these filled Paul's heart with overflowing affection and prompted his prayer for them. Thank God for the faculty of memory that can reproduce the past and prompt us to love and prayer.

At greater length and depth we see the love of God at prayer in Paul providing the motive to write as he did to the Christians in the church at Ephesus. As we will be using this key Scripture again we just make reference to it here. "For this reason I bow my knees before the Father[4]... that Christ may dwell in your hearts through faith; and that you, being rooted and grounded in love, may be able to comprehend with all the saints what is the breadth and length and height and depth, and to know the love of Christ which surpasses knowledge, that you may be filled up to all the fullness of God."[5] When the prayer of love is answered the way is open for the impossible to become possible, miracles to happen, the super-natural to be revealed and prayers answered above and beyond all that we ask or think.

Thus moved by the love of God we will pray all the time with all prayer for all kinds, classes and conditions of people. "First of all, then, I urge that entreaties and prayers, petitions and thanksgivings, be made on behalf of all men, for kings and all who are in authority, so that we may lead a tranquil and quiet life in all godliness and dignity. This is good and acceptable in the sight of God our Savior, who desires all men to be saved and to come to the knowledge of the truth."[6] This leads us to the prayer ministry of intercession.

Let us then end on a personal note which could be construed as selfish but isn't: "I love the Lord, because He hears My voice and my supplications. Because He has inclined His ear to me, Therefore I shall call upon Him as long as I live."[7]

APRIL 29 – LOVE AND THANKSGIVING – Part One

One of the simplest forms of expressed appreciation is the two monosyllable phrase:

"Thank you."

We teach our children early in life to say it; to be thankful for gifts and services lovingly given. Therefore how much more should the children of the loving heavenly Father respond to His loving gift with thanksgiving?

"Thank You Lord for saving my soul,
Thank You Lord for making me whole.
Thank You Lord for giving to me,
Thy greatest salvation, so rich and so free."
Seth (1892 – 1950) and Bessie Sykes,

The attitude of gratitude glorifies and praises God. He is exalted by the praise and thanksgiving of His people. Not only is the giving of thanks the obvious response of love, it is the will of God; the command of His Word. "In everything give thanks; for this is God's will for you in Christ Jesus."[1]

One Sunday morning in Toronto, Canada, I was scheduled to preach at a certain church on Thanksgiving Sunday. As I entered the pulpit, I picked up the bulletin containing the order of service and noticed that the front page was given over to the theme of the day: "Thanksgiving," and quoted the text above on which I planned to speak. The bulletin made one point; the word "In" was emphasized; "In everything give thanks..." and then the statement was made "It does not say: 'For everything give thanks.'" But, as I told the people that though the text does not use "For," another one does, and, as I also mentioned, "I am using two texts this morning;" and then read "always giving thanks for all things in the name of our Lord Jesus Christ..."[2] It is not really important as to which of them is used. I think Paul is using them almost as synonyms.

A few years ago a number of "Praise in, and for, everything" books flooded Christian bookstores. The subject was Scriptural, but some of the conclusions were debateable. Truth pushed to extremes can lead to untruth that unsettles the faith of some. The works of Satan are not only described in Scripture, they are damned, not praised. We don't thank God for the Devil or his deceits. But we do thank God, as Job finally did, for permitting Satan to try us, and express our gratitude for the Lord's ruling over on the kind and length of tests. He provides the way of escape. He turns the evil events into good ends, as He did in Joseph's life. We give grateful thanks for His all sufficient grace, in all situations.

Love and thanksgiving are easy when our views of God are scriptural. Love in thanksgiving glorifies Him, when like Paul we can praise Him, in and for our suffering. Paul thanked God for and in, not only his own afflictions, but also for all the saints in similar circumstances.

APRIL 30 – LOVE AND THANKSGIVING – Part Two

"Oh give thanks to the Lord, for He is good, For His lovingkindness is everlasting."[1] "O give thanks unto the Lord, for he is good: for his mercy endureth for ever."[2] "Oh that men would praise the Lord for his goodness, and for his wonderful works to the children of men!"[3] "Let them give thanks to the Lord for His lovingkindness, And for His wonders to the sons of men!"[4]

This latter verse is repeated four times on Psalm 107. God has met, delivered and saved people in different and distressing circumstances. These deliverances should call for grateful love and thanksgiving. Apparently they were slow to give it and the Psalmist exhorts them, and us, to always be ready with gratitude born of love. We have seen that this attitude, and these actions, should be in and for everything and continuous; without ceasing. We say thanks: by the loving sacrifice of praise; by the loving commitment of our lives; by the sacrificial love giving of our substance; and by our loving acceptance of all He permits in our lives.

The characteristics of love in thanksgiving are many. Dr. T. S. Rendall, former President of Prairie Bible Institute, has listed some of them in an acrostic titled "Test of Thanksgiving." What should our thanksgiving be like?

T – Therapeutic – Nothing lifts the spirit like the voice of thanksgiving.
H – Habitual – For the believer thanksgiving should become a habit of the soul.
A – Automatic – Thanksgiving should be the spontaneous response of the heart when it perceives new blessings and recalls past mercies.
N – Necessary – Thanksgiving is no option. We are required to come before God's presence with thanksgiving.
K – Knowledgeable – The eyes of the soul should always be on the lookout to discover and determine new mercies.
S – Sincere – If forced, thanksgiving loses its value. It must proceed from an honest and sincere heart.
G – Glad – There ought to be a note of gladness accompanying our gratitude.
I – Individual – Let each soul bring its offering to the King of Kings.
V – Vocal – Let the voice of thanksgiving be heard. Don't mumble your response but let it ring out as the affirmation of the soul.
I – Incessant – Our thanksgiving should never have a last chapter. Let it go on and on.
N – Normal – There's something wrong when the believing heart fails to respond with gratitude. What health is to the body, thanksgiving is to the soul.
G – Glorifying – Above all, let our thanksgiving glorify our Father in heaven. His are the gifts; His be the glory.

Ingratitude is born of lovelessness. Ingratitude towards God and His gifts was one of the first steps downward for civilizations past as Romans chapter one indicates. Love says thank you for all His gifts. "Thanks be to God for His indescribable gift!"[5]

MAY 1 – LOVE CAME DOWN AT PENTECOST

Love personified was born in Bethlehem; Love grew up in Nazareth; Love preached by Galilee; Love died on Calvary; Love rose in triumph from Joseph's tomb. Risen Love was manifested in Jerusalem and ascended to heaven from the Mount of Olives to which, one day that same Love personified, Jesus Christ the Lord, will return. As Love visible left this earthly scene Love invisible came and has acted ever since as love enabling and love directing Love's visible body on earth.

Love came down at Pentecost; Love poured out without measure; Love baptising, uniting and energizing that little band of believers into a witnessing force that turned the world upside down and right side up. Love controlled their entire post-Pentecostal world.

There are at least seven symbols of invisible love in the Bible. These indicators of the Holy Spirit are: oil for anointing; the dove for peace; water for life; light for revealing; wind for power; fire for zeal and cleansing; and tongues for worship and witness. Our Lord was anointed by the Spirit; the dove of the Spirit of peace sat upon Him; from Him the water of the Spirit of life flowed; the Spirit of light illumined Him; the wind of the Spirit enabled Him; the Spirit of fire burned in Him; and the Spirit of tongues controlled His speech. From His birth to His resurrection all the works of our Lord were done through the Spirit. The Spirit of love directed all the seven areas of his life indicated by the symbolism. In like fashion the same Spirit controls us in these seven areas.

On the day of Pentecost three of these symbols were present; wind, tongues and fire. "When the day of Pentecost had come, they were all together in one place. And suddenly there came from heaven a noise like a violent rushing wind, and it filled the whole house where they were sitting. And there appeared to them tongues as of fire distributing themselves, and they rested on each one of them. And they were all filled with the Holy Spirit and began to speak with other tongues, as the Spirit was giving them utterance. Now there were Jews living in Jerusalem, devout men from every nation under heaven... each one of them was hearing them speak in his own language."[1] Tongues which were divided by God at Babel to confuse the pride and arrogance of men were used at Pentecost to proclaim "...the mighty deeds of God,"[2] and they will be united in heaven to magnify and glorify Him. Dozens of tongues were used at Pentecost as the Gospel was declared in the power of the Spirit, and in many more tongues since then, all compelled and controlled by Love poured out at Pentecost.

"Come down, O Love divine, seek Thou this soul of mine,
And visit it with thine own ardour glowing;
O comforter, draw near, within my heart appear,
And kindle it, thy holy flame bestowing.

And so the yearning strong, with which the soul will long,
Shall far outpass the power of human telling;
For none can guess its grace, till he become the place
Wherein the Holy Spirit makes his dwelling."
Bianco da Siena (? – 1434)

MAY 2 – LOVE'S INFLUENCE

There is a hymn which has a line in it that has always troubled me. In speaking of the Holy Spirit's coming the words in question are: "He came sweet influence to impart." Surely in the light of Pentecost He came to do much more than that! More mature reflection and looking at that line in context I need to make the confession that I was wrong. I don't know whether the author, long dead Harriet Auber (1773 – 1862) will ever hear of this, but she was right.

"Our blest Redeemer, ere he breathed
His tender last farewell,
A Guide, a Comforter, bequeathed
With us to dwell.

He came in semblance of a dove
With sheltering wings outspread,
The holy balm of peace and love
On earth to shed.

He came in tongues of living flame
To teach, convince, subdue,
All powerful as the wind He came
As viewless too.

He came sweet influence to impart,
A gracious, willing Guest,
While He can find one humble heart
Wherein to rest.

And His that gentle voice we hear,
Soft as the breath of even,
That checks each fault, that calms each fear,
And speaks of heaven.

And every virtue we possess,
And every conquest won,
And every thought of holiness,
Are His alone.

Spirit of purity and grace,
Our weakness, pitying, see:
O make our hearts thy dwelling place
And worthier thee."

All His might and majesty are there, as well as His guiding ministries. "The holy balm of peace and love" introduce beautifully the truth which is so essential. I have only recently, late in life, come to appreciate the power of love's influence. It is not one of the spectacular, seen powers, but it is none the less mighty. Silent and unseen, love's influence goes its quiet and steady way. In the end analysis at the great accounting day we shall see what it produced. "Canst thou bind the sweet influences of Pleiades...?"[1] "Can you bind the chains of the Pleiades...?"[2] Influences or chains? Cyclones or breezes? "All powerful as the wind." But the wind can be a zephyr. "Soft as the breath of even." Elijah heard and saw both when distressed. But it was the sound of the still small voice that recommissioned him.

I have been thinking of the kinds of people who have affected our lives and work for God and I believe that these quiet sweet influencers will rank amongst the most effective. Influence is not easy to measure, but it is pervasive and persuasive. In an article entitled "Where Do Sermons Go?" the writer wrote:

"After a preacher died, his relatives found his many sermon manuscripts neatly tied and filed away. On top of them was a card with this inscription: 'Where has the influence gone on these sermons I have preached?' On the other side was the answer. He had written: 'Where are last year's sunrays? They have gone into fruits and grain and vegetables to feed mankind. Where are last year's raindrops? Forgotten by most people, of course, but they did their refreshing work, and their influence still abides.' In conclusion the preacher said, 'So too, my sermons have gone into lives and made them nobler, more Christ-like, and better fitted for heaven.'" <u>Our Daily Bread</u>

MAY 3 – POURED OUT LOVE

"…the love of God has been poured out within our hearts through the Holy Spirit who was given to us."[1] The verb poured in the perfect tense indicates that this is the permanent endowment of the Holy Spirit to the believer. It is the tremendous outpouring of the Spirit promised by Joel and fulfilled at Pentecost. That was where the window of heaven opened to pour out the blessings of love, holiness, authority, boldness, courage and compassion. As there was not enough room to contain all this, it had too, and did overflow. The saints were the earthen overflow vessels.

When I was young I worked on a dairy farm and, often when thirsty, poured milk from a ten gallon can into a cup. The undesired result was frequently a flood on the dairy floor. My little cup overflowed. This was the desired effect at Pentecost. The hundred and twenty disciples were to be filled, flooded and overflowed; for it's in the overflow that others are blessed. In a certain sense Pentecost was unique. The Spirit's coming, in fullness of availability to all at that time, had depended upon our Lord going to glory after His finished work. Since then the Spirit is present in the world and Pentecost is a permanent, personal possibility. "One baptism, many fillings" used to be the key phrase in my youth. Thank God it became a reality for me and not just a slogan.

"God fills the soul that it may pour
The fullness on another heart;
Not that the filled with good may store,
The good God giveth to impart".
(Author unknown)

We read that those disciples, who were filled at Pentecost, were filled again a few days later. All through the Acts they are described as fill, filled or being filled with the Spirit. The love walk, the love words, the love work and the love warfare was manifest everywhere. Stephen was filled with the Holy Spirit and was poured out unto death.

"Love will melt us, make us and move us to do what no other force in the universe can do.
Love will fill us, fire us, flood our lives and fit us for doing the seemingly impossible.
Love sacrifices, suffers and serves as naturally as we breathe.
Love never thinks the price too great to pay or the work too hard to perform.
Love needs no outside inspiration to move it. It needs only information.
Love goes and gives without asking where or to whom. It is no respecter of persons.
Love is the founder of every great missionary movement. It sent God's great Son into the world to seek and to save, and it sends God's lesser sons on the same mission.
Love is today praying, sending, spending, giving, going and working throughout the whole world, in and through every willing channel.
Dear Lord, give us this love." Selected

MAY 4 – LOVE'S GIFTS – Part One

"Gracious Spirit, Holy Ghost,
Taught by Thee we covet most
Of Thy gifts of Pentecost
Holy, heavenly Love.

Love is kind, and suffers long
Love is meek, and thinks no wrong,
Love than death itself more strong;
Therefore, give us Love.

Prophecy will fade away,
Melting in the light of day,
Love will ever with us stay;
Therefore, give us Love.

Faith will vanish into sight;
Hope be emptied in delight;
Love in heaven will shine more bright;
Therefore, give us Love.

Faith and Hope and Love we see
Joining hand in hand agree;
But the greatest of the three,
And the best, is Love.

From the overshadowing
Of Thy gold and silver wing
Shed on us, who to Thee sing,
Holy, heavenly Love."
Christopher Wordsworth (1807 – 1885)

We have endeavoured, along with Bishop Wordsworth, to hymn the theme of holy heavenly love. He calls it rightly, a Pentecostal gift. This is so as the verse: "…the love of God has been poured out within our hearts through the Holy Spirit who was given to us"[1] makes clear. We have also noted that love, the gift of God, is also love, the grace of God. We are not being pedantic when we emphasize another side of truth. Here we want to discuss how love, the gift-grace, governs all the other gifts. The good Bishop's hymn to love shows the primacy of love over all the other gifts.

"If I speak with the tongues of men and of angels, but do not have love, I have become a noisy gong or a clanging cymbal."[2] Tongues, as always, have been, and still are a source of division. On the positive side they were used to edify the crowds at Pentecost. Paul said there are "…various kinds of tongues…"[3] "…All do not speak with tongues…"[4] "…do not forbid to speak in tongues."[5] "…I speak in tongues more than you all."[6] and with that balance of truth about tongues he also stated: If I speak with tongues terrestrial and tongues celestial and am lacking in love, I'm like a noisy gong, or a clanging cymbal. Just noisy. The Corinthian church strong in gifts was lacking in grace; loud in tongues; low on love. Love should control the tongue, and tongues.

Love should also control the gift of prophecy, which is the forth telling of the Word of God as well as the foretelling, by revelation, of future events. Agabus did the latter; Peter at Pentecost the former. He took the great prophetic truths from Joel and David concerning the Holy Spirit, and Christ and His death and resurrection, and interpreted and applied them to those listening. This is prophecy at its finest, by one full of the Spirit and fearless love. Had love been lacking his teaching would have been mere words. The conversions that followed were the result of the Spirit enabling Peter to teach from a heart overflowing with love.

So it also should be with the gift of faith, the mountain moving variety. The one who has this gift and exercises it without love may do a lot of moving and shaking but it will all come to nothing. For faith must work through love.

And so it should be with all the other gifts of the Spirit. Love is the unifying force controlling this diversity of gifts.

MAY 5 – LOVE'S GIFTS – Part Two

We began to look at love's gifts as seen in the great love chapter. We saw the gift and grace of love governing the gifts of tongues, prophecy and faith. In this second part we want to again take a general look at love's gifts and things to note about them in 1ˢᵗ Corinthians Chapter Twelve. They are spiritual gifts found in the body of Christ for ministry and worship. Their diversity is noted, but they are not divisive, for all are gifts from the same Spirit. They should complement and unite, not make individuals superior and separatist. They are granted sovereignly and no believer has all of them.

"Now there are varieties of gifts, but the same Spirit. And there are varieties of ministries, and the same Lord. There are varieties of effects, but the same God who works all things in all persons."[1] Note again it is the triune God at work in spiritual gifting for varieties of ministries with varieties of effects. The same Spirit; the same Lord; the same God are all working together to work all the necessary things in each one. Trinitarian love is in charge of the distribution of the spiritual gifts.

The general listing of the spiritual gifts is as follows: "But to each one is given the manifestation of the Spirit for the common good. For to one is given the word of wisdom through the Spirit, and to another the word of knowledge according to the same Spirit; to another faith by the same Spirit, and to another gifts of healing by the one Spirit, and to another the effecting of miracles, and to another prophecy, and to another the distinguishing of spirits, to another various kinds of tongues, and to another the interpretation of tongues. But one and the same Spirit works all these things, distributing to each one individually just as He wills."[2] (Romans Chapter Twelve and Ephesians Chapter Four list other gifts.)

There are nine gifts of the Spirit listed. It is interesting to place them alongside the nine graces of the Spirit as described in Galatians. While no believer has all nine gifts, every child of God should have all the nine graces. Sovereign Love distributes the gifts according to his will. Sovereign love wills that all the graces be demonstrated in the life of every saint.

To keep us in balance we should remember that: "Now you are Christ's body, and individually members of it. And God has appointed in the church, first apostles, second prophets, third teachers, then miracles, then gifts of healings, helps, administrations, various kinds of tongues. All are not apostles, are they? All are not prophets, are they? All are not teachers, are they? All are not workers of miracles, are they? All do not have gifts of healings, do they? All do not speak with tongues, do they? All do not interpret, do they?"[3] Seven questions to which the answer is "No." While we are exhorted to go after the best gifts Paul suggests that there is something better yet to come.

MAY 6 – LOVE'S GIFTS – Part Three

In Romans Chapter Twelve the opening verses are an urgent appeal to us to dedicate ourselves completely to the Lord - as living holy sacrifices acceptable to God. This is part of our spiritual service of worship. We are not to be conformed to the world, but transformed by mind renewal; thus we will prove experientially that the will of God is good, always acceptable and perfect.

Then, because we are what we are by the grace of God, our transformed minds will think rightly about ourselves. We will not be those who over-rate themselves, nor be full of ourselves in our self-evaluations. Instead, our thinking about love's gifts will be with humility and sound judgment. We see the diversity of the gifts as a unity which ministers to the body of Christ.

To start with "...God has allotted to each a measure of faith."[1] This appears to be a working for God faith rather than saving faith. We should then be led as the disciples were to pray for an increase in our faith. In Hebrews Chapter Eleven the measure of faith given corresponds to the task to be accomplished. This truth, "...according to the proportion of his faith"[2] is related to the "charismata", the different grace-gifts, each believer has received. They should all be exercised in grace, through faith, and that faith, as we are told elsewhere, is always exercised by love. So let us exercise our gifts in this fashion; whether serving, teaching, exhorting, giving, leading or showing mercy. Our gift of giving should be with liberality, our leading with diligence, and our mercy with cheerfulness. Love makes all this easy, just as grace in faith makes it all possible. "Let love be without hypocrisy. Abhor what is evil; cling to what is good. Be devoted to one another in brotherly love; give preference to one another in honor; not lagging behind in diligence, fervent in spirit, serving the Lord."[3]

Gifts given by grace are also people; people, as gifts to the church for spiritual offices. Spiritual offices are positions in the church for the administration of its affairs, whether for spiritual oversight of the flock as elders or spiritual oversight of administrative matters as deacons. Not all believers will hold spiritual offices. A longer list of Christ's gifts of people to His church is given in Ephesians. "And He gave some as apostles, and some as prophets, and some as evangelists, and some as pastors and teachers, for the equipping of the saints for the work of service, to the building up of the body of Christ; until we all attain to the unity of the faith, and of the knowledge of the Son of God[4]... speaking the truth in love[5]... causes the growth of the body for the building up of itself in love."[6] Thank God for the people in His church who have these gifts given in love and grace.

MAY 7 – LOVE AND THE GIFT OF PROPHECY

The gift of prophecy is, perhaps, one of the most important gifts. It must be governed by love to be of value. "Pursue love, yet desire earnestly spiritual gifts, but especially that you may prophesy. For one who speaks in a tongue does not speak to men but to God; for no one understands, but in his spirit he speaks mysteries. But one who prophesies speaks to men for edification and exhortation and consolation. One who speaks in a tongue edifies himself; but one who prophesies edifies the church. Now I wish that you all spoke in tongues, but even more that you would prophesy; and greater is one who prophesies than one who speaks in tongues, unless he interprets, so that the church may receive edifying."[1]

This lengthy quote is important to our understanding of the relative merits of prophecy and tongues. The fear of facing this issue, the controversies and division which arise, and all the endless pros and cons in books and articles have certainly created more heat than light. If only we would let the Word of God be heard, and not our biases, we would be better people and our churches more in tune with the New Testament ideal.

The words great, greater and greatest are comparatives. The superlative "greatest" is used of love, and on this I major, not only in this book of readings, but I trust in life practice. This grace-gift is for all of us. We have it in Christ by His Spirit. If we always go for it in all its fullness, we will glorify God, bless people and be blessed ourselves. The word "greater" is used of the one who prophesies and, ergo, of the gift itself, as compared with the tongues speaker and the gift of tongues, unless there is interpretation with subsequent edification. The term "great" may be applied to all the gifts.

Prophecy may be defined not only as the ability to foretell future events but also the ability to forth tell the good news of the Gospel. Agabus did the former when he foretold Paul's future. Peter did the latter in his sermons at Pentecost. While the ability to both foretell and forth tell is granted to a few, all can witness to the saving good news. Prophecy in the latter aspect has a threefold ministry of edification, which is building up people in their faith and love; exhortation, which includes challenge and rebuke; and encouragement, which is consolation and comforting help. The value of this gift, and its ministry to individuals and the church is self evident. If you seek a gift then let prophecy be first and foremost. "...desire earnestly spiritual gifts, but especially that you may prophesy..."

On a personal note, I'm grateful that God in His sovereign grace has enabled me to exercise this gift of prophecy in its forth telling of the good news for nearly fifty years. Later in life a gift of teaching became evident. I give all the glory to our gracious Lord who gave these good gifts to me.

Finally, it must be noted that, from the Old Testament prophecy regarding the outpouring of the Spirit and His graces and gifts, to the fulfillment in Acts and subsequently, gender is not a barrier. Philip, the evangelist had four virgin daughters who were prophetesses.

MAY 8 – LOVE AND THE GIFT OF FAITH

"Now there are varieties of gifts, but the same Spirit. And there are varieties of ministries, and the same Lord. There are varieties of effects, but the same God who works all things in all persons. But to each one is given the manifestation of the Spirit for the common good. For to one is given the word of wisdom through the Spirit, and to another the word of knowledge according to the same Spirit; to another faith by the same Spirit..."[1] I have repeated this key passage again because these truths are so important that a second or even third reading is warranted.

There are two words used concerning spiritual gifts in the 1st Corinthians Chapter Twelve and Romans Chapter Twelve passages. The first is "pneuma" - the Spirit or wind by whom we are born again, baptized into the body and are being continually filled. The spiritual gifts come from Him. The second is "charis" - grace, and from that comes charismata or the gifts given by grace. The New Testament teaches that we all should be pneumatics and charismatics, but not fanatics with an over-emphasis on any one gift.

Having said that I would suggest that the only gift of the Spirit we should over- emphasize is love. After long study of the Word of God it is my view that faith would come a strong second. Faith pleases God as love pleases Him. Both are gifts of His grace mediated by His Spirit. Both work together and no one should seek to do one without the other. "...faith working through love."[2]

Now we will look at faith separately without seeking to wrongly divide it from its control. First of all there is saving faith which is also the gift of His love in grace. "For by grace you have been saved through faith; and that not of yourselves, it is the gift of God."[3] Then there is working faith, given to all believers, a capital grant which can be increased by usage and prayer.

Thirdly, there is the special spiritual gift of faith which seems to be the gift that, like saving faith and working faith, must also be governed by love. Paul reminded the Corinthians with this gift that: "... if I have all faith, so as to remove mountains, but do not have love, I am nothing."[4] All believers have saving faith; all have working faith, but all do not have this gift of "all faith." This, like all the other gifts of the Spirit, is distributed sovereignly and I think is closely connected with the gift of miracles.

I will close by briefly mentioning three people who stand out as so gifted. George Müller (1805 – 1895) had the gift of faith that miraculously fed thousands of orphans without one appeal to men. Hudson Taylor (1832 – 1905), the father of modern faith missions, whose faith saw thousands of workers given and supplied for China. Charles T. Studd (1860 – 1931) was over fifty when he went to Africa and founded the Worldwide Evangelization Crusade by faith and love for God and the lost.

MAY 9 – LOVE AND THE GIFT OF TONGUES

"But now, brethren, if I come to you speaking in tongues, what will I profit you unless I speak to you either by way of revelation or of knowledge or of prophecy or of teaching? Yet even lifeless things, either flute or harp, in producing a sound, if they do not produce a distinction in the tones, how will it be known what is played on the flute or on the harp? For if the bugle produces an indistinct sound, who will prepare himself for battle? So also you, unless you utter by the tongue speech that is clear, how will it be known what is spoken? For you will be speaking into the air. There are, perhaps, a great many kinds of languages in the world, and no kind is without meaning. If then I do not know the meaning of the language, I will be to the one who speaks a barbarian, and the one who speaks will be a barbarian to me. So also you, since you are zealous of spiritual gifts, seek to abound for the edification of the church. Therefore let one who speaks in a tongue pray that he may interpret. For if I pray in a tongue, my spirit prays, but my mind is unfruitful. What is the outcome then? I will pray with the spirit and I will pray with the mind also; I will sing with the spirit and I will sing with the mind also. Otherwise if you bless in the spirit only, how will the one who fills the place of the ungifted say the "Amen" at your giving of thanks, since he does not know what you are saying? For you are giving thanks well enough, but the other person is not edified. I thank God, I speak in tongues more than you all; however, in the church I desire to speak five words with my mind so that I may instruct others also, rather than ten thousand words in a tongue."[1]

This lengthy quote is deliberately included in order to give Scriptural authority and the balanced views that are Biblical, especially in dealing with this controversial gift. And it is that, despite the Corinthian distortions and over-magnifying of its importance and, ipso facto, their superiority complex and denigration of those who didn't so speak. As we have seen, Paul is at pains to point out that speaking in tongues without love is as valueless as any other gift. Spiritualized verbosity, parading its special gift of unknown tongues, is resoundingly rebuked in the introduction to the love chapter. Just preceding that Paul stresses that tongues, like all the gifts, are distributed by the Spirit and that not all speak with tongues.

It is evident that tongues at Pentecost were known foreign languages. This gift of immediate knowledge and use of foreign languages is still claimed by some today, but I have observed that the majority of missionaries have to sweat at learning native languages.

But tongues have other meanings. There is the private and personal speaking in the Spirit to God in an unknown, but known to God language, as well as speaking in one's native tongue. Paul practiced both. However, in the public ministry of the church tongues were not to be used unless an interpreter was present, and even then it was to be limited and orderly, as also with prophesy and the other ministries. "Therefore, my brethren, desire earnestly to prophesy, and do not forbid to speak in tongues. But all things must be done properly and in an orderly manner."[2]

MAY 10 – HOLY, HEALING LOVE

There is little argument that we live in a sick world. This is a world of sin-sick people who are by no means sick of their sin. In fact the majority suffer from one of the worst forms of the disease; they don't even know they are ill! When we are at last brought, by whatever means, to a personal realization that we are sick unto death, and even sick of our sins, then we have made the first step towards healing. This step is towards the great Physician who came not to minister to the self-satisfied well, but to the sick.

This great Healer has two major medicines with which He carries on His ministry of healing. They are two combination restoratives, bitter-sweet remedies. The first is righteousness-peace and the second is love-truth. The first was wrought at the Cross where "…righteousness and peace have kissed each other."[1] This is the basic medicine for sin-sick souls. The second is the foundation for the first and it is the very nature of God Who is love and truth and, because He is, He found the way to be just and yet justify the ungodly. Not only does love-truth produce righteousness-peace, it reproduces it in healed sinners.

"What has to be healed in us is our true nature, made in the likeness of God. What we have to learn is love. The healing and the learning are the same thing, for at the very core of our essence we are constituted in God's likeness by our freedom, and the exercise of that freedom is nothing else but the exercise of disinterested love – the love of God for His own sake, because He is God. The beginning of love is truth, and before He will give us His love, God must cleanse our souls of the lies that are in them. And the most effective way of detaching us from ourselves is to make us detest ourselves as we have made ourselves by sin, in order that we may love Him reflected in our souls as He has re-made them by His love…Our happiness consists in sharing the happiness of God, the perfection of His unlimited freedom, the perfection of His love." Thomas Merton (1915 – 1968)

Merton learned these truths the hard way, as many of us do. Regrettably many turn away from love-truth because its application is too hard. Its dosage as healthful medicine is too bitter. The rich young ruler, keeper of all the commandments, was one of these who rejected the truth spoken in love. He would not give up his wealth, forsake all and follow Christ. He went away sorrowful, sick at heart, turning his back on healing love. "Looking at him, Jesus felt a love for him…"[2] and that's why He told him the truth, "One thing you lack…"[2] That same look of love-truth healed Peter who was following from a distance, after denying his Lord three times. In Gethsemane Peter had used his sword in defence of Christ by taking a swipe at Malchus the high priest's slave. Jesus, in love, healed and restored the sliced off ear, and told Peter to put his sword away. Later, as He heard Peter's three denials, "The Lord turned and looked at Peter. And Peter remembered the word of the Lord[3]… And he went out and wept bitterly."[4] Love-truth had begun its healing work.

MAY 11 – LOVE AND THE GIFTS OF HEALINGS

They are described in the plural, as "gifts of healings" and, it should be noted that "All do not have gifts of healings…"[1] Peter and John exercised the physical healing gift. The two apostles were on their way to the temple for the regular prayer hour. They were not going to, nor conducting mass healing services. At the gate they were accosted by a beggar, who had been lame for more than forty years. He asked for money but, as was the case with most of the apostles, they had none. They had assumed poverty like their Lord. "But Peter, along with John, fixed his gaze on him and said, 'Look at us!' And he began to give them his attention, expecting to receive something from them. But Peter said, 'I do not possess silver and gold, but what I do have I give to you: In the name of Jesus Christ the Nazarene— walk!' And seizing him by the right hand, he raised him up; and immediately his feet and his ankles were strengthened. With a leap he stood upright and began to walk; and he entered the temple with them, walking and leaping and praising God."[2] There is no doubt about this physical restoration!

These two apostles, who had known love theoretically; who had seen it fully manifested in Christ; and who had experienced it personally at Pentecost; now demonstrated it in the exercise of the love gifts of healing. Apostolic healers! Healing is a love ministry of the Holy Spirit. Divine healing is miracle healing, evident to all. Peter and John claim no credit for gifts given and gifts used. "Men of Israel, why are you amazed at this, or why do you gaze at us, as if by our own power or piety we had made him walk? The God of Abraham, Isaac and Jacob, the God of our fathers, has glorified His servant Jesus…"[3] Then Peter went straight on to preach the Gospel, calling the crowd to return, repent and to know forgiveness of sins through Christ. And about five thousand men, hearing the message believed. "Gifts of healings," plural, include the major healing ministry to sin-sick souls. The minor, physical healing, was an unscheduled though providential, love service. On a scale of one to five thousand we see the relative importance of these "gifts of healings." I don't deny that the lesser is contained in the greater, but I do know that all believers while not having the gift of physical, faith healing, do have the power of witness, and are called to give testimony to Christ's saving power.

It is true that the healing, and the man's testimony to that fact, helped pave the way for a wider hearing of the Gospel, but we should not make this the norm. The Good News, preached in the power of the Spirit, by people motivated by the love of Christ, is God's main means for the healing of souls. Healing of bodies, by the various means included in the "gifts of healings," is finally but a temporary respite before death claims the earthly body. The Gospel brings eternal healing and glory to God. Peter, when questioned about the benefit done to the sick man, magnified the Name of Jesus. "…on the basis of faith in His name, it is the name of Jesus which has strengthened this man whom you see and know; and the faith which comes through Him has given him this perfect health[4]… And there is salvation in no one else; for there is no other name under heaven that has been given among men by which we must be saved."[5] And that is the Gospel we all can proclaim.

MAY 12 – LOVE AND BODY HEALINGS

We now enter into another area regarding the many splendoured theme of love and healing. The body emphasis here is not the physical body, but is rather the corporate body, the church. In 1ˢᵗ Corinthians Chapter Twelve there is a long description of this body and the relationship of its members, à propos the love gifts of the Spirit, and their coordinated love ministries to the whole body. Here, however, we will focus on what James teaches concerning the loving care and responsibility the body should be showing to its sick members. This is the corporate healing ministry instead of the individual "gifts of healings." "Is anyone among you suffering? Then he must pray. Is anyone cheerful? He is to sing praises. Is anyone among you sick? Then he must call for the elders of the church and they are to pray over him, anointing him with oil in the name of the Lord; and the prayer offered in faith will restore the one who is sick, and the Lord will raise him up, and if he has committed sins, they will be forgiven him. Therefore, confess your sins to one another, and pray for one another so that you may be healed. The effective prayer of a righteous man can accomplish much."[1] These instructions are still valid and should be accepted practice by sick believers, appointed elders and the church as a whole. This is love and body healing for those who are spiritually, mentally and physically sick. Holistic health is surely included in the healing of the sick.

The order and responsibilities of the participating people are clear in this ministry. The sick person has the responsibility to call for the elders. This is an acknowledgement of, and agreement with, God's ordained authority in the church and an act of faith. The elders' responsibilities are to pray over the sick person, anointing that one with oil in the name of the Lord. The prayer of group faith, combined with the faith of the sick person, and the prayer of the whole body of believers (if the anointing and prayer is carried out in a public meeting) will result in restoration of various kinds. This is the promise of the Lord. If there is sin in connection with the sickness, then confession is indicated and forgiveness promised. The ministries of love in healing are manifold and mutual in the body of Christ. "Pray for one another so that you may be healed." This loving ministry of the body to the tripartite being of the believer is being practiced more in these days, and rightly so. He restoreth my body, soul and spirit.

The promise of restoration is not always answered immediately, or in the way we expected. There are sicknesses, not unto death and sicknesses unto death. If the latter is ordained and departure time has come, then it is futile and very unwise to pray that life be prolonged. We believe that eternal Love knows best and that to depart and be with Christ is far better than to be here on earth. But how do we know? We often don't, so we pray and wait. Our cry for physical restoration is sometimes reflective of our unlove and unbelief. That the Lord's will be done should always be in our thinking and praying especially in this area of sickness or healing. Remember Hezekiah. At thirty-nine years of age he was told to put his house in order. He was about to die. This seemed to be God's first and best will. Hezekiah didn't think so and said so in prayer. He was granted a fifteen year extension and died at age fifty-four, but during that time fathered Manasseh, the worst king in the history of Judah.

MAY 13 – DIVINE LOVE AND HEALTH – SPIRITUAL AND MENTAL

"Heal us, Immanuel, here we are
We wait to feel thy touch.
Deep-wounded souls to thee repair,
And Savior, we are such.

Our faith is feeble, we confess,
We faintly trust thy word;
But wilt thou pity us the less?
Be that far from thee, Lord!

Remember him who once applied
With trembling for relief:
'Lord, I believe,' with tears he cried,
'O help my unbelief.'

She, too, who touched thee in the press
And healing virtue stole,
Was answered, 'Daughter, go in peace
Thy faith has made thee whole.'

Like her, with hopes and fears
We come to touch thee if we may
O send us not despairing home;
Send none unhealed away
William Cowper (1731 – 1800)

William Cowper's life is still a puzzle and an enigma. Cowper, out of his darkness, the poet of the dawn, found light and love. Elizabeth Barrett Browning (1806 – 1861) perhaps sums him up best:

"O poets from a maniac's tongue was poured the deathless singing!
O Christians, at your cross of hope a hopeless hand was clinging!
O men, this man in brotherhood your weary paths beguiling,
Groaned inly while he taught you peace, and died while ye were smiling!"

We previously noted the relationship between divine love and healing. In effect we said that God can heal and God does heal, but this doesn't mean that God always heals. His love allows Him to heal or not to heal as He sees fit. Omnipotence is always able to do anything. Omniscience, again governed by love, sees the big picture and knows the best means to use to achieve the end result. Healing love, drawn from Immanuel's veins, is first and foremost redeeming love.

There are mental diseases that need his healing touch. Cowper struggled most of his life in this area. The causes were complex. His mother died when he was very young and at age six, this frail little lad was shipped off to a harsh boarding school. There he was bullied and his sensitive spirit broken. A melancholic temperament as well led to depression, despair drove him to repeated attempts at suicide and ended in a lunatic asylum. How did he receive the double healing for the mind and soul?

Surprisingly it began in Dr. Cotton's private lunatic asylum. As Dr. Frank W. Boreham, D. D. (1871 – 1959) reminds us:

"in those days such asylums usually broke the bruised reed and quenched the smoking flax. But happily for William Cowper and the world Dr. Cotton is himself a kindly, gracious and devout old man and he treats his poor patient with sympathy and understanding. And under this treatment the change comes…"

Hear Cowper himself:

"The happy period which was to shake off my fetters and afford me a clear opening of the free mercy of God in Jesus Christ has now arrived…seeing a Bible…full of the unspeakable happiness that comes with calm after storm, with health after the most terrible of maladies, with repose after the burning fever of the brain."

MAY 14 – HEALTH AND LOVE-HATE CONFLICTS

Dr. Jonathon Swift (1667 – 1745) was the dean of St. Patrick's Cathedral, Dublin, Ireland in the early 1700's.

"He was at this time far gone in the love-hate conflicts that were later to madden him. Reversal of political fortunes had pursued his family, who were of the Royalist party during the civil war of the previous century. His was an unhappy childhood of poverty and neglect. He harboured countless grudges caused by slights to his voracious pride. He was afflicted by dizziness that modern medicine has diagnosed as Ménière's disease. Frustration, disappointment, deafness and pain lashed Swift into a chronic rage that would now be called paranoia. He exemplified the negative idealism which is so widely practiced by the revolutionaries of today. Because society is not perfectible it should be loathed. Humanity's failures in justice, sincerity, intelligence and cleanliness were equal objects of his fury. St. Patrick's was, in terms of the so-called Church of Ireland, as potent as symbol of English power (in the 18th century) as Dublin Castle. It was part of the apparatus of oppression. Swift, knowing it as such, hated himself for representing the oppressors." (Alice Hufstader)

Self-love plus self-hate in the one individual can be a destructive disease indeed. Yet Swift wrote wisely and satirically and with vivid imagination. He made a memorable statement about health and a trio of doctors.

"The best doctors in the world are Dr. Diet, Dr. Quiet and Dr. Merryman."

Unfortunately these couldn't cure Dr. Swift. "Physician heal thyself" they might have said of him. But he couldn't.

The first king of Israel could not heal himself either. Self-love and self-hate resided increasingly in that troubled monarch and spilled out of him in the love-hate relationships he had with his family, particularly his son Jonathon, and Jonathon's friend David. The violent rages that made Saul into a murderous, calculating "mad-man" were the outward expression of his inner turmoil, his frustrations, his wounded pride and his disappointments in loss of kingdom and reversal of position. David's star was rising as his own was setting. His son loved David more than he loved his father, or so the parent thought. What were the root causes of his paranoia, mental sickness, delusions of grandeur and persecution? Undoubtedly these causes were spiritual. His disobedience by his usurping of Samuel's priestly office by forcing himself to offer sacrifices through impatience was one example. God had to remove the kingdom from him. Saul hated himself for the things he had done to David; throwing a javelin at him while he was trying to soothe the king with music; hunting and hounding David over mountain and desert. David manifested love and loyalty and refused to harm Saul when he had Saul in his power. Saul, oozing self-pity born of self-love, "confessed" his sin to David and acknowledged how wrong he was. He later continued the process all over again.

Dr. Swift and King Saul destroyed themselves with self-love and self-hate. "…I have sinned… Behold, I have played the fool and have committed a serious error."[1] Had he acknowledged his state earlier he might have known healing of the mind and spirit. Swift had the remedy at hand in the Gospel he was paid to preach. Christ and His Gospel could have saved him.

MAY 15 – DIVINE LOVE AND HEALTH – PHYSICAL – Part One

Every Friday, during Bible College days, we heard messages from missionaries. Some of them were not so memorable and others I have never forgotten. Amongst the latter was a talk by Len Twyman from Papua New Guinea in 1937. He was down to earth, practical and quite humorous. I talked with him afterwards, in the limited time between classes. Later I wrote to him with a list of questions about pioneer missionary work, about personal health and other potential problems that I foresaw. Len took time out from his busy deputation ministry to answer me at length. The only reply I mention here concerns physical health. He made two points which I've never forgotten, which apply to us all, not only missionaries.

"John, if you are sick on the field you will need faith healing. I take all wise precautions that are possible in a primitive environment and try to stay well and so first and foremost I practice faith health. This is just as glorifying to God as faith healing."

This struck me as practical wisdom. Len's second piece of advice tied in with it.

"We also need to know the difference between self-pity and foolhardiness. Self-pity which produces fear of catching some tropical disease, or fear of eating local food and getting sick, or the foolhardiness which neglects mosquito nets and anti-malaria tablets etc., etc. Either way you will nullify your effectiveness and destroy yourself…"

This loving advice often stood me in good stead - when I practiced it! Our bodies are temples of the Holy Spirit to be presented to Him in worship and for use in His service.

During Bible College days I attended tropical medicine lectures at Sydney University. I was thankful to the doctors who lectured on malaria. It was prevalent in our early days on the island of Dominica and when I first came down with it I was able to diagnose my condition and treat it. I've never forgotten one other piece of advice from a Sydney university doctor.

"Gentlemen and ladies, be very careful about putting drugs about which you know little, into bodies about which you know less."

What wisdom for all of us when we are often being drugged to death.

God was showing His love through a missionary giving me some bodily health principles. God was showing His love through doctors who volunteered, at no charge, to give their expert knowledge and share their experiences with us.

But there is one more person to whom I'm greatly indebted, who helped nurse me back to health when I was shipped back to Roseau, the capital of Dominica, practically unconscious and apparently dying. I had been alone in an isolated part of the island and had run out of quinine (it was difficult to get during WWII) and malaria was wracking my body. In the capital I was taken to a boarding house run by a Dominican lady named Miss Emmanuel (what a wonderful name!) She cooked the island specialty for me: mountain chicken, "crapaud" large frogs. Boiled down, I was fed this nutritious soup and in other ways nursed back to health. This loving service made the third cord supplied by divine love to keep on the field for another thirty years. Divine love teaches us the principles for physical well being; divine love supplies faith healing, with or without means; and divine love through people often helps us to maintain faith health.

MAY 16 – DIVINE LOVE AND HEALTH – PHYSICAL – Part Two

"And it happened that the father of Publius was lying in bed afflicted with recurrent fever and dysentery; and Paul went in to see him and after he had prayed, he laid his hands on him and healed him. After this had happened, the rest of the people on the island who had diseases were coming to him and getting cured."[1] The unconverted natives of Malta were recipients of divine love in healing. Epaphroditus "...was sick to the point of death, but God had mercy on him, and not on him only but also on me, so that I would not have sorrow upon sorrow."[2] This sickness was not unto death, for love intervened. "...Trophimus I left sick at Miletus."[3]

Is it permissible to ask why? But the answers usually given are not often convincing. Why didn't Paul heal him? Why didn't God heal him? The only answer, as I see it, is that in the inscrutable will and sovereignty of God, He chose not to do so. Divine love is still present in the absence of health and healing. Love's purposes are not always seen immediately. Faith accepts. Love sees.

"No longer drink water exclusively, but use a little wine for the sake of your stomach and your frequent ailments."[4] Paul here deals with a health problem by the use of surprising means. "Because of the surpassing greatness of the revelations, for this reason, to keep me from exalting myself, there was given me a thorn in the flesh, a messenger of Satan to torment me, to keep me from exalting myself! Concerning this I implored the Lord three times that it might leave me. And He has said to me, 'My grace is sufficient for you, for power is perfected in weakness.' Most gladly, therefore, I will rather boast about my weaknesses, so that the power of Christ may dwell in me. Therefore I am well content with weaknesses, with insults, with distresses, with persecutions, with difficulties, for Christ's sake; for when I am weak, then I am strong."[5] After dealing in various ways with other people's health problems, divine love through Paul now concentrates on his own problem.

In all the cases mentioned above we can see divine love in action: healing and not healing; alleviating sickness and allowing it; and now in Paul's case, permitting Satan to afflict him with a thorn in the flesh, which became a permanent weakness that couldn't be removed by pleading prayer.

In a letter I received today, a Christian friend writes:

"God's hurtful but not harmful in His dealings with us. Warren Wiersbe says it well I think. 'God hurts us but never harms us. Amen. A loving parent does that to his child.'"

How we need to face this truth in the realm of physical sickness or health problems at any age. It was accepted in love as Joni Eareckson Tada (1950 -), in her second book Joni, describes her unsuccessful prayers for healing and her resolution of the problem. Loving the glory of God; loving the hand that afflicts; loving the loss of movement as a quadriplegic; loving her wheelchair; loving her new ministries; loving her new audiences and loving the husband that the loving God gave her is Joni's response.

MAY 17 – LOVE'S GRACES

Love's graces, or love's fruit, follow a list of unlovely things which are the deeds of the flesh. "Now the deeds of the flesh are evident, which are: immorality, impurity, sensuality, idolatry, sorcery, enmities, strife, jealousy, outbursts of anger, disputes, dissensions, factions, envying, drunkenness, carousing, and things like these, of which I forewarn you, just as I have forewarned you, that those who practice such things will not inherit the kingdom of God. But the fruit of the Spirit is love, joy, peace, patience, kindness, goodness, faithfulness, gentleness, self-control; against such things there is no law."[1] What a contrast! The Spirit instead of the flesh; fruit instead of works and a list of lovely virtues instead of the vices listed. Nine graces are contrasted with fifteen disgraces.

This nine-fold cluster was once seen in perfection in one life that graced this planet for thirty-three years. A life wholly controlled by the Spirit and fully manifesting love in all its forms and graces. His joy, peace patience kindness, goodness, faithfulness, gentleness and self-control, all combined in His love, have all been gifted to us in Himself by His Spirit. These grace-gifts are all included in the one love gift, Jesus Christ the Lord.

Charisma is a lovely New Testament word meaning a "gift of grace." The word has been wrongly applied to politicians, movie stars and others who seem to scintillate a bit more than the rest of us. Charisma has been given a bad press also by a few charismatic fanatics. But don't miss out on all the grace-gifts He has for His own.

"Charisma, a gift involving grace (charis) on the part of God as the donor, is used (a) of His free bestowments upon sinners, (b) of His endowments upon believers by the operation of the Holy Spirit in the churches, (c) of that which is imparted through human instruction, (d) of the natural "gift" of continence, consequent upon the grace of God as Creator, (e) of gracious deliverances granted in answer to the prayers of fellow believers" W. E. Vine - Expository Dictionary of New Testament Words

Every believer should show that he or she is being possessed by, and a possessor of, all nine of the graces of love. Not only should they be showing, they should go on growing as life goes on and we go on with God. We saw from Scripture that not every believer has all the gifts. Love control is here as in all areas of Christian living.

Joy is love rejoicing. Peace is love resting. Patience is love enduring. Kindness is love being. Goodness is love doing. Faithfulness is love serving. Gentleness is love radiating. Self-control is love ruling. That's quite a list of grace-gifts.

"Love enriches everything we do,
Its innate nature, patient, humble, kind,
Not grasping, selfish, never proud or rude,
When treated wrongly hardly seems to mind.

All special gifts from God will one day end,
And prophecy and knowledge pass away,
Yet love alone goes on for evermore,
Perfected when we reach eternal day."
Ruth McGaby

MAY 18 – LOVE'S NINE-FOLD CLUSTER

It is not easy to teach children abstract concepts like the fruit of the Spirit. Yet under the guidance of the Spirit, it can be, and has been done. I remember the pure delight on the faces of our grandchildren when we gave them their own recording of "The Music Machine." This is "A musical adventure teaching the fruit of the Spirit" to children, and as the author-producers say, "to all ages." I know we grandparents, were, and still are, blessed by it. In fact we have our own copy and listened to it again last night. It starts in a land called love, Agapé-land, and in introducing this word the writers set the tone and get to the heart of the matter.

"Love is real and love is true; there's a land called love for you…
It's not a land of make believe.
It's very real, and you can feel
Something you've never felt before
The love of God and so much more…"

I watched and listened, as our daughter and her husband taught their young children these great truths about the love-fruit, and I was happy to see the response by the little ones. Let's go over the nine, courtesy of "The Music Machine." I hope you will enjoy the words and trust you can get your own copy. Here are some extracts:

"Love, love, love makes people free,
Love makes people do the things they know they ought to do…
Love, love, love makes people friendly.
Love, love, love makes people kind…
Love is helping those who fall behind.
Love, love, love makes people thankful.
Love, love, love makes people share…
Llove is showing others that you care."

"Joy from me, joy from you
Joy is something that we do.
Joy to me, joy to you
And others too.
Give away pure delight
Make someone fell alright.
That's what joy really is, let's learn to give.
Everybody seems to want to have joy everyday.
Lot's of folks don't even know it was made to give away."

"Peace is when the wind stops blowing.
Peace is where the sun is showing.
Knowing that my Daddy's home, God gives me peace.
Peace, peace, I think I understand. Peace, peace is holding Jesus' hand."

Herbert the snail and love-patience demand special and separate attention later.

MAY 18 - CONTINUED

"Isn't God good when He asks us just to love like He does?
Isn't God good when He asks us just to be so kind?
When I treat you kindly, it makes you happy,
Changes you inside.
Makes you feel important, loved and special and it makes you kind…"

"Goodness, goodness is God's idea you see.
He tells you in the Bible, how good, being good can be…
and you'd be good if you could see, how good, being good can be."

The final three, faithfulness, gentleness and self-control are hymned like this by "The Music Machine," but it would spoil their song to curtail them here so they along with patience will be reviewed in the next pages (May 21). So meanwhile sing with Herbert.

"Have patience, have patience
Don't be in such a hurry,
When you get impatient you only start to worry.
Remember, remember that God is patient too.
And think of all the times when others have to wait for you."

MAY 19 – LOVE AND JOY

"…let them also that love thy name be joyful in thee."[1] Beethoven's "Hymn to Joy" is the music for the following verses which are an example of the joy, adoration and worship heard when love sings. Love's joy, rejoicing, praising and singing are divinely related and the hymn stresses their relationship to God and each other.

"Joyful, joyful, we adore Thee, God of glory, Lord of love;
Hearts unfold like flowers before Thee, opening to the sun above.
Melt the clouds of sin and sadness; drive the dark of doubt away;
Giver of immortal gladness, fill us with the light of day!

All Thy works with joy surround Thee, earth and heaven reflect Thy rays,
Stars and angels sing around Thee, center of unbroken praise.
Field and forest, vale and mountain, flowery meadow, flashing sea,
Singing bird and flowing fountain call us to rejoice in Thee.

Thou art giving and forgiving, ever blessing, ever blessed,
Wellspring of the joy of living, ocean depth of happy rest!
Thou our Father, Christ our Brother, all who live in love are Thine;
Teach us how to love each other, lift us to the joy divine.

Mortals, join the happy chorus, which the morning stars began;
Father love is reigning o'er us, brother love binds man to man.
Ever singing, march we onward, victors in the midst of strife,
Joyful music leads us Sunward in the triumph song of life."
Henry J. van Dyke (1852 – 1933)

This Spirit generated love-joy for Jesus is seen clearly in the lives of Paul and Silas. Stripped and beaten with rods, then thrown into prison and immobilized in the stocks, they began to sing their song of joy. "It came upon the midnight clear, That glorious song of old…" Edmund H. Sears (1810 – 1876) which refers to the angelic song at the birth of Jesus. I think it could well apply to the midnight prison rejoicing of Paul and Silas. "But about midnight Paul and Silas were praying and singing hymns of praise to God, and the prisoners were listening to them; and suddenly there came a great earth-quake…"[2] This heavenly grace-gift of joy is much more than the happiness which depends on our circumstances. Its fruit is surprising and soul-saving. The joy shown here is no superficial emotional substitute. J for Jesus; always first. O for others; always second. Y for yourself; in the place of humility always last. That spells JOY; love-joy the fruit of the Spirit.

Is it any wonder that when Paul and Silas were released, and went on their way preaching and rejoicing that the converts were of the same calibre? Like begets like and the Thessalonian church, begun after their Philippian ordeal, displayed the same fruit of love-joy. "We give thanks to God always for all of you[3]… constantly bearing in mind your work of faith and labor of love[4]…You also became imitators of us and of the Lord, having received the word in much tribulation with the joy of the Holy Spirit, so that you became an example to all the believers in Macedonia and in Achaia."[5]

MAY 20 – LOVE AND PEACE

Peace is the gift of Christ given initially by Him in promise before He left His little flock on earth. "Peace I leave with you; My peace I give to you…"[1] This promise was fulfilled when the Holy Spirit came to fill them and give the graces and gifts our Lord had promised. In the garden, at Calvary and for three days after, His disciples knew little peace because of fears without and the inward fear that they had misplaced their faith. The two walking the Emmaus Road showed this: "But we were hoping that it was He who was going to redeem Israel…"[2] They didn't realize that Calvary made peace possible. It was no make-shift peace, but was a blood bought peace, based on righteousness enabling God to justify those who believe. This was, and is, the basic peace with God all originating in His heart of love that planned reconciliation. Another one of my father's favourite hymns that shows this was:

"There comes to my heart one sweet strain,
A glad and a joyous refrain,
I sing it again and again,
Sweet peace, the gift of God's love.

Peace, peace, sweet peace,
Wonderful gift from above,
Oh, wonderful, wonderful peace,
Sweet peace, the gift of God's love.

Through Christ on the cross peace was made,
My debt by His death was all paid,
No other foundation is laid.
For peace, the gift of God's love

When Jesus as Lord I had crowned,
My heart with this peace did abound,
In Him the rich blessing I found,
Sweet peace, the gift of God's love.

In Jesus for peace I abide,
And as I keep close to His side,
There's nothing but peace doth betide
Sweet peace, the gift of God's love."
Peter P. Bilhorn (1865 – 1936)

"And the peace of God, which surpasses all comprehension, will guard your hearts and your minds in Christ Jesus."[3] This surpassing peace is the inward repose that comes when Jesus is crowned Lord and Saviour.

How we need continual infusions of the grace of inner peace. Or better, how we need to allow the Spirit to manifest the peace of God in and through us. We know, we show and others know when inner repose is maintained or missing. We should see to it that this fruit of the Spirit is carried outside ourselves and shown in harmonious relationships with our families, within the family of God and as far as possible within the human family. "If possible, so far as it depends on you, be at peace with all men."[4] Let us never forget that the whole peace destroying list of the deeds of the flesh is deliberately placed as a warning before this lovely nine-fold cluster of fruit of the Spirit. "Now those who belong to Christ Jesus have crucified the flesh with its passions and desires. If we live by the Spirit, let us also walk by the Spirit. Let us not become boastful, challenging one another, envying one another."[5]

MAY 21 – LOVE AND PATIENCE

Your patience is now rewarded. Here, from "The Music Machine" is the story, loved by our grandchildren and us of Herbert, the slow, patient snail. I wish I had learned earlier about Herbert's practices. They come from his very nature and that's no secret. For us, too, it's an open secret; love-patience is the fruit of the Spirit, a real evidence of the new creation that we are in Christ. But let's hear about Herbert, his nature, and when he forgot it.

"There was a snail called Herbert who was so very slow.
He caused a lot of traffic jams wherever he would go
The ants were always getting mad the beetles they would fume
But Herbert always poked a lot and sang this little tune:
Have patience, have patience
Don't be in such a hurry
When you get impatient you only start to worry
Remember, remember that God is patient too
So think of all the times when others had to wait for you.
When Herbert was much younger
He often got in trouble
Forgetting that he was a snail he did things on the double
He crashed through every spider's web, with beetles he'd collide
Till one day Herbert's father took his speeding son aside.
Have patience, have patience
Don't be in such a hurry
When you get impatient you only start to worry
Remember, remember that God is patient too
So think of all the times when others had to wait for you.
As you can well imagine
There's a moral to this tale
Some of you may find yourselves behind a creeping snail.
So if you are impatient and you're easily disturbed,
Think about this little song and take a tip from Herb."

I took the tip a bit late in life as I am quite impatient, I confess. I have always tended to hurry. When heart problems began to make their appearance I hung in my office in Bridgetown, Barbados, a copy of these words:

"Slow me down, Lord. Ease the pounding of my heart by the quieting of my mind. Steady my hurried pace with a vision of the eternal reach of time. Give me, amid the confusion of the day, the calmness of the everlasting hills. Break the tensions of my nerves and muscles with the soothing music of the singing streams that live in my memory. Help me to know the magical, restoring power of sleep. Teach me the art of taking minute vacations of slowing down to look at a flower, to chat with a friend, to pat a dog, to read a few lines from a good book. Slow me down, Lord, and inspire me to send my roots deep into the soil of life's enduring values that I may grow toward the stars of my greater destiny." Wilfred A. Peterson

"Inspire me to send my roots deep into the soil of life's enduring values." And what are they, and what are my roots? "…rooted and grounded in love."[1] Love to God and man are obligations. Love is the essential enduring value just as it is the root and ground and fruit of all these graces. The spirit of love and patience can work this God-like characteristic deeply in the core of my being.

MAY 22 – LOVE AND PATIENCE – ENDURANCE

As was mentioned, teaching abstract concepts to children demands simplification. While this is a good thing to bear in mind also for young adults and adult youngsters in the faith, there comes a time when primary classes give way to secondary and post secondary education. The writer of the book of Hebrews puts it this way: "Therefore leaving the elementary teaching about the Christ, let us press on to maturity…"[1] This means that we must go deeper into the Scriptures and the things concerning our Christian living. So let's leave the elementary and necessary aspects of patience and move on to a deeper study of the subject. Patience-endurance means to go on under suffering and to bear up under it with the courage born of love.

How did Jesus manifest love and patient endurance under suffering? He lived all His earthly life under the control of the Holy Spirit and He personified patience and all the other fruits of the Spirit. Love endured silently when necessary. Love endured steadfastly; He set his face to go to Jerusalem and all the suffering that awaited Him there. Love endured with long-suffering. This was His manifest attitude. "For consider Him who has endured such hostility by sinners against Himself, so that you will not grow weary and lose heart."[2] And His love and patience continued right to the end, the Cross. So "…let us also lay aside every encumbrance and the sin which so easily entangles us, and let us run with endurance the race that is set before us, fixing our eyes on Jesus, the author and perfecter of faith, who for the joy set before Him endured the cross, despising the shame, and has sat down at the right hand of the throne of God."[3]

He not only exemplifies love and patient-endurance, He also empowers us to follow His example. We are "…strengthened with power through His Spirit in the inner man, so that Christ may dwell in your hearts through faith and that you, being rooted and grounded in love."[4] "strengthened with all power, according to His glorious might, for the attaining of all steadfastness and patience; joyously giving thanks to the Father, who has qualified us to share in the inheritance of the saints in Light."[5] The rooting and grounding in love is by the Spirit; the attaining of steadfastness and patient endurance is by the Spirit; and the connection of love, joy and patience is by the Spirit. The resulting thanksgiving of praise glorifies the Father who has qualified us to share in the inheritance of the saints. He lives in us by His Spirit, and will, as we permit and cooperate, show His patience through us.

MAY 23 – THE LOVE OF GOD AND PATIENCE

"And the Lord direct your hearts into the love of God, and into the patient waiting for Christ."[1] "May the Lord direct your hearts into the love of God and into the steadfastness of Christ."[2] "May the Lord direct your hearts into God's love and Christ's perseverance."[3] These three versions all refer to God's love and all ask that the Lord Himself undertake the direction of our hearts into that heavenly love. He alone as the sole source of love can confirm our hearts into Christ-like love. Conformity to His likeness is predestination's goal by Providence's guidance, in our life-long pilgrimage of grace to glory. As we look back from the end of the road of our spiritual pilgrimage, we see that it has been the God of love and the love of God in control everywhere. Our part in this is to keep ourselves in the love of God and cooperate in the circumstantial crises He allows into our lives.

The three translations all use a different word as they emphasize the second direction "into the patient waiting for Christ," "into the steadfastness of Christ" and "into God's love and Christ's perseverance." These three words together show the New Testament meaning of patience. The Greek word "hupomoné" – patience - is sometimes passive in its endurance under trials and chastisements but it is active in its "patient waiting for Christ;" in "the steadfastness of Christ;" and in "God's love and Christ's perseverance." W. E. Vine in his Expository Dictionary of New Testament Words tells us that:

"…the patience of Christ is possible of three interpretations, a) the patient waiting for Christ; b) that they might be patient in their sufferings as Christ was in His; c) that since Christ is expecting till His enemies be made the footstool of His feet, so they might be patient also in their hopes of His triumph and their deliverance. While a too rigid exegesis is to be avoided, it may, perhaps, be permissible to paraphrase: 'the Lord teach and enable you to love as God loves, and to be patient as Christ is patient.' (From 'Notes on Thessalonians by Hogg and Vine, pp. 222,285')"

To this end His love and patience is working in our bodies, minds and spirits. His love and patience have made us what we are, and has brought us to where we are, and is constantly being shown in our lives and experiences.

One other word, frequently used in connection with patience, is longsuffering from the Greek word "makrothumia." As Christians we have known of God's longsuffering and the whole world is being shown it even though it doesn't know or care about it. Why does our Lord delay His coming? Why is His judgement postponed? The mockers, following after their own desires ask, "…Where is the promise of His coming?..."[4] The answer to these questions is because of the long patience of the love of God. "The Lord is not slow about His promise, as some count slowness, but is patient toward you, not wishing for any to perish but for all to come to repentance."[5] God still loves the world, with longsuffering love but it will end. "But the day of the Lord will come like a thief…"[6] "…what sort of people ought you to be in holy conduct and godliness, looking for and hastening the coming of the day of God[7]… and regard the patience of our Lord as salvation…"[8]

MAY 24 – LOVE AND KINDNESS

Kindness is one of the characteristics of all the loves. This kindness, which is love acting with compassion, is of course supreme in agapé. Kindness ought also to be a hallmark in marital love; it's an essential quality in all the family loves, and should be prominent in friendship love. It is coupled with love and manifested in the person of Jesus Christ. "But when the kindness of God our Savior and His love for mankind appeared, He saved us...."[1]

Kindness, shown by tender loving care, marked Joseph's marital relationship with Mary. It was evident before betrothal and in all the upheavals that followed Jesus' birth including the subsequent demands of their married life, work and other children. As Joseph probably pre-deceased Mary, our Lord was careful to ensure that she had a home and would be cared for by John the beloved.

The friendship love between Jonathon and David was notable for the constant kindness which continued long after Jonathon's death. "...'Is there not yet anyone of the house of Saul to whom I may show the kindness of God?' And Ziba said to the king, 'There is still a son of Jonathan who is crippled in both feet.'"[2] And we know what love and kindness did for Mephibosheth.

But there is another, little known, Scripture story of an obscure minor official of a royal court. We will look at him again in the series on friendship love (June 9), but here we will recount his kindness. Who was this? Like the good and thankful Samaritan, commended by the lord as a kind, compassionate and thankful foreigner, this man was an Ethiopian. His name was Ebed-melech and he is briefly mentioned in the book of Jeremiah. The record of his kindness, like the unrecorded stories of millions of people who never make headlines, was noted in heaven and did not, like any kindly cup of water, go unrewarded. Jeremiah would have died by slow suffocation in the sucking mud of a pit where he had been put by his enemies except for the intervention of unknown Ebed. The love and kindness with which he extracted Jeremiah is seen in his actions. "So Ebed-melech took the men under his authority and went into the king's palace to a place beneath the storeroom and took from there worn-out clothes and worn-out rags and let them down by ropes into the cistern to Jeremiah. Then Ebed-melech the Ethiopian said to Jeremiah, 'Now put these worn-out clothes and rags under your armpits under the ropes'; and Jeremiah did so. So they pulled Jeremiah up with the ropes and lifted him out of the cistern...."[3] You can almost hear the plop as they pulled him like a cork from a bottle. But can we also see the thoughtfulness in Ebed's kindness? The ropes would have injured the prophet for the sucking mud was powerful and the strength of the men was mighty. Love and kindness were so evident in the thoughtful actions and caring concern of Ebed. This is what love and kindness is in action. It is not just talk.

MAY 25 – LOVE AND THE GOODNESS OF GOD

Many years ago, during a missionary speaking tour of New Zealand, I was a guest in a very gracious home with a most loving and hospitable Christian hostess. She, with her husband, did everything to make me feel at ease, at home and comfortable. She acted as my chauffeur driving me to services at cost of time and gas. Just previously there had been a tragic plane crash in another part of the country with great loss of life including some Christians. During my visit in that home the postman one day delivered the letters and as my hostess examined them I heard her give an exclamation. She came to me holding up a soiled and partly charred envelope and said:

"Isn't God good, this is a letter saved out of that plane wreck."
Without thinking that it might be out of place and offensive from a guest I replied:
"But Mrs. __, God is good even if this letter from your son had been burned to ashes, like the passengers."

This reply may have been out of order but it was true and Scriptural, and she received it with characteristic grace, allowing that she had spoken unthinkingly. As I do all too often.

The character of God is often impugned in the house of His friends by their lack of understanding of His nature, love and goodness. Someone will say about the incident above that my hostess was actually praising the character of God. On first sight, and by the words, this would appear so, yet we all naturally, see with, rather than through our eyes.

"This life's dim windows of the soul
Distorts the heavens from pole to pole
And leads you to believe a lie
When you see with, not through, the eye."
William Blake (1757 – 1827)

We need spiritual insight to correct our astigmatism, short-sightedness and sometimes plain blindness concerning the love and goodness of God. I have heard sermons on my hostess's theme "God is so good" (and He is) yet the emphasis is unbalanced. The message is that Christians shouldn't be sick; and that half-truth, is linked with another half-lie, the "success" syndrome. Health and wealth should be ours because God is so good! While this may sound oversimplified I have personally heard this taught as gospel. The reality in the Scriptures, and in the life of the saints, sometimes includes sickness, poverty and failure. That good can be evil, and evil good, runs across the grain of our fallen natures; that God should allow or cause ills is foreign to our sinful self.

But hear the voice of the Lord God: "…I am the Lord, and there is no other, The One forming light and creating darkness, Causing well-being and creating calamity; I am the Lord who does all these."[1] This may come as a shock to our preconceived ideas about love and a God of love but He does not need to, and doesn't, defend or explain Himself to our finite minds and futile questions. Calvary answers all as it dealt with darkness, the devil and death.

"Ill that He blesses is our good,
And unbless'd good is ill;
And all is right that seems most wrong,
If it be His sweet will."
Frederick William Faber (1814 – 1863)

MAY 26 – LOVE AND GOODNESS

Our ideas of goodness can be vague and often limited only to good works. Actually, goodness is the inner state of being good, which is the essential pre-requisite for doing good. Our lord says. "The good man brings out of his good treasure what is good..."[1] In contrast He indicted the religious leaders, the Pharisees, with confrontational language. "You brood of vipers, how can you, being evil, speak what is good?..."[2] Let us not be smug or self-righteous but rather examine ourselves as we consider love and goodness.

We have already noted the fundamental truth that the love and goodness of God provides the basis for all real love and goodness that we posses and show. We are not good by nature but are self-centered sinners who need to be made good. We used to sing a children's hymn which contains the Biblical truths concerning love and goodness.

"He died that we might be forgiven;
He died to make us good,
That we might go to heaven,
Saved by His precious blood.

There was no other good enough
To pay the price of sin,
He only could unlock the gate,
Of heaven and let us in.

O dearly, dearly, He has loved,
We must love Him too,
Trust in His redeeming blood,
And try His works to do."
Cecil Frances Alexander (1818 – 1895)

The author shows the connection between divine love and goodness on one side and our human response. Love is so many-sided that, as in these pages, we find it controlling all areas of our life. I may seem obsessed by love, and I confess that I am, seeing it everywhere, but it is a Scriptural obsession.

A good person, in the Christian sense, is one resting in and experiencing the inner goodness of Christ who indwells the personality by His Spirit. This means that we never need to be on the defensive about being and doing good. Taunts from the non-good about do-gooders and goodie-goodies need never bother us. What He is, we are, and that's good enough for me. Our good motives and actions can be misunderstood, but not to worry, He knows and will vindicate. The really good are meek, but not weak; like a child, but not childish; gentle, but never soft when righteous indignation is called for. The loving goodness of the truly good person is seen in their courage, not only of convictions and confessions, but in the courage of steady endurance that goes on despite all opposition. The good person is genuinely humble and lovingly patient; a person of good-will; loving peace, but not afraid of conflict for righteousness sake. Who can be like this? We can be! Like Barnabas "for he was a good man, and full of the Holy Spirit and of faith..."[3] Thank God for such examples. We may not realize that when we use the expression "Thank Goodness" we are using a euphemism for "Thank God." We do thank Him for His love and goodness that makes ours possible.

MAY 27 – LOVE AND FAITHFULNESS

Faith in the King James Version is faithfulness in most other versions. If it was faith in the sense that Peter uses it[1] it would head the list of grace gifts. However in the nine fold cluster Paul is stressing fidelity as the King James Version uses it elsewhere: "...shewing all good fidelity; that they may adorn the doctrine of God our Saviour in all things."[2] Some of the modern versions say "showing all good faith."

Let's listen to "The Music Machine" on faithfulness. It indirectly points out that without faith there could be no faithfulness. Also without faith there could be no pleasing God, no impossible things made possible and no rewards.

"Without faith it's impossible, it's impossible, it's impossible to please God.
He who comes to God must believe that He is and He rewards those who seek Him.
All things are possible, all things are possible, all things are possible.
Just believe that God will do everything that He says He will do, and He rewards those who seek Him."

Thus "The Music Machine" brings us to where we want to be: counting on His faithfulness. There can be no love and faithfulness on our part except from the love and faithfulness of God. No Scriptural character illustrates this better, apart from the Lord Jesus Himself, than Jeremiah. That sensitive man was called to an impossible task demanding unfaltering love and unfailing faithfulness. In his darkest hours when it seemed love and faithfulness would fail, they triumphed. Hear him in the midst of doleful Lamentations. "Remember my affliction and my wandering, the wormwood and bitterness. Surely my soul remembers And is bowed down within me. This I recall to my mind, Therefore I have hope. The Lord's lovingkindnesses indeed never cease, For His compassions never fail. They are new every morning; Great is Your faithfulness. 'The Lord is my portion,' says my soul, 'Therefore I have hope in Him.' The Lord is good to those who wait for Him, To the person who seeks Him. It is good that he waits silently For the salvation of the Lord. It is good for a man that he should bear the yoke in his youth."[3] And there we have all the principle and practices portrayed by the prophet, who, from personal experience and the Word of the Lord, was perfectly fitted to teach us about the lovingkindness and faithfulness of God.

"Great is Thy faithfulness! Great is Thy faithfulness!
Morning by morning new mercies I see.
All I have needed Thy hand hath provided;
Great is Thy faithfulness, Lord, unto me!"
Thomas O. Chisholm (1866 – 1960)

It's a long leap in time from Jeremiah to Hudson Taylor (1832 – 1905), founder of the original China Inland Mission. His life verse for service was: "...Have faith in God."[4] Taylor used to say "Have the faithfulness of God." Like his mentor, George Müller (1805 – 1895), having wholehearted trust in the love and faithfulness of God for life and service, it was no wonder his life was one of love and faithfulness. In Christian solders, love and obedience is expected. In Christian saints, love and holiness is expected. In Christian servants, love and devotion is anticipated. In all, and especially in Christian stewards, love and faithfulness must be the norm.

MAY 28 – LOVE AND GENTLENESS

The lullaby "Gentleness" from "The Music Machine" makes a lovely introduction to this topic.

"Gentle breeze, gentle breeze blowing through the trees
And the meadow filled with flowers.
Showing me your gentleness, how I love You.
Showing me your gentleness, how I love You.

In the still of the night You draw me near
Just to whisper how You care.
Showing me your gentleness, how I love You.
Showing me your gentleness, how I love You.

Your dear Son walked the earth, He was full of love.
Now He lives within my heart
Showing me your gentleness, how I love You.
Showing me your gentleness, how I love You."

The pastoral scene, with zephyrs singing through the trees, wafting the scent from flower-filled fields, lulls our mind by lovely gentleness. We sense the mildness of this summer scene in a temperate climate. I have known many such days, in my boyhood in our English garden with the woods just beyond the fence. The attribute of gentleness, part of the divine nature, must have been seen in gentle Eden's first creation. This would be before sin entered, when lions lay with lambs and fruit and flowers never knew the curse of weeds. There gentle love reigned in the garden and in the hearts of the first lovers. There gentle love from the Creator produced reciprocal love from the blessed couple. "How we love You as You show us your love and gentleness" we can almost hear them sing their rendition of the song.

How can we find gentleness in this fallen, sinful and violent world? If this tender plant exists, how long can it last? The little lullaby suggests where the right answers can be found. "Your dear Son walked the earth, He was full of love. Now He lives within my heart Showing me your gentleness..." This simplified version of redemptive love on earth was still manifested even on the violent Cross. Words of love and forgiveness; tender thoughtfulness for His mother, all flowed from this first gentleman. And by His life of love and gentleness being formed in us, and flowing from us by His Spirit, love and gentleness still walks the earth.

Gentleness is not such a tender plant as it seems. There is a resilience and tenacity about gentleness, a certain toughness if you like, for it is rooted in love and truth; tough and tender love, truth and gentleness. The juxtapositions are Biblical. They mark the true, tough and tender greatness of being in Christ. "...And Your gentleness makes me great."[1] This gentleness is yielding, persistent and urgent. "Now I, Paul, myself urge you by the meekness and gentleness of Christ..."[2] "But we proved to be gentle among you, as a nursing mother tenderly cares for her own children."[3] That is what gentleness really means.

MAY 29 – LOVE AND SELF CONTROL

As we come to the last of this nine-fold cluster a short review is in order. The fruit of the Spirit is love in various forms:

"Joy is love with gladness. Peace is love with accord. Long-suffering is love with endurance. Gentleness is love with a whisper. Goodness is love with excellence. Faith is love with confidence. Meekness is love with mildness and temperance. Self-control is love with discipline." As Edna Mast, the author of these definitions says: "The fruit of the Spirit is love in action."

Self-control is not love in outward action but love working within, disciplining body, mind and spirit by bringing our whole tripartite being under the control of the Spirit.

The New Testament states that our bodies are the temple of God and should not be defiled or self-destroyed. Over-indulgence in any of the lawful appetites can defile and destroy. Paul says he battles his body; disciplines it as athletes did in the Olympic games of his day. "Do you not know that those who run in a race all run, but only one receives the prize? Run in such a way that you may win. Everyone who competes in the games exercises self-control in all things. They then do it to receive a perishable wreath, but we an imperishable. Therefore I run in such a way, as not without aim; I box in such a way, as not beating the air; but I discipline my body and make it my slave, so that, after I have preached to others, I myself will not be disqualified."[1] Our bodies should not be polluted but should be presented to the Lord. This is love and self-control.

And what about our minds? The defiling of minds today goes on at a sickening speed. The race seems to be on as to which nation can move the fastest down the Gadarene slopes to self-destruction. Mass suicide, like the lemmings, amidst cries of liberty, meaning license to self-destruct, and freedom meaning anarchy and lawlessness. The corrupt mass media, with Mammon as its God, controls more minds than ever before. Let us turn to the Word of God for something positive. " Finally, brethren, whatever is true, whatever is honorable, whatever is right, whatever is pure, whatever is lovely, whatever is of good repute, if there is any excellence and if anything worthy of praise, dwell on these things."[2] Only in this way will we be constantly "...taking every thought captive to the obedience of Christ."[3] And self-control in the realm of our spirits has been discussed before so we will not consider it now. I want to keep my promise and let "The Music Machine" have the last easily grasped definition of self-control; starting young and starting simple.

"Once I had a knot in my shoe and it would not come loose.
I tried and tried and pried and pried,
But it would not come loose.
I got so mad I kicked the door and stubbed my little toe.
Oh, If only I had learned a little bit of self-control.
Self-control is just controlling myself.
It's listening to my heart and doing what is smart.

Self-control is the best way I can go so I think that I'll control myself.
I never liked to brush my teeth; I wished that I could stop.
I'd have more time for candy bars and drinking soda pop.
But soon my teeth would hurt so bad from all the cavities...
I'd better learn some self-control..."

And so say all of us. And now let love's nine-fold cluster "Say it with flowers" and in addition "Say it with fruit!"

MAY 30 – LOVE'S DISCERNMENT

Our Lord Jesus, on numerous occasions, showed discerning love. His spirituality and sensitivity read hearts, knew minds, discerned thoughts and intentions and answered aloud silent questions. An example of the latter is seen when the Pharisee Simon, seeing the sinful woman kissing and anointing the feet of Jesus, had a silent conversation. "Now when the Pharisee who had invited Him saw this, he said to himself, 'If this man were a prophet He would know who and what sort of person this woman is who is touching Him, that she is a sinner.' And Jesus answered him, 'Simon, I have something to say to you.'..."[1]

Let's digress for a minute. How did a silent conversation come to be public knowledge? The observer might have questioned Simon later wondering why the Lord spoke to him as He did. Or Simon might have been mouthing his thoughts and someone could lip read. Or again, he might have been muttering to himself and was overheard. What really matters is what follows. The Lord publicly answered a silent, questioning conversation. This is love's discernment in action.

Jesus' answer to Simon consisted of a parable about two debtors; one deeply, the other not so deeply, in debt. As neither could pay, the lender graciously forgave both of them their debts. Our Lord ended with a love question to Simon. "...'So which of them will love him more?' Simon answered and said, 'I suppose the one whom he forgave more.' And He said to him, 'You have judged correctly.'"[2] Then the Lord made the application. And here, perhaps, we see His loving discernment of what the woman's actions implied. He saw the torment behind her tears, the repentance that prompted her giving and the love which longed for forgiveness. Forgiven much she loved much. His discernment, governed by His love, saw it, said it and challenged Simon with it. And this is the challenge to us.

Some more than others have a measure of natural discernment. All Christians have the plus of supernatural discernment because of the Spirit's indwelling, but this must be cultivated by use and controlled by the Spirit. A. W. Tozer (1897 – 1963) was such a person who discerned the trends towards superficiality, infidelity and immorality in the church and who dared to say so in his preaching and writing.

In addition to the general gift of discernment there is the additional gift, to some, of "...the distinguishing of spirits..."[3] Regardless of whether one is specially gifted in this way or not, we are all called, in this day of increase in lying and deceiving spirits, to test them. We are told how to discern, to know, the spirit of truth and error. The discerning is to be followed by dealing, speaking and rebuking the evil spirits but differentiating between them and the possessed. This love discerns, differentiates and delivers.

MAY 31 – LOVE'S ENCOURAGEMENT

This is one of love's quiet and most needed ministries and one in which all Christians can engage. In my book, it ranks with that other lowly gift of "helps." I'm fairly sure encouragements and helps, though not platform spectaculars, will rank high when heaven hands out the rewards for faithfulness and good stewardship.

There was a Cypriot named Joseph whom the apostles renamed Barnabas which means Son of Encouragement. Barnabas loved the Lord and showed it by his giving to the church in Jerusalem. He encouraged the church and its leaders by selling a piece of land which he owned and laying the proceeds at the apostles' feet. Loving and giving are a pair which often produce a love child called encouragement.

Mr. Encouragement saw another need in the church at Jerusalem and that was to give encouragement to new converts. "When a fellow needs a friend" is an old expression. Saul of Tarsus, newly converted persecutor of the church and murderer's assistant at the stoning of Stephen, was "…trying to associate with the disciples; but they were all afraid of him, not believing that he was a disciple. But Barnabas took hold of him and brought him to the apostles…"[1] Mr. Encouragement sponsored him. His heart of love reached out and made a friend out of an outcast. He dared to believe that God could change and convert religious bigots and criminals. In our day, Charles Colson (1931 -), of "Watergate" infamy and prison, was loved and encouraged to Christ, and now in turn is engaged in a ministry of encouragement and love to prisoners.

The new Gentile church at Antioch was isolated and needed recognition and love's encouragement. Who would be the link? The church at Jerusalem didn't need to look far; they knew the one who could fill this need. Mr. Encouragement of course! "…they sent Barnabas off to Antioch. Then when he arrived and witnessed the grace of God, he rejoiced and began to encourage them all with resolute heart to remain true to the Lord; for he was a good man, and full of the Holy Spirit and of faith…"[2] And there is the source of Barnabas' love and encouragement. The fullness of the Spirit and faith which works by love. The true love-encourager Himself. This is one of His titles; helper-encourager. He didn't fail Barnabas when further need came. His nephew, John Mark, had failed, when with his uncle and Paul on their last missionary journey. Barnabas gave his nephew love and encouragement, restored him and produced a real worker for God and writer of the Gospel. Even Paul was glad to have him back in the end.

To bring this into the present, some years ago, a group of us missionaries were praying for property suitable for a Mission Headquarters. We were few in number and had no money but believing we were in the will of God we prayed and watched. Imagine the encouragement to our faith when a Christian farmer asked us if we could use fifty acres of his land for the project. His, and his wife's, loving giving was a twentieth century repetition of Barnabas' act with the same results.

JUNE 1 – LOVE'S COVENANT

It all began with a fight! David won over Goliath and at the same time won a loving, lifelong friend. Theirs was true brotherly, friendship love. It occurred over three thousand years ago and has remained one of the most notable and noble in all history. It was a pure golden love. "To the pure, all things are pure; but to those who are defiled and unbelieving, nothing is pure, but both their mind and their conscience are defiled."[1] The world today, with its condoning almost congratulating acceptance of homosexuality and lesbianism, can hardly imagine a clear, clean friendship between two men, or two women. That between Jonathon and David was a mutually healthy, helpful relationship. These men were not misogynists, they were heterosexual, attracted to, and attracted by, the opposite sex and were married men with children.

This valid and valuable friendship commenced as the rich young prince, Jonathon, watched the poor but courageous, confident young commoner, David, prepare for conflict. And he saw him win, in the name of the Lord and with only one shot from his sling. A notable victory was gained that day, not only over the giant, but also over the heart of Jonathon. "...the soul of Jonathan was knit to the soul of David, and Jonathan loved him as himself.[2]... Then Jonathan made a covenant with David because he loved him as himself. Jonathan stripped himself of the robe that was on him and gave it to David, with his armor, including his sword and his bow and his belt."[3]

That day was a memorable one not only for all Israel, but especially for these two, one a combatant and the other a bystander. That day the lifelong, and after life, covenant was established and sealed by the gift of princely accoutrements. This verbal compact, made without written legal contracts of any kind, was as binding upon these two as any Biblical vows could be. Covenants of this kind, as well as the more common marital agreements, are not to be entered lightly or frivolously but with seriousness and understanding. Jonathon and David thus contracted to encourage and help each other until death parted them, and their agreement was to continue to their children. Covenants are often sealed with gifts, and while David had nothing, he did give himself wholeheartedly, and Jonathon did the same, plus the notable and symbolic gifts mentioned.

In all this, there are many lessons for us today, along the lines advocated by John Wesley (1703 – 1791) on December 25, 1747. He strongly urged the Methodists to renew their covenant with God. His first covenant service was held in the French church, Spitalfields on August 11, 1755. An order of service was drawn up and, with modifications, is still found in the English Methodist Hymn Book. This hymn was used.

"Come, let us use the grace divine, and all with one accord,
In a perpetual covenant join ourselves to Christ the Lord;...
To each covenant the blood apply which takes our sins away,
And register our names on high and keep us to that day!"
Charles Wesley (1707 – 1788)

JUNE 2 – LOVE'S CONSECRATION

Love's consecration was built into the love covenant between Jonathon and David. They dedicated themselves to each other with a devotion illustrative of religious consecration. Then again, because it is built into love's consecration, there was the dedication of things. This twofold description of consecration never alters. There is first the dedication of self, the whole person and personality, and because the lesser is always contained in the greater, the possessions are consecrated with the person.

Jonathon immediately stripped himself and gave David his robe, armour, sword, bow and belt. These princely clothes and accoutrements were choice gifts consecrated to David for his use and symbolic of the position David was destined to take; replacing Jonathon on the throne. This love covenant was made with full knowledge and deliberate intent and contained the most complete consecration of a secular nature that the Bible records.

David also dedicated himself wholeheartedly to Jonathon, though being the youngest and poorest of a large family he had nothing to give in the secondary aspect of consecration. He had nothing, no thing, to lay at Jonathon's feet as a reciprocal seal of their covenant of consecration. But he had something. David gave his friend counsel, comfort, encouragement, help and hope in his difficult relationship with his father, King Saul. Though intangible, these were perhaps more priceless than the princely possession he received.

Love's consecration in the wider spiritual sense starts with divine initiative. The Father thought it; the Son wrought it; the Holy Spirit brought it. The Son's separation and dedication to the task of reconciliation and redemption began before time itself. He was set apart for the Cross before the foundation of the earth. And on earth He set Himself apart in time for our salvation. We are the objects of this divine consecration contained in the New Covenant. This is the first dimension in sacred consecration.

The second dimension is when we in turn are set apart by God for His glory, worship and service. "But know that the Lord has set apart the godly man for Himself..."[1]

"I am Thine, O Lord, I have heard Thy voice,
And it told Thy love to me;...
Consecrate me now to Thy service, Lord,
By the power of grace divine;..."
Fanny Crosby (1820 – 1915)

The third and fourth dimensions in love's spiritual consecration are the two illustrated in Jonathon and David; the consecration of our selves and our substance to the Lord. We do it as the hymn says:

"All for Jesus, all for Jesus!
All my being's ransomed powers:
All my thoughts and words and doings,
All my days and all my hours.

Let my hands perform His bidding,
Let my feet run in His ways;
Let my eyes see Jesus only,
Let my lips speak forth His praise."
Mary D. James (1810 – 1883)

JUNE 3 – LOVE'S COMMITMENT

Commitment is an essential ingredient for the success of any covenant. It is the foundation for the contracts and agreements that men and women make in marital union and in the affairs of business and life in general. Commitment was prominent and pre-eminent in the mutual friendship pact that Jonathon and David made. Commitment is the act of pledging or obligating oneself to responsibilities of various kinds. Jonathon and David had family, business, political and military commitments. Their family obligations entailed familial and filial loves but their covenant love was of a special kind. It was not only a pact but also a performance and a pursuit. It was a covenant pact of love containing the continuing commitment of love.

Nowhere does this element of love's commitment stand out more clearly than when the conflict ranged fiercely about them. Saul wanted to kill David. David reminded Jonathon of their covenant. Jonathon responded with word reminiscent of Joshua's command and Israel's response of commitment. The young prince said to his friend: "...Whatsoever thy soul desireth, I will even do it for thee."[1] In the newer translation it is more prosaic: "...Whatever you say, I will do for you."[2] The truth is there; love's commitment costs. Jonathon will pay any price and does what he says. Mary at the wedding in Cana expressed it thus: "...Whatever He says to you, do it."[3]

Love's spiritual commitment to Christ is a reciprocal thing. He commits Himself to us as we really, truly commit ourselves to Him. And without this mutuality there is no scriptural commitment. As in Christian marriage so it is in Christian commitment. An illustration of this mutuality is seen in John's Gospel. Jesus was in Jerusalem at Passover time. Crowds were following Him because of the miracle at the wedding and other signs, and we are told "...many believed in His name..."[4] But it was a professed belief, wrongly based on past miracles, possible material benefit (free bread etc.) and the prospect of more titillating signs to come. The same root word for believe was used by Jesus in His reply. Bluntly put: "But Jesus, on His part, was not entrusting Himself to them..."[5] The King James Version uses the word commit. "But Jesus did not commit himself unto them..."[6] because they hadn't committed themselves to Him.

Exactly. He loved us, committed Himself to us and gave Himself for us. Such love demands commitment love in return. John Chapter Two ends with: "...for He Himself knew what was in man."[7] Chapter Three begins: "Now there was a man of the Pharisees, named Nicodemus..."[8] This man, after conversation, was convinced, converted, confessed and at the Cross committed Himself publicly, thus identifying himself with the Lord.

JUNE 4 – LOVE'S CONFESSION

We have already seen some glorious strands in the love covenant between Jonathon and David, but the coloured cord of love's confession glows with a special radiance. One strand is bright with mutual praise, another shines with reciprocated support, while a third is resplendent in common defence.

Trouble arose soon after Jonathon took David into his own home. David's exploits and demeanour caused Israel to love him and sing his praises. While Jonathon rejoiced in this honour accorded his friend, his father, King Saul, was jealous. "Now Saul told Jonathan his son and all his servants to put David to death[1]... So Jonathan told David[2]... Then Jonathan spoke well of David to Saul his father..."[3] Love can never be silent. Love delights to talk to the loved one, to defend the friend before third parties from unjust criticism and, this above all, to praise the virtues and laud the character of the other. Love's confession is love's verbal witness and these two spoke for each other when it was dangerous and costly. That's when it counts, when it costs, and to continue doing it while life shall last.

Jonathon was consistent and persistent in love's confession. "Then Jonathan spoke well of David to Saul his father and said to him, 'Do not let the king sin against his servant David, since he has not sinned against you, and since his deeds have been very beneficial to you.'"[3] Jonathon's bravery and boldness never shone brighter on any battlefield than it did here in his own home in the courageous confrontation with his own father. And it gained David temporary respite from the hounding.

"Let my lips utter praise..."[4] He is not ashamed to confess or acknowledge me before His Father in heaven, nor should I be ashamed to confess Him before friend and foe here below. Equally, to deny Him will bring denial. Ashamed of Him? He will be ashamed of us. Confession or witness is an integral part of salvation. "...The Word is near you, in your mouth and in your heart, that is, the word of faith which we are preaching, that if you confess with your mouth Jesus as Lord, and believe in your heart that God raised Him from the dead, you will be saved; for with the heart a person believes, resulting in righteousness, and with the mouth he confesses, resulting in salvation."[5]

Paul was not ashamed of this Gospel; he was always eager to preach it, but at the end of his life he was almost completely deserted and alone. So many of his friends and colleagues had failed in love's confession.

"Jesus, and shall it ever be,
A mortal man, ashamed of Thee?...
Ashamed of Jesus! sooner far
Let night disown each radiant star!...
Ashamed of Jesus! that dear Friend
On Whom my hopes of Heav'n depend!...
Ashamed of Jesus! yes, I may
When I've no guilt to wash away...
And O may this my portion be,
My Savior not ashamed of me!"
Joseph Grigg (1720 – 1768)

JUNE 5 – LOVE'S CONFIRMATION AND CONTINUATION

Before their final parting through circumstances, and their permanent parting by Jonathon's premature death, these two friends had reaffirmed, in striking language, their love covenant, and ensured its extension into the next generation and beyond. Again Jonathon, perhaps with premonition, was the prime initiator of this renewal that was to be unlimited for ever. ""If I am still alive, will you not show me the lovingkindness of the Lord, that I may not die? You shall not cut off your lovingkindness from my house forever, not even when the Lord cuts off every one of the enemies of David from the face of the earth. So Jonathan made a covenant with the house of David, saying, 'May the Lord require it at the hands of David's enemies.' Jonathan made David vow again because of his love for him, because he loved him as he loved his own life.""[1]

As it must to all, and to all earth's loves, cut off time was coming, and, young as he was, Jonathon knew it. In the midst of life he knew he was in death. Hoping for length of days he put in the "if." That is why he wanted their love covenant confirmed with new extension clauses. How soon they would be called into use he could not foresee but love made him plan for the unknown, yet in some ways, predictable future. Love's foresight, faith which works by love, love for his own family all are traceable here but it was the "lovingkindness of the Lord" and David's "lovingkindness" he was counting and calling upon. And love's trust was not misplaced.

Jonathon's sudden death in battle caused panic in his household when the news was received. Fear of the victorious Philistines, who had killed Jonathon and two of his brothers and fatally wounded his father Saul, brought tragedy at second hand to Jonathon's little son. "Now Jonathan, Saul's son, had a son crippled in his feet. He was five years old when the report of Saul and Jonathan came from Jezreel, and his nurse took him up and fled. And it happened that in her hurry to flee, he fell and became lame. And his name was Mephibosheth."[2] Years later, after David had defeated the Philistines, he became king over the united nation. He was thirty-seven years old when this happened. A little later he made inquiries. "…Is there not yet anyone of the house of Saul to whom I may show the kindness of God?…"[3] He was told of the crippled youth living in barren Lodebar (place of no pasture). He was brought to the king who said: "…Do not fear, for I will surely show kindness to you for the sake of your father Jonathan, and will restore to you all the land of your grandfather Saul; and you shall eat at my table regularly."[4]

The vows made were paid. Love's confirmed and continuing covenant was kept for Jonathon's sake. Brotherly love brought the helpless cripple from exiled poverty to eat at the king's table. Kindness for another, the father, brought the son to the banquet hall of love. Friendship sought him out, restored his estate and brought him from rags to riches. The pre-mortem pact of loving friendship brought post-mortem blessing to the son. If it was possible for Jonathon to know, how pleased he would have been with the continuation of their love.

JUNE 6 – LOVE'S CRYING

Popular teaching through the film media stated:

"Love never needs to say I'm sorry."

This is not only sentimental twaddle, but it is wrong. Love needs to apologize frequently. There are several phrases that are hard to say:

"I don't know,"
"I was wrong,"
and, perhaps the hardest of all,
"I am sorry."

And harder still for some of us is this truth: Love cries, love weeps. Not the sentimental, two hand-kerchiefs, eye watering, film crying, but tears wrung from the depths of ones being. Like those shed by the sinful, loving woman who washed our Lord's feet with her tears. We who were brought up in the old and wrong tradition that it is unmanly to cry; keep a stiff upper lip; etc. still find it difficult to show our emotions. Loud emotional weeping is not right either. Susanna Wesley (1669 – 1742) taught her children that:

"If you have to cry, cry quietly."

Crying can be therapeutic, cleansing and curative.

David and Jonathon's loving friendship was destined to be very brief, but it was deep and intense. David's dirge for Jonathon and Saul, killed on a bloody battlefield, shows this. Jonathon, cut off in his prime, died because of his filial love to an unworthy father. Saul died dishonoured and deposed because of his own self love. David mourns them both. He has bared the depths of his feelings of friendship love for the son and forgiving love for the father in his lament for them. These memorial words contain the following: "…How have the mighty fallen[1]… Saul and Jonathan, beloved and pleasant in their life, and in their death they were not parted[2]… I am distressed for you, my brother Jonathan; you have been very pleasant to me. Your love to me was more wonderful than the love of women."[3]

Though it is not recorded that David wept publicly on the occasion of his friend's death, maybe he did so privately. David had wept, before this permanent parting, when circumstances forced their separation. "…And they kissed each other and wept together, but David wept the more."[4] Males engaged in mutual kissing and weeping! It was very private, very personal and very pure. There is nothing shameful or even sentimental here. It is the parting which is a little death; prefiguring the larger, longer one. It would seem that they never met again on earth after this. Love is crying because it is bereft and bereaved. Love's sorrow should be shared pre-mortem, as they did. Don't be ashamed of it. Too soon it may be too late.

This love, wonderful love, steady and true, seen through tears, is but a shadow of the higher, holier more wonderful love of our Lord. "Jesus wept."[5] The shortest verse in the Bible sums up the substance of what we have been observing about love crying. With His friends, Mary and Martha, at the tomb of Lazarus, He cried. So should we also.

JUNE 7 – LOVE'S CONSUMMATION

In retrospect, the love story of Jonathon and David was one of the most complete friendship loves that history records. Their covenant contained a high degree of the essential elements of commitment and consecration. Their love was clear, clean and consistent. It was confessed privately and publicly and the communication lines were clear of verbosity. Circumstances forced them to talk about the essentials during their brief times together. Their love was confirmed in life and continued after death by David's looking after Jonathon's crippled son. It was a courageous love of two brave, manly men who were not ashamed to let their emotions be seen. They wept at parting, though crying was not the norm or the gauge of their friendship. Their love was so unquenchable that it has withstood the test of time and has become a classic of its kind.

Though they didn't know it, their friendship was to be very short. Even had it continued the full seventy years of David's life span it would have, in the light of eternity, still been very brief. We don't have time down here to love. In a large Christian bookstore, in the heart of London, England, a man came in and asked for a book, supplies of which were expected later that day. The conversation between the male customer and the saleswoman went like this:

Male: "Do you have <u>Time to Love</u>?"
Saleswoman: "Not yet. Come back at closing time."

Unconscious humour from an ambiguous statement. But for Jonathon and David "Time to love" was running out and they were only about thirty years of age. Closing time was coming quickly. In all aspects of our love life let's always remember:

"Life at best is very brief" (Anon.)

That's why David could say, after Jonathon's unexpected death, that was a wonderful love. Once in a blue moon there is a friendship love like that. Wonderful in its intensity; wonderful in its sensitivity; wonderful in its entirety and wonderful in its brevity. David could look aback in the forty years left to him and continue to say with a sense of amazement, "...thy love to me was wonderful..."[1] Yet David was a man who could look forward as well as backward. At another crisis time in his life, and another death, this time of a baby son, he said: "...I will go to him, but he will not return to me."[2] This was not callousness but an encouraging statement of faith founded on fact. Death is conclusive but it is not the end. Death finishes but also consummates. Death ends, but completes. Death ended their great love, but also sealed it. It fixed it for time and in time, but expanded it beyond theirs and our comprehension. Eternity's consummations will be unexpectedly wonderful.

JUNE 8 – FRIENDSHIP LOVE

In 1841 Ralph Waldo Emerson (1803 – 1882) in his essay on "Friendship" wrote:

"Men are bound by every sort of tie, by blood, by pride, by fear, by hope...by circumstance and badge and title. But when a man becomes dear to me I have touched the goal of fortune...I find very little written directly to the heart of this matter."

It's taken over one hundred and fifty years but a book The Best of Friends by David Michaelis seeks to remedy this lack. He examines seven, lifelong, male friendships. One of them was between two men, George Love (1900 – 1991) and Donold Lourie (1899 – 1990). Their friendship began at Princeton University in the 1920's and there was nothing perverse about it. Both men led normal married lives. Wives and children and work occupied their rightful places. Love became head of the Chrysler Corporation and the other top man at Quaker Oats. Yet they maintained this other bond of a special loving friendship. Michaelis notes:

"Theirs was a friendship uncomplicated by demands, jealousy, competition...They understood one another with a kind of sweet simplicity..."

Isn't that refreshing! In a fairly long life I have experienced and observed friendships like this. At Bible College I found such a friend. Ron and I were inseparable. There were affinities that drew us together. It was not a case of proximity, but more the propinquity of kindred minds and spirits. We spent our vacations together in faith gospel tours on our bicycles, and in bush missions, and other Christian activities. I was very much surprised when, toward the end of college days, a teacher called me aside one day and said:

"Your friendship is dangerous; you are depending too much on each other; you know you'll have to be separated soon."

Wise words for we were soon divided by oceans and different Christian endeavours. We met again, only once, on one of my furloughs, and soon after Ron went to be with the Lord via a heart attack. But I cherish the memory of that loving friend and lovely friendship. And such friendship love is not limited to men. I have observed several friendships amongst missionary ladies which have been the genuine article, lasting decades and unto death.

"Philos," friend, is a word we will be using a lot, as the New Testament does. It is used fourteen times as a masculine noun by Luke and once as a feminine. But we will concentrate in John's Gospel. John the Baptist describes himself as the friend of the bridegroom; standing in attendance, hearing, seeing and rejoicing; almost an equivalent of our "best man." Our Lord's use of the word begins with that reference to His friend Lazarus and moves on to describe His disciples. "You are My friends if you do what I command you. No longer do I call you slaves, for the slave does not know what his master is doing; but I have called you friends, for all things that I have heard from My Father I have made known to you."[1] We sometimes refer to friendship love as one of the lower loves when compared with agapé. Yet here our Lord uses it to describe a new intimacy; an inner circle who are told His plans. It has in it the elements of comradeship and companionship. We will be returning to it later, but here in conclusion note the qualifier "If."

JUNE 9 – JEREMIAH'S LOVING FRIEND

Jeremiah, the weeping prophet, was honoured centuries later, when people likened our Lord to him. Christ's question: "…Who do people say that the Son of Man is?"[1] was answered thus: "…Some say John the Baptist; and others, Elijah; but still others, Jeremiah…"[2] Why Jeremiah? Certainly because our Lord was a Man of Sorrows and acquainted with grief as Jeremiah had been: "Is it nothing to you, all ye that pass by? behold, and see if there be any sorrow like unto my sorrow…"[3] Surely it was also because He wept over Jerusalem as the prophet had done: "For these things I weep; mine eye, mine eye runneth down with water…"[4] And definitely our Lord was valiant for the truth as Jeremiah had been: "…they are not valiant for the truth…"[5] Finally it was because the people knew He loved them despite their rejection of Him, just as they had rejected the earlier prophet. He remained their Friend also, as Jeremiah had been. "…I have loved you with an everlasting love; therefore I have drawn you with lovingkindness."[6] In the context of the times and circumstances and all the other indictments of their love, the lack and corruption of it, this truth about God's love shines all the brighter. "Now the word of the Lord came to me saying, 'Go and proclaim in the ears of Jerusalem, saying, 'Thus says the Lord, 'I remember concerning you the devotion of your youth, the love of your betrothals'"[7]…Can a virgin forget her ornaments, or a bride her attire? Yet My people have forgotten Me days without number. How well you prepare your way to seek love!…"[8] God's relationship to Israel, like our Lord's relationship to His church, is likened to the marital union. But here there is a special and beautiful emphasis. Israel's early days are referred to as a honeymoon. How sad that honeymoons have to end! How sad that they are often too short; the honeymoon is over!

And so it was Jeremiah's message to remind them of these things. Neither the message nor the messenger was received. Totally rejected, the lonely prophet on one occasion is put into a cistern. And that's when a fellow needs a friend! "…Now in the cistern there was no water but only mud, and Jeremiah sank into the mud. But Ebed-melech the Ethiopian, a eunuch, while he was in the king's palace, heard that they had put Jeremiah into the cistern…"[9] And information led to intercession. He petitioned the king for permission to organize a rescue party. The request was granted and Ebed, this foreigner, this unknown friend, with thirty others under his command, sets out to save Jeremiah from certain death. Behind this earthly friend was the Friend whose care surpasses the surprising tenderness of the unknown Ethiopian. Ebed successfully rescued Jeremiah from the mire in which he was slowly submerging; and that is friendship in action. How Jeremiah must have been encouraged, and eternally grateful. And God did not forget Ebed! In the day of disaster about to fall on the city God said to Ebed: "…'But I will deliver you on that day,' declares the Lord, 'and you will not be given into the hand of the men whom you dread. For I will certainly rescue you, and you will not fall by the sword; but you will have your own life as booty, because you have trusted in Me…'"[10]

JUNE 10 – PHILEMON – "LOVING FRIEND"

We have seen brotherly, friendship love in action in that Old Testament love story of Jonathon and David. Now we want to consider this kind of love in a New Testament action story. It is vibrant with life, high in drama and wonderfully illustrative of "philia." In fact the name Philemon is a derivative of "philos" or friend and "philia" or friendship. Philemon means "loving friend" and a more fitting name couldn't have been given to him. Paul in this short private letter which, fortunately for us, was made public, calls him beloved, brother, partner and uses love several times to make his point; for philia involves the idea of loving in return as well as being loved.

Paul, after his friendly and factual introduction and salutation, comes to the very personal problem and practical matter involving them both. And it revolves around a third party named Onesimus. This is a different kind of triangular problem; it involves three men. Onesimus had been at one time a bond slave in the house of Philemon. And here another problem arises. The Christian master and slave relationship involves not only these three men, but the whole church and the local church that met in Philemon's house. Paul does not speak out against the general institution of slavery in that era of universal bondage to Rome. However he does come to grips with this individual case and resolves it with the principle of brotherly love. This is our relationship in Christ where "...there is neither slave nor free man...for you are all one in Christ Jesus."[1] "...there is no distinction between...slave and freeman..."[2]

Onesimus was a man who had gained his freedom by running away, and had found another higher liberty through the providence of God. Certainly he was converted through Paul while he was in prison, for Paul writes "I appeal to you for my child Onesimus, whom I have begotten in my imprisonment."[3] He could have used Apostolic authority but didn't. "Therefore, though I have enough confidence in Christ to order you to do what is proper, yet for love's sake I rather appeal to you, since I am such a person as Paul, the aged, and now also a prisoner of Christ Jesus."[4] I do not coerce or compel you to do this but of your own free will.

Paul had already sent Onesimus back to Philemon, and this was the covering love letter. Onesimus "who formerly was useless to you, but now is useful both to you and to me. I have sent him back to you in person, that is, sending my very heart[5]... For perhaps he was for this reason separated from you for a while, that you would have him back forever, no longer as a slave, but more than a slave, a beloved brother..."[6] Paul adds one more appeal and offer. The appeal of imputation; accept him as myself and put any debts or damages to my account.

Does Philemon live up to his name? He certainly does. The Colossian church completes the story. "...Onesimus, our faithful and beloved brother, who is one of your number..."[7]

JUNE 11 – A MEMORIAM FOR FRIENDSHIP LOVE

It's great to have a friend but it's better to be a friend. I treasure a book <u>Poems of Tennyson</u> not only for the poetry, but because of the memories associated with it. I never knew my paternal grandparents, both of whom died before I was born. I do know however that it was the faith and prayers of my grandmother, Ellen Davey, that helped bring her son Roger, my father, to Christ. And through her and him I came to know the Lord. Like Timothy and his grandmother Lois, I owe much to this loving woman whom I never knew. She loved the Lord and she gave and received friendship love also. On the flyleaf of this book, the only memento of my godly grandmother, this is written:

"Presented to Ellen Davey on her 74th birthday from her devoted friend and admirer, Margretta F. Brutlon 3rd June 1907"

Granny was born in 1833 and died in 1916 just a few months before I was born. She lived a long life and I've heard my father speak with appreciation and admiration of her devoted life. I wish I had known her and her friend. Their friendship was evidently an enriching experience. They had found the Friend Who sticks closer than a brother. The One Who calls us His friends. The One Who lay down His life for His friends. Having found Him they also found each other. "I've found a Friend, O such a friend!..." James G Small (1817 – 1888) had a double meaning for them. They also, I'm sure, found that friendship had to be cultivated. "A man that hath friends must shew himself friendly…"[1] I also think they would have been frank and forthright in their friendship. "Faithful are the wounds of a friend…"[2] These two ladies had a pure and elevating friendship.

I also treasure this book for its poetry for there I found Alfred Lord Tennyson's (1809 – 1892) "In Memoriam". This is a memorial to his dear dead friend Arthur H. Hallam (1811 – 1833). Its full title and dedication says:

"In Memoriam A. H. H. Obit. 1833."

Tennyson's introductory poem to the longer one starts:

"Strong Son of God, immortal love,
Whom we, that have not seen thy face,
By faith, and faith alone, embrace,
Believing where we cannot prove;

Thine are these orbs of light and shade;
Thou madest Life in man and brute;
Thou madest Death; and lo, thy foot
Is on the skull which thou hast made."

This manly, male friendship was prematurely ended by Hallam's drowning. The poet recognized that though he lost his friend, Christ had His foot "on the skull" and that through and beyond death, love was sanctified and consummated.

"Forgive my grief for one removed,
Thy creature, whom I found so fair.
I trust he lives in thee, and there
I find him worthier to be loved."

Again we see the truth that all the lesser loves, noble, right and proper as they are in time and place, must suffer death. For this is the gateway to eternal life, which is love, excelling and unending. "Mors Janua Vitae" or "Death is the gateway to life."

JUNE 12 – PLATONIC FRIENDSHIP

Originally "platonic" referred to the Greek philosopher Plato or his teachings. The adjective describes love of a character and quality that is purely spiritual or free from sensual desire, as applied to love or friendship between persons of the opposite sex. It has sometimes been known to evolve from passionate love and there is always the possibility that platonic love may evolve into the passionate.

Some eras seem to make more of platonic loves or friendships than do others. Today the passionate love seems to be in vogue. How many practise the platonic? How many even know what it means? There is a place for pure platonic love that provides mental and spiritual nourishment to the participants that they do not find with their spouses, happily married though they may be. Openly, and frequently with encouragement from the marital partner, conversations and correspondence are carried on for years, sometimes for a whole lifetime. In the 18th century platonic friendships flourished, even though that era was noted for libertinism as well.

Mary Granville Delaney (1700 – 1783) was born into the upper strata of society. The unfortunate girl was married at seventeen years of age to a man of sixty, old enough to be her grandfather. It was forced upon her by relatives seeking to restore their fortunes with a money marriage. Mercifully it was of short duration as he died. Many years later she married a widowed clergyman, Dr. Delaney, in what turned out to be a very happy second marriage. Mrs. Delaney had platonic friendships with George Frideric Handel (1685 – 1759), the great composer, and Dr. Jonathon Swift (1667 – 1745), dean of St. Patrick's Cathedral, Dublin, Ireland and author of Gulliver's Travels. In that same early Georgian era, the famous literary critic, Dr. Samuel Johnson (1709 – 1784) enjoyed such a friendship with Mrs. Hester Thrale (1741 – 1821), wife of a wealthy brewer and Member of Parliament, with the approval of the brew master himself!

But one of the classic platonic friendships of the twentieth century was between Lucy Maud Montgomery (1874 – 1942), Canadian author of Anne of Green Gables, and Ephraim Weber (1870 – 1956), then an upcoming teacher and writer in Alberta. The year was 1902. Their platonic friendship continued for forty years until her death in 1942. They were pen-friends and continued so when both married. She became a Presbyterian minister's wife and busy parish worker and author, but still wrote long letters to Weber and also to George Boyd MacMillan of Scotland. Correspondence with him commenced in 1903 and again continued until her death.

We have seen how wonderful friendships can be between two men, a David and Jonathon relationship, and between two women like my grandmother Ellen Davey and her lifelong friend Margretta Brutlon. These are friendships outside the marriage union which are enhanced by friendship love. And platonic friendship between members of the opposite sex, can, when properly conducted, also enrich the individuals concerned and if married, their marriages. While the couple have a special relationship in marriage they should not live only to and for themselves but cultivate friendships of all kinds.

JUNE 13 – BROTHERLY LOVE – Part One

Why should we bother with foreign words like "philia" which demand some thought and study? Perhaps that is like the man who said he didn't know he had been talking "prose" all his life! When we use words like "Philadelphia;" "philosophy;" "philander;" "philately" we use love words.

Pennsylvania incorporates the name of the man who treated the Native Americans courteously and in a Christian way. His statue placed on the top of City Hall towers over the city of Philadelphia, which he founded and which he hoped would be the "city of brotherly love." So we are already using Greek and didn't know it! Painless isn't it; like watching the "Phillies." Learning is a lifelong process and study often a laborious but rewarding task.

Dr. Samuel Johnson (1709 – 1784) produced one of the first great English dictionaries. He laboured on it for seven years, and was always reading, tracing and learning new words, defining them and giving examples of their use. He described those years in memorable words:

"I have sailed a long and painful voyage round the world of the English language…"

His basic work, and that of other lexicographers since, has helped us. Think, every time you use a dictionary, of the labour, not always of love, that went into it. I never use my Young's Concordance without being grateful for the laborious days and years that went into producing this vital tool for Christians. That was a labour of love with words.

So, as we now start a closer look at some of the great love words of the secular and sacred world we will have to think and do a little work. The end results, I hope, will not only be gratifying but also be glorifying to God. The words friend, friendship, brother, brotherly are common enough, but they have a Greek root. W. E. Vine in his Expository Dictionary of New Testament Words tells us that:

"adelphos denotes a brother, or near kinsman; in the plural, a community based on identity of origin or life."

Philadelphos is a favourite word of Peter and comes from "phileo" or to love and "adelphos." "… love the brotherhood…"[1] "To sum up, all of you be harmonious, sympathetic, brotherly, kindhearted, and humble in spirit."[2] "…a sincere love of the brethren…"[3] It is also a favourite word of James who uses "adelpohi" fifteen times. He uses it to encourage, exhort, deter from error and to show true brotherly love in action. Paul uses "brethren" countless times and "love of the brethren" at least twice. But we should especially note his use of a warning word "pseudadelphos" or false or lying brethren." Pseudo has come into the English language to mean counterfeit, spurious or false. Let us beware of these pseudos today. Let us then, on a practical and positive note, love all the brethren who are the whole body and community of His church.

JUNE 14 – BROTHERLY LOVE – Part Two

Leigh Hunt's (1784 – 1859) poem "Abou Ben Adhem" was a compulsory in school and a favourite of a past generation. How times have changed! Who ever heard of Abou? In my youthful days I knew more poetry (I had to learn it) than Scripture, though we were given that every morning. And that was in a government Elementary school in England. But let's return to the poem. Though some of Abou's theology may be suspect, there is Biblical truth there, as we shall see. It does illustrate brotherly love of our fellow man.

"Abou Ben Adhem (may his tribe increase!)
Awoke one night from a deep dream of peace,
And saw, within the moonlight in his room,
Making it rich, and like a lily in bloom,
An Angel writing in a book of gold:

Exceeding peace had made Ben Adhem bold,
And to the Presence in the room he said,
'What writest thou?' The Vision raised its head,
And with a look made of all sweet accord
Answered, 'The names of those who love the Lord.'

'And is mine one?' said Abou. 'Nay, not so,'
Replied the Angel. Abou spoke more low,
But cheerily still; and said, 'I pray thee, then,
Write me as one who loves his fellow men.'

The Angel wrote, and vanished. The next night
It came again with a great wakening light,
And showed the names whom God had blessed
And, lo! Ben Adhem's name led all the rest!"

The apostle John made a tie-in also with love to God and love to man. "If someone says, "I love God," and hates his brother, he is a liar; for the one who does not love his brother whom he has seen, cannot love God whom he has not seen. And this commandment we have from Him, that the one who loves God should love his brother also.""[1] Abou had latched onto a key truth. Love to God the unseen, is known in heaven by the way I love my seen brother on earth. And the opposite is equally true. My love to my seen brother, seen by others on earth, witnesses to my love for my unseen God in heaven.

This kind of loving is also described by our Lord to the surprise of those involved. "Lord, when did we see You hungry, and feed You, or thirsty, and give You something to drink? And when did we see You a stranger, and invite You in, or naked, and clothe You? When did we see You sick, or in prison, and come to You?' The King will answer and say to them, 'Truly I say to you, to the extent that you did it to one of these brothers of Mine, even the least of them, you did it to Me.'"[2] Ah, say some, that limits it to my Christian brother. No, not exclusively. "Love your neighbour" must surely mean non-believing neighbours also. Scripture also says: "So then, while we have opportunity, let us do good to all people, and especially to those who are of the household of the faith."[3] There are our priorities. And thus God is glorified. "Let your light shine before men in such a way that they may see your good works, and glorify your Father who is in heaven."[4]

In Part One on "brotherly love" it was all "philia." Here in Part two it is all "agapé." John's first letter uses some form of agapé at least twenty-one times. It is John's favourite word for love. At times the two seem synonymous but agapé provides the compulsive power and the controls for true philia love.

JUNE 15 – NO FRIEND OR BROTHER LOVED LIKE THIS

"One is kind above all others,
O how He loves!
His is love beyond a brother's;
O how He loves!
Earthly friends may fall and leave thee,
One day kind, the next day grieve thee;
But this Friend will ne'er deceive thee;
O how He loves!

'Tis eternal life to know Him?
O how He loves!
Think, O think how much we owe Him;
O how He loves!
With His precious blood He bought us,
In wilderness He sought us,
To His fold He safely brought us,
O how He loves!

We have found a friend in Jesus,
O how He loves!
'Ts His great delight to bless us,
O how He loves!
How our hearts delight to hear Him
Bid us dwell in safety near Him;
Why should we distrust or fear Him?
O how He loves!

Through His Name we are forgiven,
O how He loves!
Backward shall thy foes be driven;
O how He loves!
Best of blessings He'll provide us,
Nought but good shall e'er betide us,
Safe to glory He will guide us,
O how He loves!"

Marianne Nunn (1778 – 1847), who magnifies the love of Christ, also points out the superiority of His love as a Friend, and His love as a Brother, over the best earthly love of friend or brother. And we have had a long look at these earthly loves. We have meditated on the superb friendship between David and Jonathon and have noted that as an example of friendship and brotherly love it is without parallel. While either, I'm sure, was willing to lay down his life for the other as a brother or friend, it would still be comparative love like the New Testament statements: "Greater love has no one than this, that one lay down his life for his friends."[1] "But God demonstrates His own love toward us, in that while we were yet sinners, Christ died for us."[2]

On June 6th, 1984, a day of remembrance for the fallen, and a day of rejoicing for the victory, was held on the beaches of Normandy, France. Kings, queens, prime ministers, presidents and heads of state were present; flags were raised, and anthems sung, as country after country remembered the longest day, June 6th, 1944, when the liberation of France and Europe began. But for me the most poignant scenes were on the beaches, where old men walked in solitude remembering; and in the cemeteries, where thousands of their comrades lay buried. They had all died in the bloom of youth. There the aging veterans wept as they looked at the graves of friends and brothers. How often was John 15:13 quoted? Brotherly love, friendship love and patriotic love were all present. But mostly, and it was so stated, the former enemies were not welcome. Yet over twenty thousand of them, also friends and brothers also lovers of their country lay buried in a huge cemetery on the cliffs overlooking the North Atlantic. They too fought and died there in Normandy. For both, our Saviour laid down His unique, sinless and spotless life. He died for sinners; He died for the ungodly; He died for His enemies. He died for all of us on both sides and He knows all of those in the Normandy graveyards; French, German, English, American, Dutch, Polish, Norwegians, Canadians, Australians, New Zealanders and some of my friends who loved Him as Friend, Brother, Saviour, Lord and God.

JUNE 16 – LOVERS OF GOD

W. E. Vine in his <u>Expository Dictionary of New Testament Words</u> tells us that "philotheos" means a lover of God. In the context of inordinate loves, such as lovers of self, lovers of money, lovers of pleasure etc. we read what they ought to be; lovers of God. This is the love that is demanded and commanded. "You shall have no other gods before Me"[1] and "…Thou shalt love the Lord thy God with all thy heart, and with all thy soul, and with all thy strength, and with all thy mind…"[2] And His commands are His enablings. He first loved us. His was the initiative in this greatest of love affairs. We but give Him back the love He is pouring into us. This love match seems one-sided, and relatively speaking, of course it is. Infinite, eternal love is on one hand and finite temporal love is on the other. To be a lover of God is to love Him with the love with which He loved us.

Then again we find as lovers of God an immense freedom. St. Augustine (354 - 430) has said:

"Love God and do as you like."

Meaning of course the love of God, having freed us, as it did him, from the inordinate loves, has now put us in the control of the ordinate love. And within that great field, we can do all that His love dictates, and accept all that His love sends. Writing these pages has opened up this truth to me. Love is everywhere, love is behind everything, there's no limit to love's activities. Where the Spirit of love is there is liberty, but not license.

Then again, lovers of God love to fellowship with him and one another. "Then those who feared the Lord spoke to one another, and the Lord gave attention and heard it, and a book of remembrance was written before Him for those who fear the Lord and who esteem His name."[3] The fellowship of love is reverent. Lovers of the Lord have an awe, a holy fear, as they worship Him. There is a beautiful hymn we used to sing. Its author, H. H. Booth (1862 – 1926) uses a permissive word of approach.

"Let me love Thee, Thou are claiming
Every feeling of my soul;
Let me love, in power prevailing,
Render Thee my life, my all;
For life's burdens they are easy,
And life's sorrows lose their sting
If they're carried, Lord, to please Thee,
If they're done Thy smile to win.

Let me love Thee, come revealing
All Thy love has done for me;
Help my doubt, so unbelieving
By the sight of Calvary;
Let me see Thy love despising
All the shame my sins have brought,
By Thy torment realizing
What a price my burden bought.

Let me love Thee, love is mighty,
Swaying realms of deed and thought,
By which I shall walk uprightly
And shall serve Thee as I ought.
Love will soften every sorrow,
Love will lighten every care,
Love unquestioning will follow,
Love will triumph, love will bear.

Let me love Thee, Savior,
Take my heart forever,
Nothing but Thy favour,
Lord, My soul can satisfy!"

Because our wills have been renewed, and because they are subject to His will, and because He has commanded and enabled our love we can sing: "Let me love Thee, Savior, Take my heart forever." Love is controlled by the will. I will be a lover of the Lord.

JUNE 17 – A LOVER OF GOOD AND GOOD PEOPLE – Part One

W. E. Vine in his <u>Expository Dictionary of New Testament Words</u> tells us that "philoxenos" is translated variously as "lover of strangers," "lover of foreigners," and "lover of hospitality." It is not a case of choosing between them but rather a "both" and "all included" meaning. It is used in the context of dealing with the appointment of elders and their home, family life and character. It is worth quoting in full as these New Testament standards have never been abrogated. They are high indeed and if applied would force some resignations from church boards. "...appoint elders in every city as I directed you, namely, if any man is above reproach, the husband of one wife, having children who believe, not accused of dissipation or rebellion. For the overseer must be above reproach as God's steward, not self-willed, not quick-tempered, not addicted to wine, not pugnacious, not fond of sordid gain, but hospitable, loving what is good, sensible, just, devout, self-controlled, holding fast the faithful word which is in accordance with the teaching, so that he will be able both to exhort in sound doctrine and to refute those who contradict."[1]

To be a lover of good the overseer has to be good himself. That is why that descriptive list is included in full. He has to be a good loving family man with disciplined believing children. He has to be a good loving steward and trustee of the grace, the goodness and the Gospel of God. His character must not evidence any of the five listed prohibitions. He has to be a lover of good; good men; good things; a lover of strangers with its concomitant love of hospitality. And, finally, he has to be a lover of the Word of God and is able to use it in exhortation and refutation. He loves the teachings of the Word which show him how to live and act according to the will of God.

And that teaching shows him the will of God as it relates to loving strangers, foreigners and the responsibility of showing them hospitality. Centuries of hatred have been caused by fear of other races or faces of a different colour or cast. Xenophobic fear is still seen in some Christian's actions in rejecting, not only Jesus, but some Gentiles as well. Strangers coming to Israel in the Old Testament days were to be treated kindly; not ostracised or oppressed; they were to be positively and practically loved. "He...shows His love for the alien by giving him food and clothing. So show your love for the alien, for you were aliens in the land of Egypt."[2] This was the command under the Old Covenant; how much more today under the New Covenant. "...practicing hospitality."[3] "Do not neglect to show hospitality to strangers, for by this some have entertained angels without knowing it."[4] Philoxenia is rewarded.

JUNE 18 – A LOVER OF GOOD AND GOOD PEOPLE – Part Two

In Part One we looked at "philoxenos" and its translations and implications. Here we discuss "phil-agathes" which W. E. Vine in his <u>Expository Dictionary of New Testament Words</u> defines as "a lover of good." The King James Version uses it as part of the charge to bishops and overseers as "a lover of good men." "For a bishop must be…a lover of good men…"[1]

Not many women are named Agatha today. I have only known one, and the one that springs to mind is Agatha Christie (1890 – 1976). It is a name which has for this generation lost its popularity. Agatha means good woman, and the one I know was, and is, a very good woman; kindly affectioned; helpful to others; loving her family and friends and above all loving the Lord.

Is this a digression? No. It's an illustration of "philagathes." It is composed of two words: "philos" or lover and "agathos" or good. W. E. Vine in his <u>Expository Dictionary of New Testament Words</u> once again tells us that the adjective "agathos" describes things or people, which are in "character and constitution" good.

"God is essentially, absolutely and consummately good."

No human can be so described but the adjective is rightly applied to some men and women. Barnabas was a good man for he was full of the Holy Spirit and faith. This lovely four letter monosyllable is used again concerning older women who are to be teachers of "good" to the young women. This will encourage them "…to be sober, to love their husbands, to love their children, to be discreet, chaste, keepers at home, good, obedient to their own husbands, that the word of God be not blasphemed."[2] This kind of goodness is ridiculed today in some circles, but these are the New Testament standards. The book of Titus is Paul's epistle of grace that produces all kinds of good works. Titus is to be an example of good works. Christians are to be ready for every kind of good deed. "In all things shewing thyself a pattern of good works…"[3]

We can only be lovers of good and lovers of good men, as the New Testament teaches and the letter to Titus emphasizes, by being born again. "Not by works of righteousness which we have done, but according to his mercy he saved us, by the washing of regeneration, and renewing of the Holy Ghost; which he shed on us abundantly through Jesus Christ our Saviour; that being justified by his grace, we should be made heirs according to the hope of eternal life. This is a faithful saying, and these things I will that thou affirm constantly, that they which have believed in God might be careful to maintain good works. These things are good and profitable unto men."[4] We will be lovers of all kinds of good works and lovers of all people, especially good men and women, when we are lovers of the Lord and filled with His Spirit.

JUNE 19 – PHILANTHROPY: THE LOVE OF MANKIND

There is a monument erected to perpetuate the memory of that 19th century statesman and philanthropist, Lord Shaftesbury (1801 – 1885). Today that statue of Eros is thought of in terms of sordid sex, not philanthropy. Yet, when it was erected in Piccadilly Circus, London, England, Mr. William Gladstone (1809 – 1898) was asked to draft an inscription. He wrote:

"During a public life of half a century he devoted the influence of his station, the strong sympathies of his heart and great power of his mind to honouring God by serving his fellow men, an example to his order, a blessing to his people and a name to be by them ever gratefully remembered."

That is Christian philosophy and that is the aspect of Eros the monument builders had in mind. In a great political speech delivered in the House of Lords on 1885 the Duke of Argyll (1823 – 1900) said:

"The social reforms of the past century have not been due to a political party. They have been due to the influence, the character, the perseverance of one man. I refer of course to Lord Shaftesbury."

Who was this man? What motivated him? What was his personal philosophy? It all began when, as a boy, his biography tells us, a Christian servant "would take him on her knee and tell him Bible stories, especially the sweet story of the manger of Bethlehem and the Cross of Calvary." Maria Millis, with her love for Christ and affection for that gentle, serious child, taught him to pray and introduced that seven year old to the Saviour. She was a true lover of children, a providential influence in the life of a boy destined to devote his life, his energy, his talents and his fortune to doing good for the needy. Her reward will be great. She shines in glory through the splendour of her personal love for Christ and a little lad. All Shaftesbury did later flowed from his personal love for the Lord he had found through her. His personal knowledge of the Saviour, and his desire to see others saved, fuelled his practical love for the poor; his philanthropy. His Christian philosophy was based on one chapter in the New Testament. In his journal he wrote on October 11, 1857:

"Read this afternoon Matthew 25. What a revelation of the future judgment of the human race! Those on the left hand are condemned, not for murder, robbery, debauchery, not for breaches of the Decalogue, or for open blasphemy, not for sins they have committed, but for duties they have omitted…"

Shaftesbury was then fifty-eight and had already spent a lifetime doing his duty, doing good. And because of his personal love for Christ and mankind he continued to be the greatest Christian reformer and philanthropist of his century.

Today "do-gooders" are ridiculed. The term is one of opprobrium. Yet philanthropy has a great history. It is the love of mankind, shown in practical efforts to promote the well-being of the needy. It is a New Testament word practiced by pagans! "The natives showed us extraordinary kindness; for because of the rain that had set in and because of the cold, they kindled a fire and received us all."[1] And practiced by God! "But when the kindness of God our Savior and His love for mankind appeared, He saved us…"[2]

JUNE 20 – PHILOSOPHY: THE LOVE OF WISDOM

There is one Sophia known through her movies and that is Sophia Loren (1934 -), the Italian film actress. The name has become known and possibly used by other parents because of her fame. I wonder if its meaning has become equally publicized? I don't think so. "Sophia" means wisdom and is used in the New Testament with reference to God, to human and earthly wisdom in its highest forms, and in its most debased manifestations. When our familiar word "philos" or lover is prefixed to it we get philosopher and philosophy. A philosopher is one who loves wisdom while philosophy describes the love and pursuit of it.

Paul had an encounter with both philosophers and philosophy while in Athens. At that time there were two major philosophies contending for the minds and hearts of the people. "So he was reasoning in the synagogue with the Jews and the God-fearing Gentiles, and in the market place every day with those who happened to be present. And also some of the Epicurean and Stoic philosophers were conversing with him…"[1] The Epicurean philosophers were disciples of Epicurus (341BC – 270BC) who abandoned as hopeless the search by reason for pure truth. He sought instead true pleasure (mostly sensual) through experience and luxurious living. This philosophy still has many adherents today. The Stoic philosophers were followers of Zeno (336BC - ?) who founded a sect about 294BC. It was based on human self-sufficiency and stern self-repression. It regarded virtue as the highest good and taught that one should be free from passion, unmoved by joy or grief, and indifferent to pleasure or pain. Zeno taught in a porch (Stoa) in Athens, hence the name Stoics. These two philosophies divided the apostolic world.

Paul met this wisdom by the wisdom from above exemplified in creation and redemption, and personified in Christ's death and resurrection. Paul called these philosophers to repentance along with the idolaters and other worshippers of the unknown God; whom he had made known. This former Doctor and Philosopher of Law has now become a philosopher and teacher of the heavenly wisdom of God in Christ. It was foolishness to the Greeks and a stumbling block to the Jews. Yet at the end of his message, though some sneered, others wanted to hear more and "…some men joined him and believed, among whom also were Dionysius the Areopagite and a woman named Damaris and others with them."[2] The wisdom of God triumphed in these lives. They became lovers of the heavenly wisdom.

Paul had something else to say about worldly philosophy. He warned against it as deceptive and destructive. "See to it that no one takes you captive through philosophy and empty deception, according to the tradition of men, according to the elementary principles of the world, rather than according to Christ."[3]

JUNE 21 – PHILOLOGOS: A LOVER OF WORDS

Philologos was a New Testament character and co-worker of Paul's to whom he sends greetings in his great list of commendations. What a delightful name! "Philos" or lover and "logos" or word gives us "a lover of words." Not merely a "Mr. Talkative" like Bunyan's (1628 – 1688) character. Isn't it encouraging to know that the inspired Word records this "lover of words." This is a life-long love affair for me but I recognize that it's not for everyone. I'm glad my father started me on this road. Here's how it happened:

As a young boy I was to sit for a scholarship. I passed the first part, the written tests, and was due for the second, the oral. One evening Dad "suggested" that I study the dictionary to improve my vocabulary. Frankly, I would have preferred spending the evening and successive ones, out on the village green playing cricket with my friends. Those long delightful Southern English summer evenings were made for sport not study. I could hear the solid thwack of bat on ball and hear the joyous boyish cries and I was condemned to a dictionary! Still, when Dad "suggested" I knew it meant "insisted" so I reluctantly went to work. And I became interested and then intrigued. I never got beyond the letter "A" as I remember but one of those "A" words fascinated me. It opened up my imagination to the great oceans and their mysterious inhabitants. It had to do with whales. In due course the oral exam took place before a frightening group of elderly professors and trustees. Imagine my excitement when during "the meaning of words" session "the" word was asked and I could answer it. I think that helped me win the scholarship, and though I grumbled at the time, I've always been grateful to Dad for getting me started on becoming a "lover of words." And what was "the" word? "Ambergris"; maybe you'll have to look it up too!

Lovers of words are not to be confused with those who only love long words. They are known technically as "sesquipedalian logophiles." The old, short, Saxon rooted words are often the most powerful. But occasionally a polysyllabic word is needed. The New Testament uses some long words that are exact in meaning and essential for our understanding of the whole plan of redemption. Predestination; election; propitiation; incarnation; regeneration; justification; sanctification; glorification etc. are theological words that require study and explanation. Yet, the glorious good news of our Saviour's purpose in coming was summed up by Him in sixteen monosyllables. "For the Son of Man has come to seek and to save that which was lost."[1] These are short, two, three, four and five letter words which a child can understand, and as a child I believed and was saved. As a student of the Word of God for over fifty years, I love all the words of Scripture and am still learning new ones. "Be diligent to present yourself approved to God as a workman who does not need to be ashamed, accurately handling the word of truth."[2]

JUNE 22 – PHILETUS – WORTHY OF LOVE

Smith's <u>Dictionary of Bible Names</u> gives "beloved" as the meaning of Philetus. What a name to live up to! Sometimes parents give their children names which they hope will prove true. And sometimes, in Scripture, they were commanded to name their children John, Jesus etc. because their names described their prophetic missions. The parents of Philetus were no doubt expressing the hope that he would be beloved or worthy of love. By nature we are all unworthy people yet how much love is poured upon us by parents, partners, friends and those who love us despite all our faults.

> "Indeed this very love which is my boast,
> And which, when rising up from breast to brow,
> Doth crown me with a ruby large enow
> To draw men's eyes and prove the inner cost,
> This love even, all my worth, to the uttermost,
> I should not love withal, unless that thou
> Hadst set me an example, shown me how,
> When first thine earnest eyes with mine were crossed,
> And love called love. And thus, I cannot speak
> Of love even, as a good thing of my own:
> Thy soul hath snatched up mine all faint and weak,
> And placed it by thee on a golden throne,
> And that I love (O soul, we must be meek!)
> Is by thee only, whom I love alone."
> Sonnet 12. Elizabeth Barrett Browning (1806 – 1861)

The writer here, while expressing her feelings of unworthiness, yet worth, because her lover deemed her worthy, knew it all happened and was worthwhile because of his worth. And how much more true this is in the case of Him Who alone is worthy, loving us unworthy ones. "We love, because He first loved us."[1]

And what about Philetus? He seems to be only mentioned once and unfortunately doesn't live up to his advance billing! Paul, in his charge to young Timothy, urges him to "Be diligent to present yourself approved to God as a workman who does not need to be ashamed, accurately handling the word of truth. But avoid worldly and empty chatter, for it will lead to further ungodliness, and their talk will spread like gangrene. Among them are Hymenaeus and Philetus, men who have gone astray from the truth saying that the resurrection has already taken place, and they upset the faith of some."[2]

And there we have it, straight, as Paul usually told it in love. In the context he longs for Timothy to be worthy of the trust placed in him as a trustee of the Word of truth. Philetus had proved unworthy having become, not an encourager of peoples' faith, but a disturber and upsetter of the saints. He had strayed from the truth and worse, was leading others into error. Poor Philetus, unworthy, yet I'm sure, still prayed for in the hope of restoration. Paul, who wrote the great love chapter, and dealt on that basis for the restoration of the erring Corinthians, was not likely to remove Philetus from his prayer list. We can hope that Philetus did finally live up to his name.

JUNE 23 – PATRIOTIC LOVE

Whenever we take friends to see the beautiful national parks of Banff and Jasper in the Canadian Rocky Mountains, we nearly always go to view one majestic peak that has special significance. Not for its height nor hanging glaciers and ice falls alone, but for its name, and the story behind the name which is told on a monument at its base. Mt. Edith Cavell commemorates the British nurse (1865 – 1915) who was shot in World War One, allegedly as a spy. She was actually a patriot helping wounded soldiers. Her patriotism, or love of her country and countrymen, is one of the noblest illustrations of this kind of love, which is growing rarer today. Or else it is confused with nationalism which is increasing. It has been said that:

"Patriotism is a lively sense of collective responsibility. Nationalism is a silly cock crowing on its own dunghill…" Richard Aldington (1892 – 1962)

At school we had to learn some of Sir Walter Scott's (1771 – 1832) "Lay of the Last Minstrel" particularly the patriotic bits such as:

"Breathes there a man, with soul so dead,
Who never to himself hath said,
This is my own, my native land!
Whose heart hath ne'er within him burn'd,
As home his footsteps he hath turn'd,
From wandering on a foreign strand!"

I must confess that I had memorized this without understanding its significance until I left England, as a boy, for Australia. I have come to love this sunburnt country, as well as the West Indian islands where we lived for thirty-five years, and Canada where we live now. But I've never forgotten my birth land and whenever I returned by ship the white cliffs of Dover never ceased to move me.

Doctor Samuel Johnson (1709 – 1784) was a great debunker of false, high-flown statements or claims. He is remembered for his scathing word on patriotism.

"Patriotism is the last refuge of a scoundrel."

But to keep things in balance he also said:

"That man is little to be envied, whose patriotism would not gain force upon the plain of Marathon, or whose piety would not grow warmer among the ruins of Iona."

What has Scripture to say about this love? For thousands of years Jewish patriots have composed hymns to the love of Jerusalem and country. The Babylonian exile produced laments like this: "By the rivers of Babylon, There we sat down and wept, When we remembered Zion"[1] or psalms of praise like this: "…when the Lord brought back the captive ones of Zion, We were like those who dream. Then our mouth was filled with laughter And our tongue with joyful shouting."[2] Here, as D. D. Field (1882 – 1950) wrote:

"Patriotism has its roots deep in the instincts and the affections. Love of country is the expansion of dutiful love."

JUNE 23 - CONTINUED

But action is called for as well as emotion.

"He loves his country best who strives to make it best." Robert G. Ingersoll (1833 – 1899)

Long ago Thomas Jefferson (1743 – 1826) warned:

"I tremble for my country when I reflect that God is just."

How up to date! What is the Christian position? What can and should we do about these things? We show patriotic love by obeying its just laws and authorities and by taking stands like Peter took when forbidden to preach Christ and His Gospel. We love the whole wide world too while also remembering that "…our citizenship is in heaven…"[3]

JUNE 24 – SINCERE AND FERVENT LOVE

"Since you have in obedience to the truth purified your souls for a sincere love of the brethren, fervently love one another from the heart, for you have been born again..."[1] As is so often the case in Scripture much truth is compressed into little space. This is a digest of important facts and for our understanding it is necessary to look at key phrases and words. "You have" is used twice; once at the beginning and again at the ending. We are reminded of personal events in the past which are fundamental to what is possible in the present. The first "you have" deals with obedience. This word in the New Testament is frequently allied with believing. In some cases it is used as a synonym. It is heart obedience and commitment. It is hearing and heeding the glad tidings of good things. These believers obeyed the truth as it is in Christ.

And because they had truly done so the second "you have" took place. "You have been born again." The connection is Scriptural; inherent in the very nature of true believing and real regeneration. Receiving Christ; believing in His name; being born of God and thus being given the right to be God's children are all connected, synonymous and essential. We have spent a little time on these "you haves" because without the experience they represent there would be no present expression of that sincere, fervent love which is our theme.

Obedience to the truth purifies the soul. Peter put the same thing again when he said of the convert Cornelius and other Gentile believers: "And God, which knoweth the hearts, bare them witness, giving them the Holy Ghost, even as he did unto us; And put no difference between us and them, purifying their hearts by faith."[2] The pure in heart see God who is love, and show sincere love to the brethren. There is a guilelessness about the newborn soul; insincerity is absent because all things are new. Truth is embodied in the children of Him who is truth personified. His true love flows into and out of born again people of God in all their present, personal and practical encounters with each other. This sincere and unfeigned love is important and relevant to us all.

"Fervently love one another from the heart." Past experience with God in regeneration makes possible the present expression of sincere love plus prospective anticipation that fervent heart love will continue to be demonstrated in the future. "Fervent" was a favourite word of Peter. He used it again with the same noun: "Above all, keep fervent in your love for one another, because love covers a multitude of sins."[3] Fervour is usually associated with fire, heat, passion, ardour or zeal. It is a "hot" word commonly coupled with all kinds of love. Here, while not losing its original meaning, it has the additional thought of love on the stretch, extended and reaching out to others. Fervid love embraces all. Only the new birth and present continuous filling of the Spirit makes this possible.

JUNE 25 – LOVE BUILDS UP

One of the worst habits is to consciously, or unconsciously, "put down" people. It is a reflection of one's own condition of pride or superiority and is definitely damaging to the self-esteem of the other party. Both parties are being destroyed. This is not to say that frank confrontations are out. These are face to face and quite different from the former, which is destructive criticism. The latter kind of truth spoken in love is healthy and helpful.

"...Knowledge puffeth up, but charity edifieth"[1] says the King James Version, while another translation states: "...Knowledge makes arrogant, but love edifies."[2] One tendency in some of those who have a little or a lot of learning is to become full of themselves. Real scholars show humility knowing as Isaac Newton (1643 – 1727) is reputed to have said:

"He was like someone on the sea-shore picking up pebbles while the whole unexplored ocean of knowledge lay ahead of him."

There are certainly dangers, overt and covert, in the field of academe; while the pursuit and practice of agapé in any field of life is relatively danger free. Love edifies and builds up both the giver and receiver.

The context of our theme verse goes on to say: "If anyone supposes that he knows anything, he has not yet known as he ought to know; but if anyone loves God, he is known by Him."[3] The love of God must always be the basis upon which we build and build up. His enabling, energising and motivating love moves us into doing the right things in the right way. This is especially true in the context of "weaker" brothers and sisters. Weaker is used in the sense of having less knowledge of certain matters, such as things sacrificed to idols. This was a problem to the early church. It didn't bother "strong" believers who knew idols were nothing and could eat with impunity the food offered to them. They knew and so were liberated, but were they loving?

St. Augustine (354 - 430) is quoted as saying:

"Love God and do as you like."

This statement starts with the qualifier which we have just considered. "If anyone loves God." Yes we do. So do we have the liberty to do as we like? Again, yes we do, so long as it is what the love of God dictates and which includes the love of my neighbour who here is a weaker brother!

If I turn my liberty into license or use my liberty in a thoughtless and unloving way I am sinning against Christ because I am ruining my brother. As a strong proponent of liberty I'm not building up my brother, I'm pulling him down, causing him to stumble thereby destroying him. The love of God controlling us as it controlled Paul, can cause us to say with him: "...if food causes my brother to stumble, I will never eat meat again..."[4] A loving example becomes the best type of building material.

JUNE 26 – LOVE WITHOUT HYPOCRISY

"Let love be without hypocrisy. Abhor what is evil; cling to what is good. Be devoted to one another in brotherly love; give preference to one another in honor."[1] Professing love without practicing it is hypocritical. This is a problem in relationships. We say we are devoted to each other in brotherly love. This generalization is exposed for the hypocrisy it is when we come down to close relationships in our Christian organizations, in our missions, and in the local church.

Love is demonstrably not hypocritical when it gives preference to the other, when it honours another above itself, when it seeks to silently do good to the brother or sister, and when it is devoted to another in brotherly or true friendship love. These are all evidences of love without hypocrisy.

Paul faced the problem of hypocritical love amongst the Christian leaders of the early church. Peter, who by heavenly revelation concerning Cornelius, that Gentile centurion of the Italian cohort, finally agreed with God that salvation was possible for the Gentiles. He seemed to have learned the lesson, but later there were lingering doubts. "But when Cephas came to Antioch, I opposed him to his face, because he stood condemned. For prior to the coming of certain men from James, he used to eat with the Gentiles; but when they came, he began to withdraw and hold himself aloof, fearing the party of the circumcision. The rest of the Jews joined him in hypocrisy, with the result that even Barnabas was carried away by their hypocrisy."[2]

There are insights here we don't want to miss. The first church council at Jerusalem met to consider and settle the question of circumcision as necessary for salvation for the Gentiles. Peter and James played prominent parts there as did Paul and Barnabas. The conference debated the issue and dealt with it clearly; assuring the Gentiles that circumcision was not a requisite for salvation. I have found by experience that unanimous conference decisions are not always unanimous and often have repercussions when implemented. This was the case here where fear of man, fearing to face issues, and fearing to offend all played a part in hypocrisy. Hypocrisy is contagious. Peter's hypocrisy infected other Jews and even Barnabas caught the disease. Hypocrisy is partial and prejudiced in favour of one side.

Real love confronts this hypocrisy face to face and deals with it as Paul did with Peter. This love overcomes the fear of man. Even men in high positions. True love operates to cut out the cancer before it spreads. Love deals with partiality, whether it be of race, place, preference or nepotism. It does not dissimilate, is neither devious nor hypocritical. On the contrary it is free, full, frank and forthright; concerned and caring; it clings to what is just and abhors what is evil. Agapé controls brotherly love, governing and purifying it from all hypocrisy.

JUNE 27 – LOVE AND CONTENTMENT

If I know and trust the love of God for me, then the essential foundation of contentment is laid. If I continue, in all my circumstances, to believe in that love and return it, then continuing contentment should be my experience and expectation. If also, on the human level, there is someone who loves me and believes in me, and I respond and return this love, then there is an earthly ground for contentment in addition to the eternal. Eternal contentment is indispensable for there are some who know none of the earthly loves. But if they know the God of love and the love of God they can know satisfaction in the spiritual sense. After all, earthly contentment is relative, a matter of degree. We need to remember that contentment, like serenity, which is a higher stage, is possible because:

"He is not a disappointment;
Christ has saved my soul from sin;
All the guilt and all the anguish which oppressed my heart within.
He has banished, by His presence, all that stole my inner peace;
And He gives me full assurance that His love will never cease."
Mary W. Booth

We sing and quote these Scriptural truths, but are they heartfelt? Am I displaying divine love and contentment or showing discontentment? Where we do not find the "doctrine conforming to godliness"[1] we can be certain of finding "…morbid interest in controversial questions and disputes about words, out of which arise envy, strife, abusive language, evil suspicions, and constant friction between men of depraved mind and deprived of the truth, who suppose that godliness is a means of gain."[2] One of today's common falsehoods is that of:

"Be saved and you will be financially successful and satisfied!"

"But godliness actually is a means of great gain when accompanied by contentment. For we have brought nothing into the world, so we cannot take anything out of it either. If we have food and covering, with these we shall be content."[3] Love's contentment accompanies godliness and cures acquisitiveness.

To know real love and contentment we must curb our love for material things. We live in a world of materialistic capitalism. As we consider the above Scripture we find "but those who want to get rich fall into temptation and a snare and many foolish and harmful desires which plunge men into ruin and destruction. For the love of money is a root of all sorts of evil, and some by longing for it have wandered away from the faith and pierced themselves with many griefs. But flee from these things, you man of God, and pursue righteousness, godliness, faith, love, perseverance and gentleness."[4] "Make sure that your character is free from the love of money, being content with what you have…"[5]

Love and contentment in these areas is a learning process. First we have to unlearn the false philosophies of the world and then we learn the contentment that comes from the acceptance of our state or condition in which we find ourselves.

"I take, O cross, thy shadow for my abiding place;
I ask no other sunshine than the sunshine of His face;
Content to let the world go by to know no gain or loss,
My sinful self my only shame, my glory all the cross."
Elizabeth C. Clephane (1830 – 1869)

JUNE 28 – LOVE AND SERENITY

At first glance this juxtaposition seems incongruous. Love is disturbing in its activity and fervour. Where is the serenity in all this physical emotion, mental feverishness and spiritual stirring? Can love produce serenity? Can they be harmonized? We must clarify our thinking by distinguishing between things that differ. We have previously stated that there is a difference between agapé and eros; between philia and storgé. What we are really asking in these questions about love and serenity is this: Can there be serenity in any, or all of these four loves; in the love of God; in the love between a man and woman; in the love between friends and brothers and in the affectionate love found in families? The New Testament answer is yes! But in this answer we need to distinguish between the kind of serenity found in the natural loves and that found in the love of God. There is serenity of satisfaction without the Supreme control of the higher love, but without it there can't be perfect peace amongst the participants in the lower loves. There are too many warring elements and natures involved.

Serenity is really peace, tranquility, calmness and quietness. It is a placid, unruffled and undisturbed state that is only possible because of our Lord's parting gift of peace and His promise that in Him we would have peace. It is one of love's last bequests, fulfilled by the coming of the Spirit. And as Scripture reminds us, dying to the flesh and living in the Spirit is the way to serenity. "For the mind set on the flesh is death, but the mind set on the Spirit is life and peace."[1] Self on the throne destroys serenity in any of the loves. That's why it's obviously absent even in some Christian unions. This is especially true in the early years. It also takes time to harmonize in body, mind and spirit; to find the balance essential for tranquility. As married couples age and the fires of youth are somewhat quenched there is often a marked increase of serenity in the union. In our experience, the stages of life do have a part in determining the degree and depth of serenity in our life. That serenity at all times is desirable no one will gainsay; that it is not always visible or practiced no one will argue.

As in the other spheres of life, only when the love of God completely controls us is serenity possible. Do bachelors and spinsters have more likelihood of serenity in their earthly lives? This would seem debateable, but Paul points out that married people have much more to distract them than do singles in the service of Christ. "But I say to the unmarried and to widows that it is good for them if they remain even as I. But if they do not have self-control, let them marry; for it is better to marry than to burn with passion[2].... But if you marry, you have not sinned...Yet such will have trouble in this life[3]...But I want you to be free from concern. One who is unmarried is concerned about the things of the Lord, how he may please the Lord; but one who is married is concerned about the things of the world, how he may please his wife, and his interests are divided."[4] Will love for the Lord like this result in serenity? Is the price too high?

JUNE 29 – THE LOVE OF GOD AND OUR TEMPERAMENTS

Dr. Ole Hallesby (1879 – 1961), one of Norway's leading Christian teachers and evangelical writers, was a seminary professor in Oslo, Norway until his death. He is the author of <u>Temperament and the Christian Faith</u> and in it helps us see the special possibilities and dangers in our own personalities. He uses the four classical temperament types of sanguine, melancholic, choleric and phlegmatic to show how our dispositions shape our lives. In describing the strengths and weaknesses of each type, Hallesby challenges us to change and grow into the people God intends us to be. Some denigrate, while others completely deny this four-fold division. While new insights have made their appearance and which help us to know ourselves by their psychological differentiations, the old classics still seem to have a lot of validity. I'm personally glad to testify here that my reading Hallesby's book years ago helped me to understand my temperamental type or types. It also helped me to understand, in retrospect, my parents and grandparents and above all to see that the love of God controls temperament.

The Rev. Tim LaHaye (1926 -) has further developed Dr. Hallesby's thesis and added additional insights in his book <u>Transformed Temperaments</u> which has helped thousands of people. His psychological portraits, or better, <u>Temperamental Biographies</u> on Peter the Sanguine, Paul the Choleric, Moses the Melancholic and Abraham the Phlegmatic are interesting and helpful studies. LaHaye brings fresh views of the weaknesses and strengths of each of these great leaders.

But as far as I'm concerned his best book on this theme was his first, <u>Spirit Controlled Temperament</u>. He shows there that the temperament transforming power of God's Holy Spirit is just as available and effective today as it has ever been. The Holy Spirit has been given to make the love of God effective in us. This love, mediated by the Spirit, really controls and transforms our temperaments.

While one of the four is usually predominant, we all have secondary temperaments, with strong dashes of the other two. I have self-diagnosed myself as a choleric-melancholic and that is not an easy combination. But it does have its strengths and joys as well as its weaknesses and sorrows.

It is interesting to note that the classic description of Elijah by James lists him as "…a man subject to like passions as we are…"[1] "Elijah was a man with a nature like ours…"[2] The Living Bible paraphrase puts it like this: "Elijah was completely human as we are…" He had his highs and lows, but heavenly love transformed his temperament.

JUNE 30 – LOVE AND THE APOSTLE OF LOVE

The apostle of love is not Paul, much as he deserves the title, for his labours of love, his writings of love and his sufferings of love all qualify him for the accolade. Next to his Lord many would give him the position of prominence. But there is another apostle, whose physical proximity to the Lord Jesus during his three year apprenticeship in love, also wrote of love and experienced its sufferings. In fact he is spoken of several times as the disciple whom Jesus loved. This is John the beloved. Our Lord loved all his own and He them to the end. Did He have favourites? We dare not accuse Him of such a thing as God is not a respecter of persons; but He did have an inner circle of three: Peter and the brothers James and John, the sons of Zebedee. Of these three John, by his own choice like Martha's sister, chose the better part. He loved proximity and to be close to the One he loved and adored. He leaned on Jesus' breast at the last supper. He remained close at the Cross; close enough to receive a personal commission of love. And twice more, in proximity to the risen Lord, the words "the disciple whom Jesus loved"[1],[2] are used. That they are used by John himself to describe himself, does not validate their truth. There was modesty and humility in this euphemism for his own name. Yet there is also rightful delight in the description. We too can follow afar off, or we can choose nearness to Jesus, as John did.

Temperamentally, what kind of man was this beloved disciple, this apostle of love, whose Gospel and letters overflow with agapé? Surprisingly, the major temperamental strain in his life seems to mark him as a choleric. He, in his apprenticeship days, had a hot under the "choler" streak in him. He was desirous that the Lord do an Elijah act on those who appeared to be rejecting Him. The Lord had an apt, descriptive name for him and his brother: "Sons of Thunder." It is also not surprising that Paul is a choleric. Cholerics are practical and pragmatic. They are strong willed, often leaders, usually optimistic, who can blow their tops with volcanic outbursts, but cease erupting just as suddenly. They do not hold grudges. They can be cutting and caustic and the tongues of some crack like a bull whip. Not nice to be around! Yet as Tim LaHaye reminds us:

"they make good supervisors, generals, builders and crusaders."

Let us think a little of one contemporary choleric. Charles T. Studd (1860 – 1931), (a hero of mine in my youth, and I still admire him), was a choleric crusader in labours of love, writings of love and sufferings of love. Note how the choleric traits come through in all three areas, just as with Paul and John.

What made the change in John? He didn't change! His temperament was controlled and redirected by the Holy Spirit. He was still John Blunt as he expounded real Holy Spirit, Christlike, New Testament love. "If someone says, 'I love God,' and hates his brother, he is a liar…"[3] he reiterates in his wonderful first letter on love. When the Lord described in Revelation how He would deal frankly with the churches and also warn the world of His impending wrath, he chose the disciple whom he loved to carry the message.

JULY 1 - "CUPID"

Are people stupid who believe in Cupid? Yes and no! Who was Cupid? He is the god of love known by his Latin name. The Greeks called him Eros. We have all seen him depicted as a round, rosy, curly locked cherub, blindfolded, with his bow, winging his arrows into human hearts. As to the question, let's answer it with another one. Was Plato (427BC – 347BC) stupid? Hear him on the matter:

"Eros makes his home in men's hearts, but not in every heart, for where there is hardness he departs. His greatest glory is that he cannot do wrong nor allow it; force never comes near him. For all men serve him of their own free will. And he whom love touches not walks in darkness."

Are people stupid who believe in Cupid? Are people stupid who believe in love? We have not really answered yet. Here is a different view from a later poet:

"Evil his heart, but honey-sweet his tongue. No truth in him, the rogue. He is cruel in his play. Small are his hands, yet his arrows fly far as death. Tiny his shaft, but it carries heaven-high. Touch not his treacherous gifts, they are dipped in fire."

Are people stupid who see through false love?

So much for Eros, Aphrodite's son or companion. This beautiful, serious youth who gives good gifts to men! Two views. Two answers. A balance. They were not stupid in the eyes of their contemporaries but they believed in the god of love and the goddess Venus or Aphrodite, the goddess of love and beauty.

Some reader will say:

"Why waste time on gods who don't exist? Anyone who does so is stupid."

Paul and Barnabas had a confrontation with the devotees of pagan mythology and had to deal with them. They met people where they were and faced the fact that wrong beliefs are widely held. Hear the Scripture. It sounds like an extract on pagan pantheism. "…The gods have become like men and have come down to us. And they began calling Barnabas, Zeus, and Paul, Hermes, because he was the chief speaker. The priest of Zeus, whose temple was just outside the city, brought oxen and garlands to the gates, and wanted to offer sacrifice with the crowds."[1] Read the context for the cause and conclusion. This is living involvement with fiction based on fact and dealt with by preaching and applying the Gospel.

There is but one God. Yet, He, in the first commandment said: "You shall have no other gods before Me."[2] In reality there are none. Yet Baal became a god to Israel as did Zeus to the Greeks. False gods; substitute gods; impostor gods; no gods. Yet real to the devotees.

In Barbados I had regular visits from a salesman from a large English publishing house. I sought to witness to this young man, an Oxford graduate. When I mentioned God, he said: "Ah, yes, Zeus!" Where did I go from there? Where Paul and Barnabas went! All through the Greek and Roman world, Christ was presented in the presence of mythology. Diana, daughter of Zeus, caused Paul trouble in Ephesus. Cupid governed lives then as today. God, the true God, is the one and only God of love. In Him love is personified.

JULY 2 – FALSE LOVES

We noted false loves in the study on Cupid and will say more when we consider Eros. But there are other erroneous areas; false loves posing as true loves and marriage unions that have a surface reality but subterranean falsity. Sometimes this is the product of a "familiarity which breeds contempt" but oftimes it is caused by false ideas about love and wrong motives concerning marriage. George MacDonald (1824 – 1905) points this out in his poem about "A Mammon Marriage."

"The croak of a raven hoar!
A dog's howl, kennel-tied!
Loud shuts the carriage-door:
The two are away on their ghastly ride
To Death's salt shore!

Side by side, jarring no more,
Day and night side by side,
Each by a doorless door,
Motionless sit the bridegroom and bride
On the Dead–Sea-shore."

Materialism dooms many a marriage as well as paganism. The love of mammon is their true and false love. And there are others, much more common. The wrong thinking about love that produces stalemates and checkmates. Selfishness in love is the root cause. Silences follow, loud with self pity.

"Talking in bed ought to be easiest
Lying together there goes back so far
An emblem of two people being honest.
It becomes still more difficult to find
Words at once true and kind
Or not untrue and not unkind."
"Talking In Bed" Philip Larkin (1922 – 1985)

"So they were married- to be the more together-
And found they were never again so much together,
Divided by the morning tea,
By the evening paper,
By children and tradesmen's bills.
Waking at times in the night she found assurance
Due to his regular breathing but wondered whether
It was really worth it and where
The river had flowed away
And where were the white flowers."
"Les Sylphides" Louise MacNeice (1907 – 1963)

The poets touch the disappointment, and disillusion, that derives from false notions and emotions about Eros.

There is a right Eros, as we shall see, and a wrong one which leads to false and pagan eroticism. The world of Noah's day, the cities of Sodom and Gomorrah; and the aberrations that destroyed former civilizations are examples enough. These are the false loves of depravity, the product of diseased minds doomed for destruction today as certainly as they were in the past. Paganism, materialism; eroticism with all their falsehoods and false hopes are manifestly productive of false loves. But they can also mar and destroy what began as true family loves. These three destroyed Lot's family. He was saved at the last minute from the flames that engulfed Sodom. He lost his wife who looked back to where her heart and love were. His two daughters got out of Sodom but Sodom didn't get out of them. Their incest produced the Ammonites and Moabites.

"Farewell false love, the oracle of lies, A mortal foe and enemy to rest... A poisoned serpent covered all with flowers, Mother of sighs, and murderer of repose... A school of guile, a net of deep deceit, A gilded hook that holds a poisoned bait... A siren song, a fever of the mind, A maze wherein affection finds no end... A path that leads to peril and mishap, A true retreat of sorrow and despair... False love, desire, and beauty frail, adieu. Dead is the root whence all these fancies grew." Sir Walter Raleigh (1552 – 1618)

JULY 3 – "EROS"

Pantheism reigned supreme in the world to which Christ and the Gospel came. Pantheism is derived from "pan" or all and "theos" or god. Leaving aside its philosophical meanings, it is the worship of "all the gods." Pantheon or a temple dedicated to all the gods was the place of this worship. The Parthenon, the temple of Athene located on the Acropolis in Athens, Greece was completed about 438BC. It was already old when Paul, preaching practically under its shadow, confronted pantheism graciously, yet boldly by presenting the one God who is Creator, Saviour, Lord and Judge. These three Greek words provide the context for the contemporary Gentile world of Paul's day. And there was a fourth word Eros, which had a lot to do with its morality.

Eros, the god of love, was the most important god after the first twelve great Olympians as they were called. Eros, or Cupid in Latin, concerns us today as he concerned the world of the apostles and the first Christians. These were Jews and the first church in Jerusalem was wholly Jewish. Then came the outreach of the Gospel to the Gentiles who found a common meeting place with the Jews in Christ. The church in the Greek city of Corinth was founded by Aquila, Priscilla and Paul. This church, well known for its gifts of the Spirit, is equally well known for its carnality. Deep divisions and contentions arose from its Greek background. Greek admiration of earthly wisdom, human eloquence and erotic carnality found its way into the church. Even incest was permitted. Christians have had to face Eros, not only in the first century but ever since and increasingly more so now.

Eros today is usually seen as a synonym for "making love." Originally it included very much more; it meant other aspects of love as well. Perhaps the fullest explanation of what eros contained is found in Anders Nygren's (1890 – 1978) classic Agapé and Eros. Also C. S. Lewis (1898 – 1963), in his The Four Loves, points out the wider meanings and then deals with sex by terming it "Venus in Eros." Plato (427BC – 347BC) stresses the point that there are two loves, the popular and the heavenly. It is the heavenly that is pure eros. Plato had a point!

Heavenly eros is a good term for what God created and ordained in all human loves. He purposed pleasure and procreation. Holy heavenly love planned and provided holy heavenly eros. Though the word eros is not found in the New Testament it is evidenced and illustrated. John White – (1924 – 2002) in his recommended book Eros Defiled says:

"Something happened to love, Eros, physical love when mankind fell. The beauty was marred. The joy was tinged with sadness. Eros was defiled."

But Eros need not be defiled or destructive. It can be pure and life producing bringing fulfillment to the union. It is the earthly benediction of heavenly eros.

JULY 4 – WARNINGS ABOUT LOVE

C. S. Lewis (1898 – 1963) has been one of my mentors in love. In his book <u>The Four Loves</u> he deals with the ambivalence of love. Ambivalence is the co-existence of contradictory feelings about a particular person, object or action. We have all had such feelings even though we couldn't put them into words. In the case of love and its actions Lewis points out the seeming contradiction that "love begins to be a demon when he begins to be a god." He is speaking of the natural loves.

"Every human love, at its height, has a tendency to claim for itself a divine authority. Its voice tends to sound as if it were the will of God Himself. It tells us not to count the cost, it demands of us a total commitment, it attempts to over-ride all other claims and insinuates that any action which is sincerely done 'for love's sake' is thereby lawful and even meritorious. That erotic love and love of one's country may thus attempt to 'become gods' is generally recognized. But family affection may do the same. So, in a different way, may friendship...Now it must be noticed that the natural loves make this blasphemous claim not when they are in their worst, but when they are in their best, natural condition; when they are what our grandfathers called 'pure' or 'noble.' This is especially obvious in the erotic sphere. A faithful and genuinely self-sacrificing passion will speak to us with what seems the voice of God. Merely animal or frivolous lust will not..."

These warnings are now more than ever necessary in these days of both the idolatry and the debunking of human loves and affections. <u>Situation Ethics: The New Morality</u> by Joseph Fletcher (1905 – 1992) says that:

"Nothing is intrinsically good, but the highest good, the summum bonum, the end of all ends, love...love only is always good."

Buried under this verbiage is the more simplistic, "If it feels good, do it!" Free love is all the rage, but participants in that, even in companionate or open ended marriage, find out sooner or later that it is neither truly free, nor really love. Douglas N. Morgan in <u>Love: Plato, the Bible and Freud</u> as quoted by Dr. Leon Morris (1914 -)

"protests against 'maudlin love' which he sees as 'ignorant, misdirected and undisciplined love.' He also says forthrightly, 'When sentimentality replaces sentiment, muddle-headedness replaces reason and we wallow. Much or even most of what has been popularly written about love is nonsense.'"

Ambivalent loves; amoral loves; immoral loves; idolatrous loves; inordinate loves; maudlin loves; muddle-headed loves can all become demonic loves. No wonder John Donne (1573 – 1631), from experience and Scripture warns us to beware: "That our affections kill us not, nor die." In the preface to this book I wrote: "There will be odd juxtapositions: the loves will be frequently falling over each other; seeming to sometimes trip each other up or deliberately contradict each other." There are, in these words, veiled warnings. Those whose eyes are opened by holy, heavenly love will not be led astray. There are dangers in the poets as well as the authors and writers of prose. Lewis notes this when he says:

"Idolatry both of erotic love and of the domestic affections was the great error of 19th century literature. Browning, Kingsley and Patmore sometimes talk as if they thought that falling in love was the same thing as sanctification..."

JULY 5 – LOVE AND THE NEW MORALITY

Sir Arnold Lunn (1888 – 1974) speaks of a sermon preached in Oxford on the subject "Why not, if we're in love?" on which a Mr. John Davies commented:

"Love is supposed to be the most Christ-like of all the human virtues. Because he was attacking a desire to express this feeling the Rector's speech on Sunday was neither a very humble nor a very compassionate one."

Sir Arnold goes on:

"Nothing as silly as this was published in any undergraduate paper…before the First World War. Even those who described themselves as agnostics would not have risked ridicule by attacking a Christian clergyman for preaching chastity to the young. In the Oxford of my youth the hedonists suffered from no missionary urge to impose on others their own way of life. The frankly immoral were far less censorious of the moral than those prigs of the new morality who are forever holding forth on the prurience of the pure and the inhibitions of the chaste." Arnold Lunn and Garth Lean in The New Morality. Quoted by Dr. Leon Morris (1914 -)

The new morality is only the old morality gone aggressively public via all the media. In the process of coming out of the closet it is intolerably intolerant of those who march to the Christian drummer, Christ. It is also, in accusing Christian moralists of self-righteousness, insufferably self-righteous, while denying and castigating Christ's righteousness and those who practice and preach it. The new morality practices unrighteousness, defends its position vigorously, and denigrates those who publicly disagree. These are they who dare to maintain that there are divine standards of love and morality and that there are built in laws which will eventually destroy those who break them. They are also bound by the command of Christ and the law of love to neighbours, to warn the wicked of the end results of their wicked ways. Every born again Christian is called to be a witness to Christ's saving power, and to proclaim the good news of the Gospel to the ungodly. For the godly were once without God and without hope and without help. Many of the new godly were once practitioners of the new morality which is thousands of years old. Scripture has this to say about the new morality: "Or do you not know that the unrighteous will not inherit the kingdom of God? Do not be deceived; neither fornicators, nor idolaters, nor adulterers, nor effeminate, nor homosexuals, nor thieves, nor the covetous, nor drunkards, nor revilers, nor swindlers, will inherit the kingdom of God. Such were some of you; but you were washed, but you were sanctified, but you were justified in the name of the Lord Jesus Christ and in the Spirit of our God."[1]

Holy, heavenly love hates the sin but loves the sinner enough to confront him, to call him to repentance and faith in Christ and thus free him from the bondages of that catalogue of evil. Praise God, some of those corrupted by the old morality of Corinth were saved and became proponents of the only really true new morality, by becoming new creations in Christ. Christians, during the centuries since Corinth, who have been saved, who know it, show it, and say it, are not parading a holier than thou attitude. They are demonstrating by life and lip, holy heavenly love in all of earth's relationships.

JULY 6 – LOVE AND THE OLD-NEW IMMORALITY – Part One

Eric Blair's (1903 – 1950), (pen name George Orwell), <u>1984</u> did not envisage the kind of abomination printed Canada wide in daily newspapers on Saturday, March 31, 1984. I quote at length from the "Calgary Herald." "Homosexual Clergy Backed" reads the headline.

"Rev. William Phipps, executive secretary of the Alberta Conference of the United Church of Canada, agrees with a report which says the church should allow homosexuals to become ministers. The report, released this week by the church's division of ministry, personnel and education, says there is 'no biblical, theological, moral or health arguments to support the exclusion of gays or lesbians' from the ministry. Phipps said the report, to be submitted to the church's general council this summer, may generate some negative reaction but it is 'a clear and positive statement people can respond to.' He said 'it is a mistake to 'single out any group of people' and prevent them from entering the ministry'...But Rev. Christopher Lilly of Fairview United Church in Red Deer, said any decision to ordain homosexuals could cause 'an explosion' in the church. 'The Scriptures clearly and consistently say that those who practise homosexual behaviour will not enter the Kingdom of God,' he said. Lilly, a member of the United Church Renewal Fellowship, a conservative group within the church, said if homosexuals are ordained the church will be rejecting its fundamental doctrine of belief in the Bible as a guide for faith and morals."

There, thank God, is one voice raised in protest.

The agnosticism, apostasy and amorality evident in the above report is not unexpected from the aggressive gay and lesbian liberation movement, However, that a professedly Christian denomination should stand with such is an abomination. A later comment by a Winnipeg, Manitoba minister of the same church states:

"We feel probably we aren't ready for it, but probably the disciples weren't ready for the resurrection either."

Here blasphemy is added to apostasy.

In any wide ranging consideration of the theme "Love" we, like the Bible itself, have to face the false ideas on the subject, expose the aberrations, present holy, heavenly love in its fullness and forgiveness and its bearing upon all the natural loves. It may seem incongruous to place so much emphasis here on the false and wrong, but the "old-new" immorality was confronted and challenged by the early Christian church. As converts from corruption, they proclaimed Christ as their Liberator from Satan, and their Emancipator from sin and the world.

The April 12th 1984 edition of the "Edmonton Journal," in response to the United Church's position, has an article entitled: "A New Beginning for our Times." This article should perhaps be retitled "The New Beginning of the End Times" for the Bible states that there will be many who will teach falsely during this time. It appears to me that the task force of the United Church of Canada has presented a false teaching in its report "Sexual Orientation and Eligibility for the Order of Ministry." Hatred toward those who are homosexuals is wrong, for we are to hate the sin and love the sinner.

JULY 7 – LOVE AND THE OLD-NEW IMMORALITY – Part Two

"…Christ himself showed His love for the sinner yet nowhere does He condone the sins which they commit. The United Church of Canada has proposed that in order to love the sinner we must also love the sins which they commit. They condone homosexuality. To say that homosexual 'Christians' have a gift and calling from God to use their homosexuality on leadership is outright heresy. Timothy states the qualifications of a church leader. Homosexuals are not mentioned. In fact, the opposite is suggested (a good standing husband with but one wife). Nowhere, to my knowledge, does it say that a homosexual will advance the Kingdom of God or be a leader in the church. I would like to conclude by saying that 'all have sinned and fallen short of the glory of God,' yet 'while we were still sinners, Christ died for us,' and 'we have now received reconciliation.' For this reason Christians should be reaching out in love to the person who commits the sin of homosexuality, so that he too might be saved from his sins, including homosexuality."

Here is one evangelical, who knows true love from false, and does something positive. Larry Hayashi, of Edmonton, Alberta, who wrote the above, has availed himself of the publicity of the letters column of a public newspaper to present truly and lovingly the New Testament Gospel. He has a wider ministry than many a minister who says the same behind a pulpit on Sunday morning. Thank God for such as Larry and that we live in a country with a free press, and for a letters editor who is willing to publish the New Testament evangelical point of view.

The love of God works, woos, weeps, warns and wars as shown in the earthly life of our Lord and through the convicting work of the Holy Spirit. God uses His disciples in this working, wooing, weeping, warning, and warring ministry of love. There is no contradiction in terms, as later studies will show there is constancy, consistency and persistence in love's use of these five W's. Here we need to issue in love a Scriptural warning on the "old-new" immorality.

"Therefore God gave them over in the lusts of their hearts to impurity, so that their bodies would be dishonored among them. For they exchanged the truth of God for a lie, and worshiped and served the creature rather than the Creator, who is blessed forever. Amen. For this reason God gave them over to degrading passions; for their women exchanged the natural function for that which is unnatural, and in the same way also the men abandoned the natural function of the woman and burned in their desire toward one another, men with men committing indecent acts and receiving in their own persons the due penalty of their error"[1]

The "gay" world has been shocked since the disease A.I.D.S. has struck and killed many. There may be no hope for some physically, but in the love and power and grace of God there is eternal salvation for any kind of sinner who repents and receives Him.

JULY 8 – INORDINATE LOVES

We have been discussing the ordinate loves; the regular, ordered and proper loves; the natural loves and the supernatural love. (We see their coordination with each other). But there are inordinate affections and loves which must be noted in this wide ranging study of love. Inordinate means irregular, disorderly, improper, unnatural or unbalanced. It is not limited to immoral love though this is one area where Scripture speaks out strongly. The word inordinate is used only twice in the King James Version; once in each of the testaments.

The Old Testament use occurs in a parable of two sisters Aholah and Aholibah, depicting Samaria and Jerusalem. It is a sordid story of inordinate love, harlotry etc. picturing the spiritual adultery of idolatry. "And Aholah played the harlot when she was mine; and she doted on her lovers, on the Assyrians her neighbours[1]... And when her sister Aholibah saw this, she was more corrupt in her inordinate love..."[2] Idolatry is an inordinate love and Israel was guilty of it again and again. It is not limited to the Old Testament nor the Israel of those days. Idolatry can take many forms and is indicted in the New Testament. Sacrifices to idols were still made in New Testament days and Gentile converts were warned to abstain from such.

Today there is another form of idolatry which is also an inordinate love. It was widespread in New Testament times and is epidemic today. And that is covetousness or greed. It is in a list of inordinate loves, and is called idolatry. "Mortify therefore your members which are upon the earth; fornication, uncleanness, inordinate affection, evil concupiscence, and covetousness, which is idolatry."[3] Covetousness is as much a sin as immorality. The love of things is born of acquisitive desire, which is greed. God knows we have need of things in order to live; it is the inordinate desire for them; the amassing of the unnecessary; the abuse, not the right use of things which is condemned.

"To call covetousness idolatry is not too strong if we realize that, when we strongly desire to own a thing, it actually owns a part of us." A. W. Tozer (1897 – 1963)

From that inordinate love stems the love of money. This love is the root of all evil and is so prevalent that it will be considered separately. The inordinate love of pleasure also demands fuller examination. The inordinate love of self is the source of so many of these other irregular loves. It too will be treated separately. The inordinate love of position and power is so deluding and destructive that Lord Acton (1834 – 1902) said of it:

"Power corrupts, and absolute power corrupts absolutely."

Where is the answer to these inordinate loves? "If ye then be risen with Christ, seek those things which are above, where Christ sitteth on the right hand of God. Set your affection on things above, not on things on the earth. For ye are dead, and your life is hid with Christ in God."[4] This is the explosive power of the new affection.

JULY 9 – CALL IT LUST NOT LOVE

A lusty person is one characterized by life, spirit, vigour, vitality and virility. Robustness, heartiness as evidenced by good health and spirits are other indications of a lusty type. It is not an adjective that is necessarily evil or sinful; nor is the adverb lustily; no, not even the noun, lustiness; or even the other noun, lust. Lust, in some of the other languages from which it found its way into English, originally meant strong desire, and that could be for God and righteousness as well as for wrong and wicked things. The word has degenerated over the centuries and now has mostly evil connotations. The lust for power; the lust for money are common expressions; but lust today usually means only one thing; immoral sexual desires that demand satisfaction. The evil damages to others, as well as the damages to oneself are rarely considered, while in the amoral times in which we live "anything goes." All is condoned amongst consenting adults. Lust then, understood like this, stands high amongst the inordinate affections. It has built in penalties for the person now, and future judgments for the soul.

To confuse lust with love, or to even think of them as connected in any way seems ludicrous, yet the words have been linked for centuries. The Bible is a frank book when it deals with sexual matters. It tells some terrible and true stories about sexual aberrations and abnormalities in both Old and New Testaments. It records these deviations from the moral loving standards that God has set, not to pander to perverted minds, but to warn the wicked "lusters" and call them to repentance and save them from the death which is the wages of sin.

There is one dreadfully sad story in the Old Testament that concerns David's children and has a connection with his own sexual sin and punishment. Part of that dread legacy was to take place in his own family. "Now therefore, the sword shall never depart from your house…"[1] Absalom, David's spoilt and rebellious son, who was later to be killed, had a beautiful sister named Tamar. Amnon, another son of David, loved and longed for this beautiful young virgin. But it was lust for her, not love and let's call it by its right name. He manoeuvered this pure, innocent girl into his bedroom by feigning sickness. Then he forcibly raped her and afterwards ejected the violated girl from his room and person. "Then Amnon hated her with a very great hatred; for the hatred with which he hated her was greater than the love with which he had loved her."[2] Absalom bided his time, but later avenged his sister by killing Amnon.

Lust affects and destroys so many others besides the original luster. The New Testament tells that "…God gave them over in the lusts of their hearts to impurity…"[3] to the degrading passions of lesbianism and homosexuality with the resulting penalties in their own bodies. These are not optional lifestyles; these are lusts which are condemned by God. Some lusters like these have been converted and now pant with righteous love and desire for God and good.

JULY 10 – LUST IS AN INORDINATE AFFECTION AND DESTROYER

Love builds up, edifies, strengthens and preserves life, while lust pulls down, misleads, weakens and destroys life. The Word of God, in its terribly true telling of things as they are, recounts shameful episodes in the lives of three leaders in Israel. This is done to educate, warn and lead us away from the pitfalls in the paths of righteousness. "Now these things happened as examples for us, so that we would not crave evil things as they also craved."[1] As the epigraph also says:

"Nuptial love maketh mankind; friendly love perfecteth it; but wanton love corrupteth, and embaseth it." From Essays of Love Francis Bacon (1561 – 1626).

While these quotations refer to Israel's idolatry, immorality and unbelief, they apply equally to the lust sins of Samson, David and Solomon which felled these three strong men. Samson was the strongest physically; David was the strongest, in his day, spiritually; and Solomon was the strongest mentally. They are brought to light again here so that we may be reminded of what we know. Lust does destroy the witness and testimony of anyone of us and gives cause for the enemies of the Lord to blaspheme.

Samson's strength came, not from his size, but from his lifelong Nazarite vow. From womb to tomb no razor was to come upon his head; no strong drinks or wine were permitted; and no unclean thing was to be eaten. Samson's lust life is seen in the kind of women he sought. The first was a forbidden Philistine, who he married. The second was a harlot. The third was Delilah. Their story is well known and ended with shorn Samson, blinded and bowed, grinding the mill wheel in a Philistine prison, forced to make sport in the house of Dagon their god. Is their mercy for Samson? Yes, repentant, with hair grown, he called on the Lord and ended up in the Hebrew's hall of fame.

David's sin with Bathsheba started as lust, not love. It had dreadful consequences, but these two were forgiven by God and David did marry Bathsheba and loved her truly until the end of his days. She is one of the five women mentioned in the Matthew genealogy of Christ.

Solomon, the son born of their union, was loved by God and designated King of Israel. This wisest of men started his reign so well but ended so badly. Why? One of the reasons was his lust for foreign wives. "Now King Solomon loved many foreign women[2]... his wives turned his heart away after other gods; and his heart was not wholly devoted to the Lord his God."[3]

In conclusion three things should be stressed. First: "Therefore let him who thinks he stands take heed that he does not fall."[4] Second: "No temptation has overtaken you but such as is common to man; and God is faithful, who will not allow you to be tempted beyond what you are able, but with the temptation will provide the way of escape also, so that you will be able to endure it."[5] The warning and a way of escape. But what if you have fallen? Third: "I do not condemn you, either. Go. From now on sin no more."[6]

JULY 11 – IRRATIONAL LOVES

Dr. John Donne, (1573 – 1631) poet, preacher and dean of old (pre 1666 fire of London) St. Paul's Cathedral, in his youth was ardent in the pursuit of love. His love poetry still ranks high in English literature. His life and loves show him to have been, like so many before and since, a fool in love. He said so himself in some succinct lines in his poem "The Triple Fool".

"I am two fools, I know,
For loving, and for saying so
In whining poetry;
But where's that wise man, that would not be I…
To love and grief tribute of verse belongs…
Both are increasèd by such songs,
For both their triumphs so are published,
And I, which was two fools, do so grow three…"

He loved; he said so; and he published it! Triple fool he called himself. But he later found a true love, a romantic love, that wasn't irrational.

As Izaak Walton, (1593 – 1683) a contemporary and writer of the <u>The Life of Dr. John Donne</u> tells us:

"he fell into such a liking, as, with her approbation, increased into a love with a young gentlewoman…" They made "some faithful promises which were so interchangeably passed, as never to be violated by either party. These promises were only known to themselves; and the friends of both parties used much diligence, and many arguments, to kill or cool their affections to each other; but in vain…"

So they married secretly and when it became known he was dismissed from his position as secretary to the Lord Chancellor of England. Walton tells us again:

"Immediately after his dismission from his service, he sent a sad letter to his wife to acquaint her with it; and after the subscription of his name, writ, 'John Donne, Anne Donne, Un-done'"

Some of Donne's contemporaries called this marriage an irrational love, and in some ways it seemed so. But things are often in reality not what they seem. This love marriage started him back on the road to the union with the heavenly Beloved, of whom Donne became such an adoring worshipper and witness. But it was his wife's death that set him "wholly in heavenly things," as he wrote:

"Since she whom I lov'd hath paid her last debt
To nature, and to hers, and my good is dead,
And her soul early into heaven ravished,
Wholly in heavenly things my mind is set.
Here the admiring her my mind did whet
To seek thee, God; so streams do show the head…"

JULY 11 - CONTINUED

Walton says:

"He became crucified to the world, and all those vanities, those imaginary pleasures, that are daily acted on that restless stage, and they were as perfectly crucified to him."

Donne's mind set, to love God wholly and "...seek those things which are above[1]... set your affection on things above..."[2] was not folly but wisdom from above. It was not irrational love but rational folly. Whole hearted lovers of God have been called fools, crazy or mad. Oh yes there are irrational loves and rational ones, but love for God is the wisest and most rational of them all. We will hear more from Donne again on love and death. (December 19)

JULY 12 – IRRESPONSIBLE LOVES

There always have been irresponsible loves, but it seems to me that this century, with its modern love morals, manners and mores, is coming close to an all time low in irresponsibility. Not perhaps in short term intensity, but in the rejection of life time commitment. We are coming close to the standards of immorality and amorality that marked the end times of the antediluvians. That century saw the cup of iniquity filled to the brim. Judgment was inevitable. God spoke to Noah and between the age of 500 and 600 years, while he was building the ark, the long patience and grace of God was continued. Coupled with that was the witness to impending doom as Noah warned of righteous wrath to come. "Then the Lord saw that the wickedness of man was great on the earth, and that every intent of the thoughts of his heart was only evil continually."[1] The imagination, will, purpose and desire of that age was irredeemably corrupt. Our Lord made the connection between those end times and the last end times. And, curiously, He stressed only two things. "For the coming of the Son of Man will be just like the days of Noah. For as in those days before the flood they were eating and drinking, marrying and giving in marriage, until the day that Noah entered the ark."[2] It all sounds very natural and normal. But it was actually very unnatural and abnormal. Like Sodom later, gross immorality was linked with "arrogance, abundant food and careless ease, but she did not help the poor and needy."[3] Pride, gluttony, drunkenness, affluence, pleasure and lack of social conscience were the order of the day. Sounds familiar, doesn't it? Irresponsibility was present in every area.

But it is irresponsibility in love and marriage that concerns us here. Behind the apparent normalcy of "marrying and giving in marriage" there is the abnormality present today in ever increasing measure; divorcing and exchanging of mates; trial marriages; living together without church or civil ceremony; open ended unions; short term commitments etc., etc. Is our age incapable of or unqualified for responsibility? Sweeping generalizations are usually proven wrong by many exceptions, but irresponsible loves are more the norm today. Men and women are walking out on their family responsibilities and refusing to pay for the care of the children they brought into the world. They think only of their personal pleasure in indiscriminate sex, without care, concern or accountability for the consequences of unwanted children.

Thank God for those who still uphold the old standards; who are responsible in love and Christian marriage; who still make lifetime commitments; who are not carried away by the so called evangelical leaders who divorce and remarry as the world does. The discharge of duty is not always easy, but it is possible through grace. Marks of the responsible person, Christian or non Christian are that they meet their obligations and have a sense of accountability and trustworthiness in the areas of manners, courtesy, kindness, thoughtfulness, and gentlemanly or ladylike behaviour. We must be responsible lovers.

211

JULY 13 – DEMAS, A LOVER OF THE WORLD

"For Demas, having loved this present world, has deserted me and gone to Thessalonica..."[1] "Ye adulterers and adulteresses, know ye not that the friendship of the world is enmity with God? Whosoever therefore will be a friend of the world is the enemy of God."[2] The world is not the created universe or the inhabited earth. It is the present world system under the control of the ruler or prince of this world. Since the chaos the fall made of the moral, ethical and social order God had established, Satan has had dominion through disobedience. So the world, in this wrong sense, is the domain of the Devil's darkness over the minds and hearts of men. It refuses the Sovereign creative and redemptive rights of God in Christ; its values are satanically inspired and has force, greed, selfishness, pleasure and power as its principles. "Do not love the world nor the things in the world..."[3]

This is the present world and the then "present" world that Demas loved, the love of which caused him to desert Paul and Christ. The tragedy of Demas was that he was a professed lover and servant of the Lord. He is first mentioned as he joins with the physician Luke in sending greetings to the Colossian church. And he again is linked with Luke as a fellow worker in the lovely little letter Paul sent from prison to his friend Philemon. Demas had run well; had he become weary in well doing? Had the price of discipleship proved too high? We do know the love of the world had cooled his love for Paul; cooled his love for the work; and caused him to leave his first love for Christ. "...If anyone loves the world, the love of the Father is not in him."[4]

We do not sit in judgment on Demas; the world is ever with us. The prince is working overtly and covertly to entice us back to the world, or seduce us as we make our way through "Vanity Fair" as Bunyan called this world. In his famous "Pilgrim's Progress" he graphically pictures Satan pouring water on the fire of a Christian's love to diminish or douse it. And as Bunyan said from personal experience, Satan would come to him saying:

"I'll cool you, I'll cool you."

And then reverting to the allegory he takes us behind the scenes and shows us holy love pouring in the holy oil of the Spirit to keep the fire burning despite all of Satan's efforts to extinguish it. And Satan and Vanity Fair combined didn't overcome Pilgrim and his friend though it killed Faithful. The way to the Celestial City lies through the Vanity of Vanities which is this world's systems. Bunyan's two, like us, have to be in it, but we don't have to be of it. We can pass through it without being caught up in it. We don't have to be involved in it as Lot was in Sodom. He was corrupted by it as his children were. His wife loved it, looked back longingly towards it and lost her life.

Love of the world is one of the inordinate loves. The way to overcome it is to increase our love for Christ and have a right love of the world - the love for lost people who need his love.

JULY 14 – LIVING IN AND LOVING THE WORLD

We can't help being in the world, but we must not be of it. That is, we must not love it or be friends with it. "Ye adulterers and adulteresses, know ye not that the friendship of the world is enmity with God? Whosoever therefore will be a friend of the world is the enemy of God."[1] And that, as we saw, is what Demas did.

But there is a right kind of world loving. Christians should be, in the right way, a world loving people. Doing the will of God, paradoxically demands that we, at the same time, both love the world and not love it. An example of this is better than a lot of explanation.

Many years ago I stood beside the grave of Dwight Lyman Moody (1837 – 1899) in Northfield, Massachusetts. Moody was the Billy Graham of the 19th century and was the foremost evangelist of that era. He was used to bring the wealthy, worldly Englishman, Edward Studd (? – 1879) to Christ and, through him, his sons. As I stood by Moody's grave I had in my hand the short autobiography he had written:

"Some day you will read in the papers that D. L Moody, of East Northfield, is dead. Don't you believe a word of it! At that moment I shall be more alive than I am now. I shall have gone up higher, that is all, out of this old clay tenement into a house that is immortal; a body that death cannot touch, that sin cannot taint, a body fashioned like unto his glorious body. I was born of the flesh in 1837. I was born of the Spirit in 1856. That which is born of the flesh may die. That which is born of the Spirit will live forever."

He died in 1899 and as I stood, nearly half a century later, by the spot where lay his earthly remains, I thought of what he had written, and what he had wished as his epitaph. On that simple grave marker was written just his name, year of birth and death, and a text: "And the world passeth away, and the lust thereof: but he that doeth the will of God abideth for ever."[2] The context of that verse shows what lust of the world means, wrongly. Moody's text, by implication, shows what love of the world means, rightly.

From that time in 1856 that he was saved out of the world, D. L. Moody went back into the world to save souls out of the world. He knew the world was destined for burning and he plucked souls as brands from the burning. He began in the fires of the American Civil War. He plucked them in ever increasing numbers as his mission grew. He snatched them, in a Crusade in Chicago, even up to the night of the great Chicago fire that destroyed the city. He sailed the seas several times to seek souls in his campaigns in England, Scotland and Ireland. Moody founded, helped by money from C. T. Studd (1860 – 1931), the Moody Bible Institute which multiplied his ministry.

And that is how D. L. Moody lived in, and loved the world, rightly. And the Lord wishes all His children to so love the world by witness and works. The one who so lives and loves, like Moody, will live forever.

JULY 15 – LOVERS OF PLEASURE

We read: "But realize this, that in the last days difficult times will come. For men will be lovers of self, lovers of money, boastful, arrogant, revilers, disobedient to parents, ungrateful, unholy, unloving, irreconcilable, malicious gossips, without self-control, brutal, haters of good, treacherous, reckless, conceited, lovers of pleasure rather than lovers of God, holding to a form of godliness, although they have denied its power; avoid such men as these."[1] There can be no true study of our great theme love without some consideration of the false, wrong and inordinate loves. It is a truism to say what we all know, but we'll say it anyway, that the wrong, unbalanced loves are the enemy of and destructive of the right and true loves. And they can and do keep us from the highest love of all; the love of God. In the list above several of these wrong and unbalanced loves are mentioned. Lovers of self. Lovers of money. Lovers of pleasure. All combining against becoming lovers of God. We live in a selfish, brutal, anarchic and unloving age when the false gods and goddesses of love are rampant and ruling. In the King James Version we are warned against "inordinate affection." A modern rendering of the verse is: "Therefore consider the members of your earthly body as dead to immorality, impurity, passion, evil desire, and greed, which amounts to idolatry."[2]

Pleasure, that which is pleasing, is ordained of God, make no mistake about that. Those who would deny even legitimate pleasures build on a false premise. Some of the Puritans seemed to err here, particularly when they had political power in England. He, the Creator, made all things, and all things He made were good, proper and pleasing. Pleasures are built into all created things and it doesn't take extrasensory perception to see and enjoy them. Our senses are given us for, amongst other things, to enjoy right, wholesome and holy pleasures. We are promised that: "…in Your right hand there are pleasures forever"[3] but there are plenty of preliminary ones now.

It is the perverting and subverting of proper pleasures that is indicted. Hedonism is the enemy. This is the teaching that the chief good and man's primary purpose lies in the pursuit of pleasure. It is a doomed quest as Robert Burns (1759 – 1796) lamented:

"But pleasures are like poppies spread;
You seize the flower, its bloom is shed.
Or like the snow falls in the river,
A moment white, then melts forever."

As sure as the pursuit of pure and proper pleasure satisfy, so also will the pursuit of impure and improper pleasure destroy. The indictment of past civilizations and the individuals who comprised them is described by God who "gave them over."[4] And with history repeating itself as it does, we see the same things happening today. The lovers of pleasure are still self-destructing.

JULY 16 – LOVERS OF POWER

Lovers of power, power brokers or power manipulators are not described in Scripture by one word, but they are there. This wrong love and abuse of power is one of the inordinate loves that destroys many in its passing. It will be dethroned and in the end destroy the ambitious and arrogant wielder. The dangers for us as Christians exercising power in lowly circumstances, or Christian leaders using it in higher circles, are as real for us today as they were for King Saul, a thousand years or more before Christ. The problems arising from the use and abuse of power in the church, Christian organizations and the many para-church service societies are still present and sometimes paramount. What are sometimes called "personality problems" in reality are "power problems."

We are now faced with another difficulty. How is it that good, God given power in its twofold meaning of authority and ability, right and might, the power of the Holy Spirit anointing for service, can exist with, and permit, the abuse of authority in bad ways to bad ends? A review of the life of Saul provides answers. When small and humble at his youthful beginning he was loved, chosen by God and anointed with the Spirit. Later, as earthly power with its tendency to corrupt began to do its deadly work, he usurped the priestly office, disobeyed the commands of God and was deposed from his king-ship and deprived of the divine authority. The Holy Spirit left him. Samuel delivered the leadership death notice long before Saul died physically at the hands of the Philistines. Samuel was distressed and cried all night when given the deposition message from God, but he delivered it. "Samuel said, 'Is it not true, though you were little in your own eyes, you were made the head of the tribes of Israel? And the Lord anointed you king over Israel, and the Lord sent you on a mission[1]... Why then did you not obey the voice of the Lord[2]...For rebellion is as the sin of divination, And insubordination is as iniquity and idolatry. Because you have rejected the word of the Lord, He has also rejected you from being king.'"[3] Power is heavenly and is worked out on earth. Without humility, holiness and love, the wielder of this dual authority is doomed to be destroyed by the lesser ousting the greater.

It was so in the early church. A little brief authority went to the head of one Diotrephes. John tells of him: "I wrote something to the church; but Diotrephes, who loves to be first among them, does not accept what we say. For this reason, if I come, I will call attention to his deeds..."[4] This abuse of power has to be dealt by confrontation in a spirit of love, meekness and self judgment. We all need to heed these matters.

A Diotrephan spirit is not far below the surface in any of us. When I try to ram through, by direct or devious means, what I want as a leader, then I am being corrupted by the love of power. Once as Field Leader directing an Annual Staff Conference I was personally and publicly put on the spot by a fellow worker.

"John says: 'This is not a dictatorship, this is a fellowship' but he still says 'now you go here and you go there' and we are expected to go!"

I accepted it, for I was guilty. This is right love correcting the wrong use of power.

JULY 17 – LOVERS OF MONEY

"Philaguria" literally is a love of silver, but that doesn't limit it to the silversmiths who caused Paul, by their love of money, so much trouble. That occasion makes a good starting point and illustration of our word and theme.

The Gospel was revolutionizing Ephesus. Fear fell upon them as the people saw miracles performed and evil spirits exorcised. Many who practiced magic brought their books and burned them. This was no mandatory book burning, but the compulsive inner power of conviction that led to the voluntary destruction of evil books to the value of 50,000 pieces of silver. And that was a lot of books and a lot of money! Would that such public, voluntary burnings could take place today with the tons of pornographic material flaunted everywhere. What a bonfire that would be! But the "love of money" then, as now, "a root of all evil," can only be rooted out by real regeneration. The danger is that it creeps and corrupts its way back in.

That was also the start of a reaction which was carried a stage further by one named Demetrius. He was a silversmith who, along with others made silver shrines of Artemis. It was big business and big money to these craftsmen. When they saw their cash flow threatened there was an immediate consultation. "…Men, you know that our prosperity depends upon this business. You see and hear that not only in Ephesus, but in almost all of Asia, this Paul has persuaded and turned away a considerable number of people, saying that gods made with hands are no gods at all."[1] Watch out Paul, trouble is coming. Your Gospel is affecting the marketing of unholy religious hardware. When religion and moneymaking are married there is bound to be trouble. Our concern is not with worldly, but Christian, church, and religious love of money today.

Then Demetrius piously continues: "Not only is there danger that this trade of ours fall into disrepute, but also that the temple of the great goddess Artemis be regarded as worthless and that she whom all of Asia and the world worship will even be dethroned from her magnificence."[2] This great rabble rousing speech ought to do the trick. It did. "When they heard this and were filled with rage, they began crying out, saying, 'Great is Artemis of the Ephesians!'"[3] Then the city was filled with confusion. Religious rioting broke out and Paul and his companions were roughed up.

It's time to look at the text where our word is found. "For the love of money is a root of all sorts of evil, and some by longing for it have wandered away from the faith and pierced themselves with many griefs."[4] There's the application to us Christians in these days of "bigger is better," "cost doesn't matter." "financial success is the criterion" and "poverty for Christ's sake is passé." Mammon is the idol which is consciously or unconsciously worshipped today. The subtitle of John White's book The Golden Cow is "Materialism in the 20th Century Church." It is a must read. Of course money is needed to live and do His work but the love of it is an inordinate love. It was the Pharisees' problem.

JULY 18 – LOVE AND RICHES

Count Leo Tolstoy (1828 – 1910) was a rich Russian landowner before Communism took over. In his later life he gave away some of his wealth and estates to his peasants. He also preached a gospel of love derived from Christianity, and, in a sense, sought to try to bring in the Kingdom of Heaven on earth by these actions. He was a religious philanthropist. The sincerity of his efforts is not in question. Had the Russian Orthodox Church repented and returned to the true Gospel of Christ and divested itself of its wealth it might have forestalled the bloody revolution of 1917 which destroyed both the Czar and Church. What concerns us here regarding Tolstoy is the sad, bad and mad ending to his life. In the diaries of Tolstoy and his wife for 1910, the year in which he died, there is the record of the old disappointed and disarranged man running away from home. And why did this preacher of love and practitioner of giving flee? For the proverbial reason! A nagging wife and his own frustrations. It is sad to read of this 82 year old and his nagging wife wrangling and shouting at each other. If she desired to get back on his lap, she had, like other naggers, to start by getting off his back! Instead she continued carping and sought to confine him, instead of loving him. It doesn't seem that the gospel of love had caught on at home. They increasingly fought. Oh the tragedy of lost love.

Leaving the Tolstoys and their arguments and the rights or wrongs of his preaching and practices let us take a look at some other New Testament rich men and their problems. There are three of them. Combined, they portray the tragedy of wealth selfishly used; of the blindness that often makes fools of the rich; and of the love of money that inhibits wholehearted commitment to Christ. Our Lord told the story of the rich and foolish farmer. He was not mentally deficient, but spiritually dense. He was a fool because he did not acknowledge God as the giver of sent rain that produced the beautiful harvest. He was a fool because he gave no tithes to God of all his increase. He was a fool because he made future plans without God. He was a fool because he had made no preparations to meet God. He was a fool because he laid up treasure on earth and not in heaven. He loved wealth, which left no room for God.

Our Lord also told the story of the rich man and the poor man Lazarus. This is a callous, carefree, careless and utterly selfish rich man. He was probably religious and knew Moses. He was indifferent to the poor man at his feet. The rich man, in his purple and fine linen, was gaily living in splendour every day. The poor man lay in his rags with the only ointment for his sores the tongues of dogs applying their saliva. And then came the great reversal. The poor man, a lover of God, went to be with Him. The rich man, a lover of mammon, went to hell. "How hard it is for those who are wealthy to enter the kingdom of God!"[1] said the Lord. Too late, the rich man, remorseful now, begged Lazarus to come with water to quench the fire.

The third rich man was the young lawyer, no doubt inheritor of wealth, who still yearned for what money could buy. He was a practicing religious Jew and keeper of the law. Yet again with him love of money triumphed over love for Christ. Looking at him, the Lord loved him even as the young man went away sorrowful. Selling all and laying up treasure in heaven was too high a price to pay.

JULY 19 – LOVERS OF SELF

"…in the last days difficult times will come. For men will be lovers of self…"[1] though the time frame listed for this display of self-love is the last days, love of self has always been a mark of the natural man since the fall. And it is certainly manifest in these days of "I'm right, Jack, too bad about you!" All this is self-evident. Selfishness is a mark of unregenerate mankind. The thing that rightly concerns us as Christians is the evidence of it in us, the born again people of God.

"My Saviour, Thou hast offered rest:
Oh! give it, then, to me;
The rest of ceasing from myself,
To find my all in Thee.

This cruel self, oh, how it strives,
And works within my breast,
To come between Thee and my soul,
And keep me back from rest!

How many subtle forms it takes
Of seeming verity,
As if it were not safe to rest
And venture all on Thee."
Eliza H Hamilton

"For the flesh sets its desire against the Spirit, and the Spirit against the flesh; for these are in opposition to one another, so that you may not do the things that you please."[2] The Corinthian believers, who had all the gifts of the Spirit, were still a very carnal church. It is a continuing problem causing concern in many different church circles today. Paul expressed his concern to the church at Corinth. "And I, brethren, could not speak to you as to spiritual men, but as to men of flesh[3]… For since there is jealousy and strife among you, are you not fleshly, and are you not walking like mere men? For when one says, 'I am of Paul,' and another, 'I am of Apollos,' are you not mere men?"[4] Continued immaturity, ungodly jealously, pernicious strife, acute divisions and glorying in men, were some of the carnal fleshly indicators prominent in these lovers of self. For this is the inordinate love which is the foundation for all the others.

Self-love; the wrong love of self, is seen in quite another, and unexpected area of natural love. We know that natural loves can become inordinate and selfish, but here's a young lady showing cruelty in love and likening it to mother love. Elizabeth Barrett Browning (1806 – 1861), who was no novice in her understanding and writing of love, tells us about it in a poem: "Amy's Cruelty."

"Fair Amy of the terraced house,
Assist me to discover,
Why you who would not hurt a mouse
Can torture so your lover.

They say, Love gives as well as takes;
But I'm a simple maiden,
My mother's first smile, when she wakes,
I still have smiled and prayed in.

I only know my mother's love,
Which gives all and asks nothing:
And this new love sets the groove
Too much the way of loathing."

This young lady seems ignorant of needing love, which is reciprocal. The mother both needs and gives love. All giving would be smother love not mother love. Perhaps this is the kind she received; if so this is self-love in the mother. Did that produce this self-love in the daughter? It only confirmed what she was by nature: a lover of self. What is the way of deliverance? Death is the divine way. Love in death as we shall see. (December 19)

JULY 20 – SELF LOVE

Let's commence by clearing the ground. We are not speaking of right and proper self-esteem when we speak of self-love. We are not denying correct self-evaluation, but we are decrying the false emphasis, particularly today in some evangelical circles, which majors on "love yourself." The natural man or woman is born in sin, a fallen being. The result is universal worship of the self. Self-love is like Narcissus gazing in his pool, with conceited pride and admiration, at the self reflected there. The central self, the ego, spins off all the horde of other selfs: selfishness, self-pity, self-absorption, self-admiration, self-aggrandizement, self-assertion, self-conceit, self-deceit, self-dramatization and the dozens of other manifestations of self-love often ending in self-delusion and self-destruction.

I recently read a true but terrible book called Last Rites by Aram Saroyan (1943 -). It concerns the life and death of the famous writer, William Saroyan (1908 – 1981) it is a pitilessly honest record of the son's efforts to break down and break through the wall of self which the father had erected in his private life. Publicly, he was the wonderful, zany American author and lover of life and people. To quote the book's jacket:

"This is very much the story of a man behind a mask; the sweet and gentle poet shedding light and happiness, who is, in fact, some kind of darkness itself…"

And that darkness is revealed in part by the father himself:

"The only person I have ever really loved is Saroyan…"

This deadly poison of self-love had destroyed his wife and marriage and was destroying his son and daughter, whom he refused to see, even as he lay dying of cancer. The son, through filial love, did break through the barrier of lifelong rejection, and in the last days helped his dying father to peace and forgiveness.

That tragic story is perhaps not the norm, but it does show for us all the darkness, destructiveness and death inherent in this cruel self-love. There is only one full and final remedy for it and that is death through identification and involvement with Christ in His death and resurrection. There is a place for denial of self, but that is another matter. The Scriptural essential is identification in death.

A man, in the old days of transatlantic liners, was travelling in first class and had his dog with him. Walking with the captain, while also promenading his dog, the animal got loose and fell in the sea. The man appealed for the ship to be stopped. The captain refused saying:

"I can't turn the ship around for a dog."

The man then asked:

"Would you turn the ship around and rescue me if I fell overboard"

"Yes" was the answer, upon which the man promptly jumped into the sea and swam to his dog and the ship's crew rescued them both. That is identification and involvement. That's what Christ's identification and involvement with our sin on the Cross really means. And that's what our identification and involvement with Him on the Cross also means. Not a willingness only, but actual death.

JULY 21 – SELF-LOVE AND SELFISHNESS

We have talked a lot about thus deadly, demonic self-love and selfishness that shrivels and destroys souls. "Amour propre" indeed. "Love of self." The late L. E. Maxwell (1895 – 1984) of Prairie Bible Institute used to say "The flesh is an I specialist." He had a little list (a long one actually) which he had compiled over the years from his own life experience and the observations of thousands of Bible College students. It is revealing, soul searching and a very honest description of this cruel, devious self-love and selfishness.

"We shall discover:
In our service for Christ, self-confidence and self-esteem;
In the slightest suffering, self-saving and self-pity;
In the least misunderstanding, self-defense and self-vindication;
In our station in life, self-seeking and self-centeredness;
In the smallest trials, self-inspection and self-accusation;
In the daily routine, self-pleasing and self-choosing;
In our relationships, self-assertiveness and self-respect;
In our education, self-boasting and self-expression;
In our desires, self-indulgence and self-satisfaction;
In our successes, self-admiration and self-congratulation;
In our failures, self-excusing and self-justification;
In our spiritual attainments, self-righteousness and self-complacency;
In our public ministry, self-reflection and self-glory;
In life as a whole, self-love and selfishness."

This hydra-headed monster develops and reveals more heads, the more they are cut off. Crucifixion is the only way. It is God's way of dealing with this monumental 'I." the applied death of the Cross; the inward control of the Spirit, and manifestation of the life of Jesus by the Spirit are the Scriptural ways of victory. Some assert the annihilation way; others the sublimation route; while others give up, give in and give way, and let self-love rule and reign in their lives. I believe co-crucifixion, co-resurrection and co-reigning is the way of victory.

In Romans 5 the love of God, the love of Christ and the love of the Spirit at Calvary and Pentecost are seen. This is fundamental to salvation's deliverance from sin and self. In Romans 6 we are seen as buried with him through baptism into death and raised with him to walk in newness of life. "For if we have become united with Him in the likeness of His death, certainly we shall also be in the likeness of His resurrection, knowing this, that our old self was crucified with Him..."[1] In Romans 7 the recurring "I" is shown as the problem while in Romans 8 the life in the Spirit is the way of victory. Count the "I's" in Romans 7, then count the references to the Spirit in Romans 8. In Christ, by the Spirit we find the way of conquering self.

JULY 22 – THE NEW LOVE-LIFE

St. Augustine (354 - 430) had been as he frankly tells us in his "The Confessions" a worldly, licentious young man. Later, this previous libertine, now a new creation in Christ, was accosted by one of his former mistresses. She, perhaps not knowing of his changed life, sought to seduce him again by calling out:

"Augustine, it is I,"

to which he replied truly, but to her mysteriously,

"Yes, but it is not I."

Whether he had a chance "to follow her up" in the Christian sense, and explain what he meant, we are not told. However, we do know the source of his quotation.

"I have been crucified with Christ; and it is no longer I who live, but Christ lives in me; and the life which I now live in the flesh I live by faith in the Son of God, who loved me and gave Himself up for me."[1] This gives the full substance to Augustine's cryptic and calculated reply and the solid standing for his statement. He had become a Christian because the love of Christ had caused the Saviour to give Himself up to the shame, ignomy, curse and suffering of the Cross. This has been stated many times, and in many ways in these pages, because it is so central in the New Testament and so essential for us to personally accept this saving truth. His love makes the new life possible. He loved me and gave Himself for me.

However there is another point in this verse and we place the emphasis where the inspiring Spirit puts it. The old "I" has been crossed out, crucified with Christ, it is no longer "I" who live. Our co-crucifixion doesn't receive the attention it should by teachers of the Word. Yet it is the key to the practical outworking of the new love life. This is not only the song of the soul set free in salvation; it is the true liberation theology of the sanctification of the self through death. We are slaves chained with our own self-love bonds until He frees us for life and love. He came to set the prisoner free.

This co-crucifixion with Christ is positional truth. In the divine purpose of the Cross we died there, whether we know it or not. Once realized it becomes the liberating law that releases the love-life of Christ risen in us. It is the expulsive power of the new affection. When the true love comes, the false loves go. And this new love-life rises Phoenix like from the ashes of the burnt offering at the place of death, Calvary.

This identification with Christ in His death and resurrection is positional, practical and complete yet needs continual outworking. "If you have died with Christ to the elementary principles of the world, why?..."[2] "Therefore if you have been raised up with Christ, keep seeking the things above, where Christ is, seated at the right hand of God. Set your mind on the things above, not on the things that are on earth. For you have died and your life is hidden with Christ in God."[3] And because this is a fact, we build our faith on it. It is no longer "I" but Christ. We are liberated to live the life of love.

JULY 23 – LOVE'S REST

"Lord, I believe a rest remains
To all Thy people known,
A rest where pure enjoyment reigns,
And Thou art loved alone.

A rest where all our soul's desire
Is fixed on things above;
Where fear, and sin, and grief expire,
Cast out by perfect love.

O that I now the rest might know,
Believe, and enter in!
Now, Savior, now the power bestow,
And let me cease from sin.

Remove this hardness from my heart,
This unbelief remove:
To me the rest of faith impart,
The Sabbath of Thy love."

Charles Wesley (1707 – 1788), the sweet singer of the 18th century revival which carries the Wesley name was a happily married family man. He knew love on several levels. His brother John (1703 – 1791) had made a very unfortunate marriage. This became one of the elements, a spur in his side that kept him in the saddle, in constant travel and preaching throughout the British Isles. God overruled this loveless union for the good of many who found the love of God through John. Not many read John's journal today, or his sermons, but Charles's hymns are sung still, every Sunday, in some part of the world. His hymns on the love of God in Christ are still better, in my opinion, than the best of today's! His hymn on "Love's Rest" deals with the causes of our restlessness and lack of abiding in the love of Christ.

"Just as the Father has loved Me, I have also loved you; abide in My love. If you keep My commandments, you will abide in My love; just as I have kept My Father's commandments and abide in His love."[1] The word abide has the thought of remaining, continuing or resting. There is a deeper abiding, resting, in Christ and His love than many of us have known, and He has pointed the way by example and precept. Obedience to Him, shown by the keeping of His commandments, results in abiding and resting in His love. Belief that has no obedience in it is unbelief. We have to cease from this sin; unbelief has to be removed. Only then can we truly believe and enter into this Sabbath rest of love in a fuller way than we have ever known. This is so very personal and so very practical.

Keep our lord's commands; they are all contained in His one new commandment. "Whoever believes that Jesus is the Christ is born of God, and whoever loves the Father loves the child born of Him. By this we know that we love the children of God, when we love God and observe His commandments. For this is the love of God, that we keep His commandments; and His commandments are not burdensome."[2] They are joyous; closely related to joy. "These things I have spoken to you so that My joy may be in you, and that your joy may be made full."[3]

"A heart in every thought renewed
And full of love divine,
Perfect and right and pure and good,
A copy, Lord, of thine.

Thy nature, gracious Lord, impart;
Come quickly from above;
Write thy new name upon my heart,
Thy new, best name of Love."
Charles Wesley (1707 – 1788)

JULY 24 – LOVING OUR BONDAGE

This is a natural phenomenon often wondered at. We love our sins and bad habits though we know perfectly well that they are destroying us. Drink, drugs, smoking, fornication, homosexuality and lesbianism are but a few of the vices that are loved by the natural man and woman. The lust for wealth, power, fame and materialism is equally pursued though its destructive effect is perhaps not as fully recognized. The pleasures of sin, on a certain level, are real and their loss sadly mourned. Truly we are living in an upside down world with false values being dominant. The true values are decried or jeered at. When as a youth I began to witness for Christ in the open air, one of my workmates in the crowd was heard to say:

"I'd like to punch in the jaw the person responsible for Jack being the way he is now."

When I was gambling and sinning with my old companions, I was:

"Hail fellow good guy."

Now that I was converted and had stopped destroying myself I had become a:

"Bad guy."

But we are not going to discuss that kind of loving our bondage. There is a positive truth we need to explore and affirm. Let Scripture speak and introduce the subject. It deals with the bored ear, and not the kind that may have come first to your mind! This "bored ear" story comes from the ancient days of slavery. A Hebrew slave was to serve for six years and in the seventh year he was to be freed without payment. However, there was a provision made for an exception to this rule. "But if the slave plainly says, 'I love my master, my wife and my children; I will not go out as a free man,' then his master shall bring him to God, then he shall bring him to the door or the doorpost. And his master shall pierce his ear with an awl; and he shall serve him permanently."[1]

This ear piercing ceremony was not for earrings. It was symbolic of servitude gladly given, born of the master's love and returned as love for the master. The details need not detain us; the substance is all there; the implications can be imagined. Yet we do need to note one thing. Before being brought to the door for the piercing ceremony, he was brought before God as witness to his loving dedication. He was brought as a personal act of consecration to God first. Priorities must be right. They elevate and purify the whole transaction. We first give ourselves to Him in love's bondage. We in turn are set apart by God and that is ratified on earth by ourselves in a similar act. Not outward ear piercing, but perhaps by a personal witness of some kind, which is helpful to mark the act and the fact that we love this bondage which is perfect freedom. Its relevance is also seen in the loving servitude of matrimony, raising a family and all the other voluntarily chosen bindings of love. Through all these, and for as long as life shall last, we show our love for our loving Master.

JULY 25 – LIBERATING LOVE

We saw, in the story of the slave who refused emancipation, the truth of love's bondage. Here are two lovely hymns with their fulfillment in Christ.

"I love, I love my Master,
I will not go out free,
For he is my Redeemer;
He paid the price for me.

Rejoicing and adoring,
Henceforth my song shall be:
I love, I love my Master,
I will not go out free!"
Frances Ridley Havergal (1836 – 1879)

"I've found a Friend, oh, such a Friend!
He loved me ere I knew Him,
He drew me with the cords of love,
And thus He bound me to Him;

And round my heart still closely twine
Those ties which nought can sever,
For I am His, and He is mine,
For ever and for ever."
James Grindley Small (1817 – 1881)

However, the other side of the truth must be kept in mind. Love liberates as well as binds. Perhaps our Lord's question to Peter: Do you love me more than you love these other people and other things? will open this thought to us. Liberating love In its first instance is well known. It buys us back and sets us free. That is the necessary start, but there are deeper aspects to this truth, as our Lord indicates by His question. Many of our discipleship problems are caused by possessions, occupations and relations. Peter had faced and given up his boats, fishing business, home, father, family and friends. He had forsaken them and followed the Lord, yet their proximity meant he could, and did, return to them when he pleased. His own house, wife and mother-in-law were, rightly, at hand and he was often at home. All these are legitimate loves. They can however be the enemy of the highest love. Hence the Lord's question and His shocking statement made at another time. Liberating love frees us to hold all these good things very lightly as there is always danger in them. Peter was liberated, later, in this area.

Peter, like us, had a still deeper problem, himself. This was the root cause of his fall, his denials and his following afar off. The Lord had kindly warned him, but he, again like us, could only learn some lessons by experience. Pride goes before a fall. How often I've proved it! Praise him, liberating love delivers us from our own worst enemy, ourselves. Peter was liberated by love in this area also.

"My Saviour, Thou hast offered rest:
Oh! give it, then, to me;
The rest of ceasing from myself,
To find my all in Thee.

This cruel self, oh, how it strives,
And works within my breast,
To come between Thee and my soul,
And keep me back from rest!

How many subtle forms it takes
Of seeming verity,
As if it were not safe to rest
And venture all on Thee.

O Lord, I seek a holy rest,
A victory over sin!
I seek that Thou alone should'st reign
O'er all, without, within.

In Thy strong hand I lay me down
So shall the work be done;
For who can work so wondrously
As the Almighty One?"
Eliza H Hamilton

JULY 26 – LIBERATED BY THE LORD OF LOVE

Love has freed us; is freeing us and will finally and forever free us. The love that has no beginning or ending knows not time's tenses. Past, present and future are all alike to heavenly love. As Jesus' love never gave up on Peter it never lets up on us. It freed us from the law and the law of sin; it freed us from sin's dominion; it freed us by crisis and is freeing us by process from the despotism of self; it is freeing us from the bondage of possessions and is freeing us from all the lesser loves into the glorious freedom of the children of God. Liberating love is in the process of delivering us by death from that last enemy, death itself. "So if the Son makes you free, you will be free indeed."[1]

We saw Peter in the process of being liberated by love. We need to take the matter to its conclusion. When our Lord said to Peter, "Do you love me?" this question, thrice repeated, contains much more than is indicated by a surface reading. In the background is Peter's threefold denial. His remorse, repentance, return and restoration had been prompted by the Lord's look and His words. The Lord's lovingkindness, first in forewarning him, then in following him by eye and message, resulted in forgiveness. Now in this post- resurrection scene the Lord will lovingly draw out Peter's true heart feelings and lead him on from failure and defeat to new possibilities. (The physical foreground, the seaside; Peter's all night fishing trip; unsuccessful until the Lord took command; breakfast cooked by His own pierced hands and the welcome call "Come and have your breakfast.") All provide the setting for His after breakfast talk with Peter.

J. B. Phillips in his <u>The New Testament in Modern English</u> is one of the few translators who give the literal meanings and show the play on the words "love" and "friend" in this portion. Our Lord in His three questions is not reiterating for emphasis. He is repeating and differentiating to reveal Peter's heart. The passage quoted here will show what we mean. "When they had finished breakfast Jesus said to Simon Peter, 'Simon, son of John, do you love me more than these others?' 'Yes, Lord,' he replied, 'you know that I am your friend.' 'Then feed my lambs,' returned Jesus. Then he said for the second time, 'Simon, son of John, do you love me?' 'Yes, Lord,' returned Peter. 'You know that I am your friend.' 'Then care for my sheep,' replied Jesus. Then for the third time, Jesus spoke to him and said, 'Simon, son of John, are you my friend?' Peter was deeply hurt because Jesus' third question to him was 'Are you my friend?', and he said, 'Lord, you know everything. You know that I am your friend!'"[2]

We have quoted this in full for it is self explanatory and clears up the ambiguities in the other versions. Compare them and see. Phillips is translating literally the conversation with its play upon agapé and philia. Agapé, "...the love of God has been poured out within our hearts through the Holy Spirit..."[3] and philia, friendship love, brotherly love. Our lord finally used Peter's own word to make His point. Friendship love is fine and that's all Peter knew until Pentecost made possible what the Lord wanted Peter to know. Agapé is not possible until the Holy Spirit fills and possesses us. Peter loved like this after Pentecost.

JULY 27 – LOVE'S LAST LIBERATION

Peter, writing probably thirty years after Pentecost, showed he remembered the great lesson by the seashore when the Lord pointedly illustrated the difference between agapé and philia, between holy, heavenly, self-sacrificing and serving love and friendship or brotherly love. Though they are connected and complementary they are separate. Peter reminds us that the former has also to be added to the latter. "...in your faith supply moral excellence, and in your moral excellence, knowledge, and in your knowledge, self-control, and in your self-control, perseverance, and in your perseverance, godliness, and in your godliness, brotherly kindness, and in your brotherly kindness, love.'[1] He uses the same two words the Lord used; agapé and philia. As his Lord did, Peter distinguishes between things that differ, puts them in right relationship and makes sure that agapé controls the list. The lesson had been well learned. Thirty years later he could "tell it like it is' and teach it like his Lord. Pentecost had produced permanent fruit, not only in remembered doctrine, but in practical outworking.

By that seashore the Lord had shown Peter that his ministry should be feeding the Lord's lambs and caring for His sheep. Again the Holy Spirit's filling, and frequent refilling, was the enabling power for loving, demanding service like that. He had a little trouble fitting the Gentile lambs and sheep into this commission, but even here the Spirit and agapé finally triumphed. He went on his missionary journey to Caesarea, a Roman political and military center, and there preached Christ to Cornelius and his household. Brotherly love also received a new dimension in his life for he prefaced his message with these words: "...You yourselves know how unlawful it is for a man who is a Jew to associate with a foreigner or to visit him; and yet God has shown me that I should not call any man unholy or unclean. That is why I came without even raising any objection when I was sent for..."[2] God had convinced him that racial distinctions did not count; the Gospel was for the Gentiles also. In this case Peter seemed to add philia to agapé instead of what he exhorted in his second letter, his last letter.

Last words, writings and letters are treasured as of special importance. Just after urging his readers to ad love to brotherly love he wrote: "...the laying aside of my earthly dwelling is imminent..."[3] His death, as described by the Lord at the seashore, is about to take place. Tradition, for what it is worth, tells us that Peter was crucified upside down by the Romans. Be that true or not, he is about to die. And here the whole love drama of Peter's life comes to its destined earthly end.

As we have seen, the whole of his life, as with ours, is a process of liberating us from all the lesser loves. Our parents and all that generation pass from the scene. We pass from our children. We face the fact, if we are married, that one of us will probably predecease the other. In the end all the earthly loves are gone. Agapé remains. Death is the final liberation into the love that never ends. Our heavenly Lover desires the perfection of His beloved. This requires the liberation of the beloved from all the lesser loves. He oversees what He decrees.

JULY 28 – "LORD, ENABLE ME TO LET GO, AND LOVE"

Missionary Amy Wilson Carmichael (1867 – 1951), formerly of India, now of glory, still speaks to us by her writings and particularly her writings on love. I am still being blessed, humbled and challenged by her sayings on love, particularly by this quote from her book If.

"The more we ponder our Lord's words about love, and the burning words the Spirit gave to His followers to write, the more acutely do we feel our deadly lack...But the light is not turned upon us to rob us of our hope. There is a lifting up. If only we desire to be purged from self with its entangling nets, its subtleties, its disguises (falsehoods truly), its facile showing of brass for gold, as the Tamil says: 'if, hating unlove from the ground of the heart, we cry to be delivered then our God will be to us a God of deliverance.' No vision of the night can show, no word declare, with what longings of love divine love waits till the heart all weary and sick of itself, turns to its Lord and says, 'Take full possession.' There is no need to plead that the love of God shall fill our heart as though He were unwilling to fill us: He is willing as light is willing to flood a room that is opened to its brightness; willing as water is willing to fill an empty channel. Love is pressing round us on all sides like air. Cease to resist, and immediately love takes possession."

And there, Carmichael, with her spiritual insight and pointed pen, has outlined our most frequent problem. We wish, we even ask, for that life that is full of holy, heavenly love, but we want at the same time to hold onto the inordinate loves of pleasure, power, affections or passions that inhibit the true. "Therefore consider the members of your earthly body as dead to immorality, impurity, passion, evil desire, and greed, which amounts to idolatry."[1] St. Augustine (354 - 430) in his The Confessions puts it frankly and honestly as he prayed in effect:

"Lord deliver me from myself and my inordinate affections, but not yet!"

Carmichael and St. Augustine; from the mouth of two or three witnesses truth is established; and added to these are multitudes more who also testify to the fact of the "not yet" syndrome. And, before God, who knows our hearts, we also have to acknowledge that this is the crux of our own problems. Deliver me Lord, but not yet. I love You, Lord. Enable me to let go and love.

Is there deliverance? Yes, oh yes! "For I joyfully concur with the law of God in the inner man, but I see a different law in the members of my body, waging war against the law of my mind and making me a prisoner of the law of sin which is in my members. Wretched man that I am! Who will set me free from the body of this death? Thanks be to God through Jesus Christ our Lord!..."[2] He can make me willing to be made willing. He can wash my sins away. He can deliver me. He can free my will to will His will. He can enable me to love as He loved with Calvary love.

We will conclude with Carmichael.

"As the 15th century poem 'Quia amore langues' says: Long and love thou never so high, My love is more than thine may be. More, far more. For as His abundance of pardon passes our power to tell it, so does His abundance of love: it is as far as the East is from the West, high as the heaven is above the earth. But words fail: Love soars above them all. To look at ourselves leads to despair. Thank God, the Blood cleanseth."

JULY 29 – "LORD, WHAT IS LOVE?"

Miss Carmichael's (1867 – 1951) messages on love are so deep and true that I make no apology for bringing some of them to a new generation. She answers the question "Lord, what is love?" by her life's example on the mission field, and in the conflicts and pressures upon her as leader of a close knit missionary fellowship and finally from the pain and confinement of years of suffering. Bed bound physically, her soaring spirit and her impassioned writings on Calvary love, went to the ends of the earth and blessed us as a team of young missionaries in the West Indies. Hear her again from <u>If</u>.

"There is no force strong enough to hold us together as a company, and animate all our doings, but this one force of Love; and so there is a constant attack upon the love without which we are sounding brass and tinkling cymbal. That explains why every now and then those who want to live the life of love seem to be constrained to seek the searching and the cleansing of the Spirit of God, first (it has often happened so) in the secret of our own hearts, and then together; and we know how graciously God has answered us, so that though our word must always be, 'not as though I had already attained,' we do, by His enabling, press on. There is another reason why the adversary attacks love. It is this: Far out on our uttermost rim a thing may occur which is the reflection, so to speak, of something that was nourished in the heart of one who is in the very centre. I have always known it to be so. Perhaps it was never expressed in act or word, the eye did not see it, the ear did not hear it. But spiritual influences move where sight and hearing have no place; and unloved in any one of us, or even an absence of the quality of love of which we have been thinking, is enough to cause the slow stain to spread till it reaches some soul in a moment of weakness. And irreparable damage may result."

With the Psalmist we have to allow, even invite, the searchlight of God's Word, the spotlight of His love, to illumine the recesses of our hearts. Following the revelation of wrong, there ought to be confession and cleansing. J. Edwin Orr (1912 – 1987), back in the same era in which Miss Carmichael was writing, put the Psalmists words to the lilting refrain of the lovely Maori tune and we often sing it:

"Search me, O God, and know my heart today;
Try me, O Savior, know my thoughts I pray.
See if there be some wicked way in me;
Cleanse me from every sin, and set me free.

Lord, take my life, and make it wholly Thine;
Fill my poor heart with Thy great love divine.
Take all my will, my passion, self and pride;
I now surrender Lord - in me abide."

Only thus can our sins against love be dealt with. And when they are forgiven, we will still find that love in fellowship will not be easy, for there is suffering built into it. Natural love will never suffice. Only Calvary love conquers all. And in answer, finally, to the question "Lord, what is love?" let Miss Carmichael reply in the words of the Lord of love:

"Love is that which inspired my life, and led me to the Cross, and held me on my cross. Love is that which will make it thy joy to lay down thy life for thy brethren. Lord ever more give me this love. Blessed are they which do hunger and thirst after love for they shall be filled."

JULY 30 – LOVE'S CONFESSION AND TESTIMONY

"It passeth knowledge, that dear love of Thine,
My Jesus, Saviour; yet this soul of mine
Would of Thy love, in all its breadth and length,
Its height and depth, its everlasting strength,
Know more and more."

In this seven stanza hymn the writer, Mary Shekleton (1827 – 1883) struck the notes that find responsive chords in my own heart. I have written of my fifty year exploration and experience of that which is still unsearchable and unknowable fully in any of its dimensions. But I press on to know more and in so doing my soul is strengthened in love.

"It passeth telling, that dear love of Thine,
My Jesus, Saviour; yet these lips of mine
Would fain proclaim to sinners far and near
A love which can remove all guilty fear,
And love beget."

For five decades I have told of the untellable love of my Saviour. Inadequately, I confess, but as fully and personally as my experience and the Holy Spirit enabled me. If I ever have an epitaph or a tombstone it is my desire that the words spoken of John the Baptist might be mine. "…While John performed no sign, yet everything John said about this man (Jesus) was true."[1]

"It passeth praises, that dear love of Thine,
My Jesus, Saviour; yet this heart of mine
Would sing that love, so rich, so full, so free,
Which brings a rebel sinner, such as me,
Nigh unto God."

When the Holy Spirit poured the love of God into my heart in 1935 I went back that night to "Navua" my farm home on the banks of the Grose River, New South Wales, Australia, with an accompanying song of praise that has never ceased. Love is a fruit of the Spirit producing joy as I have proven.

"But though I cannot sing, or tell, or know
The fulness of Thy love, while here below,
My empty vessel I may freely bring:
O Thou, who art of love the living spring,
My vessel fill."

Since that first love-filling I have known many more over the years replenishing my so quickly emptied vessel. The supplies of yester-year do not suffice for today but I'm still drawing from the Living Spring, the Source of unfailing love. "…If anyone is thirsty, let him come to Me and drink."[2]

JULY 30 – C0NTINUED

"I am an empty vessel - not one thought,
Or look of love, I ever to Thee brought;
Yet I may come, and come again to Thee,
With this, the empty sinner's only plea –
Thou lovest me."

I don't know when the author wrote these lines but I know the day I read them and rewrote them here. It was a grey winter's day; it was a down day; I was drained, empty and unloving. The words met me where I was and I came, not with any love offering to Him, but with the plea, "Thou lovest me" and He met me.

"Oh, fill me, Jesus, Saviour, with Thy love!
Lead, lead me to the living fount above;
Thither may I, in simple faith, draw nigh,
And never to another fountain fly,
But unto Thee."

In this page of personal confession and testimony I admit that at times I have done as Israel did: "…They have forsaken Me, The fountain of living waters, To hew for themselves cisterns, Broken cisterns That can hold no water."[3] But now? None but Christ can satisfy.

"And when my Jesus face to face I see,
When at His lofty throne I bow my knee,
Then of His love, in all its breadth and length,
Its height and depth, its everlasting strength,
My soul shall sing."

To see Him thus in all His glory will mean that I will then fully know, now unknowable love, and be like Him.

JULY 31 – LOVE AND COMPASSION

"And Jesus called His disciples to Him, and said, 'I feel compassion for the people, because they have remained with Me now three days and have nothing to eat; and I do not want to send them away hungry, for they might faint on the way.'"[1] "Moved with compassion, Jesus stretched out His hand and touched him, and said to him, 'I am willing; be cleansed.' Immediately the leprosy left him and he was cleansed."[2]

Compassion is a composite word from the Latin "com" or with and "pati" or suffer. In the Old Testament the word is frequently connected with mercy, grace and love. "Who is a God like You, who pardons iniquity and passes over the rebellious act of the remnant of His possession? He does not retain His anger forever, because He delights in unchanging love. He will again have compassion on us..."[3] In the New Testament it is again a close companion of the love of Christ. "Therefore if there is any encouragement in Christ, if there is any consolation of love, if there is any fellowship of the Spirit, if any affection and compassion, make my joy complete by being of the same mind, maintaining the same love..."[4]

While Biblical compassion is a sympathetic emotion, a pitying feeling caused by the misfortunes or needs of others, it is also much more. While our Lord felt compassion for the multitude, that same compassion, born in His heart of love, led Him to do something for those hungry bodies. Compassion, flowing from the love of God, always leads to action. "Moved with compassion, Jesus stretched out His hand" and healed the leper. Our Lord exemplified this love in action for the three areas of people's bodily, mental and spiritual needs. And He expects His own followers to be people full of compassion, tender, merciful, loving and helpful. He told the story of the Priest, the Levite and the Samaritan to drive home the negative and positive sides of the theme. Both these religious leaders stopped, looked at the wounded wayfarer, and, because they lacked compassion they crossed the road and ignored him. The Samaritan "had compassion on him" and, from common brotherhood love, helped the injured and robbed man. Compassion is the key word in this story as it is in another the Lord told. The parable of the Compassionate Father (usually known as the parable of the Prodigal Son) whose looking, longing love, waited and watched and then ran to meet the repentant returning son. "...But while he was still a long way off, his father saw him and felt compassion for him, and ran and embraced him and kissed him."[5]

That is compassion in action. That is love in action. That is trinitarian compassionate love, in action. "The Lord's lovingkindnesses indeed never cease, for His compassions never fail. They are new every morning..."[6] To the sick; to the sorrowing; to the sinners and to the saints our Lord showed compassion, while here in person. And He still shows His love and compassion from the throne.

AUGUST 1 – LOVE'S COMING

How does romantic love happen? Many have asked, and many have been asked this question? Here are a few answers. They boil down to "It just happens" and "You'll know when it happens." As Nellie Forbush and her Emile sing about it in their famous duet from Rodgers and Hammerstein's "South Pacific:" "Some enchanted evening you may see a stranger…" and lo and behold the line changes "Some enchanted evening when you find your true love…" How come the stranger turns out to be the true love? Even the singer-lovers seemed to give up trying to answer that; saying so again in song: "…Fools give you reasons Wise men never try." Nellie seemed quite satisfied with the results; no need to ponder the reasons for: "…I'm in love, I'm in love, I'm in love, I'm in love, I'm in love with a wonderful guy!" Yes, it's better "felt" than "telt" as most of us would agree.

The places where romantic love happens make a fascinating list. Such meeting places. On ships. Sir Wilfred Grenfell (1865 – 1940) of Labrador fame, met love, as he tells us "on the quarterdeck." A real shipboard romance (not the ersatz "Love Boat" stuff on TV) that led to rugged mission work from boats on that cold Canadian coast. Dr. Frank W. Boreham, D.D. (1871 – 1959) tells of an intriguing story of where it happened to the Russian novelist, Fyodor Dostoyevsky (1821 – 1881).

"In the novels of Dostoyevsky there is no prettier story than the story of the meeting of his wife to be. He was forty-five at the time. Through voluntary taking over the debts of his dead brother, his finances had become involved…Somebody advised him to get a stenographer…A girl of nineteen knew shorthand (and was appointed). At first he treated her as a kind of Remington typewriter…Little by little, Dostoyevsky became conscious that his Remington machine was a charming young girl and an ardent admirer of his genius…And, shortly afterwards he married her."

Only fifteen years together as he died on their 15th anniversary, but it was a real Christian union. There is no doubt about the "how" or "where" of heavenly love's beginning and manifestation of the time and place of our encounter with it. "We love, because He first loved us."[1] "We know love by this, that He laid down His life for us…"[2] "…the love of God has been poured out within our hearts through the Holy Spirit…"[3]

"Jesus comes with power to gladden,
when love shines in,
Every life that woe can sadden,
when love shines in.
Love will teach us how to pray,
Love will drive the gloom away,
Turn our darkness into day,
when love shines in.

How the world will grow with beauty,
when love shines in,
And the heart rejoice in duty,
when love shines in.
Trials may be sanctified,
And the soul in peace abide,
Life will all be glorified,
when love shines in.

Darkest sorrow will grow brighter,
when love shines in,
And the heaviest burden lighter,
when love shines in.
'Tis the glory that will throw
Light to show us where to go;
O, the heart shall blessing know,
when love shines in.

We may have unfading splendor,
when love shines in,
And a friendship true and tender,
when love shines in.
When earth's vict'ries shall be won,
And our life in Heav'n begun,
There will be no need of sun,
when love shines in."
Carrie Beck (1855 – 1934)

AUGUST 2 – FIRST LOVE

Christina Rosetti (1830 – 1894) writes wistfully of "The First Day" of love's meeting and regrets that she can't remember the season, nor the day or hour. Her love came unaware, silently and slowly.

"I wish I could remember the first day,
First hour, first moment of your meeting me;
If bright or dim the season, it might be
Summer or winter for aught I can say.
So unrecorded did it slip away,
So blind was I to see and to foresee,
So dull to mark the budding of my tree
That would not blossom yet for many a May.
If only I could recollect it! Such a day of days!
I let it come and go
As traceless as a thaw of bygone snow.
It seemed to mean so little, meant so much!
If only now I could recall that touch,
First touch of hand in hand! - Did one but know!"

There's a poignancy in this poem that finds an echo, I'm sure, in many a heart that has found and been found by, true love that at first went unrecognized. In some cases, as above, first love comes as a dropped seed needing time to germinate, develop, bud and blossom before fruitage. Others find first love at first sight. Eye to eye instant recognition; this is him, this is her, this is it! How do they know? I don't know! Ask the next ones you hear make such declarations! But many have said it happens and much poetry has immortalized the sudden spark that ignites the internal combustion that melts two psyches into one love fire. It must be wonderful! For most the slower course is usual. It is a more prosaic rather than poetic happening. But first love does come to most; though sometimes it is not true first love, but just a first preamble. "Calf love" to use a common, but rather crude and cruel, expression for young loves. These first raptures mean much to adolescents.

Leaving the first coming, the first days of first love in the romantic realm, let us consider the coming of first love in the spiritual sphere. Here again the heavenly has similarities with the earthly in the sense that it is sudden and dramatic to some like Saul on the Damascus Road. Or it comes to others more slowly, like Lydia whose heart the Lord opened, like a flower opens to the sun. Yet others need years of patient prayer, and sometimes shattering circumstances and sufferings, before love inexorable wins an entry and gains the day. In the first coming of first spiritual love there is no question as to where the initiative lies. "...He first loved us."[1] From eternity past he loves us; from the foundation of the world He loves us; from the first coming of His Son to His second coming He loves us. Ours it is to respond to love's first initiative and to be receptive to His first moves of love in our earthly lives. He usually makes these moves through other love touched lives; parents who know Christ, preachers, teachers, evangelists or even some unknown lover of the Lord, doing a kindness, speaking a word or leaving a printed message. Thus first love comes sweeping all before it and sweeping all through us.

AUGUST 3 – LOVE'S SWEET YOUNG DREAM

It is said that "All the world loves a lover", especially young lovers. Young love is dream time. As the Good Book says about dreams and visions of a different kind: "…Your old men will dream dreams, Your young men will see visions."[1] The truth remains that old folks dreams are often retrospective and nostalgic while young people frequently dream and see visions of the near, middle and distant future. It's right and proper for young lovers and young marrieds to build their castles on the "main" or "the plain in Spain" as long as they are not building castles in the air. Wishful thinking, dreams and fantasies have a way of multiplying. Upon our illusions we build our conclusions and end with delusions. Keep one long leg on the ground.

"Love's Young Dream" by Thomas Moore (1779 – 1852) catches the note that charms us all, while at the same time reminding us that dreams, like all things below, "come to pass."

"Oh! the days are gone, when Beauty bright
My heart's chain wove;
When my dream of life, from morn till night,
Was love, still love.
New hope may bloom,
And days may come,
Of milder calmer beam,
But there's nothing half so sweet in life
As love's young dream:
No, there's nothing half so sweet in life
As love's young dream.

No, that hallow'd form is ne'er forgot
Which first love traced;
Still it lingering haunts the greenest spot
On memory's waste.
Twas odour fled
As soon as shed;
Twas morning's winged dream;
Twas a light, that ne'er can shine again
On life's dull stream:
Oh! 'twas light that ne'er can shine again
On life's dull stream."

Another kind of teenage dreamer was Joseph. God gave him the sort of dreams which Joel had in mind. Wild seeming dreams, which, in the recounting brought mockery and trouble from his own family. It's an old but up-to-date story "My folks don't understand!' God was telling, in dreams of heavenly bodies and earthly harvests, of his plans for the future blessing of mankind. They were dreams that would take decades to fulfill. Who could dream fiction like this? A journey at seventeen from which he would never return except in death. Hate, not love from his brothers. Put in a pit. Sold into slavery. Prosperity with Potiphar. Temptation overcome at cost of prison. From there to Pharaoh's palace and Prime Minister of Egypt at thirty. And God was with him through all the thirteen years of toil, trial, tragedy and triumph. And what about his personal dreams? He was human; he had needs and desires for a wife and family and home of his own. And God had planned a fulfillment beyond his wildest imagination. As a youth in Canaan, this Hebrew couldn't have pictured an Egyptian bride, daughter of a priest! Or of the two sons Manasseh (forgetting) and Ephraim (fruitful). The "Dreamer" as his brothers called him, with them saw his dreams fulfilled. Never knock young dreamers. Or love's sweet young dream. Remember Joseph.

AUGUST 4 – TRUTH IN WORLDLY LOVE SONGS

In some of the nice popular love songs of a few decades ago there were underlying truths which discerning writers had observed and which "rang bells" when people recognised their verity. For instance, symptoms of "being in love", and "being seen to be in love" by others, when the young lovers want it kept secret, is told beautifully in Rogers & Hammerstein's "Oklahoma."

"Why do they think up stories that link my name with yours?
Why do the neighbors chatter all day, behind their doors?
I know a way to prove what they say is quite untrue
Here is the gist, a practical list of 'don'ts' for you.
Don't throw bouquets at me
Don't please my folks too much
Don't laugh at my jokes too much
People will say we're in love!
Don't sigh and gaze at me
Your sighs are so like mine
Your eyes mustn't glow like mine
People will say we're in love!
Don't start collecting things
Give me my rose and my glove
Sweetheart they're suspecting things
People will say we're in love…
Don't praise my charm too much
Don't look so vain with me
Don't stand in the rain with me
People will say we're in love!
Don't take my arm too much
Don't keep your hand in mine
Your hand feels so grand in mine
People will say we're in love…"

And finally the lovers don't care, unashamed they sing.

"Let people say we're in love!
Who cares what happens now.
Just keep your hand in mine Your hand feels so grand in mine
Let people say we're in love.
Starlight looks swell on us
Let the stars beam from above!
Who cares if they tell on us!
Let people say we're in love!"

Does defense of our heavenly Lover testify strongly that we're in love with Him? Do we speak out for Him? Does our speech betray us? For a period of about five years in my teens I was silent in my love, with a wrong kind of silence. To put it bluntly it was a silence born of fear of man, fear to testify and fear of consequences. I was ashamed of him, not in my heart, but publicly. I'm glad the day came when "…perfect love casts out fear…"[1] His love triumphed in me, transformed me and testified through me veritably and vocally.

AUGUST 5 – WHAT IS LOVE? WHAT IS A LOVE POEM?

Many have tried to define these, and their definitions range from "daffy-nitions," to wise explanations that end up as a mass of contradictions. Jon Stallworthy (1935 -), in his introduction to <u>A Book of Love Poetry</u> assembles a few of the latter.

"What is love? 'tis not hereafter. Love is heaven, and heaven is love. Love is a sickness full of woes. Love is a growing or full constant light. Love, it is but lust. Love is more cruel than lust. Love is not love which alters when it alteration finds. Love is like linen often chang'd, the sweeter."

Perhaps paradox is a better word. Love is here and hereafter. Love is weal and woe. Love is heavenly and earthly. Love is, and love is not lust. Love is sickness and health. Love is poor and rich. Love alters and remains constant. Dr. James Orr's definition says:

"Love, generally, is that principle which leads one moral being to desire and delight in another, and reaches its highest form in that personal fellowship in which each lives in the life of the other, and finds his joy in imparting himself to the other, and in receiving back the outflow of that other's affection unto himself."

And this is one of the finest definitions I know. Stallworthy points out:

"Love of the beloved accounts for many of the most intense moments in most lives; moments generating the emotion that, recollected in tranquillity, may crystallize into poems. For these reasons, poets through the ages have written so much, so variously, and so well on this particular subject. But if they cannot themselves agree on a definition of love, no one else is going to be able to agree on any definition of a love poem other than one, like a seine net, large enough to take in all. So I consider a love poem to be not only the lover's 'ballad made to his mistress' eyebrow,' but any poem about any aspect of one human being's desire for another. Love is a country where anything can happen, and among the multitudes who have crossed its shimmering frontiers since first 'Imperial Adam, naked in the dew, felt his brown flanks and found the rib was gone...' there have always been poems of what they found."

As can be easily seen the questions here about "love poems" are limited to physical, human, earthly, romantic love. The many other aspects such as patriotic love, love of nature, friendship love etc. are considered elsewhere; while the ultimate love, the eternal love of God, is the major theme of these pages. Agapé love, holy, heavenly love is defined fully and finally for us in the pages of Holy Writ as we have seen. There we have not only a definition but also a description and demonstration of it. Abstract and concrete, theory and practice are married giving us something to see as well as to think about. Our Lord Jesus Christ is the personification, and living definition, of this love divine.

We will now consider definitions of love and love poems in perhaps the greatest love poem ever written; "Song of Solomon." This is the inspired Biblical story of two human lovers. It depicts romantic, physical and marital love, while at the same time portraying by illustration the love of Christ for His bride the church. The next pages will be devoted to the Song of Solomon. There we will find some of the questions asked here: What is love? What is a love poem?

AUGUST 6 – ON BEING "IN LOVE"

"Eros" has his statue in Piccadilly Circus, London, England. The dedicatory words written around its base are not a celebration of erotic love, but to honour philanthropic love. They commend and commemorate the life of Lord Shaftesbury (1801 – 1885), the Christian politician and statesman whose career was devoted to the uplifting of the downtrodden and disenfranchised. This monument had, in the minds of those who erected it, something of agapé as well as philanthropic love. While this Greek word for love, Eros, as noted, has other connotations besides sex, it does include it. Romantic, physical, sexual love. It is still the kind of love that makes the population world go round and has been with us from the beginning.

God, the creator of our first fore-parents and sponsor of the first marriage union, ordained sexual intercourse as an integral part of the man-woman marital relationship making them one flesh. He stated it again when He told them to "…be fruitful and multiply…"[1] and it is clear, without equivocation, in the words: "Now the man had relations with his wife Eve, and she conceived and gave birth to Cain…"[2] In the older versions the euphemistic word "know" is used. We have no record of their courtship if any, or romantic feelings if any, or even of their being "in love." What we do have is God ordaining this relationship and indicating what results were intended. Perhaps, as in many Eastern parentally arranged marriages, being "in love" came later. Either way, the thing that really matters is that our heavenly Father should be, not only consulted, but in control over our "falling in love" and following through with all that is included in it. While it is true that "falling in love" can be subsequent in a union, Jacob and Rachel were an early Biblical illustration of being "in love" before marriage. This is really too staid a statement to illustrate the emotional flame that was lit in Jacob when he met Rachel; "falling head over heels in love" is more like it.

There is another book in the Bible which devotes its eight chapters to intimate descriptions of what this emotional, mental and physical way of being "in love" really means. This is the book called the Song of Solomon or The Song of Songs. It is first a love song, really a duet with an occasional chorus, wherein the two lovers extol each other's charms and rejoice in all the joys of marital love. In addition to the clear surface meaning, there is also a very special application in the realm of spiritual love. It is the love of the heavenly Bridegroom, Christ, for His beloved bride, the church.

In the New Testament this parallel of marital love and heavenly spiritual love is all drawn together. The being "in love" of "falling in love" stage is to be continually practiced after marriage in the deeper and more demanding circumstances of twenty four hour proximity and presence of children. Time must not deaden nor rust destroy this love for it is symbolic of His unchanging and eternal love.

AUGUST 7 – IDYLLIC, PASTORAL LOVE

Christopher Marlowe (1564 – 1593) is best remembered for the simplicity and sweetness of his poem "The Passionate Shepherd to His Love."

"Come live with me and be my Love,
And we will all the pleasures prove
That hills and valleys, dale and field,
And all the craggy mountains yield.

There will we sit upon the rocks
And see the shepherds feed their flocks,
By shallow rivers, to whose falls
Melodious birds sing madrigals."

An idyll, like Marlowe's, is a short poem or prose work describing idealized scenes or events from rustic life, but it has also come to mean a picturesque or charmingly simple scene or a romantic pastoral interlude.

And there is one book in the Bible which contains all these descriptions. It is first of all an idyllic, pastoral love story of a shepherd and his sweetheart; a shepherd husband and his beloved bride. But he was also more than a country man, he was a king. The book is called by two names: "Song of Songs" is the literal one, the noun repeated to bring out its special and superlative character. It is the best or most excellent of songs. The other title "The Song of Solomon" also derives from the opening verse. "The Song of Songs, which is Solomon's."[1] He is traditionally viewed as the author though the verse can also be read: "The Song of Songs, which is about or concerning Solomon." But never forget "...a greater than Solomon is here."[2] in wisdom, wealth and works. And love. It is obviously a poem about love and the first interpretation of the book must follow the natural or literal view. There are other interpretations, and of course applications. It is best to read it right through following this best of songs in its country love scenes and settings. It is the Garden of Eden all over again except that the results of the fall are now evident, in the separation, lost and bereft scenes which will be looked at later.

Love in the country! It evokes memories and brings to mind personal experiences. It's June, July and summer in the Northern hemisphere where the principal singers of this song were celebrating spring love, summer love, midst flowers, fruits, the song of birds and the baaing of lambs and bleating of sheep. An ideal idyll. But this is no fairy story. Here, idyllic idealism is tempered by romantic realism. "Tell me, O you whom my soul loves, Where do you pasture your flock, Where do you make it lie down at noon?...if you yourself do not know, Most beautiful among women, Go forth on the trail of the flock And pasture your young goats By the tents of the shepherds."[3]

There is a "shepherd hypothesis" view of this book which introduces a third person, a young shepherd, the "goodie" against the "baddie." For me, Solomon the shepherd-king suffices. The application to Jesus, the Shepherd-King, is not fanciful or far fetched. He is the lover of the bride. He is the good Shepherd who laid down His life for the sheep. He is the great Shepherd living, caring for the sheep. And the chief Shepherd is coming for His sheep.

AUGUST 8 – REALITY VERSUS ROMANTICISM IN LOVE

Marlowe's (1564 – 1593) poem about idyllic, pastoral, shepherd love and its invitation to the young lady to "Come live with me and be my Love" brought answers by two other poets. One, surprisingly, was by Sir Walter Raleigh (1552 – 1618) who flung his coat to cover a puddle for Queen Elizabeth the first (1533 – 1603). Sir Walter gives an unromantic answer by the young invitee. The balance of truth is never more necessary than in the lists of love. It is not all sweetness and light. Raleigh's young lady takes a sceptical tone in her reply to the glib shepherd. She feels he is painting too pretty a picture of love in the country. Realism is needed to temper romanticism. There's winter as well as spring.

"If all the world and love were young,
And truth in every shepherd's tongue,
These pretty pleasures might me move
To live with thee and be thy Love.

But Time drives flocks from field to fold;
When rivers rage and rocks grow cold;
And Philomel becometh dumb;
The rest complains of cares to come.

The flowers do fade, and wanton fields
To wayward Winter reckoning yields
A honey tongue, a heart of gall,
Is fancy's spring, but sorrow's fall…"

Marlowe met his match in his contemporary Raleigh. I like his down to earth reply.

Four centuries later Cecil Day Lewis (1904 – 1972), (not C. S. Lewis), wrote another poetic answer to Marlowe and his shepherd. Lewis faces reality by placing his poem in the city where many now live. And not in the affluent suburbs either. The hero is probably a dock worker with only part time employment. He is honest as he paints a picture of life as it really is and will be. Can love face unpleasant facts? Is love, stripped of the romantic, possible in such circumstances, with hunger a present factor? The young man issues his invitation in a most unusual love proposal.

"Come, live with me and be my love,
And we will all the pleasures prove
Of peace and plenty, bed and board,
That chance employment may afford.

I'll handle dainties on the docks
And thou shalt read of summer frocks:
At evening by the sour canals
We'll hope to hear some madrigals.

Care on thy maiden brow shall put
A wreath of wrinkles, and thy foot
Be shod with pain: not silken dress
But toil shall tire thy loveliness.

Hunger shall make thy modest zone
And cheat fond death of all but bone
If these delights thy mind may move,
Then live with me and be my love."

This is reality, not romanticism. Not moonlight and roses, but daylight, diapers and dirty dishes. Better this is made clear before than after. "Love is blind" they say "but marriage is an eye opener." True love can live in country or city. True love can survive plenty or penury. True love can endure prosperity or adversity. For true love is not blind in the natural or spiritual. Scripture always balances truth as is pointed out in that love poem or series of love poems, known as the Canticles, or Song of Solomon. There is, as we have seen, idyllic love in the country, and there is also a very different and difficult love in the city, as we shall note. True love's survival quotient is very high, very strong and triumphant.

AUGUST 9 – MY BELOVED

In the Song of Songs the word "beloved" is used twenty-six times, most of them by the Shulamite about her shepherd-spouse and king. It is her favourite expression and description of him. His descriptions of her are even more endearing. "My love" "My spouse" are some of his expressions of love. She says, with all the love of her heart "My beloved is mine, and I am his..."[1] and in a parallel passage "I am my beloved's and my beloved is mine..."[2] But note the change of emphasis and contrast in these couplets. In the first the bride emphasizes her grasp on her beloved and then rejoices that she is his. In the second she stresses his hold of her before affirming her grasp of and her belonging to him. She held him, he held her. They belonged to each other, bound with the bonds of love. Her admiring, adoring love is an inspiration.

But it is also an illustration. There are a number of current interpretations of this superlative song. It is clearly first of all a love song; literal, down to earth, describing natural, romantic, marital love in frank and free fashion. This is right and proper human love; honoured by having its rightful place in the canon of Scripture. Never forget this. Scofield in his <u>Reference Notes</u> says its interpretation is twofold but:

"Primarily, the book is the expression of pure marital love as ordained of God in creation, and the vindication of that love as against both asceticism and lust—the two profanations of the holiness of marriage."

There is the dramatic interpretation which views the Song as drama. Then there is the allegorical view. This was common amongst the Jews who regarded the Song as an expression of their love relationship between God and His chosen people. The Christian allegorical interpretation sees it as the love reflected between Christ and His church. The typical interpretation says that the Song portrays King Solomon as a type of Christ the heavenly Bridegroom and the Shulamite spouse is a type of the bride, the church. We will be following this typical interpretation.

Scofield says:

"the saintliest men and women of the ages have found it a source of pure and exquisite delight. That the love of the divine Bridegroom should follow all the analogies of the marriage relation seems evil only to minds so ascetic that marital desire itself seems to them unholy."

I delight in the writings of one of these saintly men and he expresses my feelings for my Beloved. Samuel Rutherford (1600 – 1661) loved his Beloved with an adoring love. Some of his last sayings on the subject were arranged by Anne Cousin (1887 – 1960) in a beautiful hymn.

"O Christ, He is the fountain, the deep, sweet well of love!
The streams of earth I've tasted more deep I'll drink above...

O I am my Beloved's and my Beloved's mine!
He brings a poor vile sinner into His "house of wine...

The Bride eyes not her garment, but her dear Bridegroom's face;
I will not gaze at glory but on my King of grace.
Not at the crown He giveth but on His pierced hand;
The Lamb is all the glory of Immanuel's land."

AUGUST 10 – LOVE'S UNION AND COMMUNION

Memory is love's handmaiden. It brings to our minds "…whatever is true, whatever is honorable, whatever is right, whatever is pure, whatever is lovely, whatever is of good repute, if there is any excellence and if anything worthy of praise, dwell on these things."[1] And my mind is dwelling on something lovely at this moment. It was a little book, which the worms destroyed years ago on the mission field. But not before I had devoured its content. It was written by Hudson Taylor (1832 – 1905). The title of the book was Union and Communion and it drew lessons and parallels from the "Song of Songs" and applied them to the Lord and ourselves; the heavenly Lover and His church and people. At least this is what memory, love's handmaiden, brings to my mind now after nearly forty years since first reading it. And I want to think again, let my mind dwell, on these things.

"The Song of Songs" could have been sung in Eden before the fall broke the union and communion of love on both the earthly and heavenly levels. Unquestionably this superlative song is first of all a hymn extolling human love. And, we only have to go back to the beginning to see it is a song which Adam could have sung when the Lord in His wise providence brought Eve to him to be his wife. Let our minds dwell for a moment on that lovely happening. God saw in His unfallen creation that everything He had made was "good:" right, pure, perfect, lovely, things of beauty and things for utility. Except in one area where He Himself said "It is not good." And to explain by completing the quote: "…It is not good for the man to be alone; I will make him a helper suitable for him."[2] As Matthew Henry (1662 – 1714) in his Complete Commentary on the Whole Bible says:

"…woman was made of a rib out of the side of Adam; not made out of his head to rule over him, nor out of his feet to be trampled upon by him, but out of his side to be equal with him, under his arm to be protected, and near his heart to be beloved."

And God, who had made her, brought her to Adam. "The man said, 'This is now bone of my bones, And flesh of my flesh; She shall be called Woman, Because she was taken out of Man.'"[3] No union could have been closer, nor more complete than that one. As they walked and talked in that pure nude state no union could have been more intimate. Nor, as God also walked and talked with them in the Garden, could love's union and communion have been closer on the higher level.

But sin spoiled it all: disobedience to love's light demand, broke that perfect union and communion on both levels. And God had to put it together in both areas. He made reunion with Himself possible through love's redeeming grace. Fellowship has been re-established. Reconciliation is proclaimed. Love found a way - the way of the Cross. And love is the way for union and communion in marriage today, even fallen as we are. Love's union and communion is seen on the natural level in the Song of Songs as the lovers walked and talked together. Solomon: "How beautiful and how delightful you are, My love, with all your charms!"[4] While his sweetheart and spouse replies: "I am my beloved's, And his desire is for me. Come, my beloved…"[5] and that is love's union and communion, on both levels, literally and typically.

AUGUST 11 – LOVE'S SEPARATIONS

"Dear as remembered kisses after death,
And sweet as those by hopeless fancy feigned
On lips that are for others; deep as love,
Deep as first love, and wild with all regret;
O Death in life, the days that are no more."
Alfred Tennyson (1809 – 1892)

There is a torment in separation for two who love without reserve; a bereftness; a death in life as Tennyson calls it. In the Song of Songs the bride's longing, yearning desire for her absent beloved is seen in her disturbing dreams and in her desperate night search for him in the city. "On my bed night after night I sought him whom my soul loves; I sought him but did not find him. 'I must arise now and go about the city; In the streets and in the squares I must seek him whom my soul loves.'..."[1] "The watchmen who make the rounds in the city found me, They struck me and wounded me; The guardsmen of the walls took away my shawl from me. I adjure you, O daughters of Jerusalem, If you find my beloved, As to what you will tell him: For I am lovesick."[2] The sufferings of this lover seeking her beloved, calling for him in the mid watches of the night, portray what separation means when any of life's loves go, are called or taken away.

Mary and Martha and their loss and separation by death from the brotherly love of Lazarus, is one such case. Their sorrow was solaced by the Saviour in that wonderful restoration scene and by His words: "...Did I not say to you that if you believe, you will see the glory of God?"[3] And they saw it in the resurrection of their love.

Poets have pondered and put into words the emotions at work when the loved one is far away.

"I love him, I dream of him,
I sing of him by day;
And all the night I hear him talk
And yet he's far away.

I love him, I trust him;
He trusteth me alway
And so the time flies hopefully,
Although he's far away."
Barry Cornwall (1787 – 1874)

This separated sweetheart has a tranquility, peace and serenity that the disturbed bride in the Song of Songs seems to lack. Yet her troubled dreams, torment in separation and suffering in the search are perhaps the reactions of a more intense temperament and deeper more impassioned love. She was lovesick! What is this sickness? It is of the mind and heart and it has often been noted that it can affect ones health for good or ill. Mostly it makes people better; a sparkle in the eye; a zest for living; all "bright eyed and bushytailed" as one lover expressed it. Paradoxically this sickness is health. And when in the Song the anguished one found her spouse, all was well in every part of her tripartite being.

The disciples faced with the supreme case of love's separation, their Lord's departure, were deeply disturbed. He counselled them: "Therefore you too have grief now; but I will see you again, and your heart will rejoice..."[4] Love's separations, like most things, come to pass, not to stay. The bitterness of Marah was sweetened by the tree thrown into its waters and that is symbolic of the tree, the Cross, which can sweeten the sorrow and alleviate the grief of those bereft of love. Elim with its palms and springs is just ahead and the Lord our healer is there.

AUGUST 12 – LOVE'S REUNIONS

William Shakespeare (1564 – 1616) has a lot to say about love in his plays and sonnets. In Feste's song from "Twelfth Night" he has the happy phrase "Journeys end in lovers meeting" and surely this is the enabling hope that helps lovers endure separations. The thought of unions past and reunions future makes time fly and waiting possible. But hear the Bard of Avon on the matter.

"O mistress mine, where are you roaming?
O, stay and hear! your true-love's coming,
That can sing both high and low.
Trip no further, pretty sweeting;
Journeys end in lovers meeting,
Every wise man's son doth know."

Proximity, presence, the beloved person is what lovers desire most. Having known this blessedness and now, for shorter or longer seasons, having no physical or personal contact with the partner, this separation sharpens the senses and sweetness of anticipated reunion. Imagination may seem a poor substitute for possession, but the mind can fulfill functions of preserving love, and even increasing it, when bodies are separated by time and space. There is much truth in the old saying "Absence makes the heart grow fonder" despite the inevitable cynic who chimes in with "Yes, of someone else!" Allowing one's memory to minister in loving thoughts of past experiences with the dear one will usually be of more use than counting the minutes, hours, days, weeks, months or years that remain until reunion is possible.

During World War II some lovers were separated for periods of one, two, three, four, even five years, the whole length of the war from 1939 to 1945. Doctor Ben Wheeler (1911 – 1964) in his secret wartime diaries, which were a whole war-long, love letter to his wife Nell, often cried, "How long?" "Let me count the days" he seemed to say, as they took their slow journey in the prisoner of war camps. The future was dark; the end never seemed to come, but come it did and the reunion of love finally took place. Ben Wheeler sought, by intensity of living and loving and serving to survive the horrors of those Japanese death camps (and he did). And knowing that his life, because of malnutrition, sickness and suffering, would be foreshortened (as it was), he determined to live and love to the full during the time left to him (and he did). He loved wisely and he loved well, not only with his beloved Nell and family, but in his medical career that increased in responsibility and loving service to the sick and suffering. In thus giving of himself both during the war and afterwards he discovered what God had promised through the prophet Joel. "Then I will make up to you for the years that the swarming locust has eaten…"[1]

Love's reunions lead to love's restorations. The losses become gains and another Scriptural paradox is explained by experience. "Journeys end in lovers meeting" and so they will, and so we will. Down here it is a consummation that is deeply desired, but not always granted. But up there, in that day, reunion with and restoration to loved ones is assured. And best of all, this long night's journey into day will end in that face to face meeting with the beloved lover of our souls.

AUGUST 13 – LOVE'S PERJURIES

"...at lover's perjuries they say love laughs. O gentle Romeo, If thou dost love, pronounce it faithfully..." "Romeo and Juliet", William Shakespeare. (1564 – 1616)

Juliet, (the young lady in this story of romance and tragedy,) knew of lover's, (or love's,) lies. She, young as she was, had heard of these youthful promises of "eternal undying love," "I will love you forever" pledges that are so lightly, glibly given in courting days. Both sexes are prone to it but the male is the master of it.

"The Bedouin Love-Song" by Bayard Taylor (1825 – 1878) is an example of love's perjuries or love's hyperbole.

"From the Desert I come to thee
On a stallion shod with fire;
And the winds are left behind
In the speed of my desire.
Under thy window I stand,
And the midnight hears my cry:
I love thee, I love but thee,
With a love that shall not die
Till the sun grows cold,
And the stars are old,
And the leaves of the Judgement Book unfold!

My steps are nightly driven,
By the fever in my breast,
To hear from thy lattice breathed
Thee word that shall give me rest.
Open the door of thy heart,
And open thy chamber door,
And my kisses shall teach thy lips
The love that shall fade no more
Till the sun grows cold,
And the stars are old,
And the leaves of the Judgement Book unfold!"

That, in its genre, will take some beating! Poor fellow; despite his protestations it looks like a case of unrequited love.

Do they expect to be believed? Do they expect to keep these vows? Why yes, of course, we both believe them! Love like ours is unique! It can't; it won't; it will never die! The young fellow who wrote his girlfriend the poetic perjury of saying he would go through fire and water for her, added the prosaic post script:

"See you on Saturday night, if it's not raining."

Was it unconscious or deliberate humour? Or said with tongue in cheek? Whatever, it was down to earth.

We move forward in time. Where are these young lovers and the vows said at the altar? Wonder of wonders. They have survived the eye-opening realities of love that was blind. Dirty dishes, socks, shorts, shirts, diapers and faces have all been overcome and transmuted by love that faced reality, into the solid gold of a lasting, loving family relationship. But a high percentage don't make it today. Divorce is the easy way out. Love's exaggerations have a way of finding us out.

Christian young people who make and exchange vows of love have divine love on their side. And this divine love is His and only His. "...I have loved you with an everlasting love..."[1] No perjury or hyperbole here and with such love in their hearts Christian couples can rightly expect His love to endure to the end of the road.

AUGUST 14 – LOVE AND KISSES

Many a love letter has had these capitals S. W. A. K. or S. W. A. L. K. at the end, or even on the outside flap of the envelope, to the delight of the recipient. "Sealed with a Kiss" or "Sealed with a Loving Kiss" has been the nearest thing to the real thing. This romantic, lovers kissing is the best known, commonest, sweetest kind and sometimes, and sometimes not, a prelude to engagement and marriage. It can be:

"Kiss me, Kate, we will be married o' Sunday" "The Taming of the Shrew" William Shakespeare (1564 – 1616)

"One fond kiss, and then we sever! One farewell, and then forever!" Robert Burns (1759 – 1796).

This manner of kissing and this matter of romantic kisses has honourable mention in the Scriptures. "May he kiss me with the kisses of his mouth! For your love is better than wine."[1] "Your lips are like a scarlet thread, And your mouth is lovely…"[2] Such kisses are the endearments that unite and bind.

Then the Bible has a lot of references to family kissing. It can be a perfunctory cheek dampener or a very meaningful relative's kiss. Such was the first kiss with which Jacob greeted Rachel, for she was a relation. But it wasn't long until his kisses grew warmer and developed into romantic lip caressing for he fell in love with her and they were married seven years later.

Friendship kisses are frequent in Holy Writ. These are not of kinship but of companionship and comradeship developing from the relationship formed in common causes and shared interests. The kisses of men like Jonathon and David were honourable not homosexual. Such kissing is common amongst the Latin peoples and often mentioned in the Romance languages. It was once common in England. Horatio Nelson (1758 – 1805), that one-armed, one-eyed sailor hero of Copenhagen, the Nile and Trafalgar as he lay dying in the cockpit of "Victory," gasped with his dying breath "Kiss me, Hardy." And his captain did. Watching sportsmen in action today seems to indicate it's making a comeback.

One of the great kisses of love is that of forgiveness and reconciliation. Such was the kiss bestowed by the loving, waiting father upon his prodigal, repentant, returning son. It calls forth responsive returns of the same nature, like the love and kisses showered upon the feet of the forgiving Lord by the woman who was a sinner. The Word of God uses "kisses and kissing" in a metaphorical fashion in the matter of the kind of reconciliation needed for the salvation that made forgiveness possible. "Lovingkindness and truth have met together; Righteousness and peace have kissed each other."[3] These all met and were reconciled by the love of God in Christ on the Cross. It is now incumbent upon us to "Kiss the Son, lest he be angry…"[4] The way is open, be reconciled.

Fellowship kissing was common in the early church. "Greet one another with a holy kiss…"[5] The manner of it, male with male, female with female, or mixed we don't know. We do know it was the kiss of agapé, which was symbolic of the true fellowship and deep affection they felt for one another.

AUGUST 15 – LOVE'S TOKENS

Love's tokens were spoken of in Rogers & Hammerstein's popular song "People Will Say We're in Love: from "Oklahoma." A glove, the hand that lived in the glove:

"Don't keep your hand in mine… People will say we're in love."

A hundred years before that song about love's tokens indicating a state of love, it was put poetically, (by one who knew romantic love, and love's tokens) in a deeper, truer way than by the lovers in imaginary "Oklahoma."

"I never gave a lock of hair away
To a man, Dearest, except this to thee,
Which now upon my fingers thoughtfully,
I ring out to the full brown length and say
'Take it.' My day of youth went yesterday;
My hair no longer bounds to my foot's glee,
Nor plant I it from rose or myrtle-tree,
As girls do, any more: it only may
Now shade on two pale cheeks the mark of tears,
Taught drooping from the head that hangs aside
Through sorrow's trick. I thought the funeral-shears
Would take this first, but Love is justified,
Take it thou, finding pure, from all those years,
The kiss my mother left here when she died."
Sonnet XVIII from "Sonnets from the
Portuguese" by Elizabeth Barrett Browning (1806 – 1861)

Pictures, a curl, a kiss, some words, all are lover's tokens; like, rings for fingers and ears, and lockets for bosom and breast. Exchanged love tokens, for it seems she also received from Robert Browning (1812 – 1899)

"…curl for curl upon that mart,
And from my poet's forehead to my heart…" Sonnet XIX

Be that as it may, tokens have also been seals for many centuries. "Put me like a seal over your heart, Like a seal on your arm…"[1]

And the oft repeated question "Do you love me?" is also a much desired verbal token, to be continued, not only in romantic but in marital love. Mrs. Browning, with her usual perception, also writes of this token.

AUGUST 15 - CONTINUED

"Dost thou love me, my beloved?
Who shall answer yes or no? what is prov'd or disprov'd
When my soul inquireth so,
Dost thou love me, my beloved?
I have known how sickness bends,
I have known how sorrow breaks,
How quick hopes have sudden ends,
How the heart thinks till it aches
Of the smile of buried friends.
Do not blame me if I doubt thee,
I can call love by its name
When thine arms are wrapt about me;
But even love seems not the same,
When I sit alone without thee…"

Tokens are not tokenism, but they can be superstitious. When Alessandro Gavazzi (1809 – 1889), a converted Italian monk of the 19th century was a baby, his mother placed a locket charm around his neck to drive away malignant powers. When he found the Saviour, his mother's gift troubled him. As a charm it was valueless. He had the Lord's grace to sustain and succour him. And yet, for his mother's sake, and to honour her love, he continued wearing it, but with this difference, he put Scripture verses inside it which were found when he died, an old man of eighty. And what were those verses? "Who will separate us from the love of Christ?…[2](nothing) will be able to separate us from the love of God…"[3] These promises of God are eternal love's true tokens.

AUGUST 16 – LOVE, AND THE MOON

In some cynics' views love and the moon, and love and madness are synonymous! Just a few decades sago the thought of a man on the moon was limited to mythology. When H. G. Wells (1866 – 1946) wrote his science fiction account, <u>The First Men in the Moon</u>, of the men who invaded the moon, he anticipated the kind of criticism we have been, and still are, hearing concerning modern man and the moon. Wells describes a conversation between the invaders and the Grand Lunar. He asks the travellers many questions about the earth, some of which they are unable to answer.

"I understood the Grand Lunar to ask why had I come to the moon seeing we had scarcely touched our own planet yet…"

A good question even if it's spoken by that mythical man in the moon, the Grand Lunar! "Moon madness" may be a just term but the nations will increasingly engage in it just as modern day lovers will continue to gaze at it and wander together arm in arm under its silvery gleams. But moon madness is still considered by some to be a literal disease. The full moon is dangerous; it has powers besides its ocean pulling, tide causing effects. Oh yes, the moon can charm and do you harm! Especially the June moon, beloved of the romantic poets in Northern climes. You can be carried away by that seductress of the night.
Sir Richard F. Burton (1821 – 1890) wrote:

"That gentle Moon, the lesser light,
The Lover's lamp, the Swain's delight,
A ruined world, a globe burnt out,
A corpse upon the road of night."

William Shakespeare (1564 – 1616) in "Romeo and Juliet" has this dialogue:

Romeo: "Lady, by yonder blessed moon I swear that tips with silver all these fruit-tree tops"
Juliet: "O, swear not by the moon, the inconstant moon, that monthly changes in her circled orb, lest that thy love prove likewise variable."

Not only does the moon change, she has a darker side, seen only by astronauts. And that darker side has been seen in the Scripture references to that "queen of heaven"[1] and the peoples love for, and worship, of that false goddess. And over the centuries from those far off days, there has arisen another false love and worship of, the one today called Mary "Queen of Heaven" by the Roman Catholic Church. Mariolatry is still rife and rampant in these circles.
"God made the two great lights, the greater light to govern the day, and the lesser light to govern the night…"[2] Literally, we know that the sun is our life. We are children of the day, not nocturnal beings. And symbolically the sun stands for the Son of God, our lover and giver of life, light, health and all things bright and beautiful. Nowhere in Scripture, to my knowledge, is the moon a metaphor or simile for spiritual things. The moon shines with borrowed, reflected light, from the sun and is a dead, dry, barren, rocky, dusty and lifeless orb. Our sun is vibrant with pulsing energy, fire and light. "But for you who fear My name, the sun of righteousness will rise with healing in its wings…"[3] We do not denigrate the lesser light; we magnify the greater light.

AUGUST 17 – LOVE LETTERS – Part One

Love letters have been treasured down the ages; their fading ink and unfading vows have come down to descendents in bundles bound with silk and have sometimes found their way into permanent book form. These communications of love have often blessed subsequent generations.

One very different kind of love letter came to my attention recently as a special feature in the August 1983 edition of "Reader's Digest." It first appeared as a National Film Board award winning film entitled "A War Story." It is a sensitive, 82 minute documentary on the life of Dr. Ben Wheeler (1911 – 1964) written by his daughter Anne, and based on her father's secret war-time diary written when he was a prisoner of the Japanese from 1942 to 1945. Some of his fellow prisoners were to later call him "a man sent from God" because of his incredible feats of medicine (without medicine), his enduring hope (in hopeless circumstances) and his unfading love. His diary is an extraordinary love letter. Its yellowing pages were not discovered by his daughter until long after her father's death, at the age of 53, when he was chief of medicine at the Royal Alexandra Hospital, Edmonton, Alberta, Canada. It is a 4 years long love letter, so true that the very worst of war could not destroy it.

"Night after night Ben Wheeler, 31 in 1942, talked on paper to his beloved wife Nell in Alberta, just as though she was there with him. He poured out his love, his yearnings and the day's happenings in small, lined notebooks, scribbling in pencil or pen with ink concocted from bugs, mud and leaves. Keeping a diary was punishable by, at the very least, a savage beating so Wheeler hid his among the medical records that his captors allowed."

Ben Wheeler and Nell Pawsey were childhood friends who married at the age of 21. The year was 1932. The Depression didn't deter the young lovers and after graduation from the University of Alberta they went to England for a course in tropical medicine and then as a family to India in 1937. The idyll ended in 1941 with the bombing of Pearl Harbour and early in 1942 Ben Wheeler was posted to Singapore, two weeks before it fell. And from then on it was one P. O. W. camp after another.

"September 27, 1942 Nell is 32 today, my darling. If I could only be with her... I gave my honey's and the boys' photos a thorough cleaning yesterday, all fresh for Nell's birthday...January 24, 1943...Nettie dear. We cannot be kept apart forever. How I love you....February 18 1944 Darlings! The biggest day since I have been a POW. Three letters from you...July 9 1945... The 5th, dear. No, I didn't forget. Got out your photo and the boys..."

(This was their wedding anniversary). And the next month the war was over. Wheeler weighed 100 pounds, but survived and saved many others too. Saved by love.

These few extracts from "A man sent from God" introduce us to a far greater, eternal love letter. The Bible is God's love letter to the human race. The Old Testament is a prophetic love letter; while the New Testament is the fulfillment of these love promises, in the life of His Son; "The Man Sent from God"

AUGUST 18 – LOVE LETTERS – Part Two

In the New Testament, which is part of God's love letter to mankind, there are twenty-seven other love letters. These, plus the thirty-nine in the Old Testament, make the library of love, called the Bible. In that we have seen all kinds of love; in fact it is the greatest book on true love the world has ever known. There are two special writers of love letters in the New Testament who have been our instructors in these pages. Let us listen again to John the Beloved and Paul the writer of that great chapter on agapé.

John is called the disciple whom Jesus loved. John is described thus four times. Once at the Last Supper as he leaned on Jesus' breast; again, as from the Cross, our Lord committed His mother to John's care; and twice after His resurrection. John was a very loving man and in his first love letter he wrote this: "Beloved, I am not writing a new commandment to you, but an old commandment which you have had from the beginning...[1] The one who loves his brother abides in the Light and there is no cause for stumbling in him[2]...whoever keeps His word, in him the love of God has truly been perfected..."[3] John's whole first letter is one of the greatest love letters in the New Testament. And this is the man who once urged the Lord to rain down fire on a Samaritan village! The Lord had to rebuke this "Son of Thunder" as John was then called. Mr. Love and Mr. Thunder! What kind of a Jekyll and Hyde personality is this? When and how did love triumph in him? How did he become such a writer of love letters? For he wrote a second one also. "The elder to the chosen lady and her children, whom I love in truth...[4] And this is love, that we walk according to His commandments..."[5] What made John a writer like this? The Spirit of Love outpoured at Pentecost; He made the difference. He enabled John to write unparalled love letters.

And He did the same thing for Saul of Tarsus, the hater of Jesus and murderer of his followers. Saul became Paul, now a lover of the Lord and Christians. He wrote at least two love letters to the Corinthian church in which truth and love and the rebukes of love round out that great chapter on the excellence of agapé. He concludes the first love letter with these words: "My love be with you all in Christ Jesus. Amen."[6] And then early in his second letter to them he reveals his heart of love "For out of much affliction and anguish of heart I wrote to you with many tears; not so that you would be made sorrowful, but that you might know the love which I have especially for you."[7] He was "...jealous for you with a godly jealousy; for I betrothed you to one husband, so that to Christ I might present you *as* a pure virgin."[8] This second love letter to the church at Corinth is a commentary on love that gives. "I will most gladly spend and be expended for your souls. If I love you more, am I to be loved less?"[9] And Paul ends it with a lovely benediction. "The grace of the Lord Jesus Christ, and the love of God, and the fellowship of the Holy Spirit, be with you all."[10] How Christ-like to be able to write love letters like these; and how fortunate and blessed are the recipients, including ourselves to read and heed them.

AUGUST 19 – "I GAVE GOD TIME" – A LOVE STORY

Many have been blessed by the writings of Ann Kiemel (1945 -). But she wrote one very personal and very special book that must have cost her perhaps more than some of her others. In I Gave God Time she tells intimately and honestly a love story which is all that one would expect, and yet it is much more. She gives principles which are Biblical and of universal worth, one of which is the importance of waiting on God about this all important matter of a partner for life. And not only waiting on, but waiting for, God; even though the years pass and it seems the single state may be her lot. She knows that if that is God's will then all will be well. There had of course been suitors, but to her they were unsuitable. Like the statement made by someone else:

"Those available are not desirable and those desirable are not available so I wait."

Ann had written in one of her earlier books:

"Jesus, if this is your will, then yes to being single. In my deepest heart I want to marry, to belong to a great man, to know I am linked to his life…and he to mine…following Christ and our dreams together but you know what I need. If I never marry, it is yes to you."

God knows the deepest desires of our hearts and if we "Trust in the Lord and do good; Dwell in the land and cultivate faithfulness. Delight yourself in the Lord; And He will give you the desires of your heart. Commit your way to the Lord, Trust also in Him, and He will do it."[1] These great Biblical truths were, in effect, what Ann Kiemel was believing and practicing. Trust…Delight…Commit…Trust "and He will do it."

And God was doing it.

"On a potato farm in Idaho, a young man knelt in a small bunkhouse and prayed, 'Father God, give me a woman of God. A woman committed to you…someone strong where I am weak. Make me the man she needs, build her…guide her…prepare her, bless her."

And God answered the prayer desire of Ann Kiemel in Boston and the specific request of William Earle Anderson in Idaho. Their desires were His desires. "Moreover, I will give you a new heart and put a new spirit within you; and I will remove the heart of stone from your flesh and give you a heart of flesh. I will put My Spirit within you and cause you to walk in My statutes, and you will be careful to observe My ordinances."[2] And so He did and so they did. Miraculously He brought them together.

I Gave God Time tells the whole story, full of suspense, humour, deep spiritual warmth, and romance, of how God guided this couple's whirlwind courtship all the way to the altar of Park Street Church in Boston in June 1981.

Ann Kiemel Anderson's love story, and some of her love letters, are shared with the reader as a praise testimony to answered prayer for guidance and provision. And what of all those whose prayers along these lines are not answered? "…My grace is sufficient for you…"[3]

AUGUST 20 – LOVE'S HONEYMOON

Love's honeymoon is the special time for the newly wed "honies" to moon and spoon to their heart's content. It is actually the time honoured period for the couple to make physical, mental and spiritual adjustments away from family, work and other distractions. Short honeymoons are better than no honeymoons, but long honeymoons are best of all. A year would be fine, wouldn't it? Yes it would, and I say that with Biblical approval. "When a man takes a new wife, he shall not go out with the army nor be charged with any duty; he shall be free at home one year and shall give happiness to his wife whom he has taken."[1] Circumstances permitted a year's honeymoon in those far off leisurely agricultural, pastoral societies such as Israel was. Even if the couple were urban dwellers, towns were small, family allotments were near and every family had an inheritance of land. One could wish that, instead of the rushed two weeks or so of travel, from which frazzled honeymooners return, there could be some arrangement for a long, leisurely "lune de miel" today. But only "the idle rich" it seems, can take a year away from responsibility nowadays.

But just imagine you had had a year for your honeymoon! How would you and your spouse have planned and, finances permitting spent it? Why a trip around the world would be fine for starters! No way could the Biblical couple do that. Horsepower was literal in those days and wind power was limited to travel by water over the lake or more daringly if one put out into the Mediterranean Sea.

Anyway the Bible advises they stay at home; but be free at home. Who got the meals? Did their families look after them? The "freedom" at home was not, I think, personal freedom from practical, personal responsibilities in the home, but freedom from military service. The army couldn't come in and say "your military call up date has arrived, we are conscripting you now." "He shall not go out with the army." That was nice to know during the honeymoon year. Not "just married, just killed" as we have seen so often in recent wars. And the freedom from business clause was neat. "Nor be charged with any duty" (except of course bringing her goat's milk in bed in the morning!) His major purpose for that honeymoon year was clearly stated: "He shall give happiness to his wife." For the whole year the onus seems to be on him to be thoughtful, considerate, understanding and kind to his wife. By that time it might become habitual! Hopefully there was mutuality on the honeymoon. The key element is personal, practical love.

We have had to forget the thought of long honeymoons and settle for short ones. But isn't the major emphasis on quality of love given in the set apart period, rather than quantity of time permitted? For both to love each other personally, practically, mentally, spiritually, as well as physically is surely the implication behind "he shall give happiness to his wife."

AUGUST 21 – NEED LOVE – Part One

The "need" element in human love is, in its place, quite right and proper and God implanted. The instinctive desires placed in the genes of the human race by the Creator were all part of love's purposeful planning. The mutual needs of husband and wife in the physical, sexual and emotional areas of their lives were all previously thought of and provided for by God. Paul in his advice about marriage is quite frank about this. There is no false modesty about the rights and mutual needs of the partners in the sexual area of their relationship. "The husband must fulfill his duty to his wife, and likewise also the wife to her husband. The wife does not have authority over her own body, but the husband does; and likewise also the husband does not have authority over his own body, but the wife does. Stop depriving one another, except by agreement for a time, so that you may devote yourselves to prayer, and come together again so that Satan will not tempt you because of your lack of self-control."[1] There is reciprocal love.

There is better, up-to-date and clearer teaching in the Scriptures than in many a modern sex manual. The Word of God has been saying for millennia what is now being hailed as a great breakthrough; mutuality of male and female needs and fulfillments! The privileges and responsibilities are clearly stated. There can never be the withholding of the person as either a persuader or for punishment. In the mutual need of giving and receiving both are satisfied.

Arthur L. Gillom was a poet who knew "need love."

"I want you when the shades of eve are falling
And purpling shadows drift across the land;
When sleepy birds to loving mates are calling
I want the soothing softness of your hand.

I want you when the stars shine up above me,
And Heaven's flooded with the bright moonlight;
I want you with your arms and lips to love me
Throughout the wonder watches of the night.

I want you when in dreams I still remember
The lingering of your kiss-for old times' sake
With all your gentle ways, so sweetly tender,
I want you in the morning when I wake.

I want you when the day is at its noontime,
Sun-steeped and quiet, or drenched with sheets of rain;
I want you when the roses bloom in June-time;
I want you when the violets come again.

I want you when my soul is thrilled with passion;
I want you when I'm weary and depressed;
I want you when in lazy, slumberous fashion
My senses need the haven of your breast

I want you when through field I'm roaming,
I want you when I'm standing on the shore;
I want you when the summer birds are humming
And when they've flown-I want you more.

I want you, dear, through every changing season;
I want you with a tear or with a smile;
I want you more than any rhyme or reason
I want you, want you, want you-all the while."

AUGUST 22 – NEED LOVE – Part Two

It is wonderful to be wanted and needed and to be able to meet the desires of the loved one and in turn to have one's own wishes and requirements recognized and met. The element of pleasure in this mutual need love covers physical, mental, emotional, social and spiritual areas, but the unifying pleasure lies in the pleasuring of the partner. Peter reminds us of this reciprocity in his beautiful phrase "...heirs together of the grace of life..."[1] However the context of the words must not be ignored. "You husbands in the same way, live with your wives in an understanding way, as with someone weaker, since she is a woman; and show her honor as a fellow heir of the grace of life, so that your prayers will not be hindered."[2] Because the wife is usually physically lighter and lacking the strength of the husband, understanding is demanded. Need love must be governed by love for the partner. Need love though reciprocal is different for the woman than the man because God designed us that way; and as the French say "Vive la différence!" Conjugal rights that are forced are conjugal wrongs. Let love control here, as Scripture says it should, with the husband leading the way. And this will foster not hinder our prayers.

When these things are understood and practiced; when the wife is honoured and loved by the husband she in turn will have no problem in loving and honouring him. I recently read a Father's Day card which sums it up. The wife, after more than forty years of marriage had written at the bottom of the printed card:

"To my dear husband who still gives me protection, attention, security, grocery money and...goose bumps!!"

What a lovely appreciation of the supply in five areas of need love. Senior citizens still meeting each others needs. There is ginger there, not geriatrics! All their personal living has shone with the splendour of need love, seen and supplied, both on the spiritual and natural levels.

Plato (427BC – 347BC), whose name is perpetuated in the term platonic love, had some pre-Christian insights into need love. He said it is "the son of poverty." How descriptive and how true. Moving to the area of our spiritual needs, we know how these were met. "...He was rich, yet for your sake He became poor, so that you through His poverty might become rich."[3] We, sons of poverty, have had all our past needs supplied by the Son who submitted to poverty. And now, returned to home and wealth, "...God will supply all your needs according to His riches in glory in Christ Jesus."[4] Our "need love" fully met on all levels by "gift love" has only to be appropriated and it is "received love." This is full salvation – past, present, and future.

There remains the problem of reciprocating this love. He has need of nothing; God is fully contained in the world of the Trinity. The disparity between His riches and our poverty is so great that it would seem to preclude any thought of mutuality. What can He need? What can we give Him? We can give Him back the life and love He has given us. "We love, because He first loved us."[5]

AUGUST 23 – LOVE IS A "TWOSOME"

It takes "two to tango" so they say and it certainly takes two to "fall in," "be in," and "make love." We have seen that God has ordained it so, created it so and continues it so. And we also know that these two, united in marriage are "one" in His sight; and they become one in the sight of man when they make their vows and consummate their union.

Yet, despite all this being true, they are still "two." Two personalities; two temperaments; two sets of genes; two backgrounds etc., etc. That these two need to be integrated; their differences accepted; their goals defined; their conflicting drives correlated; and their conflicts sublimated, no one will gainsay. This a part of the process of marriage. They are two, the two becoming one; they complement each other.

But there are some very positive reasons why it is good that they are, and in certain areas, always will be, separate. Hear this Scripture so truly applicable to a really loving marriage: "Two are better than one because they have a good return for their labor. For if either of them falls, the one will lift up his companion. But woe to the one who falls when there is not another to lift him up. Furthermore, if two lie down together they keep warm, but how can one be warm alone? And if one can overpower him who is alone, two can resist him…"[1]

In these verses some notable facts stand out, very practical matters, which we will focus on by isolating and combining them. Mutual help in the area of work. Mutual assistance in the sphere of walk. Mutual aid in the realm of warmth. Mutual support in the arena of war. Romantic love may have brought the couple together but it is romantic love plus practical love that will keep them together. How glad they are that they are "two" when mutual assistance is needed. Though certain "work" ought to be understood as being the major responsibility of one or the other this doesn't mean the husband shouldn't help his wife or vice versa. They are co-workers wherever it is applicable. Togetherness in work strengthens the union. This is practical love. And what about mutual aid in the sphere of marital walk together? "Can two walk together, except they be agreed?"[2] Step by step is the way of steady progress in marital life and love. When one stumbles or falls the other is there with the lift of love and restoration in major or minor falls. This is practical love. And what about the mutual comfort and togetherness of lying together?

"My feet are cold darling, be my hot water bottle!"

Beyond the physical and personal warmth of marital embracing, there is the other warmth of love given and received when there is a mental "down" or a "spiritual coldness" in either partner. Pray you are not both "down" or "cold" at the same time. This is practical love. But what do we mean by mutual support on the arena of war? No, we are not referring to disagreements or even confrontations within the marriage. If they occur there are Scriptural ways to settle them. We are referring to the Christian warfare; the conflict outside; the spiritual warfare. Sometimes one partner might be wounded. Then practical love binds up. Together they can triumph through Christ. They will be "heirs together" forever.

AUGUST 24 – LOVE IS A "THREESOME"

"…A cord of three strands is not quickly torn apart."[1] This is actually the continuation and conclusion of the "two are better than one" theme and it is not a contradiction as we shall see. There are many Biblical threes; trinities, tri-unities, three-folds, tri-partites and triads but this "three fold cold", this threesome has special relevance to a loving marriage. Firstly, while apparently, but not actually, contradicting the "twosome" emphasis, married people should early stop stressing "me and I" or "you and I" thus reinforcing the separateness of wills, wishes and wants. The emphasis should be moved to "us." There are times when the personal pronouns can be used, but the "ego/I" can cause trouble. "Us" marks the new entity, sweetening and strengthening the marriage, not distancing and separating like "I, me my and mine" can. And "us" makes room for others.

Triangles are an old and wrong geometric pattern in marriage, but here's a lovely and right threesome. As the old song puts it:

"Just Mollie and me, and baby makes three; we're happy in our blue heaven." (George Whiting and Walter Donaldson)

This third strand is another strengthening factor helping to unite the partners in even closer bands of love. This makes possible a new language of love. Father, mother, baby are an improvement on the lovely words of husband and wife. Don't delay too long in bringing, if possible, this third person into the family. If this should prove to be impossible then try to add a child by adoption. Become surrogate parents of even a needy third world child. This is family love too.

There is still another, the most important, cord that will support and sanctify any marriage. Invite this third Party to not only the pre-nuptial planning, but further back still to the pre-courting days. Ask Him to guide you to Mr. or Mrs. Right. If this is done He'll do His part, He'll engineer your circumstances and direct your paths. And of course you will invite Him to the wedding as they did at Cana of Galilee. He will not only grace the ceremony He can make it miraculous. He even became the Master of ceremonies and finally Host to that ceremony, saving the day from disaster. If "me and you" becoming "us" is good and if husband and wife becoming father, mother and child is better, then parents, children, plus Christ is best of all. Heavenly Love is now presiding. He is the high Angle of this triangle. Any Christian marriage can sour if He is not the high Point, holy third Party, outside it and in it. He is the reference Point, the Adjudicator, the Advocate to whom the other parties go, for counsel, comfort and courage when earthly support seems to fail. Our very present Intercessor, high Priest, and Help in trouble is there, closer than hands or feet; closer than breathing. He is as close now spiritually, as He was then physically, at Cana. That couple never regretted inviting Him. Nor will you as you make Him the third Party in completing the "threesome."

256

AUGUST 25 – TENDER LOVING CARE

"The smallest details of economy become noble and delicate when they are lighted by sentiments of tenderness. To furnish a room is not to furnish a room, it is rather to adorn a place where I await my lover; to order supper is not simply to give orders to my cook, it is to amuse myself with delighting him I love; these necessary occupations as seen by one who loves are pleasures a thousand times more lively and touching than the shows and the gambling that constitutes the happiness of those incapable of real love."

These sentiments by Lady Mary Wortley Montagu (1689 – 1762) indicate her idealism regarding marriage.

"She viewed husband and wife as married lovers, a theory not then widely held or admired in the world of marriage à la mode. Her summation of the duties and privileges of the married state are variations on the vows she and Edward had repeated so many years ago. Viewed in the light of their bankrupt union, these lines are as wistful as they are idealistic." Sisters of the Quill Alice A. Hufstader.

Lady Mary, unfortunately, had made a mercenary marriage to a very wealthy, insensitive and older man who turned out to be an indifferent husband. Like her, many today start with high hopes and ideals of domestic married love, full of reciprocal caring and sharing.

Lady Mary uses a word which is a key to happy domestic love. "Tenderness" is what she had hoped for; instead she found her "Prince of the Pits" (he was an owner of coal pits) preoccupied with business and politics. Today we would use the term "tender loving care" as indicative of what Lady Mary had desired and never received. And many a marriage today, even Christian ones, lacks this essential ingredient. Tender loving care is comprised of thoughtfulness, gentleness, and caring love and should be mutual. It is full of understanding and is undemanding. The partner's welfare and pleasure are put before one's own. Tenderness is not weakness or wrong softness, it is strength, governed by love, dedicated to the well-being of the beloved. Are there living examples of tender loving care in the orbit of your knowledge, or even better, in the circle of your experience? And are there examples in Scripture which can aid us in the understanding and practice of it? Yes!

In the area of domestic love I think Joseph, the husband of Mary, and foster father of the baby Jesus, was a good example of tender loving care. His sensitivity is seen in his responses to all the divine commands concerning her, from the time of their engagement, through the journey to Bethlehem, and the later one to Egypt and finally to Nazareth. Tender loving care was exemplified and magnified in dozens of ways. This combination of love and tenderness is Trinitarian in source. The Father exhibits it in countless ways for His family. It is notable in Jesus who showed tender loving care for all His earthly family. We have previously noted that tenderness and love, tender loving care, are a fruit of the Spirit, shown in the marital, domestic realm, and the human family, and in the family of God. So "Be kind to one another, tender-hearted..."[1] Tender loving care saves relationships while its absence destroys them.

AUGUST 26 – CALLED APART BY TENDER LOVING CARE

"…Come away by yourselves to a secluded place and rest a while." (For there were many people coming and going, and they did not even have time to eat.) They went away in the boat to a secluded place by themselves."[1] Our Lord's concerned love for His disciples on this occasion is but an example of his tender loving care for all His servants from then until now. His love is so personal and practical; so knowledgeable and understanding; and so attuned to our physical, mental and spiritual breaking points that He arranges vacation times. If we refuse, for any of many so called reasons, to respond to His loving call to "come apart" then only too often and too sadly we "come apart" in the form of breakdowns, or break ups! The continuing needs of the people and work are often raised as excuses for our inability to cease activities, but deeper down the underlying, and maybe unconscious, thought is my indispensability. Things can't, or won't, go on without me, or they certainly won't go on as well. It is revealing to see that they sometimes go on better. He also in love, called His own apart in preparation for better, deeper and fuller future service. Wrong reasoning aside, there are times when it seems impossible to escape for a needed vacation or for a period of rest, recuperation and reassessment. But we must make and take time out. He has many ways of enforcing it if we don't respond voluntarily to His signals and loving invitations. The reasons behind His loving care in laying us aside are not immediately evident but finally we see and understand. An anonymous writer posed the questions and gave some of the answers for us who may be forcibly sidelined by sickness, circumstances or age's limitations.

"Did He set you aside when the fields were ripe
And the workers seemed so few?
Did He set you aside and give someone else
The task you so longed to do?

Did He set you aside when the purple grapes
Hung low in the autumn sun?
And did hands not your own just gather them in;
The trophies you'd almost won?

Did He set you aside on a couch of pain;
There where all you could do was pray?
And then when you whispered, 'Oh, please let me go.'
Was His answer always, 'Stay'?

Did he set you aside with no plan at all;
With no reason that you could see
While your heart cried out. 'In this limited space,
Lord, how can I work for Thee'?

Did He set you aside with a heavy cross,
And was your heart filled with despair?
Did you think He had gone and left you alone,
Then suddenly He was there?

And there in the shadows, the world all shut out,
Just kneeling alone at His feet,
Did you learn the answers (though not all yet)?
Say weren't His reasons sweet?"

With hindsight we answer "Yes". How much better if, by faith, we respond immediately and gladly to His call to come aside into a "lonely" place and rest awhile. This isolation often results in a deeper spiritual service. We know that He is planning for us in love. "'For I know the plans that I have for you,' declares the Lord, 'plans for welfare and not for calamity to give you a future and a hope.'"[2]

AUGUST 27 – LOVE'S TOUCH

Touching is one of the therapies advocated today in certain circles for certain cases. Perhaps these cases had overdoses of "don't touch" when they were small! Whatever the causes of their inhibitions, right and wrong touching has been with us since Eden. God told the first couple that they could touch, take, and taste anything in the Garden except for the fruit of the tree of the knowledge of good and evil. Up to that time I don't read of even a prohibition against touching the tree of life! After the fall of course that was forbidden, lest the guilty pair take of it and live forever in their fallen estate. So "do touch, don't touch" teaching has been around for a long time.

The word touch in the New Testament has a number of meanings from the usual finger or hand touch, to hold on or even embrace. And another word, sometimes translated touch, has the thought of "feeling with;" our word sympathy comes from this. "For we have not an high priest which cannot be touched with the feeling of our infirmities…"[1] He touched untouchable lepers; touched the sick of all kinds, including the sin sick; touched Peter's mother-in-law and healed her of a fever; touched coffins and dead bodies; touched the eyes of the blind and the ears of the deaf. And He took infants and children into His arms and embraced them. His touch was the all encompassing and all embracing touch of love.

Our Lord once reclined at a table and touched food without ceremonially washing first. This led to His 'woes' upon the Pharisees and Scripture lawyers. "…Woe to you lawyers as well! For you weigh men down with burdens hard to bear, while you yourselves will not even touch the burdens with one of your fingers."[2] The word for touch used here is touch lightly. Those like the Priest and Levite on the Jericho road, wouldn't touch a problem that meant the costly involvement of love, but left that to the Samaritan! Are love-touched Christians touching people?

"'Twas battered and scarred and the old auctioneer
He thought it scarcely worthwhile
To waste much time with the old violin
But he held it up with a smile.

What am I bidden, good folk, he cried
Who'll start the bidding for me
A dollar, a dollar, come, who'll make it two
Two dollars, now who'll make it three.

Three dollars once and three dollars twice
And going for three, but no
From the back of the room a grey haired man
Stepped forward and picked up the bow.

And brushing the dust from the old violin
And tightening up the loose strings
He played a melody pure and so sweet
Sweet as the angels sing.

When the music ceased the old auctioneer
In a voice that was quiet and low
Asked, 'What am I bidden for the old violin?'
And he held it up with the bow.

A thousand dollars — come, who'll make it two
Two thousand, and who'll make it three
Three thousand once and three thousand twice
And going and gone, cried he.

And the people shouted, and some of them cried
We do not quite understand
What changed its worth; swift came the reply
The touch of the master's hand."
Myra Brooks Welch

AUGUST 28 – LOVE'S EXTRAVAGANCE

There are differing accounts by Matthew, Mark and Luke, of the woman whose love caused her to break her alabaster box of costly perfume and pour it out upon the Lord. Some think John's record also refers to the same woman and the same incident. While some details indicate they were not the same, the main emphasis is the same; an expensive gift from an expansive nature showed love's extravagance. For our purpose we will use all four accounts as a composite picture and portrayal of the theme.

Love motivated her to act as she did. Her need, and her knowledge of the Lord's love for sinners, prompted her to go weeping to Him. She not only poured out her tears, but poured out her treasure, without restraint, upon Him. This abandoned extravagance brought high praise from the Saviour and heavy criticism from the unloving and mean-spirited observers which included His own disciples. "Why this waste? For this perfume might have been sold for a high price and the money given to the poor…"[1] Judas the treasurer and betrayer, "knowing the cost of everything but the value of nothing," was even more vehement and detailed. "Why was this perfume not sold for three hundred denarii and given to poor people? Now he said this, not because he was concerned about the poor, but because he was a thief, and as he had the money box, he used to pilfer what was put into it."[2]

Love's extravagance poured out upon the Beloved is never lost. The love, wealth and laid down lives of over two millennia, from the wise mens' gold to the latest martyr, is not, never has been, never will be waste, for love's generosity is never wasted. The love that breaks the box and breaks the bank and pours all on Him bears great interest. Brushing aside their hypocritical concern about the poor He praised the woman's deep love, real faith and prophetic insight. She had anointed Him beforehand for His burial. There was no post-mortem loving here!

"Do not keep the alabaster box of your love and tenderness sealed up until your friends are dead. Fill their lives with sweetness. Speak approving, cheering words while their ears can hear them, and while their hearts can be thrilled and made happier. The kind things you mean to say before they are gone say before they go. The flowers you mean to send for their coffin send to brighten and sweeten their homes before they leave them. If my friends have alabaster boxes laid away, full of fragrant perfumes of sympathy and affection, which they intend to break over my body, I would rather they bring them out in my weary and troubled hours and open them, that I may be refreshed and cheered while I need them. I would rather have a plain coffin without flowers, a funeral without an eulogy, than a life without the sweetness and love emanating from sympathy. Let us learn to anoint our friends, while they are yet among the living. Post-mortem kindness does not cheer the burdened heart; flowers on the coffin cast no fragrance backward over the weary way." George W. Childs

AUGUST 29 – LOVE'S FRAGRANCE

"And when we obey Him, every path He guides us on is fragrant with His lovingkindness and His truth."[1] "But thanks be to God, who always leads us in triumph in Christ, and manifests through us the sweet aroma of the knowledge of Him in every place. For we are a fragrance of Christ to God among those who are being saved and among those who are perishing; to the one an aroma from death to death, to the other an aroma from life to life…"[2] Taken together these portions from the Old and New Testaments teach us some precious truths concerning love's fragrance.

"When we walk with the Lord
In the light of His Word,
What a glory He sheds on our way!
While we do His good will,
He abides with us still,
And with all who will trust and obey.

But we never can prove
The delights of His love
Until all on the altar we lay;
For the favor He shows,
For the joy He bestows
Are for them who will trust and obey."
John Sammis (1846 – 1919)

And we have not only seen the Glory on our way we have smelt the fragrance of His presence and His lovingkindness. Truly we can say, sense and smell with the Psalmist, what he stated about Christ: "You have loved righteousness and hated wickedness; Therefore God, Your God, has anointed You with the oil of joy above Your fellows. All Your garments are fragrant with myrrh and aloes and cassia. Out of ivory palaces…"[3] The great hymn "Out of the Ivory Palaces" Henry Barraclough (1891 – 1983) describes and gives meaning to the essential essences that made this fragrance so rich and rare. In the path of loving duty we are greeted by the delightful aroma of love's fragrance.

The Levitical sweet fragrance offerings are so called because they typify Christ in all His own perfections, and in His loving obedience and affectionate devotion to His Father's will. And because we are in Him the sweet fragrance of Christ should be given forth by us. Years ago in the city of Melbourne, Australia, I was riding in one of the old city tram cars which was packed with passengers, sitting and standing. Suddenly the car was filled with the sweet smell of violets. Near me, an apologetic man got up from a lady's lap where he had fallen after a jolting stop. In falling, he had crushed a bouquet of violets she was carrying which immediately gave out their essential, innate perfume. I thought to myself: "I wonder if the sweet aroma of the love of Christ issues from me when I am sat upon or "set upon?" He manifests through us the sweet aroma of the knowledge of Him in every place. For we are a fragrance of Christ to unsaved and saved alike. They not only see us, they use that other sense; the sense of smell. Am I a stench or a sweet savour? Love is sometimes stern but always sweet. It is honest and loving; it speaks truth in love. A well known evangelist is reputed to have replied, when asked why, as an old man and a widower, he had married a very young Christian lady "I wanted to smell perfume not liniment!" Whatever we make of this answer there will be, in the truly Christian love fragrance, both the smell of perfume and liniment. The balm of Gilead is a balsam; our lives and message are an aroma from death to death for some, and life to life for others. Love is both a pungent and an unguent.

AUGUST 30 – LOVE AND WORSHIP – Part One

The adoration of love on the human level is to revere the partner by regarding her, or him, with the utmost respect, devotion, esteem and honour. It is to love the lover with the highest degree possible and permissible as man to woman and woman to man. Is this sort of language inappropriate? Is it too strong for this most universal of the lesser loves? Hear the Scriptural commands again. "Husbands, love your wives, just as Christ also loved the church and gave Himself up for her[1]...each individual among you also is to love his own wife even as himself, and the wife must see to it that she respects her husband."[2] The King James Version uses the word reverence. It is the same godly fear, reverential awe, rightful respect that on the higher level is demanded and given to God as we worship Him. "I love you" and "I adore you" and "I worship you" and "I respect and reverence you" are the highest tributes that a man can pay a woman and vice versa. The older form of the marriage service contained these words "And with my body I thee worship." It's a pity it was discontinued.

The love that produces the worship of God is the highest level love. It is His gift of His Son by His Spirit, inducing and producing love and worship in us and from us. "But an hour is coming, and now is, when the true worshipers will worship the Father in spirit and truth; for such people the Father seeks to be His worshipers. God is spirit, and those who worship Him must worship in spirit and truth."[3] The Saviour of the world gave these words to the sinful, Samaritan woman to whom He had shown courtesy, kindness and love. He corrected her wrong notions about worship and put His finger on the sin in her life and she became a saved woman, a spiritual worshipper and a splendid witness. Personal salvation produces deep love in the deeply forgiven; this in turn produces loving spiritual worship, heart to heart communion, followed by the outward devotional acts of giving. Thus did this other sinful, weeping, loving, forgiven, woman who anointed Christ's feet with the perfume from her alabaster box. This is love and worship. This is love worshipping the One of worth, the worth One; for worship derives from "worth-ship."

"With my body I Thee worship" is another act of this high level holy devotion. "Therefore I urge you, brethren, by the mercies of God, to present your bodies a living and holy sacrifice, acceptable to God, which is your spiritual service of worship."[4] As on the lower level the body presented is an act of worshipful love so it is, and much more so, on the highest. This brings glory to God and is the goal of love and worship. The loving worshipful sacrifice of our selves, our songs and our substance all done in the Spirit, is the highest praise and the chief good we can render and offer to God.

AUGUST 31 – LOVE AND WORSHIP – Part Two

"More love to Thee, O Christ, more love to Thee!
Hear Thou the prayer I make on bended knee.
This is my earnest plea: More love, O Christ, to Thee;
More love to Thee, more love to Thee!

Once earthly joy I craved, sought peace and rest;
Now Thee alone I seek, give what is best.
This all my prayer shall be: More love, O Christ to Thee;
More love to Thee, more love to Thee!"
Elizabeth P Prentiss (1818 – 1878)

John Donne (1573 – 1631) was led to the love of God by way of the love of a woman, his beloved Anne, who became his wife. He was not the first, nor will he become the last, to be so led. Led via the lower to the higher. And in one sense we all come this way. A mother's love, or another's love, is the first we know; sometimes these loves are like John the Baptist, way-preparers for the Christ and His love. These lesser loves must be careful, as John was, not to usurp the bridegroom's position. The best man is really only second best. John knew this and was careful to state it "…After me comes a Man who has a higher rank than I, for He existed before me."[1] "He who has the bride is the bridegroom; but the friend of the bridegroom, who stands and hears him, rejoices greatly because of the bridegroom's voice. So this joy of mine has been made full. He must increase, but I must decrease."[2] We must learn and apply what John knew and stated. The lesser is contained in, and blessed by, the greater. Lesser loves have their place but must never usurp the higher. Before he found his true earthly love, who helped him on to the heavenly Love, Donne was undone by previous loves who led him away from, not up to, the Highest. Let us heed the warning; wrongful worship of the lower loves can destroy the faculty for true love and worship of Christ.

Another warning is needed today for some who are misled by the increasing worshipful love of Mary making her a mediatrix and calling her the Queen of Heaven. This latter title has had bad antecedents in Scripture. The Word of God says of Mary through Spirit filled Elizabeth: "…Blessed are you among women, and blessed is the fruit of your womb!"[3] "And Mary said: 'My soul exalts the Lord, And my spirit has rejoiced in God my Savior.'"[4] She worshipped God with devoted triune love, as she presented her body to Him for His holy use, as she exalted Him in her soul, and exalted in Him with her spirit. Her love and worship of Him should be an example for us. We should not exalt her to the Trinity and the Throne, nor love and worship her; even with "lutria" which is described as a lower form of worship, something between the lower worship love of man for woman and the highest love and worship of God by humans. Christ is the only mediator between God and man. "…'Who is My mother and who are My brothers?' And stretching out His hand toward His disciples, He said, 'Behold My mother and My brothers! For whoever does the will of My Father who is in heaven, he is My brother and sister and mother.'"[5] As the Lord commanded, we must "hate" any rightful lower loves or worship that would distract, disrupt or destroy the higher loves and worship.

SEPTEMBER 1 – AN ARRANGED LOVE MARRIAGE

Does God go before the godly in the very important area of love and marriage? There is a Scripture promise which guides us and answers in the affirmative. "Trust in the Lord with all your heart and do not lean on your own understanding. In all your ways acknowledge Him, and He will make your paths straight."[1] And then there is the direct promise of faith which Abraham gave to his servant on finding a bride for Isaac. This is, in its happy outcome of divine guidance in the quest, a promise which we can also take for ourselves today. The servant took Abraham's word as the Word of God to him and acted upon it. We can do the same. "…go to my country and to my relatives, and take a wife for my son Isaac.[2]… He will send His angel before you, and you will take a wife for my son from there."[3] This promise is amplified in the New Testament to cover all the manifold areas of our living including love, marriage and a life partner. "When he puts forth all his own, he goes ahead of them…"[4]

The story of the servant's journey, his faith and prayer and the miraculous timing of events that followed, makes thrilling reading. Abraham's desire for the right kind of wife for his son, is surely echoed by all Christian parents for their children. While that was an arranged marriage it was certainly "arranged" from heaven as well as on earth. Our children make their own choices; we give them the principles and pray for their submission to God's will and direction. As that faithful steward's stewardship was wonderfully rewarded, so today we dare to believe that the same will be so in our stewardship. Bethuel and Laban saw divine providence at work and were quick to agree that the decision was out of their hands. In the end Rebekah made the decision. Her glad and immediate "I will" has been echoed by millions since.

Several areas of love came together as Rebekah said that. Abraham's love for his son; the servant's love for Abraham; her family's love for Rebekah and God's love for them all. The choice was made by love involving all parties including the girl who loved "by faith" in the description of the faithful witness. And the groom was waiting to love; sight unseen! It was a good choice - she got a good, gentle, and loving man. A man who goes out to the field to meditate in the evening is becoming almost as rare as the fields. A quiet, peace loving, country loving, God loving man is a treasure. And what kind of person did Isaac get? A good, friendly, capable, decisive, full of faith, hospitable, second miler (one of the servant's tests) and a beautiful young girl.

So they met in the field, wed in his mother's tent, and commenced their married life with these lovely words: "…she became his wife, and he loved her…"[5] And that's where the fadeout usually comes with the cliché "And they lived happily ever afterwards." They should have, for any marriage conceived and consummated under such circumstances, should end well. That it didn't is not to deny the divine love, guidance and providence shown. "Made in heaven" and "made for each other" was true, but marriage is also "made on earth" and sometimes "unmade on earth." Why did it go wrong? We will look again at Isaac and Rebekah.

SEPTEMBER 2 – WHAT WENT WRONG IN THIS LOVE MARRIAGE?

Love, like life, sometimes starts well but ends badly. And, thank God, the reverse is also true. Why did the marriage of Isaac and Rebekah seem to run out of love? It began as a really "made in heaven" marriage. It began so well. True it was an arranged affair, as most were in those days. But people can and do fall in love in arranged marriages as well as in the Jacob and Rachel case of falling in love before marriage. We don't have all the facts, but we see enough in Scripture to give some answers. God forbid that this should be looked upon as an autopsy on the marriage of Isaac and Rebekah. After all they didn't divorce or separate. But there was division at the end in some areas and seeming disappointment. What we are doing is looking at the anatomy of this relationship for our own edification. We are told that Old Testament happenings are given as examples for us and are written for our instruction.

So we start where we left them: "Just Married." Did any couple get off to such an apparently good start? There are several factors to note at the outset. There was an age differential, Isaac was forty when he married and sixty when his twin sons were born. Rebekah was a very much younger woman. Many a December – June marriage has turned out happily. There had been real love at the beginning of Isaac's and Rebekah's marriage. But a large difference in age can certainly test love in the later years of marriage. Isaac at sixty, when his first and only children came, was not old for those days, but by the time his sons were forty and marrying, he was one hundred and almost blind. Children coming late, though long desired, prayed for and loved can be a strain and in this case were a cause of division. Need this be so? No! Is it so? Too often, yes!

The second point to note is this. Isaac had been intensely, possessively loved by his mother Sarah. We are told that at the marriage "Then Isaac brought her into his mother Sarah's tent, and he took Rebekah, and she became his wife, and he loved her; thus Isaac was comforted after his mother's death."[1] His mother's funeral and his own wedding coming so close upon it, and the use of his mother's tent, raises this question. Did he really leave his mother and cleave to his wife as Scripture enjoins? Despite all the love, on so many levels, that brought this couple together, marriage has to be worked at practically in so many down to earth areas. This is one such area.

The third point to note has to do with the child loving and rearing stages. Here there was partiality and favouritism. "… Isaac loved Esau…but Rebekah loved Jacob."[2] This can be psychologically damaging to the children and destructive to the marriage. Parents don't play favourites; love all equally. The children will know it and show it if you don't.

There remains one more thing to look at in answer to "What went wrong?" Isaac was a placid, peace loving man willing to be acted upon rather than acting and he was incapacitated. Rebekah was a manager, able, decisive, loving her boy and getting him what she felt he deserved. She had her way, but lost her husband's and also Jacob's esteem.

SEPTEMBER 3 – MISMATCHED AND MISMATED LOVE

These pages have sought the linkages between love in the Bible and love in the human condition. Because the Bible is the book of eternal life and also describes our life on earth the connections are not hard to see. Again and again the Biblical illustrations have leapt to mind when we have sought to examine these themes. But before giving the Scripture stories on mismatched and mismated love let us hear a poet on the subject and make some other observations on it.

"Why have such scores of lovely, gifted girls
Married impossible men?
Simple self-sacrifice may be ruled out,
And missionary endeavor, nine times out of ten.

Repeat "impossible men": not merely rustic,
Foul-tempered or depraved
(Dramatic foils chosen to show the world
How well women behave, and always have behaved).

Impossible men: idle, illiterate,
Self-pitying, dirty, sly,
For whose appearance even in City parks
Excuses must be made to casual passers-by

Has God's supply of tolerable husbands
Fallen, in fact, so low?
Or do I always over-value woman
At the expense of man?"
Robert Graves (1895 – 1985)

Two world wars killed millions of potentially "tolerable husbands." I have heard women say that they lost lovers and fiancés in these conflicts. These women never married choosing the single state over a relationship with "impossible men." But surely the main reason for mismatches and mismating must be the "love is blind" syndrome. I know it's a cliché, but there's a lot of truth in clichés. Blindness sees no faults, no flaws and no failings. Blind obsession cannot reason nor understand incompatibilities of body, mind and spirit. Love's loss of sight so often brings the blight of mismatching and mismating. Short-sighted blindness cannot see the distant scenes when passion cools and reality sets in.

This is particularly so in the case of the "unequal yoke." "Do not be bound together with unbelievers…"[1] The context gives the reasons why; how can professed believers be so blind and disobedient? You'll hear infatuation say:

"He (she) loves me; he (she) promises to go to church. I'll convert him (her)!"

It often works the other way!

There is the classic story in the Old Testament of a lovely, gifted, gracious, capable woman married to a selfish, short sighted, narrow minded, arrogant boor who happened to be wealthy in flocks and lands. How come she married him? Abigail was married to Nabal and finally frustrated with him explains: "Please do not let my lord pay attention to this worthless man, Nabal, for as his name is, so is he. Nabal is his name and folly is with him…"[2] Why did she marry a fool? Perhaps she had no choice as marriages in those days were mostly arranged. Or he may have changed through avarice coupled with drink for he was a drunk. He had also insulted David and only Abigail's wise intervention and actions saved her and her husband. Later shock and fear caused him to have a heart attack and he died. Thus the mismatch ended. There is a happy conclusion to the story. Abigail became the wife of David.

SEPTEMBER 4 – MARRIAGE DISABILITIES – Part One

Disabilities in marriage can become apparent early, even in those which begin by the couple "being in love". There are built in impediments which neither discovers until after the honeymoon. There are incompatibilities of background and person; of mind and spirit. Disagreements arise over roles; money; life styles; division of work and responsibilities in the home; the number and raising of children. These can develop in the nitty gritty of day to day living together. We have seen, in the Biblical examples of Isaac and Rebekah, of Nabal and Abigail, that love in the beginning is no guarantee of its continuing without work and effort, and that its loss, including loss of respect, can have tragic outcomes. In looking dispassionately at love and disabilities in marriage we have left romanticism for realism. Can friendship love alone sustain a marriage?

Elizabeth Robinson Montagu (1720 – 1800) though well known in her age is not known now. She was very down to earth and did not live on cloud nine. "Fidget" Robinson, before marriage was very observant.

"When nineteen, with smallpox stalking the land, Elizabeth whose health was never robust, was sent from home to be quarantined among strangers. She describes her surroundings: 'The Goodman and his wife snored, the little child cry'd, the maid screamed, one little boy had whooping cough, another screamed with chilblains'. Equally courageous was the philosophy she brought to bear upon her privation. 'I endeavour…to be wise when I cannot be merry, easy when I cannot be glad, content with what cannot be mended and patient when there is no redress.'" Sisters of the Quill Alice A. Hufstader

What did "Fidget," the girl with her eyes open, think about love and marriage, and how did she fare in the marriage mart of those days? Elizabeth knew her mind and rejected love in the romantic sense. Her friends declared her to be an ignoramus in love.

"Lacking an emotional view of matrimony, she planned her marriage in a business like spirit…Setting aside tenderness for a cheerful materialism, she pronounces that 'Gold is the chief ingredient in the composition of worldly happiness.' (One of the early Goldiggers. 'Diamonds are a girl's best friend!') Living in a cottage on love is certainly the worst diet and the worst habitation one can find…"

So she married when she was twenty-three, wealthy Edward Montagu, who was fifty-one! It was not a merely mercenary marriage à la mode. Theirs was the love of friendship rather than passion. Did it work? Yes, after a fashion. He became a kindly recluse, she a very capable manager of his collieries and farms. She wrote to her husband:

"In a good marriage each has the credit of the other's virtues; they have double honour, united interests… This, my dearest, is my happier lot, enriched by your fortune, enabled by your virtues, graced by your character and supported by your interest."

A bit fulsome and smug this! But the twenty-eight year span between Mrs. Montagu in her early fifties and "His honour" (as she called her husband when he annoyed her) now began to make itself felt. She found herself responsible for a peevish old man who objected to her comings and goings. She wrote an angry letter to her sister about him objecting to her visiting…(to be continued)

SEPTEMBER 5 – MARRIAGE DISABILITIES – Part Two

(continued)

"Do you not admire these lovers of liberty! What do the generality of men mean by a love of liberty but the liberty to be saucy to their superiors, and arrogant to their inferiors, to resist the powers of others over them, and to exert their powers over others."

She's not only having a dig at the upstart colonials in America in 1772, soon to turn a domestic disagreement with the motherland into a revolution, she was letting off steam concerning domestic differences with "His honour", he husband now not so doting, but in his dotage. As her aging husband declined into senility she cultivated platonic friendships with well known contemporaries through conversation and correspondence.

"Mr. Montagu died just after the outbreak of the American Revolution. His last illness was long and difficult, with the result that his harassed wife wrote more of the sick rook than of Concord and Lexington. She was left an extremely rich widow and mistress of all her husband's holdings."

And that's where we leave her.

This examination of friendship love and disabilities in the Montagu marriage began with a question: Can friendship love alone sustain a marriage? The answer would seem to be a qualified "Yes" if both partners work at it; if they go their own ways and if there's lots of money to play with! A very iffy proposition and answer.

But the question must be broadened. Can any kind of natural love maintain and fulfill the expectations humans have in the institution of marriage? I answer with an unequivocal "No". Exceptions come to mind and I will be challenged on this. I repeat what these pages have emphasized. Only the love of God continually filling our hearts by the Holy Spirit can sanctify and enable romantic and friendship loves, and enable and enrich them in matrimony. Marital love becomes what our Maker meant it to be when agapé governs it. And governs it until the end when duty often replaces delights and when disparities, disabilities and disappointments could destroy it. Then heavenly love really comes into its own, and lightens and brightens the difficulties that often crowd in towards the end. Dismaying diseases, dotage, senility, all have to be faced as possibilities, probabilities or realities. Who or what is sufficient for these things? Human resources and all the natural loves are not sufficient. One partner has often to bear the burdens alone; yet he or she is not alone; we can cast all our cares on Him; His grace is, and will be sufficient; His love and His promises will never fail.

Some passages in Hebrews can help us in these very practical down to earth, down to the finishing circumstances of our life and loves. "Marriage is to be held in honor among all, and the marriage bed is to be undefiled…"[1] "Make sure that your character is free from the love of money, being content with what you have; for He Himself has said, 'I will never desert you, nor will I ever forsake you,' so that we confidently say, 'The Lord is my helper, I will not be afraid…'"[2] "Through Him then, let us continually offer up a sacrifice of praise to God, that is, the fruit of lips that give thanks to His name."[3] "Let love of the brethren continue."[4]

SEPTEMBER 6 – DISAPPOINTED IN LOVE?

We cannot be human without sometimes disappointing others, and being disappointed by them, in many areas of love. To face these facts, built into human nature and the human condition, is a first step in our delivery from false romantic love notions and nonsense. There is plenty of room and need for progress and maturing in love in the manifold meanings of that word both in and outside of marriage. We have seen how two people, Isaac and Rebekah, began well in the affairs of the heart but later in their own marriage and family relationships there was much disappointment. Many marrieds in our day, it would appear, are both disappointed and disillusioned in their love life after the first novelty wears off. The reasons are many and known, and it is not our purpose to turn this page into a marriage counselling column. Lots of singles have also been disappointed in love; in parental, social, friendship loves as well as the jilting, jolting affects of romantic love gone wrong.

What we want to emphasize here is the fact that divine love is never a disappointment. We may not understand or appreciate the ways of agapé's planning or working in our lives, but we must hold fast to the truth that the God of love, who wills only good for His children, cannot deny His nature, nor disappoint them in any realm of love. The fault and disappointment is in us.

J. N. Darby (1800 – 1882) carried in his Bible an article, which had been translated from French, and bore the title "Disappointments?" and a Scriptural statement: "…this thing is from Me…"[1]

"The disappointments of life are in reality only the decrees of love. I have a message for thee today. My child, I will whisper it softly in thine ear, in order that the storm clouds which appear may be gilt with glory, and that the thorns on which thou mayest have to walk be blunted. The message is but short, a tiny sentence, but allow it to sink into the depths of thine ear, and be to thee as a cushion on which to rest thine weary head: 'This thing is from Me.'"

Disappointments are the decrees of love. That phrase should be memorized and called up whenever circumstances or people disappoint us. Mrs. Frankie Brogan received this message as she tells us in her book, The Snare of the Fowler. Her son had been brainwashed by the Children of God movement under the leader David Berg (1919 – 1994) (who called himself Moses David) and his infamous "Mo" letters. During the years of praying, waiting and working for her son's deliverance she came to the end of herself and was helped there by this word: "This thing is from Me," and the message of the whole long article.

"I continued to read…Hast thou never thought that all which concerns thee, concerns Me also? He that toucheth thee toucheth the apple of mine eye. That is why I take a special interest in thine upbringing…I am the God of circumstances. Thou hast not been placed where thou art by chance, but because it is the place I have chosen for thee…Art thou passing through a night of affliction? 'This thing is from Me'…The sting will go in the measure in which thou seest Me in all things. Therefore set your heart unto all the words that I testify among you this day. For it is your life."

She was not disappointed in love.

SEPTEMBER 7 – JACOB "FALLS IN LOVE"

The love story of Jacob and Rachel is so real, romantic and relevant that we must explore it in more detail and follow it, in its ups and downs, "until death did them part." They were married for less than twenty memorable years. Rachel was Jacob's first, and in the romantic sense, his only love. Her loss was traumatic and he mourned her until his dying day nearly eighty years later. Let's examine this intense love story for our own edification. The lessons are many.

It is, in its manners, morals and mores, a very different marriage than we would expect. Yet as always with Bible stories, it is important that we remember their era and geographical location. This desert love song was sung, seventeen hundred years before the birth of Christ, in the plain of Aram, the land between the great Tigris and Euphrates rivers. This Eastern romance was very different in setting and standards from what we know and experience in our Western culture today. Yet there is one unchanging similarity. Human nature has not changed. Jacob "fell in love" with an ardour like a consuming flame. The language of love bridges the millennia, and the experience of love is as up-to-date as today.

There is another underlying truth that is unchanging. When God is recognized as "Chargé d' affaires" of the heart and life, happy outcomes can be expected. This romance was divinely planned. Jacob's long lonely journey had a marvellous intervention and revelation in which Jacob came to see that God was all knowing, everywhere present and all powerful. With such a God in charge no wonder Jacob's quest had such a miraculously happy ending. Jacob and Rachel's first meeting was arranged by the One who had gone before them. They came together as two merging flames leap to embrace. She was "...beautiful of form and face,"[1] while he, though over forty, was as smitten as a teenager.

His feelings of love can be deduced from the beautiful description of his emotional state. It is memorable in language and depicts a love of quality and depth that is rare and real in its willingness to wait and sacrifice for the loved one. "Now Jacob loved Rachel, so he said, (to Laban, her father) 'I will serve you seven years for your younger daughter Rachel.'[2]... So Jacob served seven years for Rachel and they seemed to him but a few days because of his love for her."[3] Finally, the self-inflicted servitude ended, and Jacob, now nearing fifty, claimed his bride. Despite another setback, this marriage, made in heaven, was consummated on earth.

Their love, after long waiting, produced two sons, Joseph and Benjamin. The latter's birth caused his mother's tragic death. She was buried on the road to Bethlehem by her grieving sixty year old husband. Suddenly bereft of his beloved Rachel, he lived on until he was one hundred and forty seven years old, but never forgot her.

SEPTEMBER 8 – HANNAH, LOVED AND LOVING

My mother's Christian names were Mary Hannah, and they could not have been more Biblical; one from the Old Testament and one from the New. I have often wondered why my maternal grandparents chose those names for their first born. I don't think in 1880 they were any more popular than in 1974 when mother died in her ninety-fifth year. I like to think that Grandma and Granddad chose them because they were Christians and wanted their daughter to have really Christian and Biblical names, and to grow up to be like those Biblical namesakes. She did. Mary is the Greek form of the Hebrew Miriam and has, we are told, the meaning "bitter." When we think of the bitter experiences of the New Testament "Marys," especially of our Lord's mother, we can see the appropriateness of the name of that especially chosen and choice one. Mary suited one side of my mother's nature for she was, I see in retrospect, in temperament mainly a melancholic, like her father. She was a quiet, thoughtful, loving person, who, in her later years especially, chose, like that other Mary, to be at Jesus' feet waiting, watching, worshiping and listening. But it is the Hannah character that we want to discuss now. The name means "grace." It was prophetically given to my mother for she became what she was finally, because of the grace of God. I honour my mother Hannah as a gracious and above all a loving woman.

The Biblical Hannah was loved and loving. Unfortunately she was in an invidious, impossible situation. Her bitter circumstances arose because God's will, as was commonly the case in those days, concerning marriage had been disobeyed. Monogamy had given way to polygamy. Elkanah, the husband, had two wives, Hannah and Peninnah. The latter had children; the former none. Elkanah was a good husband and loving father, generous, and saw to it that the family worshipped and sacrificed regularly at Jerusalem. To Hannah, the childless, he gave double portions, because he loved her. Her longing love drove her to prayer; to the God she loved. She asked from distress, with bitter weeping, a specific request for a son, and made accompanying vows, that if granted, the boy would be dedicated to lifelong Levitical service and would be a Nazarite. She made this prayer in the temple on one of their annual pilgrimages. And on their return home to Ramah "…Elkanah had relations with Hannah his wife, and the Lord remembered her. It came about in due time, after Hannah had conceived, that she gave birth to a son; and she named him Samuel, saying, 'Because I have asked him of the Lord.'"[1] She loved this baby with a special love that gave him back, literally, to God whom she loved more. She took him back to the temple and gave him to the high priest Eli, saying: "For this boy I prayed[2]…so I have also dedicated him to the Lord…"[3] And that is Hannah, loved and loving on the highest plane.

SEPTEMBER 9 – LOVE'S SERENDIPITIES

Some of us know by experience the joy of being surprised by love. Suddenly it came; out of the blue. We were smitten unexpectedly by the arrow with the sweetened tip. Unquestionably we have fallen in love; blessed surprise, beautiful fall! We are scornful of the bruises and ignorant of the blindness that beclouds our eyes; we see only the beauty and bounty of the beloved. Others may wonder, doubt and query - let them. For us beauty is in the eye of the beholder and bliss in the arms of the holder. And then there are the numerous other felicitous surprises that come our way seemingly, though not by chance or happenstance. As Helen Steiner Rice (1900 – 1981) tells us:

"Into our lives come many things
To break the dull routine.
The things we had not planned on
That happen unforeseen.

The unexpected little joys
That are scattered on our way.
Success we did not count on
Or a rare, fulfilling day.

A catchy, lilting melody
That makes us want to dance.
A nameless exaltation
Of enchantment and romance.

An unsought word of kindness,
A compliment or two
That sets the eyes to gleaming
Like crystal drops of dew.

The unplanned sudden meeting
That comes with sweet surprise
And lights the heart with happiness
Like a rainbow in the skies...

Now some folks call it fickle fate
And some folks call it chance,
While others just accept it
As pleasant happenstance

But no matter what you call it
It didn't come without design,
For all our lives are fashioned
By the Hand that is divine.

And every happy happening
And every lucky break
Are little gifts from God above
That are ours to freely take."

These are the serendipities of love. Serendipity is a word coined by Horace Walpole (1717 – 1797) in 1754. It comes from "Serendip" the old name for Ceylon, now Sri Lanka.. I learned the word in this fashion. I used to ride a bicycle from the Mission Headquarters in Bridgetown, Barbados to the Christian Literature Crusade store. Everyday I passed a tourist guest house with the intriguing name "Serendipity." Finally, I satisfied my curiosity and dispelled my ignorance, by going to the dictionary. That inn-keeper must have been kept busy explaining "Serendipity." The serendipities flowing from the love of God are constantly surprising us. What a happy day when we discovered Christ's saving power. That curious, concerned, little man Zaccheus, climbing his tree to see Jesus was happily, unexpectedly, called to come down and receive Christ into his heart and home. He had no idea as the day dawned, that the supreme serendipity of meeting the Saviour and experiencing His salvation would be his lovely lot. Our God is the serendipitous source of all the other lovely, unexpected, joyous events that delight our days. He prompts loved ones, friends and acquaintances to think and plan pleasant surprises for us. And even apart from these secondary sources we are continually making happy, seemingly accidental, discoveries of heavenly origin hid in earth. Pharaoh's dreams; the cup-bearers jogged memory combining under God brought thirty year old Joseph from prison to palace. The serendipities of love sublime surprised him that day.

SEPTEMBER 10 – WHAT A LOVELY DAY

The Lord has made every day, so each can be lovely. A dreary day can be brightened by the trite, though kind, expression:

"Have a nice day!"

It is a common saying of store clerks or others who had served you on any capacity. Some grouches resented it but most people were appreciative and responded accordingly. As confession is good for the soul I will state that temperamentally I am a mixture of the choleric and melancholic which I described in the reading "The Love of God and Our Temperaments" (June 29). As my wife, so patient can attest, in my early days I allowed my moods to darken, not only my day, but hers and the children's as well.

Early in my Christian life I found, with a friend, a simple and lovely way to change a down-beat attitude or mood, into an up-beat one. It's a pity I didn't practice more what I learned with my friend Ron Maxwell. He was my closest friend at Bible College in the 1930's and we spent our vacations together in country mission work. We would pack our bicycles and set off, by faith, on gospel tours, trusting the Lord for a sleeping spot in church halls (prayer cushions make a good mattress if they are not fixed on the kneeling stands); also looking to Him to supply meals and, or, money. We may have been naïve, but we were simple souls, intent on witnessing for the Lord in nightly open-air meetings. We drummed or rang up (we carried a bell!) our own congregation. All this was good preparation for the foreign field. But the best preparation was a self-discovery I made. I found out that circumstances seemed to affect my emotions and moods and Ron's also to a degree. We were, under these conditions, and in these moods, hardly a victorious team ready to go out and fight the battles of the Lord. And then we made a happy discovery. During prayer sessions together we found that if we prefaced these with a chorus or a hymn then gloom had to go. Moodiness sometimes needs a swift loving kick, or a laughing at, not soppy commiseration; temperaments need the changing power of the Spirit, while both moods and attitudes can be altered by music that can help the saints in their day to day battles. Ludwig van Beethoven's (1770 – 1827) magnificent music still moves us mightily! His "Hymn to Joy" with words by Henry van Dyke (1852 – 1933), says it all.

"Joyful, joyful, we adore Thee,
God of glory, Lord of love;
Hearts unfold like flowers before Thee,
Opening to the sun above.

Melt the clouds of sin and sadness;
Drive the dark of doubt away;
Giver of immortal gladness,
Fill us with the light of day!

Thou art giving and forgiving,
Ever blessing, ever blessed,
Wellspring of the joy of living,
Ocean depth of happy rest!

Thou our Father, Christ our Brother,
All who live in love are Thine;
Teach us how to love each other,
Lift us to the joy divine."

What a day for love! What a day to be loving! What a day to be loved! "A man that hath friends must shew himself friendly…"[1] If I personally complain that "no one loves me!" then why is that? Perhaps I am not loving or friendly. Perhaps I only want to receive love and affection, not give it. I respond: "How can I give what I don't have?" Right. And here's the remedy as stated by the great, good and loving Physician: "But for you who fear My name, the sun of righteousness will rise with healing in its wings; and you will go forth and skip about like calves from the stall."[2]

SEPTEMBER 11 – MARRIAGES

Marriages come in all kinds. There are serene or stormy ones. They are sometimes long, or short, or in between. Some are loving and some are hateful. They can be blissful or blightful. Some are growing and expanding, others shrinking and drying up. Some breathe life, others reek of death. "They lived happily ever after" used to be the trite ending to some Victorian novels, but false romanticism will not make a happy marriage. That has to develop by mutual work, understanding and short account keeping. Confession, forgiveness and forgetting are all essential elements. Of course, both being born again Christians as the marriage commences will be a distinct advantage, but disasters and divorces are not unknown in these circles. The lordship of Christ in both lives is necessary for success as is a heart acceptance of the Biblical principle regarding the roles of husband and wife.

Two modern books by William J. Petersen tell the stories of six couples, five from the past and one famous contemporary marriage, that of Billy (1918 -) and Ruth (1926 -) Graham, and in this case her own book <u>It's My Turn</u> is highly recommended reading. The two books are: <u>Martin Luther had a Wife</u> and <u>Harriet Beecher Stowe had a Husband</u>. Most of us have read about Luther (1483 – 1546) but know little about his ex-nun wife. Calvin Stowe (1802 – 1886), Harriet Beecher's (1811 – 1896) husband, was much more than that! John Calvin's (1509 – 1564) wife was a widow named Idolette and they buried all three children born in the nine years of their marriage. She was a loving, calming wife. William Carey (1761 – 1834) married three times. His first wife, Dorothy, went insane. Adoniram Judson (1788 – 1850), another missionary, and his wife Anne overcame awesome problems in overseas service in the nineteenth century and achieved a successful, but short, marriage.

The refreshing thing about these five stories about people long dead is that the portrayals tell things like they were. They do not gloss over faults and failures, but point out, for our encouragement and edification, why things went wrong, and, thank God, why things went right. The Word of God has a lot to say about love and marriage and it gives living examples of marriages like Abraham and Sarah, Isaac and Rebekah, Jacob and Rachel, with their calms and storms, successes and failures. These are told at length, with a wealth of detail, with lessons for all of us in the married state today. The circumstances are different, but human nature has not changed, and neither has the grace, goodness and love of God. When He guided these marriages He used the human elements and allowed their free wills to, sometimes seemingly, frustrate His will. Yet, in the end, His over-ruling worked out His purposes for His glory and their good.

Scripture also gives short, sharp, portraits of marriages that were not only difficult but doomed. We noted Abigail's marriage to a man whose name described him, Nabal or fool. The ending was sudden and severe for him, but the aftermath was surprising and joyous for her. In contrast, the short, sweet, record of Ruth and Boaz is a heart warming love story of a June to December relationship that went on from strength to strength and merged into the human lineage of Christ. We will look more at these Biblical relationships.

SEPTEMBER 12 – LOVE'S GIVING IN THE BOOK OF RUTH

The four chapters in the little book of Ruth are a love story on many levels in many lives. The word love is found only once in the book but it is present everywhere. Elimelech and Naomi, husband and wife, evidently had a loving marriage but we are told only of the hardship and losses including the death of Elimelech. There two sons married in Moab but we are not told of their romance or love; only that Mahlon and Chilion died and left Orpah and Ruth widows. The story at its commencement is more funeral than wedding match.

However, the basic theme of self giving love begins to shine forth in motivation and action as Naomi plans her return to Judah. She urges the young widows to remain in their own land and their own homes. They will be happier there with more possibilities for remarriage. Naomi thinks with her heart and head for the welfare of her daughters-in-law. Orpah accepts the wise love-inspired advice and returns, and that is the end of her story.

Ruth, by love's inspiration, made her choice in the memorable words: "…Do not urge me to leave you or turn back from following you; for where you go, I will go, and where you lodge, I will lodge. Your people shall be my people, and your God, my God. Where you die, I will die, and there I will be buried. Thus may the Lord do to me, and worse, if anything but death parts you and me."[1] This expression of love's loyalty and sacrificial giving ranks with the marriage vows with their pledge of love's fidelity "till death do us part." This young Gentile woman has known love and shows love. There is a mutuality about this love of Naomi for Ruth and Ruth for Naomi. Poverty stricken as they were, love made their little house beautiful. Their sharing concern for each other was a benediction, and all without seeming to ever use the word love. There is a lesson here. Love speaks more loudly and clearly in deeds than in words. As Ruth gleans grain and garners survival rations for them both, Naomi is praying, and planning in love, for her daughter's (for she is surely this now) future.

The love story of Ruth and Boaz, a June – December romance indeed – is again carried out without love song or verbiage in a courtship peculiar to that time and place. It featured a loving concern and practical considerations. Boaz commanding that grain be left on purpose for Ruth to glean; his handling of the legal matters as kinsmen redeemer; his care of her in the threshing floor episode when she takes the initiative on Naomi's advice; his concern for her reputation and generosity all say yes, this is love in action, not word. So the marriage took place and a son Obed was born to them. He became the grandfather of King David. Yes, love in action is actively rewarded.

Loving giving can never out give our loving Giver who plans all. Ruth has a book in the Bible, countless girls named after her, and a place in the royal lineage of Christ.

SEPTEMBER 13 – PROVIDENTIAL LOVE IN THE LIFE OF RUTH

"She stood breast-high amid the corn,
Clasp'd by the golden light of morn,
Like the sweetheart of the sun,
Who many a glowing kiss had won.

On her cheek an autumn flush,
Deeply ripen'd; such a blush
In the midst of brown was born,
Like red poppies grown with corn.

Round her eyes her tresses fell,
Which were blackest none could tell,
But long lashes veil'd a light,
That had else been all too bright.

And her hat, with shady brim,
Made her tressy forehead dim;
Thus she stood amid the stooks,
Praising God with sweetest looks:

Sure, I said, Heav'n did not mean,
Where I reap thou shouldst but glean,
Lay thy sheaf adown and come,
Share my harvest and my home."

The poet, Thomas Head (1799 – 1845), has imaginatively and beautifully portrayed Ruth as also did Geoffrey T. Bull (1921 -) in his book <u>Love Song in Harvest</u>. He retold the Scriptural story of this loving, grateful young woman and painted the prophetic portrait of Boaz as the forerunner of Christ our Kinsmen Redeemer. This short story of mature and mutual love, and love's provisions on several levels, is also a picture of the Lord's providential love in all the lives of the main characters, Naomi, Ruth and Boaz. As for the word "providence" itself it only appears once in Scripture and there refers to human providence or forethought. The word is derived from "provide." Divine providence is divine forethought making provision for His own.

In the lives of these three people we see the divine forethought in the providential timing of all the events in their lives. Providential love was at work in the famine that drove Naomi and her family from Bethlehem to Moab; in the deaths of her husband and sons; in the timing of the rains and good harvest that ended the ten year exile; in the timing that brought the two women into the life of Boaz at harvest time; in the timing of love's providence that put Ruth in the right field at the right time. "…her hap was to light on a part of the field belonging unto Boaz…"[1] and he was a good and godly relative of Naomi's with the rights and responsibilities of caring for the widows' interests. Providential love and foresight provided for all the material needs of the two women and all the romantic, physical and marital needs of both Ruth and Boaz. It is an exciting love story and a wonderful expression of providential love.

"God moves in a mysterious way,
His wonders to perform;
He plants his footsteps in the sea,
And rides upon the storm….

Judge not the Lord by feeble sense,
But trust Him for his grace;
Behind a frowning providence,
He hides a smiling face."
William Cowper (1731 – 1800)

To fully enter into and enjoy the fruits and sweets of all the sovereign, divine providential love is planning for us, we must love Him and be fully committed to His will. He will do His part; let us do ours, as did Naomi, Ruth and Boaz.

SEPTEMBER 14 – LOVE NOT LUCK

"What the unbeliever calls good luck the believer calls God's love."

This quote from the end of a message by Henry G. Bosch in <u>Our Daily Bread</u> is part of his testimony. Our brother begins with a title "I'm Never Lucky!" and a text "…who works all things after the counsel of His will."[1] He goes on to say:

"On one occasion as a young man I was very happy about a blessing the Lord had given me. without thinking I exclaimed, 'Boy, was I ever lucky!' Hearing this a brother in Christ rebuked me with three small words I've never forgotten. He said, 'I'm never lucky!' He meant that everything comes to us from God, even as Paul said in his famous sermon on Mars Hill. I quickly realized how out of character my remark had seemed."

This testimony points out what evangelical Christians thought and taught in my young days. I also can remember, after using the words "luck" and "lucky," being told that for the Christian there was no such thing as luck. There was love and the sovereignty and providence of God. All things bright and beautiful, all things dark and dreary, yes all things come from God's good hands. No change or chance, as the world saw it, could alter this truth. The world is ever with us and as Bosch writes:

"We so easily fall into the jargon of the world, for we constantly rub elbows with the unsaved and are influenced by their thinking. The Scriptures clearly teach that blessings are not the result of chance, but that every good gift and every perfect gift comes from above. We should be especially careful, therefore, to give our heavenly Father the glory for all the kindnesses He showers upon us. Our lives are in His hands. Every joy that delights our hearts has been planned by Him who directs "all things after the counsel of His own will." He withholds nothing from us that is truly desirable, and even works for our own good through things that appear disastrous."

And they not only "appear disastrous" they are real disasters. Job's tragedies were real; and so was his attitude towards them, and his recognition that the sovereignty and providence of God gave, and took away; gave good and gave evil. He learned later, what we know theoretically and have proved experientially, that all things work; that all things work together; and that "…all things to work together for good to those who love God, to those who are called according to His purpose."[2] And that good, is character good, Christlike character; conformity to the image of His Son. There is no such thing as luck in all of this; there is only and always love. Job from his distress rebuked his unbelieving wife: "…'You speak as one of the foolish women speaks. Shall we indeed accept good from God and not accept adversity?' In all this Job did not sin with his lips."[3]

It is noticeable that luck is bad or good to the worldly Christian, while for the taught believer the truth is, God is always love. There is no such thing with Him as "bad love" nor "bad good" nor "bad providence" nor "bad sovereignty." Bosch continues to say:

"Although we may not mean to dishonour the Lord or deny his loving providence when we use words like 'chance' and 'luck' we are actually giving the impression that His many benefits are the result of a blind but pleasant fate. As Christians we should always say, 'Isn't the Lord good!' Personally, I'm never lucky but I'm divinely blest!"

SEPTEMBER 15 – LOVE AND THE SOVEREIGNTY OF GOD

In the bad old days of the perversion called the "Divine Right of Kings" evil men could be elevated to the throne; absolute powers of life and death were theirs and it was all supposedly sanctioned by God. When Israel wanted to change from a theocracy to a monarchy and become like the nations around them, God warned them of the consequences. He allowed it, but it was His permissive will, not His directive, first, best and sovereign will. How blinded Israel was by the tinsel trappings, puny powers and the false favours these arrogant kings could grant. To exchange the loving benevolence of the Sovereign of the Universe for the malevolence of human despots and dictators was folly of the worst kind, but My people will have it so. So they shall have their wish and when heaven would punish self-willed nations or individuals, it is let them have what they want. "…Now appoint a king for us to judge us like all the nations[1]… The Lord said to Samuel, 'Listen to the voice of the people in regard to all that they say to you, for they have not rejected you, but they have rejected Me from being king over them[2]…Now then, listen to their voice; however, you shall solemnly warn them and tell them of the procedure of the king who will reign over them.'"[3] And then followed an awful list of atrocities their kings would, and did, commit. They regretted bitterly afterwards for having exchanged the benign sovereignty of God for the malign devilishness of men.

Letting them have their way was not an abrogation of the supreme sovereignty of God but rather it was love allowing them to learn lessons the hard way. Sovereign love for rebellious Israel was always ruling over and over-ruling in their affairs. The historical illustration that will illustrate this concerns Balak, the Moabite who ordered the mercenary prophet Balaam to curse Israel. But he wasn't allowed to do it but was compelled, three times, to bless Israel. Love is still on the throne.

The sovereignty of God in creation and His continued control over His Universe is not questioned by born again, Bible believing saints. Nor is his sovereignty questioned in the spiritual realm; he purposed. Planned and in due course performed, the essential acts of redemption and salvation for "whosoever will." We sinners are the objects of that sovereign love. Why then, having experienced the blessings of sovereign love in Christ, do we, by our words and deeds, dare to doubt His sovereign beneficence in our day to day affairs?

"God moves in a mysterious way
His wonders to perform;
He plants His footsteps in the sea
And rides upon the storm.

Deep in unfathomable mines
Of never failing skill
He treasures up His bright designs
And works His sovereign will.

His purposes will ripen fast,
Unfolding every hour;
The bud may have a bitter taste,
But sweet will be the flower.

Blind unbelief is sure to err
And scan His work in vain;
God is His own interpreter,
And He will make it plain."
William Cowper (1731 – 1800)

SEPTEMBER 16 – LOVE'S UNDERSTANDING

"Poor soul, in this thy flesh what dost thou know?
Thou know'st thyself so little...
Thou art too narrow, wretch, to comprehend
Even thyself; yea though thou wouldst but bend
To know thy body...
What hope have we to know our selves, when we
Know not the least things, which for our use be?...
Thou look'st through spectacles; small things seem great
Below; but up unto the watch-tower get,
And see all things despoiled of fallacies:...
In heaven thou straight know'st all..."

John Donne (1573 – 1631), through a good education, continued reading and study, and very wide continental travels and immersion in other cultures, knew a lot about a lot of things. He was also wise enough to know how little he knew. The fool knows not and knows not that he knows not; the wise man knows not and knows that he knows not. His exhortation to mount the watchtower of God and learn is sound advice. There we learn truth "despoiled of fallacies."

In the great love chapter we are reminded "For we know in part[1]...but when the perfect comes, the partial will be done away."[2] That, of course, is when perfect love comes in the returning Person of our Lord, and when we are perfected, seeing Him face to face. "In heaven thou straight know'st all." But now! How many go through life either not understood or misunderstood?

We ought to be, we need to be, diligent students in the school of understanding love. We need to know ourselves with right love's understanding. We need to know our spouses with understanding love. We need to know our children, parents, friends, workmates, associates and sinners of every kind with understanding love. Love studies and is considerate of the other person. Love considers the others well being, welfare and needs as well as learning about their circumstances. Love's understanding particularizes, one at a time, and makes allowances.

Love's understanding is essential in the marriage relationship. The "urge to merge" sometimes changes to "desperate to separate." The course of true love does not run smooth but the oil of love's understanding does help in the rough spots. Even after a long courtship each lover is constantly surprising the other with fresh revelations. The joke is told that one poor man misheard his wedding vows as "Four richer, four poorer, four better, four worse" and relied "I didn't know I was marrying sixteen women!" While this is funny, even frivolous, it could be frightening! There is some truth here which applies to both genders. But understanding love will not falter under all sixteen faces of Adam or Eve!

And there is one even more important area for understanding love. "...What I do you do not realize now, but you will understand hereafter."[3] The ways of holy love are difficult to understand at times. But understanding will be given, if not in this life, in the next.

SEPTEMBER 17 – THE SIXTEEN PEOPLE WE MARRIED

As noted, one man is said to have been shocked when, for the first time in the rehearsal for the wedding, the words "for richer, for poorer, for better, for worse" sounded like the numeral "four!" "Four richer, four poorer, four better, four worse!" Whether prophetic or not, there is an element of truth here for all of us whether courting, engaged or married couples or even singles. Who really knows himself or herself? Who really knows the partner they married? The title of this book: "Partners In God's Love," while majoring on knowing God and His love and being partners with Him and His purposes, also emphasizes our partnership in all the natural loves, including that of marriage. Knowing, and understanding with love, our mates in the marriage relationship is a lifelong undertaking.

Now let's enlarge on this humorous title "The Sixteen People We Married." To have a fair warning is also to be forewarned and forearmed. It will also help explain why some marriages fail. We didn't make allowances for the sixteen faces of Adam or Eve! There used to be a TV program which went something like this. Before a live studio audience a panel of three people all professed to be a certain person. One was actually the real person. Each one would be interviewed by the Master of Ceremonies and given an opportunity to prove why and how he, or she, was the real person. Meanwhile the audience was evaluating the attitudes, answers and affirmations made. Then the audience voted. The punch line came when the Master of Ceremonies said "Now, will the real 'John Doe' stand up!" audience assessments were often wrong. People were fooled and how often have people been fooled before and after marriage, with delights as well as defects!

Speaking personally, I'm sure people say of me:

"Truly, is that the real John L. Davey standing up?"

I sometimes have to stop and ask the question of myself. My parents made their estimates of me. my brothers and sister had their views. At school, through kindergarten, elementary, junior, high and Bible College my teachers made their evaluations, not always, as I thought, with love. I think of the headmaster who had me up on the carpet and gave me six across the seat. My friends, through the various age groups also gave their "guesstimates' as to the real JD. And my brother-in-law, and other bosses for whom I worked, gave me or withheld "testimonials." And finally, my wife, of almost forty-five years, my children and my grandchildren "know me" and their judgments are tempered by love. But how deeply am I seen and known? The real me; not my sixteen faces; not my facades; not my masks; not my intentional or unintentional cover-ups; not my manifestations of my mixed temperaments; not my misunderstood personality traits or motives; not my better side; not my gifts or virtues. None of these, alone or together constitute the unrevealed reality which is the real, unique me. Only One really sees me, knows me, and, knowing all, yet loves me.

"…Thou God seest me…"[1] is not the indictment of a super secret Detective in the skies but it is the all knowing love of Christ. May we love with His insightful love all the sixteen facets of our love partners, in all areas and ages and stages of life.

SEPTEMBER 18 – CIRCUMCISED TO LOVE

Don't be misled by this title. We are not talking about physical circumcision. This is the more important theme of spiritual circumcision and its relationship to the love of God. Scripture uses this terminology and in fact has quite a bit to say about the subject. "Moreover the Lord your God will circumcise your heart and the heart of your descendants, to love the Lord your God with all your heart and with all your soul, so that you may live."[1] Circumcision of the heart is obviously a spiritual operation, performed by the loving hands of the divine Surgeon. It is a major spiritual heart operation to remove, in a spiritual sense, the very heart itself and replace it with a new one. It is not merely doctoring up, or by-passing the old natural heart, but taking it right out and putting in a spiritual one. This is drastic surgery.

What grounds do we have for such statements? God, in the book of Ezekiel, frequently makes such promises to Israel. "…I will take the heart of stone out of their flesh…"[2] "Moreover, I will give you a new heart and put a new spirit within you; and I will remove the heart of stone from your flesh and give you a heart of flesh. I will put My Spirit within you and cause you to walk in My statutes…"[3]

And what is the supreme importance of this spiritual circumcision, this spiritual heart surgery? It is to enable them "to love the Lord…and to live." We are circumcised to love and to live the life of love in Christ. Do these truths apply to us today as Christians under the New Covenant? They certainly do. We are the children of Abraham by faith and we are called to spiritual circumcision, the new heart, that pulses with the divine animation of love. His love enables us to love Him back with the same love that He loved us. The heart and love of Christ is ours. "…in Him you were also circumcised with a circumcision made without hands…by the circumcision of Christ."[4] Paul, a circumcised Jew who boasted of it, became a converted and spiritually circumcised Christian and wrote of it. "…beware of the false circumcision; for we are the true circumcision, who worship in the Spirit of God and glory in Christ Jesus and put no confidence in the flesh."[5] This twice circumcised man glorified God for his spiritual circumcision of love and life. His new heart of love constrained and compelled him to a life of loving service and suffering. It also enabled him, through his inspired writings, to show us what this new agapé heart was really like.

SEPTEMBER 19 – LOVE'S COURAGE

There can be little argument about the connection here. Love makes meek mothers, self-forgetful bold defenders of their babies, in both the animal and human worlds. The charred corpse of a prairie chicken found after a sweeping grassland fire showed love and courage. When the burnt body was moved a little brood of chicks ran from under the blackened sheltering wings. That mother hen faced the onrushing flames without stirring to save herself. That is love's courage.

The supreme example of this love and courage is seen and heard in Gethsemane. "...My soul is deeply grieved, to the point of death[1]... My Father, if this cannot pass away unless I drink it, Your will be done."[2] Love's courage was also seen and heard on the Cross as an illustration of what was sneeringly said below the Cross. "He saved others; He cannot save Himself. He is the King of Israel; let Him now come down from the cross..."[3] Love's courage couldn't save Him if it was to save others. It could have come down, but it couldn't! For He was the One who said, using the mother hen illustration, in His loving, longing lament over Jerusalem. "Jerusalem, Jerusalem...How often I wanted to gather your children together, the way a hen gathers her chicks under her wings, and you were unwilling."[4]

His supreme courageous love sets a standard for His children. While His love and courage, like Himself are unique, we must translate it into action, however humbly and obscurely, in our daily lives. Suddenly, silently, without observers, opportunities will come when we are faced with choices; to save ourselves, or to save others; to come down from our cross or to remain there. Love for the Lord and His lost sheep will produce, by the Spirit, courage suited to the occasion, thus enabling us to do, or take a stand, or face an issue, or say what has to be said. David's courage, born of love for his God, his sheep, his family and Israel, enabled him to face and fight a lion, a bear and a giant. Love and courage are united and they increase in strength when practiced.

But it is in facing ourselves and putting the finger on our own sin that love's courage is seen in its most personal way and shines forth in its holy nature. Here we see the difference between the natural loves and their courage, and holy heavenly love that enables us to courageously face the facts concerning the true nature of sin and forgiveness in our own lives, and to deal with the sin and receive forgiveness. He loves and convicts us so that we will convict ourselves. He loves us and hates our sin. His forgiveness is just in dealing with and destroying sin. And only by, and because, His love has been poured into our hearts by the Holy Spirit can we be truly loving and courageous in dealing first with ourselves and then others. Pentecost made all this possible. The courage of the love of God made the timid confident and the fearful valiant. It gave speech to silent Peter who then proclaimed salvation and forgiveness with courage and conviction for he had been himself a recipient of love. This Holy Spirit love gave the courage to face and deal with race and social issues in the church and above all to face themselves and each other.

SEPTEMBER 20 – LOVE'S LIFTING POWER

Elizabeth Barrett (1806 – 1861) was headed for what seemed a premature grave. She was for many years an invalid in her home at 50 Wimpole St., London, England. The exact nature of her illness is uncertain. G. K. Chesterton (1874 – 1936) says of her:

"She was an invalid, and an invalid of a somewhat unique kind, and living beyond all question under very unique circumstances...But her illness, whatever it may have been, was real enough to her, and dangerously so at times."

She calls herself:

"The picture of helpless indolence; sublimely helpless and impotent; I had done living I thought; was ever life so like death before? My face was so close against the tombstones, that there seemed no room even for the tears."

She speaks always of life before the meeting with Robert Browning (1812 – 1899) as one of sadness. At the age of fifteen the illness which was to haunt her life began. While saddling her pony she injured herself in some way which was thought to have affected her spine. The theme of death often comes through in her sonnets.

"...Betwixt me and the dreadful outer brink
Of obvious death, where I, who thought to sink..."

And then love came in the person of Robert Browning, the knight in shining armour, to joust with and defeat her depressions, doubts and death itself. Love is really life giving and afforded a marvellous cure in Elizabeth's body, mind and spirit. She never ceased to marvel at it.

"My poet, thou canst touch on all the notes God set between His After and Before..."

"Beloved, my Beloved, when I think That thou wast in the world a year ago,
What time I sat alone here in the snow..."

"A heavy heart, Beloved, have I borne
From year to year until I saw thy face..."

"I lived with visions for my company
Instead of men and women, years ago..."

"My own Beloved, who hast lifted me
From this drear flat of earth where I was thrown...
Before thy saving kiss! My own, my own,
Who camest to me when the world was gone,
And I who looked for only God, found thee! I find thee;
I am safe, and strong, and glad...
Make witness, here, between the good and bad,
That Love, as strong as Death, retrieves as well."

SEPTEMBER 20 - CONTINUED

"...Then, love me, Love! Look on me—breathe on me!
As brighter ladies do not count it strange,
For love, to give up acres and degree,
I yield the grave for thy sake, and exchange
My near sweet view of Heaven, for earth with thee!"

This reversed reasoning is not false or wrong. Love gave her new life to live on earth instead of early heaven; heaven before the appointed time. Paul was in two minds once; heaven now or later or earth for now to help and benefit others? How often, too, was Paul comforted by human companionship when restless, afflicted, depressed and in constant conflict without and fears within. And every sinner knows the life giving, saving, lifting power of love.

"I was sinking deep in sin,
Sinking to rise no more..."

Then came the miraculous rescue:

"Love lifted me!
Love lifted me!
When nothing else could help,
Love lifted me!"
James Rowe (1865 – 1933)

SEPTEMBER 21 – HOW DO I LOVE THEE?

As already mentioned, one of the great and true love stories of the 19th century was that of Robert Browning (1812 – 1899) and Elizabeth Barrett (1806 – 1861). It is stranger, truer and more romantic than fiction. She was a confirmed, couched invalid, partly through a fall and partly through her father's obsessive love and coddling. Drawn by poetry the two young people corresponded. Then he visited her in her sick room, properly chaperoned of course, and began to encourage her to get up and walk. And then, wonder of wonders, to even go outside. The often objecting father was hovering in the background, and too often in the foreground. Their proximity, poetry, kindred minds and compatible spirits brought about the inevitable; they fell in love. Her father had feared this possibility, frowned upon their increasing closeness, and finally forbade their meeting. But love will find a way. The rejuvenated Elizabeth, healthy through liberating love, yet still frail, overcame the fear of her father and secretly married Robert at a nearby church and then eloped with him to Italy. There they lived most of their lives and there their son was born.

Elizabeth Barrett Browning later wrote the famous "Sonnets from the Portuguese" which of course have nothing to do with Portugal or the Portuguese! Because of her dark complexion, the imaginative Robert called his wife endearingly his "little Portuguese," and thus she called herself. Her "sonnets from the Portuguese" to her beloved, whose love had brought wholeness to her heart and body, are amongst the classic lines in the language of love.

> "How do I love thee? Let me count the ways.
> I love thee to the depth and breadth and height
> My soul can reach, when feeling out of sight
> For the ends of being and ideal grace.
> I love thee to the level of everyday's
> Most quiet need, by sun and candle-light.
> I love thee freely, as men strive for right;
> I love thee purely, as they turn from praise.
> I love thee with the passion put to use
> In my old griefs, and with my childhood's faith.
> I love thee with a love I seemed to lose
> With my lost saints, I love thee with the breath,
> Smiles, tears, of all my life! and, if God choose,
> I shall but love thee better after death." Sonnet 43

One day she came with her sheaf of sonnets, and offered them shyly to him as her tribute of love's adoration, from his "Portuguese." He was overwhelmed, as any husband would be, and felt that because they were so good they should be shared with a wider audience. So we have come to be blessed by them. They show us a standard and an ideal for romantic love, maintained in marriage, which often seems unsustainable. They also point in the title, and by direct quote and indirect reference, to greater questions about the greatest love.

SEPTEMBER 22 – LOVE'S RIVALRIES

"If thou must love me, let it be for nought
Except for love's sake only.
Do not say 'I love her for her smile, her look, her way
Of speaking gently, for a trick of thought
That falls in well with mine, and certes brought
A sense of pleasant ease on such a day'
For these things in themselves, Beloved, may
Be changed, or change for thee, and love, so wrought,
May be unwrought so.
Neither love me for Thine own dear pity's wiping my cheeks dry,
A creature might forget to weep, who bore
Thy comfort long, and lose thy love thereby!
But love me for love's sake, that evermore
Thou mayst love on, through love's eternity." Sonnet 14

Elizabeth Barrett Moulton-Barrett (1806 – 1861), to give her maiden name in full, had two earthly loves which she lost. Love for her brother Edward was cut off by his premature death by drowning. His death devastated her. Her brother had loved her for herself alone.

"…my brother whom I loved so…he was the dearest of friends and brothers in one…better than us all, and kindest and noblest and dearest to me, beyond comparison, any comparison…" "…the spring of life…seemed to break within me then…when…I lost what I loved best in the world…"

In that loss she was drawn closer to her father to whom she was genuinely devoted though he was a despot who became increasingly strange as he aged.

"…I felt that he stood the nearest to me on the closed grave…he was generous and forbearing in that hour of bitter trial…"

She dedicated her first book of poems to him and that dedication was reprinted in all editions of her poems until her death; long after she had left him, never to be forgiven. In 1841 she was in her room in her home at 50 Wimpole St., London, England, shut in by increasing invalidism with "Flush, my dog" her chief companion and "loving friend." At least Flush loved her for herself alone. In winter she never left her room "…we all get used to the thought of a tomb…" and her father was content to have it so. His possessive, obsessive love was about to be challenged.

1845 was the year love's rivalries came to a head. Robert Browning (1812 – 1899) came into her life and loved her as she desired and later wrote "If thou must love me, let it be for nought Except for love's sake only." And he did and as we know, displacing her father. How sad her words "…I had believed Papa to have loved me more than he obviously does…"

SEPTEMBER 23 – LOVE IN SINCERITY

Insincerity in love, in all the realms where that word applies, is a common failing, yea worse, a callous sin. The man in the man-woman relationship is notorious for insincere promises, ulterior motives and a flattering line all to gain their nefarious ends. Is this too hard on men? The history of romantic love and ruined women prove it. The poets rhyme it and love songs lament it. It breeds a cynicism in some women; breaks others up; and yet makes a few face these unpleasant facts, acknowledging them as the lady does in Rogers & Hammerstein's "Oklahoma" about being jilted.

"Why should a woman who is healthy and strong
Blubber like a baby if her man's goes away?
A weepin' an' a whalin' that he's done her wrong
That's one thing you'll never hear me say!
Never gonna think that the man I lose is the
only man among men!
I'll snap my fingers to show I don't care
I'll buy me a brand new dress to wear
I'll scrub my neck
And I'll brush my hair
And start all over again!

Many a new face will please my eye
Many a new love will find me
Never have I once looked back to sigh
Over the romance behind me
Many a new day will dawn before I do!

Many a like lad may kiss and fly
A kiss gone by is bygone.
Never have I asked an August sky
'Where has last July gone?'
Never have I wandered through the rye
Wondering 'where has some guy gone?'
Many a new day will dawn before I do.

Never have I chased the honeybee
Who carelessly cajoled me
Somebody jist as sweet as he
Cheered me and consoled me.
Never have I wept into my tea
Over the deal someone doled me."

But let us lift sincerity in love to a higher plane. "The sincerity of your love" is Paul's theme, "But just as you abound in everything, in faith and utterance and knowledge and in all earnestness and in the love we inspired in you, see that you abound in this gracious work also. I am not speaking this as a command, but as proving through the earnestness of others the sincerity of your love also."[1] The selfishness of so called love in the popular song contrasts with the selflessness of the giving love that Paul is calling for here. He has already commended the Macedonian Christians on their dual love and double giving. "...they first gave themselves to the Lord and to us..."[2] and they gave liberally out of their poverty for saints' support. He now urges the Corinthians to show the sincerity of their love by doing what the Macedonians had done. The sincerity of our love for Christ is shown by our actions towards others.

And finally, Paul in his benediction, at the close of his letter to the Ephesians, says: "Peace be to the brethren, and love with faith, from God the Father and the Lord Jesus Christ. Grace be with all them that love our Lord Jesus Christ in sincerity. Amen."[3]

SEPTEMBER 24 – LOST LOVE

William Wordsworth (1770 – 1850) laments a lost love in his ode to "Lucy"; whether of family, friend or a lover we'll never know. Whether or not it's just a poetic fancy and figure of his imagination, the words are lovely.

"She dwelt among the untrodden ways
Beside the springs of Dove,
Maid whom there were none to praise
And very few to love:

A violet by a mossy stone
Half hidden from the eye!
Fair as a star, when only one
Is shining in the sky.

She lived unknown, and few could know
When Lucy ceased to be;
But she is in her grave, and, oh,
The difference to me!"

Lost love, of whatever kind and from whatever cause, is a bereaving experience. Even partings are such sweet sorrow. But the permanent separation of lovers by death is desolating. Unrequited love is a grievous thing to the one loving in vain. The usurpation of love, by any means, is devastating to one of the partners and destructive to both. The loss of human love, while still in life, is always regrettable. But love in the grave is the inevitable end of all the natural loves.

Yet even the higher love can be lost by leaving and the loss of this is eternally impoverishing. Hear our Lord on this matter: "But I have this against you, that you have left your first love. Therefore remember from where you have fallen, and repent and do the deeds you did at first; or else I am coming to you and will remove your lampstand out of its place, unless you repent."[1] This was spoken by the risen Lord to John who was instructed to write it in a letter and send it to the church at Ephesus. This was a model church. Its birth and development is recorded in the book of Acts and in the Ephesian epistle. At the time of that writing it had reached its apogee and at the time of the Lord's indictment it was at its perigee. And all this happened in a time frame of about thirty to thirty-five years; one genera-tion; AD 62 to AD 95 as <u>Wycliffe Bible Commentary</u> suggests. In that short period the church was born, matured and decayed. Oh not to the outward eye. It still maintained high standards in ethics, morals, walk, work, discerning of false apostles and teachers, and in preserving endurance; high praise from the risen Lord Himself. Yet His eye had discerned the inner flaw, the worm in the woodwork. All was in danger of being lost because they had left their first love. He calls it a fallen church and that means the individuals who comprise it.

To leave one's first love, and the deeds of first love, is clearly explained in Scripture. "…I remember concerning you the devotion of your youth, The love of your betrothals, Your following after Me in the wilderness, Through a land not sown."[2] First love is the love of the first espousal, betrothal, engage-ment and the first tender, devoted embrace of the newly wed. This illustration from marital love is used by God about Israel in the Old Testament and the Lord about His church and people under the New Covenant. Oh the difference lost love makes on the natural and spiritual levels. The causes and cure should concern us.

SEPTEMBER 25 – RESTORED LOVE

The Ephesian church as a collective group and as individuals had left, and so lost, their first love to their Lord. Their whole testimony, outwardly healthy and strong, was carrying an inner disease which would prove fatal unless discussed and dealt with. The Lord had discerned it and faithfully pointed it out via letter dictated from heaven, to be delivered to the presiding elder. The disease was loss of first love, their glowing inner devotion to Him, likened unto the worshipful and rightful adoration of human lovers for each other, as the old English form of marriage vows used to include:

"With my body I thee worship."

The Lord, while on earth, had indicated some of the causes of this falling away from first love. "Because lawlessness is increased, most people's love will grow cold."[1] This statement was made in the context of a threefold question of the disciples and His own lengthy answer. Their question had to do with signs of His coming and the end of the age as well as their practical query about the destruction of the Jewish temple. His answer on the end time signs was full and contains the quote that we are discussing. In the end times lawlessness will increase and this will be the cause of love growing cold and so being left and lost. Whether this is lost by love growing cold, or loss by leaving and not cleaving, the same sad result occurs. Love is lost. The age in which He came to earth was wicked but not lawless. The Romans ruled with a cruel, dictatorial rod of iron. They were the iron civilization portrayed by the fourth element in Daniel's great image. They imposed a harsh rule of law over all the then known world which they conquered. I think we are living now in the days of the feet and toes of the great prophetic image. Democracy, with all its benefits, is being destroyed by the inner decay of individualism and lawlessness inherent in it. Since the French revolution this has been the norm. Lawlessness and anarchy is creeping around the globe. Criminals are coddled; death penalties are abolished in the "civilized" world; drink, drugs, homosexualism and abortion are legalized. Through it all the church is seemingly innocuous and worse the love of Christians will grow cold and even be contaminated by this ages' amorality and immorality.

Is there any hope? Yes, there is and what He tells us about the cure applies to our natural and spiritual lives. The causes for leaving love, and losing the warmth of love, are manifold. The cure for the first century Asian churches and those today are clearly given by the risen Lord. Remember, repent, return and I will restore you, or else I will remove your witness from the earth. This message was emphasized to individuals in these churches. The Spirit gave special promises to overcomers. He still does today to those who return to him and allow Him to renew and restore their lost love.

SEPTEMBER 26 – LAST LOVE

In the realm of marital love, the first love is not necessarily the last love. Many people, because of deaths, have two or three loves in their earthly lives. It is not uncommon for the saints of God to follow this pattern. In our days Mrs. Elisabeth Elliott Gren is a well known example. She was first married and briefly to the missionary martyr Jim Elliott (1927 – 1956) and then later married a Christian educator who died of cancer. She is now married to a Christian teacher. Three marriage partners in one lifetime is not the norm but not unknown. In the last century, that great man of faith George Müller (1805 – 1895), married twice. His first wife was the ideal help-mate during the strenuous years of the building of the orphan homes on Ashley Down, Bristol, England and of the caring for thousands of children during the forty years of their marriage. He later remarried and enjoyed another, almost quarter century of marital bliss. Together, he and the second Mrs. Müller travelled extensively in world-wide ministry. At ninety years of age, Müller preached the funeral sermon for his second wife, as he had also done, in the chapel and at the grave, for his first wife. The first love, middle love, and last love of saints is sometimes spread out over more than one marriage.

Mockers of the married state query the sanity of anyone, once released from what they call the bondage of unholy deadlock, ever wanting to bind themselves again. They have never known true love, and the bliss of real union. They can't understand that happy married experience makes the state desirable a second and even a third time. This has nothing to do with the false loves and cynical marrying, divorcing and remarrying of today's world! "Desiderata" by Max Ehrmann (1872 – 1945) reminds us to:

"not feign affection. Neither be cynical about love; for in the face of all aridity and disenchantment it is as perennial as the grass."

The first love of Abraham was not his last. Sarah was a remarkable woman. She followed her husband faithfully in all his wanderings and fulfilled all the duties of her role. She, with God's blessing, performed the paradox of submission to the lordship of her husband while at the same time expressing herself forcefully and acting as a liberated woman in those unliberated times. Their marriage was child-less until Isaac was born to them in their old age. She was ninety and he a hundred! That set everyone laughing and gave them a second spring which lasted thirty-seven more years. Sarah died and Abraham took another wife whose name was Keturah and she gave him six more children. His last love was no placid eventide rest! Abraham lived one hundred seventy-five years "…and died in a ripe old age, an old man and satisfied with life…"[1] Sometimes a last love can prove to be a good love. Remarriage after the death of a spouse is Scriptural.

"Love at the closing of our days is apprehensive and very tender.
Glow brighter, brighter, farewell rays of one last love in its evening splendor.
Blue shades takes half the world away: through western clouds alone some light is slanted.
O tarry, O tarry, declining day, enchantment, let me stay enchanted.
The blood runs thinner, yet the heart remains as ever deep and tender.
O last belated love, thou art a blend of joy and of hopeless surrender."
Fyodor Tyutchev (1803 – 1873)

SEPTEMBER 27 – PASSION AND PURITY

"The only place outside of heaven where you can be perfectly safe from all the dangers and perturbations of love is hell." The Four Loves by C. S. Lewis (1898 – 1962)

In her book Passion and Purity author Elisabeth Elliot brings a unique experience to the subject. Married originally to martyr Jim Elliot (1927 – 1956) she, with her husband, was a missionary to the Indians of South America. She told the story in Through Gates of Splendour of an unusual depiction of a human love story, secondary to Jim's passionate love for Christ and the souls of the Auca Indians. Later Elisabeth Elliot became Mrs. Addison Leitch. He was a Christian academic, professor and teacher in a university, but again, like her marriage to Jim, it was brief, less than five years due to his death from cancer. These marriages and bereavements did not deter her from marrying again. She is now Mrs. Lars Gren. She knows by experience the two levels of meaning in the words passion and purity.

I haven't read her book, but the title set me thinking of passion as a word allied to the Greek "pathos" or suffering. Even on the level of physical love and passion, that compelling emotion of ardent affection and amorous desire, there is built in suffering. As we have seen none "can be perfectly safe from all the dangers and perturbations of love." On the highest level, the passion, is the suffering and death of Jesus Christ, described in the Gospels, where in His eternal love, He suffered for our sins and sinners on Calvary. The zeal, ardour and avid desire of Jim Elliot to respond to that passion and love can only be described in the words already used: passionate love.

Love like that is truly pure love, for there is purity of motive and a pure single eye to God's glory. "Blessed are the pure in heart, for they shall see God."[1] These are they, like Jim Elliot, whose moral being is free from contamination by impurity, whose eye is single and without divided loyalties or interests. To be pure like this one must be, as John Donne (1573 – 1631) said "ravished by love."

"…Love loves unto purity… Therefore all that is not beautiful in the beloved, all that comes between and is not of love's kind, must be destroyed." George MacDonald (1824 – 1905)

The two levels of purity like the two levels of passion are bound, from time to time, to be in conflict. The highest must prevail.

"O Lord and Master of us all,
Whate'er our name or sign,
We own Thy sway, we hear Thy call,
We test our lives by Thine.

Thou judgest us; Thy purity
Doth all our lusts condemn;
The love that draws us nearer Thee
Is hot with wrath to them."
John Greenleaf Whittier (1807 – 1892)

Yes, there is suffering in purity as there is in passion; in all the levels of meaning in these words. Our Lord suffered at the highest levels, and he lifted His disciples there also. The loving Lord "…presented Himself alive after His suffering…"[2] These passionate, pure, loving, suffering men were made so by his pure and passionate love.

SEPTEMBER 28 – LOVE'S LAMENT FOR A LOST WIFE

Alfred Lord Tennyson's (1809 – 1892) lost two loves. One was his dearest friend, Arthur H. Hallam (1811 – 1833), drowned at sea. The other was his true love. We have already discussed Tennyson's tribute to Hallam (June 11). Now hear his lament for his lost love, his bride, his wife.

"O that 'twere possible
After long grief and pain
To find the arms of my true love
Round me once again!

When I was wont to meet her
In the silent woody places
By the home that gave me birth,
We stood tranced in long embraces
Mixt with kisses sweeter sweeter
Than anything on earth.

A shadow flits before me,
Not thou, but like to thee:
Ah Christ, that it were possible
For one short hour to see
The souls we loved, that they might tell us
What and where they be…

But she tarries in her place
And I paint the beauteous face
Of the maiden, that I lost,
In my inner eyes again,
Lest my heart be overborne,
By the thing I hold in scorn,
By a dull mechanic ghost
And a juggle of the brain.

I can shadow forth my bride
As I knew her fair and kind for my wife;
She is lovely by my side
In the silence of my life…"

Tennyson's lament for the loss of his wife, the love of his life, is a late echo of the cry of another bereaved but at the time, strangely silent husband. We saw earlier what a romantic love match there was between Jacob and Rachel. We noted how he fell in love and was not mute about it. Why then, at her early and unexpected death in childbirth, did he not express himself with concern? The record seams too casual, too cold as we read: "It came about as her soul was departing (for she died), that she named him Ben-oni; but his father called him Benjamin. So Rachel died and was buried on the way to Ephrath (that is, Bethlehem). Jacob set up a pillar over her grave; that is the pillar of Rachel's grave to this day."[1] The Bethlehem Road was to herald a great joy in the centuries ahead but here it is first recorded as the road of great grief. For despite appearances of calm acceptance of his wife's death, and even callousness in denying her last request regarding the naming of her son, Jacob was grieving deeply as he journeyed on. Life has to go on, and the loss of his beloved Rachel had shocked him, silenced him and driven his sorrow inward.

Are we being presumptuous here and reading into Scripture what is not there? I don't think so. Israel, to use his other name, was about sixty years old when Rachel died. Eighty-seven years later he died at age one hundred forty-seven. Up to the end of his life he carried an inner shrine in his heart where he remembered Rachel with love, and lamented her still with faithfulness. At his last sickness, down in Egypt, talking to his beloved Joseph, the first born child of his marriage with Rachel, he suddenly spoke his love lament for his lost wife. "Now as for me, when I came from Paddan, Rachel died, to my sorrow, in the land of Canaan on the journey, when there was still some distance to go to Ephrath; and I buried her there on the way to Ephrath (that is, Bethlehem)."[2] Not a detail is forgotten as everything is etched permanently in his mind and heart. This sick and dying man had written his lament for his lost love indelibly within. There would be but one word: Rachel.

SEPTEMBER 29 – SATISFYING LOVE

"O Christ in Thee my soul hath found,
And found in Thee alone,
The peace, the joy, I sought so long,
The bliss till now unknown.

I sighed for rest and happiness
I yearned for them not Thee;
But while I passed my Saviour by,
His love laid hold on me.

The pleasures lost I sadly mourned,
But never wept for Thee,
Till grace the sightless eyes received,
Thy loveliness to see.

Now none but Christ can satisfy,
None other name for me!
There's love and life and lasting joy,
Lord Jesus found in Thee." Unknown

The search for satisfaction, the quest for love, is a demanding drive leading so often to disappointment and disillusion. Like many, I sought it for a time in pleasure and self-gratification, only to find fleeting fulfillment of my desires and needs. It was like a will o' the wisp or the luring, seducing mirages of the desert that drew the desperate on to destruction. I have told in "Something Personal" (January 2) about finding and being found by the lasting love of God and how it laid hold of me. That was bliss, the really satisfying love of Christ. The bliss was until then unknown. I look back with gratitude to that baptism of heavenly love, that filling and overflowing of the Spirit of Christ, which altered the course of my life. Writing now, almost fifty years later I can see, with the 20 – 20 vision of hindsight, how that holy, heavenly love has guided, guarded and given nothing but good, even when it didn't seem so. "…all things to work together for good to those who love God…"[1] And that "good" is the pre-destined conformity to the character and image of Christ. It takes a lifetime to bring to maturity the love of Christ in and through us and enroute we discover what St. Bernard of Clairvoux (1090 - 1153) wrote of centuries earlier.

"Jesus, Thou Joy of loving hearts,
Thou Fount of life, Thou Light of men,
From the best bliss that earth imparts,
We turn unfilled to Thee again."

During these almost fifty years I have known the best bliss that all the lesser loves can give, and they have been, and are God's good lesser gifts. I have also found that they all, in their turn, leave us. Our parents and their parental love are gone. Our own children, rightly so, go, though their love does not. Our friends whom we have loved are gone, or are going one by one. One of us in the partnership of marital love will go before the other. All the lesser loves are passing, temporal, ephemeral leaving their memories of bliss and blessing. I thank God that they are being banked in heaven in transfigured forms. These truths have been repeatedly stressed, in varied ways, and without apology. Desires of the temporal kind are recognized that they have their temporal satisfaction but, and we all know it, "from the best bliss that earth imparts, we turn unfilled to Thee again." Even these fresh, satisfying fillings of Divine love are but a taste of what lies ahead.

SEPTEMBER 30 – WAITING LOVE

During our years in Barbados our family came to know two widows. The first, Mrs. Hilda Taylor, lost her husband a few years after our arrival in that island in 1957. The Taylors were so kind and helpful to us in our early days, easing our settling into life there. John Taylor was a sick man and soon went to be with the Lord. We attended his funeral. Hilda's love, practical love, for the Lord seemed to increase as she grew older. She ran a Bible class for many years where we were frequently asked to speak. She loved souls. The launch of the magazine "Caribbean Challenge" coincided with our arrival in Barbados, and from the beginning Aunt Hilda, as everyone called her, showed her interest by becoming a distributor. It was a means of reaching souls for Christ. Over the years she increased the distribution by many hundreds. In her seventies this widow multiplied her ministry of love in this area by organizing other sub-distributors in her district. What a joy it was to drive into her yard and leave a number of boxes of this Good New magazine. "She hath done what she could..."[1] is a verse that describes Hilda Taylor. She would type my Bible class outlines and pass them on to others. She was loved because she loved:

"Si vis amari, ama - If you wish to be loved, love" to quote Benjamin Franklin (1706 – 1790).

Hilda was also a waiting lover; waiting with loving anticipation for the return of her Lord, or for His coming for her. And the day came when He did. I was back in the island when she was called home in 1977. And I was honoured by being asked to bring the message at her funeral. "Precious in the sight of the Lord is the death of His godly ones"[2] seemed most fitting for Aunt Hilda. She awaits in His presence for the resurrection redemption of her body, from the Westbury Cemetery, Bridgetown, Barbados.

The other widow was dear little Daisy Browne. She was a lover of the Lord and a quiet doer of good works; a regular attendee at the Bible classes; a helper of the servants of the Lord. I was again on a visit to Barbados, arriving on Friday, September 4, 1981 to be the speaker at the annual Christian Literature Crusade area conference. The next day I was taken to a nursing home to see Daisy who was obviously dying. She was conscious and cognisant of us as we quoted the Scriptures and prayed with her; so frail, so small, and yet rejoicing in the Lord. She went to be with Him a day or two later and on Wednesday, September 9, I brought the message at her funeral in James St. Methodist Church. I spoke on aged Anna, the prophetess widow, who waited, watched and served in the Temple. Daisy was eighty-seven and had only lived with her husband for seven years before he had died. I described Anna and Daisy as lonely widows, living witnesses and loving women. At the gravesite I discovered something I had not known about Daisy. She was buried beside her husband. His stone read:

"In loving memory of Archibald A. Browne. Fell asleep March 1930. Aged 37. What I do thou knowest not but thou shalt know hereafter. Until we meet."

Daisy had been a widow in waiting love for fifty-one years. She had been waiting for her beloved Lord and waiting for reunion with her loved husband. Their waiting days are over now.

OCTOBER 1 – HUSBAND: "LOVE YOUR WIFE"

"Husbands, love your wives, just as Christ also loved the church and gave Himself up for her."[1] "So husbands ought also to love their own wives as their own bodies. He who loves his own wife loves himself; for no one ever hated his own flesh, but nourishes and cherishes it, just as Christ also does the church."[2] "For this reason a man shall leave his father and mother and shall be joined to his wife, and the two shall become one flesh."[3] "Nevertheless, each individual among you also is to love his own wife even as himself…"[4] These words can be quickly written and read; preaching on them is relatively easy; practicing them takes conscious, deliberate acts of the will and is hard and lifelong. It just cannot be done in one's own energy or by human effort. The enabling power to live Christlike love for one's partner must be supernatural. That is why at the commencement of this family relationship section the paramount command is given. "…be filled with the Spirit."[5] Obedience to this command makes possible obedience to the other command: "Husbands, love your wives, just as Christ also loved the church and gave Himself up for her." This is impossible to do for the natural man and the carnal Christian. It is practically possible for the Spirit controlled husband. Because he is subject to the Spirit who has made Christ Lord in him, he can, and will, subject himself to a lifetime of giving unto death for his wife, as Christ did in the power of the Spirit for the church.

The substance of the teaching for Christian husbands, the complete New Testament doctrine, is summarized in the connected key words: "leave" and "be joined"; "two" and "one"; "nourishes" and "cherishes"; "love" and "gave"; "his own wife" and "his own flesh"; "husbands" and "wives"; and "Christ" and "church." These seven couplets portray the union of Christian marriage as it ought to be, and as it really is in the union of the Bridegroom and the bride; Christ and His church. The love initiative in both cases comes from the head. The Head of the church and the head of the wife, in practical and positional roles, initially and continually, will the acts of love. He loved the church because He willed to do so; He gave His life for her because He willed to do so; He nourishes and cherishes her because He wills to do so. Likewise the similar acts of the truly loving husband must be willed into reality.

Romantic love necessarily is emotion and feeling to a large degree, but as the novelty wears off and the reality and practicality of marital love is revealed, more and more it is the will to love that counts. Not by any means is passionate, emotional, feeling love passé - far from it, but the kind of love being discussed for husbands is mental, spiritual as well as physical.

"In contrast the infatuated person wants to perceive and respond only to stimuli which are in accordance with his wishes. He wants the other person to be available to him. Responsibility is being available for the other. But the infatuated person wants the partner to be as he imagines her and does not want her to behave in accord with herself and her peculiarities. He wants the other as the object of his wishes; wants to bend the other to his intentions; wants to use the other." Karl von Heigel (1835 – 1905)

Am I an infatuated lover or do I love with agapé, as a true husbandly lover?

OCTOBER 2 – WIFE: "LOVE YOUR HUSBAND"

"...encourage the young women to love their husbands..."[1] "They should school the young women to be affectionate to their husbands and to their children, to be sober-minded, pure in their lives, industrious in their homes, kind, submissive to their husbands, so that the Christian teaching may not be exposed to reproach."[2] The text is taken in its context to show the practicalities of this wifely love. It is not popular theology in some Christian circles today, but I believe the Word is given to control, correct and judge me. I am not to criticize or correct it. Its purpose is to bring me into conformity to the character of Christ and to do the will of God. This will is perfect love, perfect good and ought to be perfectly acceptable and accepted.

To put this in the context of the human and church family we must repeat and enlarge. Titus the teacher, like all true teachers of the Word, was to preach and teach the truth, that which was in accordance with sound doctrine. He was to instruct the whole church in Crete. "Older men are to be temperate, dignified, sensible, sound in faith, in love, in perseverance. Older women likewise are to be reverent in their behavior, not malicious gossips nor enslaved to much wine, teaching what is good, so that they may encourage the young women to love their husbands, to love their children, to be sensible, pure, workers at home, kind, being subject to their own husbands, so that the word of God will not be dishonored. Likewise urge the young men to be sensible; in all things show yourself to be an example of good deeds, with purity in doctrine, dignified, sound in speech which is beyond reproach..."[3]

The mixture of agapé and philia through this section shows that these loves complement each other and are intensely practical. We are not discussing romantic love, emotions and feelings here, but that love which flows from the will. I will love like this. I will accept the demands, duties and submissions of love. I will, by the grace of God, practice them in daily down to earth living, through example and by precept whatever age bracket I am in.

"Love is the ability to bestow upon one's partner responsible care, respect and understanding. Care means looking after the loved one and aiding the latter's growth and development. Responsiveness means readiness to respond to stimuli; expressions and needs of the partner and to every manifestation of animation in the other. Respect means that one must have regard for the other and take into account his qualities, loving him, not only for his good ones (this is usually easy) but also his shortcomings and weaknesses. Respect means recognizing the other as a person." Karl von Heigel (1835 – 1905)

The will to love the husband practically like this, with caring concern, ready responsibility and loving respect for him as a person, and for his role in the family and church, presupposes a worthy husband, a loving giving husband. What if you married a dud? A worthless type? The answers have ranged from "how sad, too bad"; "you've got to live with it"; to "get rid of him!" What does Scripture say? It says several relevant things.[4]

OCTOBER 3 – LOVE WINS!

Love wins; not always; not always right away; but it wins much more frequently than it loses in this vale of tears and one day, in the land where all tears have been wiped away, it will eternally triumph. We have seen the permanence of love; it never fails nor ceases in its activity; for love is eternal. Never failing, never ceasing in its activity is not of course the same as never losing. Win some. Lose some would seem to fit love's battles on earth.

The great love chapter's teaching in the context of the conflicts in the Corinthian church, triumphed in the case of gross immorality. The sinning brother was disciplined. Discipline in love did its chastening restorative work. Love of this kind is not gullible. It, win or lose, faces the fight. As we saw earlier love did win in the conflict over partisanship; divisions in the church; the arrogance of gifts over grace; lawsuits before unbelievers. The love chapter was given in these contexts; it certainly by Paul's reaction in his second letter to them, triumphed in some, if not all.

There is one area where conflict of views and values is inevitable. It is sometimes the sad result of disobedience; in others through ignorance; and yet again because of grace and the conversion of one partner and not the other. A believer who marries an unbeliever is sinning against life and light and love. Disobedience is not justified by the siren song that says:

"You love him or her. Love is good. Love will win the unbeliever. Marry and you will see!"

And do they ever see! Everyone sees the sad results of disobedience to the known will of God. Others, who love the Lord, yet are untaught and ignorant, and stumble into such marriages, have also to suffer many a heartbreak. Yet other happy worldlings, blithely wed, get on very well until one of them gets converted.

Is there a word of hope, of encouragement for any of these? Can heavenly love in the Christian spouse ever win in a situation like this? Hallelujah, yes! Peter has a very relevant and encouraging word. "In the same way, you wives, be submissive to your own husbands so that even if any of them are disobedient to the word, they may be won without a word by the behavior of their wives, as they observe your chaste and respectful behavior."[1] Peter's practical word has meaning for marriage partners who are burdened with this unequal yoke. And these truths apply to either gender. The positive promise is clear and concise. "Won without a word." Win him or her by loving behaviour, not by "ear bashing" nor by "Bible banging" to use a couple of colourful Australian expressions. The time will come for verbal witness but it is best to be silent in your love at first and let your actions speak. Christian behaviour by the wives and husbands of unconverted partners has triumphed as many can testify. It may take years, but stand upon this promise. The love of Christ in you, shining through you, shining in the dark days, will win for you every day. And who knows will yet win the lost loved one.

OCTOBER 4 – A LOVING WORTHY WIFE

"An excellent wife, who can find? For her worth is far above jewels. The heart of her husband trusts in her, and he will have no lack of gain. She does him good and not evil all the days of her life."[1] The King James Version says "Who can find a virtuous woman? For her price is far above rubies." Ruth was such a woman and such a wife. "…for all my people in the city know that you are a woman of excellence."[2] Or as the King James Version puts it "…for all the city of my people doth know that thou art a virtuous woman." Ruth was a woman of worth who married Boaz, a man of wealth; and worth and wealth are the same word here. There is also a paradox and as has been said:

"A paradox is a truth standing on its head to gain attention."

Ruth was poor yet wealthy. Her worth was her wealth. The expressions "virtuous," "of worth," "of excellence," denotes ability, efficiency or attainment in any one of a number of areas. The word denotes comprehensive excellence. She is the ideal woman and the ideal wife. The word "virtuous" includes the commonly understood sense of moral probity and has its roots in inner goodness which in turn is the fruit of vital godliness and holy, heavenly love.

We have seen Ruth as one who gave herself, her energy and strength of body, mind and heart in loyalty and loving service to her mother-in-law and her second husband. Using Ruth here as an illustration of the wife of Proverbs 31 paints a real picture of her. The eulogy of one fits both. As the writer extols the virtues of the exemplary wife and the virtuous woman we can picture Ruth in her various spheres of activity while her husband Boaz is occupied in civic affairs; ruling and judging in the gate of the city. Both of these women had goodness and the love of God. Both were worthy women and worth wives. Both were worth coming home to. Both loved their husbands, their children and their households. Both were good workers in the house and in the fields and this latter occupation is as honourable as it is ancient. A woman who can plant and care for fruit, vegetables and flowers is excellent indeed. And when this is coupled with business acumen she becomes almost too good to be true; a paragon of perfection. Happy indeed is the man who has found such a woman!

The dangers of course are apparent. Ability and acumen are some of the qualities that make for leadership and authority. These women could have easily crossed the line and worn the pants in the house! But they didn't. They fortunately had able, authoritative husbands who led in the Divinely ordained areas of headship. The secret, an open one, is apparent in both these women, their husbands and the families; just the one word secret, love. They loved and were loved. "Strength and dignity are her clothing, and she smiles at the future. She opens her mouth in wisdom, and the teaching of kindness is on her tongue."[3] "Her children rise up and bless her; Her husband also, and he praises her, saying: 'Many daughters have done nobly, but you excel them all.'"[4] These are sincere and loving compliments from and admiring and adoring husband and loving grateful children for a woman who feared and loved the Lord.

OCTOBER 5 – HUSBANDLY AND WIFELY LOVE

And here, in this family series on the different aspects of love, is perhaps the best place to pay my tribute of love to the one, who for almost forty-five years, has shown, and grown in, that special love called wifely love. As we considered the commands in the area of love in marriage we saw that a Christian husband's love was to be Christlike, in the same way in which He loved the church and gave Himself for it. It is a demanding, self-sacrificing love which, I confess, I have often failed to live up to. But that is the norm, the Scriptural standard, which is constantly before me. The Christian wife's love is to be submissive and revering. This is equally demanding and not easy in fulfillment. In both cases these kinds of love are only possible as the love of Christ in each partner continues to have first place, and to grow in each life. Fortunately for us we started our relationship on that Christian love basis; the love of God was being poured into our hearts by the Holy Spirit. We had experience of the love that must be first. But we had mainly theoretical knowledge of the other loves so essential to a happy and successful marriage. Here we were learners in love. We are still learning! We did learn. First about romantic love. Our romance was not normal by any means but it was, to us, miraculous.

I met Ethel Kathleen Rodway in Toronto, Canada in July 1940, at Worldwide Evangelization Crusade Headquarters, then at 163 College St. She was secretary to Canadian Director Alfred Roscoe. I was enroute to the West Indies. She arranged a Canadian tour for me and "we entered into correspondence!" By the time I left for Dominica I had fallen in love with my correspondent, but didn't tell her so! No, not for lack of courage but Mission principles! We were warned that there was "many a slip 'twixt the call and the ship!" And I felt I should keep on to the field and then write back! So I did and we courted by mail! If anyone would like hints on courtship by correspondence perhaps we can help! The Lord overcame all the obstacles and Ethel with three other single missionaries arrived in Dominica in December 1941. One week later, on Christmas Day, we were married in the Mission House I had rented. On her arrival I queried her:

"I hope you brought a ring and I hope you brought some money? I only have a dollar. I spent all I had getting the Mission house ready for you and our family of three grown children!"

She replied:

"I brought two rings and I have $100!"

And on that, this new bride began housekeeping on $5 a week! I take my hat off to a real pioneer missionary and help meet. I will tell later of the children God gave us. She stood by my side through thick and thin; travelled in canoes and sloops and sailing vessels while disliking the sea and a non-swimmer. She set school lessons for the children in back rooms of Christian Literature Crusade book-stores while also serving alone in the front of the stores. She went with me, by faith, into every new island advance and didn't complain. She has been longsuffering, forgiving and loving. And here I give "honour to whom honour is due:" To a good and loving wife; to a good and loving mother; to a good and loving grand-mother; to a good and loving worker; to a good and loving missionary; and to a good and loving woman who is a lover of Christ. Believing, as I do, that we should give bouquets to the living rather than flowers to the dead, I pen this heartfelt acknowledgement and appreciation of a virtuous woman and spouse like the proverbial one,[1] Scripture's highest accolade for wifely love.

OCTOBER 6 – LOVE'S SUBMISSION – Part One

Love submits to love; i.e. love, in the Son and sons and daughters, submits to the love of the Father. Love submits to the loving will of God. In the very nature of final Authority this must be, and is, so. Take the chain of authority and work down and we will see the principle and the process repeated.

First there is the love relationship of the Father, the Son and the Holy Spirit. They are equal members of the Godhead; workers together in creation and redemption; using the plural "we" and "us." "Then God said, "Let Us make man in Our image, according to Our likeness…"[1] Then switching from singular to plural, "…Whom shall I send, and who will go for Us?…"[2] when it was a case of a service decision. It was not a dilemma nor was it resolved by arbitrary fiat but was in the nature of an appeal. Isaiah heard it and responded. "…Here am I. Send me!"[2] And "He said, 'Go…'"[3] God usually sends the one who is willing to go.

Which brings up the matter of independent will; submission of will and love in the Godhead. We will not surmise but state the facts as given in Scripture. The Son came to do His Father's will. He delighted in it. It was the loving bondage of the pierced ear voluntarily chosen. That will was to cost Him dearly, but He knew that his Father's lovingkindness would preserve Him. The whole prophetic section of the Messianic Psalm 40 was fulfilled in Him.

The Son was given; the Son was sent; and the Son was loved; all three by the Father. And the Son submitted to the Father; cooperated with the Father; did no work separate from the Father; and only once asked if there was the possibility of another way other than via the Cross; yet still said "…yet not as I will, but as You will."[4] From the cradle through the Cross to the crown, the Son submitted His will to the Father. It was love's submission to love's authority for love's purposes of salvation.

In turn, upon His return, the Father and the Son sent the Spirit who came, like the Son, voluntarily, submissively, not to glorify Himself but to magnify and exalt the Son and glorify the Father. The separating of the members of the Godhead and their submission to each other, while actual and factual, is only part of the truth of the Trinity working in unity. The Father was in the Son reconciling the world to Himself. The Spirit is the Spirit of Christ. The Son indwelling us is the same as the Spirit indwelling us. Language can confuse us. But the love of the Father, Son and Holy Spirit, submitting for our redemption helps us to understand love's submission when we are called to it.

There are still final acts of love and submission to take place, the Son is to be sent and will come again; and finally, having seen all submit to Him, He in turn will be subject.

OCTOBER 7 – LOVE'S SUBMISSION – Part Two

The mystery of love's submission in the Godhead, past, present and future is not easily understood though clearly indicated in Scripture as we have seen.

"The statement that the Son also Himself shall be subject to God has been thought by some to lower the dignity of the Son of God, as well as possibly, to cast a reflection on His Deity. The subjection however, is not that of the Son as Son, but as the incarnate Son, this, of course, does not involve inequality of essence. The son of a king may be officially subordinate and yet equal in nature to his father."

These helpful words from Wycliffe Bible Commentary will also introduce us to the problem of love's personal submissions as required in the descending scale of authority. "But I want you to understand that Christ is the head of every man, and the man is the head of a woman, and God is the head of Christ."[1] We have seen the sense in which God is the head of Christ; it does not indicate inequality. It does show difference of role. And His role is supreme. Christ is the head of all things. He is the head of the Church. And Christ is the head of man. He is the federal head, the last Adam of the new humanity and the head of the new body, the Church. He is also literally the head of every man. Man is under Christ. Man is subordinate. Man is subject. Man is in submission. Reject this truth as we will, or rebel against it, it still stands. But why rebel against love? All the order that requires submission, all the authority that necessitates it, and the will that demands it, is good, acceptable and perfect. And love's submission finds the truth of it. Submit and we find we are submitting to agapé; self-giving, self-sacrificing, serving love.

This is equally so with the headship of man in relation to woman. In God's order the woman is under the man. This is denied today both outside and even inside some churches. Rebellion against and rejection of divine love's law of order only brings disorder and worse, destruction of the woman's divinely ordained role. Subordination here does not imply gender inequality; nor does it involve inequality. In Christ "There is neither Jew nor Greek, there is neither slave nor free man, there is neither male nor female; for you are all one in Christ Jesus."[2] This is positional relationship where there is no racial discrimination; no social distinction; no sexual differentiation. Yet of course the roles, as well as our bodies, are different. The role of men and women differ in the church and in the family. There are four orders in the Word: personal, family, ecclesiastical and governmental. Truths relating to each must be carefully distinguished. In some areas we are all required to submit. And again to submit to each other. In marriage, final authority, headship, is vested in the husband. Two heads would make a monstrosity out of marriage. But headship is not the same as dictatorship. Love governs this submission as it does with the authority of parents and children and servants and masters. It is all outlined in love. All that's needed is love's submission.

OCTOBER 8 – LOVE, RESPECT, SUBMISSION

When a lady is in charge! Is this a mistake? A misprint? No, just a Scriptural description of certain facts of life, at certain times, and in certain circumstances. "Now Deborah, a prophetess, the wife of Lappidoth, was judging Israel at that time. She used to sit under the palm tree of Deborah between Ramah and Bethel in the hill country of Ephraim; and the sons of Israel came up to her for judgment. Now she sent and summoned Barak the son of Abinoam from Kedesh-naphtali, and said to him, 'Behold, the Lord, the God of Israel, has commanded, 'Go and march to Mount Tabor, and take with you ten thousand men from the sons of Naphtali and from the sons of Zebulun. I will draw out to you Sisera, the commander of Jabin's army, with his chariots and his many troops to the river Kishon, and I will give him into your hand.'"[1] Three thousand years later, Israel was led in peace and war, for some crucial years, by a courageous and beloved, modern Deborah, Mrs. Golda Meir (1898 - 1978).

Queen Elizabeth I (1533 – 1603) said she couldn't have governed without the "loves" of the people. She had a way with words too, defending her sex, demanding loyalty, respect and submission in an autocratic age of powerful men.

To one such group she said "Had I been crested, not cloven, my lords, you had not treated me thus."

Speaking to her troops at Tilbury on the approach of the Spanish Armada in 1588 she said: "I know I have the body of a weak and feeble woman, but I have the heart and stomach of a king, and of a king of England too; and think foul scorn that Parma of Spain or any prince of Europe, should dare to invade the border of my realm."

To another rebel this: "I will make you shorter by the head."

And to a bishop: "Proud prelate, do what I tell thee, or I'll make thee what thou wert, before I made thee what thou art!"

And on her death bed to Robert Cecil (1563 – 1612): "Must! Is must a word to be addressed to princes? Little man, little man! Thy father, if he had been alive, durst not to have used that word."

Quite a lady! Quite a leader! Perhaps that's why she remained single.

Margaret Thatcher (1925 -) former Conservative Prime Minister of England was called the "Iron Lady" by her detractors. She put dictators down to the cry of "Thatcher, Thatcher, there's not a man to match her!" And what did husband Denis think about her activities? He was secure in his person and position and backed his wife with love and respect.

And what about Deborah and her husband? And Barak her general? Lappidoth seems to have been sensibly silent, at least as far as the Scripture records. And Barak, summoned and commanded and directed under divine authority, through Deborah in her role as prophetess, he obeyed with a proviso: "...If you will go with me, then I will go; but if you will not go with me, I will not go."[2] She agreed but pointed out that he would get no honour out of it as another woman would.

When the men won't go to the Mission Field the women must. When husbands abdicate their role wives have to make decisions alone. The Spirit filled ministry of women was prophesied by Joel and fulfilled at Pentecost and portrayed in Phillip's four daughters who prophesied. Can we today, love and respect such servants, and submit to the Lord's message through them.

OCTOBER 9 – FATHER LOVE: YEARNING AND WAITING

Father love provides and protects when the child is young; but when it comes of age a new learning process begins. The cruel, cold world must be the teacher. There is a very contemporary chorus on this theme of the Father heart of love that yearns over the child:

> "Like a Father You yearn to protect me
> Yet I must learn on my own;
> Until I've made my choice
> To follow Your voice…"

This is a concept of Father love that is often overlooked in that familiar story, told by our Lord Jesus, and known to us as the story of the prodigal son. When that self-willed man wanted freedom and the money to pay for it, the father gave him both liberty and his share of the estate. Remonstrance would have been of little use, as the father knew. The young man's mind was made up, and, presumably being of age, love let him go. Putting myself, as a father, in that father's shoes I have often wondered what I would have done. Knowing myself, I'm pretty sure I would have had my say about things, and probably withheld the cash! Jesus, knowing His Father, and that Father heart of love, told it truly and exactly as the father does with his prodigal son. Love, while yearning over them, lets them go in order to learn, often the hard way, that liberty, when it becomes license and self-indulgence, is bondage; slavery that is self inflicted. The young man of the parable, getting as far away from home and its influences, as he could journey, gave himself up to the proverbial wine, women and song. As long as the money lasted, hangers on and layabouts of both sexes leeched onto him and then left having sucked him dry. And then what? That youth found, that having left home, the memories of it and his father's love hadn't left him. He began to think, which is a first step to repentance; this is a change of mind leading to a change of course, and a change of action. "I considered my ways and turned my feet to Your testimonies. I hastened and did not delay to keep Your commandments."[1]

And so in repentance, brought about by desperate need and remorse over rejected love, he returned with speeches of self-abnegation all prepared, to find, what? He found watching, waiting love that went out to meet and greet the returned prodigal. Love silenced his speeches; love, that had run to embrace and kiss him, ordered replacement robes for his rags, riches for his poverty, the ring of relationship and coverings for his calloused feet. Father love ordered the feast of the fattened calf with music and merriment. "For this son of mine was dead and has come to life again; he was lost and has been found…"[2] Yearning, waiting love had won. As it did for us because of the Cross.

We commenced with a contemporary song of the soul set free and conclude with it. Did that one who said "I've made my choice to follow Your voice" really make it? Whether the ignorance or arrogance of rebellious youth, or the right yearning for learning prompted this young person, he or she did come back saying:

> "You, You are my wholeness
> You are my completeness
> My soul, my thirsty soul can
> Rest in the depths of Your love."

OCTOBER 10 – FATHER LOVE: FREELY GIVING

We have seen, in connection with father love, a prodigal son under grace, in this age of grace. It is salutary to consider a prodigal son under law, in the age of law. I might suggest that the reader review the story again for it is not my purpose to review it here. But remember, even in this day of grace, prodigals who refuse to repent and return to yearning, waiting love, condemn themselves to love's wrath. As holy love has a holy heaven, it also has a holy hell for all the unholy, unrepentant and unbelieving. Our Lord Jesus is the One who warns of this awful place. He died to save us from this place where the fire never goes out because in the nature of holy, heavenly love, it can't be extinguished. And it was Father love, holy, heavenly love that found the way, at an awful cost, to justify the ungodly and still be just. Philip Doddrige (1702 – 1751) sings of Father love that saves and seals. And to this end Father love is bringing us. He has provided in himself, through the Son, by the Spirit, for all our need.

"Father of peace, and God of love,
We own Thy pow'r to save,
That pow'r by which our Shepherd rose
Victorious o'er the grave.

Him from the dead Thou brought'st again,
When by His sacred blood,
Confirmed and sealed forevermore
Th'eternal cov'nant stood.

O may Thy Spirit seal our souls,
And mold them to Thy will,
That our weak hearts no more may stray,
But keep Thy cov'nant still.

That all we think and all we do
Be pleasing in Thy sight,
Through Jesus Christ, to Whom be praise
In endless glory bright."

The analogy between our heavenly Father's love and a human father's love, parallel each other in many ways, but in other areas it falls far short. One such case is in the area of giving. "Now suppose one of you fathers is asked by his son for a fish; he will not give him a snake instead of a fish, will he? Or if he is asked for an egg, he will not give him a scorpion, will he? If you then, being evil, know how to give good gifts to your children, how much more will your heavenly Father give the Holy Spirit to those who ask Him?"[1] How much more! How much more? The difference is as great as the heavens are above the earth. His love in giving is beyond compare. His love gifted to us in His Son. "But God demonstrates His own love toward us, in that while we were yet sinners, Christ died for us. Much more then, having now been justified by His blood, we shall be saved from the wrath of God through Him. For if while we were enemies we were reconciled to God through the death of His Son, much more, having been reconciled, we shall be saved by His life."[2] How much more! How much more? All that, and still there's more to follow! His love gifted to us by His Spirit, and, with Him, all His graces and gifts. The Father's love giving goes on and on.

"He giveth more grace as our burdens grow greater,
He sendeth more strength as our labors increase;
To added afflictions He addeth His mercy,
To multiplied trials he multiplies peace."
Annie Flint (1866 – 1932)

OCTOBER 11 – FATHER LOVE

"Just as a father has compassion on his children, So the Lord has compassion on those who fear Him. For He Himself knows our frame; He is mindful that we are but dust."[1] Love and compassion are always together. Love may be the "silent" partner, but it is certainly not a "sleeping" partner. Love moves people into compassionate action as we have seen in these pages. Heavenly Father love has been considered previously. This time we are going to look at earthly father love like the "as" in the verse indicates. The "so" of comparison is understood and underlies the story of father love I am about to tell. It is the one I know by blessed experience, and my memories of it, with all its blemishes, are as vivid now as it was the last time I saw my dad.

It was September 15, 1938 and he was vigorously waving his hat and shouting farewell words of encouragement as I sailed from the old wharf, where today, within a couple of hundred meters, stands the white winged Sydney Opera House on Benelong Point. I didn't know at the time that dad was within less than two years of home call. Roger Thomas Davey was called up higher on August 15, 1940 at Richmond, New South Wales, Australia. He was sixty-six years of age. As I look at this moment at the memorial card that mother had printed I read the words: "Faith Triumphant" summing up the text: "Blessed are the dead who die in the Lord from now on! 'Yes,' says the Spirit, 'so that they may rest from their labors, for their deeds follow with them.'"[2]

Father was a man who loved the Lord; having been converted as a young man through evangelistic meeting in the North of England conducted by a lady worker of the, then young, Salvation Army. He had been brought up as an Anglican. Later, when the family moved to Kent in the South of England and I joined them there, we went to a Primitive Methodist Sunday School, a Baptist Mission Hall, and occasionally Plymouth Brethren meetings. Quite a background! An early remembrance of father's love was experienced during the long walks to some of these meetings. Dad would carry the tired boy on his back for miles. This was practical fatherly love but more than natural love was behind it. We were on the way to a gospel meeting and the love of Christ in dad was carrying his son there. He wanted to see me saved. Heavenly Father love moved him. "…In His love and in His mercy He redeemed them, and He lifted them and carried them all the days of old."[3] And father love kept on "carrying" me under the sound of the gospel after we had emigrated to Australia in 1929. My parents joined the Carlton Baptist Church in Kogarah, and took me and my brother to a mission there conducted by the Rev. Wilfred Jarvis in June of 1930. I had made a child's profession of Christ at home earlier in England. But at that mission I was converted, made a public confession of Christ in baptism and became a member of Carlton Baptist Church. Father's love went beyond the physical caring and carrying; it cared and carried spiritually. I am forever grateful. I don't want to paint a picture of unflawed fatherly love though. Father, in temperament, was a choleric with the accompanying strengths and weaknesses as I observe and experience in myself. But the love of God triumphed in dad right up until the end. Now he dwells in his Father's love.

OCTOBER 12 – MOTHER LOVE

"Can a woman forget her nursing child and have no compassion on the son of her womb? Even these may forget, but I will not forget you. Behold, I have inscribed you on the palms of My hands…"[1] Compassionate love in the Lord's case is unending, while even the most noble love on earth, compassionate maternal love, can cease. Undoubtedly the greatest lovers are mothers. A father's love is strong, but mother's is stronger. A father's love is long, but mother's is longer. Mother love has a large measure of mystery in it; there is a great mixture of pleasure-pain in it; it not only suffers, it suffers long, life long in some cases. Mother love is not governed by sex; nor is it time's fool. It does not change with the seasons nor fade with the years. But, and we have it on good authority, the Word of God, that not all mothers are paragons of perfection, while even some good mothers, are not always good at "mothering." Mother love is the inner motivating force; mothering consists not only consists of the acts of love common to most mothers, but that extra, that special something, a mixture of attitude, affection, authority, ability to anticipate and share in all the woes, wonders, welts and worries the child may meet. But again not all have it either.

A comic strip called "Grumps" (now, like so many other good things, it has gone with the wind) had a memorable scene. The baby was bawling its heart out. The visiting grandma finally asked the mother if the baby's condition and crying didn't bother her. "Not a bit" replied the mother. "I've taken Valium." "But the baby must be upset over something" persisted grandma. "Let it get its own Valium," said this cartoonist caricature of a modern, misfit, misnamed mother. The exaggeration makes a valid point. But such are the bad exceptions, not the norm. Mother love, the good and true is rightly celebrated on Mother's Day, and should be done so every day. And here, I wish to publicly pay a tribute to my mother and her love.

What kind of a mother, was, is, my mother we ask ourselves? And I ask myself? I am looking now at two pictures of her. The first is of her in a flouncy, flowing wedding gown on her wedding day in 1902. She was twenty-two. The second, in my Bible where I have pasted it, is her in the nursing home in Richmond, New South Wales, Australia where she died November 10, 1974 in her ninety-fifth year. She had been a widow for thirty-four years. Mary Hannah Davey (nee Swinburn) was a loving mother. If there was one characteristic above others that I remember, it was her self-sacrifice. She gave herself and her substance unstintingly for the nearly sixty years I knew her. In the lean depression years she went without, often at mealtimes. In her long widowhood she gave liberally, from the poverty of her widow's pension, to our young family on the mission field. In Roseau, Dominica, West Indies, there stands a Mission building into which mother gave of her penury. Widow's mites multiply miraculously because they are born of love for the Lord. Mother knew the Lord as a young woman but it was not until later in life that she came into deep commitment to Christ. On a Sunday night at a Keswick deeper life convention mother came into a richer experience of the love of Christ. Katoomba, in the Blue Mountains was a place of sacred memories to her, as it is to her son. She is buried in St. Peter's Church yard cemetery, Richmond, with her daughter Marie Eleanor Biddle overlooking the Hawkesbury River and in sight of those same Blue Mountains.

OCTOBER 13 – SMOTHER LOVE

Though at first it might not be apparent, at the heart of smother love, is self love. This smother love pampers, spoils, gives in, gives way, gives everything and refuses to say "No"; will not, cannot discipline. Because it fears the loss of the love that ministers to the ego; the love that builds the pride and vanity of the self love; the selfishness that is rarely reckoned in these sorry travesties of real love. Earlier this poem by Elizabeth Barrett Browning (1806 – 1861) was used from the daughter's side, as we dealt with the cruelty of self love. But here I will repeat it, and use it from the mother's side, as an illustration of smother love. It is the wrong kind of love and is present in mothers, aunts, and particularly grandmothers and grandfathers. It smothers with wrong kindness; inhibits the development of true relationships and often ends in love-hate situations which are mutually destructive.

"Fair Amy of the terraced house,
Assist me to discover,
Why you who would not hurt a mouse
Can torture so your lover.

They say, Love gives as well as takes;
But I'm a simple maiden,
My mother's first smile, when she wakes,
I still have smiled and prayed in.

I only know my mother's love,
Which gives all and asks nothing:
And this new love sets the groove
Too much the way of loathing."

Poor Amy! Everything is lavished on them. Poor rich children! How frequently their sad lives and sad ends disgrace the headlines. They are without responsibility or accountability; and not only rich kids; ordinary middle class ones, with their "gimme, gimme, gimmes" are often the product of smother love of one kind or another. We don't glorify the poet, nor extol poverty by, or for itself but, the long and illustrious roll call of poor children, who by struggle have triumphed and blessed their day and generation, makes encouraging reading. Think of just one. George Washington Carver (1864 – 1903) of peanut fame. Frequently such children know real love from struggling parents.

Some examples of spoiled, smothered, indulged and over privileged children from Scripture will surprise us. From the homes of priests, prophets and kings come the sad records of undisciplined, disobedient (to God and parents) children. They destroyed themselves and brought disgrace to their parents and shame upon the name of the Lord. Smother love was not the only cause, but surely part of it. Think of these three names: Eli, Samuel and David. They glorified God in many ways but Scripture indicts them for the upbringing of their children. These are cases of father's smother love. Eli's sons, Hophni and Phineas abused their positions in abominable and arrogant ways and were destroyed. Their old father died the day they did. Samuel, surprisingly, observing these things from close up, failed in the same way, in the same areas. David's indulgent affection destroyed Absalom. David wept wrongly and too late for him. Adonijah was another spoiled, arrogant, rebellious son, also cut off in his prime. Scripture does not cover up but relates these examples for our benefit.

OCTOBER 14 – SISTER LOVE

My sister, Marie Eleanor, was the first born in our family and the only girl (another had died in her first year) in a family of boys. As she was about fourteen years older than I, she often looked after me, and from this caring, I learned about sister love. I knew it by experience before I had heard of the term. And I received that love all through life. She has been with the Lord for many years and it is, in memory, her love for the Lord which most moves me, for she loved me, not only with sister's love but the love of a Christian sister. She used to teach me in Sunday School, and I remember the first Bible I had was won in her class. I have to state that it was gained for perfect attendance not good behaviour. Regrettably I was not a model brother or example in class. But she still loved me, and I have kept, for over sixty years, the flyleaf from that first Bible, for not only was it written in her hand, it contains a verse which became very important in my life. During my wandering teens, I always carried that Bible with me, though I didn't read it. I wanted it with me, not for sentimental reasons, but because of the truth of that text. "Thy word is a lamp unto my feet, and a light unto my path."[1] In northern New South Wales to which I had journeyed by pony and sulky there came a time when I stopped running and started thinking of returning home. My sisters gift of love and text of truth, helped at a cross-roads of life. I thank God for sister's love.

As I'm sure Moses did also. I always think of Miriam as Moses' guardian angel during those crucial days when his life was in the balance as he floated and cried in his rocking cradle on the Nile. That story is well known but the faithful sister's love and watch care for her baby brother is rarely given the attention it deserves. She had been given a charge by her mother Jochebed, to keep a vigilant eye on that frail vessel and its precious cargo, saved by ingenuity and love from Pharaoh's death sentence on all Jewish baby boys. The decree, of that Egyptian despot and hater of Israel, said: "…Every son who is born you are to cast into the Nile…"[2] Mother love, while obeying the letter of the law, found a way to save her beautiful boy. After hiding him for three months she made a waterproof reed basket and "cast" her son into the Nile. Miriam was posted as caretaker, observer, reporter and fulfilled her guardian duties with sister love and holy boldness. When the basket and baby were found by Pharaoh's daughter and the bathing party, Miriam approached and said: "…Shall I go and call a nurse for you from the Hebrew women that she may nurse the child for you?"[3] Given the "go ahead" the girl went and called her mother who came and was told: "…Take this child away and nurse him for me and I will give you your wages…"[4] This true story of Providential love, parental love, and sister's love, has its hinge in the latter love, of a sister. What a key player she was; not just a bit player, in these love scenes. And despite some inevitable disagreements, personality clashes and power struggles, Miriam continued to play an important role in Moses' life. Sister love was never lost and brother love never ceased.

OCTOBER 15 – BROTHER LOVE

I have known three brothers. The eldest has gone to be with the Lord I trust; the youngest is still searching but I believe and pray that the love of God, my father's and mother's love and prayers, and his own knowledge of the way will bring him back. Now it is my middle brother, of whom I wish to write and his brother's love to me when I was a youngster. George was born in the same month, October, but eight years earlier than I; 1908 to be exact. I did not see too much of him until 1929. After that I saw even less, for he was based in England while we (father, mother, with younger brother and myself) had moved to Australia. George had gone to sea, and all I saw of him was during the time his ship was back in port. But those visits, though rare, were greatly anticipated by me. George would often bring home a case of grapefruit from Africa or something else exotic from some where else. But it wasn't for his gifts that I appreciated him; it was for his, what I now know to be, brother's love. One early incident, apparently insignificant, stands firm in my memory. It was early in 1928, and I had already sat for and passed, my written examinations for a scholarship. Now the time for the oral tests had arrived and that day coincided with George's homecoming. Learning where I was going he immediately looked me over and smartened me up! With his own brilliantine he settled my unruly hair, and generally tidied me up for the visual and verbal exams that awaited me that day. I won the scholarship, not because of my older brother's simple loving concern and care, but I'm sure it helped. Appearance counted as well as the right answers. Later this loving brother gave me my first watch and first double breasted suit. I still, occasionally when in England go and stay with him and his wife and on one occasion we had a long walk and talk in the North London suburb where he is now retired. Brother love on my part was concerned about George's spiritual welfare. So I chatted with him, and witnessed about Christ and he assured me that he "believed on the Lord" as his Saviour.

We have seen sister's love in Scripture in the case of Miriam and Moses. But there was an older brother too, in that family and his name was Aaron. Miriam was the oldest child of Amram and Jochebed. Aaron came next, three years older than Moses, and evidently born before the decree to drown the Jewish boys in the Nile. Due to Moses' adoption and Egyptian upbringing the first forty years of the brother's lives were lived in separation and the next forty in isolation, for Moses fled Egypt. So they only experienced brother love in theory and at a distance until God's time was ripe. Moses, at eighty years of age, prayed that God would excuse him when told that he would lead Israel out of Egypt. Then God called the older brother into the act. Aaron was to act as Moses' mouthpiece before Pharaoh. They were then eighty-three and eighty years of age respectively. It was not an ordinary background of brother love or an auspicious age at which to start living it. Yet they worked closely together for the next forty years until Aaron died at age one hundred twenty-three. They had their problems but brother love did prevail and continue until the end. One of the most touching evidences of this brother love is seen in the small incident when Aaron, the older brother, physically supported the arms of his younger brother until Israel prevailed in the battle. Supportive love is one of the loveliest forms of brother love.

OCTOBER 16 – AFFECTIONATE LOVE

A fanciful myth using etymology as a reason, or excuse, associates the "Stork" and all the stork stories about babies with the Greek word "Storgé." The Greek lexicon defines it as "Affection, especially of parents to offspring and of course equally of offspring to parents." C. S. Lewis (1898 – 1963) in his helpful book <u>The Four Loves</u> describes it as one of the natural loves found not only in the human family but also in the animal world.

"The image we must start with is that of a mother nursing a baby, a bitch or a cat with a basketful of puppies or kittens, all in a squeaking, nuzzling, heap together; purrings, lickings, baby-talk, milk, warmth, the smell of young life."

This is family love, though we must not limit it to the human and animal families. It is needed and shown in the wide spiritual family; the whole church; the family of God.

The word is used three times in the New Testament; twice with regret for its lack and once in combination with another "love" word, when it is urged upon us. On the first occasion it is in the context of a list of abominations that helped destroy nations now long gone. Amongst these degrading depravities our word is in the three fold family context. "…haters of God, insolent, arrogant, boastful, inventors of evil, disobedient to parents, without understanding, untrustworthy, unloving, unmerciful."[1] Other versions render "unloving" as "heartless," "without natural affection" which is exactly what it is. This affection love or affectionate love is largely lacking in our uncivil civilization.

Again, among the long list of signs of the last times which Paul tabulates, is the lack of this down to earth, personal, practical family love, family affection. We find our word here and again it is in the negative context. "In the last days… men will be lovers of money, boastful, arrogant, revilers, disobedient to parents, ungrateful, unholy, unloving…lovers of pleasure rather than lovers of God."[2] "Without natural affection" says the King James Version. Parents may or may not have lavished affection upon their children but it is not being reciprocated. Ingrates indeed. In close needy family cases, in cases in the wider family, and in the church family, affectionate love is so desperately needed and so callously withheld. Why? The reasons are many, some no doubt reasonable sounding, but the three inordinate loves also on this list; "lovers of self, lovers of money, lovers of pleasure" while not being "lovers of God" are the major causes.

The third New Testament usage is a positive note. It is a lovely combination of "philos" and "storges" giving us "philostorges" or tenderly loving, tenderly affectioned. "Be devoted to one another in brotherly love…"[3] When brotherly love is married to kindly love, affectionate love we have a union that blesses the physical family, the world family and the spiritual family. We are blessed and again, because of love like this, God is glorified. Nurture affection, natural affection, need affection can be regularly supplied through us, as well as to us, by the super natural affection of God.

OCTOBER 17 – LOVE'S FRUIT

We now look at love's fruit on the human level. This could cover a wide range through all the lesser loves, but that has been done under other titles. We will review marital love; from falling in love, through being in love to first married love, hopes and expectations run high. The expected results can be called love's fruit. And what sweet fruitage it can be. Then comes the normal, next expected fruit; the fruit of the womb, a baby, love's lovely new life. A child, desired and prayed for, is, as we have seen in the case of Samuel, a crowning joy and blessing to any couple. I have called such as him and before him, Isaac, Joseph, Benjamin and Obed, love children. A "love child" today often refers to a baby born out of wedlock, and many of these are loved and frequently by a single parent. Yet again, inside and outside of marriage, there are too many children unwanted and unloved. Poor little ones who are sinned against before they are born and sinned against afterwards. Thank God He loves "all" the children of the world; heavens streets are filled with them.

"…I heard the children singing…it was the New Jerusalem…" Frederick Weatherly (1848 – 1929)

And we parents again and again thank God for the fruit of the womb.

There is much more to be said about love's fruit. We see the fruit develop and mature and someone else pluck it! As the man said, after giving away his daughter in marriage: "I have paid all the bills to raise her, now I give her away, and have to pay for the privilege of doing that in this reception!" Too bad! It is still more blessed to give than to receive. Had he not heard of planting fruit trees for other generation's benefit? He must have plucked some other parent's darling! Now he could look forward to the next crop of love fruit; the grandchildren. Love is wonderful, especially in its human fruitage.

We move higher to "love's fruit" in the realm of the Spirit. "But the fruit of the Spirit is love, joy, peace, patience, kindness, goodness, faithfulness, gentleness, self-control…"[1] We have had an in depth look at these under the title "Love's Graces" (May 17) and I mention them again here because they are part of what our Lord meant when He spoke of "fruit, more fruit, much fruit and fruit that remains." This is love's spiritual fruit, and it is in line with this that He concludes His message on increasing fruitfulness with these words: "This I command you, that you love one another."[2]

Then there is love's fruit, through us, in other lives, seeing others receive a blessing and seeing love being reproduced as fruit in other saints. Paul was always looking for this kind of love's harvest, for God, for himself and for others.

And last but by no means least. Love's fruit in the salvation of sinners. This is soul winning fruit. There's joy in heaven, joy on earth, and joy in the soul winner's heart because of love's fruit.

OCTOBER 18 – LOVE YOUR CHILDREN

"…encourage the young women to…love their children."[1] The older women were to do this encouraging, which on the surface hardly seems necessary. Surely young mothers do this? They must love their offspring? We all know some, or know of some, who don't. The reasons vary, but today child neglect and child abuse must be widespread, for we read so much about it. It has always been prevalent in every age, but improved world wide communication technology keeps us better informed. Selfish, pleasure loving, or even over tired young working mothers are amongst the guilty. Young children were left for hours outside a gambling casino while their married and single parents were inside wasting their time and money. This was given banner headlines by the concerned editor of our local paper. Unloved children are frequently unwanted children; unwanted from conception and unwanted when they are born. We frequently saw, while on the mission field, that grannies seemed to be left with the raising of their grandchildren, and perhaps it was so in Paul's day.

The mothers of Salem, who brought their children to Jesus, were loving young women who wanted the best for their little ones. They knew He loved children and that He was willing to bless theirs. Moved by love, these mothers acted, only to receive a rude rebuff, and rough handling from a surprising quarter. His disciples were the ones rebuking the mothers and refusing to permit the children to come near him. Those who should have been foremost in loving children were actually rejecting them. Why do our children feel rejected? Why do they not come to Christ? He is willing. Are we the stumbling blocks? Maybe we merit the indignation and displeasure He showed His disciples. He was vexed with them, grieved and much displeased. He also said: "…Permit the children to come to Me; do not hinder them; for the kingdom of God belongs to such as these[2]… And He took them in His arms and began blessing them, laying His hands on them."[3]

Hannah's son was desperately desired, joyfully received and lovingly cared for. The love she had for God was shown in the name she gave the boy, Samuel, "asked of God", and in her love act of devoting him back to God and His service. This is how to love your children. Give them to God before they are conceived; dedicate them to him publicly at birth and prepare them for His lifelong service. Encourage your children in their turn to do likewise.

Encourage them to love Him; encourage them to thank Him for dying for them. Grandmothers encourage your daughters by example and precept to love their children. Young mothers you will find that the love investment, of time, patience, energy and caring, you put into your children will be returned a hundredfold in this life and in the life to come. They whom you have brought to Christ will rejoice together with you.

OCTOBER 19 – CHILDREN'S LOVE

To have an unthankful child gives pain worse than a scorpion's sting. To have raised rebellious offspring causes suffering worse than the childless can ever know. But to have loving children who seek to follow the Lord is one of life's greatest joys. And we have been blessed.

Our first daughter was born to other parents in the island of Dominica. Soon after our marriage there on Christmas Day, 1941, the Lord gave us another gift, a lovely Dominican child, who needed a home and help. Her father, who had polio, and a large family, was finding it difficult to make ends meet in wartime; while the brave mother struggled to garden, and feed and clothe the children. We were holding meetings in that country village up in the mountains and in the end it was arranged that we would look after Cornelia, one of the smallest and younger members of the family. The Lord gave us a promise: "…Take this child away and nurse her for me and I will give you your wages…" in a slight gender adaptation from the Moses story. So our first child was an "adopted daughter." What a blessing Cornelia has brought to us and so many others. Her life of love for the Lord and people continues today as she carries on the work commenced by her adoptive parents. Over forty years have passed but love continues to grow and flow between us. Children's love is a many splendoured thing.

Then on a wild, windy, wet night in December, 1944, in Roseau, the capital, our son was born in most difficult circumstances in the mission house we were renting. Complications at birth had me on my knees at one time, thanking God as Job did. The same Lord gives, and takes away. I thought our first born was dead at birth. But he lived and became our miracle child. Like Cornelia he too was saved as a child and learned to love the Lord, his parents, and people, and to show it in practical ways. The first Biblical way was by obedience to his parents and lawful authority. Obedient love is the hallmark of children's love. Again over forty years have passed but love continues to grow and flow between us as we worked together in a local church extension work here in the City of Edmonton. It is wonderful to be able to play together also. We have occasional golf games. Father, son, son-in-law and grandsons! No generation gap here.

I was on tour in New Zealand in April, 1949, expecting to be back in Sydney, Australia, for the birth of another child. Then came an emergency call:

"Return immediately, baby girl born April 25, thought to be a blue baby."

I was put on a Clipper flying boat which ultimately splashed down in Rose Bay. I hurried to the nursing home to be greeted at the door by an Australian matron who looked me over while listening to my name. She said, surprising me:

"With your complexion, that's one reason why the baby's so dark."

The baby's condition righted itself and I tell the story of our "Anzac" in "Nurse's Love."

Cornelia, John, Susanne; each name stirs memories, loving thoughts; with occasional wondering about my failures. Believing strongly, as I do, in the Scriptural principles of obedience in love, and the disciplines of love plus disciplinary love, I was perhaps too heavy handed with the children when they were young. But recently on a visit to us, Cornelia said: "Thank you Dad for your loving discipline when I was small."

OCTOBER 20 – NURSE'S LOVE

To love is even more wonderful than to be loved. And, to my mind, nowhere is this self-less love more evident than among nurses. Perhaps, because we have a daughter who is a nurse, I am biased. I watched the development of this special nurse from her infancy. Early on she expressed what she felt her vocation would be and at school prepared for it. During school vacations she worked in a hospital kitchen and became acquainted with the hard, behind the scenes, work of practical duties. Then came the years of nursing school training and finally graduation and ward service. Just this past week, while talking to our own doctor, he enquired after Susanne.

"She used to work with me in surgery" he said "and I wish there were more like her."

This may seem out of place, and immodest parental love glaringly paraded, but I offer the excuse that she is a good illustration of "nurse's love" and the only one I know intimately. Love for her profession and love for her patients is, for me anyway, the supreme evidence in one serving in this high calling.

It is evident that a Christian nurse has inborn love, as well as innate, natural humanitarian love. Inborn love is the love of Christ dwelling in the heart by faith. And I know from observation (from hospital beds!) that only the love of Christ can make a nurse truly empathetic, really understanding of a patient's holistic needs, and lovingly caring and responsive during the long hours of the night watch duty. I know well enough that many a nurse, who is not a Christian, is dedicated, loving and caring, but there is a difference between natural love and Christ's love. The former will "run out" sooner than the latter which is supernatural. The motto of one Christian Nurse's Association is: "Caritas Christi Urget Nos," which is Latin for that tremendous verse: "For the love of Christ controls us…"[1] "constrains us," "urges us on," and "motivates us." This is not only the compulsion of our love for Christ, but more truly the love of Christ for us. His love comes first; is foremost and forever; unflagging, unfaltering and unaffected by time or circumstances. Dr. Alexander Maclaren (1826 – 1910) points out that this love is independent of time and space; is not turned away by unworthiness; not repelled by failure to respond; not disgusted by any sin; unwearied by any failings of its approach, however numerous. The love of Christ never loses its intensity.

There is a Scripture which in the King James Version adds another dimension. "But we were gentle among you, even as a nurse cherisheth her children," and lest we are carried away by the picture of a nurse on the children's ward the modern versions make clear the special emphasis. "But we proved to be gentle among you, as a nursing mother tenderly cares for her own children."[2] These verses taken together give the full picture of "nurse's love." From a regular nurse's love for children; through a nurse who is caring for her own children; to a nursing mother lovingly giving of herself for her little ones.

OCTOBER 21 – LOVE'S DISCIPLESHIP

"When I was one-and-twenty
I heard a wise man say,
'Give crowns and pounds and guineas
But not your heart away;
Give pearls away and rubies
But keep your fancy free.'
But I was one-and-twenty,
No use to talk to me.

When I was one-and-twenty
I heard him say again,
'The heart out of the bosom
Was never given in vain;
'Tis paid with sighs a plenty
And sold for endless rue.'
And I am two-and-twenty,
And oh, 'tis true, 'tis true."
A. E. Housman (1859 – 1936)

This is from a worldly wise man, but worldly wisdom is not always foolish. I know from experience the truth of some of the things he writes. At nineteen years of age, had things continued as they were heading I could have become engaged and married. It would have been premature and foolish and in the mercy of God it was prevented by His move on me in that same year, challenging me to love's discipleship and discipline on a higher plane. December 7, 1935 was a memorable day indeed as I responded to his call to forsake all and follow Him. When I was "one-and-twenty" I was in the Missionary and Bible College, Croydon, New South Wales, Australia. That was a grand place to celebrate my twenty-first birthday. When I was "two-and-twenty" I was on a French ship enroute to Britain and France for further training and preparation for the mission field. How glad I am that love's discipleship triumphed over natural love's desires. I am not decrying that which is honourable and divinely decreed. When I was five-and-twenty I was married on the mission field; finding, following and fulfilling His will.

Love's discipleship, as we saw in "Love Plus Hate" (February 11), is demanding and divisive. Discipline and discipleship are connected in language and even more so in their Scriptural union. Our Lord treats "would be," "could be" and "should be" disciples with severe doses of the "cannots." Possessions, occupations and relations are amongst the prime preventatives keeping us from wholly following the Lord in love's discipleship. We see it written large in the Word and it has loomed large in our past experience and is ever liable to attack again and seek to divert us from the demanding course. Lesser loves can be enemies of the higher.

John the Baptist made and had disciples. Disciple simply means pupil or student and was usually applied to those who attached themselves to a teacher. What John had to do and what all teachers of the Word have to do, is to transfer the affection and allegiance of the scholars from themselves to the Master. This problem is not new. The Corinthian church was carnal in this and other areas. People became followers and disciples of their favourites; Apollos the golden tongued; Cephas or Peter, "primus inter pares" or first among equals; and Paul, a man given to seeing things as they were. John rejoiced as he saw his disciples following the Lord. We must train and make disciples who love their Lord above all other loves and who will then, themselves, become teachers, trainers and makers of others who will follow the Lord's discipleship.

OCTOBER 22 – LOVE'S DISCIPLINE

"...My son, do not regard lightly the discipline of the Lord, nor faint when you are reproved by Him; for those whom the Lord loves He disciplines, and He scourges every son whom He receives."[1] This New Testament quotation from the Old Testament book of Proverbs shows the continuity and acceptance from generation to generation of this truth, that true love disciplines. Some generations in some countries are more self-indulgent in the areas of personal and family life and loving, while others at other times have been too harsh. We may be awakening to the fact that we have lacked in the discipline of love. Our heavenly Father, whose name is love, shows us the difference between the false love that indulges itself, its children at home, at school, at work and at play. This will be increasingly true in the last days. "For men will be lovers of self, lovers of money, boastful, arrogant, revilers, disobedient to parents, ungrateful, unholy, unloving, irreconcilable, malicious gossips, without self-control, brutal, haters of good, treacherous, reckless, conceited, lovers of pleasure rather than lovers of God."[2] This recitation of the harvest from false loves drives us to a consideration of the true love and its fruitful discipline.

A father, writing to his son, urges him to consider several things about the Lord's loving discipline. Don't treat it lightly; don't laugh it off as old fashioned. God has ways of regulating conduct that are impossible for parents. He can chasten through circumstances that are painful, powerful and salutary. When these start to bite, don't complain, but recognize them as the reproofs of the love that won't let you go. Don't faint or falter; they can be a proof of sonship; you are not unique; every son in His family is subject to the scourging discipline of love. You are illegitimate without it! "Those whom I love, I reprove and discipline..."[3]

Francis Thompson (1859 – 1907), described by Dr. Frank W. Boreham, D.D. (1871 – 1959) as "one of England's purest poets and choicest souls" first conceived and drafted his classic The Hound of Heaven in the days of his raggedness and wretchedness. This lilting lyric to the heavenly love that would not let him go, recognizes the same scourging discipline of "love's uplifted stroke."

> "Naked, I wait thy Love's uplifted stroke!
> My harness, piece by piece,
> Thou hast hewn from me
> And smitten me to my knee;
> I am defenceless, utterly."

The heavenly Father's hounding, chastening love, gained the victory and Thompson became a disciple. This is one of the results of disciplinary love; it produces disciples. Discipline and disciples are joined by God, let no man sever them. The finest fruit from love's discipline is described in the context of our text. "All discipline for the moment seems not to be joyful, but sorrowful; yet to those who have been trained by it, afterwards it yields the peaceful fruit of righteousness."[4] Let us, as earthly parents, use love's discipline as our heavenly Father does.

OCTOBER 23 – LOVE'S ACCEPTANCE

Love's acceptance of holy love's discipline, testing and suffering is much deeper and more meaningful than resignation to these things. Acceptance is a positive attitude of affirmation that God in his love knows best and is planning a harvest. Resignation seems to have something negative in it; I may be resigned to it or resigned from it; opting out can follow with critical results. Job and his wife are examples of acceptance and opting out of God's drastic dealings with their lives and family and fortune. After a series of dreadful disasters and the death of all of their children, "Then Job arose and tore his robe and shaved his head, and he fell to the ground and worshiped. He said, 'Naked I came from my mother's womb, and naked I shall return there. The Lord gave and the Lord has taken away. Blessed be the name of the Lord.' Through all this Job did not sin nor did he blame God."[1] Here is acceptance, with worshipful reaffirmation of trust in God.

Then, as ills have a way of doing, more came his way in the form of an awful and painful and foul attack of boils covering him from head to foot. The distraught man needed now, as never before, the love, acceptance and comfort of his wife. She, who had probably been resigned to all the other losses, now faced with the loss of her husband's health and the consequences, has had enough and opts out of any semblance of even resignation to the will of God. "Then his wife said to him, 'Do you still hold fast your integrity? Curse God and die!' But he said to her, 'You speak as one of the foolish women speaks. Shall we indeed accept good from God and not accept adversity?' In all this Job did not sin with his lips."[2]

We know from the beginning the reasons for this series of calamities. The war in heaven was being worked out on earth. Heavenly love believed in Job and was sure of his love in return, come what may. Satan was permitted to test Job up to the limit that the removal of the hedge of love allowed. Job was being made a spectacle to heaven, hell, earth, angels fallen and unfallen and men.

Dr. T. S. Rendall, former President of Prairie Bible Institute, writing in the <u>Prairie Overcomer</u> suggests:

"When crushed by a sorrow or confined by a sickness, we often respond, 'Why me, O Lord?' But there are good reasons for suggesting the question ought to be, 'Why not me, O Lord?' We do not raise the issue foolishly or flippantly. Given his understanding of the heavenly Father's use of weakness, loss, sickness, etc., as a means of loving discipline, should not the believer willingly place himself in God's hands…? …To respond 'Why me, O Lord?' is to end up in the slough of self pity; to respond 'Why not me, O Lord?' is to walk the highway of victory."

Miss Amy Wilson Carmichael (1867 – 1951) spent the last years of her missionary life in India, bedridden. She wrote a poem entitled "In Acceptance Lieth Peace." The verses state:

"Not in forgetting lieth peace…
Not in endeavor lieth peace…
Not in aloofness lieth peace…
Not in submission lieth peace…

He said, 'I will accept the breaking sorrow
Which God to-morrow
Will to His son explain.'
Then did the turmoil deep within him cease.
Not vain the word, not vain;
For in Acceptance lieth peace."

OCTOBER 24 – LOVING OTHER PEOPLE'S CHILDREN

The word "philoteknous" means "child-lovers." It is not the debased kind of 'child-loving' practised blatantly in some places today by pornographic paedophiles. They were even publishing their own magazine when we lived in Toronto. The police and the courts were hampered in their efforts against such people and publications by the advocates of "civil liberties" and "civil rights" to use and abuse other people's children. It is appalling to think how far our civilization has gone down the demonic path to self-destruction. Even the euphemism (and abuse of a lovely word) "gay" is used instead of the obloquy of a term like "pederast" for these perverts. Today, when one calls it what Christ and Scripture calls "sin" instead of "just another life-style," the accusation is immediately levelled that one is unloving, hyper critical, behind the times, from the Bible belt or a bigoted fundamentalist! The same kind of people say the same kind of things when one dares to support the "pro-life" movement in the case of unborn babies who are murdered at public expense, because some demand the "right" for unlimited abortions on demand. Oddly again, these same people are found in more public protests demanding this time for the abolition of the death penalty for murderers. Their credo is kill the unborn, but don't judicially execute the murders of children!

Here "philoteknous" means "child-lovers" of the good and godly kind which in the context has to do with parental child loving. The young wives and mothers were being exhorted to love their children. "Can a woman's tender care, Cease toward the child she bare? Yes, she may forgetful be..." William Cowper, (1731 – 1800), and, even worse, uncaring and brutal towards the child. This of course is not limited to women as the men in the relationship are as bad if not worse.

Who will love and care for other people's unloved, even abused children? The response is: "That's the government's responsibility; let the official social workers do it; we have enough to do looking after our own children!" Even some Christians talk like this, saying in effect: "I am not my brother's keeper!" We are not all called to fulltime counselling and care of juvenile delinquents, or other people's unwanted children, or young rebels fighting authority. This is true, but we are called to be a caring, sharing, paying and praying people, who stand with those serving and loving such young people.

Fred and Dorothy Peterson is one such couple. We have known them since, as young newly weds, they came to serve in the "Peace Corps" in Barbados where we were missionaries. Their love for the Lord and people was evident. They were teaching in the public schools but their care and concern for the young people went beyond school hours and their students' mental development. They lived in a village with them and entered into their social life. They were concerned for the salvation of the whole person. Fred, in a recent letter to me, says:

"We introduce them to the Good Shepherd by seeking to be real shepherds ourselves."

OCTOBER 25 – RETURNED LOVE

Here is a family love story, as told by Rev. Paul Van Gorder, with whom we worked in a crusade in Trinidad and Tobago, West Indies, in 1952.

"The following incident portrays the power of love to stimulate love in return. A mother was busily writing letters at her desk as her little girl played in another room with a doll. After some time, she called her daughter to come and sit on her lap. The little girl said:

'Mommy, I'm glad you called for me. I love you so much.'

'Do you, darling?' she asked as she tenderly hugged her beaming five year old. 'I am glad you love me. You weren't lonely while I was writing, were you? You and your dolly seemed to be having such a good time together.'

'We were having fun, but I got tired of loving her. She never loves me back.'

'Is that why you love me?'

'That's one reason, Mommy; but not the best.'

'And what is the best?' Her bright blue eyes were earnest as she replied, 'O Mommy, can't you guess? I love you now because you loved me and took care of me when I was too little to love you back.'"

He went on to say:

"What indescribable joy fills the heart of a mother and father when their little child responds to their love by freely showing them affection."

On the human, romantic love level, it sometimes happens that love on one side will beget love on the other but frequently there is no reciprocation. Unrequited love can sometimes be a shattering experience to the party suffering it. It is a sad traumatic time for the rejected lover. In an extension of this thought, even if there is a responsive return of love it is rarely of the intensity and ardour of the initiator who is completely, overwhelmingly in love. This can cause problems in a relationship when one loves so much more ardently than the other.

We have stated the problem. The answer is found in honest evaluation, communication, and a desire on the part of the one lacking whole-hearted love, to find the way to an increase in ardour and intensity. We pray for an increase in faith; we can also pray for an increase in love. If this is the handicap in a Christian marriage where love has been lopsided then a deepening of one's love for the Lord will quicken love to the partner.

In like fashion, but on a larger scale, how the heart of our heavenly Father must rejoice when we return his love and tell Him so with pure affection and agapé love. In the course of these pages we have gone back to the Source of our love in the words of the inspired writer on agapé; the apostle John. "In this is love, not that we loved God, but that He loved us and sent His Son to be the propitiation for our sins."[1] "We love, because He first loved us."[2] He is the most patient, longsuffering lover since man was placed on love's probation and fell in Eden. Since then our Father's love plans and Person have been largely rejected. Unrequited love has been the response. "How oft have I…and you would not" has been the heavenly Lover's lament.

OCTOBER 26 – LOVE GIVES BEFORE IT'S TAKEN

"…God tested Abraham…'Take now your son, your only son, whom you love, Isaac…and offer him there as a burnt offering…'"[1] God the Maker and Sustainer of all things is also the Undertaker. I use this word in two senses: undertaking and caring for us in all the affairs of life and secondly undertaking and planning our transition to the next world. The nature of our circumstances and our times are in his sovereign control. The century in which we were born, the country of our birth, parents and genes are all matters over which we have no control. We have no choice in any of them as we enter into this world or, (for those who leave their exit from it in His hands alone) do we decide the time and manner of our demise. Euthanasia and suicide excluded, all affairs from womb to tomb are, for His children, directed by the heavenly Undertaker.

Yet in between the beginning and ending of our earthly pilgrimage we are constantly called to make choices. The committed Christian makes them in the light of the principles of God's Word which are all designed by holy love for His people's welfare, and the wider good, which He alone can see. His children's most cherished plans and hopes, their prized possessions, and beloved family and friends should all be given back, really returned, to the Undertaker whose purposes and planning are from His heart of love. Our Lord Himself, after expressing His personal desire still said: "…yet not as I will, but as You will."[2] He, in love, had given His will and His life back to his loving Father, before it was taken. This doesn't cut the nerve of faith, it nourishes it.

Abraham, in the case of his beloved Isaac, did the same. He knew that God, who had given Isaac, had the right of recall. Abraham, who loved this miracle child of his old age; who had in a sense received him out of death; held him very lightly in terms of "ownership." He had, I believe, already given the love-gift back to the Giver. He believed God could, and would if necessary, give him another resurrection for Isaac. This seems to me to be the underlying reason why he, as a father, could so speedily, so joyfully and so unregretfully take his son to the place of sacrifice and personally raise the knife to slay him. He, in love, had already, by faith, given Isaac back before he was taken. Abraham had already "banked" Isaac in heaven.

We must also give our "Isaacs" back to the undertaker who has the power of resurrection. Sometime, somewhere, someway they will be given back by him who takes and undertakes. This is the way of peace. One of our beloved grand-daughters was desperately ill after two major stomach operations. We prayed and agonised for her restoration, but no peace came until we faced the worst, and the best. She was His gift to her parents and us. He had the right of early recall. We could, and did, give her back. In the wider application, as Jim Elliott (1927 – 1956) the mid-century martyr said:

"He is no fool, who gives what he cannot keep, to gain that which he cannot lose."

OCTOBER 27 – LOVE CALLS CHILDREN HOME – Part One

The beloved granddaughter whose illness brought us to recognise God's right of recall, was restored to her parents and to us. However, worldwide, myriads of children are not given back, they are taken; perhaps picked as lovely fresh flowers might be a better analogy. The heavenly Gardener is an amazing Florist. He has cultivated variety, beauty and loveliness in the earthly blooms. In the gardens of love in glory, that amazing group of little children from all age groups form a living, singing choir of youth.

Scripture indicates that there is an age (it must vary somewhat and God knows it) in childhood which can hardly be called innocency, but rather an age of unaccountability. This is an awkward phrase but it is based on these words from the Word of God: "Moreover, your little ones who you said would become a prey, and your sons, who this day have no knowledge of good or evil, shall enter there, and I will give it to them and they shall possess it."[1] The occasion was the Israelites sin of unbelief that refused to allow them into Canaan and caused a whole generation to die in the wilderness. Their little ones, who were then too young to understand good or evil, God did not judge with their parents, nor did He forbid them entry into the land of promise. What is the connection between that and love calling children home to heaven? The relevance lies here: If children up to a certain age are judged unaccountable because of ignorance of good or evil, then will not the Judge of all the earth do right in taking them home to heaven? Though I know of no Scripture that states this explicitly, there seems room in "…we have fixed our hope on the living God, who is the Savior of all men, especially of believers."[2] to support this. There is coverage in the blood of Christ for babies and the mentally handicapped, who can't believe that He is the Christ, the Saviour of the world. It is our responsibility to teach our children the difference between right and wrong and of the necessity of believing in Jesus.

The last Adam, Christ, undid the tragedy of Eden. The first Adam's sin was that of disobedience. This is an inherited bias in all descendants of Adam. Christ's obedience and death undid the Edenic wrong and made possible salvation from both the inherited bias through to personal sin and unbelief. Starting from the premise that "…God demonstrates His own love toward us, in that while we were yet sinners, Christ died for us,"[3] Paul moves into the great passage of Adam's disobedience and Christ's obedience. This does not mean that all will be saved. Everyone is responsible for their own sin and unbelief. Each must receive the abundance of grace and the righteousness that God makes available. While everyone must give an account of himself to God, what of those who can't be accountable? The Wycliffe Bible Commentary says:

"All men sin, except for infants dying in infancy…"

Therefore love calls the little ones home. Love has made provision through Christ. Loves own country is full of these fairest flowers. Love has prepared a place for them.

OCTOBER 28 – LOVE CALLS CHILDREN HOME – Part Two

Yesterday, we likened heaven to a garden, with the fairest flower of all being the fairest Lord Jesus. We saw the gardens, flowering in all their loveliness and fragrance, as a picture of young children of all ages, all colours and from all the centuries, gathered by the heavenly Florist. They have been selected purposefully according to His love plan.

This time we will change the picture and use the City instead of the country. (The Bible begins in a Garden and ends in a City!)

On the Open Air Campaigns in 1938 we used an amplifier with gospel records to attract a crowd. One favourite record, with almost any crowd, was "The Holy City" by Frederick Weatherly (1848 – 1929). People would say:

"Play that one about the city, the New Jerusalem."

And we would play:

"Last night I lay a-sleeping…
I saw the Holy City…
It was the New Jerusalem…
I heard the children singing…"

The voices of angelic children thronged the streets of the city of God, the city of love, singing the songs of Zion; praising the Lord. Yes, people then, and I still do, love that song.

"And the streets of the city will be filled with boys and girls playing in its streets."[1] The City will have no pain; no suffering; tears all wiped away. Joy and singing only will be there, for the former things are passed away. Bereft parents, comfort yourselves with these things. The little ones are not lost; love has called them home.

Here is a relevant word of consolation sent to the newspaper by a bereaved grandmother:

"I lost my grandson last year and found great comfort in this poem."

"'I'll lend you for a while a child of mine,' He said.
'For you to love the while he lives and mourn for when he's dead.
It may be six or seven years, or twenty-two or three,
But will you, till I call him back, take care of him for me?
He'll bring his charms to gladden you, and should his stay be brief,
You'll have his lovely memories as solace for your grief.

I cannot promise he will stay; since all from earth return,
But there are lessons taught down there I want this child to learn.
I've looked the wide world over in My search for teachers true
And from the throngs that crowd life's lanes I have chosen you.
Now will you give him all your love, not think the labor vain,
Nor hate Me when I come to call to take him back again?'

I fancied that I heard them say, 'Dear Lord, Thy will be done!
For all the joy Thy child shall bring, the risk of grief we run.
We'll shelter him with tenderness, we'll love him while we may,
And for the happiness we've known, forever grateful stay;
But should the angels call for him much sooner than we've planned,
We'll brave the bitter grief that comes and try to understand!'"
Edgar Guest (1881 – 1959)

OCTOBER 29 – GRANDPARENTS' LOVE

Can old dogs learn new tricks? Can people in their sixties, seventies and eighties have new learning experiences? Can grandparents start to love all over again? From this new state of experience, this state of living and learning and loving, my wife and I shout a joyous, positive "Yes" to the questions posed. Grandparents' love is only possible because of grandchildren and their love! How wonderful! For fourteen years we have been on the receiving end of this love. 1970 saw the birth of what were to be four grandchildren during the decade of the 1970's. As each one changes so has the measure of their love and affection. Grandchildrens' love is marked by a special trust relationship and I think my wife has received blessed reciprocal love here. As she has acted as a baby sitter, to all four at different times, I have noticed the response and affection they return to her. She has also acted as a surrogate mother when the children's own mothers were unavoidably absent. I have seen also the loving efforts and responses as she has sought to pass on the love of Jesus to them. By example, by teaching choruses, and Scriptures, she has sought to express, through her grandmotherly love, the truth about heavenly love and its meaning. She has an additional opportunity to relate with one of the girls who is in her Sunday School class.

So we have found that grandparent and grandchildren loves are mutual, reciprocal loves, changing as the teenage years are here for some and fast approaching for others. Fascinating areas for love lie ahead! This week, as a special treat, I took one of our granddaughters to the circus. Earlier we had taken all four to the very unusual Grand Circus from China. But this other was the usual animals, clowns, aerial high wire and trapeze kind of show. It was a little love gesture on grandpa's part for a granddaughter on a special occasion. We do not want to appear partial. Our goal is to love them all equally and to seek that all will early, through their parents' efforts, and our back-up assistance, come to the Lord of love. We press on, praying and loving them into the way of love as taught in the Book and the hymn.

"I am so glad that our Father in Heav'n
Tells of His love in the Book He has giv'n;
Wonderful things in the Bible I see,
This is the dearest, that Jesus loves me.

Jesus loves me, and I know I love Him;
Love brought Him down my poor soul to redeem;
Yes, it was love made Him die on the tree;
Oh, I am certain that Jesus loves me!

In this assurance I find sweetest rest,
Trusting in Jesus, I know I am blessed;
Satan, dismayed, from my soul now doth flee,
When I just tell him that Jesus loves me.

Oh, if there's only one song I can sing,
When in His beauty I see the great King,
This shall my song through eternity be,
'Oh, what a wonder that Jesus loves me!'"
Philip Bliss (1838 – 1876)

Yes, we are so glad that He loves us as individuals and families and that we can pass on this love to the next generation. Grandparents' love has privileges and responsibilities.

OCTOBER 30 – FAMILY LOVES

In family love, and the family loves, there are often overlooked and rarely mentioned members; mothers-in-law, fathers-in-law, daughters-in-law and sons-in-law. Frequently, amongst these, there are choice souls, despite all the mother-in-law jokes. My own mother-in-law was a very sweet lady whom, unfortunately, we got to see quite infrequently, as missionary furloughs were ten years apart in those times. My wife's mother-in-law was also a special person. I have written already of her and her love (October 12).

Scripture speaks of Peter's mother-in-law, and I have often wondered about her. She lived, evidently, in the same home with her daughter and son-in-law which speaks well of her as being welcome in Peter's home. For in that home, so often given to hospitality, she must have served the Lord, and then one day she was taken ill. "And immediately after they came out of the synagogue, they came into the house of Simon and Andrew, with James and John. Now Simon's mother-in-law was lying sick with a fever; and immediately they spoke to Jesus about her. And He came to her and raised her up, taking her by the hand, and the fever left her, and she waited on them."[1] There was a lot of love in that home. The Lord was there; the love of Christ was manifest there to a beloved woman, whose serving love is described. That lady's son-in-law was learning, and was to become famous in the way of love also.

We have told the story of Ruth and her mother-in-law Naomi. What a love relationship was there, and theirs. Mother-in-law and daughter-in-law loved each other with serving and caring love. And, moving to the present, I have observed at close hand, for some years now, this same beautiful kind of sharing love between our daughter-in-law Sharon, and her mother-in-law, and also her father-in-law! I ought to know, she doesn't only call me "Dad;" she loves me; she loves us as Ruth loved Naomi, practically and steadily. Boaz not only loved Ruth, he loved her mother-in-law. "...for he said, 'Do not go to your mother-in-law empty-handed'"[2] as he sent six measures of barley to her.

Mothers-in-law yes, but what about fathers-in-law? Moses got off to a good start with his future father-in-law Reuel (or Jethro). While going into exile in Midian, Moses exhibited the nobility of his character in helping the daughters of Jethro water their flocks and in defending them from the other shepherds. Moses was given hospitality in Jethro's home and later married Zipporah, one of the daughters. After the exodus, Jethro, who was a priest in Midian, came to meet and greet his son-in-law and brought his wife and children to him and gave him good counsel which he heeded, father-in-law and son-in-law had a lot of love and respect for each other. And the same is true for me today as I thank God for a son-in-law Roy, who loves the Lord and his family including his mother and father-in-law.

OCTOBER 31 – SINGLE LOVERS OF THE WORD

In October, 1947, at a Worldwide Evangelization Crusade (W.E.C.) missionary conference in Chicago, Illinois, a lady made a special journey from Minneapolis, Minnesota, to visit me. She was almost sixty years of age and I was thirty-one. She was a librarian due for retirement and I was a missionary on furlough. In our interview she told me that God had called her to work with us in the island of Dominica in the West Indies. There was one little problem; God hadn't told me! The Mission's policy at that time was not to encourage older people to become first-termers on the foreign field. But this lady, Miss Olea Solheim, had a stubborn Scandinavian streak in her (i.e. a very strong will). She insisted and I resisted (wrongly as it turned out). Finally, in consultation with Mr. Norman Grubb, then Secretary of W.E.C. and others, we reached this agreement. If Miss Solheim should ever come to Dominica outside Mission channels, then this would be an indication of God's seal on her call and no doubt there would be work for her to do.

About three years later, one a moonlit night, a rowboat made its way ashore from the steamer anchored in the bay off Roseau, the capital of Dominica. I met it as two of our missionaries were returning. Imagine my surprise when another voice out of the moonlit boat said:

"Hello, I made it!" and there was Olea!

Her arrival was in the will and timing of God. As part of our W.E.C. mission work we had opened a Christian Literature Crusade (C.L.C.) bookshop in Dominica in 1947 and now we needed someone to manage it as we were moving on to Trinidad & Tobago, West Indies. Olea was God's person, prepared and called for just such a ministry. She gave more than ten years of devoted service to the Lord in the island. And she brought an assistant with her, another senior citizen, her friend, Miss Helga Hotvedt. Together these two put the work of C.L.C. in Dominica on a solid foundation. They were real sacrificial missionaries; single lovers of the Lord. I honour their memory and their labour of love when they could have been retired.

This week their saga came to an earthly end. Olea had gone to her reward some years before and now Helga has gone.

"From death to life" says the card. "In memory of Helga Oline Hotvedt born in Decorah, Iowa, December 27, 1900. Passed away July 21, 1983 at the age of 82 years, 6 months, 24 days."

The Scripture was "Nay, in all these things we are more than conquerors through him that loved us. For I am persuaded, that neither death, nor life, nor angels, nor principalities, nor powers, nor things present, nor things to come, Nor height, nor depth, nor any other creature, shall be able to separate us from the love of God, which is in Christ Jesus our Lord."[1] Both of these single ladies, lovers of the Lord, have now heard "...Well done, good and faithful servant..."[2]

The service of the Lord around the world knows many of such devoted single ladies, lovers of the Lord, who have given up their rights to a husband, home, children, security and comfort. Single lovers of the Lord, have the right to forego their rights, and, like Olea and Helga, have done so because of love.

NOVEMBER 1 – LOVE'S VOICE

'Twas the voice of love that said: "…It is not good for the man to be alone; I will make him a helper suitable for him."[1]

"The voice that breathed o'er Eden, that earliest wedding day,
The primal wedding blessing, it hath not passed away.
Still in the pure espousal of Christian man and maid
The Holy Three are with us, the threefold grace is said.

Be present, awful Father, to give away this bride
As Thou gav'st Eve to Adam, a helpmate at his side.
Be present, Son of Mary, to join their loving hands
As Thou didst bind two natures in Thine eternal bands.

Be present, Holy Spirit, to bless them as they kneel,
As Thou for Christ, the Bridegroom, the heav'nly Spouse dost seal.
O spread Thy pure wing o'er them, let no ill power find place
When onward to Thine altar their hallowed path they trace.

To cast their crowns before Thee in perfect sacrifice,
Till to the home of gladness with Christ's own Bride they rise.
To Father, Son, and Spirit, eternal One and Three,
And was and is forever, all praise and glory be."
John Keble (1792 – 1866)

'Twas the voice of love that was heard above the cacophony of noise that surrounded His Cross. Hear again these seven words, these seven words of love voiced from the Cross by dying, undying Love. "…Father, forgive them; for they do not know what they are doing…"[2] He said to His killers while saving and assuring the thief with the words of love: "…Truly I say to you, today you shall be with Me in Paradise."[3] Loving and caring for His mother He committed her to John the beloved "…Woman, behold, your son!"[4] Then out of the darkness of love's separation He cried "…My God, my God, why have You forsaken Me?"[5] and as His suffering increased "…I am thirsty"[6] was wrung from Him. Then came the shout of victor, not victim "…Father, into your hands I commit my Spirit…"[7] and "…It is finished…"[8] The work He came to do, He did, He died for us, as He dismissed His Spirit into His Father's hands of love.

"O let me kiss thy bleeding feet,
And bathe and wash them with my tears!
The story of thy love repeat…
O let thy love my heart constrain!
Thy love for every sinner free,
That every fallen soul of man
May taste the grace that found out me;
That all mankind with me may prove
Thy sovereign everlasting love."
Charles Wesley (1707 – 1788)

Charles Wesley's song of loving gratitude together with John Keble's reminder of the voice of love in Eden, combine in the voice of thankful love. Let us add our voice of praiseful love also.

NOVEMBER 2 – LOVE'S COMMUNICATION AND COMPANIONSHIP

Love's communication and companionship can be seen in all the loves. We see it in the friendship love of David and Jonathon; and we see it in all true friendship loves today. We see it in the brotherly love of the early Christians and we see it today in the brotherhood of believers. There is also communication, companionship and comradeship outside the fellowship of faith. Worldly unbelievers have their friendships, fellowships, brotherhoods, clubs, etc. where communication and comradeship of a certain kind of love is given reciprocally. It is the same in all the earthly family relationships. The world rightly loves its own, but the family loves of Christians are marked by that additional holy, heavenly love which enables, enriches and sanctifies them. Love's communication and companionship with the Lord by His own disciples, while He was on earth, is continued by Him and His people today. The world-wide fellowship of the people of God is unique in love's union and communion.

"I am Thine, O Lord, I have heard Thy voice,
And it told Thy love to me;
But I long to rise in the arms of faith
And be closer drawn to Thee.

O the pure delight of a single hour
That before Thy throne I spend,
When I kneel in prayer, and with Thee, my God
I commune as friend with friend!

There are depths of love that I cannot know
Till I cross the narrow sea;
There are heights of joy that I may not reach
Till I rest in peace with Thee.

Draw me nearer, nearer blessed Lord,
To the cross where Thou hast died.
Draw me nearer, nearer, nearer blessed Lord,
To Thy precious, bleeding side."

This prayer of that loving communicator, blind but beloved Fanny Crosby (1820 – 1915), is given a glad "Amen" by all His own today, who are living in love's communication and companionship. Lord we long to know more of these delights as we walk and talk with You.

We must also talk about the need for love's communication and companionship in the area of marriage. It is sad to see, and hear, married couples publicly state:

"We have nothing to say to each other."

What a dreadful confession. What has gone wrong? I'm sure they communicated and enjoyed companionship when they were getting acquainted and in the early stages of their marriage. The causes are numerous and cases vary as will the cures. Counselling of the right kind can help. Right silences can resonate with love, but wrong silence can sound harsh. Talking things over is a necessary first step; the major one is the renewal of the relationship and return to mature loving communication and adult loving companionship.

NOVEMBER 3 – COMPLIMENTARY LOVE

"Compliment" and "complement" differ not in pronunciation but in meaning. Change but one letter and we have an entirely different word. The first as defined by "Merriam – Webster" is "an expression of esteem, respect, affection or admiration." The second is "something that fills up or makes perfect." Things which when added make a whole. Curiously, they both come from the same Latin root and originally compliment was synonymous with complement. Compliment was used with the meaning "to complete." This is not only interesting, it is instructive. While our present theme is complimentary love the other is inextricably bound with it. In life and love both are needed in their modern meanings and necessary in their original united emphasis of completeness. While courting the swain is lavish in his compliments to his sweetheart. With word, deed or gift he woos her; yet when he has won her the courting compliments languish and the wooing flowers often cease. You and I have heard the excuses and reasons why this is so, but our concern here is to get them flowing and flowering again.

Compliments ought to increase rather than decrease; love ought to increase in depth and maturity after marriage, marking the "completement," the whole, the "one" which the "two" have become. Keep the compliments sincere and keep them coming. A new dress, a nice meal, some special effort by the spouse, ought to be noticed, appreciated and complimented. It should also be mutual. Hard work in the marketplace, help in the home and with the children ought equally to be commended. Wives and husbands in so doing, (i.e. engaging in complimentary love) are equally, though perhaps unconsciously engaged in complementary love. This is making a whole. While Adam was a complete man and Eve a complete woman, paradoxically they were incomplete. They were made for each other and each needed the other. While life, circumstances or choice keep some men and women single, and they can find and do live complete lives, the ordained plan for us, for our comfort and full "completement," is to have one of the other gender in our lives. We are happy when we find our alter egos.

Whether married or single, compliments of respect and praise, sincerely felt and expressed, are positively life building. Their absence, lack of appreciation, or even worse depreciation and deprecation, are deadeningly destructive. One of the characteristics of the Christ-like person, the Spirit controlled person, is kindness. Love is kind and one of its evidences in the marriage relationship is shown in the speech pattern between the partners. Conversational compliments should flow freely.

NOVEMBER 4 – COMPLEMENTARY LOVE

Algernon Charles Swinburne (1837 – 1909) is not an authority on Biblical love or holy matrimony. However, in his poem "A Match" he does say, and say well, some true things about "complementary love." His "Ifs" introduce complementary things and ideas, stressing also the point that opposites are often essential to completeness in life and love.

"If love were what the rose is,
And I were like the leaf,
Our lives would grow together
In sad or singing weather,
Blown fields or flowerful closes,
Green pleasure or gray grief;
If love were what the rose is,
And I were like the leaf.

If I were what the words are,
And love were like the tune,
With double sound and single
Delight our lips would mingle,
With kisses glad as birds are
That get sweet rain at noon;
If I were what the words are,
And love were like the tune.

If you were life, my darling,
And I your love were death,
We'd shine and snow together
Ere March made sweet the weather
With daffodil and starling
And hours of fruitful breath;
If you were life, my darling,
And I your love were death.

If you were thrall to sorrow,
And I were page to joy,
We'd play for lives and seasons
With loving looks and treasons
And tears of night and morrow
And laughs of maid and boy;
If you were thrall to sorrow,
And I were page to joy.

If you were April's lady,
And I were lord in May,
We'd throw with leaves for hours
And draw for days with flowers,
Till day like night were shady
And night were bright like day;
If you were April's lady,
And I were lord in May.

If you were queen of pleasure,
And I were king of pain,
We'd hunt down love together,
Pluck out his flying-feather,
And teach his feet a measure,
And find his mouth a rein;
If you were queen of pleasure,
And I were king of pain."

There is a lament here for something missing. Complementary love is seen but not experienced. Swinburne's life lacked the true loves that complete, satisfy and make life whole. His was really a sad life, existing on the ersatz loves, the substitutes that cloy and turn to bitterness. We, who have found the divine love that unites us to our Maker, should be grateful and also sympathetic to those seeking satisfaction in substitutes.

The complementary principle is built into the universe by the God who Himself exemplifies complementary love. His fatherhood is everywhere extolled in Scripture and it also uses motherhood to extol His care. "…And you will be nursed, you will be carried on the hip and fondled on the knees. As one whom his mother comforts, so I will comfort you…"[1] He has ordered and ordained the father-mother family love principle and together they illustrate complementary love.

When we lived in Barbados a new restaurant opened called "Yin-yang." I asked the owner what it meant and he said that "yin" in Chinese philosophy is the passive, female force while "yang" is the active, male force whose manifestations are opposite and complementary. We are complementary in our persons, in fit, form and function. Paul uses the marriage relationship as exemplifying the complementary love of Christ and His church.

NOVEMBER 5 – LOVE SAYS "I'M SORRY"

We have noted the falseness of the statement "Love never needs to say I'm sorry." (June 6) That is modern, sentimental, liberal talk and has nothing to do with true love. It is typical of our times and misleads the younger generation to whom it is proffered as modern wisdom! True love knows when it has sinned and though sometimes slow to say "I'm sorry" it does apologize. No one said that apologies are easy for they, if they are real, contain a confession that includes a repentance born of love. "I'm sorry" ought also to include reparations where possible.

It took David almost a year to admit his sin and to, in effect, say "I'm sorry" to God and Bathsheba. God had to use the prophet Nathan and the parable of the one little lamb to produce righteous indignation in David and make him open himself to the application "...You are the man!..."[1] The divine conviction had been going on for most of the year of David's silence and he reveals the inner turmoil that was rending him and finally drove him to confession "...I will confess my transgressions to the Lord..."[2]

Oh the relief and blessing: "...How blessed is he whose transgression is forgiven, whose sin is covered! How blessed is the man to whom the Lord does not impute iniquity..."[3] These words of grateful praise show the happy results of acknowledgement of guilt and confession of sin from a repentant heart. This brings in turn love's forgiveness.

These are the deeper implications of saying, with sincerity, "I'm sorry" to God. It brings salvation originally, and the restored joy of salvation, to a backslider now returning. David's Psalm 51, written as the heading tells us, "...when Nathan the prophet came to him, after he had gone in to Bathsheba."[4] tells of this joy. David said "I'm sorry" to Bathsheba. David did love her, care for her, marry her and honour her until the end of his life. They experienced other joys including their peace-child, Solomon.

Love saying "I'm sorry" ought to apply also to the matters of: impatience, sharpness, unkindness, thoughtlessness, cutting and inconsiderate comments, or being uncommunicative, withdrawn or withholding of speech or person. These not only mar marriages and friendships but can, cumulatively destroy them. When realized, love saying "I'm sorry" ought also to imply "I won't do it again." But alas we often do. That's why we have to, all through life, keep saying "I'm sorry." That's why we also, when the offended party, have to jeep on graciously accepting the apologies and forgiving the offender. Accounts should be kept short and settled swiftly. Scripture says so: "...do not let the sun go down on your anger."[5]

NOVEMBER 6 – LOVE AND THE TONGUE

"Let's contend no more,
Love, Strive nor weep:
All be as before,
Love, Only sleep!

What so wild as words are?
I and thou
In debate, as birds are,
Hawk on bough!

See the creature stalking
While we speak!
Hush and hide the talking,
Cheek on cheek!

Teach me, only teach,
Love As I ought
I will speak thy speech,
Love, Think thy thought.

Must a little weep,
Love, (Foolish me!)
And so fall asleep,
Love, Loved by thee."
"A Woman's Last Word"
Robert Browning (1812 – 1889)

The expression "mosquito net lectures", no doubt originating in the tropics, maybe on some mission field, has always fascinated me. The lady in the poem had evidently been listening to such a lecture and wisely ended it by loving action. She was following a Biblical principle whether she knew it or not. "...do not let the sun go down on your anger."[1] The wider context of the text refers to speaking truth with our neighbour, but it certainly has application to married couples. Speak the truth in love to each other. Keep short accounts and "be kind to one another, tender-hearted, forgiving each other, just as God in Christ also has forgiven you."[2] A kind and tender tongue is a tongue controlled by love.

The tongue can be a deadly destructive force as James tells us at length and as we know only too well by experience and observation. He also has positive instruction about it: "...everyone must be quick to hear, slow to speak and slow to anger."[3] There is a silence which is born of ignorance. As the young parliamentarian, when asked why he was delaying delivery of his maiden speech, replied:

"If I don't speak, the opposition might think I'm stupid; if I do I'm afraid they will be sure of it."

He might have been "putting himself down" or it might have been a case where silence is cowardly. But there is also a silence which is golden. There's "...A time to be silent and a time to speak"[4] and the loving heart knows these time zones in marriage or in any relationship. The Lord was often silent in His love; even in His silence for several days after He received the news of Lazarus' death. That silence may have seemed callous but it wasn't, as events proved. He was silent under provocation; love held His tongue. He was not silent about injustice and hypocrisy. Love loosed His tongue.

The tongue is double barred by teeth and lips. There are other check gates also as we ask ourselves:

"Is it true?" "Is it kind?" "Is it necessary?"

These three barriers will kill gossip before it starts but only the truly loving heart will think first and possibly refrain from speaking.

NOVEMBER 6 - CONTINUED

"When you have nothing to say, say nothing." Charles Caleb Colton (1780 – 1832)

This is love's silence.

"Under all speech that is good for anything there lies a silence that is better. Silence is deep as eternity; speech is shallow as time." Thomas Carlyle (1795 – 1881)

That's a good word for preachers, who can always say something; prophets have something to say.

"Lord, fill my mouth with worthwhile stuff and nudge me when I've said enough." Author unknown.

NOVEMBER 7 – LOVE COVERS

"Cover-ups" have always sounded unlawful and have become more prevalent in our times. The "Watergate Cover-up" named after the building complex in Washington, D.C., USA, brought about the resignation of President Nixon (1913 – 1994) on August 9, 1974. The shame and ignomy was not limited to him; others went to prison because of it. That illegal break-in to steal political secrets and the subsequent "cover-up" rocked the United States and made "cover-up" a worse expression than it was before.

Can the phrase be rehabilitated? (Love Covers by Paul E. Billheimer is a book that amplifies this subject.) God engaged in a good and symbolic cover-up. After Adam and Eve sinned they tried to hide from God and covered themselves with fig leaves. This was the first wrong cover-up. God called them, found them and reclothed them with animal skins. This was symbolic of the atonement covering that sacrificed animals were to make in the millennia ahead until the Lamb of God would come. He then put away sin by the sacrifice of Himself and the shedding of His blood and He clothes believers in the garments of His righteousness. What a gracious and glorious cover-up, all prompted by love.

Noah's sons engaged in a right, proper and good cover-up motivated by filial love. After the Flood Noah planted a vineyard and became the first in that new world to succumb to intemperance. In his drunken state he became exposed and Shem and Japheth covered him with a blanket in a kind and loving fashion. Another "cover-up" prompted by love.

Our theme, though, comes from an Old Testament book that is quoted in the New Testament. "Hatred stirs up strife, but love covers all transgressions."[1] "Above all, keep fervent in your love for one another, because love covers a multitude of sins."[2] We have seen how God in love covered the guilty pair and made provision in love for the temporary covering of their sins by animal sacrifice. Yet,

"Not all the blood of beasts
On Jewish altars slain
Could give the guilty conscience peace
Or wash away the stain.

But Christ, the heav'nly Lamb,
Takes all our sins away;
A sacrifice of nobler name
And richer blood than they.

My faith would lay her hand
On that dear head of Thine,
While, like a penitent, I stand,
And there confess my sin."
Isaac Watts (1974 – 1748)

When we as Christians are commanded by love to "cover" are we being invited to go another way than God has shown? "No!" We preach the Good News to sinners; we urge saints to put things right with God and their neighbours; but we quietly "draw the blanket" of privacy and silence over episodes that have been dealt with. "He who conceals a transgression seeks love, but he who repeats a matter separates intimate friends."[3] There is a time to uncover and a time to cover-up. Love will control both.

NOVEMBER 8 – LOVE BURIES

After love buries or covers confessed and forgiven sin, don't disinter it. Whether it concerns me, you or someone else don't uncover it again; keep it buried "tale" and all. Don't discuss it again; nor discredit the person, or yourself, who has had forgiveness from God and dealt with the matter. I think this is one of the applications of the Scripture which says: "The mouth of the righteous is a fountain of life...But love covers all transgressions. On the lips of the discerning, wisdom is found..."[1] Love controls the lips because of its deeper control of the heart and mind. As we saw, divine love does not gloss over sin; it judges it; it has paid the penalty for it and now demands that it be confessed and forsaken. Then it is forgiven, pardoned and put away forever. And the forgiven sinner, in whom this holy love abides, will in turn forgive others for Christ's sake. Be silent about it, and, better still, forget it. And this raises another matter.

Gossip, or character assassination, is one of the deadly sins, and unbelievably, some Christians indulge in it. Even a seemingly right prayer request can, consciously or unconsciously, imply or uncover things that should not be mentioned. Gossip can be revealed in: "Please pray for...who is...who has... who needs...etc." it is better to pray privately when doubtful about the results of publicity even in the public prayer meeting. Gossip is idle talk; repeated rumour; scandalous speech; and slanderous innuendo of a derogatory nature. Insinuations are usually part of gossip and Scripture condemns the whole sorry list in no uncertain terms. "Women must likewise be dignified, not malicious gossips..."[2] "For men will be...malicious gossips..."[3] "Older women likewise are to be reverent in their behavior, not malicious gossips..."[4] In some versions it is translated "slanderers"; those given to finding fault, and given to spreading innuendoes and criticisms in the church. In the Greek it is "diabalos" and yes, it means exactly like it looks and sounds! Its root is in, and its fruit is from, the devil, the false accuser of, and calumniator of the brethren. Beware lest we be caught in his common, cruel, snare of slander. Don't be a scholar in his school of slander.

Love is aware of this snare and avoids it. Love buries and covers it but more positively love "does not rejoice in unrighteousness, but rejoices with the truth."[5] We have been "born again" into the Father's family of holy love and are also disciples and learners in His school of disciplined love. We are learning how to speak the "truth in love"[6] as we take His love yoke upon us and learn of Him. Our Lord Jesus Christ, holy love personified, not only teaches us by example and precept, he has given us the Enabler to work love in us, and work it out through us, in all the positive, practical ways and personal areas mentioned above. "...because the love of God has been poured out within our hearts through the Holy Spirit who was given to us."[7] This enabling love empowers us to bury the wrong and resurrect and rejoice in the right.

NOVEMBER 9 – A CLOUDBURST OF LOVE

The Rev. John G. Ridley MC (1896 – 1974) is mentioned in these pages (February 16). He was an inspiration to me, a friend of my family, used in blessing to my mother and a constant challenge to all of us. Occasionally, while on furlough in Australia, I was privileged to be on the same platform with him, and I noticed that his constant theme, illustrated and introduced in many and varied ways, was the love of God. The last address I heard him give was on: "We love, because He first loved us."[1] It was given at the Mission Headquarters of the Worldwide Evangelization Crusade in Strathfield, Sydney. John loved missions and missionaries as part of his love for his Lord and love of souls everywhere. Australia's greatest evangelist was great because he loved greatly and was greatly loved. A long time before the Strathfield address, one of the most memorable, of his many messages on love was entitled: "Caught in a Cloudburst!" The text was: "But God commendeth his love toward us, in that, while we were yet sinners, Christ died for us",[2] but John used the beautiful French rending of this verse: "But God causes to burst like a cloudburst His own love, because while we were still sinners, Christ died for us."

"Caught in a Cloudburst!" "Caught in a Cloudburst of Love." To anyone who has ever been drenched, almost drowned, in a torrential, tropical storm, a "cloudburst" is not only an unforgettable experience, it is an apt, and exact description of the event. It is a beautiful translation in relation to the love of God. Soaked in love! Drenched and almost drowned in love. We are caught and drenched daily in this cloudburst of love and loving-kindness. His love for us was real long before we were born. His Son was given from the world's birth. All this "while we were still sinners."

There is a long-lived lie which says:

"Love God and He will love you."

This is not only a canard but a caricature of the character and nature of God, somewhat like its equivalent:

"God doesn't love sinners."

This verse and many others give the lie to these untruths. "For God so loved the world…"[3] "Herein is love, not that we loved God, but that he loved us…"[4] "But God commendeth his love toward us, in that, while we were yet sinners, Christ died for us"[2] "…He Himself is the propitiation for our sins; and not for ours only, but also for those of the whole world."[5] The whole world is the actual beneficiary of this "cloudburst of love." As literally, God makes His rain to benefit both just and unjust, so, in the love-death of His Son there is potential salvation for every lost son of Adam's fallen race. For God is "…not wishing for any to perish but for all to come to repentance."[6] With this worldwide cloudburst of love come the worldwide, full circle rainbow of promise. But remember, He is the actual Saviour only of those who believe.

NOVEMBER 10 – LOVE CALLING

It was a sunny Sunday in Barbados, West Indies, January 21, 1968 to be exact. I was assisting in a service where a new Canadian friend was to give his testimony. I had met him just previously when, with his party of colleagues, he attended a Bible class I was conducting. Tom McCormack was a big man in several senses of the word "big." At six feet four inches tall he had a breadth of mind and capacity of heart that matched his physical stature. He was a very successful business man being at that time President of the Dominion Food Stores chain in Canada. His company had four hundred stores with sixteen thousand employees and six hundred million in sales. But bigger than all this was Tom's love for the Lord; love for His people and love for His work all over the world. He loved people and young people in particular. As an example: The year before Canada celebrated its Centenary with Montreal's Expo 67, Tom wanted, as President of the company to do something special for Canadian High School students. He was guided to promote, in every Canadian province, an essay competition on:

"Why I would like to go to Expo '67!"

A number of the winning essay writers would be selected by an impartial panel of judges to receive air fare, a week at Expo with all expenses paid and spending money. A selected number of prizes were allocated to each province and one of the Alberta winners was our own daughter. A year later I met Tom and learned of this background and saw the love of Christ shining through him. Now I was hearing his testimony for the first time. He gave it in the form of a poem.

"I had walked life's way with an easy tread,
Had followed where comforts and pleasure led,
Until one day in a quiet place
I met the Master face to face.

With station and rank and wealth for my goal,
Much thought for my body, but none for my soul,
I had entered to win in life's mad race,
When I met the Master face to face.

I had built my castles and reared them high,
With their towers had pierced the blue of the sky,
I had sworn to rule with an iron mace,
When I met the Master face to face.

I met Him and knew Him and blushed to see
That His eyes, full of sorrow, were fixed on me;
And I faltered and fell at His feet that day,
While my castles melted and vanished away.

Melted and vanished and in their place
Naught else did I see but the Master's face.
And I cried aloud, 'Oh, make me meet
To follow the steps of Thy wounded feet.'

My thought is now for the souls of men,
I have lost my life to find it again,
E'er since one day in a quiet place
I met the Master face to face."
Author Unknown

That reminded me that when love comes and when love calls our response should be like Tom's and Mary's! "Now Jesus loved Martha and her sister and Lazarus."[1] But death had come to this family which He loved. Martha came to Him, but Mary waited until the summons came. "…The Master is come, and calleth for thee. As soon as she heard that, she arose quickly, and came unto him."[2] He loves; He calls; be like Tom and Mary; come quickly.

NOVEMBER 11 – FLYING FROM LOVE

"I Fled Him, down the nights and down the days;
I fled Him, down the arches of the years;
I fled Him, down the labyrinthine ways
Of my own mind; and in the mist of tears
I hid from Him, and under running laughter.
Up vistaed hopes I sped;
And shot, precipitated,
Adown Titanic glooms of chasmed fears,
From those strong Feet that followed, followed after..."
"The Hound of Heaven"
Francis Thompson (1859 – 1907)

Francis Thompson was one of England's great poets; standing on par with John Milton (1608 – 1674) and others of whom the "sceptred isle" has produced so many. Critic J. L. Garvin describes him as "...an argonaut of literature, far travelled in the realm of gold..." "The Hound of Heaven" is the most wonderful lyric in the language.

Who was Francis Thompson? Who was this poet, who in his short life achieved such fame; who climbed so high after falling so low? He spent years of his life in escapism. He failed his college exams; he fled from family and friends and tried to fly from love. He became an opium addict and a derelict, sleeping on the embankment of the Thames River, while still reading Aeschylus and Blake, and scribbling his own thoughts on scraps of paper. One night when Francis, only in his twenties, was cold and starving a hand was placed on his shoulder and a voice said: "Is your soul saved?" "What right have you to ask me that question?" was the angry retort. "Ah well" said Mr. McMaster, a Christian shoemaker out seeking the lost, "if you won't let me save your soul, let me save your body!" and he took Francis home and cared for him. Run away as we will we are hounded by love.

Many have fled, for various motives, from the natural loves of romance, family and friends. These motives include self-love, fear of commitment or an unwillingness to pay the cost and accept the consequences of loving and being loved. Most of us, wittingly or unwittingly, fly from the presence and the love of God, like our fore parents, because of their sin. But where can we hide? Under the fig leaves of our own coverings? Or by flying to far off places? For a few years I tried to do this. What folly! Who can escape omnipresence? Who can outwit omniscience? Who can avoid omnipotence? These three majestic "O's" of eternal love will find us and find us out. "Where can I go from Your Spirit? Or where can I flee from Your presence? If I ascend to heaven, You are there; If I make my bed in Sheol, behold, You are there. If I take the wings of the dawn, If I dwell in the remotest part of the sea, Even there Your hand will lead me, And Your right hand will lay hold of me."[1] Thus Thompson, fleeing, hears the following footsteps of this "Tremendous Lover" and His voice.

"But with unhurrying chase,
And unperturbed pace,
Deliberate speed, majestic instancy,
They beat, and a Voice beat
More instant than the Feet,
'All things betray thee, who betrayest Me.'...

Across the margent of the world I fled...
From this tremendous Lover...
Whom wilt thou find to love ignoble thee,
Save Me, save only Me?...
Rise, clasp My hand, and come!"

NOVEMBER 12 – LOVE, IN JONAH

Jonah was another who fled from love, but his reasons for running were very different from those of Francis Thompson. Jonah knew God; was a prophet of God; with a commission from God which he didn't like. Told to go east, to the great city of Nineveh on the banks of the Tigris River he decided to go west, as far as he could go across the length of the Mediterranean Sea. Tarshish, his destination, is thought, by some commentators, to have been a then Semitic mining colony located west of the Rock of Gibraltar at the mouth of the Guadalquiver River in Spain. These geographical details are given to show the determination of Jonah to distance himself deliberately from Nineveh, God's destiny for him. His larger folly, like Thompson's, was to try and flee from "the presence of the Lord;" and the "love of God;" and the "Hound of Heaven."

In this little book we have Jonah's perversity, prayer, preaching and petulance. "Where can I go from Your Spirit? Or where can I flee from Your presence? If I ascend to heaven, You are there; If I make my bed in Sheol, behold, You are there. If I take the wings of the dawn, If I dwell in the remotest part of the sea, Even there Your hand will lead me, And Your right hand will lay hold of me."[1] We quoted this Scripture in connection with the fleeing poet on the banks of the Thames River, and twenty-seven centuries before him, it is seen in vivid application to the runaway prophet in the Mediterranean. God, in love, moves to head him off by a series of miraculous events. The great storm, the great fish, the great sojourn in the depths of the sea, the great deliverance and the great second chance given to Jonah were all part of the lengths to which God would go. These included not only turning a wilfully disobedient servant around, but his ultimate aim of love for a great and wicked Gentile city. Eternal love was desirous, not of their destruction, but of their deliverance and salvation.

Here is the crux of Jonah's problem. He was in disagreement with God's worldwide mission policy. It is the policy of covenant love to Israel for the whole world, as outlined in the bottom line of God's covenant with Abraham. "...by your descendants all the nations of the earth shall be blessed."[2] Through Israel, Christ would come as Saviour of the world. Bigotry doesn't alter this! So Jonah, though recommissioned, went with very bad grace; still he went and delivered a brief but powerful message to high and low in Nineveh. Repent or in forty days judgment will destroy you. Though Jonah's heart attitude had not been changed to love for lost Gentiles, his message, no doubt reinforced by his appearance, and the story that went before him of his three days in the deep, and then deliverance, had the desired effect. The whole city repented, turned to God and was saved. (Incidentally our Lord put His seal upon the historicity of Jonah by likening Jonah's resurrection to His own).[3] The love of God triumphed in the case of Nineveh and persevered to convince the petulant prophet. "Should I not have compassion on Nineveh, the great city in which there are more than 120,000 persons who do not know the difference between their right and left hand, as well as many animals?"[4]

NOVEMBER 13 – LOVE AND "MISSIONS"

The first "mission" to which divine love leads us is "admission." This is the admission of our sin and guilt and need.

This in turn should move us to the Person and place where "remission" can be justly and lovingly granted. "...without shedding of blood is no remission."[1] Coming to Christ in repentance and faith we receive Him, and with Him, the divine forgiveness which He purchased with His own blood.

His love should then compel us to the third love mission; "submission." This is submission to the Son of God, our Saviour, as Lord in all areas of our life. "Therefore I urge you, brethren, by the mercies of God, to present your bodies a living and holy sacrifice, acceptable to God, which is your spiritual service of worship. And do not be conformed to this world, but be transformed by the renewing of your mind, so that you may prove what the will of God is, that which is good and acceptable and perfect."[2]

These three missions are really parts of the whole salvation mission of the Son of God. Admission; remission; submission; they ought not to be separated into categories as we are so prone to do. This trinity of love "missions" are interrelated and dependent on each other. Without admission there can be no personal remission of sin. The New Testament leaves no room for the false dichotomy, so prevalent today, of separating remission from submission. To claim Him as Saviour but refuse to crown Him as Lord is often done, but is unscriptural. "...that if you confess with your mouth Jesus as Lord, and believe in your heart that God raised Him from the dead, you will be saved."[3] "Who are You, Lord?"[4] "What do You want me to do?" These two questions from smitten Saul are fundamental for vital relationship with Christ in His Person and saving work and subsequent service. The answers, and Paul's obedient love submission, made him the greatest missionary of the age.

This brings us to the fourth "mission" to which divine love urges us; the "Great Commission." His love mission, which is wrapped up in the first three words, now causes us to put forward into the well known areas described as "Missions" or the taking of the Gospel to others. This includes personal, door to door, city wide, provincial or state, national, overseas or foreign missions. The "Great Commission" has never been withdrawn or abrogated. This mission is still incumbent upon the whole church and every one of us who claims to know Jesus Christ the Lord. His mission set the standard for the saint's personal love mission in the world. It is our love response to His love initiative. The Christ-like loving missions of individuals in the New Testament are examples for us today. Sadly, we often use them as illustrations and leave them there. "If you love Me, you will keep My commandments"[5] applies to this last command equally as to the first. When the full history of love and missions is revealed in heaven, what a spectacular story it will be. Illustrative of this is the life of William Cameron Townsend (1896 – 1982). He, in his love for God and man, sought out the overlooked cultures and tongues and founded Wycliffe Bible Translators, through which thousands have been brought to Christ.

NOVEMBER 14 – LOVE'S EXPECTATIONS

When travelling by bus to the centre of the City of Edmonton, Alberta, Canada, I pass a store named "Great Expectations." Below the name in smaller letters is the explanation: "Everything for the mother to be." The owner had borrowed the title from Charles Dicken's (1812 – 1870) book Great Expectations. That famous novel, his last, and left unfinished when he died, tells the story of Pip and Estella. His obsessive love for one "beyond his station" and her calculating "blow hot, blow cold" strategy sets the background for Dicken's convoluted story. Poor boy Pip had great expectations of becoming a gentleman and marrying the rich and beautiful lady Estella. Great expectations kept turning out as poor realizations, which is not unknown in real life and love. The happy ending strikes a false note. It was written by someone else after the novelist's death and there has been much speculation as to how he would have ended it. But that is not our concern here. There are two areas though where this theme concerns us and they are the expectations we have of our heavenly Lover and His expectations of His earthly lovers.

When, almost fifty years ago, I responded to God's missionary call and started out literally on a life of faith, I had never heard William Carey's (1761 – 1834) challenge:

"Attempt great things for God; expect great things from God."

Now, in retrospect, I can see and say I have had a half-century of great realizations from my great expectations from Him. Carrying on mission work and marriage in wartime with new converts and new babies and new workers gave my dear wife and me (beginners ourselves) great opportunities to prove Him. Our expectations of Him have never been failed.

But what about His expectations of us? "But this man, after he had offered one sacrifice for sins for ever, sat down on the right hand of God; from henceforth expecting till his enemies be made his footstool."[1] What about our heavenly Lover's expectations of us in the light of His Word just quoted? Had we done all we could and should have, even in the missionary aspects of playing our part in the Great Commission, we would have only been fulfilling our duty of love. But looking back over five decades we see faith that faltered and missed opportunities. His great expectations of us have, in comparison, been poor realizations. He has never been a disappointment though we have been to Him.

"He expecteth, He expecteth,
Down the stream of time,
Still the words come softly ringing
Like a chime,
Oftimes faint, now waxing louder
As the hour draws near,
When the King, in all His glory,
Shall appear.

He is waiting with long patience
For His crowning day,
For that Kingdom which shall never
Pass away.
And till every tribe and nation
Bow before His throne,
He expecteth loyal service,
From His own.

He expecteth, but He heareth
Still the bitter cry
From earth's millions, 'Come and help us,
For we die.'
He expecteth, doth He see us
Busy here and there,
Heedless of these pleading accents
Of despair.

Shall we, dare we disappoint Him?
Brethren, let us rise;
He who died for us is watching
From the skies.
Watching till His royal banner
Floateth far and wide,
Till He seeth of His travail
Satisfied." Anon.

NOVEMBER 15 – LOVE: CONTROLLING AND COMPELLING

"For the love of Christ controls us, having concluded this, that one died for all, therefore all died; and He died for all, so that they who live might no longer live for themselves, but for Him who died and rose again on their behalf."[1] To be filled with the Spirit is to be controlled by Him and as He pours Himself into us, He is pouring the love of God in Christ into us. The Spirit filled life is the love controlled life; true for every Christian and true for all time, everywhere. The Spirit is the Executive Director of Missions, local and foreign, and of every real "sent" one. This is clear in the "Acts" of the Holy Spirit, and in the long continuation, and as yet unfinished, story of His doings, in conjunction with Christ, in His people. The book of Acts begins with Christ's ascension, the promise of empowerment for witness, the descent of the Holy Spirit and the baptism of all the one hundred twenty or so gathered in the upper room. All this was made possible by the death, resurrection and ascension of Christ to the throne. Thus the promise was fulfilled and the promised One sent.

Death and love; death and the Spirit controlled life; death and missions are inextricably linked. They are as united as the Trinity. The New Testament tells it exactly as it is. He died, we died; He lives, we live; He did all His work through the Spirit, so must we. We are to be constrained, controlled and compelled by love as our theme text tells us. However, we cannot be like this unless the Spirit of love, who is the Spirit of Christ, enables us.

He is not only the enabler He is the motivator. The motivation for missions is love. It is often the missing motive. There are so many mixtures in our own motives that it ill behoves us to judge others. Yet, generally speaking, we can say that as far as missionary motivation goes "need" is not equated with "call." Need is put forward as a motive. I doubt, from long observation, that going anywhere, any distance, because of people's needs will suffice to keep us there and keep us pegging away. Need calls from every quarter; only the specific direction of the Spirit, plus His motivating and energizing can lead us to needs that He can meet through us. Only God can bear the burdens and sins of the whole world and they killed His Son. But we can and must, through the compulsion of love, meet the near and far needs to which He directs the giving of ourselves, our substance and our intercession.

Death to personal desire will often be demanded as the will of God is walked and worked out; but resurrection life and love in the Spirit will prevail, even if shortened physical life through deprivation, disease or martyrdom should result. After the "Boxer" rebellion (1899 – 1901) took place in northern China, Marshall Broomhall (1866 – 1937) wrote a book detailing the role of the China Inland Mission during those troubled times. The title says it all: By Love Compelled

NOVEMBER 16 – THIRTEEN VERSES FOR MISSIONARIES

Charles Willoughby, who, if not a missionary, certainly knew a lot about them, and the problem areas where love would be tested, wrote a series of thirteen verses based on the thirteen verses of 1 Corinthians 13.

"If I speak with the tongues of nationals and of senior missionaries, but have not love, I am become a blaring trumpet or a clanging cymbal.

And if I have great administrative ability, and understand all doctrines and all customs; and if I have all faith so as to remove obstinate government officials, but have not love, I am nothing.

And if I give up all the comforts of the homeland to minister to the heathen, and if I am martyred on the field, but have not love, it profiteth me nothing.

Love is patient and kind to fellow missionaries; love is not envious of another's support; love does not boast of many deputation meetings, is not inflated with pride,

Does not become arrogant to fellow workers, does not insist on its own methods, is not provoked by trying personalities, takes no thought of self;

Rejoices not in the shortcoming of others, but rejoices in their triumphs;

Bears all the hardships of the life, believes even when everything goes wrong; hopes in the 'hopeless' situations, endures through everything.

Love never fails; as for administrative abilities, they shall fail; as for language schools, they shall cease; as for beautiful outfits, they shall vanish away

For now we know missionary principles imperfectly, and we practice them imperfectly

But when perfection comes, these imperfections shall be put away.

When I was a child, my talk was childish, my thoughts were childish, my reasoning was childish; but when I became a missionary, I laid aside my childish ways. (or did I?)

Now we see God's nature and ways very dimly, but then face to face; now my knowledge is imperfect, but then I shall know fully, even as I am fully known.

Now abideth fundamentalism, premillenialism and love, these three, but the greatest of these is love."

As a result of having spent almost fifty years in close connection with many missionaries of many missions in many lands, and also in contact with many mission circles in the homelands, I know the truth of these words by Willoughby. Thirteen sentences that convict me in retrospect and challenge me in the present in their extension and application. Daily reading of, and prayerful consideration, and specific application over one month, of these verses, should make love more real in all our relationships. As the Holy Spirit convicts us in an area, put it right, and experience afresh Romans 5:5

NOVEMBER 17 – BY LOVE SENT FORTH

"By this all men will know that you are My disciples, if you have love for one another."[1] "As You sent Me into the world, I also have sent them into the world."[2] We have noted that holy heavenly love is the compelling, propelling force in the universe. It formed the planets and the stars and set them on their courses. It sustains the creation that it caused. It created and walked and talked with man in his innocency. It planned and produced the incarnation and redemption that brought back and released the fallen, but believing, members of the human race. It sent from heaven "...the Spirit of His Son into our hearts, crying, 'Abba! Father!'"[3] It continues to intercede for us from the throne. It continues to thrust forth labourers into the harvest field of this world. It continues to build the Church which is His body. Holy, heavenly love is eternally active in the continuing work of His Son through His sons and daughters. The mystery and mastery of love as described by our Lord must result in loving, sacrificial service in, and to, the world of our day and generation. Love's consecration says:

"Take my life...Take my hands...Take my feet...Take my voice...Take my intellect...Take my will...Take my heart...Take my love...Ever, only, all for Thee." Frances Ridley Havergal (1836 – 1879)

As our Lord was sent forth in this manner by love, so we are sent forth by Him today. This "as so" or "as also" is very simple in language, easily understood (at least superficially) but profoundly significant and full of important truths. This applies not only to official foreign or home missionaries but for all believers who are also his witnesses. The verse is repeated again after his resurrection. "...as the Father has sent Me, I also send you."[4] Here it is prefaced with the gift of his peace; followed by the promise of the Holy Spirit as He breathed on them; and concluded with their entrustment with the message of forgiveness. Everything is to be motivated by holy, heavenly love. For as He was compelled by agapé in His coming and going so we must be propelled by it. Love personified and performing was His manner and ministry in the first century and thus it must be today. Agapé resulted in brotherly love in the early church; towards each other in practical ways, and to the world in the preaching of the Gospel. This uncompromising love, proclaimed by people propelled by love, produced miracles of repentance and faith.

"So send I you-by grace made strong to triumph
O'er hosts of hell, o'er darkness, death, and sin,
My name to bear, and in that name to conquer,
So send I you, My victory to win.

So send I you-to take to souls in bondage
The word or truth that sets the captive free,
To break the bonds of sin, to lost death's fetters,
So send I you, to bring the lost to Me.

So send I you-My strength to know in weakness,
My joy in grief, My perfect peace in pain,
To prove My power, My grace, My promised presence,
So send I you, eternal fruit to gain." Margaret Clarkson (1915 -)

NOVEMBER 18 – THE "IF" OF LOVE

Here are some modern writings about that greatest love chapter, 1 Corinthians 13. These are very personal, practical missionary applications of agapé love. The first was written by a student in an Indian language school, who no doubt had been observing missionaries and Christian workers.

"If I have the language ever so perfectly and speak like a pundit and have not love that grips the heart, I am nothing.

If I have decorations and diplomas and am proficient in up-to-date methods and have not the touch of understanding love, I am nothing.

If I am able to worst my opponents in argument so as to make fools of them, and have not the wooing note, I am nothing.

If I have all faith and great ideals and magnificent plans and wonderful visions, and have not the love that sweats and bleeds and weeps and prays and pleads, I am nothing.

If I surrender all prospects, and leaving home and friends and comforts, give myself to the showy sacrifice of a missionary career, and turn sour and selfish amid the daily annoyances and personal slights of a missionary life, and though I give my body to be consumed in the heat and sweat and mildew of India, but have not the love that yields its rights, its coveted leisure, its pet plans, I am nothing. Nothing.

Virtue has ceased to go out of me.

If I can heal all manner of sickness and disease, but wound hearts and hurt feelings for want of love that is kind, I am nothing.

If I write books and publish articles that set the world agape, but fail to transcribe that word of the Cross in the language of love, I am nothing.

Worse, I may be competent, busy, fussy, punctilious, and well-equipped, but like the church at Laodicea, nauseating to Christ."

In contrast to this, here is a positive example. There was a missionary to India whose writings were a real inspiration and challenge to us as beginning missionaries. I refer to Miss Amy Wilson Carmichael (1867 – 1951). Her books like <u>Gold Chord</u>, <u>Meal in a Barrel</u>, <u>Windows</u> and many others encouraged us in a life of faith and to build a work that lasts with gold, silver and precious stones, not wood, hay or stubble. She said you can build quickly and cheaply with the latter materials but they perish just as quickly. Gold, silver and precious stones are costly materials and building with them is slow arduous work, but it is work that lasts and can endure the fire. The heart of her work and the strength of it was love. It was a love that was pure gold, silver and precious stones. She wrote one little book devoted to this theme and which repeats the emphasis of the Indian student. It is titled <u>If</u> and each page consists of a challenging "if" thought about love and ends with "Then I know nothing about Calvary love." Miss Carmichael said the thoughts came to her with this emphasis and she dared not soften them even though some might not understand or even be offended. She was following the Pauline pattern of 1 Corinthians 13 and the Indian student's challenge. I believe Miss Carmichael was a shining example of Calvary love.

NOVEMBER 19 – THE "THOUGH" OF PARTNERSHIP LOVE –
Part One

We have given an abbreviated version of the "If" that was born in the heart of a missionary in an Indian language school. The full text is even stronger and worth repeating in this section on love and missions and missionaries. The principles are valid for all of us and in this book, <u>Partners in God's Love,</u> nowhere is the emphasis more needed than on the home front mission field.

"Though I speak in the dialect of the people I serve and can preach with the eloquent power of a fiery evangelist; though as a surgeon I can operate with skill; though as an agriculturist I can raise acres of high-grade river rice; though as a teacher I can deliver learned lectures, but do not have love, my message is empty.

And though I have the talent of a diplomatic organizer and administrator in councils and meetings; though I have all the confidence that I need to raise large funds, but do not have love, I am good for nothing.

And though I share my possessions and give money to the poor, but do not help my brother and sister to become strong, independent followers of Christ, I achieve absolutely nothing.

Love, if it is genuine in the life and work of a missionary, is patient and constructive; it does not seek for position and prestige. Love is glad to see a competent national in charge, and envies not. Love seeks to train an indigenous leadership; it does not cherish inflated ideas of its own importance; it is never anxious to impress. Love tries to identify itself with people and is never puffed up.

Love that is genuine does not belittle. It does not compile statistics of another's mistakes. Love seeks to bear joy and sorrow, failure and success, in helpful ways. Love is not easily provoked when there is difference of opinion; and when rumours are spread, love believes the best.

Love that is genuine is a partner. It is better to fail with a national in charge than to succeed without him. Love is not touchy; it never hides hurt feelings. Love never barricades understanding; it rejoices in sharing the truth.

Love keeps an open mind; is willing to attempt new methods and ways of doing things. Love does not consider the past so precious that it limits new vision. Love gives courage to change old ways when necessary. Unless we are prepared to adapt and change, we shall have defenders of an old system but no new voice. We shall have preachers, but not prophets. We shall keep the bush neatly pruned by hired hands with expensive equipment. But within the bush there will be no burning fire.

Love that trusts like little children never fails. Large institutions may cease; even heavily subsidized schools and colleges that impart knowledge may close. If wisdom gained there fails to lead students to Christ the Savior, it would be better to entrust such education to the government; for our knowledge is always incomplete without Him who is 'the way, the truth and the life.' Love that has no other desire but to trust never fails.

We are in a period of change and transition. Who knows exactly where we are going and what will happen?

But now here on earth, we can comprehend only in part..."

NOVEMBER 20 – THE "THOUGH" OF PARTNERSHIP LOVE –
Part Two

"When missions were yet at the stage of childhood, the methods of proclaiming Christ's gospel were simple. Authority was in the hands of a few. But now that missions have grown for over a century into maturity, they must put away childish dependence. There must be on each of the fields abroad a new, strong, independent church of the Master that is self-supporting, self-administering, and self-propagating.

But whatever happens, whatever direction the winds of change may take, there is this certainty: Our Lord will not leave Himself without a witness. He is perfecting His plan in and through history, though everything now looks confused and baffling.

Be sure of this: institutions will pass away, but labor wrought by hands that have shared with those in need, and proclaimed the message of the saving love of Christ, who died and rose again and lives as Lord of life, will never, never pass away. In this life there are only three enduring qualities: faith, hope, and love; these three. But the greatest of these is love."

This amplification and application of 1 Corinthians 13 by this anonymous writer is full of vision and verity and one senses the vigour and vitality of the Spirit Himself in this missionary, be he or she, expatriate or national. The Holy Spirit's motivating power of love that sent apostles to martyrdom in the Book of Acts, and made loving witnesses and workers of all church members in that same period, is still at work today. The missionary principles and practices described in this 20th century writing were practiced in the 1st century.

Two things, amongst others, are apparent in the Acts. People took note of those ambassadors "… that they had been with Jesus."[(1)] They were Christ-like in love. Secondly, they were continually, filled, controlled and guided by the Spirit of love. Souls were saved and churches were established during the chaotic times of persecution and extreme poverty amongst the new converts. These kinds of circumstances were normal for the first three centuries when Christians were hated and hunted. The open secret of their growth had been given by their Lord: "Truly, truly, I say to you, unless a grain of wheat falls into the earth and dies, it remains alone; but if it dies, it bears much fruit."[(2)] The high cost of loving, as He loved, was understood and paid by these early Christians and churches. And, thank God, these tremendous principles became transferable concepts; not to be given mental assent only but to become active in multitudes of the Lord's people since then.

I had a valued copy of a book called Fenton Hall – Pioneer to the Amazon Indians which I gave away to other missionary colleagues before I retired. Fenton Hall, who was an airman in WW1, carried the same intrepid, courageous, self-sacrificing spirit of the flyers, to Brazil. His love for the Lord and the Amazon Indians made him a literal corn of wheat kind of pioneer. He died early, but the harvest still comes home.

NOVEMBER 21 – CARMICHAEL'S "IFS" ON CALVARY LOVE

Amy Wilson Carmichael (1867 – 1951) was the founder of the Donhavur Fellowship in south India. I have before me now her little book entitled simply <u>If</u>. Written then by a missionary for fellow missionaries, or better, given by God for herself and shared with others, we today are also blessed and challenged by these "Ifs." I call them "A Missionary's 'Ifs'" because of their background and because the field is the world and we are all servants of His in it. We will be more profitable, better "sent ones" if we heed these very Scriptural "Ifs." Don't let the heat of love keep you away from the fire. I hope the selected extracts will encourage you to get a copy for yourself. Miss Carmichael tells how it came to be written.

"One evening a fellow worker brought me a problem about a younger one who was missing the way of love. This led to a wakeful night, for the word at such times is always, 'Lord, is it I? Have I failed anywhere? What do I know of Calvary love?' and then sentence by sentence the 'Ifs' came, almost as if spoken aloud to the inward ear…Some of the 'Ifs' seem to be related to pride, selfishness or cowardice, but digging deeper we come upon an unsuspected lovelessness at the rest of them all…And in case any true follower be troubled by the 'then I know nothing', I would say the thought came in this form, and I fear to weaken it. But here, as everywhere, the letter killeth…"

"If I have not compassion on my fellow servant, even as my Lord had pity on me, then I know nothing of Calvary love.

If I belittle those whom I am called to serve, talk of their weak points in contrast perhaps with what I think of as my strong points; If I adopt a superior attitude, forgetting 'Who made thee to differ? And what hast thou that thou hast not received?' then I know nothing of Calvary love.

If I am perturbed by the reproach and misunderstanding that may follow action taken for good of souls for whom I must give account; if I can not commit the matter and go on in peace and in silence, remembering Gethsemane and the Cross, then I know nothing of Calvary love.

If I have not the patience of my Saviour with souls who grow slowly; if I know little of travail (a sharp and painful thing) till Christ be fully formed in them, then I know nothing of Calvary love.

If I sympathize weakly with weakness, and say to one who is turning back from the Cross 'Pity thyself'; if I refuse such a one the sympathy that braces the brave and heartening words of comradeship, then I know nothing of Calvary love.

If I say, 'Yes, I forgive, but I cannot forget,' as though the God, who twice a day washes all the sands on all the shores of all the world, could not wash such memories from my mind, then I know nothing of Calvary love.

If I refuse to be a corn of wheat that falls into the ground and dies (is separated from all in which it lived before), then I know nothing of Calvary love.

That which I know not, teach Thou me, O Lord, my God."

NOVEMBER 22 – LOVE IN REVOLUTION

The English started modern revolutions rolling when the Puritans under Cromwell (1599 – 1658) and his Roundheads, won the civil war (1642 – 1651) and sent King Charles I (1600 – 1649) head rolling. That revolution had a number of major causes, one of which was the demand for freedom of conscience in religion and tolerance for the evangelical minority. Intolerance soon defeated the victors and what was heralded as the triumph of the love of God turned into hatred, factionalism and self destruction. This in turn paved the way for the restoration of the Stuart monarchy. Under King Charles II (1630 – 1685) liberty turned to license, and libertinism and licentiousness became rampant, masquerading under the name of love. During the next century the Wesley-Whitfield revolution, through the Holy Spirit preaching of the love of God in Christ, with its call to repentance, brought a revival of Gospel truth in England. Thousands were brought into the Kingdom and historians are on record as saying that that religious revolution saved Britain from the horrors of the soon to come French Revolution.

But the American Revolution (1775 – 1783) came first with the rise of the thirteen colonies against the mother country, its crazy King George III (1738 – 1820) and its stubborn politicians. "No taxation without representation" became one of the watchwords along with "Give me liberty or give me death." "Democracy" became a buzz word and the new American Constitution, framed by deists and humanists became the modern "Magna Carta." In the meantime, humble backwoods preachers went on preaching the love of God.

The bloody French Revolution (1789 – 1799), with its cry of "Liberty, Fraternity, Equality" ended the monarchy and attacked the Roman Catholic Church allied to the establishment. In the name of brotherly love the guillotine knifed its way through the aristocracy, including King Louis XVI (1754 – 1793) in its carnage, and soon began to devour its own children. The dictator Napoleon (1769 – 1821) ended the anarchy.

The Russian Revolution of 1917 ended the reign of Tsar Nicholas II (1868 – 1918) and the rule of the established church. Evangelicals, in Russia, though few, grew under persecution, and the Lord has many people there. The love of God, through the preaching of the Gospel, still triumphs in individual lives despite revolution.

The Chinese Revolution (1927 – 1949) and Communist takeover was followed by the ouster of missionaries with statements like this:

"The traders and the missionaries came together to China. Imperialist and cultural exploitation, preaching and robbery, walked hand in hand. Together they must go."

And go they did! But the true church, born of the deep, deep love of Jesus, stayed. It has grown through persecution. Meanwhile the masses were indoctrinated in new love. Emotions had to be reordered. Love was a difficulty. Love was a problem and love of family and ancestors had to be redirected to love of the state.

This one page covers over three hundred years of revolution and love in revolution. Love in tribulation would perhaps be a better word. Tribulation can diminish love. It can also foster love. Tribulation can never, ever sever His own from the love of Christ.

NOVEMBER 23 – LOVE AND LIBERATION THEOLOGY

I now wish to discuss a relevant, practical topic. For how long should Christian love suffer oppression? How far should Christian love go in resisting it? Should Christian love engage in revolution against a lawful but awful rightist or leftist authority? Should Christian love take up arms in pursuit of liberty? These and similar questions are very relevant today. There are pro and con voices but liberation theology seems to prevail today, but on a positive note I sense its day has come and gone.

The view of Christ as a nationalist, revolutionary leader of an oppressed people seeking confrontation with Rome in armed revolt is not very Scriptural. "The Spirit of the Lord is upon me, because He anointed me to preach the Gospel to the poor. He has sent me to proclaim release to the captives and recovery of sight to the blind, to set free those who are oppressed, to proclaim the favorable year of the Lord..."[1] It is wrong exegesis to say that this prophecy, which He applied to Himself, speaks of freeing the downtrodden by His followers' armed intervention. He did it by love, living and dying love, on Calvary.

It is true that there were some, at His first coming, who thought He had come as a King to overthrow Rome's rule by force and restore the kingdom to Israel. There were also armed bands leading revolts. But He was not such a practitioner or preacher. He preached the bad news about sin's bondage and the Good News of redemption and release from Satan, sin and self if they would repent. It was a message of love's liberation and was the liberation theology of the kind He proclaimed and practiced. It wasn't very popular then!

It is still not popular, but it is very personal and very practical. Ask any really born again believer! They sing the song of the soul set free from sin's shackles and the Satanic strong man's strength.

On the Damascus road (yes it's still there) a bloodthirsty, hateful religious zealot, was on another murderous mission. His liberation theology taught him that he was acting in God's name until God stopped him. Then Saul became Paul and a loving exponent of New Testament liberation theology with good social works as evidence. He spoke the truth and suffered all his life for it personally, by imprisonment and persecution. His commission is found in Acts 26:14-18.

Our Lord, as Son of God could have called for heavenly legions; one word from Him threw soldiers on the ground, but His personal answer, to all the questions posed above, was unequivocal, clear and concise: "...My kingdom is not of this world. If My kingdom were of this world, then My servants would be fighting so that I would not be handed over to the Jews; but as it is, My kingdom is not of this realm."[2]

NOVEMBER 24 – REVOLUTIONARY LOVE

Revolutionary Love is the title of a book by Bishop Festo Kivengere (1919 – 1988) of Uganda. He was a man who knew what he was talking about having suffered under the brutal dictatorship of Idi Amin (1924 – 2003). In fact Kivengere had even gone so far as to say, and write,

"I love Idi Amin!"

The good Bishop had either lost his mind or he was a good bishop, elder and overseer. He, of course, was the latter and was telling the world that, hounded as he and his family had been, he could, and would, love his enemy. Revolutionary Love is his mature witness to the power of God's love in all circumstances. Revolutionary times demands revolutionary love.

We are considering this subject as a continuation of the theme "Love and Liberation Theology." There we asked a number of questions and sought some answers. Quite frankly, I believe the answer to liberation theology and practice lies in the two words: "Revolutionary Love." The proponents of "Christian" revolution by terrorism and bloodshed have misunderstood and misapplied Christian love in both its meaning and application. Evangelical proponents of Christian New Testament love have been warned by Dr. Paul S. Rees in his book Don't Sleep Through the Revolution.

This Christian love is revolutionary love of a different kind and is applied in a very different kind of way. It has to do with loving one's enemies and doing good to them, while being rejected, persecuted and even martyred. It is the reverse of the other. There, while the revolutionaries are also willing to die for what they believe, they also make countless innocent people suffer in the process. There seems to be callousness about this kind of revolution for political power, while professing love for the common man. Selfishness has been the prime motivation of mankind since the Fall; only the new birth alters that. For while there have been many selfless and dedicated revolutionaries, their love, aims and means are not the same as those of revolutionary Christian lovers. The first seven beatitudes sum up the difference.

The love of Christ is revolutionary love and it continues its revolutionary way by suffering for righteousness sake and by laying down its life for others. This does not mean that His people are indifferent to social injustice, anymore than Christ, His apostles and His people were in the first century. Do good to all, love all was their guideline within the parameters of the wider truth:

"…that until Christ's return the tares and the wheat grow up together, and that salvation must be measured in terms more enduring and holistic than those of socio-economic liberation." Dr. W. Dayton Roberts, Vice-President, Latin American Mission, San Jose, Costa Rico.

NOVEMBER 25 – LOVE AND CONFLICT – Part One

The next three readings are about a topic which I have finally come to realize is central to our Christian walk and that is, that where love is there is going to be conflict. I recognize that I will only scratch the surface in these brief pages but I encourage the reader to delve into the Word for further edification.

The love of Christ compelled the body of Christ (about one hundred twenty members) into all manner of conflicts after Pentecost. As Spirit filled witnesses, speaking the truth about Christ, they took opposition and persecution as part of their commitment to Him. The real miracle was that they rejoiced in it; prayed for their enemies and went back for more. One would have expected that Christians filled with the spirit of love would have won their way into the hearts of people without any conflict. However, such was not the case for two major reasons. First, there is a war in the unseen spirit world. "For our struggle is not against flesh and blood, but against the rulers, against the powers, against the world forces of this darkness, against the spiritual forces of wickedness in the heavenly places."[1] Secondly, our Gospel is hidden from the unbelieving. "And even if our gospel is veiled, it is veiled to those who are perishing, in whose case the god of this world has blinded the minds of the unbelieving so that they might not see the light of the gospel of the glory of Christ, who is the image of God."[2] The fall of angelic beings in heaven preceded and precipitated the fall of the human race on earth. The continuing conflict there caused, and continues to cause, the conflict here. This overall view is necessary for an understanding of the local scene.

This conflict climaxed at Calvary. There the enemy was defeated but he is not yet destroyed. At Calvary the Gospel was made possible; it was purchased at an awful price. When Christ in his Gospel of love and truth is proclaimed in the power of the Spirit of love and truth, there is bound to be conflict. From Acts 2 onwards, until today there has been a "Holy War" to use Bunyan's phrase. Peter, James, John, Stephen, Paul and all the others whose stories are recorded, fought the good fight of faith. Victories were gained. Souls were saved. Churches were planted. But they knew they had been in war. Their battle wounds and scars showed it. The truth spoken in love is still not loved, as relatively few truly repent and respond.

And so the conflicts continue as meaningful, forward moves on reformation and revival in the church started with one or two obedient ones praying and paying the price. Martin Luther (1483 – 1546), John (1703 – 1791) and Charles (1707 – 1788) Wesley, George Whitfield (1714 – 1770) and the holy band at Oxford, Jonathon Edwards (1703 – 1758), Charles Finney (1792 – 1815), William Booth (1829 – 1912) and others all knew that the love of God poured out in them, was to be poured out through them and they knew it would result in conflict. Wesley's journals are but a continuation of the Book of Acts. The early history of The Salvation Army is the story of Spirit filled men and women moved by holy love, going out to engage the enemy, wherever he may be entrenched. The fight for souls is fierce. Love and conflict are inevitable; love and truth are unconquerable.

"Fierce may be the conflict, strong may be the foe,
But the King's own army none can overthrow;
'Round His standard ranging, victory is secure,
For His truth unchanging makes the triumph sure."
Frances Ridley Havergal (1836 – 1879)

NOVEMBER 26 – LOVE AND CONFLICT – Part Two

There is plenty of evidence to show that the Salvation Army was born of love for Christ and love for men and women. It expected conflict as it sought to release souls from Satan and sin. After all, that's what armies engage in. In reading the history of General William Booth (1829 – 1912) and his wife Catherine (1829 – 1890), their own family and their wider family of "Salvationists" we note that it is a story of continual conflict between truth and righteousness battling error and evil. These soldiers of Christ saw the power of Satan and sin broken by the power of His love, working through them. They believed and preached the blood of the Lamb for cleansing and the fire of the Holy Spirit for fighting. The Booth family are gone but not their descendants or the work they founded.

In the 1930's in Sydney, Australia I attended an evangelistic campaign conducted by Mrs. Catherine Booth-Clibborn (1858 – 1955), or "the Maréchale" as she was advertised. She had resigned from the Army in 1902 to become an independent evangelist. She was the oldest daughter of William and Catherine Booth. Night after night I listened to, what was to me a very old lady, giving out the good news with energy and fervour. She called men and women to repentance as she had been doing since thirteen years of age. Under the banner of love young Catherine, her three sisters and the rest of the Booth family, poured forth the message of redeeming love. The struggle, then as now, is fought on two levels, the earthly and the heavenly.

One night in the Sydney campaign, she told some of her life story and in particular the start of the Army in France. In 1881, Captain Catherine Booth and three courageous young lady lieutenants commenced Army work in Paris. They sought out an arena of poverty, squalor and vice and from the first word of the Gospel uttered in French, the fight was on and it was fierce. People came and souls were won. Someone addressed her as "Madame la Maréchale" (Madam, the Marshall, quite a promotion in rank!) and the name stuck. In 1883 the Maréchale became the centre of a "cause célèbre" in Switzerland. The issue was freedom of worship and she argued the case in a Swiss courtroom. She won and by 1889 the "Armée du Salut" was recognized as a religious institution. But Catherine had suffered imprisonment first. I am glad, that as a young man, I had heard that veteran of love and conflict for Christ.

I'm glad too I knew another who understood the meaning of conflict. I was a contemporary and friend in the 1930's of a young man, born in China and planning to return there. R. Arthur Mathews and I were together in Open Air Campaigner Gospel Route marches in the state of New South Wales, Australia. He was destined for long imprisonment by the Communists in China. Arthur died in 1978 but left behind a life long testimony of love and conflict and a book Born for Battle. I encourage you to read its thirty one studies on spiritual warfare.

NOVEMBER 27 – LOVE AND CONFLICT – Part Three

Thus far we have been discussing the external conflicts with which Christian love must contend. However, our fight is also with the unseen spiritual adversaries of God and good. These adversaries are the powers of darkness and their earthly emissaries and those in "…the snare of the devil, having been held captive by him to do his will."[1] The weapons at our disposal for use in our warfare are not carnal or fleshly but mighty under God and include prayer, faith, the sword of the Spirit, which is the Word of God and love. We fight not for the victory, but in victory. We fight from the throne where we are seated spiritually with the risen Christ. We fight from the heavenly heights in the authority and power He gives us by His Spirit. We fight the good fight of faith.

Moving closer to home, how are the internal conflicts in the churches to be resolved? We again turn to Scripture for our guidance. In Christian love, of course, but with the kind of Christian love shown by the first church in Jerusalem. There were incipient racial problems in that church despite its Pentecostal experience and its apostolic leadership. They were all converted Jews, but as in the nation of Israel today where there is conflict between European and Asiatic Jews, so there was conflict between "…the Hellenistic Jews against the native Hebrews…"[2] How did Christian love handle this? In a very practical way! While the apostles continued to preach, teach and pray, seven Spirit filled people were chosen to impartially serve the daily meals to all the widows. Thus the first "deacons' began their work of love. When moral, doctrinal and liberal problems began to arise in the seven churches in Asia, the risen Lord instructed John to send letters of both commendation and criticism to them. The letters praised what was praiseworthy and also pointed out the errors of their ways and called them to return and repent, or else. This was all done in true love by the One who said: "For those whom the Lord loves He disciplines and He scourges every son whom He receives."[3]

I sense that today there is a civil war between Christian groups and that must delight Satan. For example, in a report entitled "Cooperating in World Evangelization" (published as Lausanne Occasional Paper No. 24) these topics of conflict are listed in five major categories. They are: "Dogmatism about Nonessentials and Differing Scriptural Interpretations; The Threat of Conflicting Authorities; The Harmfulness of Strained Relationships; The Rivalry between Ministries; and The Suspicion about Finances." There is potential here for many problems! How do they advocate handling them? "Truth and love then, need to be kept in balance…*not* an emphasis on love (or rather, a caricature of it) at the expense of truth…*nor* an emphasis on truth (pursued relentlessly) at the expense of love…" How true!

In the first arena of external conflict with Satan we must be prepared to lay down our lives, in love. In the second arena of internal evangelical church frictions we must be prepared to lay down our differences, in love.

In closing, as I indicated at the outset, I have barely scratched the surface and have done so at the risk of perhaps being overly simplistic. However, my purpose was to introduce the reader to this most important topic and encourage further research.

NOVEMBER 28 – LOVE AND THE MID-LIFE CRISIS

Moses, at eighty years of age, could hardly be described as being in mid-life! He had a crisis at forty years of age when he made his great renunciation of love. The next forty years in Midian seemed settled middle years as family, and tending sheep didn't produce many mid-life crises! He had given up on "crusading." His one effort in the flesh had ended badly. Mocked by the Hebrews and hounded by the Egyptians, his exile now seemed permanent. He had settled down and was satisfied. "Don't disturb me" seemed to be his retirement philosophy. But watch out Moses, you are in for a real mid-life crisis! God is moving to stir up your nest; disturb your rest; cause havoc in your family; and alter your attitudes and lifestyle. The great revelation and annunciation from the burning bush ushered in this crisis. God's time had come to move in the liberation of Israel. But Moses didn't want any part of it. Excuses tumbled out of him. But patient heavenly love that had preserved the baby in the Nile; prepared him in forty years of primary school in Egypt; and given forty years of quiet secondary school in the desert was not about to give up on Moses. Though he seemed to have given up on himself, persevering love prevailed.

We cannot avoid or evade sovereign love when it calls us in crises, small though they may be. Ours are much more mundane, but heavenly love will see us through. Mid life is a time for evaluation, self examination and overcoming of our personal, family, business, career and other crises which seem to come along.

I was interested to read in Brian Booth's (1933 -) autobiography (January 24) the following when he had to hang up his bat:

"If you take seventy as the average life span, then you are middle aged at thirty five. At fifty you are close to the final third of your life. Crisis thinking comes at forty five and sixty five. 'What have I achieved and what was its value?' becomes the questioning thought, and what of the future? I write this" continues Booth "at the fifty year stage…My cricket may be finished but I'm not…I had set myself the task of writing this book…As a teacher who trains teachers to be…my thinking is people centred…The physical side is important but…there is a mental and spiritual facet also…When I put my life into Jesus Christ's hands as a nineteen year old it was not a passing whim…Thirty years later I see it as the most important event of my life." From Booth to Bat

That's the way to face a mid-life crisis, with Christ. His love will enable us to triumph over any and all of our crises. "Above all, keep fervent in your love for one another, because love covers a multitude of sins."[1] Love says the best is yet to be. Moses came through his crisis. His last forty years changed the world. Our last years are also full of love and promise.

NOVEMBER 29 – COVERED BY LOVE

"Then Moses said, 'I pray You, show me Your glory!' And He said, 'I Myself will make all My goodness pass before you, and will proclaim the name of the Lord before you; and I will be gracious to whom I will be gracious, and will show compassion on whom I will show compassion.' But He said, 'You cannot see My face, for no man can see Me and live!' Then the Lord said, 'Behold, there is a place by Me, and you shall stand there on the rock; and it will come about, while My glory is passing by, that I will put you in the cleft of the rock and cover you with My hand...'"[1] This is what we need; to see His glory.

We have seen how Moses was called to serve at eighty years of age! Now we see this servant of God covered by the loving hand of God. Moses prayer to be shown the glory of God was, as is so often the case, answered exceedingly abundantly beyond all he asked or thought. Love showed him the goodness of God; Love proclaimed the name of the Lord before him; Love chose the rock; Love cleft the rock; Love covered him there while Love in all His glory was passing by. The symbolism of the cleft rock and the covering of love has wider implications.

Blind Fanny Crosby (1820 – 1915) "saw" this scene and captured for herself, and us, the essential elements as they concern us in Christ. She made the applications in her wonderful Gospel hymn concerning the depths of His love that covers. She saw herself, her soul, hidden in the cleft rock, Christ; hidden in the depths of His love. She "saw" other rock scenes in that dry thirsty wilderness. She "saw" a thirsty multitude calling for water, and she "saw" Moses strike that rock and from the cleft came the life giving water. That Sinai scene has spiritual significance: "...all drank the same spiritual drink, for they were drinking from a spiritual rock which followed them; and the rock was Christ."[2]

"A wonderful Saviour is Jesus my Lord,
A wonderful Saviour to me,
He hideth my soul in the cleft of the rock,
Where rivers of pleasure I see.

He hideth my soul in the cleft of the rock
That shadows a dry, thirsty land;
He hideth my life in the depths of his love,
And covers me there with his hand."

Augustus Montague Toplady (1740 – 1778), more than a century before Crosby, also "saw" prophetically and scripturally, other aspects of that cleft rock and the covering of love.

"Rock of Ages, cleft for me,
Let me hide myself in Thee;
Let the water and the blood,
From Thy wounded side which flowed,
Be of sin the double cure;
Save from wrath and make me pure.

Nothing in my hand I bring,
Simply to the cross I cling;
Naked, come to Thee for dress;
Helpless look to Thee for grace;
Foul, I to the fountain fly;
Wash me, Savior, or I die.

Not the labor of my hands
Can fulfill Thy law's demands;
Could my zeal no respite know,
Could my tears forever flow,
All for sin could not atone;
Thou must save, and Thou alone.

While I draw this fleeting breath,
When mine eyes shall close in death,
When I soar to worlds unknown,
See Thee on Thy judgment throne,
Rock of Ages, cleft for me,
Let me hide myself in Thee."

NOVEMBER 30 – LOVE FOR THE GLORY OF GOD

We have noted the high place love holds personally in our tripartite beings. For body, soul and spirit love is our life. We have seen the even higher place it has as the enabling motivator, for all kinds of service for others. It fills, controls and compels us. We need to see love now, in every realm, occupying the highest place and kept as resident there. The love of God in us, and its flow through us, should converge and coalesce into this superlative: "Love for the Glory of God." For instance, consider all that has been said on the subject of missions as an ongoing command; as an outcome of loving obedience; as a grateful response to God's love for us and a response to the needs of others. All these are motivators for missions, but are they in themselves sufficient for the task? After years of holding them forth as the prime reasons I have come to see, that good as they are, they are not quite good enough unless the highest motivator of all, love for the glory of God, controls them and us. We are not being pedantic or quibbling over words. The love of God in us must be translated into love for the glory of God through us. This is the highest form love can take and is not limited to "missions." It must be the motivating force for all of life in all its facets, in all places and at all times. My original title for this page was "Love and the Glory of God", but I changed it to "Love for the Glory of God" to better describe the subject.

What does Scripture mean by the glory of God? In the Old Testament it has the thought of beauty and majesty, but it usually means honour. In the New Testament "glory" or "glorious" comes from the Greek word "doxa" and from which we get our English word "doxology." W. E. Vine in his Expository Dictionary of New Testament Words tells us that "doxa" "signifies an opinion, estimate, and hence, the honor resulting from a good opinion. It is used of the nature and acts of God in self-manifestation...and particularly in the person of Christ, in whom essentially His 'glory' has ever shone forth and ever will do... it was exhibited in the character and acts of Christ in the days of His flesh... His grace and His power were manifested..." in His life, death, resurrection, ascension and present ministry. Thus together Deity, grace and power constitute His glory. His Deity will be manifested fully in power and great glory at His second coming. We love the glory, the honour of God. We love and praise the majesty of His might. We love Him in whom all honour resides. Love for the glory of God should be the goal of our lives; to know God; to glorify God; to honour and magnify Him forever. Love for the glory of God should be the motivation behind every message we give and every mission we undertake. Love for the glory of God should be the first thought in prayer.

"When the glory of the Father
Is the goal of every prayer:
When before the throne in heaven
Our High Priest presents it there;

When the Spirit prompts the asking,
When the waiting heart believes:
Then we know of each petition
Everyone who asks receives." Anon

Isaiah saw the Lord, sitting on His throne, lofty, exalted; he heard the seraph saying: "Holy, Holy, Holy, is the Lord of hosts, The whole earth is full of His glory."[1] The heavenly host praised God at the birth of Christ saying: "Glory to God in the highest..."[2] as the glory of the Lord shone on the shepherds. And around the throne, all give honour and glory to the Lamb. "For from Him and through Him and to Him are all things. To Him be the glory forever. Amen."[3]

DECEMBER 1 – "LOVES" IN HOSEA

Marital love between husband and wife is God ordained, necessary, important and lovely. The Old Testament writers used it as an illustration of the relationship between God and Israel and the analogies are carried on in the New Testament in the love relationship between Christ as Bridegroom and the Church as Bride.

The book of Hosea uses the marital imagery in unusual ways. God literally moves in a very unorthodox way in the life of the prophet Hosea as it relates to marriage. Put bluntly, as W. G. Cole does in his book <u>Sex and Love in the Bible</u>, the major problem is outlined:

"Any discussion of love in the Old Testament must begin with Hosea, the prophet who married a whore."

Whether a reformed or practicing one commentators differ, but the command says: "...'Go, take to yourself a wife of harlotry and have children of harlotry; for the land commits flagrant harlotry, forsaking the Lord.' So he went and took Gomer the daughter of Diblaim, and she conceived and bore him a son."[1] Go and marry a prostitute! Why? The answer is in the book and in the whole history of Israel and her love relationship with God. Gomer's and Israel's unfaithfulness in going after other lovers goes through the cycle of judgment, return and restoration because love is loathe to lose that upon which so much love has been lavished. The constancy of Hosea's love for Gomer, despite all the neglect and rejection, is meant to, and does, portray God's love, not only for Israel, but for the world and individuals, for me and you.

The story of Hosea's second symbolic marriage raises other problems which are evident, but can't be dealt with here. Suffice it to say that the major themes of the book are carried on by way of a new illustration, which is actually just a repeat of the first; God's yearning love for His people. "When Israel was a youth I loved him...I led them with cords of a man, with bonds of love... How can I give you up...?How can I surrender you...?How can I make you like...?How can I treat you like...?All My compassions are kindled."[2] Dr. Leon Morris (1914 – 2006) in his <u>Testaments of Love</u> says:

"Hosea does not use the precious word 'love' lavishly...(he) uses it in order to say three principal things: first, it is a demanding love...second, it is a wrathful love...and third, it is a merciful love."

It's a long way and a long time between Hosea and his message and the American poet, John Greenleaf Whittier (1807 – 1892) and his themes of love and grace.

"Thou judgest us; thy purity
Doth all our lusts condemn;
The love that draws us nearer thee
Is hot with wrath to them;

Forever round the mercy seat,
The guiding lights of love might burn;
But still, if habit-bound, the feet
Would lack the will to turn.

What if thine eye refuse to see,
Thine ear of Heaven's free welcome fail,
And thou a willing captive be,
Thyself thy own dark jail?"

DECEMBER 2 – THE BONDS OF LOVE IN HOSEA

Here is another of those paradoxes; love liberates while at the same time love binds. It gives liberty yet constricts. It is all-inclusive while being extremely exclusive. This is true of all the loves, but mainly of holy, heavenly love as found in Christ. The Christian's life and love has been described by Jean Pigott (1845 – 1882) in the words:

"My freedom is Thy grand control."

His control frees us to love all within the parameters set out in His Word. We have seen Hosea bound in an unusual, unorthodox marriage; yet, dishonoured as he was, the bonds of love controlled him from seeking freedom. He was shackled by love on one level, and his life was an illustration of how God was bound by love to wayward Israel and how He used those bonds to draw the nation back to Himself. We have already noted some of the references to "love" in Hosea. Collectively, they form an impressive illustration of Hosea's, Israel's and God's love. "Then the Lord said to me, 'Go again, love a woman who is loved by her husband, yet an adulteress, even as the Lord loves the sons of Israel, though they turn to other gods and love raisin cakes.'"[1] "Their liquor gone, they play the harlot continually; their rulers dearly love shame."[2] "…You have loved harlots' earnings on every threshing floor."[3] "…And they became as detestable as that which they loved."[4] "When Israel was a youth I loved him…"[5] "I led them with cords of a man, with bonds of love…"[6] Bonds of love; bands of love; ropes of love; cords of love; in any translation you pick up they use synonyms for the binding, unbreakable union of love.

That is one emphasis, but there is another. These bonds of love are lead ropes, halters, or leading lines that He uses. "I led them…" they can also be guide lines or reins to direct or guide us from behind. So whether led or drawn by the bond of love, or steered by them, and, on occasion having our ribs tickled with them, love holds the ropes. We cannot escape and finally we don't want to.

"I've found a Friend, O such a friend! He loved me ere I knew Him;
He drew me with the cords of love, and thus He bound me to Him;
And round my heart still closely twine those ties which naught can sever,
For I am His, and He is mine, forever and forever.
I've found a Friend, O such a friend! So kind and true and tender,
So wise a Counselor and Guide, so mighty a Defender!
From Him who loves me now so well what power my soul can sever?
Shall life or death, shall earth or hell? No! I am His forever."
James Small (1817 – 1888)

There is a further reference by Hosea that implies the bondage of the bond slave's service. "Ephraim is a trained heifer that loves to thresh, but I will come over her fair neck with a yoke…"[7] Accepting the yoke of love we find:

"In service which Thy love appoints
There are no bonds for me,
For my secret heart has learned the truth
Which makes Thy children free,
And a life of self-renouncing love
Is a life of liberty."
Anna Lititia Waring

DECEMBER 3 – WHOLE HEARTED LOVE IN HOSEA

"…I will love them with all my heart, for my anger has turned from them. I will fall like dew on Israel. He shall bloom like the lily, and thrust out roots like the poplar, his shoots will spread far; he will have the beauty of the olive and the fragrance of Lebanon. They will come back to live in my shade; they will grow corn that flourishes; they will cultivate vines as renowned as the wine of Helbon. What has Ephraim to do with idols when it is I who hear his prayer and care for him? I am like a cypress evergreen, all your fruitfulness comes from me. Let the wise man understand these words. Let the intelligent man grasp their meaning. For the ways of Jehovah are straight and virtuous men walk in them, but sinners stumble."[1]

The Jerusalem Bible says: "I will love them with all my heart." This is God's wholehearted love for repentant and returning Israel whom He has healed from apostasy, idolatry and unfaithfulness. Because He had first, and forever, loved them with all His heart, He could, and did, command a reciprocal response. "And you shall love the Lord your God with all your heart…"[2] And as it was for Israel so it is today for the Church and Christians. Another translation of Hosea's final word on divine love's wholeheartedness is: "…I will love them freely…"[3] These two versions imply limitless, lasting love boundless and free. Hosea's last word on love is the loveliest of all the "loves" in his book. The hymn writer W. E. Littlewood (1831 – 1886) puts it well.

"There is no love like the love of Jesus,
Never to fade or fall,
Till into the fold of the peace of God
He has gathered us all.

Jesus' love, precious love,
Boundless and pure and free;
O turn to that love, weary, wand'ring soul:
Jesus pleadeth with thee!

There is no eye like the eye of Jesus,
Piercing so far away;
Never out of sight of its tender light
Can the wanderer stray.

There is no voice like the voice of Jesus,
Tender and sweet its chime,
Like musical ring of a flowing spring
In the bright summertime.

There is no heart like the heart of Jesus,
Filled with a tender love;
No throb nor throe that our hearts can know,
But He feels it above.

Oh, let us hark to the voice of Jesus!
Then we shall never roam;
And we shall rest on His loving breast,
All the way to our heavenly home."

Hosea's love for his roaming, straying spouse, though disappointed, was not denied, for it was whole-hearted. God's love for backslidden Israel, though stern and disciplinary, was consistently and persistently whole-hearted. Christ's love for His Church and churches, while both commendatory and condemnatory was, and is, continuously whole-hearted. His love for straying, denying Peter was as eternally whole-hearted as it is for us, yes, even when we wander or roam or are led astray. This whole-hearted love leads on to His other "I wills" resulting in the "he will" and "they wills" of blooming flowers, spreading roots, shoots and fruits as "all your fruitfulness comes from me."

DECEMBER 4 – LOVE CAME LATE

Romantic love came late in life to C. S. Lewis (1898 – 1963). He knew it theoretically, he wrote of it prosaically and poetically, long before it came so personally and so suddenly. Yes, love came late to him, as it does to so many. Yet coming late, but lovely, it burned more fiercely and consumed itself briefly and completely. Years before, in his incomplete autobiography, he had borrowed three words from William Wordsworth's (1770 – 1850) ode to one, loved long since, and lost awhile.

"Surprised by joy, impatient as the Wind
I turned to share the transport. Oh! with whom
But Thee, deep buried in the silent tomb,
That spot which no vicissitude can find?
Love, faithful love, recalled thee to my mind.
But how could I forget thee? Through what power,
Even for the least division of an hour,
Have I been so beguiled as to be blind
To my most grievous loss? That thought's return
Was the worst pang that sorrow ever bore,
Save one, one only, when I stood forlorn,
Knowing my heart's best treasure was no more;
That neither present time, nor years unborn
Could to my sight that heavenly face restore."

C. S. Lewis' book Surprised By Joy tells of his slow conversion to Christ as his Lord and his God. He truly loved the Lord but it did not come early or easy to him. But thank God it came in 1931. Lewis, in 1936 wrote a celebrated book about love entitled The Allegory of Love. It is not easy reading. We are grateful that he later wrote what has since become a classic, The Four Loves. Affection. Friendship. Eros. Charity. His studies on these four loves were first published in 1960 and have helped many of us in our quest to understand the relationship, meaning and application of "storgé," "philia," "eros" and "agapé." I'm grateful to him for these writings.

Late in his physical life romantic love came to Lewis. Curiously he was again "Surprised By Joy" this time by a widow whose name was Joy Davidman (1915 – 1960). It began quietly as a friendship. Then, as a practical aid to this lady, who was in Lewis' opinion being politically persecuted for past affiliations, he married her, much to the surprise and disapproval of many of his colleagues. It was no love match, but an act of philanthropy and friendship. He provided for her and cared for her children. Out of this unlikely ground, true romantic love sprang up. Love came in the sunset years of his life and warmed and gave him a new wonder. Alas this late love blooming was destined, all too soon, to shed its petals. Joy developed cancer and despite hopeful remissions and renewals of the pleasures of love, she died, as must all earthly loves. Lewis wrote another book about this rending ending of his late love. A Grief Observed makes fascinating reading as it is one of the most accurate accounts of the devastation brought about in a life bereaved by love.

Boaz knew a late love and described her thus: "…you are a woman of excellence."[1] Aging Boaz, to whom love came late with Ruth, found his Joy also.

DECEMBER 5 – LOVE'S OLD SWEET SONG

There was a song, popular in my father's day, which I, when a boy, used to hear him sing frequently. "Just a song at twilight, when the lights are low; And the flick'ring shadows softly come and go…." C. Clifton Bingham (1859 – 1913) (and here memory has failed me, though I do believe its title was "Love's Old" or "Love's Own Sweet Song." Everyone must have heard another of those nostalgic "old timers", a sentimental song indeed. "When your hair has turned to silver, I will love you just the same; I will only call you sweetheart, That will always be your name…." Charles Tobias (1898 – 1970) Are you feeling turned off? I'm sure that most who have discarded Victorian sentiment and mores will be. I have also inveighed against sentimentality where these kinds of statements are used to wrongly describe the strong, sure, sacrificial, serving agapé of God. Yet I do not want to be misunderstood. There is a place for nostalgia and sentimental trips down memory lane. Thomas Moore (1779 – 1852), as usual, has something sensible and sweet to say about this state.

> "Believe me, if all those endearing young charms
> Which I gaze on so fondly today
> Were to change by tomorrow and fleet in my arms
> Like fairy gifts fading away,
> Thou wouldst still be adored as this moment thou art
> Let thy loveliness fade as it will
> And around the dear ruin each wish of my heart
> Would entwine itself verdantly still.
>
> It is not while beauty and youth are thine own
> And thy cheeks unprofaned by a tear
> That the fervor and faith of a soul can be known
> To which time will but make thee more dear.
> No, the heart that has truly loved never forgets
> But as truly loves on to the close
> As the sunflower turns to her God when he sets
> The same look which she turned when he rose."

But the Old Book said it first; said it best; said it briefly. "…And rejoice in the wife of your youth."[1] Say what you like about the Victorians, my Victorian grand parents, on both sides, stayed with the same partners right through their long married lives. My parents married the year after Queen Victoria died and lived together till death divided them. Today people change partners as casually as they trade in their vehicles. Divorce is not unexpected in the world, but the shocking thing today is the way it is invading the church. Some "evangelical" leaders are misleading others by their marrying, unmarrying (discarding, dissolving, and divorcing) and re-marrying. It would appear that the old views and vows are being watered down. They enter marriage without lifelong commitment. If it doesn't work out we can always get out. The cynic calls it "unholy deadlock." It is still "holy wedlock" to some Christians. But enough of my editorializing.

It is good and God-glorifying to see the "golden oldies" still hanging in there. Through thick and thin their life long love commitment may have faltered, but it never failed. Their children and grand children rise up to honour them.

DECEMBER 6 – LOVE AMONG THE RUINS

"Love Among the Ruins" is the title of a Robert Browning (1812 – 1899) poem. In it he describes the title's meaning.

"Where the quiet-colored end of evening smiles…
Was the site once of a city great and gay,
(So they say)…
Now, the single little turret that remains
On the plains…
Marks the basement whence a tower in ancient time
Sprang sublime…
And I know, while thus the quiet-colored eve
Smiles to leave…
That a girl with eager eyes and yellow hair
Waits me there
In the turret whence the charioteers caught soul
For the goal,
When the king looked, where she looks now, breathless, dumb
Till I come…
When I do come, she will speak not, she will stand,
Either hand
On my shoulder, give her eyes the first embrace
Of my face,
Ere we rush, ere we extinguish sight and speech
Each on each."

With apologies to him I use that intriguing title to describe the life situation of aging love amongst the geriatric group. It can also be truly, not unkindly, spoken of as "Love Among the Ruins." Thomas Moore (1779 – 1852) started it with his loving lines:

"Let thy loveliness fade as it will,
And around the dear ruin each wish of my heart
Would entwine itself verdantly still."

Everyone wishes to live a long time, but no one wants to grow old. Despite our desires for perennial youth (hair pieces, hair dyes, face lifts, supports, etc.) the best that we can hope for these clay caskets is that they will grow old gracefully, decay with decorum, disintegrate with dignity, and be allowed to die with decency. There is no escaping the ravages of time; the sagging and the bagging; the shrinking and the wrinkling; the swelling and the bloating; the swinging hammocks of slackened skin or the once strong muscles now like string; big veins, blue veins, no veins. We know that mortality is upon us. The appointed time is rapidly approaching for all unless He should come! Then, for just that one generation of believers, the appointment with the undertaker will be replaced by the appointment with the "upper taker." That will be love reclaiming the ruins. But it's not all gloom and doom while we wait and watch and work if we are able. Let's enjoy each other's company like Robert Burns (1759 – 1796) wrote:

DECEMBER 6 - CONTINUED

"John Anderson, my jo, John,
When we were first acquent;
Your locks were like the raven,
Your bonie brow was brent;
But now your brow is beld, John,
Your locks are like the snaw;
But blessings on your frosty pow,
John Anderson, my jo.

John Anderson, my jo, John,
We clamb the hill thegither;
And mony a cantie day, John,
We've had wi' ane anither:
Now we maun totter down, John,
And hand in hand we'll go,
And sleep thegither at the foot,
John Anderson, my jo."

And that's love among the ruins! We may potter and totter and drool and dodder, but if we are not senile we can love. Married love, friendship love and, brotherly love among the ruins. We stand upon the promises of love come what may. "…though our outer man is decaying, yet our inner man is being renewed day by day."[1] And the best is yet to be; departure, either way to be with Christ.

DECEMBER 7 – LOVE AND CHANGE

"I hear the words of love,
I gaze upon the blood,
I see the mighty sacrifice,
And I have peace with God.

'Tis everlasting peace,
Sure as Jehovah's name;
'Tis stable as His steadfast throne,
Forevermore the same.

The clouds may come and go,
And storms may sweep my sky,
This blood-sealed friendship changes not:
The cross is ever nigh.

My love is ofttimes low,
My joy still ebbs and flows;
But peace with Him remains the same,
No change Jehovah knows.

I change, He changes not,
The Christ can never die;
His love, not mine, the resting-place,
His truth, not mine, the tie."

Horatio Bonar (1808 – 1889) has been our mentor and guide in other areas of Christian love, and here, he again ministers. Love overcomes the fear of change. In the midst of changing circumstances and changing self, Bonar points to the unchanging Cross and the unchanging Christ. These are the centres of unchanging love, the focal point and Person of stability and security. We know that change is the law of earth and the law of our development and maturity in the Christian life here below. Physically, mentally and spiritually we should and must change, but this growth depends on the eternal unchangeables of the nature and character of God. His eternal love and holiness are not variables. Though His revelation of Himself in the Old Testament was a preparatory and progressive unveiling, culminating in the New Testament incarnation of His Son, there was no change in His nature and character of holy love. It was the priesthood, the law, and the offerings for sin that changed. Our Lord Jesus Christ as a man came not from the tribe of Levi, but Judah. He came not of the order of the Levitical priesthood through Aaron, but through Melchizedek, King of Salem and priest of the most high God. This Melchizedek was Abraham's priest and superior and blessed him. "For when the priesthood is changed, of necessity there takes place a change of law also."[1] A change in the priesthood ushered in His unchangeable priesthood. "…the Lord has sworn and will not change His mind 'You are a priest forever.'"[2] And so of course the sacrifices, which were many, continual and temporary, had to change too. Love changed the tribe, the priesthood, the law and the sacrifices. Love's preparatory types gave way to the Antitype; the One who brought in the unchanging sacrifice, the once and for all salvation. "Every priest stands daily ministering and offering time after time the same sacrifices, which can never take away sins; but He, having offered one sacrifice for sins for all time, sat down at the right hand of God…"[3] Eternal holy love made on the Cross the supreme manifestation of unchanging saving love. "Therefore He is able also to save forever those who draw near to God through Him, since He always lives to make intercession for them."[4] This is holy, unchanging, living love, saving us, changing us, unchangeably. It is on these unvariables that we depend on to handle in a practical fashion all the inevitable changes that life will bring. Rightly taught we can rightly live knowing that "Jesus Christ is the same yesterday and today and forever."[5]

DECEMBER 8 – LOVE AND FEAR

"O love that casts out fear,
O love that casts out sin,
Tarry no more without,
But come and dwell within.

True sunlight of the soul,
Surround us as we go;
So shall our way be safe,
Our feet no straying know.

Great love of God, come in!
Well-spring of heavenly peace;
Thou Living Water, come!
Spring up, and never cease.

Love of the living God,
Of Father and of Son;
Love of the Holy Ghost,
Fill thou each needy one."
Dr. Horatius Bonar (1808 – 1889)

Beside the Royal Mile in Edinburgh, Scotland, there is a small church. In the graveyard alongside and behind it are tombs of famous people but on my personal pilgrimage there I was looking for the grave of Dr. Horatius Bonar. As I stood before the stone I thanked God for the memory and continuing influence of that lover of the Lord. Horatius Bonar was one of Scotland's beloved men of the kirk. Bonar was the exponent of holy love, sunlight love, surrounding love, indwelling love and the love that casts out fear and sin. Beyond the Great Castle and Holyrood Palace, the visit to that church and grave was the most memorable event of my pilgrimage.

Dr. Bonar says of this love:

"True sunlight of the soul,
Surround us as we go;
So shall our way be safe,
Our feet no straying know."

But he had already introduced the Scriptural truth; that it is a love that casts out fear, the fear that kills is part of the sin that love casts out. It is the sin of unbelief where fear is fostered. Fear of the past; fear of the present; fear of the future; fear of poverty in old age; fear of debilitating illness at any age; fears without and fears within destroy our peace, disturb our relationship with the Lord, and one another, and profoundly affect us on our pilgrimage. Wrong fear is one of our worst enemies. This kind of fear centers on the areas of "it might happen; what if that came on me" and all the other possibilities that the "if" of fear opens up. They are often illusory. We worry about things that may never happen, and should they be sent or permitted, He has provided the answer, which is love.

"There is no fear in love; but perfect love casts out fear, because fear involves punishment, and the one who fears is not perfected in love."[1] When two people really love each other, on this level love casts out fear. Many a fearful bride has found her fears of marriage removed by a loving husband whose own fears of responsibility and inadequacy have been removed by a loving wife. And if these fears are controlled by holy love, then what have we to fear? His perfect love has taken care of the past, is caring for the present, and we are promised that same perfect love care for all our unknown tomorrows. Yet still we sometimes fear. Ask forgiveness and claim His promise. Thus He reassured the church at Smyrna, the suffering church, the martyr church. "…The first and the last, who was dead, and has come to life, says this[2]… Do not fear what you are about to suffer… Be faithful until death, and I will give you the crown of life."[3]

DECEMBER 9 – PERFECT LOVE

Dorothy Gurney (1858 – 1932) wrote a beautiful hymn that is still sung occasionally at Christian weddings. It expresses the vows and hopes of the bride and groom uniting their lives in holy matrimony. It is also the desire of believing parents and friends assembled to wish them the highest happiness and to continue to know more fully Him who is personified in the hymn as "Perfect Love."

"O perfect Love, all human thought transcending,
Lowly we kneel in prayer before thy throne,
That theirs may be the love which knows no ending,
Whom thou forevermore dost join in one.

Grant them the joy which brightens earthly sorrow;
Grant them the peace which calms all earthly strife,
And to life's day the glorious unknown morrow
That dawns upon eternal love and life.

Hear us, O Father, gracious and forgiving,
Through Jesus Christ, Thy coeternal Word,
Who, with the Holy Ghost, by all things living
Now and to endless ages art adored."

Perfect love in all its perfections and manifestations is trinitarian love; the love of the Father, the love of the Son and the love of the Holy Spirit. All the desired blessings flowing from perfect love, as requested in the hymn, are born in heaven and made real in our hearts through the person and work of the Son. There are no imperfections in trinitarian love. It is perfect love and it was once perfectly personified on earth in the Person of the perfect Son. Trinitarian love is now working in us to multiply, here and now, the manifestations of that perfect love in us, His people.

And here lies the problem and the paradox. How can that which is perfect be perfectly manifested by those who are imperfect? The answers will show more of the glories of many splendoured love. John affirms that it is so: "…if we love one another, God abides in us, and His love is perfected in us[1]…God is love, and the one who abides in love abides in God, and God abides in him. By this, love is perfected with us, so that we may have confidence in the day of judgment; because as He is, so also are we in this world."[2] The perfect One and perfect love live in the born again believer giving assurance of this indwelling by the gift of His Spirit because we have believed and confessed that Jesus is the Son of God. We are human habitations of perfect trinitarian love because of our love for one another. Here's where the paradox and the imperfect become apparent. John again not only expresses the paradox, but he provides an answer to the problem. "There is no fear in love; but perfect love casts out fear, because fear involves punishment, and the one who fears is not perfected in love."[3] When we fear the costs of loving involvement with one another, or fear the future there cannot be perfect, complete, mature love. But as we allow perfect love to have His perfect way in us we have confidence regarding the Judgment Seat of Christ. We are imperfect, but are being perfected in perfect love forever.

DECEMBER 10 – LOVE CAN SAVE THE OLD

In January 1959, I was speaking at a Keswick Summer Convention in the sea side city of Albany, Western Australia. Albany is a beautiful place with many attractions, including fishing, which draws large numbers of vacationers during the season. Conversely it is not an easy place to hold a deeper Christian life convention, in a tent, in the heat, amongst the holidaymakers, most of whom are intent on sport. But "he who watches the wind will not sow and he who looks at the clouds will not reap,"[1] and "sow your seed in the morning and do not be idle in the evening, for you do not know whether morning or evening sowing will succeed, or whether both of them alike will be good."[2] So we sowed twice a day beside the sea. It was not an evangelistic campaign as the ministry was largely to Christians who were taking holidays at Albany. But "just as you do not know the path of the wind…so you do not know the activity of God who makes all things."[3] God was blowing as the wind, and working mysteriously in one life that week in Albany. Divine love was about to triumph again.

I was giving a series of messages on the natural man, the carnal man and the spiritual man using Bible characters to illustrate the themes. I believe that Gospel preaching is included in Bible teaching so I was using the natural man as an obvious opportunity to present the Good News. And Bible teaching evangelism was again to be used by the Spirit of God in the deliverance of a soul. Later I learned that story from the person concerned.

Bob and his wife had come to Albany for a fishing vacation. His "cobber" or "buddy", who owned a boat, could not go out one day, but told Bob:

"There is another fellow who will take you out fishing."

Unknown to Bob this fellow was a Christian and he witnessed for the Lord and lovingly invited Bob to the Keswick meeting. He went, he told me, because he wanted to keep in with this fellow and keep the way open for more fishing! He little knew that the Fisher of souls already had His hook in him! The love of God over-rules ulterior motives. I was unaware that he attended several services coming under deeper and deeper conviction. The Spirit brought him to repentance and public commitment and confession of Christ one night when the opportunity was given.

"Oh, the love that sought me!
Oh, the blood that bought me!
Oh, the grace that brought me to the fold…"
W. Spencer Walton (1850 – 1906)
was later Bob's testimony.

He was then 67 years of age, married for 40 years and in a very close relationship with his wife. Now this greater love brought division into his home. His wife rejected his Christ and her husband. Later he told me:

"Since my conversion I have been a boarder in my own home."

And this went on for years. In 1966 I revisited Perth in Western Australia, and Bob, now 74, had become a worker at the People's Church Christian Centre. He gave me his card and on the back was a poem commemorating his conversion.

DECEMBER 10 - CONTINUED

"He's found you now, this loving Christ of mine.
So long He sought, but you would wander on, unheeding love's approach…"

But finally love won in Bob and began to win at home. In 1974 I was again in Perth speaking at the Orange Grove Keswick Convention. Bob, now in his 82nd year, still loving and serving the Lord, with tears in his eyes, said of his wife:

"John, she kissed me for the first time in years. She is going to be saved even after the Lord calls me home!"

DECEMBER 11 – LOVE AND OVERCOMING

"And they overcame him because of the blood of the Lamb and because of the word of their testimony, and they did not love their life even when faced with death."[1] Love is the basis of, and makes possible, the overcoming life. Love led Christ to Calvary; love caused Him to shed His blood for sin and sinners. This trinitarian love has death built into it, plus resurrection which made Christ the first Overcomer of Satan, sin and the grave. Included in His overcoming love are both the possibility of, and the way of, our own overcoming. "He who overcomes, I will grant to him to sit down with Me on My throne, as I also overcame and sat down with My Father on His throne."[2] Love overcoming all obstacles and all enemies made Him the supreme witness and His testimony as truth, and to truth, made love and truth supreme. It is the way the Master walked; should not the servant tread it still?

Trinitarian love overcomes the world, the flesh and the devil (the trinity of evil). The threefold way of overcoming is by the blood of the Lamb; the witness of our life and words of love; and the kind of love that recognizes death as an integral part of this overcoming life. "...they did not love their life even when faced with death." Such was the message again of the risen Lord to the church and individual Christians at Smyrna. "Do not fear what you are about to suffer. Behold, the devil is about to cast some of you into prison, so that you will be tested, and you will have tribulation for ten days. Be faithful until death, and I will give you the crown of life. He who has an ear, let him hear what the Spirit says to the churches. He who overcomes will not be hurt by the second death."[3]

It was from this verse that John Bunyan drew his immortal character "Faithful." Faithful, who was faithful until death, and through love for the lord and His truth, overcame all that the Vanity Fair of this world could do to him. He and Pilgrim overcame by the blood of the Lamb, by the word of their testimony, and they loved not their lives unto death. Both were bold love witnesses; both were willing for death as the end price and bottom line of love. Faithful was called upon and paid the supreme price of love's overcoming. After they had rejected the wares, manners and morals of Vanity Fair, they were imprisoned and Faithful was condemned to death by the jury whose names speak for themselves; Mr. Blindman, Mr. No-good, Mr. Malice, Mr. Love-lust, Mr. Live-loose, Mr. Heady, Mr. Highmind, Mr. Enmity, Mr. Liar, Mr. Cruelty, Mr. Hate-light and Mr. Implacable. The verdict was a foregone conclusion. He was condemned to death; "they burned him to ashes at the stake. Thus came Faithful to his end." Faith, which walks and works and talks by love, overcame the trinity of evil. For all of us, at all times, this is love's way.

"Lord Crucified, O mark Thy holy Cross
On motive, preference, all fond desires,
On that which self in any form inspires
Set Thou that sign of loss.

And when the touch of death is here and there
Laid on a thing most precious in our eyes,
Let us not wonder, let us recognize
The answer to this prayer."
Amy Wilson Carmichael (1867 – 1951)

DECEMBER 12 – HYPER-CONQUERORS THROUGH HIM WHO LOVED US

The word hyper, from the Greek "huper," is used quite often today. Hyper-acidity, hyper-tension and hyper-thyroidism are fairly common ailments. Numerous parents know what it means to have a hyper-active child. Hyperbole, or deliberate exaggeration, extravagant statements or excessive verbiage may be used for rhetorical effect, but such expressions can also be a form of lying. We have all known hyper-critics or hyper-perfectionists. All these, and many more, "hyper" words as used in daily life serve to remind us that "hyper" is also a Scriptural word. Our Lord used it in connection with the comparative loves. "He who loves father or mother more than Me is not worthy of Me; and he who loves son or daughter more than Me is not worthy of Me."[1] Here "huper" stands alone and means "above," "beyond," or "more than." Love for our spouse, parents or children that goes "beyond the bounds" of love for the Lord is unworthy of Him Who loved us and gave Himself for us. Discipleship love is "more than" love. It is hyper-love.

"Huper" as used as a prefix in conjunction with "nikao" or "to overcome" is what our discussion will concentrate on. Nikao also means "to prevail" or "to be victorious" in the field as David was when he felled Goliath. Yes, and to be a "hupernikao;" a hyper-conqueror as he stood on the fallen giant and destroyed him with his own sword. But David was a super-conqueror before he ever fought. He had faith in God to declare the victory beforehand, not in a proud or presumptuous way, but affirms it for the glory of God. "This day the Lord will deliver you up into my hands, and I will strike you down and remove your head from you. And I will give the dead bodies of the army of the Philistines this day to the birds of the sky and the wild beasts of the earth, that all the earth may know that there is a God in Israel, and that all this assembly may know that the Lord does not deliver by sword or by spear; for the battle is the Lord's and He will give you into our hands."[2] It was David's love for God and for his flock that inspired the courage to tackle a lion and a bear, bare handed and deliver sheep from their mouths. Love for God, Israel and his family made him a hyper-conqueror over the Philistine.

And what of us today? The same God and the super-promise is ours. In every area of earthly and spiritual life we are promised: "But in all these things we overwhelmingly conquer through Him who loved us."[3] We are hyper-conquerors over an impressive list of "whos" and "whats" which we will examine later. Suffice it to say; now we can be surpassing victors and God-glorifying witnesses as we claim our position in the all conquering Christ. We are positionally risen with Him; ascended with Him; seated with Him; reigning with Him in the Spirit. "But God, being rich in mercy, because of His great love with which He loved us, even when we were dead in our transgressions, made us alive together with Christ (by grace you have been saved), and raised us up with Him, and seated us with Him in the heavenly places in Christ Jesus..."[4] Surely this is one application of the Old Testament promise "...thou shalt be above only, and thou shalt not be beneath..."[5]

DECEMBER 13 – WHO SHALL SEPARATE US FROM THE LOVE OF CHRIST?

Romans 8, like John 3, 1 Corinthians 13 and 15, is one of the great key chapters concerned with life in the Spirit, the love of Christ, incarnate and risen, and the life and love of the Lord's people. In contrast to the "I" problems of Romans 7, this chapter has the answer to them all; life in the Spirit. "For the law of the Spirit of life in Christ Jesus has set you free from the law of sin and of death."[1] "For the mind set on the flesh is death, but the mind set on the Spirit is life and peace, because the mind set on the flesh is hostile toward God..."[2] "However, you are not in the flesh but in the Spirit, if indeed the Spirit of God dwells in you. But if anyone does not have the Spirit of Christ, he does not belong to Him."[3] Life in the Spirit, resulting in the outworking of love has been the theme in all these pages. The love of God the Father, Son and Holy Spirit is intermingling, intervening, controlling and completing all the other loves of the lovers of the Lord. "Love, the many splendoured thing" moves in Romans 8 to heights of majestic splendour and glory.

We noted the chapter's commencement and theme but did not mention the first verse. "Therefore there is now no condemnation for those who are in Christ Jesus."[4] This is taken up again in the chapter as a series of questions. "...If God is for us, who is against us?"[5] Many are but no opposition will prevail because we have the right One on our side. "Who will bring a charge against God's elect?..."[6] Many will try, including Satan the accuser of the brethren, but no accusation will stand because God has justified us. "Who is the one who condemns?..."[7] Many will, and do, make condemnatory statements (read the papers) about "evangelicals," "fundamentalists," "born again people" but no condemnation will succeed because He who died now lives and is interceding for us at the right hand of God. "Who will separate us from the love of Christ?..."[8] Life long efforts of fallen angels, the rulers of darkness, the unseen spiritual powers and the fallen prince of this world, the Devil himself will not triumph. No separation is possible because none of the above "...nor any other created thing, will be able to separate us from the love of God, which is in Christ Jesus our Lord."[9]

The eternal Lover, "...You loved Me before the foundation of the world;"[10] the eternal Lamb "...slain from the foundation of the world;"[11] Jesus, the Christ "...foreknown before the foundation of the world..."[12] was the eternal Son given in love for the world, and from out of the world He was given His church. "...He chose us in Him before the foundation of the world, that we would be holy and blameless before Him"[13] and one day from the throne of His glory, the King of glory will come and say: "...Come, you who are blessed of My Father, inherit the kingdom prepared for you from the foundation of the world."[14] The eternally foreknown, foretold and predestined course of events will be fulfilled. As we await the summons we are encouraged by the fact that no one will separate us from His love. But, "What of the "Whats?""

DECEMBER 14 – WHAT SHALL SEPARATE US FROM THE LOVE OF CHRIST?

Yes, "What of the "Whats?"" Our broad view of Romans 8 saw that no opposition could prevail; no accusation could stand; no condemnation could succeed and no separation could be possible through the efforts of any of the "Whos" natural or spiritual. The four "Who" questions and the answers showed none could "...separate us from the love of God, which is in Christ Jesus our Lord."[1] But we should review the passage again. Can the "Whats" succeed where the "Whos" failed? Can all this long list of "Whats" separate us? "...Will tribulation, or distress, or persecution, or famine, or nakedness, or peril, or sword?"[2] "But in all these things we overwhelmingly conquer through Him who loved us. For I am convinced that neither death, nor life, nor angels, nor principalities, nor things present, nor things to come, nor powers, nor height, nor depth, nor any other created thing, will be able to separate us from the love of God, which is in Christ Jesus our Lord."[3]

As Romans 8 gave a resounding "No" to the efforts of the "Whos" to separate us from eternal love, it also gives an unequivocal "No" to the attempts of the "Whats" to sever us from the love of God in Christ. We are not denying their power, their efforts and their short term, even long term successes. But there is an encouraging word for those who are tempted. "No temptation has overtaken you but such as is common to man; and God is faithful, who will not allow you to be tempted beyond what you are able, but with the temptation will provide the way of escape also, so that you will be able to endure it."[4] And again from our Lord's own lips: "For false Christs and false prophets will arise and will show great signs and wonders, so as to mislead, if possible, even the elect."[5]

John Bunyan (1628 – 1688), while convicted, but still unconverted, was often tempted and tormented. He heard one day a sermon on the love of Christ and wrote:

"My comforting time was come. I began to give place to the Word which with power did over and over again make this joyful sound within my soul: 'Who shall separate me from the love of Christ?' And with that my heart was filled full of comfort and hope, and I could believe that my sins would be forgiven me. yes, I was so taken with the love and mercy of God...that I could not tell how to contain until I got home..."

Later he tells us:

"The tempter would come upon me with such discouragements as these: 'You are very hot for mercy but I will cool you...' With this, several who were fallen off, would be set before my eyes. Then I would be afraid that I should fall away, too, but, thought I, I will watch and take care..."

Romans 8:35-39 was given to him.

"That" he says "was a good word to me."

I have, more than once, stood beside Bunyan's grave in Bunhill Fields, London, England and thought of all the "Whos" and "Whats" that beset him, in prison, and out. I rejoiced in the perseverance of that man of God and all the other saints buried around him. Life with all its "Whos" and "Whats" could not separate them from the love of Christ. Nor could death.

DECEMBER 15 – LOVE'S BEST IS YET TO BE

"Say over again, and yet once over again,
That thou dost love me. Though the word repeated
Should seem a 'cuckoo-song,' as dost treat it,
Remember, never to the hill or plain,
Valley and wood, without her cuckoo-strain
Comes the fresh Spring in all her green completed.
Beloved, I, amid the darkness greeted
By a doubtful spirit-voice, in that doubt's pain
Cry, 'Speak once more, thou lovest!' Who can fear
Too many stars, though each in heaven shall roll,
Too many flowers, tho each shall crown the year?
Say thou dost love me, love me, love me, toll
The silver iterance! only minding, Dear,
To love me also in silence with thy soul."
Elizabeth Barrett Browning (1806 – 1861)

Does love have doubts? To ask the question is to answer it. We know that true earthly love some-times has its doubts from both internal and external causes. Even a lover of the Lord like John the Baptist "In Extremis" in prison sent and said: "...Are You the Expected One, or shall we look for someone else?"[1] This appointed, anointed forerunner and protagonist of the Christ, had his moments of concern, doubt, yes, even unbelief. Like the father who said "...I do believe; help my unbelief,"[2] we need the reiterations and reassurances of love on earthly and heavenly levels. Our Lord gave John what he needed and He also healed the father's disordered son. He also gives us assurance by the Spirit witnessing to our spirits that we are His children and that His resurrection life is ours now and for all the future. We love to hear these promises repeated. We need these reminders. He gives them to us so let us in all the levels of love give them to others and to Him. "I love you."

This is love's transient, transition stage from the temporal to the eternal and all encouragements while enroute are so welcome. That's no doubt why Mrs. Browning, older than her husband, kept asking for these reassurances. She, with her intuition, said it was a two note cuckoo song, but there's no English spring without a cuckoo!

What did her Robert (1812 – 1899) think of it all? We are not told specifically, but some of his poems are revealing and we know he loved her to the end. She died many years before he did. The reality of their love survived the early romantic years and all the tragedy of her father's refusal to see his daughter or open her letters. This loss of her father's love, the earlier loss by death of her mother's and of her favourite brother's love through his premature death, probably all contributed to her continual need for reaffirmations from her one great remaining love. In his "Rabbi Ben Ezra" he saw the combi-nation of earthly and heavenly loves; he recognized the inevitability of growing old, but yet together; he contemplated the whole plan and he understood "love's best is yet to be."

Grow old along with me!
The best is yet to be,
The last of life, for which the first was made:
Our times are in his hand
Who saith, 'A whole I planned,
Youth shows but half; trust God: see all, nor be afraid!'

Not once beat 'Praise be thine!
I see the whole design,
I, who saw power, see now Love perfect too:
Perfect I call thy plan:
Thanks that I was a man!
Maker, remake, complete, I trust what thou shalt do.'"

DECEMBER 16 – NO LASTING LOVELINESS ON EARTH

There is a melancholic sadness about the fact that all of earth's lesser loves are doomed to die; all natural loveliness is ephemeral; all physical beauty is destined for dust. "A voice says, 'Call out.' Then he answered, 'What shall I call out?' All flesh is grass, and all its loveliness is like the flower of the field. The grass withers, the flower fades, When the breath of the Lord blows upon it…"[1] The loveliness of field and flower is fleeting. We are stimulated by sight and scent and then, as Scripture says, as we observe the lilies, that, "…not even Solomon in all his glory clothed himself like one of these,"[2] yet tomorrow they will wilt and die. Nothing, no thing, under the sun is forever. Life itself, all the loveliness of physical form and beauty, is but temporal and passing. The brevity of life and loveliness, the temporality of things and the loss of all of our lesser loves are meant to wean us from our false ideas about them and our dependence upon them. Their very fragility should lead us to the imperishable and their changeableness to the unchangeable love of the altogether lovely One. This old hymn of my youth is rarely sung now, but its words still ring true.

"Life at best is very brief,
Like the falling of a leaf,
Like the binding of a sheaf,
Be in time!...

Fairest flowers soon decay,
Youth and beauty pass away,
Oh, you have not long to stay,
Be in time!…

Sinner, heed the warning voice,
Make the Lord your final choice,
Then all Heaven will rejoice,
Be in time!" Anon.

So then, the sad facts of lost loves, no lasting loveliness and impermanent friendships should lead us to the glad facts which He accents in the above Scripture. The unchanging God in His unchanging Word, urges us to find in the eternal Son, eternal life and eternal love. In losing the lesser loves we gain the greater love and then, wonder of wonders, we find that the lesser loves are transmuted, transcended and transferred. Here is the blessedness of dying. In losing our lives and loves in His will, we find them again, purified and sanctified, not only on earth, but in heaven. Family love here will be transferred and transcended (exceeded and excelled) to the family of God in the life to come. Souls won here on earth because of our obedient love, will be, as Paul reminds us, found, known, loved again and our crown of exaltation. "For who is our hope or joy or crown of exaltation? Is it not even you, in the presence of our Lord Jesus at His coming? For you are our glory and joy."[3] Our loved ones, who have gone on ahead, are waiting to welcome us home into the eternal state of loving family fellowship. This is what is meant by transferred love, transcended love and transmuted love. The transmuted loves of earth, are, in and by His love, changed, transformed and transfigured loves. They are metamorphosed, which is the word used in the Transfiguration on the Mount, and in our own earthy cases. "…we all…are being transformed into the same image from glory to glory, just as from the Lord, the Spirit."[4] How? Paul again tells us![5]

DECEMBER 17 – MORS JANUA AMOR

Since I was a student in Bible College in the 1930's I have known a truth embodied in three Latin words. I used to attend occasionally, when studies permitted, a meeting held in the home of Rev. J. Pearson-Harrison, one of my lecturers. Rev. Harrison and his wife had been richly blessed through the ministry and deeper-life writings of Mrs. Jessie Penn-Lewis (1861 – 1927). The emphasis of her books is on the spiritual conflict in heaven and also on another New Testament principle; "death is the gateway to life." That is the translation of "Mors Janua Vitae" which was the masthead message on the magazine put out by the Harrisons. "Mors Janua Vitae." You can almost see it in English. Mors, death, mortician, mortuary; Janua, January, the gateway month, beginning anew; Vitae, vitality, life, life force. This is the consistent teaching of our Lord concerning the life via death. He was about to undergo on the Cross and in the tomb, the application of the principle: "...unless a grain of wheat falls into the earth and dies, it remains alone; but if it dies, it bears much fruit."[1]

Then "Mors Janua Amor" came to me. "Death is the gateway to love" was suggested by an association of ideas in my subconscious, and, I trust, by the Holy Spirit who also moves in the realm of the mind: "...taking every thought captive to the obedience of Christ."[2]. Suddenly I saw behind the truth of "Mors Janua Vitae" this other one, "Mors Janua Amor." Behind, in front of, underneath and above all is love. Love brought Him from glory; love motivated all His works and words. Love led Him to Calvary, to the grave, to resurrection, to ascension, to the throne ministry and will bring Him back to wrap up this sorry state of earthly affairs. And as it was on earth for Him and His own, it is now, and will be in the future. We have proved it previously; we are experiencing it now; we will participate in and partake of it fully in the future as we pass via death to eternal life. "Mors Janua Vitae" and "Mors Janua Amor" belong together and lead into "Mors Janua Gloria." It is the Holy Spirit who fills our hearts continually with the love of God which can minister life through death, so that we end up with even more love via this portal of glory. It is the Holy Spirit of love who makes the death of Christ, and the life of Christ and the love of Christ real to and in me. "I have been crucified with Christ; and it is no longer I who live, but Christ lives in me; and the life which I now live in the flesh I live by faith in the Son of God, who loved me and gave Himself up for me."[3] The Spirit, with my cooperation, must bring me to salvation and sanctification through identification and involvement with Christ in His Cross, resurrection life and love. Death is the ordained gateway to life. Death is the predestined gateway to love. Death is the foreordained gateway to glory.

"Christ died for me,
Christ died for me;
Oh! What a salvation this,
That Christ died for me.

I died with Christ,
I died with Christ;
Oh! What a salvation this,
That I died with Christ.

Christ liveth in me,
Christ liveth in me;
Oh! what a salvation this,
That Christ liveth in me."
Daniel Webster Whittier (1840 – 1901)

DECEMBER 18 – DEATH IN LOVE

"No man is an island, entire of itself; every man is a piece of the continent, a part of the main. If a clod be washed away by the sea, Europe is the less, as well as if a promontory were, as well as if a manor of thy friends or of thine own were: any man's death diminishes me, because I am involved in mankind and therefore never send to know for whom the bell tolls; it tolls for thee." John Donne (1573 – 1631)

John Donne, one time libertine, poet and man about London town, later faithful husband, convert and famous preacher at St. Paul's cathedral, has a lot to say, but not always easy to understand, about love and death. King James I (1566 – 1625) (of the famous, or infamous, dedication page in the 1611 Authorized Version) said:

"Donne poetry is like Paul's peace, it passeth understanding."

While acknowledging that the King had a point about his famous contemporary, the above lines can be understood by most of us. The 17th century English is impeccable for that age and stands up well today. This portion is well known and widely quoted still. Ernest Hemmingway (1899 – 1961) used five words of it for his novel "For Whom the Bell Tolls". Donne's writings, sermons and poems have often disturbed, challenged and consoled me.

I have assisted, during these past forty plus years, at the funeral services of acquaintances, friends and loved ones in a number of countries. Donne's words, once I knew them, always seemed relevant. Ask not "for whom the bell tolls; it tolls for thee." "Any man's death diminishes me, because I am involved in mankind." I am involved; in life, in love and in death. I have also learned by experience that while in some ways all this involvement in mankind diminishes me, in other senses it wonderfully enlarges me. Nowhere else does it enhance and enlarge more than the "death in love" connection.

Some years ago I attended, and assisted, at the funeral in London, England of one very near and dear to me. I called him "son" and he called me "dad." In a sense he was our son-in-law for he married the girl we had raised as our "adopted" daughter. He had also, formally and in a Christian manner, asked me for "her hand in marriage." How quaint, how odd and how old fashioned some may have thought. But Pat was a Christian gentleman. He married Cornelia in 1971, and as she told me later, they enjoyed nine years of real love for each other, for others and for the Lord. Suddenly death interrupted it all. I spoke at Pat's graveside on: "…though he is dead, he still speaks"[1] and "…blessed are the dead who die in the Lord… for their deeds follow with them."[2] His faith, which worked by love is still speaking. And so we buried him on Monday, September 29, 1980 in West Norwood Cemetery, not far from the tomb of Charles Haddon Spurgeon (1834 – 1892). A simple headstone marks the plot with these words:

"Patrick Martin. Died 21st September, 1980. Aged 41 years."

Of course his loss diminished his wife, his family, our family and many others, but how it enlarged us all in our love for the Lord, for each other and for His sheep. Some days after the funeral I attended even-song in St. Paul's Cathedral with Pat's widow and there, together, we worshipped the Lord of life, the Lord of love and the Lord of love in death.

DECEMBER 19 – LOVE IN DEATH

"Death be not proud, though some have called thee
Mighty and dreadful, for, thou art not so,
For, those, whom thou think'st, thou dost overthrow,
Die not, poor death, nor yet canst thou kill me.
From rest and sleep, which but thy pictures bee,
Much pleasure, then from thee, much more must flow,
And soonest our best men with thee do go,
Rest of their bones, and souls delivery.
Thou art slave to Fate, Chance, kings, and desperate men,
And dost with poison, war, and sickness dwell,
And poppy, or charms can make us sleep as well,
And better then thy stroke; why swell'st thou then;
One short sleep past, we wake eternally,
And death shall be no more; death, thou shalt die."
John Donne (1573 – 1631)

"Therefore, since the children share in flesh and blood, He Himself likewise also partook of the same, that through death He might render powerless him who had the power of death, that is, the devil, and might free those who through fear of death were subject to slavery all their lives."[1] Calvary love destroyed death and the Devil. Love's death was the prelude to deathless love for Him and soon will be for all of us. "For this perishable must put on the imperishable, and this mortal must put on immortality. But when this perishable will have put on the imperishable, and this mortal will have put on immortality, then will come about the saying that is written, 'Death is swallowed up in victory. O death, where is your victory? O death, where is your sting?' The sting of death is sin, and the power of sin is the law; but thanks be to God, who gives us the victory through our Lord Jesus Christ."[2] At Calvary, love drew the sting and broke the power of sin; the wages of sin are paid. Death is swallowed up by His victory. We share in that victory of love triumphant now and will share in it as we cross the river. "But in all these things we overwhelmingly conquer through Him who loved us. For I am convinced that neither death... nor any other created thing, will be able to separate us from the love of God, which is in Christ Jesus our Lord."[3] Here is love in death conquering all.

We are told that "...the day of one's death is better than the day of one's birth."[4] This is true for the born again but not for the unbeliever. As the Lord said: "...you will die in your sins; for unless you believe that I am He, you will die in your sins."[5] For the believer it is glory all the way, but only if our affections are settled there; our treasure banked there; our hopes fixed there; and our love rooted there. Charles T. Studd (1860 – 1931) had a wonderful wife named Priscilla. When he was courting her as a young missionary in China, and she accepted him, she also wrote him a reminder of the relativity of love.

"Lord Jesus Thou art to me dearer than ever Charlie can be."

Thus they lived. Loving each other passionately, but loving the Lord Jesus more. At the end of their lives they were separated for years. He was in Africa, and she was in England looking after the home end of the Mission.

DECEMBER 19 - CONTINUED

He wrote:

"There will be a funeral soon" (his wife had already gone home to glory) "mine and be sure you celebrate it scripturally and send hallelujahs all around. It is a better day than one's wedding day."

Was he right? Hear another lover. Elizabeth Barrett Browning (1806 – 1861)

"Guess now who holds thee!
'Death,' I said, But, there, the silver answer rang,
'Not death, but Love.'"

DECEMBER 20 – LOVE'S VALEDICTION

A valediction is a bidding farewell; a leave taking. The word is derived from two Latin words: "vale" or farewell and "dicere" or say. A student, chosen to be a valedictorian at the graduating ceremony of his or her class, is granted a high honour.

One of the most moving last valedictions in Scripture is Paul's goodbye to the Ephesian elders. At Miletus, while he awaited a ship, he sent for the leaders of that church to which he had given two years of his life and love. Then follows, no formal, but a very fond and final farewell. It is full of true love's strength and real love's warnings. The kindness and affection shines through every phrase as he recalls his tears and trials "…from the first day that I set foot in Asia…"[1] Paul is involved. This is a spontaneous pouring forth of deeply felt truth and real concern for the church's welfare. True love is bitter sweet, like life itself. There is death and depth in it. It comes straight from the heart of love. It heralds Christ Jesus' blessings and the way Paul proclaimed that Gospel. He did not shrink from declaring to them the whole counsel of God nor from warning these overseers of the ravening wolves that would attack the flock. Then comes the touching personal goodbye. He had no doubt about what awaited him, "…bonds and afflictions…"[2] "but I do not consider my life of any account as dear to myself…"[3] now rightful emotion is allowed its course. When he said "… that they would not see his face again…"[4] and prayed his farewell prayer with them, and said that lovely final word, "…it is more blessed to give than to receive."[5] they wept and kissed and accompanied him to the ship. This is the grief of genuine love and is love's valediction.

"God be with thee, my beloved, God be with thee!
Else alone thou goest forth,
Thy face unto the north,
Moor and pleasance all around thee and beneath thee
Looking equal in one snow;
While I, who try to reach thee,
Vainly follow, vainly follow
With the farewell and the hollo,
And cannot reach thee so.
Alas, I can but teach thee!
God be with thee, my beloved, God be with thee!

Can I love thee, my beloved, can I love thee?
And is this like love, to stand
With no help in my hand,
When strong as death I would watch above thee?
My love-kiss can deny
No tear that falls beneath it;
Mine oath of love can swear thee
From no ill that comes near thee,
And thou diest while I breathe it,
And I, I can but die!
May God love thee, my beloved,
may God love thee!"
Elizabeth Barrett Browning (1806 – 1861)

The poem I still like the best of all the valedictory love songs, is the one I heard first as a boy when the little church farewelled our family as we left England for Australia in 1929.

"God be with you till we meet again;
Keep love's banner floating o'er you,
Strike death's threatening wave before you;
God be with you till we meet again."
Jeremiah E. Rankin (1828 – 1904)

DECEMBER 21 – LOVE'S FAREWELL

"As virtuous men pass mildly away,
And whisper to their souls to go,
Whilst some of their sad friends do say,
'Now his breath goes,' and some say, 'No.'

So let us melt, and make no noise,
No tear-floods, nor sigh-tempests move;
'Twere profanation of our joys
To tell the laity our love…

Dull sublunary lovers' love
Whose soul is sense, cannot admit
Of absence, 'cause it doth remove
The thing which elemented it.

But we by a love so much refined,
That ourselves know not what it is,
Inter-assured of the mind,
Care less, eyes, lips and hands to miss.

Our two souls therefore, which are one,
Though I must go, endure not yet
A breach, but an expansion,
Like gold to aery thinness beat…"
"A Valediction Forbidding Mourning"
John Donne (1573 – 1631)

I have attended last rites, last farewells, where mourners have loudly voiced their laments like official noise makers. As though quietness, and absence of outer show would deny love and grief. Our Lord was alert to insincerity. "…a synagogue official came and bowed down before Him, and said, 'My daughter has just died; but come and lay Your hand on her, and she will live.' Jesus got up and began to follow him…[1] When Jesus came into the official's house, and saw the flute-players and the crowd in noisy disorder, He said, 'Leave; for the girl has not died, but is asleep.' And they began laughing at Him. But when the crowd had been sent out, He entered and took her by the hand, and the girl got up."[2]

There is a lot to say in favour of quiet weddings and funerals with just the family, a few friends and Jesus. Donne wanted no mourning, pointing out that:

"Dull sublunary lovers' love…cannot admit of absence," while "we by a love so much refined, that ourselves know not what it is… our two souls therefore, which are one, though I must go, endure not yet a breach, but an expansion…"

What a true view of Christian love and death. We must face inevitable fact. One partner in friendship or marital love must predecease the other. While truly bereft, grief should not distress or debilitate, for we "…sorrow not, even as others which have no hope."[3] Death is love's expansion, not love's extinction.

So "may there be no moaning of the bar when I put out to sea…" Alfred Lord Tennyson (1809 – 1892) Rather let there be praise and hallelujah which the Salvation Army introduced. Mrs. Priscilla Studd, who had been a young Salvationist, with her husband Charles maintained this attitude from the time of their marriage in China through her homecoming and his. She was suddenly called from Spain to glory and he from the Belgian Congo (now Zaire). His last words were "Hallelujah, hallelujah." The funeral was a time of celebration with converts praising the Lord. This sincere noise is pleasing to heaven, for it is the perfume of praise and prayer.

"At the very least" said Studd "let us see that the Devil holds a thanksgiving service in Hell when he hears of our departure from the field of battle."

DECEMBER 22 – LOVING COMFORT IN THE LOSS OF A LOVED ONE

"Death, as it must to all men, came to...at the age of..."

In the early days of <u>Time</u> magazine the above was the standard obituary notice for notables in its column called "Milestones". The essential facts are probably all that the readers want to know, but the bereaved need comfort.

There is a portion of Scripture which gives loving comfort in the loss of loved ones. The Thessalonian Christians, expecting the imminent return of Christ and their removal from earth, were shocked by the physical death of their loved ones. Today, like those Thessalonians, uninformed believers suffer unnecessary grief. Ignorant grief is to a large degree worldly and ungodly. Christians grieve, but it is not hopeless sorrow, like the world's grief. Because of the lack of teaching on this subject some Christians act as if their Christian loved ones are gone forever. The God of love has loving comfort in His Word for His people suffering, enduring or contemplating the loss of a loved one. "But we do not want you to be uninformed, brethren, about those who are asleep, so that you will not grieve as do the rest who have no hope. For if we believe that Jesus died and rose again, even so God will bring with Him those who have fallen asleep in Jesus. For this we say to you by the word of the Lord, that we who are alive and remain until the coming of the Lord, will not precede those who have fallen asleep. For the Lord Himself will descend from heaven with a shout, with the voice of the archangel and with the trumpet of God, and the dead in Christ will rise first. Then we who are alive and remain will be caught up together with them in the clouds to meet the Lord in the air, and so we shall always be with the Lord. Therefore comfort one another with these words."[1] There is complete loving comfort, for all sorrowing saints, of all the centuries. We are under a cloud, not of glory, but of doom.

"If we believe."

Believe what? About whom? About our Lord Jesus Christ who died and rose again and Who lives now in the power of an endless life. And because He lives, we live now, in our spirit, through death and for evermore. Such is our hope that death is transformed. It is the gateway to glory; to reunion with loved ones who have gone before and above all this: we shall see the King in all His beauty and be like Him. There is no preference or precedence: whether through the vale or via the air we shall meet together in everlasting love and bliss. This wonderful thing called love, attends and affects every aspect of life, from birth to death. Death for the believer is a conclusion; a continuation; a change of circumstances; a change of condition; a new citizenship; a confirmation of all we have believed; and most importantly a consummation of love in Christ. The very contemplation of this brings sure and certain loving comfort in the loss of a loved one. It doesn't, though death is cruel, make us callous; it makes us true comforters.

DECEMBER 23 – LOVED TO THE END

"…Jesus knowing that His hour had come that He would depart out of this world to the Father, having loved His own who were in the world, He loved them to the end."[1] And He did, until their ends. The Herod who massacred the infants at the birth of Christ; the Herod who beheaded John the Baptist; the Herod who killed James the disciple; none of these could kill His love. He loved them until the end of His own life and from the power of His endless life, and eternal love, He has gone on loving. Stephen, as the stones struck and killed him, saw heaven opened and Jesus standing to receive him. John the beloved, who outlived all his fellow apostles, from his exile on the island of Patmos, was loved until the end, and before it came wrote "…to Him who loves us…"[2] present and continuous. And so it has gone on from the 1st century until now. Two thousand plus years of love. "…having loved His own…He loved them to the end…" The other side of this concerns us. "Having loved Him… we love Him to the end." Hopefully we will do this through Him in a prayerful and humble manner.

St. Bernard of Clairvoux (1090 - 1153), wrote of Him, who having begun the work of love in us, would complete it.

"O Jesus, King most wonderful!
O Conqueror renowned!
O Source of peace ineffable,
In whom all joys are found:

When once you visit darkened hearts,
Then truth begins to shine,
Then earthly vanity departs,
Then kindles love divine.

Oh, may our tongues forever bless,
May we love you alone
And ever in our lives express
The image of your own!"

Yes, we believe, with Bernard and Paul "…that He who began a good work in you will perfect it until the day of Christ Jesus."[3] From Paul, in the first century, to Bernard, a thousand years later, loved and loving, let's hear from another witness in the nineteenth century.

"And who saith, 'I loved once'?
Not angels, whose clear eyes, love foresee,
Love, through eternity,
And by 'To Love' do apprehend 'To Be.'
Not God, called Love, His noble crown-name casting
A light too broad for blasting:
The great God, changing not from everlasting,
Saith never, 'I loved once.'"
Elizabeth Barrett Browning (1806 – 1861)

Dear Lord, enable me to keep my promise. May "he loved once" never be said of me; rather let it be, he loved the Lord and loved Him unto the end.

DECEMBER 24 – LOVE'S OWN COUNTRY

I was privileged to know, in the later years of his life, John G. Ridley, MC (1896 – 1974), once Australia's foremost evangelist. This soldier-poet, after being severely wounded in WWI, was invalided out of the Australian Army which he had hoped to make his life's career. He pioneered in "the outback" of Australia with his Gospel van and later was used Australia wide in campaigns and conventions. My own mother was deeply blessed at one of his meetings. He returned again and again to his favourite theme; the love of God. The last message I heard him give was based on "We love, because He first loved us."[1] For many years, when we were on the mission field, we received every Christmas from John a little folder with one of his poems printed as the Ridley family Christmas greeting.

I have before me, and I treasure, his card for 1966. It is worth sharing, for he, being dead, in it still speaks, and I can still hear the echo of his voice and see that man of blessed memory. He entitled that Christmas poem: "Love's Own Country" basing it upon the text: "...they desire a better country, that is, a heavenly one..."[2] and upon some of the last letters from his favourite author, Samuel Rutherford (1600 – 1661). Anne R. Cousin (1824 – 1906) used Rutherford's letters "Take Me to Love's Own Country, Unto Immanuel's Land" some two hundred years later for her hymn "The Sands of Time are Sinking."

"Tell me of 'Love's Own Country'
The landscape of my God;
Tell of that better country
Where holy feet have trod;
Tell of the Father's mansions,
Where rise the songs so sweet;
Tell of the flowing river,
And of the golden street.

Tell me of 'Love's Own Country'
Land of the hearts that love;
Home of the Saviour's lovers,
Born of the realm above.
Tell me of souls made perfect,
Now in glory bright;
Safe in that blessed country,
Where there is no night.

Tell me of 'Love's Own Country'
Tell of the angel throng,
And of the saints in splendour,
Singing the grand new song.
Tell of the hand that binds them
Into one blest accord;
Love of their loving Saviour,
Jesus the risen Lord.

Take me to 'Love's Own Country'
Saviour, for this I pray;
Take me to 'Love's own Country'
Land of the perfect day.
Hasten thy second advent,
Hope of the heaven born heart:
Take me to 'Love's Own Country'
To see Thee as thou art."

John has had his heart's desire fulfilled for some years now. Faith is fulfilled. Hope is realized. He sees the Lord of love face to face in "Love's Own Country." In life, few knew how much John suffered from his head wound, or how much he travailed for souls. He was granted a great harvest and knows now the joy of harvest home. Heaven is a wonderful place because it is "Love's Own Country." It is one of the most felicitous phrases I have ever heard for describing heaven.

John's life long earthly mentor in the language of love had lived three hundred years before him. Samuel Rutherford, writing to Colonel Ker in 1653 said quoting: "'... he that dwelleth in love dwelleth in God.'[3] O sir, what a house that must be! What is it to dwell in love; to live in God? How far are some from this, their house and home! How ill acquaint with the rooms, mansions, safety and sweetness of holy security to be found in God."

DECEMBER 25 – LOVE'S NATIVITY

"Immensity cloysterd in thy deare wombe,
Now leaves his welbelov'd imprisonment,
There he hath made himself to his intent
Weake enough, now into our world to come;
But Oh, for thee, for him, hath the Inne no roome?
Yet lay him in this stall, and from the Orient,
Starres and wise men will travel to prevent
Th'effect of Herod's jealous general doome.
Seest thou, my Soule, with thy faiths eyes, how he
Which fils all place, yet none holds him, doth lye?
Was not his pity towards thee wondrous high,
That would have need to be pittied by thee?
Kisse him, and with him into Egypt goe,
With his kinde mother, who partakes thy woe."
John Donne (1573 – 1631)

* * * * *

"Love came down at Christmas,
Love all lovely, love divine;
Love was born at Christmas,
Star and angels gave the sign.

Worship we the Godhead,
Love incarnate, love divine;
Worship we our Jesus:
But wherewith for sacred sign?

Love shall be our token,
Love shall be yours and love be mine,
Love to God and to all men,
Love for plea and gift and sign."
Christina Rossetti (1830 - 1894)

Two hundred years later the English has changed but Rossetti's hymn on love's nativity echoes Donne's. Love's great stoop from the Father's eternal love to the lowly virgin's womb is beyond our human comprehension. Its magnificence, mystery and miracle we see but cannot understand. But believing we rejoice and love the love that first loved us. We bring our love and gifts, and worship and adoration, with shepherds and wise men; with Simeon and the prophetess Anna; with poets and sages over the centuries we sing of Love's nativity.

"How silently, how silently, the wondrous Gift is giv'n;
So God imparts to human hearts the blessings of His Heav'n.
No ear may hear His coming, but in this world of sin,
Where meek souls will receive Him still, the dear Christ enters in.

O holy Child of Bethlehem, descend to us, we pray;
Cast out our sin, and enter in, be born in us today.
We hear the Christmas angels the great glad tidings tell;
O come to us, abide with us, our Lord Emmanuel!"
Phillips Brooks (1835 - 1893)

DECEMBER 26 - LOVING HIS APPEARING - Part One

"Henceforth there is laid up for me a crown of righteousness, which the Lord, the righteous judge, shall give me at that day: and not to me only, but unto all them also that love his appearing."[1] "In the future there is laid up for me the crown of righteousness, which the Lord, the righteous Judge, will award to me on that day; and not only to me, but also to all who have loved His appearing."[2] Paul, at the conclusion of his objective assessment of his life since Christ met and changed him, also rejoices in the firm assurance of an awaiting award. We note how he swiftly broadens a personal appraisal, with resulting reward, to include all lovers of his Lord, past, present and future, who also love His second coming.

What Paul did in a generalized way for us, we must do specifically and personally. We must make a correct appraisal of our attitudes and actions since we were saved, using the three "I haves." These cover warring the good warfare for Christ in the arena of this world; righteously running the Christian race on life's race course; and fully obeying the faith at all times and in all areas of life. Following this assessment, we should then consider our attitudes and actions concerning His coming and His awards for the latter depends on the former. Can we say with Paul? "I have fought the good fight, I have finished the course, I have kept the faith."[3] The qualifying words are "all" and "love." "...all them also that love his appearing." "...all who have loved His appearing." He first loved us and showed it in many ways with the greatest being the incarnation and passion where he died and rose to save us. That love continues now on the Throne in heaven where he appears in the presence of God for us. It will be completed in the future when He "...will appear a second time for salvation without reference to sin, to those who eagerly await Him."[4] This eagerness is the eagerness of reciprocal love born in us when we received the Saviour and the love of God poured into our hearts by the Holy Spirit. Do I love this past appearing for me culminating in the cross? Do I love His future appearing at the second coming? Am I included with the "all" of all ages who have wondered, watched, waited and worked for His return?

This is what "loving His appearing" means. It is not only loving thoughts and attitudes, but also love in action through words, works, witness and warfare. Love for His appearing is not soft or sentimental, nor is it limited to songs about His return. His love is strong, sacrificial and the supreme love of our lives. This love for him is translated in some versions as "longing." We not only "look," we "long" because we love. A yearning, passionate desire for the Beloved possessed aged John on Patmos, as he ended the Revelation with "...Amen. Come, Lord Jesus."[5]

DECEMBER 27 - LOVING HIS APPEARING - Part Two

"...and not only to me, but also to all who have loved His appearing."[1] This is the continuation of Paul's assessment and assurance statements about his past life, and connecting them with his future reward. He concludes these statements by including all believers "who have loved His appearing." At first glance, the past tense used in this translation, could lead us to think that the reference is to Christ's first coming. While it is true that believers love that past appearing, when he came to put away sin by the sacrifice of Himself, the context here shows that our Lord's future return is indicated. It is also true that only as we understand, and accept His salvation purchased on the Cross, will we long for and love the thought of His second coming. Love for the Lord must include both of His appearances.

The King James Version states: "Henceforth there is laid up for me a crown of righteousness, which the Lord, the righteous judge, shall give me at that day: and not to me only, but unto all them also that love his appearing." This present tense emphasizes the ongoing, ever increasing multitude of the Lord's lovers who are watching for that glorious day. The past tense included all the saints of Paul's time, and in the longer past sense, all the believers who had lived and died before Christ. In the centuries since then, millions have also longed for and loved that blessed hope. The present tense covers Christians now living and who are yearning for this appearance and fulfillment of all the promises contained in His coming. What is also implied, should He not return today, includes those yet unborn who will in their time believe in His past and future appearings. Finally there will be one generation who will behold Him coming in power and great glory. That group of believers will bypass the grave and go with Him, and all the saints resurrected from all the ages, direct to glory.

"All" is one of the operative words in the text and so is "love." Here in the Christian life, love is the qualifier. Love contains the thought of longing, eager desire and anticipation. Anyone who has known the longing of love for an absent earthly loved one will have a small idea of the passion and desire contained here in this love for our heavenly Father's visible coming. This attitude of love will produce actions of love.

"In the advent light, O Saviour,
I am living day by day;
Waiting, working, watching ever,
Knowing Thou art on the way.

In the advent light to witness
To a dark and dying world;
This the holy ordination,
May His banner be unfurled.

He is coming! He is coming!
Pass the heavenly watchword on;
Go ye forth to meet the Bridegroom,
Hail! To God's anointed Son."
Anon.

DECEMBER 28 - LOVE'S RETURN

"On that bright and golden morning, when the Son of Man shall come,
And the radiance of His glory we shall see;
When from ev'ry clime and nation He shall call His people home,
What a gath'ring of the ransomed that will be!

When the blest, who sleep in Jesus, at His bidding shall arise
From the silence of the grave, and from the sea,
And with bodies all celestial they shall meet Him in the skies,
What a gath'ring and rejoicing there will be!

What a gath'ring, what a gath'ring,
What a gath'ring of the ransomed in the summer land of love!
What a gath'ring, what a gath'ring,
Of the ransomed in that happy home above."
Fanny Crosby (1820 – 1915)

That assembly "in the summer land of love" will be the first phase of the fulfilment of all God's purposes, promises and prophecies from the foundation of the world. That gathering will be a time when realization will be far beyond the bounds of anticipation. That resurrection assembly "in the summer land of love" will be first, a reunion in the air. "For the Lord Himself will descend from heaven with a shout, with the voice of the archangel and with the trumpet of God, and the dead in Christ will rise first. Then we who are alive and remain will be caught up together with them in the clouds to meet the Lord in the air, and so we shall always be with the Lord."[1] What a rapturous reunion of love that will be to meet the Lover of our souls and loved ones gone before. Then will be love's nuptials with the marriage of the heavenly Bridegroom to His earthly bride, the Church. The wedding supper will provide occasion for more rejoicing and expressions of love. That gathering of the ransomed "in the summer land of love" will be joined by myriads of angels singing the new song "...Worthy is the Lamb that was slain to receive power and riches and wisdom and might and honor and glory and blessing."[2] In due course Love's rule and reign on earth will begin. What a day that will be when love extends its boundaries and takes back the dominion from the devil and his forces in this world. The final conflicts will be devastating and earth will know the wrath of God. Love's severity will finally replace love's long suffering. Love's retribution and rule with a rod of iron will be known and necessary. Rebellion will be put down. The new heaven and new earth will replace the ruins of sin and Satan's final uprising. Finally creation itself will be restored by regeneration and rejuvenated by the reorganization of God.

"We shall bless Thee, we shall show Thee
All our hearts could never say.
What an anthem that will be,
Ringing out our love to Thee,
Pouring out our rapture sweet
At Thine own all-glorious feet.

O the Joy to see Thee reigning,
Thee, my own beloved Lord!
Every tongue Thy Name confessing,
Worship, honour, glory, blessing,
Brought to Thee with one accord.
Thee, my Master and my Friend,
Vindicated and enthroned
Unto earth's remotest end,
Glorified, adored and owned."
Frances Ridley Havergal (1836 – 1879)

DECEMBER 29 - LOVE'S VENITÉ

"Venité," in the Latin version, is the first word of Psalm 95. "Come, let us sing for joy…"[1] with the word repeated: "Let us come before His presence with thanksgiving…[2] come, let us worship and bow down…"[3]

Some years ago, while travelling on a British ship, I used to attend the Sunday morning service. It was usually conducted by the Captain and attended by a cross section of passengers. I noticed he liked Psalm 95 and announced it first in the Anglican form and "now the venité…" In the Anglican form of service it is used at Matins, or morning prayer, frequently in a musical setting. It blessed my heart and as these readings on love conclude we will say "and now love's venité." Come, let us sing of His love as we shall with the saints in glory; as John did on Patmos. Come, let us fall down before Him; let us worship Him who is holy, heavenly love.

"…from Him who is and who was and who is to come, and from the seven Spirits who are before His throne, and from Jesus Christ, the faithful witness, the firstborn of the dead, and the ruler of the kings of the earth. To Him who loves us and released us from our sins by His blood and He has made us to be a kingdom, priests to His God and Father; to Him be the glory and the dominion forever and ever. Amen. Behold He is coming with the clouds…"[4] He is coming with the clouds that covered His ascension, and coming with the cloud of witnesses, those of whom the elders now sing: "…Thou art worthy…for thou wast slain, and hast redeemed us to God by thy blood out of every kindred, and tongue, and people, and nation."[5] No wonder John described the throne as rainbow circled, full coloured with all the races pouring out their adoring love. All that blood-washed throng is worshipping Him, who continues to love them. That glorious shining one is seated on the rainbow-encircled throne, the God who was, who is and who will forever be love.

Death is the glory portal to all this. Let us hear again John Donne (1573 – 1631) on his two main themes; love and death and death and love. Hear him sing again of the glory beyond the portal, and experienced now:

"Till God's great venité change the song…I will awake early; I will praise Thee…O glorious beauty, infinitely reverant, infinitely fresh and young, I came late to Thy love if I consider the past days of my life, but early if Thou beest pleased to reckon with me from this hour of the shining of Thy grace upon me."

But aged John must have the last venité; a series of them as he looks and longs for the coming of His Lord. Three Gospel venités: "The Spirit and the bride say, 'Come.' And let the one who hears say, 'Come.' And let the one who is thirsty come…"[6] Then in response to the Lord's "…'Yes, I am coming quickly.' Amen. Come, Lord Jesus"[7] and take me to Him Who is love and to love's own country.

DECEMBER 30 - "FINALLY...THE GOD OF LOVE...BE WITH YOU"

It seems fitting to finalize all the foregoing about love with some re-emphasis and encouragements. The laws of high, heavenly love commanding all the lower earthly loves may seem complex and their high standards impossible to fulfill. This is true regarding the "natural man". But what we cannot do, God can. This is the message of cheer, explicit and implicit in the preceding pages. The impossibility of loving God wholeheartedly, and our inability to love men and women rightly in all the arenas of life, should point us to the Enabler. Our need should force us to the source of love. All the complexities and impossibilities are resolved by the simplicity and profundity of His plan. God gave Himself, His Son, His Spirit to liberate us in body, mind and spirit by His costly Calvary redemptive love.

In all this God is the initiator. If His holy love has lawful aspects of wrath, severity and the fires of Sinai, it is also full of grace, mercy and goodness that should lead us to repentance. This love woos us to Him.

"Jesus' love, precious love,
Boundless and pure and free;
O turn to that love, weary, wand'ring soul:
Jesus pleadeth with thee!"
W. E. Littlewood (1831 - 1886)

Don't be intimidated by the implications inherent in His love but respond to the invitation and find the promises fulfilled, the powers given and the pleasures of love experienced. Instead of being natural, we are now spiritual, Spirit controlled people filled with the love of God poured into our hearts by the Holy Spirit and able to show brotherly love.

Why do people not respond? The natural man does not accept the things of the Spirit of God because he is blinded and bound by Satan, self and sin and alienated from the Lord of love. Many feel they are hopeless cases; they think they may have sinned away their day of grace or committed the unpardonable sin; they have broken almost every commandment of God and man, if not in act, then in thought. In the realm of Eros, physical and sexual love they have made shipwreck. Satan uses these hidden guilt complexes and fears to keep sinners and even fallen saints from coming to, or returning to Christ. We saw how the Lord dealt in love and grace with the woman taken in adultery. He did not condone or condemn. He counselled and forgave her. Here is hope following a catalogue of sin: "Such were some of you; but you were washed, but you were sanctified, but you were justified in the name of the Lord Jesus Christ and in the Spirit of our God."[1]

"Finally...the God of love...be with you."[2] The title in this page is a benediction. The God of love, the love of God be with you. In knowing that love, all the other loves will be right.

DECEMBER 31 - LOVE IN RETROSPECT AND PROSPECT

And so ends the year as it began, with love, the many splendoured thing we have seen in all the days past, and in all our countless ways, past. God's eternal love has enabled and enriched our lives and living by making a many splendoured thing out of all other loves. It has energised and elevated romantic and marital love; it has sanctified and sweetened friendship and platonic love; it has made human brotherly love possible and spiritual brotherly love vital; it has given grace and gifts to the people of God so that they might serve in this world; and it has sent us out in our daily ministries to be His witnesses.

For the last year we have studied this many-faceted thing called love. I am the better for the writing of it, and, I humbly hope more loving in all areas of my life. In the Preface I stated my purposes, and here, in this, which is in effect a Postscript, I give my thanks to Him who is always, and in all ways, love. This book has its share of confession of both kinds; confession of failure and confession of Christ who lives, loves, forgives and forgets. These pages are also in large part an affirmation of things believed, learned and loved over the period of years from 1935 to 1984; almost fifty years of proving and praising the love of God. And running as a connecting cord through all the writing, quoting and discussing, is the theme of aspiration. Aspiring further to become, to be, to do, to will and to obey, which is the road to love's goal; the glory of God. Love in retrospect and prospect.

Charles Wesley (1707 – 1788) has often inspired our hearts with his songs to the Lord of love. Hear him now summing up our past year.

"Sing to the great Jehovah's praise!
All praise to him belongs:
Who kindly lengthens out our days
Demands our choicest songs.

His providence hath brought us through
Another various year:
We all with vows and anthems new
Before our God appear.

Father, thy mercies past we own;
Thy still continued care;
To thee presenting, through thy Son,
Whate'er we have or own.

Our lips and lives shall gladly show
The wonders of thy love,
While on in Jesu's steps we go
To see thy face above.

Our residue of days or hours
Thine, wholly thine, shall be;
And all our consecrated powers
A sacrifice to be:

Till Jesus in the clouds appear
To saints on earth forgiven,
And bring the grand Sabbatic year,
The jubilee of heaven."

For several years, while in Barbados, I was privileged to conduct a New Year's Eve service. We always ended with this hymn by Lawrence Tuttiett (1825 - 1897). It truly describes love's prospect.

"Father, let me dedicate
All this year to Thee,
In whatever earthly state
Thou wilt have me be.
Not from sorrow, pain, or care
Freedom dare I claim;
This alone shall be my prayer:
Glorify Thy name.

If Thou callest to the cross
And its shadow come,
Turning all my gain to loss,
Shrouding heart and home,
Let me think how Thy dear Son
To His glory came
And in deepest woe pray on:
'Glorify Thy name.'"

Roger and Mary Davey Wedding - 1902

Wedding - Dec. 25, 1941

Family picture - 1955

John and Ethel Davey - 1965

ENDNOTES

January 1 - (1) 1 John 4:8; (2) Joshua 3:4
January 4 - (1) Genesis 1:1; (2) Hebrews 11:6; (3) Genesis 1:26,27
January 5 - (1) John 4:24; 1 John 1:5; 1 John 4:8; (2) 1 John 4:9; (3) 1 John 4:9,10; (4) 1 John 3:16
January 6 - (1) Romans 5:5
January 7 - (1) Isaiah 43:1-7; (2) Genesis 12:3; (3) Psalm 107:1-3: (4) Matthew 8:10-11; (5) Matthew 9:37
January 8 - (1) Matthew 9:38; (2) Romans 2:4
January 9 - (1) Hebrews 11:6; (2) 1 Peter 1:16; (3) Romans 3:26
January 11 - (1) Deuteronomy 7:7-8; (2) 2 Timothy 1:12 KJV
January 13 - (1) 1 John 3:16; (2) Isaiah 55:1; (3) Luke 23:35
January 14 - (1) Matthew 3:17; (2) Matthew 17:5; (3) Psalm 24:7-8; (4) Ephesians 1:6 KJV
January 17 - (1) Ephesians 3:17-19
January 21 - (1) John 20:19-20; (2) John 20:24-25; (3) John 20:29; (4) 1 Peter 1:7-8
January 22 - (1) Joshua 24:15; (2) Acts 16:31
January 23 - (1) John 21:15-17 Phillips "The New Testament in Modern English"
January 25 - (1) Deuteronomy 11:1; (2) Deuteronomy 11:13-14; (3) Deuteronomy 11:22-24; (4) John 14:15 (5) John 14:21 (6) John 14:23-24
January 26 - (1) Jude 21; (2) Deuteronomy 30:19-20
January 28 - (1) John 21:15; (2) Luke 17:10; (3) 1 Corinthians 12:3
January 29 - (1) Revelation 12:11
January 31 - (1) John 3:8; (2) 2 Samuel 22:11
February 2 - (1) Hebrews 2:18; (2) Hebrews 4:15; (3) John 14:30-31; (4) 1 John 2:16; (5) 1 Corinthians 10:13
February 3 - (1) Deuteronomy 13:1-3; (2) Isaiah 8:20 KJV; (3) Isaiah 8:19; 1 Samuel 28:7-10; (4) 2 Corinthians 11:14; (5) Ephesians 6:12
February 4 - (1) Romans 7:21-24; (2) 2 Corinthians 12:7
February 5 - (1) 1 Peter 4:12 KJV
February 7 - (1) Romans 8:28-29; (2) Genesis 42:36
February 8 - (1) Luke 14:26-27; John 12:25; (2) Matthew 12:48; (3) Ephesians 5:28-29
February 9 - (1) Matthew 10:34-36
February 10 - (1) Titus 3:3-5
February 11 - (1) Psalm 97:10 KJV; (2) Luke 14:26
February 12 - (1) Romans 9:13
February 13 - (1) Ecclesiastes 3:8
February 15 - (1) Romans 11:22
February 16 - (1) 1 Corinthians 16:22 KJV; (2) 1 Corinthians 16:22; (3) Galatians 1:8-9; (4) Galatians 3:13; (5) Romans 8:39 to 9:3
February 17 - (1) Jeremiah 31:15; Matthew 2:16-18; (2) Isaiah 53:3-4; (3) Psalm 126:5-6; (4) Luke 13:34-35; (5) Luke 22:44
February 18 - (1) Isaiah 5:1-7; (2) Isaiah 6:5; (3) Isaiah 42:10; (4) John 12:36-40
February 20 - (1) 1 Corinthians 5:7; (2) Psalm 45:1-2

February 21 - (1) Luke 10:27

February 22 - (1) Ephesians 5:19

February 23 - (1) Ephesians 5:19; (2) Job 38:4,7; (3) Hebrews 1:6; (4) 1 Peter 5:1

February 25 - (1) John 9:2,3

February 28 - (1) Psalm 45:1; (2) Matthew 10:8

February 29 - (1) Revelation 2:4; (2) 2 Chronicles 7:14 KJV

March 3 - (1) Revelation 22:3-4; (2) 1 John 3:1-2

March 4 - (1) Proverbs 19:21

March 5 - (1) 2 Thessalonians 3:5; (2) Hebrews 12:6-7; (3) Romans 5:2-5; (4) James 1:4; (5) Revelation 3:10; 1:9

March 6 - (1) Luke 6:35; (2) Romans 12:10 KJV; (3) 2 Corinthians 2:4; (4) 2 Corinthians 2:7-8

March 7 - (1) 1 Samuel 18:7

March 8 - (1) Song of Solomon 8:6-7; (2) Romans 8:28; (3) Psalm 69:9

March 9 - (1) 1 Corinthians 12:21-25; (2) Romans 3:27

March 10 - (1) Isaiah 14:12-14; (2) Ezekiel 28:14-19; (3) 1 Corinthians 1-5; (4) 1 Corinthians 4:7,10,14,18,19,21

March 11 - (1) Acts 28:2; (2) 1 Corinthians 7:36; (3) 1 Corinthians 7:38

March 12 - (1) 1 Corinthians 10:31-33; (2) 1 Corinthians 9:22

March 14 - (1) 1 Corinthians 3:1-3

March 15 - (1) 1 Corinthians 5:5; (2) 1 Corinthians 5:1; (3) 1 Corinthians 13:6

March 16 - (1)1Corinthians 1:1,2,4-8; (2) 2 Corinthians 2:14; (3) 2 Corinthians 3:2-3

March 17 - (1) Isaiah 34:5,6; (2) Ephesians 6:17; (3) Hebrews 4:12; (4) Ephesians 4:15; (5) 2 Thessalonians 2:10

March 18 - (1) Ephesians 4:15; (2) Ephesians 4:13; (3) John 1:16-17; (4) Luke 4:22; (5) Luke 4:28; (6) Psalm 51:6; (7) Romans 11:22; (8) Galatians 4:16; (9) 2 Thessalonians 2:9-10

March 19 - (1) 1 John 3:18; (2) 2 John 1:1; (3) 3 John 1:1; (4) 3 John 1:3; (5) 3 John 1:6; (6) 3 John 1:8; (7) 3 John1:9-10; (8) Ephesians 4:15

March 20 - (1) 1 Corinthians 13:7; (2) Song of Solomon 2:4

March 21 - (1) 1 Corinthians 1:11; (2) 1 Corinthians 1:12; (3) 1 Corinthians 11:18

March 22 - (1) Hebrews 11:1; (2) 2 Thessalonians 1:2,3; (3) 2 Thessalonians 1:9; (4) 2 Thessalonians 1:10; (5) Galatians 5:6; (6) Galatians 5:5; (7) Galatians 5:4

March 23 - (1) Luke 23:34; (2) Luke 23:43; (3) John 8:24; (4) 1 Corinthians 13:7

March 24 - (1) 2 Thessalonians 2:16-17; (2) Romans 15:13

March 25 - (1) 2 Corinthians 11:1; (2) 2 Corinthians 11:2; (3) 2 Corinthians 11:3; (4) 2 Corinthians 11:5; (5) 2 Corinthians 11:23; (6) 2 Corinthians 11:23-28; (7) 2 Timothy 4:6-7; (8) Hebrews 12:1-2

March 26 - (1) 1 Corinthians 13:8-10; (2) Luke 16:17

March 27 - (1) Hebrews 9:27; (2) 1 Corinthians 13:11; (3) 2 Thessalonians 1:3

March 28 - (1) Romans 11:22

March 29 - (1) John 13:17; (2) John 14:23; (3) John 15:10

March 30 - (1) Psalm 136:1-3; (2) Psalm 136:26

March 31 - (1) Psalm 63:3-4; (2) Ephesians 5:19; (3) Romans 13:8; (4) Ephesians 4:32; (5) Psalm 25:4-10; (6) Psalm 23:6

April 1 - (1) 1Corinthians 5:7; (2) Romans 4:25; (3) Ephesians 1:19-20; (4) Philippians 3:10-11

April 3 - (1) Ephesians 3:17-19; (2) Jeremiah 31:3

April 4 - (1) Ephesians 3:17; (2) Ephesians 3:18-19

April 6 - (1) Psalm 130:1-4,7; (2) 2 Corinthians 5:21

April 7 - (1) Ephesians 3:19; (2) Luke 5:4; (3) Galatians 5:6; (4) Psalm 107:23-24

April 8 - (1) Revelation 1:5-6; (2) Ephesians 2:6; (3) Ephesians 2:4-5; (4) 1 Corinthians 2:9

April 9 - (1) Psalm 118:27; (2) Matthew 27:46; (3) Psalm 116:3; (4) Galatians 2:20

April 10 - (1) Romans 6:23; (2) Isaiah 9:6; (3) Isaiah 53:12; (4) Galatians 2:20; (5) 2 Corinthians 9:15; (6) Matthew 10:8; (7) Romans 8:32; (8) Luke 6:38

April 11 - (1) 1 Samuel 22:2; (2) 1 Chronicles 11:19; (3) John 15:13; (4) Romans 5:7-8; (5) 1 John 3:16

April 12 - (1) Matthew 26:26-28; (2) 1 Corinthians 11:26; (3) 1 Corinthians 11:28; (4) Matthew 26:30

April 13 - (1) Jude 12-13; (2) 2 Peter 2:1-3,13-14; (3) 1 Corinthians 11:20-22; (4) 1 Corinthians 11:28-34

April 15 - (1) Matthew 5:1-12
April 16 - (1) Proverbs 21:7 The Living Bible; (2) Luke 6:35-38; (3) Matthew 5:7; (4) Matthew 18:22; (5) Luke 6:38
April 17 - (1) Mark 2:5; (2) Mark 2:7; (3) Ephesians 4:32; (4) 1 John 1:9
April 18 - (1) Matthew 23:35-40; (2) Luke 10:26; (3) Deuteronomy 6:5; Leviticus 19:18; (4) Exodus 20:3-4,7-8; (5) 1 John 4:9-10
April 19 - (1) Romans 13:8-10; (2) Ephesians 6:2; (3) Exodus 20:12; (4) Exodus 20:13 KJV; (5) John 8:11; (6) Ephesians 4:28; (7) Exodus 20:16 KJV
April 20 - (1) Luke 10:29
April 21 - (1) Matthew 5:43-45; (2) Matthew 5:45; (3) Matthew 5:48; (4) 2 Peter 1:4; (5) Luke 23:34; (6) Matthew 27:54; (7) Luke 23:47; (8) Acts 7:55; (9) Acts 7:59-60
April 23 - (1) 1 Timothy 2:2-4; (2) Luke 22:31-32; (3) Hebrews 7:25
April 24 - (1) 2 Peter 1:16-18; (2) Mark 15:39; (3) Mark 15:37-38; (4) Hebrews 4:15-16; (5) Luke 24:34
April 25 - (1) John 17:23-24; (2) John 17:25-26
April 26 - (1) John 17:11; (2) John 17:20-23; (3) Colossians 3:14; (4) Acts 5:13-14
April 27 - (1) Isaiah 59:16; (2) Nehemiah 2:4-5
April 28 - (1) Philippians 1:3-4; (2) Philippians 1:7; (3) Philippians 1:8-9; (4) Ephesians 3:14; (5) Ephesians 3:17-19; (6) 1 Timothy 2:1-4; (7) Psalm 116:1-2
April 29 - (1) 1 Thessalonians 5:18; (2) Ephesians 5:20
April 30 - (1) Psalm 107:1; (2) Psalm 107:1 KJV; (3) Psalm 107:8 KJV; (4) Psalm 107:8; (5) 2 Corinthians 9:15
May 1 - (1) Acts 2:1-6; (2) Acts 2:11
May 2 - (1) Job 38:31 KJV; (2) Job 38:31
May 3 - (1) Romans 5:5
May 4 - (1) Romans 5:5; (2) 1 Corinthians 13:1; (3) 1 Corinthians 12:10; (4) 1 Corinthians 12:30; (5) 1 Corinthians 14:39; (6) 1 Corinthians 14:18
May 5 - (1) 1 Corinthians 12:4-6; (2) 1 Corinthians 12:7-11; (3) 1 Corinthians 12:27-30
May 6 - (1) Romans 12:3; (2) Romans 12:6; (3) Romans 12:9-11; (4) Ephesians 4:11-13; (5) Ephesians 4:15; (6) Ephesians 4:16
May 7 - (1) 1 Corinthians 14:1-5
May 8 - (1) 1 Corinthians 12:4-9; (2) Galatians 5:6; (3) Ephesians 2:8; (4) 1 Corinthians 13:2
May 9 - (1) 1 Corinthians 14:6-19; (2) 1 Corinthians 14:39-40
May 10 - (1) Psalm 85:10; (2) Mark 10:21; (3) Luke 22:61; (4) Luke 22:62
May 11 - (1) 1 Corinthians 12:30; (2) Acts 3:4-8; (3) Acts 3:12-13; (4) Acts 3:16; (5) Acts 4:12
May 12 - (1) James 5:13-16
May 14 - (1) 1 Samuel 26:21
May 16 - (1) Acts 28:8-9; (2) Philippians 2:27; (3) 2 Timothy 4:20; (4) 1 Timothy 5:23; (5) 2 Corinthians 12:7-10
May 17 - (1) Galatians 5:19-23
May 19 - (1) Psalm 5:11 KJV; (2) Acts 16:25-26; (3) 1 Thessalonians 1:2; (4) 1 Thessalonians 1:3; (5) 1 Thessalonians 1:6-7
May 20 - (1) John 14:27; (2) Luke 24:21; (3) Philippians 4:7; (4) Romans 12:18; (5) Galatians 5:24-26
May 21 - (1) Ephesians 3:17
May 22 - (1) Hebrews 6:1; (2) Hebrews 12:3; (3) Hebrews 12:1-2; (4) Ephesians 3:16-17; (5) Colossians 1:11-12
May 23 - (1) 2 Thessalonians 3:5 KJV; (2) 2 Thessalonians 3:5; (3) 2 Thessalonians 3:5 New International Version; (4) 2 Peter 3:4; (5) 2 Peter 3:9; (6) 2 Peter 3:10; (7) 2 Peter 3:11-12; (8) 2 Peter 3:15
May 24 - (1) Titus 3:4-5; (2) 2 Samuel 9:3; (3) Jeremiah 38:11-13
May 25 - (1) Isaiah 45:6-7
May 26 - (1) Matthew 12:35; (2) Matthew 12:34; (3) Acts 11:24
May 27 - (1) 2 Peter 1:5; (2) Titus 2:10; (3) Lamentations 3:19-27; (4) Mark 11:22
May 28 - (1) Psalm 18:35; (2) 2 Corinthians 10:1; (3) 1 Thessalonians 2:7
May 29 - (1) 1 Corinthians 9:24-27; (2) Philippians 4:8; (3) 2 Corinthians 10:5

May 30 - (1) Luke 7:39-40; (2) Luke 7:42-43; (3) 1 Corinthians 12:10
May 31 - (1) Acts 9:26-27; (2) Acts 11:22-24
June 1 - (1) Titus 1:15; (2) 1 Samuel 18:1; (3) 1 Samuel 18:3-4
June 2 - (1) Psalm 4:3
June 3 - (1) 1 Samuel 20:4 KJV; (2) 1 Samuel 20:4; (3) John 2:5; (4) John 2:23; (5) John 2:24; (6) John 2:24 KJV; (7) John 2:25; (8) John 3:1
June 4 - (1) 1 Samuel 19:1; (2) 1 Samuel 19:2; (3) 1 Samuel 19:4; (4) Psalm 119:171; (5) Romans 10:8-10
June 5 - (1) 1 Samuel 20:14-17; (2) 2 Samuel 4:4; (3) 2 Samuel 9:3; (4) 2 Samuel 9:7
June 6 - (1) 2 Samuel 1:19; (2) 2 Samuel 1:23; (3) 2 Samuel 1:26; (4) 1 Samuel 20:41; (5) John 11:35
June 7 - (1) 2 Samuel 1:26 KJV; (2) 2 Samuel 12:23
June 8 - (1) John 15:14-15
June 9 - (1) Matthew 16:13; (2) Matthew 16:14; (3) Lamentations 1:12 KJV; (4) Lamentations 1:16 KJV; (5) Jeremiah 9:3 KJV; (6) Jeremiah 31:3; (7) Jeremiah 2:1-2; (8) Jeremiah 2:32-33; (9) Jeremiah 38:6-7; (10) Jeremiah 39:17-18
June 10 - (1) Galatians 3:28; (2) Colossians 3:11; (3) Philemon 10; (4) Philemon 8-9; (5) Philemon 11-12; (6) Philemon 15-16; (7) Colossians 4:9
June 11 - (1) Proverbs 18:24 KJV; (2) Proverbs 27:6
June 13 - (1) 1 Peter 2:17; (2) 1 Peter 3:8; (3) 1 Peter 1:22
June 14 - (1) 1 John 4:20-21; (2) Matthew 25;37-40; (3) Galatians 6:10; (4) Matthew 5:16
June 15 - (1) John 15:13; (2) Romans 5:8
June 16 - (1) Exodus 20:3; (2) Luke 10:27 KJV; (3) Malachi 3:16
June 17 - (1) Titus 1:5-9; (2) Deuteronomy 10:18-19; (3) Romans 12:13; (4) Hebrews 13:2
June 18 - (1) Titus 1:7-8 KJV; (2) Titus 2:4-5 KJV; (3) Titus 2:7 KJV; (4) Titus 3:5-8 KJV
June 19 - (1) Acts 28:2; (2) Titus 3:4-5
June 20 - (1) Acts 17:17-18; (2) Acts 17:34; (3) Colossians 2:8
June 21 - (1) Luke 19:10; (2) 2 Timothy 2:15
June 22 - (1) 1 John 4:19; (2) 2 Timothy 2:15-18
June 23 - (1) Psalm 137:1; (2) Psalm 126:1-2; (3) Philippians 3:20
June 24 - (1) 1 Peter 1:22-23; (2) Acts 15:8-9 KJV; (3) 1 Peter 4:8
June 25 - (1) 1 Corinthians 8:1 KJV; (2) 1 Corinthians 8:1; (3) 1 Corinthians 8:2-3; (4) 1 Corinthians 8:13
June 26 - (1) Romans 12:9-10; (2) Galatians 2:11-13
June 27 - (1) 1 Timothy 6:3; (2) 1 Timothy 6:4-5; (3) 1 Timothy 6:6-8; (4) 1 Timothy 6:9-11; (5) Hebrews 13:5-6
June 28 - (1) Romans 8:6; (2) 1 Corinthians 7:8-9; (3) 1 Corinthians 7:28; (4) 1 Corinthians 7:32-34
June 29 - (1) James 5:17; KJV; (2) James 5:17
June 30 - (1) John 21:7 KJV; (2) John 21:20 KJV; (3) 1 John 4:20
July 1 - (1) Acts 14:11-13; (2) Exodus 20:3
July 5 - (1) 1 Corinthians 6:9-11
July 7 - (1) Romans 1:24-27
July 8 - (1) Ezekiel 23:5 KJV; (2) Ezekiel 23:11 KJV; (3) Colossians 3:5 KJV; (4) Colossians 3:1-3 KJV
July 9 - (1) 2 Samuel 12:10; (2) 2 Samuel 13:15; (3) Romans 1:24
July 10 - (1) 1 Corinthians 10:6; (2) 1 Kings 11:1; (3) 1 Kings 11:4; (4) 1 Corinthians 10:12; (5) 1 Corinthians 10:13; (6) John 8:11
July 11 - (1) Colossians 3:1 KJV; (2) Colossians 3:2 KJV
July 12 - (1) Genesis 6:5; (2) Matthew 24:37-38; (3) Ezekiel 16:49
July 13 - (1) 2 Timothy 4:10; (2) James 4:4 KJV; (3),(4) 1 John 2:15
July 14 - (1) James 4:4 KJV; (2) 1 John 2:17 KJV
July 15 - (1) 2 Timothy 3:1-5; (2) Colossians 3:5; (3) Psalm 16:11; (4) Romans 1:24
July 16 - (1) 1 Samuel 15:17-18; (2) 1 Samuel 15:19; (3) 1 Samuel 15:23; (4) 3 John 9-10
July 17 - (1) Acts 19:25-26; (2) Acts 19:27: (3) Acts 19:28; (4) 1 Timothy 6:10
July 18 - (1) Luke 18:24
July 19 - (1) 2 Timothy 3:1-2: (2) Galatians 5:17; (3) 1 Corinthians 3:1; (4) 1 Corinthians 3:3-4

July 21 - (1) Romans 6:5-6

July 22 - (1) Galatians 2:20; (2) Colossians 2:20; (3) Colossians 3:1-3

July 23 - (1) John 15:9-10; (2) 1 John 5:1-3; (3) John 15:11

July 24 - (1) Exodus 21:5-6

July 26 - (1) John 8:36; (2) John 21:15-17 Phillips "The New Testament in Modern English" (3) Romans 5:5

July 27 - (1) 2 Peter 1:5-7; (2) Acts 10:28-29; (3) 2 Peter 1:14

July 28 - (1) Colossians 3:5; (2) Romans 7:22-25

July 30 - (1) John 10:41; (2) John 7:37; (3) Jeremiah 2:13

July 31 - (1) Matthew 15:32; (2) Mark 1:41-42; (3) Micah 7:18-19; (4) Philippians 2:1-2; (5) Luke 15:20; (6) Lamentations 3:22-23

August 1 - (1) 1 John 4:19; (2) 1 John 3:16; (3) Romans 5:5

August 2 - (1) 1 John 4:19

August 3 - (1) Joel 2:28

August 4 - (1) 1 John 4:18

August 6 - (1) Genesis 1:28; (2) Genesis 4:1

August 7 - (1) Song of Solomon 1:1; (2) Luke 11:31 KJV; (3) Song of Solomon 1:7-8

August 9 - (1) Song of Solomon 2:16; (2) Song of Solomon 6:3

August 10 - (1) Philippians 4:8; (2) Genesis 2:18; (3) Genesis 2:23; (4) Song of Solomon 7:6; (5) Song of Solomon 7:10-11

August 11 - (1) Song of Solomon 3:1-2; (2) Song of Solomon 5:7-8; (3) John 11:40: (4) John 16:22

August 12 - (1) Joel 2:25

August 13 - (1) Jeremiah 31:3

August 14 - (1) Song of Solomon 1:2; (2) Song of Solomon 4:3; (3) Psalm 85:10; (4) Psalm 2:12 KJV; (5) Romans 16:16

August 15 - (1) Song of Solomon 8:6; (2) Romans 8:35; (3) Romans 8:39

August 16 - (1) Jeremiah 7:18; (2) Genesis 1:16; (3) Malachi 4:2

August 18 - (1) 1 John 2:7; (2) 1 John 2:10; (3) 1 John 2:5; (4) 2 John 1; (5) 2 John 6; (6) 1 Corinthians 16:24; (7) 2 Corinthians 2:4; (8) 2 Corinthians 11:2; (9) 2 Corinthians 12:15; (10) 2 Corinthians 13:13

August 19 - (1) Psalm 37:3-5; (2) Ezekiel 36:26-27; (3) 2 Corinthians 12:9

August 20 - (1) Deuteronomy 24:5

August 21 - (1) 1 Corinthians 7:3-5

August 22 - (1) 1 Peter 3:7 KJV; (2) 1 Peter 3:7; (3) 2 Corinthians 8:9; (4) Philippians 4:19; (5) 1 John 4:19

August 23 - (1) Ecclesiastes 4:9-12; (2) Amos 3:3 KJV

August 24 - (1) Ecclesiastes 4:12

August 25 - (1) Ephesians 4:32

August 26 - (1) Mark 6:31-32' (2) Jeremiah 29:11

August 27 - (1) Hebrews 4:15; KJV (2) Luke 11:46

August 28 - (1) Matthew 26:8-9; (2) John 12:5-6

August 29 - (1) Psalm 25:10 Living Bible: (2) 2 Corinthians 2:14-16; (3) Psalm 45:7-8

August 30 - (1) Ephesians 5:25; (2) Ephesians 5:33; (3) John 4:23-24; (4) Romans 12:1

August 31 - (1) John 1:3; (2) John 3:29-30; (3) Luke 1:42; (4) Luke 1:46-47; (5) Matthew 12:46-48

September 1 - (1) Proverbs 3:5-6; (2) Genesis 24:4; (3) Genesis 24:7; (4) John 10:4; (5) Genesis 24:67

September 2 - (1) Genesis 24:67; (2) Genesis 25:28

September 3 - (1) 2 Corinthians 6:14; (2) 1 Samuel 25:25

September 5 - (1) Hebrews 13:4; (2) Hebrews 13:5-6; (3) Hebrews 13:15; (4) Hebrews 13:1

September 6 - (1) 1 Kings 12:24 KJV

September 7 - (1) Genesis 29:17; (2) Genesis 29:18; (3) Genesis 29:20

September 8 - (1) 1 Samuel 1:19-20; (2) 1 Samuel 1:27; (3) 1 Samuel 1:28

September 10 - (1) Proverbs 18:24 KJV; (2) Malachi 4:2

September 12 - (1) Ruth 1:16-17

September 13 - (1) Ruth 2:3 KJV

September 14 - (1) Ephesians 1:11; (2) Romans 8:28; (3) Job 2:10

September 15 - (1) 1 Samuel 8:5; (2) 1 Samuel 8:7; (3) 1 Samuel 8:9
September 16 - (1) 1 Corinthians 13:9; (2) 1 Corinthians 13:10; (3) John 13:7
September 17 - (1) Genesis 16:13 KJV
September 18 - (1) Deuteronomy 30:6; (2) Ezekiel 11:19; (3) Ezekiel 36:26-27; (4) Colossians 2:11; (5) Philippians 3:2-3
September 19 - (1) Matthew 26:35; (2) Matthew 26:42; (3) Matthew 27:42; (4) Matthew 23:37
September 23 - (1) 2 Corinthians 8:8; (2) 2 Corinthians 8:5; (3) Ephesians 6:24 KJV
September 24 - (1) Revelation 2:4-5; (2) Jeremiah 2:2
September 25 - (1) Mathew 24:12
September 26 - (1) Genesis 25:8
September 27 - (1) Matthew 5:8; (2) Acts 1:3
September 28 - (1) Genesis 35:18-20; (2) Genesis 48:7
September 29 - (1) Romans 8:28
September 30 - (1) Mark 14:8 KJV; (2) Psalm 116:15
October 1 - (1) Ephesians 5:25; (2) Ephesians 5:28-29; (3) Ephesians 5:31; (4) Ephesians 5:33; (5) Ephesians 5:18
October 2 - (1) Titus 2:4; (2) Titus 2:4-5 Weymouth New Testament; (3) Titus 2:2-8; (4) 1 Corinthians 7:10-16; 1 Peter 3:1-2; Matthew 19:3-12
October 3 - (1) 1 Peter 3:1-2
October 4 - (1) Proverbs 31:10-12; (2) Ruth 3:11; (3) Proverbs 31:25-26; (4) Proverbs 31:28-29
October 5 - (1) Proverbs 31:10-31
October 6 - (1) Genesis 1:26; (2) Isaiah 6:8; (3) Isaiah 6:9; (4) Matthew 26:39
October 7 - (1) 1 Corinthians 11:3; (2) Galatians 3:28
October 8 - (1) Judges 4:4-7; (2) Judges 4:8
October 9 - (1) Psalm 119:59-60; (2) Luke 15:24
October 10 - (1) Luke 11:11-13; (2) Romans 5:8-10
October 11 - (1) Psalm 103:13-14; (2) Revelation 14:13; (3) Isaiah 63:9
October 12 - (1) Isaiah 49:15-16
October 14 - (1) Psalm 119:105 KJV; (2) Exodus 1:22; (3) Exodus 2:7; (4) Exodus 2:9
October 16 - (1) Romans 1:30-31; (2) 2 Timothy 3:1-4; (3) Romans 12:10
October 17 - (1) Galatians 5:22-23; (2) John 15:17
October 18 - (1) Titus 2:4; (2) Mark 10:14; (3) Mark 10:16
October 20 - (1) 2 Corinthians 5:14; (2) 1 Thessalonians 2:7
October 22 - (1) Hebrews 12:5-6; (2) 2 Timothy 3:2-4; (3) Revelation 3:19; (4) Hebrews 12:11
October 23 - (1) Job 1:20-22; (2) Job 2:9-10
October 25 - (1) 1 John 4:10; (2) 1 John 4:19
October 26 - (1) Genesis 22:1-2; (2) Matthew 26:39
October 27 - (1) Deuteronomy 1:39; (2) 1 Timothy 4:10; (3) Romans 5:8
October 28 - (1) Zechariah 8:5
October 30 - (1) Mark 1:29-31; (2) Ruth 3:17
October 31 - (1) Romans 8:37-39 KJV; (2) Matthew 25:23 KJV
November 1 - (1) Genesis 2:18; (2) Luke 23:34; (3) Luke 23:43; (4) John 19:26; (5) Matthew 27:46; (6) John 19:28; (7) John 19:30; (8) Luke 23:46
November 4 - (1) Isaiah 66:12-13
November 5 - (1) 2 Samuel 12:7; (2) Psalm 32:5; (3) Psalm 32:1-2; (4) Psalm 51:1; (5) Ephesians 4:26
November 6 - (1) Ephesians 4:26; (2) Ephesians 4:2: (3) James 1:19; (4) Ecclesiastes 3:7
November 7 - (1) Proverbs 10:12; (2) 1 Peter 4:8; (3) Proverbs 17:9
November 8 - (1) Proverbs 10:11-13; (2) 1 Timothy 3:11; (3) 2 Timothy 3:2-3; (4) Titus 2:3; (5) 1 Corinthians 13:6; (6) Ephesians 4:15; (7) Romans 5:5
November 9 - (1) 1 John 4:19; (2) Romans 5:8 KJV; (3) John 3:16; (4) 1 John 4:10 KJV; (5) 1 John 2:2; (6) 2 Peter 3:9
November 10 - (1) John 11:5; (2) John 11:28-29 KJV
November 11 - (1) Psalm 139:7-10

November 12 - (1) Psalm 139:7-10; (2) Genesis 26:4; (3) Matthew 12:39-41; (4) Jonah 4:11
November 13 - (1) Hebrews 9:22 KJV; (2) Romans 12:1-2; (3) Romans 10:9; (4) Acts 9:5; (5) John 14:15
November 14 - (1) Hebrews 10:12-13 KJV
November 15 - (1) 2 Corinthians 5:14-15
November 17 - (1) John 13:35; (2) John 17:18; (3) Galatians 4:6; (4) John 20:21
November 20 - (1) Acts 4:13 KJV; (2) John 12:24
November 23 - (1) Luke 4:18-19; (2) John 18:36
November 25 - (1) Ephesians 6:12; (2) 2 Corinthians 4:3-4
November 27 - (1) 2 Timothy 2:26; (2) Acts 6:1; (3) Hebrews 12:6
November 28 - (1) 1 Peter 4:8
November 29 - (1) Exodus 33:18-22; (2) 1 Corinthians 10:4
November 30 - (1) Isaiah 6:3; (2) Luke 2:14; (3) Romans 11:36
December 1 - (1) Hosea 1:2-3; (2) Hosea 11:1,8
December 2 - (1) Hosea 3:1; (2) Hosea 4:18; (3) Hosea 9:1; (4) Hosea 9:10; (5) Hosea 11:1; (6) Hosea 11:4; (7) Hosea 10:11
December 3 - (1) Hosea 14:4-9 Jerusalem Bible; (2) Deuteronomy 6:5; (3) Hosea 14:4
December 4 - (1) Ruth 3:11
December 5 - (1) Proverbs 5:18
December 6 - (1) 2 Corinthians 4:16
December 7 - (1) Hebrews 7:12; (2) Hebrews 7:21; (3) Hebrews 10:11-12; (4) Hebrews 7:25; (5) Hebrews 13:8
December 8 - (1) 1 John 4:18; (2) Revelation 2:8; (3) Revelation 2:10
December 9 - (1) 1 John 4: 12; (2) 1 John 4:16-17; (3) 1 John 4:18
December 10 - (1) Ecclesiastes 11:4; (2) Ecclesiastes 11:6; (3) Ecclesiastes 11:5
December 11 - (1) Revelation 12:11; (2) Revelation 3:21; (3) Revelation 2:10-11
December 12 - (1) Matthew 10:37; (2) 1 Samuel 17:46-47; (3) Romans 8:37; (4) Ephesians 2:4-6; (5) Deuteronomy 28:13 KJV
December 13 - (1) Romans 8:2; (2) Romans 8:6-8; (3) Romans 8:9; (4) Romans 8:1; (5) Romans 8:31; (6) Romans 8:33; (7) Romans 8:34; (8) Romans 8:38; (9) Romans 8:39; (10) John 17:24; (11) Revelation 13:8 KJV; (12) 1 Peter 1:20; (13) Ephesians 1:4; (14) Matthew 25:34
December 14 - (1) Romans 8:39; (2) Romans 8:35; (3) Romans 8:37-39; (4) 1 Corinthians 10:3; (5) Matthew 24:24
December 15 - (1) Matthew 11:3; (2) Mark 9:24
December 16 - (1) Isaiah 40:6-7; (2) Luke 12:27; (3) 1 Thessalonians 2:19-20; (4) 2 Corinthians 3:18; (5) Romans 2:1-2
December 17 - (1) John 12:24-26; (2) 2 Corinthians 10: 5; (3) Galatians 2:20
December 18 - (1) Hebrews 11:4; (2) Revelation 14:13
December 19 - (1) Hebrews 2:14-15; (2) 1 Corinthians 15:54-57; (3) Romans 8:37-39: (4) Ecclesiastes 7:1; (5) John 8:24
December 20 - (1) Acts 20:18; (2) Acts 20:23; (3) Acts 20:24; (4) Acts 20:38; (5) Acts 20:35
December 21 - (1) Matthew 9:19; (2) Matthew 9:23-25; (3) 1 Thessalonians 4:13
December 22 - (1) 1 Thessalonians 4:13-18
December 23 - (1) John 13:1; (2) Revelation 1:5; (3) Philippians 1:6
December 24 - (1) 1 John 4:19; (2) Hebrews 11:16; (3) 1 John 4:16 KJV
December 26 - (1) 2 Timothy 4:8 KJV; (2) 2 Timothy 4:8; (3) 2 Timothy 4:7; (4) Hebrews 9:28; (5) Revelation 22:20
December 27 - (1) 2 Timothy 4:8
December 28 - (1) 1 Thessalonians 4:16-17; (2) Revelation 5:12
December 29 - (1) Psalm 95:1; (2) Psalm 95:2; (3) Psalm 95:6; (4) Revelation 1:4-7; (5) Revelation 5:9 KJV; (6) Revelation 22:17; (7) Revelation 22:21
December 30 - (1) 1 Corinthians 6:9; (2) 2 Corinthians 13:11

Printed in the United States
75823LV00005B/1-60